SOCIOLOGICAL
MEASUREMENT

CHANDLER PUBLICATIONS IN

ANTHROPOLOGY AND SOCIOLOGY

LEONARD BROOM, *Editor*

Science Research Associates, Inc., 259 East Erie Street, Chicago, Illinois 60611
Distributors   A Subsidiary of IBM

S R A

SOCIOLOGICAL MEASUREMENT

AN INVENTORY OF SCALES AND INDICES

by

CHARLES M. BONJEAN
THE UNIVERSITY OF TEXAS

RICHARD J. HILL
PURDUE UNIVERSITY

and

S. DALE McLEMORE
THE UNIVERSITY OF TEXAS

CHANDLER PUBLISHING COMPANY
124 Spear Street, San Francisco, California 94105

CONTENTS

viii · Contents

PREFACE

This reference book is intended to be an aid to those engaged in sociological research. We hope it will be especially helpful during the initial stages of research—in reviewing the literature and selecting measures of the phenomena with which an investigator is concerned. Indeed, it was while the authors were at these stages in their own research that the need for such a volume came to mind.

During the three years between the decision to compile the inventory and the completion of the manuscript, we have found the materials to be useful as have some of our colleagues. We also have found a number of limitations—some related to our organization of this material and some to the sources and span of time covered in compiling the bibiliographies. Since the procedures we employed in constructing the bibliographies presented here were not (and could not have been) exhaustive, we anticipate that some conspicuous, even surprising, omissions will be apparent to specialists in different fields. Thus, the reader should not expect our review of the literature to be as complete for the purposes of his research as we would expect his specialized review to be. The criteria used in selecting various scales and indices for inclusion in this volume (which are discussed fully in the Introduction) certainly did not include *all* of those which might be pertinent to any specific piece of research. Given the amount of sociological research published in recent years and the low degree of agreement with respect to the measurement of social phenomena, it would have been impossible to include all sources and all measures. On the other hand, we believe the volume does provide the investigator with a large body of recent, relevant literature in regard to measurement. He will be exposed in detail to some measures— those used and cited most frequently—and he will be given some information necessary to help him find other measures quickly. At best, we hope the volume will contribute to a more rational selection of scales and indices in future research and to a greater continuity of sociological measurement. At least, we hope our bibliographies will lead the investigator to sources that he may otherwise overlook.

The citations included in this volume are several steps removed from their original sources. They were copied from journals onto cards. From the cards they were collated into subject categories or conceptual classes and copied again. The categories were revised, and they were copied once more. Then they were typed in a form suitable for the publisher, and then, of course, they went from type to print. We have noticed errors at each of these stages and although substantial periods of time were devoted to proofreading and checking sources, we are certain that errors were overlooked or introduced at the stages outlined above. We are just as certain that we have not found all of them; consequently, we would be grateful to those using this volume should they call errors of fact or of omission to our attention.

Although we bear full responsibility for the contents of the volume—including the errors—it would not have been possible to complete the project without the help and support of many. We are particularly grateful to Mrs. Ann Hardy, who helped us in every stage of the endeavor from looking up original sources to typing the final draft. Her patience and persistence have been unsurpassed in our experience. Sue Johnson Jecker and Kathleen Stones Crittenden sifted through many volumes of text and footnotes, and indexed the measures they found. Also helping in various stages of the project were E. D. Anderson, Thomas Bice, Judith Bootcheck, Michael Micklin, Louie Miller, Vincent Salvo, Dennis Scheck, Sonia Scheck, James Singleton, and Jere Wysong, all of whom are or have been our students at Texas or Purdue. We also are grateful to Mrs. Viki Kowallik who did some of the typing. Finally, a grant from the University of Texas Research Institute enabled us to expedite completion of the manuscript.

CHARLES M. BONJEAN

RICHARD J. HILL

S. DALE MCLEMORE

January, 1967

CREDITS

THEODOR W. ADORNO. For suggestions and permission to use the California F-Scale developed by Theodor W. Adorno, Else Frenkel-Brunswik, Daniel J. Levinson, and R. Nevitt Sanford.

AMERICAN JEWISH COMMITTEE. For permission to use the Ethnocentrism (California E Scale) and the Authoritarianism (California F Scale) measures, from *The Authoritarian Personality* by T. W. Adorno, Else Frenkel-Brunswik, Daniel J. Levinson, and R. Nevitt Sanford. Copyright 1950 by the American Jewish Committee, New York.

THE AMERICAN PSYCHOLOGICAL ASSOCIATION. For permission to use the Stereotype Checklist, from the *Journal of Abnormal and Social Psychology*, 28 (1933), p. 283, by Daniel Katz and Kenneth W. Braly.

ROBERT F. BALES. For suggestions and permission to use his measure of Social-Emotional Reactions (in small-group situations).

BASIC BOOKS, INC. For permission to use the Dogmatism Scale, from *The Open and Closed Mind* by Milton Rokeach. Copyright 1960 by Basic Books, Inc., Publishers, New York.

EMORY S. BOGARDUS. For permission to use his Social Distance Scale.

ERNEST W. BURGESS. For permission to use the Marital Adjustment measure he developed with Leonard Cottrell and Harvey Locke, and the Marital Satisfaction measure he developed with Paul Wallin.

F. STUART CHAPIN. For permission to use his Social Participation Scale.

DONALD O. COWGILL. For suggestions concerning the Index of Segregation which he developed with Mary S. Cowgill.

KINGSLEY DAVIS. For suggestions and permission to use his Index of Urbanization.

OTIS DUDLEY DUNCAN. For suggestions and permission to use his Indices of Centralization, of Occupational Status, and of Segregation.

EDWIN A. FLEISHMAN. For material related to the measures of Consideration and Initiating Structure.

ROBERT W. HODGE. For permission to reproduce material from "Occupational Prestige in the United States, 1925–1963," co-authored with Paul M. Seigel and Peter H. Rossi.

AUGUST B. HOLLINGSHEAD. For suggestions and permission to use his measure of Occupational Status, the Two Factor Index of Social Position, the Three Factor Index of Social Position, and material from *Elmtown's Youth* and *Social Class and Mental Illness* (co-authored with Frederick Redlich).

JULIUS A. JAHN. For suggestions and permission to use the Index of

Segregation developed by Julius A. Jahn, Calvin Schmid, and Clarence Schrag.

DANIEL KATZ. For permission to use the Stereotype Checklist which he developed with Kenneth W. Braly.

WALTER C. KAUFMAN. For suggestions and permission to use his Status Concern Scale.

GERHARD LENSKI. For suggestions and permission to use his measures of Status Crystallization.

HARVEY J. LOCKE. For permission to use the measure of Marital Adjustment which he developed with Karl M. Wallace.

HERBERT McCLOSKY. For permission to use his measure of Conservatism.

RUSSELL MIDDLETON. For suggestions and permission to use the Religious Orthodoxy Scale which he developed with Snell Putney.

ARTHUR G. NEAL. For suggestions and permission to use his Powerlessness Scale.

GWYNN NETTLER. For suggestions and permission to use his Alienation measure.

F. IVAN NYE. For suggestions and permission to use the Delinquent Behavior Checklist which he developed with James Short.

MILTON ROKEACH. For permission to use his Dogmatism Scale.

WILLIAM H. SEWELL. For permission to use his measure of Socioeconomic Status of Farm Families.

ESHREF SHEVKY. For permission to use the measures of Urbanization, Social Rank, and Segregation which he developed with Marilyn Williams and Wendell Bell.

LEO SROLE. For permission to use his Anomia Scale.

STANFORD UNIVERSITY PRESS. For permission to reproduce material from *Social Area Analysis* by Eshref Shevky and Wendell Bell. Copyright 1955 by the Stanford University Press.

RALPH M. STOGDILL. For materials related to the measures of Consideration and Initiating Structure.

STANLEY H. UDY, JR. For suggestions and permission to use his measure of Administrative Rationality.

THE UNIVERSITY OF CHICAGO PRESS. For permission to reproduce Table 1 from "Occupational Prestige in the United States, 1925–1963," *American Journal of Sociology*, 70 (1964), pp. 290–292, by Robert W. Hodge, Paul M. Siegel, and Peter H. Rossi; copyright 1964 by the University of Chicago.

D. VAN NOSTRAND COMPANY, INC. For permission to use Marian Winterbottom's Achievement Training measure from John W. Atkinson, *Motives in Fantasy, Action and Society*. Copyright 1958 by D. Van Nostrand Company, Inc., Princeton, N.J.

W. LLOYD WARNER. For permission to use his Index of Status Characteristics and measure of Occupational Status.

FRANK R. WESTIE. For his "A Note to Potential Users of the Summated Differences Scales" for measuring Social Distance.

JOHN WILEY AND SONS, INC. For permission to use quotations from *Elmtown's Youth* by August B. Hollingshead. Copyright 1949 by John Wiley and Sons, Inc., New York. Also for permission to quote from *Social Class and Mental Illness* by August B. Hollingshead and Frederick Redlich. Copyright 1958 by John Wiley and Sons, Inc., New York.

SOCIOLOGICAL MEASUREMENT

INTRODUCTION

One of the major themes in the development of contemporary sociology has been a steadily increasing interest in problems of measurement. Almost every issue of our journals reveals the development of new measures as well as new uses of old ones. This proliferation of measuring instruments has led some sociologists to express fear that sociology is becoming fragmented and to raise questions concerning continuity in social research. When the investigator tries to build continuity in his research, more often than not, he is faced with one or both of two major problems. So many different measures are available for some phenomena that the selection of a scale or index may itself be a research problem of no small magnitude.[1] In other cases, an extensive search through the literature may yield no adequate description of a scale or index to measure the phenomenon of concern to the investigator.[2] The purposes of this volume are related to assessing this problem in social research more clearly and to offering some initial aids to its solution. Specifically:

1. Our first goal is to assess the extent of continuity in social research as well as its substantive location. This first purpose has been accomplished through a content analysis of four major journals for the twelve-year period 1954–1965; the method employed is described in detail below. The analysis was designed

---

[1] Examples of such variously measured phenomena include achievement, alienation, segregation, socioeconomic status, and so on.

[2] Examples are numerous. Should the reader desire verification, he should attempt to find a *complete* description of a measure of social mobility or of conservatism in our major journals.

to locate those conceptual areas which have generated the greatest empirical activity during the period reviewed and to identify the specific scales and indices that have been used and cited with greatest frequency.[3]

2. Our second goal is to present a series of bibliographies, based on the content analysis referred to above, that will serve as an aid during the initial stages of research. The bibliographies are organized by categories within the conceptual classes and include only those sources discussing or using measures of each of these concepts. The term "conceptual classes" refers, in this discussion, to the major division in the scheme by which the bibliographies are classified ("Achievement," "Achievement Motivation," and the like). The term "category" refers to the numbered entries within each of the conceptual classes.

3. Finally, where we have located continuity in regard to specific measures, descriptions of each of the measures are presented for the reader's convenience.

CONTINUITIES IN MEASUREMENT, 1954–1965

Following Lazarsfeld and Rosenberg, ". . . we use the word 'index' when we are confronted with a combination of several indicators into one measurement."[4] This definition suggests that more than one dimension of a concept may be reflected by an index. The term "scale" as used here may be thought of generally as a special type of index which is designed to reflect only a single dimension of a concept; however, it is extremely difficult to draw a sharp distinction between an index and a scale, and no such effort

[3] The importance of systematizing existing tools of sociological measurement as a step toward continuity has been suggested by William A. Faunce, "Scales and Indices: A Proposal," *American Sociological Review*, 24 (April, 1959), p. 256. Other recent efforts in this direction include Delbert C. Miller, *Handbook of Research Design and Social Measurement* (New York: David McKay Company, Inc., 1964), and Marvin E. Shaw and Jack M. Wright, *Scales for the Measurement of Attitudes* (New York: McGraw-Hill Book Company, 1967).

[4] Paul F. Lazarsfeld and Morris Rosenberg (eds.), *The Language of Social Research* (Glencoe, Ill.: The Free Press, 1955), p. 16.

will be made. Hagood and Price state in this regard that: "In sociological research the terms 'scale' and 'index' are used to refer to all sorts of measures absolute or relative, single or composite, usually indirect or partial. . . ."[5]

Measuring instruments which were classified as scales or indices for the purposes of this volume typically involved the use of more than one "piece" of information. For example, if an author measured religiosity by asking "How many times did you attend church last year?", the resulting numbers were regarded as indicators rather than as indices or scales, because they were based upon a single piece of information; and such indicators are, consequently, not included in this volume. If, on the other hand, religiosity was measured by combining information on church attendance, number of other church-related activities, proportion of income spent on religious matters, frequency of Bible reading, and so on, the measure has been included in this volume.

The most conspicuous exceptions to or departures from the above criterion for the acceptance of a measure as a scale or index occur in the bibliographies concerning "Societal Characteristics" and "Socioeconomic Status, Occupational." In the former case, marginal inclusions occur primarily because at the societal level it frequently is not feasible for researchers to array or categorize societies in terms of more than a single piece of information. Technological development, for instance, may be measured in terms of per capita coal consumption or of median income. Of course, such information may represent some underlying combination of data. This same observation applies also to occupation as an index of socioeconomic status. Although only a single piece of information is utilized for classifying respondents or subjects, in most cases the occupational categories were constructed on the basis of additional information.[6]

The *American Journal of Sociology*, the *American Sociologi-*

[5] Margaret Jarman Hagood and Daniel O. Price, *Statistics for Sociologists* (revised edition, New York: Henry Holt and Co., 1952), p. 138.

[6] For example, the North-Hatt (NORC) list of occupations by prestige was constructed from ratings by 2,920 respondents. See Cecil C. North and Paul K. Hatt, "Jobs and Occupations: A Popular Evaluation," *Opinion News*, 9 (September, 1947), pp. 3–13.

cal Review, Social Forces, and *Sociometry* were taken to be representative of the main research currents of American sociology. Every article and every research note in each issue of these four journals published from January, 1954, through December, 1965, was examined carefully. To check reliability, 20 per cent of the issues were examined independently by two readers. Still further, after the initial search was concluded all of the references cited were checked by the authors. Each attempt to measure an attribute or variable through the use of scales or indices was noted on a separate card listing the following: (1) a complete reference to the article in which the measure appeared, (2) the concept indicated by the measure employed, (3) the technique(s) of measurement employed, and (4) other uses and users of the same or similar techniques which were cited. The last point should be stressed here because even though this inventory was confined to articles published in the journals named above during a twelve-year period, the tables and bibliographies presented below reflect both a variety of other research publications and a much longer span of time.

The cards accumulated in the manner described were then classified according to (1) the concepts underlying the various measurements, and (2) the specific measures utilized. The conceptual classes employed were set up during the examination of the accumulated cards and have undergone several revisions.[7] Other concepts and criteria of classification might have been utilized. Thus, the reader is cautioned that generalizations based on the frequency of uses and citations of measures by concept as well as the number of different measures found are highly conditional. Obviously, different conceptual classes might yield different conclusions.

The criteria employed in constructing the classification scheme were (1) utility to the reader and (2) comprehensiveness. We have tried throughout to "take the role of the other" and to

[7] An earlier summary of our findings, based on an analysis of the four journals cited above over a five-year time span, employs a somewhat different set of conceptual classes. See Charles M. Bonjean, Richard J. Hill, and S. Dale McLemore, "Continuities in Measurement, 1959–63," *Social Forces,* 43 (March, 1965), pp. 532–536.

imagine the types of problems which would lead researchers to consult this book. Consequently, we have proceeded empirically and have constructed enough conceptual classes to minimize the number of entries which are treated as "Miscellaneous Categories." The result is one possible way of classifying the concepts which sociologists have found to be most useful in conducting their research. A consequence of our approach, which will become obvious to the reader, is that the constructed conceptual classes are not mutually exclusive. We hope that this departure from the strict rules of logical classification is made more palatable by the closer approximation of the classification scheme to common research interests and usage. Additionally, we have tried to coordinate the conceptual classes and the categories through the author and subject indexes and through the cross-referencing procedures which will be discussed below.

Table 1 presents a frequency distribution of measures by concept as well as the number of different measures found for each concept. The 3,609 recorded uses and citations of the 2,080 scales and indices identified in the analysis are classified by categories within the 78 conceptual classes listed. The conceptual classes are thus the bases for the organization of the bibliographies that make up the bulk of this volume. For reference purposes, they are listed alphabetically in Table 1 and are the principal headings in the bibliographic portion of the book.

As a sociologist might expect, measures of socioeconomic status were used and cited with the greatest frequency during the twelve-year period investigated. In the four journals reviewed there were noted 435 attempts to measure socioeconomic status by techniques employing either occupational status or more than one piece of information.

Table 1 also indicates those areas characterized by the greatest amount of continuity in social research. Continuity is apparently most characteristic among investigations dealing with authoritarianism, racial and ethnic stereotypes, community leadership, occupational status, reputational status, and residential segregation. On the other hand, there seems to be little or no continuity in regard to the measurement of achievement, authority, community charac-

TABLE 1. CLASSIFICATION AND FREQUENCY OF USE AND
CITATION OF SCALES AND INDICES, 1954–1965

Conceptual Class	Number of Scales and Indices	Number of Uses and Citations
1. Achievement	9	10
2. Achievement Motivation	12	45
3. Anomia and Alienation	24	71
4. Aspirations	35	46
5. Assimilation	16	16
6. Authoritarianism	6	61
7. Authority: Attitudes toward and Characteristics of	33	36
8. Class Consciousness	8	12
9. Cohesion	18	21
10. Community: Attitudes toward and Characteristics of	24	26
11. Complex Organizations: Attitudes toward and Perceptions of	42	45
12. Complex Organizations: Characteristics of	34	56
13. Complex Organizations: Informal Relations	36	46
14. Conformity and Deviance	23	29
15. Consensus	10	11
16. Crime and Delinquency	47	64
17. Education: Attitude toward and Perceptions of	16	18
18. Education: Behavior in and Characteristics of	11	12
19. Family: Interpersonal Relations and Authority	86	103
20. Family: Perceptions of and Attitudes toward	22	36
21. Family Cohesion	20	22
22. Health: Individual	10	15
23. Innovation and Diffusion	27	35
24. Interests	6	10
25. Intergroup Relations: Ethnocentrism	4	12
26. Intergroup Relations: Nonracial and Nonethnic	20	30
27. Intergroup Relations, Racial and Ethnic: Characteristics of	16	19
28. Intergroup Relations, Racial and Ethnic: Discrimination	19	26
29. Intergroup Relations, Racial and Ethnic: Group Belongingness	12	15
30. Intergroup Relations, Racial and Ethnic: Prejudice and Social Distance	37	74

Conceptual Class	Number of Scales and Indices	Number of Uses and Citations
31. Intergroup Relations, Racial and Ethnic: Stereotypes	4	18
32. Interpersonal Relations: Attitudes toward	23	30
33. Interpersonal Relations: Characteristics of	53	63
34. Job Satisfaction, Morale, and Related Measures	29	35
35. Leadership, Community and Organizational: Behavior and Characteristics of	17	32
36. Leadership, Community and Organizational: Identification of	13	54
37. Leadership, Small Group: Behavior and Characteristics of	39	52
38. Leadership, Small Group: Identification of	18	22
39. Marital Adjustment and Courtship	28	70
40. Marital and Family Roles	17	19
41. Medicine and Health: Attitudes toward	23	29
42. Medicine and Health: Behavior in and Characteristics of	34	49
43. Mental Ability	32	67
44. Miscellaneous Categories	29	32
45. Neighborhood, Attitudes toward and Characteristics of	11	16
46. Norms	22	30
47. Occupational Roles	48	56
48. Personal Adjustment	63	100
49. Personality: General	34	61
50. Personality Traits: Creativity	4	8
51. Personality Traits: Dominance	6	23
52. Personality Traits: Masculinity-Femininity	7	14
53. Personality Traits: Motives and Needs	32	56
54. Personality Traits: Sociability-Withdrawal	9	17
55. Personality Traits: Various Categories	60	101
56. Political Attitudes	49	68
57. Political Behavior	17	27
58. Religion: Attitude toward, Participation in, and Characteristics of	40	61

(continued)

Conceptual Class	Number of Scales and Indices	Number of Uses and Citations
59. Self-Image, Self-Concept, and Related Measures	55	84
60. Small Groups: Attitudes toward, Identification with, and Perceptions of	41	59
61. Small Groups: Behavior and Interaction in	80	104
62. Small Groups: Status and Status Relations in	14	55
63. Social Mobility and Related Measures	29	71
64. Social Participation	39	71
65. Societal Characteristics	59	80
66. Socioeconomic Status: Composite, Objective	68	146
67. Socioeconomic Status: Composite, Subjective and Objective	6	8
68. Socioeconomic Status: Occupational	56	270
69. Socioeconomic Status: Reputational	2	11
70. Status Concern	4	10
71. Status Consistency and Related Measures	11	21
72. Urban Areas: Metropolitan Areas and Dominance	11	13
73. Urban Areas: Segregation	10	61
74. Urban Areas: Socioeconomic Status	27	65
75. Urban Areas: Urbanization (Family Status)	1	28
76. Urban Areas: Various Categories	19	31
77. Values	63	127
78. Work-Value Orientations	44	62
Totals	2,080	3,609

teristics, attitudes toward and perceptions of complex organizations, consensus, and characteristics of education.

Indeed, Table 1 indicates that fragmentation, rather than continuity, is an important characteristic of measurement in social research. A comparison of the number of measures found for each conceptual class with the frequency of uses and citations of the measures indicates that most measures used and cited in the journals examined were developed or modified by the investigator for the specific research reported.

Continuity in social research may be assessed, at least roughly, by comparing the total number of measurement attempts to the total number of measures used and cited.[8] As noted above, there were 3,609 attempts to measure various phenomena by the use of scales or indices and 2,080 different measures were used. Of the measures used, only 589 (28.3 per cent of the total number of scales and indices) were used more than once. Even though the percentage figure is low, it may overestimate continuity in social research since in many cases a measure contrived by one investigator and used on data presented in one journal article was reported a second time by the same investigator using the same data in a different article.

The lack of continuity in social research is reflected further by the observation that of the 2,080 scales and indices appearing in the journals over the twelve-year period covered by the analysis, only 47, or 2.26 per cent, were used more than five times.

THE BIBLIOGRAPHIES AND THEIR USE

As was stated earlier, the bulk of this volume is a collection of bibliographies based on the content analysis described above. The conceptual classes, identified in Table 1, and their associated bibliographies are presented in alphabetical order. Since the concepts of our classification scheme are not mutually exclusive, as was indicated earlier, strongly related conceptual classes have been cross-referenced. For example, the class "Personality Traits: Motives and Needs" contains several references which probably would interest students of marriage and the family; hence, the classes "Marital Adjustment and Courtship" and "Family: Perceptions of and Attitudes toward" show "Personality Traits: Motives and Needs" as a cross reference. The reader who is interested in studying complementary needs in mate selection, for instance, would probably be best advised to start with "complementary

[8] The assessment is termed "rough" because uses, although they greatly outnumbered citations, were not analyzed separately here.

needs" in the Index of Topics; however, if he were to begin with one of the alphabetized conceptual classes, he probably would start with "Marital Adjustment and Courtship." There he would find "Complementary Needs" (category 5) and "Homogamy-Heterogamy" (category 7). If the reader followed the cross reference to "Personality Traits: Motives and Needs," he would find additional citations to articles concerning complementary needs in mate selection.

Still another effort to coordinate the conceptual classes is the cross-referencing of certain specific categories within given conceptual classes with specific categories within other conceptual classes. This type of cross-referencing may be illustrated as follows: Within the class "Family: Interpersonal Relations and Authority," category 17 is "Child-Rearing Practices: Independence Training" (which represents a measure devised by Marian Winterbottom). Accompanying this category is the suggestion that the reader "see also category 10" in "Achievement Motivation." At that point, the reader will find a discussion of Winterbottom's measure of Achievement Training and some items relating to independence training. If the reader consults all cross-referenced conceptual classes and categories, he may be fairly certain that he will find all scales and indices related to this concept that have appeared in the *American Journal of Sociology*, the *American Sociological Review*, *Social Forces*, and *Sociometry* from January, 1954, through December, 1965. He also will find the original source of the measure (the first item in a category) and uses reported elsewhere *if* they were cited in the articles reviewed.

Complete bibliographic information is given for each use and citation of each measure including the specific pages in the article where the measure is discussed (unless the article referred to is less than four pages long). The measures are presented alphabetically within conceptual classes. Thus, for example, should one be interested in measuring political apathy, he would first turn to the conceptual class "Political Attitudes." Given the knowledge that the measures are presented alphabetically, the reader will immediately find several measures of political apathy identified under categories 32, 33, and 34 within this conceptual class. Had there been more than one use or citation of a given political-apathy measure, the references within the appropriate category would have been ordered *chronologically*. This same general rule is followed throughout any given bibliography.

In a few cases we depart from the practice of chronological listings within categories. For example, where we describe specific measures, there are some instances in which discussions of scale or index modifications or tests of validity or reliability are of special significance. To note the special significance of these sources, they have been taken out of chronological order and presented immediately before or within our discussion of the measure. In nearly all cases, however, the original use of the measure is the first item under the category title.

Primarily to save space, if an article is cited more than once within the same conceptual class, a *complete* reference is given only for one citation (usually the first). Additional citations list the author's last name, a note telling the reader in which category he may find the full reference, the page number(s) where the measure is cited, and—in many instances—the year of publication. Since the categories are arranged *chronologically*, dates have been included in the additional citations wherever such inclusions probably would assist the reader. Thus, looking again at "Political Attitudes," one finds that the first measure presented under "political futility" is by Herbert McClosky and John H. Schaar. The reference under category 39 is: "McClosky and Schaar, pp. 24-31 and 35; see category 1 above." This indicates that the article by McClosky and Schaar was cited earlier in this conceptual class and that the complete reference can be found under category 1. If an additional article had been listed under category 1, the reference in category 39 also would have contained a date.

The basic criterion used for placing a measure within a given conceptual class was the author's use of the measure. For example, as noted previously, some measures may be found in several different conceptual classes. Thus, the North, Hatt (NORC) rankings of occupations by prestige have been used to measure socioeconomic status; consequently, under "Socioeconomic Status: Occupational" one finds this measure listed as category 6. Here the reader will find 53 uses and citations of the prestige rankings (all but one of which are listed chronologically); but this measure also has been used to assess social mobility. Therefore, under the conceptual class "Social Mobility and Related Measures," the reader will find the North, Hatt measures listed as category 11, "Occupational Mobility, Career (North, Hatt Related)" and again as category 16, "Occupational Mobility, Intergenerational (North, Hatt Related)." Under these two categories the reader will find fifteen additional citations to articles where this scale has been employed to measure slightly different phenomena.

One consequence of this criterion of classification is that, at first glance, some measures do not appear to be used as widely as they are. For example, in Table 2 are shown the 50 measures that were used and cited within a specific context more than five times each between January, 1954, and December, 1965. To continue the above example, occupational prestige was measured via the North, Hatt scale a total of 53 times; however, as was shown above, the North, Hatt scale (or modifications of it) was used an additional 15 times in relation to two other measures. The reader should bear in mind that this underenumeration occurs because a given scale or index may be utilized by different authors as measures of different phenomena. The problem of underenumeration is even more noticeable in the case of certain general techniques. For example, Bales's Interaction Process Analysis may be used to measure a number of different phenomena. We mention that it has been used six times to measure "social-emotional reactions," and it is discussed under the conceptual class "Small Groups: Status and Status Relations." Here the IPA technique is presented within a given conceptual context. That is, a description of how Interaction Process Analysis may be employed to assess social-emotional reactions is discussed. This general technique, to repeat, also has been used to measure other phenomena. For example, it is cited as category 15, "Individual Assertiveness," under "Leadership: Small Group, Behavior and Characteristics of," and as category 8, "Leader Consensus," under "Leadership: Small Group, Identification of." The reader should refer to both the Index of Topics and the Index of Names if he is interested in all of the many phenomena which have been measured by the use of some form of Interaction Process Analysis or any other general technique (as

TABLE 2. MOST FREQUENTLY USED AND CITED MEASURES, 1954–1965*

Measure	Frequency of Use and Citations
1. Occupational Status (Census, Edwards)	91
2. California F Scale and Modifications	53
3. Occupational Prestige (North, Hatt)	53
4. Leadership (Reputational Approach)	35
5. Stereotype Check List (Katz, Braly)	33
6. Indexes of Social Position (Hollingshead)	30
7. Anomia (Srole)	28
8. Social Rank (Shevky, Williams, Bell)	28
9. Index of Status Characteristics (Warner)	27
10. Urbanization (Shevky, Williams, Bell)	26
11. Segregation (Shevky, Williams, Bell)	25
12. Sociometric Status and Structure (Various Measures)	19
13. Marital Adjustment (Burgess, Cottrell, Locke)	18
14. Social Distance (Bogardus)	18
15. Social Participation (Chapin)	17
16. Achievement Motivation (Murray, McClelland, Atkinson)	16
17. Occupational Status (Census, Edwards Related)	16
18. Occupational Status (Warner)	16
19. Ethnocentrism (California E Scale)	15
20. Segregation (Duncan, Duncan)	15
21. Occupational Mobility, Intergenerational (Census, Edwards Related)	12
22. Occupational Mobility, Intergenerational (North, Hatt Related)	10
23. Social Class: Judges or Informants	10
24. Occupational Status (Duncan)	9
25. Socioeconomic Status (Sewell)	8
26. American Council on Education Psychological Examination	8
27. Centralization	8
28. Consideration (Ohio State Leader Behavior Description · Questionnaire and Related Measures)	8
29. Delinquency Proneness, Social Responsibility (Gough)	8
30. Initiating Structure (Ohio State Leader Behavior Description Questionnaire and Related Measures)	8
31. Occupational Status (Hollingshead)	8

(continued)

* The total number of measures cited in this table adds to 50, rather than the 47 cited in the text of the introduction, because several were used as indicators of different concepts. For example, the North, Hatt occupational prestige ratings (3) have been used as measures of socioeconomic status and as measures of intergenerational occupational mobility (22). The distinction is made in this table, but the prestige ratings are treated as a single measure in our discussion.

TABLE 2. *continued*

Measure	Frequency of Use and Citations
32. Status Crystallization (Lenski)	8
33. Dogmatism (Rokeach)	7
34. Segregation (Cowgill, Cowgill)	7
35. Segregation (Jahn, Schmid, Schrag)	7
36. Social Distance, Summated Differences Technique (Westie)	7
37. Achievement Training (Winterbottom)	6
38. Administrative Rationality (Udy)	6
39. Alienation (Nettler)	6
40. Alienation, Powerlessness (Neal)	6
41. California Test of Personality (Tiegs, Clark, Thrope)	6
42. Conservatism (McClosky)	6
43. Delinquent Behavior Checklist (Nye, Short)	6
44. Edwards Personal Preference Schedule	6
45. Marital Satisfaction (Burgess, Wallin)	6
46. Religious Orthodoxy (Putney, Middleton)	6
47. Social-Emotional Reactions (Bales)	6
48. Status Concern (Kaufman)	6
49. Urbanization (Davis)	6
50. Values (Allport, Vernon, Lindzey)	6

opposed to a specific measure), such as the Thematic Apperception Test (TAT), Rorschach tests, and others. Because these
techniques generally are used in different ways to measure different
phenomena, most are *not* discussed in this volume. In consequence of the "author's use" criterion, the reader is cautioned
again in regard to generalizations based on Table 1.

SPECIFIC MEASURES DISCUSSED

As stated above, in Table 2 are the 47 measures that were used
and cited more than five times each between January, 1954, and
December, 1965, in the four journals covered by our review. Discussions of each of these measures are placed within the relevant
conceptual classes under the appropriate categories. Thus, for example, Table 2 indicates that the Census (Edwards) classification

of occupations has been used most frequently as a measure of occupational status. We therefore have placed the discussion of the Edwards scheme under category 25, "Occupational Status (Census, Edwards and Modifications)," within the conceptual class "Socioeconomic Status: Occupational." The first sources listed under category 25 are those describing the Edwards measure in some detail. Following these sources is a description of the measure based primarily upon the sources cited prior to the description. The sources which follow the description of the measure are the remaining references to uses and citations of the Edwards scheme as an index of occupational status which were contained in the journals reviewed.

It should be noted again, as was done in the case of our discussion of the North, Hatt scale, that although the discussion of the Edwards measure has been placed within the bibliography denoting its most frequent use, many additional uses of the Edwards classification have occurred. For instance, 12 additional uses and citations of the Edwards classification are listed under category 13, "Occupational Mobility, Intergenerational (Census, Edwards Related)" within the conceptual class "Social Mobility and Related Measures." A complete discussion of how the Edwards classification is used as a measure of intergenerational mobility is *not* presented at this point, however, because those who have used it have not necessarily used it in the same manner. Rather than arbitrarily presenting a discussion of any given use of the Edwards scheme as a measure of intergenerational mobility, we have left it to the reader to examine the original sources and to decide which, if any, of the applications is best suited to the purposes of his research.

Some additional points relating to the discussions of specific measures deserve note. In several cases, the description of a measure which has been used and cited more than five times does not include the actual items or other elements comprising the scale or index. This departure from our general plan has occurred primarily in two types of situations: (1) Some frequently used and cited psychological instruments (among them the California Psychological Inventory and the Edwards Personal Preference Schedule) have been published already for commerical use.[9] (2) Some authors of frequently used and cited measures have advised us that certain of their scales or indices probably should not be published in their present form or at the present time. Where a complete description of a measure (including the items or other elements) has been set forth in this book, the author(s) of the measure have in most cases read and approved the presentation. In several instances, the authors of the measures have not only checked the accuracy of our descriptions but have suggested significant revisions or modifications (some of which have not been published previously). Thus, the reader may proceed with some degree of confidence that the measures presented here in full are described accurately and that the description is relatively up-to-date.

[9] The addresses of the publishers of these and the other psychological instruments which have been uncovered by our review are included in our discussions of these instruments.

ACHIEVEMENT

SEE ALSO
Achievement Motivation
Aspirations
Mental Ability
Work-Value Orientations

1. ACCESS TO MEANS FOR THE ACHIEVEMENT OF LIFE GOALS

Meier, Dorothy L., and Wendell Bell, "Anomia and Differential Access to the Achievement of Life Goals," *American Sociological Review*, 24 (April, 1959), pp. 189–212. See p. 198.

2. ACCESS TO MEANS FOR THE ACHIEVEMENT OF LIFE GOALS, REVISED

Meier and Bell, p. 200; see category 1 above.

3. ACHIEVEMENT (LINDZEY, URDAN)

Lindzey, Gardner, and James A. Urdan, "Personality and Social Choice," *Sociometry*, 17 (February, 1954), pp. 47–63. See p. 49.

4. ACHIEVEMENT (KELLY, MADDEN, GARDNER, TERMAN, RUCH)

Kelly, Truman, Richard Madden, Eric F. Gardner, Lewis M. Terman, and Giles M. Ruch, *Stanford Achievement Test*, New York: Harcourt, Brace and World, 1953.

Seeman, Melvin, "Alienation and Social Learning in a Reformatory," *American Journal of Sociology*, 69 (November, 1963), pp. 270–284. See p. 281.

5. ATTITUDE TOWARD ACHIEVEMENT

Westoff, Charles F., Robert G. Potter, Jr., Philip C. Sagi, and Elliot G. Mishler, *Family Growth in Metropolitan America*, Princeton: Princeton University Press, 1961, pp. 383–400. See pp. 383–385 and 398–399.

6. DISCREPANCY BETWEEN ASPIRATION AND ACHIEVEMENT

Hollingshead, A. B., R. Ellis, and E. Kirby, "Social Mobility and Mental Illness," *American Sociological Review*, 19 (October, 1954), pp. 577–584. See p. 581.

7. ECONOMIC ACHIEVEMENT

Bressler, Marvin, and Charles F. Westoff, "Catholic Education, Economic Values and Achievement," *American Journal of Sociology*, 69 (November, 1963), pp. 225–233. See p. 228.

8. PERCEIVED GROUP ACCOMPLISHMENT

Meltzer, Leo, "Comparing Relationships of Individual and Average Variables to Individual Response," *American Sociological Review*, 28 (February, 1963), pp. 117–123. See p. 118.

9. STATUS FRUSTRATION

McClosky, Herbert, and John H. Schaar, "Psychological Dimensions of Anomy," *American Sociological Review*, 30 (February, 1965), pp. 14–40. See pp. 30–31.

ACHIEVEMENT MOTIVATION

SEE ALSO

Achievement

Aspirations

Family: Interpersonal Relations and Authority

Personality: Motives and Needs

Values

1. ACHIEVEMENT CONCERN

Sewell, William H., and A. O. Haller, "Factors in the Relationship between Social Status and the Personality Adjustment of the Child," *American Sociological Review*, 24 (August, 1959), pp. 511–520. See p. 516.

2. ACHIEVEMENT MOTIVATION (EDWARDS)

Edwards, Allen L., *The Edwards Personal Preference Schedule*, New York: Psychological Corporation, 1959.

Cartwright, Desmond S., and Richard J. Robertson, "Membership in Cliques and Achievement," *American Journal of Sociology*, 66 (March, 1961), pp. 441–445. See p. 442.

3. ACHIEVEMENT MOTIVATION (MURRAY, MCCLELLAND, ATKINSON)

Murray, Henry A. (ed.), *Explorations in Personality*, New York: Oxford University Press, 1938.

Murray, Henry A., *Thematic Apperception Test*, Cambridge, Mass.: Harvard University Press, 1943.

McClelland, David C., John W. Atkinson, Russell Clark, and Edgar Lowell, *The Achievement Motive*, New York: Appleton-Century-Crofts, Inc., 1953.

Mills, Theodore M., "The Coalition Pattern in Three-Person Groups," *American Sociological Review*, 19 (December, 1954), pp. 657–667. See p. 660.

McClelland, David C. (ed.), *Studies in Motivation*, New York: Appleton-Century-Crofts, Inc., 1955, pp. 401–423.

Rosen, Bernard C., "The Achievement Syndrome: A Psychocultural Dimension of Social Stratification," *American Sociological Review*, 21 (April, 1956), pp. 203–211. See p. 205.

Atkinson, John W. (ed.), *Motives in Fantasy, Action and Society*, Princeton, N.J.: D. Van Nostrand, 1958. See pp. 179–204 and 685–734.

The attempt to define and measure achievement motivation has grown out of efforts to solve the more general problem of constructing a theory of human motivation. In a particularly influential work, Murray (1938, p. 164) defines the need for achievement (*n* Ach) as "the desire or tendency to do things as rapidly and/or as well as possible." In this same work (p. 164), Murray presents ten questionnaire items which he used to measure *n* Ach; however, he also utilizes other techniques, including his and Morgan's *Thematic Apperception Test* (TAT) (Christiana D. Morgan and Henry A. Murray, "A Method of Investigating Fantasies: The Thematic Apperception Test," *Archives of Neurological Psychiatry*, 34, pp. 289–306). The TAT, which consists of a series of pictures, was used "In an attempt to discover the covert (inhibited) and unconscious (partially repressed) tendencies of normal persons." (Murray, 1938, p. 529) After the respondent views a picture, he is asked to create an imaginative story which is then analyzed for motivational content.

Following Murray's leads, McClelland, Atkinson, Clark, Lowell (1953) and their associates have undertaken and assembled numerous studies of motivation. They and their followers have emphasized the achievement motive, and they have experimented broadly with techniques for arousing and manipulating achievement motivation. One of their special concerns, however, has been the measurement of achievement motivation. According to McClelland (1955, p. 401), "Contemporary psychological theory stresses the importance of motivation, but provides no satisfactory method for measuring it . . . at the human level." He observes in another place (1958, p. 685) that "Here, as elsewhere, real theoretical advance has to wait on methodological developments."

The general procedure which the authors of *The Achievement Motive* (1953, p. 107) adopt come from "the Freudian hypothesis that a good place to look for the effects of motivation is in fantasy"; consequently, they begin by showing each experimental subject a series of four pictures and asking each person to make up or tell a story about each picture (which is projected onto a screen for 20 seconds). The subjects are instructed (1953, p. 98) that "This is a test of your creative imagination," and they are given four minutes to write each story. The subjects also are instructed to be guided in their writing by the following questions:

1. What is happening? Who are the persons?
2. What has led up to this situation? That is, what has happened in the past?
3. What is being thought? What is wanted? By whom?
4. What will happen? What will be done?

After the stories are written, the content is analyzed and scored in detail according to a system devised and described by McClelland, Atkinson, Clark, and Lowell (1953, pp. 110–138; 1958, pp. 179–204). These authors report that the scoring system "can be learned with reasonable scoring reliability (over .90) in a week's time" and they observe further that "Around a minute per story is not exceptionally fast scoring." (1953, p. 110) Practice materials for scoring *n* Ach are presented by Charles P. Smith and Sheila Feld (Atkinson, 1958, pp. 685–735) and should be consulted before one attempts to analyze stories for achievement motivation.

Briefly stated, the scoring procedure is as follows: The scorer examines the story first for Achievement Imagery (AI); that is, he looks for references to achievement goals. "By achievement goal is meant *success in competition with some standard of excellence.*" (1953, p. 110) If a story contains some reference to achievement but fails to meet, either explicitly or implicitly, the criterion set forth above, then it is scored as Doubtful Achievement Imagery (TI) and it is "not scored further for achievement-related sub-categories." (1953, p. 114) If a story contains no reference, explicitly or implicitly, to an achievement goal, it is scored as Unrelated Imagery (UI). The sub-categories of AI are Instrumental Activity (I+, I?, I−, that is, the outcome is successful, doubtful, or unsuccessful); Anticipatory Goal State (Ga+, Ga−, that is, someone anticipates goal attainment or failure); Obstacles or Blocks (Bp, Bw; personal or environmental obstacles may exist); Nurturant Press (Nup; someone aids or sympathizes with the achiever); Affective States (G+, G−; the emotional states associated with goal attainment or failure); and Achievement Thema (Ach The, that is, when the AI becomes the central plot of the story). If a story is scored for UI, it receives a minus one (−1). TI is scored zero (0), and AI is scored plus one (+1). If the story is scored for AI, then the sub-categories are scored. "Each sub-category is scored only once per story and is given a weight of +1. An Achievement score is obtained by summing (algebraically) the categories for that story. The n Achievement score for any one individual is the total of the scores obtained on all stories written." (1953, pp. 147–148)

Rosen, Bernard C., "Race, Ethnicity, and the Achievement Syndrome," *American Sociological Review*, 24 (February, 1959), pp. 47–60. See p. 49.

Kerchoff, Alan C., "Anomie and Achievement Motivation: A Study of Personality Development within Cultural Disorganization," *Social Forces*, 37 (March, 1959), pp. 196–202. See p. 196.

Rosen, Bernard C., and Roy D'Andrade, "The Psychosocial Origins of Achievement Motivation," *Sociometry*, 22 (September, 1959), pp. 185–218. See pp. 188–195.

McClelland, David C., *The Achieving Society*, New York: D. Van Nostrand, 1961.

Rosen, Bernard C., "Family Structure and Achievement Motivation," *American Sociological Review*, 26 (August, 1961), pp. 574–585. See p. 576.

Crockett, Harry J., Jr., "The Achievement Motive and Differential Occupational Mobility in the United States," *American Sociological Review*, 27 (April, 1962), pp. 191–204. See p. 193.

Veroff, Joseph, Sheila Feld, and Gerald Gurin, "Achievement Motivation and Religious Background," *American Sociological Review*, 27 (April, 1962), pp. 205–217. See p. 207.

Rosen, Bernard C., "Socialization and Achievement Motivation in

Brazil," *American Sociological Review,* 27 (October, 1962), pp. 612–624. See p. 614.

Burnstein, Eugene, Robert Moulton, and Paul Liberty, "Prestige vs. Excellence as Determinants of Role Attractiveness," *American Sociological Review,* 28 (April, 1963), pp. 212–219. See p. 215.

Rosen, Bernard C., "The Achievement Syndrome and Economic Growth in Brazil," *Social Forces,* 42 (March, 1964), pp. 341–354. See pp. 344–345.

Kahl, Joseph A., "Some Measurements of Achievement Orientation," *American Journal of Sociology,* 70 (May, 1965), pp. 669–681. See p. 669.

4. ACHIEVEMENT ORIENTATION

Selvin, Hanan C., and Warren O. Hagstrom, "The Empirical Classification of Formal Groups," *American Sociological Review,* 28 (June, 1963), pp. 399–411. See p. 406.

5. ACHIEVEMENT ORIENTATION: ACCOMPLISHMENT

Cox, Henrietta, *Study of Social Class Variations in Value Orientation in Selected Areas of Mother-Child Behavior,* unpublished Ph.D. dissertation, Washington University, 1964.

Kahl (1965) p. 681; see category 3 above.

6. ACHIEVEMENT ORIENTATION: ACTIVISM

Strodtbeck, Fred L., "Family Interaction, Values, and Achievement," in David C. McClelland, Alfred L. Baldwin, Urie Bronfenbrenner, and Fred L. Strodtbeck, *Talent and Society,* Princeton, N.J.: D. Van Nostrand, 1958.

Cox (1964); see category 5 above.

Kahl (1965), pp. 674 and 681; see category 3 above.

7. ACHIEVEMENT ORIENTATION: INTEGRATION WITH RELATIVES

Strodtbeck (1958); see category 6 above.

Kahl (1965), pp. 674 and 680–681; see category 3 above.

8. ACHIEVEMENT ORIENTATION: OCCUPATIONAL PRIMACY

Kahl (1965), p. 679 and 680; see category 3 above.

9. ACHIEVEMENT ORIENTATION: TRUST

Cox (1964); see category 5 above.

Kahl (1965), p. 681; see category 3 above.

10. ACHIEVEMENT TRAINING

Winterbottom, Marian, *The Relationship of Childhood Training in Independence to Achievement Motivation*, unpublished Ph.D. dissertation, University of Michigan, 1953.

Rosen (1956), p. 211; see category 3 above.

Winterbottom, Marian, "The Relation of Need for Achievement to Learning Experiences in Independence and Mastery," in Atkinson (1958), pp. 453–478; see category 3 above.

Winterbottom's measure of achievement training has grown out of her investigations of David McClelland's hypotheses concerning "the number of experiences in independent mastery, the age at which the training is given, and the emotional accompaniments of the training as important conditions for the development of an achievement motive in the child." (1958, p. 454)

Following McClelland, Winterbottom hypothesized that high *n* Achievement is produced in the child by parental demands and rewards for early independence and mastery behavior. Data bearing on this hypothesis were gathered from a "demands" questionnaire "which included a list of twenty kinds of independence and mastery behaviors that [mothers] might consider as goals" of their training. (1958, p. 454) Mothers were asked to check each item which described a goal of her training and to state the age at which she expected each goal to have been reached. The "demands scale" (1958, p. 455) was as follows:

To stand up for his own rights with other children.
To know his way around his part of the city so that he can play where he wants without getting lost.
To go outside to play when he wants to be noisy or boisterous.
To be willing to try new things on his own without depending on his mother for help.
To be active and energetic in climbing, jumping and sports.
To show pride in his own ability to do things well.
To take part in his parents' interests and conversations.
To try hard things for himself without asking for help.
To be able to eat alone without help in cutting and handling food.
To be able to lead other children and assert himself in children's groups.
To make his own friends among children his own age.

To hang up his own clothes and look after his own possessions.
To do well in school on his own.
To be able to undress and go to bed by himself.
To have interests and hobbies of his own. To be able to entertain himself.
To earn his own spending money.
To do some regular tasks around the house.
To be able to stay alone at home during the day.
To make decisions like choosing his clothes or deciding how to spend his money by himself.
To do well in competition with other children. To try hard to come out on top in games and sports.

The demands scale may be scored for both the number of goals given and for the age at which such behavior is expected.

Two lists of possible parental emotional reactions also were utilized. These lists concerned what mothers did when their children did or did not fulfill their expectations. The "good" and "bad" performance lists (each of which was composed of three directional items and three neutral items) were as follows (1958, pp. 455–456):

["Good" List] Rewarding Reactions
    1. Kiss or hug him to show how pleased you are.
    2. Tell him what a good boy he is. Praise him for being good.
    3. Give him a special treat or privilege.
["Good" List] Relatively Neutral Reactions
    4. Do nothing at all to make it seem special.
    5. Show him you expected it of him.
    6. Show him how he could have done better.
["Bad" List] Punishing Reactions
    1. Scold or spank him for not doing it.
    2. Show him you are disappointed in him.
    3. Deprive him of something he likes or expects, like a special treat or privilege.
["Bad" List] Relatively Neutral Reactions
    4. Don't show any feeling about it.
    5. Point out how he should have behaved.
    6. Just wait until he does what you want.

Respondents were asked to make three choices from the six possible for each scale.

Winterbottom described two different measures which may

be obtained from the "good" and "bad" performance scales. The first measure was the number of rewards or punishments (which could vary from zero to three). The second measure was based on the assumption "that direct physical rewards or punishments are affectively more intense than less personal reactions" (1958, p. 456). The rewarding and punishing reactions were listed (as above) in their assumed order of intensity; however, each six-item scale was presented to respondents in randomized order.

Rosen (1959), p. 51; see category 3 above.

Rosen and D'Andrade (1959), p. 196; see category 3 above.

Rosen (1962), p. 617; see category 3 above.

11. ACHIEVEMENT VALUE (DECHARMS)

DeCharms, Richard C., H. William Morrison, Walter R. Reitman, and David C. McClelland, "Behavioral Correlates of Directly and Indirectly Measured Achievement Motivation," in David C. McClelland (ed.) (1955); see category 3 above.

Burnstein, Moulton, and Liberty (1963), p. 215; see category 3 above.

ANOMIA AND ALIENATION

1. ALIENATION (CLARK)

Clark, John P., "Measuring Alienation within a Social System," *American Sociological Review*, 24 (December, 1959), pp. 849–852. See p. 850.

2. ALIENATION (DAVIDS AND MODIFICATION)

Davids, Anthony, "Alienation, Social Apperception, and Ego Structure," *Journal of Consulting Psychology*, 19 (February, 1955), pp. 21–27. See pp. 21 and 24–26.

Davids, Anthony, "Generality and Consistency of Relations between the Alienation Syndrome and Cognitive Processes," *Journal of Abnormal and Social Psychology*, 51 (July, 1955), pp. 61–67. See pp. 63–65.

Struening, Elmer L., and Arthur H. Richardson, "A Factor Analytic Exploration of the Alienation, Anomia and Authoritarianism Domain," *American Sociological Review*, 30 (October, 1965), pp. 768–776. See pp. 772–775.

3. ALIENATION (DEAN) (SUBSCALES: POWERLESSNESS, NORMLESSNESS, SOCIAL ISOLATION)

Dean, Dwight G., "Alienation and Political Apathy," *Social Forces*, 38 (March, 1960), pp. 185–189. See p. 188.

Dean, Dwight G., "Alienation: Its Meaning and Measurement," *American Sociological Review*, 26 (October, 1961), pp. 753–758. See p. 757.

Dean, Dwight G. and Jon A. Reeves, "Anomie: A Comparison of a Catholic and Protestant Sample," *Sociometry*, 25 (June, 1962), pp. 209–212. See p. 210. (Only the Normlessness subscale is used here.)

Erbe, William, "Social Involvement and Political Activity: A Replication and Elaboration," *American Sociological Review*, 29 (April, 1964), pp. 198–215. See pp. 205–206.

4. ALIENATION (HAJDA)

Hajda, Jan, "Alienation and Integration of Student Intellectuals," *American Sociological Review*, 26 (October, 1961), pp. 758–777. See p. 764.

5. ALIENATION (LIVERANT, ROTTER, SEEMAN, AND NEAL, I-E POWERLESSNESS)

Rotter, Julian B., Melvin Seeman, and Shephard Liverant, "Internal vs. External Control of Reinforcements: A Major Variable in Behavior Theory," in Norman F. Washburne (ed.), *Decisions, Values and Groups*, Vol. 2, London: Pergamon Press, 1962, pp. 473–516.

Neal, Arthur G., and Melvin Seeman, "Organizations and Powerlessness: A Test of the Mediation Hypothesis," *American Sociological Review*, 29 (April, 1964), pp. 216–226. See p. 219.

Liverant, his colleagues, and his students see the powerlessness dimension of alienation as being related to the idea of internal-external control: ". . . internal control refers to the perception of positive and/or negative events as being a consequence of one's own actions and thereby under personal control. Whereas external control refers to the perception of positive and/or negative events as being unrelated to one's own behaviors in certain situations and therefore beyond control." (p. 499) Powerlessness, of course, would be directly related to the perception of external control and inversely related to the perception of internal control.

Internal- and external-control statements were created to fit into four specific need categories (academic recognition, social recognition, love and affection, and dominance) and two general classes (social-political and general life philosophy). An inventory of some 150 forced-choice items offering a contrast between internal and external control make up the scale, although all items are seldom used as a single scale. Rather, the numerous people working with this dimension have borrowed, modified and constructed alternative items, depending upon variations in particular research objectives and variant conceptions of the central empirical referents. Among the short forms of the I-E scale is the following, constructed by Neal and Seeman (1964).

THE POWERLESSNESS SCALE

This is a survey to find out what the public thinks about certain events which we face in our society. Each item consists of a pair of statements. Please select the one statement of each pair (*and only one*) which you more strongly believe to be true. Be sure to check the one you actually *believe* to be more nearly true, rather than the one you think you should check or the one you would like to be true. This is a measure of personal belief; obviously, there are no right or wrong answers. Again, be sure to make a choice between each pair of statements.

1. ___ I think we have adequate means for preventing run-away inflation.
   ___ There's very little we can do to keep prices from going higher.
2. ___ Persons like myself have little chance of protecting our personal interests when they conflict with those of strong pressure groups.
   ___ I feel that we have adequate ways of coping with pressure groups.
3. ___ A lasting world peace can be achieved by those of us who work toward it.
   ___ There's very little we can do to bring about a permanent world peace.
4. ___ There's very little persons like myself can do to improve world opinion of the United States.
   ___ I think each of us can do a great deal to improve world opinion of the United States.
5. ___ This world is run by the few people in power, and there is not much the little guy can do about it.
   ___ The average citizen can have an influence on government decisions.
6. ___ It is only wishful thinking to believe that one can really influence what happens in society at large.
   ___ People like me can change the course of world events if we make ourselves heard.
7. ___ More and more, I feel helpless in the face of what's happening in the world today.
   ___ I sometimes feel personally to blame for the sad state of affairs in our government.

Each of the seven items is scored dichotomously and the scores are summed. The powerlessness response is scored as "1" and the other response is scored as "0." A reproducibility coefficient of .87 (Guttman Scalogram Technique) was obtained for a community-wide sample (Columbus, Ohio) of 604 respondents.

Neal, Arthur, *Stratification Concomitants of Powerlessness and Normlessness: A Study of Political and Economic Alienation*, unpublished Ph.D. dissertation, Ohio State University, 1959.

Seeman, Melvin, and John Evans, "Alienation and Learning in a Hospital Setting," *American Sociological Review*, 27 (December, 1962), pp. 772–782. See pp. 774–775.

Neal, Arthur, and Salomon Rettig, "Dimensions of Alienation Among Manual and Non-Manual Workers," *American Sociological Review*, 28 (August, 1963), pp. 599–608. See p. 601.

Seeman, Melvin, "Alienation and Social Learning in a Reformatory," *American Journal of Sociology*, 69 (November, 1963), pp. 270–284. See pp. 272–273.

6. ALIENATION (MCCLOSKY, SCHAAR)

McClosky, Herbert, and John H. Schaar, "Psychological Dimensions of Anomy," *American Sociological Review*, 30 (February, 1965), pp. 14–40. See pp. 24, 30–31, and 37.

7. ALIENATION (MIDDLETON)

Middleton, Russell, "Alienation, Race and Education," *American Sociological Review*, 28 (December, 1963), pp. 973–977. See pp. 973–974.

8. ALIENATION (NETTLER)

Nettler, Gwynn, "A Measure of Alienation," *American Sociological Review*, 22 (December, 1957), pp. 670–677. See p. 675.

Nettler, Gwynn, Scales of Alienated Attitude, unpublished, 1964.

As used by Nettler, alienation is characteristic of an individual "who has been estranged from, made unfriendly toward, his society and the culture it carries."

Models of persons characterized by this alienated attitude were sought in the psychological literature and in belles lettres. Paradigmatic expressions of alienation were then typed on cards and presented to Nettler's colleagues and acquaintances who were asked if they knew any people, including themselves, to whom the descriptions applied. Confidential interviews were then arranged with 37 of these "known aliens." Questions were designed to "determine whether among these different individuals there was a common set of attitudes toward society and its members."

As originally set forth (1957), individuals were given single alienation scores. The revised scale (1964) measures four major cultural themes which are rejected by Nettler's "known aliens." Such people disdain mass culture, politics, religion, and "familism." Questions representing shorthand expressions of these alienated sentiments yield reliable, valid, and unidimensional scales when scored on a two-category basis. For 265 western Canadian subjects (1964) reproducibility coefficients ranged from .87 to .94.

The four subscales may be combined into a scale-of-scales that provides a measure of alienation useful for group-ordering purposes. The reported coefficient of reproducibility is 86.6 per cent; minimal marginal reproducibility is 69 per cent.

Response scores are simply summed. The higher the score the more alienated the respondent.

NETTLER'S SCALE OF ALIENATED ATTITUDE

Scale No. 1: Vs. Mass Culture (CR = 88.0%, MMR = 72.0%)

	Scale Value	
	yes	no
1. Do you read Reader's Digest?	0	1
2. Do national spectator sports (football, baseball, hockey) interest you?	0	1
	(disagree)	(agree)
3. "Our public education is in pretty sorry shape." Do you agree or disagree?	0	1
4. Do you enjoy TV?	0	1

Scale No. 2: Vs. Familism (CR = 87.0%, MMR = 72.0%)

5. Are you interested in having children? (Or would you be at the right age?)	0	1
	(married)	(single)
6. For yourself, assuming you could carry out your decision or do things over again, do you		

think a single life or a married life would be the more satisfactory?

0   1

(disagree)   *(agree)*

7. "If people really admitted the truth, they would agree that children are more often a nuisance than a pleasure to their parents." Do you agree or disagree?

0   1

8. Do you think most married people lead trapped (frustrated or miserable) lives?

0   1

Scale No. 3: A-Religiosity (CR = 94.0%, MMR = 67.0%)

(divine purpose)   *(chance)*

9. Do you believe human life is an expression of a divine purpose, or is it only the result of chance and evolution?

0   1

(truth)   *(myth)*

10. Do you think religion is mostly myth or mostly truth?

0   1

11. Do you participate in church activities?

0   1

Scale No. 4: A-Politicalism (CR = 91.5%, MMR = 72.7%)

12. Do you vote in national elections? (Or would you if of voting age?)

0   1

13. Are you generally interested in local (municipal and provincial or state) elections?

0   1

14. Looking backward, did the last national election in the United States (between Kennedy and Nixon) interest you?

0   1

(disagree)   *(agree)*

15. "In the long run, and with some rare exceptions, who gets elected, or doesn't hasn't the slightest influence upon social welfare." Do you agree or disagree?

0   1

Sommer, Robert, and Robert Hall, "Alienation and Mental Illness," *American Sociological Review*, 23 (August, 1958), pp. 418–420. See p. 418.

Nettler, Gwynn, "Antisocial Sentiment and Criminality," *American Sociological Review*, 24 (April, 1959), pp. 202–208. See p. 205.

Angell, Robert, "On Nettler's 'Antisocial Sentiment,'" *American Sociological Review*, 24 (August, 1959), p. 543.

Nettler, Gwynn, "Reply to Angell," *American Sociological Review*, 24 (August, 1959), pp. 543–544.

Simmons, J. L., "Tolerance of Divergent Attitudes," *Social Forces*, 43 (March, 1965), pp. 347–352. See p. 349.

9. ALIENATION (PEARLIN)

Pearlin, Leonard I., "Alienation from Work: A Study of Nursing Personnel," *American Sociological Review*, 27 (June, 1962), pp. 314–326. See p. 315.

Zurcher, Louis A., Jr., Arnold Meadow and Susan Lee Zurcher, "Value Orientation, Role Conflict and Alienation from Work: A Cross-Cultural Study," *American Sociological Review*, 30 (August, 1965), pp. 539–548. See pp. 542–544.

10. ALIENATION (FACTOR ANALYSIS)

(Alienation-related factors include alienation via rejection, conventionality, emotional distance, perceived purposelessness and self-determinism)

Struening and Richardson (1965), pp. 769–771; see category 2 above.

11. ANOMIA (PUTNEY, MIDDLETON)

Middleton, Russell, "Prejudice and Persuasion," *American Sociological Review*, 25 (October, 1960), pp. 679–686. See p. 681.

Putney, Snell, and Russell Middleton, "Dimensions and Correlates of Religious Ideologies," *Social Forces*, 39 (May, 1961), pp. 285–290. See p. 287.

Putney, Snell, and Russell Middleton, "Ethical Relativism and Anomia," *American Journal of Sociology*, 67 (January, 1962), pp. 430–438. See pp. 432–433.

12. ANOMIA-EUNOMIA (SROLE AND MODIFICATIONS)

Srole, Leo, "Social Dysfunction, Personality, and Social Distance Attitudes," paper read at the American Sociological Society meetings, Chicago, 1951.

Srole, Leo, "Social Integration and Certain Corollaries: An Exploratory Study," *American Sociological Review*, 21 (December, 1956), pp. 709–716. See p. 713.

The eunomia-anomia dimension, as conceived by Srole, refers to the "individual's generalized, pervasive sense of 'self-to-others belongingness' at one extreme compared with 'self-to-others distance' and 'self-to-others alienation' at the other pole of the continuum." The concept is seen as a "variable contemporary condition having its origin in the complex interaction of social and personality factors, present and past."

Although Srole has taken steps toward the purification and enlargement of the original scale, this analytical operation has not been completed. In the meantime, use of the original scale is supported by the large series of independent studies that have usefully applied it already (see the bibliography below).

The five items set forth below, each reflecting a different component of anomia, make up the scale.

THE ANOMIA SCALE

Now I'd like your opinions on a number of different things. I'm going to read you several statements. With each statement, some people agree and some people disagree. As I read each statement, will you tell me whether you *more* or *less* agree with it, or *more* or *less* disagree with it? For example, here is this statement:

1. Most public officials (people in public office) are not really interested in the problems of the average man. In general, would you agree with that statement or disagree?
2. These days a person doesn't really know whom he can count on.
3. Nowadays, a person has to live pretty much for today and let tomorrow take care of itself.
4. In spite of what some people say, the lot (situation) (condition) of the average man is getting worse, not better.
5. It's hardly fair to bring a child into the world with the way things look for the future.

Each "agree" response is given a score value of 1. Thus, respondent scores fall in a range from 0 to 5; the higher the score, the greater the anomia manifested by the respondent.

Srole has noted that ideally the items should have been so phrased that for half of them an anomic orientation would have required a "disagree" reply, but he felt that such wording would necessarily have taken the form of cultural cliches that would have elicited almost universal agreements. Thus, he suggests that the way out of the difficulty is to intersperse the items among a larger item series of *different* content, but of two format types:

1. Items bearing on recognizably controversial issues on which opinions tend to split evenly—to reinforce the point made in the instructions, "some people agree, some disagree."
2. Items that would predominantly tend to pull "disagree" responses.

He notes that the purpose of these tactics is to reduce the possibility that the respondent will operate under or develop an "acquiescence set."

Roberts, A. H., and Milton Rokeach, "Anomie, Authoritarianism and Prejudice: A Replication," *American Journal of Sociology*, 61 (January, 1956), pp. 355–358. See p. 357.

Bell, Wendell, "Anomie, Social Isolation, and the Class Structure," *Sociometry*, 20 (June, 1957), pp. 105–116. See pp. 106–107.

Freeman, Howard E., and Ozzie G. Simmons, "Wives, Mothers, and the Posthospital Performance of Mental Patients," *Social Forces*, 37 (December, 1958), pp. 153–159. See p. 156.

Rose, Arnold M., "Attitudinal Correlates of Social Participation," *Social Forces*, 37 (March, 1959), pp. 202–206. See pp. 203–204.

Meier, Dorothy L., and Wendell Bell, "Anomia and Differential Access to the Achievement of Life Goals," *American Sociological Review*, 24 (April, 1959), pp. 189–202. See p. 190.

Lenski, Gerhard E., and John C. Leggett, "Caste, Class, and Deference in the Research Interview," *American Journal of Sociology*, 65 (March, 1960), pp. 463–467. See pp. 464–465.

Mizruchi, Ephraim H., "Social Structure and Anomia in a Small City," *American Sociological Review*, 25 (October, 1960), pp. 645–654. See p. 647.

McDill, Edward L., "Anomie, Authoritarianism, Prejudice, and Socio-Economic Status: An Attempt at Clarification," *Social Forces*, 39 (March, 1961), pp. 239–245. See pp. 239–240.

Putney and Middleton (1962), p. 432; see category 11 above.

Weinstein, Eugene A., and Paul N. Geisel, "Family Decision Making over Desegregation," *Sociometry*, 25 (March, 1962), pp. 21–29. See p. 25.

Angell, Robert C., "Preferences for Moral Norms in Three Problem Areas," *American Journal of Sociology*, 67 (May, 1962), pp. 650–660. See pp. 650–651.

Killian, Lewis M., and Charles M. Grigg, "Urbanism, Race, and Anomia," *American Journal of Sociology*, 67 (May, 1962), pp. 661–665. See p. 661.

Photiadis, John D., and Jeanne Biggar, "Religiosity, Education, and Ethnic Distance," *American Journal of Sociology*, 67 (May, 1962), pp. 666–672. See p. 669.

McDill, Edward L., and Jeanne Clare Ridley, "Status, Anomia, Political Alienation, and Political Participation," *American Journal of Sociology*, 67 (September, 1962), pp. 205–213. See p. 208.

Carter, Roy E., Jr., and Peter Clarke, "Public Affairs Opinion Leadership among Educational Television Viewers," *American Sociological Review*, 27 (December, 1962), pp. 792–799. See p. 795.

Rose, Arnold M., "Alienation and Participation: A Comparison of Group Leaders and the 'Mass,' " *American Sociological Review*, 27 (December, 1962), pp. 834–838. See p. 836.

Blalock, H. M., Jr., "Making Causal Inferences for Unmeasured Variables from Correlations among Indicators," *American Journal of Sociology*, 69 (July, 1963), pp. 53–62. See p. 56.

Neal and Rettig (1963), p. 603; see category 5 above.

Photiadis, John D., and Arthur L. Johnson, "Orthodoxy, Church Participation, and Authoritarianism," *American Journal of Sociology*, 69 (November, 1963), pp. 244–248. See p. 244.

Lowenthal, Marjorie Fiske, "Social Integration and Mental Illness in Old Age," *American Sociological Review*, 29 (February, 1964), pp. 54–70. See p. 63.

Erbe (1964), p. 214; see category 3 above.

Neal and Seeman (1964), p. 220; see category 5 above.

Rhodes, Lewis, "Anomia, Aspiration, and Status," *Social Forces*, 42 (May, 1964), pp. 433–440. See p. 436.

Ehrlich, Howard J., "Instrument Error and the Study of Prejudice," *Social Forces*, 43 (December, 1964), pp. 197–206. See p. 200.

Struening and Richardson (1965), p. 769; see category 2 above.

Lipman, Aaron, and A. Eugene Havens, "The Colombian Violencia: An Ex Post Facto Experiment," *Social Forces*, 44 (December, 1965), pp. 238–245. See p. 240.

13. ANOMY (MCCLOSKY, SCHAAR)

McClosky and Schaar, pp. 23–25; see category 6 above.

14. ANTI-AUTHORITARIAN PESSIMISM

McDill (1961), p. 243; see category 12 above.

15. ECONOMIC NORMLESSNESS

Neal and Rettig (1963), p. 603; see category 5 above.

16. INEVITABILITY OF WAR

Neal and Rettig (1963), p. 604; see category 5 above.

17. MIDDLE-CLASS EUNOMIE

McDill (1961), p. 243; see category 12 above.

18. MIDDLE-CLASS MARITAL MORALITY

McDill (1961), p. 243; see category 12 above.

19. NEGATIVE WELTANSCHAUUNG

McDill (1961), p. 243; see category 12 above.

20. POLITICAL ALIENATION (THOMPSON, HORTON)

Thompson, Wayne E., and John E. Horton, "Political Alienation as a Force in Political Action," *Social Forces*, 38 (March, 1960), pp. 190–195. See pp. 191–192.

Horton, John E., and Wayne E. Thompson, "Powerlessness and Political Negativism: A Study of Defeated Local Referendums," *American Journal of Sociology*, 67 (March, 1962), pp. 485–493. See p. 489.

21. POLITICAL ALIENATION (QUINNEY)

Quinney, Richard, "Political Conservatism, Alienation, and Fatalism: Contingencies of Social Status and Religious Fundamen-

talism," *Sociometry*, 27 (September, 1964), pp. 372–378. See
p. 377.

22. POLITICAL ALIENATION (ZIMMER)

McDill and Ridley (1962), p. 208; see category 12 above.

23. POLITICAL NORMLESSNESS

Neal and Rettig (1963), p. 603; see category 5 above.

24. SOCIAL SELF-MAINTENANCE (MANY)

Many, Karen, "Indices of Social and Physical Self-Maintenance,"
Geriatrics Research Project Staff Memorandum, San Francisco, Calif.: Langley Porter Institute, June 14, 1961.

Lowenthal (1964), p. 63; see category 12 above.

ASPIRATIONS

SEE ALSO

Achievement Motivation
Personality: Motives and Needs
Values
Work-Value Orientations

1. AMBITION, COMPOSITE INDEX OF

Turner, Ralph H., "Some Aspects of Women's Ambition," *American Journal of Sociology*, 70 (November, 1964), pp. 271–285. See pp. 275–276 and 281.

2. ASPIRATION

Hollingshead, A. B., R. Ellis, and E. Kirby, "Social Mobility and Mental Illness," *American Sociological Review*, 19 (October, 1954), pp. 577–584. See p. 581.

3. ASPIRATIONS FOR RESPONSIBILITY IN WORK

Schwartz, Richard D., "Functional Alternatives to Inequality," *American Sociological Review*, 20 (August, 1955), pp. 424–430. See p. 430.

4. EDUCATIONAL ASPIRATION (NORTH, HATT)

N.O.R.C., "Jobs and Occupations: A Popular Evaluation," *Opinion News*, 9 (September, 1947), pp. 3–13.

Haller, A. O., and William H. Sewell, "Farm Residence and Levels of Educational and Occupational Aspiration," *American Journal of Sociology*, 62 (January, 1957), pp. 407–411. See p. 408.

5. EDUCATIONAL ASPIRATION, LEVEL OF

Haller, A. O., and C. E. Butterworth, "Peer Influences on Levels of Occupational and Educational Aspiration," *Social Forces*, 38 (May, 1960), pp. 289–302. See p. 292.

6. EDUCATIONAL ASPIRATION: ARITHMETIC TEST

Schiff, Herbert, "Judgmental Response Sets in the Perception of Sociometric Status," *Sociometry*, 17 (August, 1954), pp. 207–227. See p. 213.

7. EDUCATIONAL ASPIRATION: DIGIT SYMBOL TEST

Schiff; see category 6 above.

8. EDUCATIONAL ASPIRATION: READING SPEED

Schiff; see category 6 above.

9. EDUCATIONAL ASPIRATION: WIFE'S FOR HUSBAND

Turner; see category 1 above.

10. EXPECTATIONS, PLANS, AND ASPIRATIONS FOR THE FUTURE (GILLESPIE, ALLPORT)

Gillespie, J. M., and Gordon W. Allport, *Youth's Outlook on the Future*, New York: Doubleday, 1955.

Danziger, K., "The Psychological Future of an Oppressed Group," *Social Forces*, 42 (October, 1963), pp. 31–40. See p. 32.

11. GOAL DISCREPANCY

Schiff, p. 214; see category 6 above.

12. GRADES EVALUATION, CHANGE IN, AMONG FRESHMEN

Wallace, Walter L., "Institutional and Life-Cycle Socialization of College Freshmen," *American Journal of Sociology*, 70 (November, 1964), pp. 303–318. See p. 306.

13. GRADUATE ASPIRATIONS, CHANGE IN

Wallace; see category 12 above.

14. MATERIAL ASPIRATION

Turner; see category 1 above.

15. MATERIAL-EDUCATION POLARIZATION

Turner; see category 1 above.

16. MOBILITY ASPIRATION (NORTH, HATT)

N.O.R.C. (1947); see category 4 above.

Reissman, L., *Class in American Society*, New York: The Free Press of Glencoe, 1959, pp. 401–404.

Gist, Noel P., and William S. Bennett, Jr., "Aspirations of Negro and White Students," *Social Forces*, 42 (October, 1963), pp. 40–48. See p. 43.

17. MOTHER'S ASPIRATION FOR HER SON (NORTH, HATT)

N.O.R.C. (1947); see category 4 above.

Rosen, Bernard C., "Race, Ethnicity, and the Achievement Syndrome," *American Sociological Review*, 24 (February, 1959), pp. 47–60. See p. 59.

18. OCCUPATIONAL ASPIRATION (HALLER)

Haller, A. O., *Occupational Aspiration Scale*, East Lansing, Mich.: Michigan State University, 1957.

Miller, I. W., Jr., "Normalized Data for the OAS Raw Scores," mimeographed, East Lansing, Mich.: Social Research Service of Michigan State University, April, 1958.

Haller, A. O., "Planning to Farm: A Social Psychological Interpretation," *Social Forces*, 37 (March, 1959), pp. 263–268. See p. 266.

Haller and Butterworth; see category 5 above.

19. OCCUPATIONAL ASPIRATION (NORTH, HATT)

N.O.R.C. (1947); see category 4 above.

Haller and Sewell (1957); see category 4 above.

20. OCCUPATIONAL ASPIRATION (REISSMAN)

Reissman, L., "Level of Aspiration and Social Class," *American Sociological Review*, 18 (June, 1953), pp. 233–242. See p. 239–240.

Dynes, Russell R., Alfred C. Clarke, and Simon Dinitz, "Levels of Occupational Aspiration: Some Aspects of Family Experience as a Variable," *American Sociological Review*, 21 (April, 1956), pp. 212–215. See p. 212.

21. OCCUPATIONAL ASPIRATION (WILENSKY)

Wilensky, Harold L., "Mass Society and Mass Culture: Interdependence or Independence?" *American Sociological Review*, 29 (April, 1964), pp. 173–197. See p. 185.

22. OCCUPATIONAL ASPIRATION: WIFE'S FOR HUSBAND

Turner; see category 1 above.

23. PARENTAL ASPIRATIONAL MOTIVATIONS (HOLLINGSHEAD)

Hollingshead, August B., *Two-Factor Index of Social Position*, New Haven: privately mimeographed, 1957.

Bell, Gerald D., "Processes in the Formation of Adolescents' Aspirations," *Social Forces*, 42 (December, 1963), pp. 179–186. See p. 183.

24. PARENTAL DESIRE FOR HIGH ACHIEVEMENT

Haller and Butterworth; see category 5 above.

25. PARENTS' EDUCATIONAL ASPIRATIONS FOR CHILDREN

Westoff, Charles F., Marvin Bressler, and Philip C. Sagi, "The Concept of Social Mobility: An Empirical Inquiry," *American Sociological Review*, 25 (June, 1960), pp. 375–385. See p. 381.

26. PARENTS' REPORTED EDUCATIONAL ASPIRATION FOR CHILDREN

Haller (1959), p. 265; see category 18 above.

27. REALISTIC ASPIRATION SCORE

Empey, Lamar T., "Social Class and Occupational Aspiration: A Comparison of Absolute and Relative Measurement," *American Sociological Review*, 21 (December, 1956), pp. 703–709. See p. 708.

28. SOCIAL ASPIRATION

Rosengren, William R., "Social Sources of Pregnancy as Illness or Normality," *Social Forces*, 39 (March, 1961), pp. 260–267. See p. 262.

29. SOCIAL STATUS ASPIRATIONS

Westoff, Bressler, and Sagi; see category 25 above.

30. STATUS ASPIRATION, COMPOSITE INDEX OF

Swinehart, James W., "Socio-economic Level, Status Aspiration, and Maternal Role," *American Sociological Review*, 28 (June, 1963), pp. 391–399. See p. 393.

31. STATUS ASPIRATION: EDUCATIONAL DISCREPANCY

Swinehart; see category 30 above.

32. STATUS ASPIRATION: OCCUPATIONAL DISCREPANCY

Swinehart; see category 30 above.

33. STATUS ASPIRATION: SATISFACTION WITH NEIGHBORHOOD

Swinehart; see category 30 above.

34. STUDENT ASPIRATION LEVEL

Bell (1963); see category 23 above.

35. WIFE'S PERCEPTION OF HUSBAND'S MOBILITY OPPORTUNITY

Westoff, Bressler, and Sagi; see category 25 above.

ASSIMILATION

SEE ALSO

Intergroup Relations, Racial and Ethnic: Prejudice and Social Distance

1. ACCULTURATION

Roy, Prodipto, "The Measurement of Assimilation: The Spokane Indians," *American Journal of Sociology*, 67 (March, 1962), pp. 541–551. See pp. 542–543.

2. AMALGAMATION

Roy; see category 1 above.

3. AMERICANIZATION, INDICES OF

Iga, Mamoru, "The Japanese Social Structure and the Source of Mental Strains of Japanese Immigrants in the United States," *Social Forces*, 35 (March, 1957), pp. 271–278. See p. 272.

4. ASSIMILATION

Kwan, Kian M., *Assimilation of the Chinese in the United States: An Exploratory Study in California*, unpublished Ph.D. dissertation, University of California, Berkeley, 1958.

Fong, Stanley L. M., "Assimilation of Chinese in America: Changes in Orientation and Social Perception," *American Journal of Sociology*, 71 (November, 1965), pp. 265–275. See p. 268.

5. ASSIMILATION-ORIENTATION INVENTORY

Fong (1965); see category 4 above.

6. AUTHORITY OF THE SOCIALLY SUPERIOR

Iga; see category 3 above.

7. COLLECTIVITY ORIENTATION

Iga; see category 3 above.

8. CONFORMITY TO CUSTOMS

Iga; see category 3 above.

9. CONTACT WITH THE UNITED STATES, INDEX OF

Form, William H., and Julius Rivera, "Work Contacts and International Evaluations: The Case of a Mexican Border Village," *Social Forces*, 37 (May, 1959), pp. 334–339. See pp. 335–336.

10. INTERMARRIAGE, INDEX OF

Savorgnan, Franco, "Matrimonial Selection and the Amalgamation of Heterogeneous Groups," *Population Studies*, supplement (March, 1950), pp. 59–67.

Hutchinson, Bertram, "Some Evidence Related to Matrimonial Selection and Immigrant Assimilation in Brazil," *Population Studies*, 11 (November, 1957), pp. 149–156.

Lieberson, Stanley, "The Old-New Distinction and Immigrants in Australia," *American Sociological Review*, 28 (August, 1963), pp. 550–565.

11. JAPANESENESS

Uyeki, Eugene S., "Correlates of Ethnic Identification," *American Journal of Sociology*, 65 (March, 1960), pp. 468–474. See pp. 469–470.

12. MARRIAGE PATTERN

Iga; see category 3 above.

13. OBLIGATION AND EXTERNAL SANCTION

Iga; see category 3 above.

14. PATERNAL AUTHORITY

Iga; see category 3 above.

15. SEX FORMALITY

Iga; see category 3 above.

16. SOCIAL INTEGRATION

Roy; see category 1 above.

AUTHORITARIANISM

1. CALIFORNIA F SCALE AND MODIFICATIONS

Adorno, Theodor W., Else Frenkel-Brunswik, Daniel J. Levinson, and R. Nevitt Sanford, *The Authoritarian Personality*, New York: Harper and Brothers, 1950, pp. 222–279.

The frequently used California F Scale was developed on the basis of a set of hypotheses which emerged from the investigation of ethnocentrism and anti-Semitism. The original motivation underlying the construction of the F Scale was the desire to "measure prejudice without appearing to have this aim and without mentioning the name of any minority group." (p. 222) Consideration of this problem led the researchers to study a more fundamental issue: "At this point the second—and major—purpose of the new scale began to take shape. Might not such a scale yield a valid estimate of antidemocratic tendencies at the personality level?" (pp. 222–223) The second objective did not supersede the first in the minds of the researchers. Rather, the attempt was made to achieve the first goal by realizing the second objective.

The instrument is not strictly unidimensional in the usual meaning of this measurement concept. Instead, the effort was made to tap nine central "personality trends." These variables, along with the authors' definitions of them, were as follows:

a. *Conventionalism*—rigid adherence to conventional, middle-class values.
b. *Authoritarian Submission*—submissive, uncritical attitude toward idealized moral authorities of the in-group.
c. *Authoritarian Aggression*—tendency to be on the lookout for, and to

condemn, reject, and punish people who violate conventional values.

d. *Anti-intraception*—opposition to the subjective, the imaginative, the tender-minded.

e. *Superstition and Stereotypy*—the belief in mystical determinants of the individual's fate; the disposition to think in rigid categories.

f. *Power and "Toughness"*—preoccupations with the dominance-submission, strong-weak, leader-follower dimension; identification with power figures; overemphasis upon the conventional attributes of the ego; exaggerated assertion of strength and toughness.

g. *Destructiveness and Cynicism*—generalized hostility; vilification of the human.

h. *Projectivity*—the disposition to believe that wild and dangerous things go on in the world; the projection outwards of unconscious emotional impulses.

i. *Sex*—exaggerated concern with sexual "goings-on."

The discussion in *The Authoritarian Personality* includes three forms of this scale (Form 78, Form 60, and Forms 45 and 40 combined). Most of the studies employing the instrument have relied on all or part of the combined Forms 45 and 40, and it is this set of items which is reported below. Shorter forms for measuring authoritarianism have been devised (see, for example, Sanford and Older, 1950, below), and several critical studies of the original instrument have been reported (see, for example, Camilleri, 1959, below). Despite the modifications and criticisms that have been offered, the original items continue to be used heavily.

The original authors report reliabilities ranging from .81 to .97 with the average reliability being .90. The F Scale also correlates highly with the California Ethnocentrism and Anti-Semitism Scales. (See, for example, Christie and Jahoda, 1954, and Christie, Havel, and Seidenberg, 1958, below.)

The items included in the F Scale have been used with a variety of introductions and with several methods of obtaining responses. In the following reporting of the scale, the introduction originally employed is presented along with a response procedure that has been found useful by several researchers. The items are clustered according to the dimension they reportedly tap. In the actual use of the scale, these items should be randomized. Nonresponse to a particular item is scored "0."

THE F SCALE (FORMS 40 AND 45)

SURVEY OF GENERAL PUBLIC OPINION: INSTRUCTIONS

We are trying to find out what the general public feels and thinks about a number of important social questions.

We are sure you will find the enclosed survey interesting. You will find in it many questions and social issues which you have thought about, read about in newspapers and magazines, and heard about on the radio.

This is *not* an *intelligence test* nor an information test. There are no "right" or "wrong" answers. The best answer is *your personal opinion*. You can be sure that, whatever your opinion may be on a certain issue, there will be many people who agree, many who disagree. And this is what we want to find out: how is public opinion really divided on each of these socially important topics?

It must be emphasized that the sponsors of this survey do not necessarily agree or disagree with the statements in it. *We have tried to cover a great many points of view.* We agree with some of the statements, and disagree with others. Similarly, you will probably find yourself agreeing strongly with some statements, disagreeing just as strongly with others, and being perhaps more neutral about still others.

We realize that people are very busy nowadays, and we don't want to take too much of your time. All that we ask is that you:

(a) Read each statement carefully and mark it according to your first reaction. It isn't necessary to take a lot of time for any one question.

(b) *Answer every question.*

(c) *Give your personal point of view.* Don't talk the questions over with anyone until you have finished.

(d) Be as *sincere, accurate,* and *complete* as possible in the limited time and space.

This survey works just like a Gallup Poll or an election. As in any other secret ballot, the "voters" who fill it out do not have to give their names.

Mark each statement in the left margin according to how much you agree or disagree with it. Please mark every one. Write $+1, +2, +3,$ or $-1, -2, -3,$ depending on how you feel in each case.

$+1$: I agree a little -1: I disagree a little
$+2$: I agree on the whole -2: I disagree on the whole
$+3$: I agree very much -3: I disagree very much

a. *Conventionalism*

1. Obedience and respect for authority are the most important virtues children should learn.

2. A person who has bad manners, habits, and breeding can hardly expect to get along with decent people.
3. If people would talk less and work more, everybody would be better off.
4. The businessman and the manufacturer are much more important to society than the artist and the professor.

b. *Authoritarian Submission*

5. Obedience and respect for authority are the most important virtues children should learn.
6. Science has its place, but there are many important things that can never possibly be understood by the human mind.
7. Every person should have complete faith in some supernatural power whose decisions he obeys without question.
8. Young people sometimes get rebellious ideas, but as they grow up they ought to get over them and settle down.
9. What this country needs most, more than laws and political programs, is a few courageous, tireless, devoted leaders in whom the people can put their faith.
10. No sane, normal, decent person could ever think of hurting a close friend or relative.
11. Nobody ever learned anything really important except through suffering.

c. *Authoritarian Aggression*

12. A person who has bad manners, habits, and breeding can hardly expect to get along with decent people.
13. What the youth needs most is strict discipline, rugged determination, and the will to work and fight for family and country.
14. An insult to our honor should always be punished.
15. Sex crimes, such as rape and attacks on children, deserve more than mere imprisonment; such criminals ought to be publicly whipped, or worse.
16. There is hardly anything lower than a person who does not feel a great love, gratitude, and respect for his parents.
17. Most of our social problems would be solved if we could somehow get rid of the immoral, crooked, and feebleminded people.
18. If people would talk less and work more, everybody would be better off.
19. Homosexuals are hardly better than criminals and ought to be severely punished.

d. *Anti-intraception*

20. When a person has a problem or worry, it is best for him not to think about it, but to keep busy with more cheerful things.

21. Nowadays more and more people are prying into matters that should remain personal and private.
22. If people would talk less and work more, everybody would be better off.
23. The businessman and the manufacturer are much more important to society than the artist and the professor.

e. *Superstition and Stereotypy*

24. Science has its place, but there are many important things that can never possibly be understood by the human mind.
25. Every person should have complete faith in some supernatural power whose decisions he obeys without question.
26. Some people are born with an urge to jump from high places.
27. People can be divided into two distinct classes: the weak and the strong.
28. Some day it will probably be shown that astrology can explain a lot of things.
29. Wars and social troubles may some day be ended by an earthquake or flood that will destroy the whole world.

f. *Power and "Toughness"*

30. No weakness or difficulty can hold us back if we have enough will power.
31. What the youth needs most is strict discipline, rugged determination, and the will to work and fight for family and country.
32. An insult to our honor should always be punished.
33. It is best to use some prewar authorities in Germany to keep order and prevent chaos.
34. What this country needs most, more than laws and political programs, is a few courageous, tireless, devoted leaders in whom the people can put their faith.
35. People can be divided into two distinct classes: the weak and the strong.
36. Most people don't realize how much our lives are controlled by plots hatched in secret places.

g. *Destructiveness and Cynicism*

37. Human nature being what it is, there will always be war and conflict.
38. Familiarity breeds contempt.

h. *Projectivity*

39. Nowadays when so many different kinds of people move around and mix together so much, a person has to protect himself especially carefully against catching an infection or disease from them.

40. Nowadays more and more people are prying into matters that should remain personal and private.
41. Wars and social troubles may some day be ended by an earthquake or flood that will destroy the whole world.
42. The wild sex life of the old Greeks and Romans was tame compared to some of the goings-on in this country, even in places where people might least expect it.
43. Most people don't realize how much our lives are controlled by plots hatched in secret places.

i. *Sex*

44. Sex crimes, such as rape and attacks on children, deserve more than mere imprisonment; such criminals ought to be publicly whipped, or worse.
45. The wild sex life of the old Greeks and Romans was tame compared to some of the goings-on in this country, even in places where people might least expect it.
46. Homosexuals are hardly better than criminals and ought to be severely punished.

In the preceding listing of items, a number of items appear under more than one category. In the following table, the first place an item appears is given under the heading, "Original Item." Repetitions of this item are listed under "Repeated Item."

Original Item	Repeated Item	Original Item	Repeated Item
1	5	14	32
2	12	15	44
3	18, 22	19	46
4	23	21	40
6	24	27	35
7	25	29	41
9	34	36	43
13	31	42	45

Sanford, Fillmore H., and H. J. Older, A *Short Authoritarian-Equalitarian Scale*, Progress Report No. 6, Series A., Philadelphia: Institute for Research in Human Relations, 1950.

Srole, Leo, "Social Dysfunction, Personality, and Social Distance Attitudes," paper read before the American Sociological Society, Chicago, 1951.

Christie, Richard, and J. Garcia, "Subcultural Variation in Authoritarian Personality," *Journal of Abnormal and Social Psychology*, 46 (October, 1951), pp. 457–469. See p. 458.

Christie, Richard, "Changes in Authoritarianism as Related to Situational Factors," *American Psychologist*, 7 (October, 1952), pp. 307–308.

Eager, Joan, and M. B. Smith, "A Note on the Validity of Sanford's Authoritarian-Equalitarian Scale," *Journal of Abnormal and Social Psychology*, 47 (April, 1952), pp. 265–267.

Christie, Richard, and Marie Jahoda, *Studies in the Scope and Method of "The Authoritarian Personality,"* Glencoe, Ill.: The Free Press, 1954.

O'Neil, W. M., and Daniel J. Levinson, "A Factorial Exploration of Authoritarianism and Some of Its Ideological Concomitants," *Journal of Personality*, 22 (June, 1954), pp. 449–463. See pp. 451–456.

Hollander, E. P., "Authoritarianism and Leadership Choice in a Military Setting," *Journal of Abnormal and Social Psychology*, 49 (July, 1954), pp. 365–370. See p. 365.

Allen, Dean A., "Antifemininity in Men," *American Sociological Review*, 19 (October, 1954), pp. 591–593. See p. 591.

Bass, Bernard M., "Authoritarianism or Acquiescence," *Journal of Abnormal and Social Psychology*, 51 (November, 1955), pp. 616–623. See p. 616.

Roberts, Alan H., and Milton Rokeach, "Anomie, Authoritarianism, and Prejudice: A Replication," *American Journal of Sociology*, 61 (January, 1956), pp. 355–358. See p. 357.

MacKinnon, William J., and Richard Centers, "Authoritarianism and Urban Stratification," *American Journal of Sociology*, 61 (May, 1956), pp. 610–620. See p. 611.

Srole, Leo, "Social Integration and Certain Corollaries: An Exploratory Study," *American Sociological Review*, 21 (December, 1956), pp. 709–716. See p. 713.

Sutcliffe, J. P., and M. Haberman, "Factors Influencing Choice in Role Conflict Situations," *American Sociological Review*, 21 (December, 1956), pp. 695–703. See p. 700.

Chapman, Loren J., and Donald T. Campbell, "Response Set in the F Scale," *Journal of Abnormal and Sociol Psychology*, 54 (January, 1957), pp. 129–132. See p. 129.

Jackson, Douglas N., and Samuel J. Messick, "A Note on 'Ethnocentrism' and Acquiescent Response Sets," *Journal of Abnormal and Social Psychology*, 54 (January, 1957), pp. 132–134. See pp. 132–133.

Jackson, Douglas N., Samuel J. Messick, and Charles M. Solley, "How Rigid Is the Authoritarian?" *Journal of Abnormal and Social Psychology*, 54 (January, 1957), pp. 137–140. See p. 138.

Kaufman, Walter C., "Status, Authoritarianism, and Anti-Semitism," *American Journal of Sociology*, 62 (January, 1957), pp. 379–382. See p. 381.

Campbell, Donald T., and Thelma H. McCormack, "Military Experience and Attitudes toward Authority," *American Journal of Sociology*, 62 (March, 1957), pp. 482–490. See pp. 482–483.

Pettigrew, Thomas F., "Desegregation and Its Chances for Success: Northern and Southern Views," *Social Forces*, 35 (May, 1957), pp. 339–344. See p. 339.

Smith, Charles U., and James W. Prothro, "Ethnic Differences in Authoritarian Personality," *Social Forces*, 35 (May, 1957), pp. 334–338. See pp. 334–335.

MacKinnon, William J., and Richard Centers, "Social-Psychological Factors in Public Orientation Toward an Outgroup," *American Journal of Sociology*, 63 (January, 1958), pp. 415–419. See p. 416.

Christie, Richard, Joan Havel, and Bernard Seidenberg, "Is the F Scale Irreversible?" *Journal of Abnormal and Social Psychology*, 56 (March, 1958), pp. 143–159. See p. 143.

Pettigrew, Thomas F., "Personality and Sociocultural Factors in Intergroup Attitudes: A Cross-National Comparison," *Journal of Conflict Resolution*, 2 (March, 1958), pp. 29–42. See p. 33.

Freeman, Howard E., and Ozzie G. Simmons, "Mental Patients in the Community: Family Settings and Performance Levels," *American Sociological Review*, 23 (April, 1958), pp. 147–154. See p. 150.

Chapman, Loren J., and Darrell R. Bock, "Components of Variance Due to Acquiescence and Content in the F Scale Measure of Authoritarianism," *Psychological Bulletin*, 55 (September, 1958), pp. 328–333. See p. 328.

Freeman, Howard E., and Ozzie G. Simmons, "Wives, Mothers, and the Posthospital Performance of Mental Patients," *Social Forces*, 37 (December, 1958), pp. 153–159. See pp. 156–158.

Camilleri, Santo F., "A Factor Analysis of the F-Scale," *Social Forces*, 37 (May, 1959), pp. 316–323. See p. 316.

Chapman, Loren J., and Donald T. Campbell, "The Effect of Acquiescence Response-Sets upon Relationships among the F Scale, Ethnocentrism, and Intelligence," *Sociometry*, 22 (June, 1959), pp. 153–161. See p. 154.

Middleton, Russell, "Negro and White Reactions to Racial Humor," *Sociometry*, 22 (June, 1959), pp. 175–183. See p. 177.

Lipset, Seymour Martin, "Democracy and Working-Class Authoritarianism," *American Sociological Review*, 24 (August, 1959), pp. 482–501. See pp. 486–487.

Martin, James G., and Frank R. Westie, "The Tolerant Personality," *American Sociological Review*, 24 (August, 1959), pp. 521–528. See p. 525.

Harvey, O. J., "Reciprocal Influence of the Group and Three Types of Leaders in an Unstructured Situation," *Sociometry*, 23 (March, 1960), pp. 57–68. See p. 60.

Mogar, Robert E., "Three Versions of the F Scale and Performance on the Semantic Differential," *Journal of Abnormal and Social Psychology*, 60 (March, 1960), pp. 262–265.

Pettigrew, Thomas F., "Social Distance Attitudes of South African Students," *Social Forces*, 38 (March, 1960), pp. 246–253. See p. 249.

Small, Donald O., and Donald T. Campbell, "The Effect of Acquiescence Response-Set Upon the Relationship of the F

Scale and Conformity," *Sociometry*, 23 (March, 1960), pp. 69–71. See p. 70.

Friedrich S., Robert W., "Alter Versus Ego: An Exploratory Assessment of Altruism," *American Sociological Review*, 25 (August, 1960), pp. 496–508. See p. 499.

Glaser, William A., "Doctors and Politics," *American Journal of Sociology*, 66 (November, 1960), pp. 230–245. See p. 242.

McDill, Edward L., "Anomie, Authoritarianism, Prejudice, and Socioeconomic Status: An Attempt at Clarification," *Social Forces*, 39 (March, 1961), pp. 239–245. See p. 240.

Putney, Snell, and Russell Middleton, "Dimensions and Correlates of Religious Ideologies," *Social Forces*, 39 (May, 1961), pp. 285–290. See p. 287.

Dean, Dwight G., "Alienation: Its Meaning and Measurement," *American Sociological Review*, 26 (October, 1961), pp. 753–758. See p. 756.

Fishman, Joshua A., "Some Social and Psychological Determinants of Intergroup Relations in Changing Neighborhoods," *Social Forces*, 40 (October, 1961), pp. 42–51. See p. 47.

Photiadis, John D., and Jeanne Biggar, "Religiosity, Education, and Ethnic Distance," *American Journal of Sociology*, 67 (May, 1962), pp. 666–672. See p. 669.

Rhyne, Edwin Hoffman, "Racial Prejudice and Personality Scales: An Alternative Approach," *Social Forces*, 41 (October, 1962), pp. 44–53. See pp. 45–48.

Steiner, Ivan D., and Homer H. Johnson, "Authoritarianism and Conformity," *Sociometry*, 26 (March, 1963), pp. 21–34. See p. 23.

Photiadis, John D., and Arthur L. Johnson, "Orthodoxy, Church Participation, and Authoritarianism," *American Journal of Sociology*, 69 (November, 1963), pp. 244–248. See p. 244.

Bell, Gerald D., "Processes in the Formation of Adolescents' Aspirations," *Social Forces*, 42 (December, 1963), pp. 179–186. See p. 182.

Berkowitz, Norman H., and George H. Wolkon, "A Forced Choice Form of the F Scale—Free of Acquiescent Response

Set," *Sociometry*, 27 (March, 1964), pp. 54–65. See pp. 55–59.

Kutner, Bernard, and Norman B. Gordon, "Cognitive Functioning and Prejudice: A Nine-Year Follow-Up Study," *Sociometry*, 27 (March, 1964), pp. 66–74. See p. 68.

Tuckman, Bruce W., "Personality Structure, Group Composition and Group Functioning," *Sociometry*, 27 (December, 1964), pp. 469–487. See p. 478.

Lipsitz, Lewis, "Working-Class Authoritarianism: A Re-evaluation," *American Sociological Review*, 30 (February, 1965), pp. 103–109. See pp. 105 and 107.

Struening, Elmer L., and Arthur H. Richardson, "A Factor Analytic Exploration of the Alienation, Anomia and Authoritarianism Domain," *American Sociological Review*, 30 (October, 1965), pp. 768–776. See p. 769.

2. EQUALITARIANISM-AUTHORITARIANISM

Adams, Stuart, "Social Climate and Productivity in Small Military Groups," *American Sociological Review*, 19 (August, 1954), pp. 421–425. See p. 422.

3. FASCISM

McClosky, Herbert, and John H. Schaar, "Psychological Dimensions of Anomy," *American Sociological Review*, 30 (February, 1965), pp. 14–40. See pp. 32–33.

4. INTOLERANCE OF AMBIGUITY (MCCLOSKY, SCHAAR)

McClosky and Schaar, pp. 28–29, 35, 37 and 38; see category 3 above.

5. INTOLERANCE OF AMBIGUITY (WEBSTER, SANFORD, FREEDMAN)

Webster, Harold, R. Nevitt Sanford, and Mervin Freedman, "A New Instrument for Studying Authoritarianism," *Journal of Psychology*, 40 (July, 1955), pp. 73–84. See pp. 77–81.

Harvey, O. J., "Reciprocal Influence of the Group and Three Types of Leaders in an Unstructured Situation," *Sociometry*, 23 (March, 1960), pp. 57–68. See p. 60.

Harvey, O. J., "Personality Factors in Resolution of Conceptual

Incongruities," *Sociometry*, 25 (December, 1962), pp. 336–352. See p. 339.

6. RELIGIOUS AUTHORITARIANISM

Allen, Mark K., *Personality and Cultural Factors Related to Religious Authoritarianism*, unpublished Ph.D. dissertation, Stanford University, 1955.

Canning, Ray R., and James M. Baker, "Effect of the Group on Authoritarian and Non-Authoritarian Persons," *American Journal of Sociology*, 64 (May, 1959), pp. 579–581. See p. 580.

AUTHORITY: ATTITUDES TOWARD AND CHARACTERISTICS OF

SEE ALSO

Complex Organizations: Attitudes toward and Perceptions of

Complex Organizations: Characteristics of

Leadership, Community and Organizational: Behavior and Characteristics of

Leadership, Community and Organizational: Identification of

Leadership, Small Group: Identification of

1. AUTHORITY (BORGATTA)

Borgatta, Edgar F., "Attitudinal Concomitants to Military Statuses," *Social Forces*, 33 (May, 1955), pp. 342–347. See p. 345.

2. AUTHORITY (WILENSKY)

Wilensky, Harold L., "Orderly Careers and Social Participation: The Impact of Work History on Social Integration in the Middle Mass," *American Sociological Review*, 26 (August, 1961), pp. 521–539. See p. 529.

3. AUTHORITY, ATTRIBUTED

Grusky, Oscar, "A Case for the Theory of Familial Role Differentiation in Small Groups," *Social Forces*, 35 (March, 1957), pp. 209–217. See pp. 212–213.

4. AUTHORITY, BYPASS OF

Borgatta; see category 1 above.

5. AUTHORITY, GENERAL

Freeman, Howard E., and H. Ashley Weeks, "Analysis of a Program of Treatment of Delinquent Boys," *American Journal of Sociology*, 62 (July, 1956), pp. 56–61. See p. 58.

6. AUTHORITY, GENERALIZED ACQUIESCENCE WITH

Abegglen, James C., "Subordination and Autonomy Attitudes of Japanese Workers," *American Journal of Sociology*, 63 (September, 1957), pp. 181–189. See p. 182.

7. AUTHORITY, HIERARCHY OF

Hall, Richard H., *An Empirical Study of Bureaucratic Dimensions and Their Relation to Other Organizational Characteristics*, unpublished Ph.D. dissertation, Ohio State University, 1961.

Hall, Richard H., "The Concept of Bureaucracy: An Empirical Assessment," *American Journal of Sociology*, 69 (July, 1963), pp. 32–40. See p. 35.

8. AUTHORITY, OBEISANCE TO

Pearlin, Leonard I., and Morris Rosenberg, "Nurse-Patient Social Distance and the Structural Context of a Mental Hospital," *American Sociological Review*, 27 (February, 1962), pp. 56–65. See p. 61.

9. AUTHORITY RELATIONS, EXPECTED

Turk, Herman, "Social Cohesion through Variant Values: Evidence from Medical Role Relations," *American Sociological Review*, 28 (February, 1963), pp. 28–37. See p. 34.

Turk, Herman, and G. Robert Wills, "Authority and Interaction," *Sociometry*, 27 (March, 1964), pp. 1–18. See p. 6.

10. CENTRALIZATION (VOLUNTARY ASSOCIATIONS)

Simpson, Richard L., and William H. Gulley, "Goals, Environmental Pressures, and Organizational Characteristics," *American Sociological Review*, 27 (June, 1962), pp. 344–351. See p. 348.

11. CONTROL

Tannenbaum, Arnold S., "Control and Effectiveness in a Voluntary Organization," *American Journal of Sociology*, 57 (July, 1961), pp. 33–46. See p. 39.

12. CONTROL, ACTIVE

Tannenbaum, Arnold S., and Basil S. Georgopoulos, "The Distribution of Control in Formal Organizations," *Social Forces*, 36 (October, 1957), pp. 44–50. See p. 46.

13. CONTROL, ORIENTATION OF

Tannenbaum and Georgopoulos, p. 48; see category 12 above.

14. CONTROL, PASSIVE

Tannenbaum and Georgopoulos; see category 12 above.

15. CONTROL, SOURCE OF

Tannenbaum and Georgopoulos, p. 48; see category 12 above.

16. DECISION CENTRALITY

Mulder, Mauk, "Communication Structure, Decision Structure and Group Performance," *Sociometry*, 23 (March, 1960), pp. 1–14. See p. 4.

17. DISCIPLINE-INITIATIVE

Borgatta; see category 1 above.

18. INFLUENCE, GLOBAL

Patchen, Martin, "Alternative Questionnaire Approaches to the Measurement of Influence in Organizations," *American Journal of Sociology*, 69 (July, 1963), pp. 41–52. See pp. 43–44.

19. INFLUENCE, GROUP

Williams, Lawrence K., L. Richard Hoffman, and Floyd C. Mann, "An Investigation of the Control Graph: Influence in a Staff Organization," *Social Forces*, 37 (March, 1959), pp. 189–195. See p. 190.

20. INFLUENCE, INDIVIDUAL

Williams, Hoffman, and Mann; see category 19 above.

21. INFLUENCE, SPECIFIC

Patchen; see category 18 above.

22. INFLUENCE OF UPPER SUPERVISORY LEVELS ON RANK-AND-FILE

Smith, Clagett G., and Oguz N. Ari, "Organizational Control Structure and Member Consensus," *American Journal of Sociology*, 69 (May, 1964), pp. 623–638. See p. 628.

23. MULTI-DIRECTIONAL DISTRIBUTION OF COMMUNICATION

Smith, Clagett G., and Michael E. Brown, "Communication Structure and Control Structure in a Voluntary Association," *Sociometry*, 27 (December, 1964), pp. 449–468. See pp. 455–456.

24. POWER HIERARCHY

Thompson, James D., "Authority and Power in 'Identical' Organizations," *American Journal of Sociology*, 62 (November, 1956), pp. 290–301. See p. 295.

25. PRESSURE FROM SUPERIORS TO PARTICIPATE

Meltzer, Leo, "Comparing Relationships of Individual and Average Variables to Individual Response," *American Sociological Review*, 28 (February, 1963), pp. 117–123. See p. 118.

26. RELATIVE HIERARCHICAL DISTRIBUTION OF CONTROL

Smith and Brown, p. 456; see category 23 above.

27. SATISFACTION WITH REGIONAL MANAGER

Bowers, David G., "Organizational Control in an Insurance Company," *Sociometry*, 27 (June, 1964), pp. 230–244. See p. 234.

28. SLOPE OF THE CONTROL CURVE

Smith and Ari, pp. 627–628; see category 22 above.

29. TOTAL AMOUNT OF CONTROL

Smith and Ari, pp. 627–628; see category 22 above.
Smith and Brown, pp. 456–457; see category 23 above.

30. VERTICAL DISTRIBUTION OF COMMUNICATION

Smith and Brown, p. 455; see category 23 above.

31. WORK-GROUP CONSENSUS REGARDING ADEQUACY OF SUPERVISORY PLANNING

Smith and Ari, pp. 629–630; see category 22 above.

32. WORK-GROUP CONSENSUS REGARDING INFLUENCE DESIRED FOR VARIOUS LEVELS

Smith and Ari, pp. 629–630; see category 22 above.

33. WORK-GROUP CONSENSUS REGARDING TRUST AND CONFIDENCE IN SUPERVISORS

Smith and Ari, pp. 629–630; see category 22 above.

CLASS CONSCIOUSNESS

SEE ALSO

Status Concern

1. CLASS BARRIER CONSCIOUSNESS

Landecker, Werner S., "Class Crystallization and Class Consciousness," *American Sociological Review*, 28 (April, 1963), pp. 219–229. See p. 225.

2. CLASS CONSCIOUSNESS (GLANTZ)

Glantz, Oscar, "Class Consciousness and Political Solidarity," *American Sociological Review*, 23 (August, 1958), pp. 375–383. See pp. 377–378.

3. CLASS CONSCIOUSNESS (MANIS, MELTZER)

Manis, Jerome G., and Bernard N. Meltzer, "Some Correlates of Class Consciousness among Textile Workers," *American Journal of Sociology*, 69 (September, 1963), pp. 177–184. See pp. 178–179.

4. CLASS SELF IDENTIFICATION

Svalastoga, K., E. Høgh, M. Pedersen, and E. Schild, "Differential Class Behavior in Denmark," *American Sociological Review*, 21 (August, 1956), pp. 435–439. See p. 436.

5. CLEAR AWARENESS OF SOCIAL CLASS

Haer, John L., "An Empirical Study of Social Class Awareness," *Social Forces*, 35 (December, 1957), pp. 117–121. See p. 119.

6. SOCIAL CLASS RATING

Leslie, Gerald R., and Arthur H. Richardson, "Life-Cycle, Career Pattern and the Decision to Move," *American Sociological Review*, 26 (December, 1961), pp. 894–902. See p. 897.

7. STATUS SENSITIVITY INDEX

Svalastoga, Hogh, Pedersen, and Schild, p. 436; see category 4 above.

8. WORKING-CLASS CONSCIOUSNESS

Leggett, John C., *Working-Class Consciousness in an Industrial Community*, unpublished Ph.D. dissertation, University of Michigan, 1962, pp. 54–72.

Leggett, John C., "Uprootedness and Working-Class Consciousness," *American Journal of Sociology*, 68 (May, 1963), pp. 682–692. See pp. 685–686.

Leggett, John C., "Working-Class Consciousness, Race, and Political Choice," *American Journal of Sociology*, 69 (September, 1963), pp. 171–176. See p. 173.

Leggett, John C., "Economic Insecurity and Working-Class Consciousness," *American Sociological Review*, 29 (April, 1964), pp. 226–234. See pp. 228–229.

Landecker, p. 228; see category 1 above.

COHESION

SEE ALSO

Family Cohesion

1. AMBIENCE, DENSITY OF

Caplow, Theodore, "The Definition and Measurement of Ambiences," *Social Forces*, 34 (October, 1955), pp. 28–33. See p. 30.

2. CLASSROOM AGREEMENT

Muldoon, J. F., "The Concentration of Liked and Disliked Members in Groups and the Relationship of the Concentrations to Group Cohesiveness," *Sociometry*, 18 (February, 1955), pp. 73–81. See p. 74.

3. COHESION BETWEEN PROFESSIONALS

Turk, Herman, "Social Cohesion through Variant Values: Evidence from Medical Role Relations," *American Sociological Review*, 28 (February, 1963), pp. 28–37. See pp. 31–32.

4. COHESIVENESS (SUCHMAN)

Suchman, Edward A., "Sociomedical Variations among Ethnic Groups," *American Journal of Sociology*, 70 (November, 1964), pp. 319–331. See pp. 323–324.

5. COHESIVENESS (THEODORSON)

Theodorson, George A., "The Relationship between Leadership and Popularity Roles in Small Groups," *American Sociological Review*, 22 (February, 1957), pp. 58–67. See p. 63.

6. COHESIVENESS OF CLASSROOM

Muldoon, p. 75; see category 2 above.

7. COMMUNITY INTEGRATION

Anderson, C. Arnold, "Community Chest Campaigns as an Index of Community Integration," *Social Forces*, 33 (October, 1954), pp. 76–81. See p. 76.

8. CORRESPONDENCE PLUREL

Gross, Edward, "Primary Functions of the Small Group," *American Journal of Sociology*, 60 (July, 1954), pp. 24–29. See pp. 25–26.

9. CREW ATTRACTIVENESS

Hall, Robert L., "Social Influences on the Aircraft Commander's Role," *American Sociological Review*, 20 (June, 1955), pp. 292–299. See p. 295.

10. CREW COHESIVENESS

Berkowitz, Leonard, "Group Norms among Bomber Crews: Patterns of Perceived Crew Attitudes, 'Actual' Crew Attitudes, and Crew Liking Related to Air Crew Effectiveness in Far Eastern Combat," *Sociometry*, 19 (September, 1956), pp. 141–152. See p. 144.

11. GROUP COHESIVENESS

Shelley, Harry P., "Focused Leadership and Cohesiveness in Small Groups," *Sociometry*, 23 (September, 1960), pp. 209–216. See p. 211.

12. GROUP SOLIDARITY

Rosengren, William R., "Symptom Manifestations as a Function of Situational Press: A Demonstration in Socialization," *Sociometry*, 22 (June, 1959), pp. 113–123. See pp. 114–115.

13. INTEGRATION

Gross (1954); see category 8 above.

Gross, Edward, "Symbiosis and Consensus as Integrative Factors in Small Groups," *American Sociological Review*, 21 (April, 1956), pp. 174–179. See p. 176.

14. RESTRAINING FORCES

Hall; see category 9 above.

15. SOCIAL CLASS COHESION

Loomis, Charles P., and colleagues, "Social Status and Communication in Costa Rican Rural Communities," in Olen E. Leonard and Charles P. Loomis (eds.), *Readings in Latin American Social Organization and Institutions*, East Lansing, Mich.: State College Press, 1953, p. 186.

Ellis, Robert A., "Social Stratification and Social Relations: An Empirical Test of the Disjunctiveness of Social Classes," *American Sociological Review*, 22 (October, 1957), pp. 570–578. See p. 575.

16. SOCIAL SATISFACTION

Hagstrom, Warren O., and Hanan C. Selvin, "Two Dimensions of Cohesiveness in Small Groups," *Sociometry*, 28 (March, 1965), pp. 30–43. See pp. 33–38.

17. SOCIOMETRIC COHESION

Selvin, Hanan C., and Warren O. Hagstrom, "The Empirical Classification of Formal Groups," *American Sociological Review*, 28 (June, 1963), pp. 399–411. See p. 405.

Hagstrom and Selvin (1965); see category 16 above.

18. SOLIDARITY ORIENTATION

Street, David, "The Inmate Group in Custodial and Treatment Settings," *American Sociological Review*, 30 (February, 1965), pp. 40–55. See p. 52.

COMMUNITY: ATTITUDES TOWARD AND CHARACTERISTICS OF

1. CIVIC-EDUCATION NORMS

Litt, Edgar, "Civic Education, Community Norms, and Political Indoctrination," *American Sociological Review*, 28 (February, 1963), pp. 69–75. See pp. 70–71.

2. COMMUNITY ATTACHMENT

Wilensky, Harold L., "Orderly Careers and Social Participation: The Impact of Work History on Social Integration in the Middle Mass," *American Sociological Review*, 26 (August, 1961), pp. 521–539. See p. 528.

Wilensky, Harold L., "Mass Society and Mass Culture: Interdependence or Independence?" *American Sociological Review*, 29 (April, 1964), pp. 173–197. See p. 186.

3. COMMUNITY DEVELOPMENT PROGRAM, ATTITUDE TOWARD

Young, James N., and Selz C. Mayo, "Manifest and Latent Participators in a Rural Community Action Program," *Social Forces*, 38 (December, 1959), pp. 140–145. See p. 144.

4. COMMUNITY DEVELOPMENT PROGRAM, KNOWLEDGE OF

Young and Mayo, pp. 143–144: see category 3 above.

5. COMMUNITY IDENTIFICATION

Stone, Gregory P., "City Shoppers and Urban Identification: Observations on the Psychology of City Life," *American Journal of Sociology*, 60 (July, 1954), pp. 36–45. See p. 44.

6. COMMUNITY IDENTIFICATION INDEX

Fanelli, A. Alexander, "Extensiveness of Communication Contacts and Perceptions of the Community," *American Sociological Review*, 21 (August, 1956), pp. 439–445. See p. 442.

7. COMMUNITY INTEGRATION

Anderson, C. Arnold, "Community Chest Campaigns as an Index of Community Integration," *Social Forces*, 33 (October, 1954), pp. 76–81. See p. 76.

8. "COMMUNITYNESS"

Sutton, Willis A., Jr., and Jiri Kolaja, "Elements of Community Action," *Social Forces*, 38 (May, 1960), pp. 325–331. See pp. 326–327.

9. COMMUNITY ORGANIZATIONS, PRESTIGE OF

Young, Ruth C., and Olaf F. Larson, "A New Approach to Community Structure," *American Sociological Review*, 30 (December, 1965), pp. 926–934. See pp. 931–932.

10. COMMUNITY SATISFACTION

Omari, Thompson Peter, "Factors Associated with Urban Adjustment of Rural Southern Migrants," *Social Forces*, 35 (October, 1956), pp. 47–53. See p. 49.

11. COMMUNITY-SERVICE GOAL SCALE

Danziger, K., "The Psychological Future of an Oppressed Group," *Social Forces*, 42 (October, 1963), pp. 31–40. See p. 37.

12. CURRENT PREVALENCE OF PSYCHIATRIC CONDITIONS IN A COMMUNITY

Hollingshead, August B., and Frederick Redlich, "Social Stratification and Schizophrenia," *American Sociological Review*, 19 (June, 1954), pp. 302–306. See p. 302.

13. ENDOGAMY-EXOGAMY

Janes, Robert W., "A Technique for Describing Community Structure through Newspaper Analysis," *Social Forces*, 37 (December, 1958), pp. 102–109. See p. 107.

14. FACTOR ANALYSIS OF COMMUNITY (COUNTY) VARIABLES

Provides information for construction of scales for urbanism, welfare, influx, poverty, magni-complexity, educational effort and proletarianism.

Jonassen, Christen T., and Sherwood H. Peres, *Interrelationships among Dimensions of Community Systems: A Factorial Analysis of Eighty-two Variables*, Columbus, Ohio: Ohio State University Press, 1960.

Jonassen, Christen T., "Functional Unities in Eighty-eight Community Systems," *American Sociological Review*, 26 (June, 1961), pp. 399–407. See pp. 401–406.

15. INSTITUTIONAL COMPLETENESS OF ETHNIC COMMUNITIES

Breton, Raymond, "Institutional Completeness of Ethnic Communities and the Personal Relations of Immigrants," *American Journal of Sociology*, 70 (September, 1964), pp. 193–205. See p. 195.

16. INSTITUTIONAL CONSERVATISM

Rubin, Morton, "Localism and Related Values among Negroes in a Southern Rural Community," *Social Forces*, 36 (March, 1958), pp. 263–267. See p. 264.

17. LOCALITY ORIENTATION

Rubin, p. 264; see category 16 above.

18. LOCALITY SATISFACTION

Rubin, p. 264; see category 16 above.

19. PROJECTION OF LOCAL OPPORTUNITIES

Rubin, p. 264; see category 16 above.

20. SATISFACTION WITH CITY'S GOVERNMENT

Hetzler, Stanley A., "Social Mobility and Radicalism-Conservatism," *Social Forces*, 33 (December, 1954) pp. 161–166. See p. 161.

21. SATISFACTION WITH CITY'S INDUSTRIES

Hetzler, p. 161; see category 20 above.

22. SATISFACTION WITH GENERAL ECONOMIC OPPORTUNITIES WITHIN CITY

Hetzler, p. 161; see category 20 above.

23. SATISFACTION WITH TOWN

Hetzler, p. 161; see category 20 above.

24. SOCIAL CLASS OF COMMUNITIES

Pinard, Maurice, "Structural Attachments and Political Support in Urban Politics: The Case of Fluoridation Referendums," *American Journal of Sociology*, 68 (March, 1963), pp. 513–526. See p. 522.

COMPLEX ORGANIZATIONS: ATTITUDES TOWARD AND PERCEPTIONS OF

SEE ALSO

*Job Satisfaction, Morale,
and Related Measures*

1. **ABSENCE OF CONFLICT, PERCEIVED CONSENSUS OF**
Smith, Clagett G., and Oguz N. Ari, "Organizational Control Structure and Member Consensus," *American Journal of Sociology*, 69 (May, 1964), pp. 623–638. See p. 630.

2. **ACTIVE SKILLS IRRELEVANT TO THE ORGANIZATION**
Meltzer, Leo, "Comparing Relationships of Individual and Average Variables to Individual Response," *American Sociological Review*, 28 (February, 1963), pp. 117–123. See p. 118.

3. **ACTIVE SKILLS RELEVANT TO THE ORGANIZATION**
Meltzer; see category 2 above.

4. **ATTRACTION TO THE ORGANIZATION**
Back, Kurt W., "Influence through Social Communication," *Journal of Abnormal and Social Psychology*, 46 (January, 1951), pp. 9–23. See pp. 10–15.
Jackson, Jay M., "Reference Group Processes in a Formal Organization," *Sociometry*, 22 (December, 1959), pp. 307–327. See p. 311.

5. **BIG BUSINESS, ATTITUDE TOWARD (COMPOSITE INDEX)**
Steiner, Ivan D., "Primary Group Influences on Public Opinion," *American Sociological Review*, 19 (June, 1954), pp. 260–267. See p. 265.

6. **BIG BUSINESS, ATTITUDE TOWARD (CONTENT ANALYSIS)**
Steiner; see category 5 above.

7. **BIG BUSINESS, ATTITUDE TOWARD (SELF-RATING)**
Steiner, p. 263; see category 5 above.

8. CHURCH ANTI-UNIONISM

Dornbusch, Sanford M., and Roger D. Irle, "The Failure of Presbyterian Union," *American Journal of Sociology*, 64 (January, 1959), pp. 352–355. See p. 353.

9. COMMITMENT TO AIR DEFENSE GOALS

Davis, F. James, "Conceptions of Official Leader Roles in the Air Force," *Social Forces*, 32 (March, 1954), pp. 253–258. See p. 256.

10. COMPANY AND SUPERVISOR, EMPLOYEES' ATTITUDE TOWARD

Sirota, David, "Some Effects of Promotional Frustration on Employees' Understanding of and Attitude toward Management," *Sociometry*, 22 (September, 1959), pp. 273–278. See p. 275.

11. CONTACT BENEFITS OF MEMBERSHIP

Meltzer; see category 2 above.

12. DISADVANTAGES OF MEMBERSHIP

Meltzer; see category 2 above.

13. ECONOMIC BENEFITS OF MEMBERSHIP

Meltzer; see category 2 above.

14. EVALUATION OF MEMBERSHIP

Fishbein, Martin, "The Perception of Non-members: A Test of Merton's Reference Group Theory," *Sociometry*, 26 (September, 1963), pp. 271–286. See p. 276.

15. EVERYDAY OPERATIONS, PERCEIVED CONSENSUS REGARDING

Smith and Ari; see category 1 above.

16. INFLUENCE DESIRED, HIERARCHICAL CONSENSUS REGARDING

Smith and Ari, pp. 629–630; see category 1 above.

17. INFORMATION PASSED DOWN FROM ABOVE, SATISFACTION OF EMPLOYEES WITH

Henry, Andrew F., "An Empirical Study of Attitude Components," *Social Forces*, 36 (October, 1957), pp. 26–31. See p. 27.

18. INFORMATION PROCESS, SATISFACTION WITH

Robinson, James A., "Process Satisfaction and Policy Approval in

State Department-Congressional Relations," *American Journal of Sociology*, 67 (November, 1961), pp. 278–283. See p. 280.

19. INFORMATION WANTED FROM ABOVE, PERCEPTION OF

Henry; see category 17 above.

20. INSTITUTION AND STAFF, PERSPECTIVE ON

Street, David, *Inmate Social Organization: A Comparative Study of Juvenile Correctional Institutions*, unpublished Ph.D. dissertation, University of Michigan, 1962, pp. 213–224.

Street, David, "The Inmate Group in Custodial and Treatment Settings," *American Sociological Review*, 30 (February, 1965), pp. 40–55. See pp. 46–47.

21. INVOLVEMENT IN THE ORGANIZATION

Meltzer; see category 2 above.

22. INVOLVEMENT (OF MEMBERS)

Simpson, Richard L., and William H. Gulley, "Goals, Environmental Pressures, and Organizational Characteristics," *American Sociological Review*, 27 (June, 1962), pp. 344–351. See p. 348.

23. JOB RELATIONS ATTITUDE SCALE

Abegglen, James C., "Subordination and Autonomy Attitudes of Japanese Workers," *American Journal of Sociology*, 63 (September, 1957), pp. 181–189. See p. 182.

24. KNOWLEDGE (ABOUT AN AGRICULTURAL COOPERATIVE)

Clark, John P., "Measuring Alienation within a Social System," *American Sociological Review*, 24 (December, 1959), pp. 849–852. See p. 851.

25. KNOWLEDGE OF ORGANIZATION PRIOR TO JOINING

Meltzer; see category 2 above.

26. LABOR-ATTITUDE SCALE

Liu, William T., "The Marginal Catholics in the South: A Revision of Concepts," *American Journal of Sociology*, 65 (January, 1950), pp. 383–390. See p. 386.

27. LEGITIMACY OF ORGANIZATIONAL INFLUENCE

Schein, Edgar, and J. Steven Ott, "The Legitimacy of Organizational Influence," *American Journal of Sociology*, 67 (May, 1962), pp. 682–689. See pp. 683–684 and 689.

28. MILITARY MANAGEMENT PROBLEMS

Davis; see category 9 above.

29. OIL COMPANIES, ATTITUDE TOWARD

Lazarsfeld, Paul F., "Recent Developments in Latent Structure Analysis," *Sociometry*, 18 (December, 1955), pp. 647–659. See p. 651.

30. ORGANIZATION'S PROGRAM, ATTITUDE TOWARD

Meltzer; see category 2 above.

31. PROMOTIONAL FRUSTRATION INDEX

Sirota; see category 10 above.

32. REWARDS, ASSESSMENT OF

Borgatta, Edgar F., "Attitudinal Concomitants to Military Statuses," *Social Forces*, 33 (May, 1955), pp. 342–347. See pp. 345–346.

33. SATISFACTION SCALE OF AGRICULTURAL COOPERATIVE MEMBERS

Clark, p. 851; see category 24 above.

34. SEDENTARY SKILLS IRRELEVANT TO THE ORGANIZATION

Meltzer; see category 2 above.

35. SEDENTARY SKILLS RELEVANT TO THE ORGANIZATION

Meltzer; see category 2 above.

36. SELF-DEVELOPMENT BENEFITS OF MEMBERSHIP

Meltzer; see category 2 above.

37. SENSITIVITY TO SANCTIONS (2 MEASURES)

Borgatta; see category 32 above.

38. STATUS COMMITMENT (IN HOSPITAL)

Seeman, Melvin, and John W. Evans, "Apprenticeship and Attitude Change," *American Journal of Sociology*, 67 (January, 1962), pp. 365–378. See p. 368.

39. UNDERSTANDING OF ORGANIZATIONAL PURPOSES

Meltzer; see category 2 above.

40. WORK DEPARTMENT, EVALUATION OF

Garbin, A. P. and John A. Ballweg, "Intra-Plant Mobility: Volitional versus Non-Volitional," *Sociological Inquiry*, 33 (Spring, 1963), pp. 197–206.

Garbin, A. P., and John A. Ballweg, "Intra-Plant Mobility of Negro and White Workers," *American Journal of Sociology*, 71 (November, 1965), pp. 315–319. See pp. 317–318.

41. WORK STANDARDS, HIERARCHICAL CONSENSUS REGARDING

Smith and Ari, pp. 629–630; see category 1 above.

42. WORTH OF AN ORGANIZATIONAL POSITION

Keuth, James L., and Bernard Levenson, "Conceptions of Organizational Worth," *American Journal of Sociology*, 70 (November, 1964), pp. 342–348. See pp. 342–344.

COMPLEX ORGANIZATIONS: CHARACTERISTICS OF

1. ADMINISTRATIVE COMPONENT

Terrien, Frederic W., and Donald L. Mills, "The Effect of Changing Size upon the Internal Structure of Organizations," *American Sociological Review*, 20 (February, 1955), pp. 11–13. See p. 12.

2. ADMINISTRATIVE RATIONALITY

Udy, Stanley H., Jr., " 'Bureaucratic' Elements in Organizations: Some Research Findings," *American Sociological Review*, 23 (August, 1958), pp. 415–418.

Udy, Stanley H., Jr., *Organization of Work*, New Haven, Conn.: HRAF Press, 1959, pp. 139–158.

Udy, Stanley H., Jr., "Administrative Rationality, Social Setting and Organizational Development," *American Journal of Sociology*, 68 (November, 1962), pp. 299–308.

Udy's measure of administrative rationality has been developed out of his comparative analysis of work organization in non-industrial societies. The beginnings of this measure of one dimension of bureaucratic structures are reported in Udy's 1958 article. Continued refinement of the measure has led to the development of a "seven-item" cumulative scale.

The unit of observation employed in this measure is an organization engaged in the production of material goods. For each organization, the presence or absence of seven characteristics is noted. The characteristics as specified by Udy (1962) are as follows (pp. 301–302):

1. *Limited objectives*—objectives explicitly restricted only to the production of certain products.
2. *Segmental participation*—explicit definition of the terms of participation by some mutual contractual agreement.
3. *Performance emphasis*—expected dependence of the quantity of the reward on the amount and/or quality of work done.
4. *Specific job assignment*—continuous assignment by management of particular people to particular roles.
5. *Specialization*—the concurrent performance of three or more qualitatively different operations by different members.
6. *Compensatory rewards*—allocation of money or goods in kind by members of higher authority to members of lower authority in return for participation.
7. *Central management*—the existence of a single internal source of ultimate authority.

Udy (1962) has examined thirty-four work organizations in nonindustrial societies using data from the Human Relations Area Files. For these thirty-four organizations, the presence of the above seven characteristics was found to form a cumulative scale having a coefficient of reproducibility of 0.95.

Udy, Stanley H., Jr., "Technical and Institutional Factors in Production Organizations: A Preliminary Model," *American Journal of Sociology*, 67 (November, 1961), pp. 247–254. See p. 248.
Stinchcombe, Arthur L., "Comment," *American Journal of Sociology*, 67 (November, 1961), pp. 255–259.
Udy, Stanley H., Jr., "Rejoinder," *American Journal of Sociology*, 67 (November, 1961), pp. 259–260.

3. AGENCY (INSURANCE) EFFECTIVENESS

Factor analysis: agency development; factor A; agency development, factor B; business costs; growth of business; manpower turnover; regional manager's personal preference; and volume of business.

Bowers, David G., "Organizational Control in an Insurance Company," *Sociometry*, 27 (June, 1964), pp. 230–244. See p. 234.

4. BUREAUCRACY

Hall, Richard H., "The Concept of Bureaucracy: An Empirical Assessment," *American Journal of Sociology*, 69 (July, 1963), pp. 32–40. See p. 34–36.

5. BUREAUCRATIC COMPETITIVENESS

Blau, Peter M., "Cooperation and Competition in a Bureaucracy," *American Journal of Sociology*, 59 (May, 1954), pp. 530–535. See p. 531.

6. CHURCH-SECT

Riley, Matilda White, *Sociological Research*, New York: Harcourt, Brace and World, 1963, p. 342.

Demerath, N. J., III, *Social Class in American Protestantism*, Chicago: Rand McNally and Co., 1965, Chapter III.

Scanzoni, John, "Innovation and Constancy in the Church-Sect Typology," *American Journal of Sociology*, 71 (November, 1965), pp. 320–327. See p. 320.

7. COMBAT EFFICIENCY

Chesler, David J., Neil J. Van Steenberg, and Joyce E. Brueckl, "Effect on Morale of Infantry Team Replacement and Individual Replacement Systems," *Sociometry*, 18 (December, 1955), pp. 587–597. See p. 590.

8. COMPLEXITY

Udy, Stanley H., Jr., "The Structure of Authority in Non-Industrial Production Organizations," *American Journal of Sociology*, 64 (May, 1959), pp. 582–584. See p. 582.

Anderson, Theodore R., and Seymour Warkov, "Organizational Size and Functional Complexity: A Study of Administration in Hospitals," *American Sociological Review*, 26 (February, 1961), pp. 23–28. See p. 25.

Udy (1961), p. 248; see category 2 above.

Stinchcombe (1961), see category 2 above.

Udy (1961), pp. 259–260; see category 2 above.

9. CREDIT STANDING OF RETAIL ESTABLISHMENTS

Hochbaum, Godfrey, John G. Darley, E. D. Monachesi, and Charles Bird, "Socioeconomic Variables in a Large City," *American Journal of Sociology*, 61 (July, 1955), pp. 31–38. See p. 33.

10. DIVISION OF LABOR

Hall, Richard H., *An Empirical Study of Bureaucratic Dimensions and Their Relation to Other Organizational Characteristics*, unpublished Ph.D. dissertation, Ohio State University, 1961.

Hall (1963), p. 35; see category 4 above.

11. EFFECTIVENESS (GRUSKY)

Grusky, Oscar, "Corporate Size, Bureaucratization, and Managerial Succession," *American Journal of Sociology*, 67 (November, 1961), pp. 261–269. See p. 267.

12. EFFECTIVENESS (WESCHLER, TANNENBAUM, TALBOT)

Weschler, Irving R., Robert Tannenbaum, and Eugene Talbot, "A New Management Tool: The Multi-Relational Sociometric Survey," *Personnel*, 29 (July, 1952), pp. 85–94.

Massarik, Fred, Robert Tannenbaum, Murray Kohanc, and Irving R. Weschler, "Sociometric Choice and Organizational Effectiveness: A Multi-Relational Approach," *Sociometry*, 16 (August, 1953), pp. 211–238. See pp. 214–217.

Shepherd, Clovis, and Irving R. Weschler, "The Relation between Three Interpersonal Variables and Communication Effectiveness," *Sociometry*, 18 (May, 1955), pp. 103–110. See p. 105.

13. EFFICIENCY OF AIR DIVISION SQUADRONS

Medalia, Nahum B., and Delbert C. Miller, "Human Relations Leadership and the Association of Morale and Efficiency in Work Groups: A Controlled Study with Small Military Units," *Social Forces*, 33 (May, 1955), pp. 348–352. See p. 350.

14. EMPLOYEE INFORMATION (THREE MEASURES)

Sirota, David, "Some Effects of Promotional Frustration on Employees' Understanding of and Attitudes toward Management," *Sociometry*, 22 (September, 1959), pp. 273–278. See p. 275.

15. FLEXIBILITY

Georgopoulos, Basil S., and Arnold S. Tannenbaum, "A Study of Organizational Effectiveness," *American Sociological Review*, 22 (October, 1957), pp. 534–540. See p. 538.

16. GOALS, FOCUSED OR DIFFUSE

Simpson, Richard L., and William H. Gulley, "Goals, Environmental Pressures, and Organizational Characteristics," *American Sociological Review*, 27 (June, 1962), pp. 344–351. See p. 346.

17. IMPERSONALITY

Hall (1961); see category 10 above.

Hall (1963), p. 35; see category 4 above.

18. INTERNAL COMMUNICATION

Simpson and Gulley, pp. 348–349; see category 16 above.

19. INVOLVEMENT, INTERNAL OR EXTERNAL

Simpson and Gulley; see category 16 above.

20. MEMBERSHIP PARTICIPATION

Tannenbaum, Arnold S., "Control Structure and Union Functions," *American Journal of Sociology*, 61 (May, 1956), pp. 536–545. See p. 538.

21. PERFORMANCE RATING OF BOMBARDMENT CREW

Adams, Stuart, "Social Climate and Productivity in Small Military Groups," *American Sociological Review*, 19 (August, 1954), pp. 421–425. See p. 423.

22. PERFORMANCE RATING OF ORGANIZATIONAL STATIONS

Georgopoulos and Tannenbaum, p. 537; see category 15 above.

23. POWER DISTRIBUTION IN UNIONS

Raphael, Edna E., "Power Structure and Membership Dispersion in Unions," *American Journal of Sociology*, 71 (November, 1965), pp. 274–283. See p. 276.

24. PRESSURE TO SUPERSEDE SCHEDULE

Borgatta, Edgar F., "Attitudinal Concomitants to Military Statuses," *Social Forces*, 33 (May, 1955), pp. 342–347. See pp. 345–346.

25. PRESTIGE RANKING OF STRATEGIC AIR COMMAND SQUADRON (TWO MEASURES)

Mack, Raymond W., "The Prestige System of an Air Base: Squadron Rankings and Morale,"*American Sociological Review*, 19 (June, 1954), pp. 281–287. See p. 283.

26. PRODUCTIVITY OF PUBLIC EMPLOYMENT AGENCY

Blau; see category 5 above.

27. RESPONSIBILITY

Borgatta, p. 345; see category 24 above.

28. SCOPE OF REWARD

Stinchcombe (1961), see category 2 above.
Udy (1961), pp. 249, 259–260; see category 2 above.

29. SOCIAL INVOLVEMENT OF ORGANIZATIONS

Stinchcombe (1961), see category 2 above.
Udy (1961), pp. 249, 259–260; see category 2 above.

30. STATION PRODUCTIVITY (GEORGOPOULOS, TANNENBAUM)

Georgopoulos and Tannenbaum, p. 537; see category 15 above.

31. STATION PRODUCTIVITY (SMITH, ARI)

Smith, Clagett G., and Oguz N. Ari, "Organizational Control Structure and Member Consensus," *American Journal of Sociology*, 69 (May, 1964), pp. 623–638. See p. 631.

32. SYSTEM OF PROCEDURES

Hall (1961); see category 10 above.
Hall (1963), p. 35; see category 4 above.

33. SYSTEM OF RULES

Hall (1961); see category 10 above.
Hall (1963), p. 35; see category 4 above.

34. TECHNICAL COMPETENCE

Hall (1961), p. 35; see category 10 above.
Hall (1963), p. 35; see category 4 above.

COMPLEX ORGANIZATIONS:
INFORMAL RELATIONS

1. AGGRESSION TOWARD SUPERVISOR AND CO-WORKERS, VERBAL

Day, Robert C., and Robert L. Hamblin, "Some Effects of Close and Punitive Styles of Supervision," *American Journal of Sociology,* 69 (March, 1964), pp. 499–510. See p. 505.

2. AGGRESSIVE FEELINGS TOWARD SUPERVISORS AND CO-WORKERS

Day and Hamblin, see category 1 above, pp. 504–506.

3. ASSUMED SIMILARITY

Osgood, C. E., and G. Suci, "A Measure of Relation Determined by Both Mean Differences and Profile Information," *Psychological Bulletin,* 49 (May, 1952), pp. 251–262. See pp. 252–259.

Fiedler, F. E., and Kate Senior, "An Exploratory Study of Unconscious Feeling Reactions in Fifteen Patient-Therapist Pairs," *Journal of Abnormal and Social Psychology,* 47 (April, 1952), pp. 446–453. See pp. 446–448.

Hutchins, Edwin B., and Fred E. Fiedler, "Task-Oriented and Quasi-Therapeutic Role Functions of the Leader in Small Military Groups," *Sociometry,* 23 (December, 1960), pp. 393–406. See p. 394.

4. ASSUMED SIMILARITY OF GROUPS

Fiedler and Senior (1952); see category 3 above
Hutchins and Fiedler (1958); see category 3 above.

5. ASSUMED SIMILARITY BETWEEN OPPOSITES

Osgood and Suci (1952); see category 3 above.

Fiedler, F. E., *Leader Attitudes and Group Effectiveness*, Urbana, Ill.: University of Illinois Press, 1958.

Hutchins and Fiedler (1958); see category 3 above.

6. ATTRACTION

Blau, Peter M., "Patterns of Choice in Interpersonal Relations," *American Sociological Review*, 27 (February, 1962), pp. 41–55. See p. 44.

7. ATTRACTION TO A PERSON'S WORK GROUP

Back, Kurt W., "Influence through Social Communication," *Journal of Abnormal and Social Psychology*, 46 (January, 1951), pp. 9–23. See pp. 10–15.

Jackson, Jay M., "Reference Group Processes in Formal Organization," *Sociometry*, 22 (December, 1959), pp. 307–327. See p. 311.

8. AVERAGE ASSUMED SIMILARITY TO THE GROUP

Fiedler and Senior (1952); see category 3 above.

Hutchins and Fiedler (1958), p. 398; see category 3 above.

9. CHOICE OF SURVIVAL COMPANIONS-LEADERS

Levi, M., E. P. Torrance, and G. Pletts, "Sociometric Studies of Combat Air Crews in Survival Training," *Sociometry*, 17 (December, 1954), pp. 304–328. See p. 306.

10. COHERENCE AND INTEGRATION OF PRIMARY AND SECONDARY ROLES (THREE MEASURES)

Wilensky, Harold L., "Orderly Careers and Social Participation: The Impact of Work History on Social Integration in the Middle Mass," *American Sociological Review*, 26 (August, 1961), pp. 521–539. See p. 529.

11. COMBAT PROFICIENCY

Levi, Torrance, and Pletts, p. 307; see category 9 above.

12. CONSULTATION

Blau; see category 6 above.

13. CORRESPONDENCE PLUREL SCORE

Gross, Edward, "Primary Functions of the Small Group," *American Journal of Sociology*, 60 (July, 1954), pp. 24–29. See p. 25.

14. CREW EFFECTIVENESS

Berkowitz, Leonard, "Group Norms among Bomber Crews: Patterns of Perceived Crew Attitudes, 'Actual' Crew Attitudes and Crew Liking Related to Air Crew Effectiveness in Far Eastern Combat," *Sociometry,* 19 (September, 1956), pp. 141–152. See p. 144.

15. ENJOYMENT OF RELATIONSHIP

Turk, Herman, and G. Robert Wills, "Authority and Interaction," *Sociometry,* 27 (March, 1964), pp. 1–18. See p. 8.

16. FRIENDSHIP INVOLVEMENT

Wheeler, Stanton, "Socialization in Correctional Communities," *American Sociological Review,* 26 (October, 1961), pp. 697–712. See p. 703.

17. GROUP ADJUSTMENT

Hutchins, and Fiedler (1958), p. 399; see category 3 above.

18. GROUP SANCTIONS, EXTENT OF

Meltzer, Leo, "Comparing Relationships of Individual and Average Variables to Individual Response," *American Sociological Review,* 28 (February, 1963), pp. 117–123. See p. 118.

19. HETEROSEXUAL RELATIONS, ATTITUDES TOWARD

Abegglen, James C., "Subordination and Autonomy Attitudes of Japanese Workers, "*American Journal of Sociology,* 63 (September, 1957), pp. 181–189. See p. 182.

20. INFLUENCE EXERCISED BY RANK-AND-FILE MEMBERS UPON THEMSELVES

Smith, Clagett G., and Oguz N. Ari, "Organizational Control Structure and Member Consensus," *American Journal of Sociology,* 69 (May, 1964), pp. 623–638. See p. 628.

21. INFLUENCE OF MEN UPON UPPER SUPERVISORY LEVELS

Smith and Ari; see category 20 above.

22. INFORMAL ACCEPTANCE

Blau; see category 6 above.

23. INFORMAL APPROACHABILITY

Blau, pp. 52–54; see category 6 above.

24. INFORMAL STATUS

Blau, pp. 52–54; see category 6 above.

25. INTERACTION, CONTENT AND FEELING TONE

Banks, E. P., "Methodological Problems in the Study of Psychiatric Wards," *Social Forces*, 34 (March, 1956), pp. 277–280. See p. 279.

26. OBJECTIVE GROUP RATING OF INDIVIDUAL

Reeder, Leo G., George A. Donohue, and Arturo Biblarz, "Conceptions of Self and Others," *American Journal of Sociology*, 66 (September, 1960), pp. 155–159. See p. 154.

27. PERSONAL CONTACT, CHECKLIST

Stogdill, R. M., "The Sociometry of Working Relationships in Formal Organizations," *Sociometry*, 12 (November, 1949), pp. 276–286. See pp. 278–279.

Jacobson, Eugene, and Stanley E. Seashore, "Communication Practices in Complex Organizations," *Journal of Social Issues*, 7 (No. 3, 1951), pp. 28–40. See pp. 33–36.

Weiss, Robert S., and Eugene Jacobson, "A Method for the Analysis of the Structure of Complex Organizations," *American Sociological Review*, 20 (December, 1955), pp. 661–668. See pp. 662–663.

Jackson (1959), p. 310; see category 7 above.

28. PERSONAL CONTACT, DEGREE OF

Back, Kurt W., Robert E. Coker, Thomas G. Donnelly, and Bernard S. Phillips, "Public Health as a Career of Medicine: Secondary Choice within a Profession," *American Sociological Review*, 23 (October, 1958), pp. 533–541. See p. 537.

29. POWER INDICES FOR SUB-GROUPS (THREE MEASURES)

Grusky, Oscar, "A Case for the Theory of Familial Role Differentiation in Small Groups," *Social Forces*, 35 (March, 1957), pp. 209–217. See pp. 212–213.

30. PRESSURE FROM NONSUPERIORS TO PARTICIPATE

Meltzer; see category 18 above.

31. PRISON-CAMP OFFICERS, ATTITUDES TOWARD

Grusky, Oscar, "Organizational Goals and the Behavior of Informal Leaders," *American Journal of Sociology*, 65 (July, 1959), pp. 59–67. See p. 63.

32. RELATIVE INFLUENCE OF MEMBERS UPON EACH OTHER

Bass, Bernard M., "Measures of Average Influence and Change in Agreement of Rankings by a Group of Judges," *Sociometry*, 23 (June, 1960), pp. 195–202. See pp. 197–201.

33. RESPECT

Blau; see category 6 above.

34. SOCIABILITY AND SYMPATHY

Wispe, Lauren G., "A Sociometric Analysis of Conflicting Role-Expectations," *American Journal of Sociology*, 61 (September, 1955), pp. 134–137. See pp. 135–136.

35. SOCIAL INTERACTION, EXTENT OF

Turk and Wills, pp. 7–8; see category 15 above.

36. SOCIOMETRIC INDEX (CONCERNING INTERACTIONS AMONG SUPERIORS AND SUBORDINATES)

Stogdill, Ralph, "Interactions among Superiors and Subordinates," *Sociometry*, 18 (May, 1955), pp. 552–557. See p. 553.

CONFORMITY AND DEVIANCE

SEE ALSO
Crime and Delinquency

1. ADHERENCE TO REGULATIONS

Davis, F. James, and Robert B. Hagedorn, "Testing the Reliability of Systematic Field Observations," *American Sociological Review*, 19 (June, 1954), pp. 345–348. See p. 345.

2. ALCOHOL INTAKE, QUANTITY-FREQUENCY INDEX OF

Straus, Robert and Selden Bacon, *Drinking in College*, New Haven, Conn.: Yale University Press, 1953, pp. 60–75.

Mulford, Harold, and Donald Miller, "Drinking Behavior Related to Definitions of Alcohol: A Report of Research in Progress," *American Sociological Review*, 24 (June, 1959), pp. 385–389. See pp. 387–388.

3. ALCOHOL USE

Nettler, Gwynn, "Antisocial Sentiment and Criminality," *American Sociological Review*, 24 (April, 1959), pp. 202–208. See p. 205.

4. ALCOHOL USE, DEFINITIONS OF

Kuhn, Manford H., and Thomas McPartland, "An Empirical Investigation of Self-Attitudes," *American Sociological Review*, 19 (February, 1954), pp. 68–76. See pp. 69–70.

Mulford and Miller (1959), p. 386; see category 2 above.

5. CONFORMISTS-DEVIANTS, PERSONAL TRAITS OF

Riley, Matilda W., John W. Riley, Jr., and Jackson Toby, *Sociological Studies in Scale Analysis*, New Brunswick, N.J.: Rutgers University Press, 1954, pp. 126–149. See p. 128.

Riley, Matilda W., and Richard Cohn, "Control Networks in Informal Groups," *Sociometry*, 21 (March, 1958), pp. 30–49. See pp. 34–35.

6. CONFORMITY (BELL)

Bell, Gerald D., "Processes in the Formation of Adolescents' Aspirations," *Social Forces*, 42 (December, 1963), pp. 179–186. See p. 182.

7. CONFORMITY (KELLEY, SHAPIRO)

Kelley, Harold H., and Martin M. Shapiro, "An Experiment on Conformity to Group Norms Where Conformity is Detrimental to Group Achievement," *American Sociological Review*, 19 (December, 1954), pp. 667–677. See p. 671.

8. CONFORMITY (WILLIS)

Willis, Richard H., "Two Dimensions of Conformity-Nonconformity," *Sociometry*, 26 (December, 1963), pp. 499–513. See pp. 500–507.

9. CONFORMITY, TO A FICTITIOUS NORM

Emerson, Richard M., "Power-Dependence Relations: Two Experiments," *Sociometry*, 27 (September, 1964), pp. 280–298. See p. 284.

10. CONFORMITY, TO GROUP PRESSURE (CANNING, BAKER)

Canning, Roy R., and James M. Baker, "Effect of the Group on Authoritarian and Non-Authoritarian Persons," *American Journal of Sociology*, 64 (May, 1959), pp. 579–581. See p. 580.

11. CONFORMITY, TO GROUP PRESSURE (GOLDMAN, HAKERLEIN, FEDER)

Goldman, Morton, Bernard J. Hakerlein, and Gloria J. Feder, "Conformity and Resistance to Group Pressure, " *Sociometry*, 28 (June, 1965), pp. 220–226. See p. 223.

12. CONFORMITY, INEQUALITY OF

Steiner, Ivan D., and Homer H. Johnson, "Authoritarianism and Conformity," *Sociometry*, 26 (March, 1963), pp. 21–34. See p. 28.

13. CONFORMITY, SOCIAL

Pettigrew, Thomas F., "Personality and Sociocultural Factors in Intergroup Attitudes: A Cross-National Comparison," *Journal of Conflict Resolution*, 2 (March, 1958), pp. 29–42. See p. 33.

Pettigrew, Thomas F., "Social Distance Attitudes of South African Students," *Social Forces*, 38 (March, 1960) pp. 246–253. See p. 246.

Feagin, Joe R., "Prejudice, Orthodoxy and the Social Situation," *Social Forces*, 44 (September, 1965), pp. 46–56. See p. 47 and 53–54.

14. CONFORMITY, TO STAFF ROLE-EXPECTATIONS

Wheeler, Stanton, "Socialization in Correctional Communities," *American Sociological Review*, 26 (October, 1961) pp. 697–712. See pp. 699–700.

15. CONFORMITY, TOTAL

Steiner and Johnson, pp. 27–28; see category 12 above.

16. DEVIANT ACTS, SERIOUSNESS OF

Sutcliffe, J. P., and M. Haberman, "Factors Influencing Choice in Role Conflict Situations," *American Sociological Review*, 21 (December, 1956), pp. 695–703. See p. 697.

17. EXTERNAL CONFORMITY

Peterson, Richard A., "Dimensions of Social Character: An Empirical Exploration of the Riesman Typology," *Sociometry*, 27 (June, 1964), pp. 194–207. See p. 200.

18. INHIBITION

Slater, Philip E., "Contrasting Correlates of Group Size," *Sociometry*, 21 (June, 1958), pp. 129–139. See p. 136.

19. NARCOTICS INDEX

Nettler; see category 3 above.

20. NORMS, INFLUENCE OF, ON INDIVIDUAL JUDGMENT

Sherif, Muzafer, "A Study of Some Social Factors in Perception," *Archives of Psychology*, 27 (July, 1935). See pp. 27–42.

Walter, Norman, "A Study of the Effects of Conflicting Suggestions upon Judgments in the Autokinetic Situation," *Sociometry*, 18 (May, 1955), pp. 138–146. See pp. 138–139.

21. PEER GROUP CONFORMITY

Back, Kurt W., and Keith E. Davis, "Some Personal and Social Situational Factors Relevant to the Consistency and Prediction of Conforming Behavior," *Sociometry,* 28 (September, 1965), pp. 227–240. See pp. 232–235.

22. PERCEIVED PRESSURES, STRENGTH OF

Steiner, Ivan D., "Primary Group Influences on Public Opinion," *American Sociological Review,* 19 (June, 1954), pp. 260–267. See p. 263.

23. SUICIDE INDEX

Nettler; see category 3 above.

CONSENSUS

1. CONSENSUS (BACKMAN, SECORD, PEIRCE)

Backman, Carl W., Paul F. Secord, and Jerry R. Pierce, "Resistance to Change in the Self-Concept as a Function of Perceived Consensus among Significant Others," *Sociometry*, 26 (March, 1963), pp. 102–111. See p. 106.

2. CONSENSUS (JONES)

Jones, James A., "An Index of Consensus of Rankings in Small Groups," *American Sociological Review*, 24 (August, 1959), pp. 533–537. See pp. 534–535.

3. CONSENSUS (THOMPSON)

Thompson, James D., "Authority and Power in 'Identical' Organizations," *American Journal of Sociology*, 62 (November, 1956) pp. 290–301. See p. 295.

4. CONSENSUS AND DISSENT WITH REFERENCE TO SUPREME COURT DECISIONS

Snyder, Eloise C., "Uncertainty and the Supreme Court's Decisions," *American Journal of Sociology*, 65 (November, 1959), pp. 241–245. See p. 243.

5. GROUP CONSENSUS REGARDING SOLUTIONS TO PROBLEMS

Borgatta, Edgar F., Robert F. Bales, and Arthur S. Couch, "Some Findings Relevant to the Great Man Theory of Leadership," *American Sociological Review*, 19 (December, 1954), pp. 755–759. See p. 758.

6. INDIVIDUAL-GROUP SIMILARITY

March, James G., "Influence Measurement in Experimental and Semi-Experimental Groups," *Sociometry*, 19 (December, 1956), pp. 260–271. See p. 262.

7. INDIVIDUAL-GROUP SIMILARITY, OVER-ALL

March; see category 6 above.

8. ROLE CONSENSUS

Thomas, Edwin J., "Role Conceptions and Organizational Size," *American Sociological Review*, 24 (February, 1959), pp. 30–37. See p. 32.

9. STAFF CONSENSUS IN MENTAL HOSPITALS

Wallace, Anthony F. C., and Harold A. Rashkis, "The Relation of Staff Consensus to Patient Disturbance on Mental Hospital Wards," *American Sociological Review*, 24 (December, 1959), pp. 829–835. See pp. 830 and 833.

10. VALUE CONSENSUS

Farber, Benard, "An Index of Marital Integration," *Sociometry*, 20 (June, 1957), pp. 117–134. See pp. 119–120.

Kerckhoff, Alan C., and Keith E. Davis, "Value Consensus and Need Complementarity in Mate Selection," *American Sociological Review*, 27 (June, 1962), pp. 295–303. See p. 297.

CRIME AND DELINQUENCY

SEE ALSO

Conformity and Deviance
Urban Areas: Metropolitan Areas and Dominance
Urban Areas: Segregation
Urban Areas: Socioeconomic Status
Urban Areas: Urbanization (Family Status)
Urban Areas: Various Categories

1. CRIME, SERIOUSNESS OF

Rose, Arnold M. , and Arthur E. Prell, "Does the Punishment Fit the Crime? A Study in Social Valuation," *American Journal of Sociology*, 61 (November, 1955), pp. 247–259. See p. 251.

2. CRIME PATTERN, ATYPICAL

Schmid, Calvin, "Urban Crime Areas: Part I," *American Sociological Review*, 25 (August, 1960), pp. 527–542. See pp. 537–538.

3. CRIMES OF DECEIT

Nettler, Gwynn, "Antisocial Sentiment and Criminality," *American Sociological Review*, 24 (April, 1959), pp. 202–208. See p. 205.

4. CRIMINALITY

Nettler; see category 3 above.

5. CRIMINALITY, OFFICIAL

Nettler; see category 3 above.

6. DELINQUENCY PRONENESS, SOCIAL RESPONSIBILITY (GOUGH)

See also category 7 below.
Gough, Harrison G., and Donald R. Peterson, "The Identification

and Measurement of Predispositional Factors in Crime and Delinquency," *Journal of Consulting Psychology,* 16 (June, 1952), pp. 207–212. See pp. 207–208.

Gough, Harrison G., *California Psychological Inventory,* Palo Alto, Calif.: Consulting Psychologists Press, 1956.

Two of the 18 subtests of the *California Psychological Inventory* (CPI) have been used frequently to measure delinquency proneness. These two subtests are the Responsibility (Re) and Socialization (So) components of the CPI.

The 18 subtests of the CPI (which, in addition to Re and So, measures dominance, capacity for status, sociability, social presence, self-acceptance, sense of well-being, self-control, tolerance, good impression, communality, achievement via conformance, achievement via independence, intellectual efficiency, psychological mindedness, flexibility, and femininity) consist of varying numbers of true-false statements describing personal opinions and the behavior of self and others. If the subject agrees with a statement or feels that it is true about himself, he is to answer "true." The Re scale consists of 42 such statements, and the So scale contains 22 statements. These 64 items are derived from a similar list of 64 items published in an earlier paper by Gough and Peterson (1952).

Copies of the CPI may be purchased from the Consulting Psychologists Press, Inc., 577 College Avenue, Palo Alto, California, 94306. For an extensive bibliography (144 citations) and reviews of the CPI, see Oscar K. Buros, *The Sixth Mental Measurements Yearbook,* Highland Park, New Jersey: The Gryphon Press, 1965, pp. 166–170.

Lindzey, Gardner, and James A. Urdan, "Personality and Social Choice," *Sociometry,* 17 (February, 1954), pp. 47–63. See p. 49.

Reckless, Walter C., Simon Dinitz, and Ellen Murray, "Self Concept as an Insulator against Delinquency," *American Sociological Review,* 21 (December, 1956), pp. 744–746. See p. 744.

Reckless, Walter C., Simon Dinitz, and Barbara Kay, "The Self

Component in Potential Delinquency and Potential Non-Delinquency," *American Sociological Review*, 22 (October, 1957), pp. 566–570. See p. 567.

Scarpitti, Murray, Dinitz, and Reckless (1960); see category 10 below.

Vincent, Clark E., "Socioeconomic Status and Familial Variables in Mail Questionnaire Responses," *American Journal of Sociology*, 69 (May, 1964), pp. 647–653. See pp. 647–649.

McClosky, Herbert, and John H. Schaar, "Psychological Dimensions of Anomy," *American Sociological Review*, 30 (February, 1965), pp. 14–40. See pp. 30–31.

7. DELINQUENCY PRONENESS, SOCIALIZATION

See also category 6 above.

Gough and Peterson (1952); see category 6 above.

Gough (1956); see category 6 above.

Reckless, Dinitz, and Murray (1956); see category 6 above.

Gough, Harrison G., "Theory and Measurement of Socialization," *Journal of Consulting Psychology*, 24 (February, 1960), pp. 23–30.

Scarpitti, Murray, Dinitz, and Reckless (1960); see category 10 below.

Landis, Judson R., and Frank R. Scarpitti, "Perceptions Regarding Value Orientation and Legitimate Opportunity: Delinquents and Non-Delinquents," *Social Forces*, 44 (September, 1965), pp. 83–91. See p. 85.

8. DELINQUENT ACTS AFFECTING INTERPERSONAL RELATIONS

Scott, John Finley, "Two Dimensions of Delinquent Behavior," *American Sociological Review*, 24 (April, 1959), pp. 240–245. See p. 241.

9. DELINQUENT ACTS NOT AFFECTING INTERPERSONAL RELATIONS

Scott; see category 8 above.

10. DELINQUENT BEHAVIOR CHECKLIST

Nye, F. Ivan, and James F. Short, Jr., "Scaling Delinquent Behavior," *American Sociological Review*, 22 (June, 1957), pp. 326–331. See pp. 328–329.

The approach of Nye and Short to the measurement of delinquency represents an effort "to avoid the socioeconomic and other biases which appear inseparable from official records or institutionalized populations. They attempt to avoid such biases by going directly to the behavior involved rather than employing the actions taken by enforcement agencies as criteria." (F. Ivan Nye, personal communication, November, 1966).

To achieve this purpose, Nye and Short have constructed a list of 21 items of criminal and anti-social behavior (p. 328) "which would (1) provide a range from trivial to serious crimes, (2) be committed by an appreciable segment of the population, and (3) be admitted under favorable circumstances." The constructed items were administered as part of a questionnaire to samples of urban, suburban, and rural public high school students and to boys and girls in state training schools. The data gathered from these questionnaires were then utilized to study the scalability of the delinquency checklist items.

Nine items were selected for the initial scaling effort, and from them a seven-item Guttman scale emerged which (p. 330) "satisfactorily ordered the non-institutional population." In order to create an instrument which might be more suitable for populations of official delinquents, four items involving more serious offenses were added to the seven-item scale; however, it was found that the seven-item scale differentiated boys in training school and public school more clearly than did the eleven-item scale.

The authors caution that "obtaining valid data is contingent on anonymity, positive motivations to cooperate and partial disguise of the nature of the list of items." (F. Ivan Nye, personal communication, November, 1966). They conclude (p. 331) that "These delinquency scales are in no case presented as final or definitive," and they, in fact, have continued to experiment with the items in some of their subsequent publications (see for example Nye, Short, and Olson, below). The seven-item scale is as follows:

DELINQUENT BEHAVIOR CHECKLIST

1. Driven a car without a driver's license or permit? (Do not include driver training courses) (1) very often ___, (2) several times ___, (3) once or twice ___, (4) no ___.
2. Taken little things (worth less than $2) that did not belong to you? (1) no ___, (2) once or twice ___, (3) several times ___, (4) very often ___.
3. Bought or drank beer, wine, or liquor? (Include drinking at home) (1) no ___, (2) once or twice ___, (3) several times ___, (4) very often ___.
4. Purposely damaged or destroyed public or private property that did not belong to you? (1) very often ___, (2) once or twice ___, (3) several times ___, (4) no ___.
5. Skipped school without a legitimate excuse? (1) no ___, (2) once or twice ___, (3) several times ___, (4) very often ___.
6. Had sex relations with a person of the opposite sex? (1) no ___, (2) once or twice ___, (3) 3 or 4 times ___, (4) 5 or 6 times ___, (5) 7 or 8 times ___, (6) 9 times or more ___.
7. Defied your parents' authority (to their face)? (1) no ___, (2) once or twice ___, (3) several times ___, (4) very often.

Short, James F., Jr., and F. Ivan Nye, "Reported Behavior as a Criterion of Deviant Behavior," *Social Problems*, 5 (1957–1958), pp. 207–213.

Nye, F. Ivan, James F. Short, Jr., and Virgil J. Olson, "Socioeconomic Status and Delinquent Behavior," *American Journal of Sociology*, 63 (February, 1958), pp. 381–389. See p. 384.

Nye, F. Ivan, and James F. Short, Jr., *Family Relationships and Delinquent Behavior*, New York: John Wiley and Sons, Inc., 1958. See Chapter II.

Scarpitti, Frank R., Ellen Murray, Simon Dinitz, and Walter C. Reckless, "The 'Good' Boy in a High Delinquency Area: Four Years Later," *American Sociological Review*, 25 (August, 1960), pp. 555–558. See p. 556.

Smith, David O., and Desmond S. Cartwright, "Two Measures of Reported Delinquent Behavior," *American Sociological Review*, 39 (August, 1965), pp. 573–576. See pp. 573–574.

11. GANG DELINQUENCY DIMENSIONS: AUTHORITY PROTEST

Short, James F., Jr., Ray A. Tennyson, and Kenneth I. Howard, "Behavior Dimensions of Gang Delinquency," *American So-*

ciological Review, 28 (June, 1963), pp. 411–428. See pp. 417–421.

12. **GANG DELINQUENCY DIMENSIONS: CONFLICT**

Short, Tennyson, and Howard; see category 11 above.

13. **GANG DELINQUENCY DIMENSIONS: RETREATIST PATTERN**

Short, Tennyson, and Howard; see category 11 above.

14. **GANG DELINQUENCY DIMENSIONS: STABLE CORNER ACTIVITIES**

Short, Tennyson, and Howard; see category 11 above.

15. **GANG DELINQUENCY DIMENSIONS: STABLE SEX PATTERN**

Short, Tennyson, and Howard; see category 11 above.

16. **ILLEGAL BEHAVIOR**

Clark, John P., and Eugene P. Wenninger, "Socio-Economic Class and Area as Correlates of Illegal Behavior among Juveniles," *American Sociological Review*, 27 (December, 1962), pp. 826–834. See pp. 829–830.

Clark, John P., and Eugene P. Wenninger, "Goal Orientations and Illegal Behavior among Juveniles," *Social Forces*, 42 (October, 1963), pp. 49–59. See p. 52.

17. **LARCENY**

Nettler; see category 3 above.

18. **OPPORTUNITY, LIMITED AWARENESS OF**

Landis, Judson R., Simon Dinitz, and Walter C. Reckless, "Implementing Two Theories of Delinquency: Value Orientation and Awareness of Limited Opportunity," *Sociology and Social Research*, 47 (July, 1963), pp. 408–416. See pp. 411–413.

Landis and Scarpitti (1965); see category 7 above. See pp. 84–85.

19. **OPPORTUNITY STRUCTURES: ADULT "CLOUT"**

Short, James F., Raymond Rivera, and Ray A. Tennyson, "Perceived Opportunities, Gang Membership and Delinquency," *American Sociological Review*, 30 (February, 1965), pp. 56–67. See pp. 61 and 63.

20. **OPPORTUNITY STRUCTURES: ADULT HELPFULNESS**

Short, Rivera, and Tennyson; see category 19 above.

21. OPPORTUNITY STRUCTURES:ADULT POWER AND HELPFUL-
NESS

Short, Rivera, and Tennyson, p. 63; see category 19 above.

22. OPPORTUNITY STRUCTURES: CRIMINAL, ELITE INCLUSIVE

Short, Rivera, and Tennyson, p. 65; see category 19 above.

23. OPPORTUNITY STRUCTURES: CRIMINAL, ELITE LESS INCLU-
SIVE

Short, Rivera, and Tennyson, p. 65; see category 19 above.

24. OPPORTUNITY STRUCTURES: CRIMINAL LEARNING

Short, Rivera, and Tennyson, pp. 60 and 63; see category 19 above.

25. OPPORTUNITY STRUCTURES: ILLEGITIMATE

Short, Rivera, and Tennyson, p. 63; see category 19 above.

26. OPPORTUNITY STRUCTURES: ILLEGITIMATE, LESS INCLUSIVE

Short, Rivera, and Tennyson, p. 63; see category 19 above.

27. OPPORTUNITY STRUCTURES: INTEGRATION OF THE CARRIERS
OF CRIMINAL AND NONCRIMINAL VALUES

Short, Rivera, and Tennyson, pp. 60 and 63; see category 19 above.

28. OPPORTUNITY STRUCTURES: LEGITIMATE EDUCATIONAL

Short, Rivera, and Tennyson, pp. 60 and 63; see category 19 above.

29. OPPORTUNITY STRUCTURES: LEGITIMATE EDUCATIONAL
AND OCCUPATIONAL

Short, Rivera, and Tennyson, p. 63; see category 19 above.

30. OPPORTUNITY STRUCTURES: LEGITIMATE OCCUPATIONAL

Short, Rivera, and Tennyson, pp. 60 and 63; see category 19 above.

31. OPPORTUNITY STRUCTURES: PERCEPTION OF ILLEGITIMATE

Short, Rivera, and Tennyson, p. 63; see category 19 above.

32. OPPORTUNITY STRUCTURES: PERCEPTION OF ILLEGITIMATE,
LESS INCLUSIVE

Short, Rivera, and Tennyson; see category 19 above.

33. OPPORTUNITY STRUCTURES: TOTAL CRIMINAL

Short, Rivera, and Tennyson, p. 63; see category 19 above.

34. OPPORTUNITY STRUCTURES: VISIBILITY OF CRIMINAL CAREER

Short, Rivera, and Tennyson; see category 19 above.

35. PAROLE VIOLATION

Kirby, Bernard C., "Parole Prediction Using Multiple Correlation," *American Journal of Sociology*, 59 (May, 1954), pp. 539–550. See p. 542.

36. PREDICTION OF SUCCESSFUL TREATMENT FOR DELINQUENT BEHAVIOR

Freeman, Howard E., and H. Ashley Weeks, "Analysis of a Program of Treatment of Delinquent Boys," *American Journal of Sociology*, 62 (July, 1956), pp. 56–61. See p. 58.

37. RATTING

Street, David, "The Inmate Group in Custodial and Treatment Settings," *American Sociological Review*, 30 (February, 1965), pp. 40–55. See p. 44.

38. SEX OFFENSE, "ABNORMAL"

Nettler; see category 3 above.

39. SEX OFFENSE, "NORMAL"

Nettler; see category 3 above.

40. STAFF PERSPECTIVES OF DELINQUENTS: BELIEF IN CLOSE RELATIONSHIP

Street; see category 37 above.

41. STAFF PERSPECTIVES OF DELINQUENTS: BELIEF IN DISCIPLINE

Street; see category 37 above.

42. STAFF PERSPECTIVES OF DELINQUENTS: BELIEF IN IMPORTANCE OF UNDERSTANDING

Street; see category 37 above.

43. STAFF PERSPECTIVES OF DELINQUENTS: BELIEF IN STRONG SANCTIONS

Street; see category 37 above.

44. STEALING, ATTITUDE TOWARD

Smigel, Erwin O., "Public Attitudes toward Stealing as Related to the Size of the Victim Organization," *American Sociological Review*, 21 (June, 1956), pp. 320–327. See p. 321.

45. SUBSCRIPTION TO PRISON CODE

Tittle, Charles R., and Drollene P. Tittle, "Social Organization of Prisoners: An Empirical Test," *Social Forces*, 43 (December, 1964), pp. 216–221. See p. 218.

46. THEFT

Dentler, Robert A. and Lawrence J. Monroe, "Social Correlates of Early Adolescent Theft," *American Sociological Review*, 26 (October, 1961), pp. 733–743. See p. 734.

47. THEFT, EFFECT OF, ON INTERPERSONAL RELATIONS

Turner, Ralph H., "Self and Other in Moral Judgment," *American Sociological Review*, 19 (June, 1954), pp. 249–259. See p. 259.

EDUCATION: ATTITUDE TOWARD AND PERCEPTIONS OF

1. CIVIC EDUCATION NORMS, ATTITUDE TOWARD

Litt, Edgar, "Civic Education, Community Norms, and Political Indoctrination," *American Sociological Review*, 28 (February, 1963), pp. 69–75. See p. 71.

2. EDUCATION, ATTITUDE TOWARD

Weinstein, Eugene A., and Paul N. Geisel, "Family Decision Making over Desegregation," *Sociometry*, 25 (March, 1962), pp. 21–29. See p. 25.

3. EDUCATION, CRITICISM OF

Horton, John E., and Wayne E. Thompson, "Powerlessness and Political Negativism: A Study of Defeated Local Referendums," *American Journal of Sociology*, 67 (March, 1962), pp. 485–493. See p. 489.

4. GREEK ORGANIZATIONS, ATTITUDE TOWARD

Scott, William A., "Cognitive Consistency, Response Reinforcement and Attitude Change," *Sociometry*, 22 (September, 1959), pp. 219–229. See pp. 222–223.

5. "HOW MUCH SCHOOL IS POSSIBLE" SCALE

Tumin, Melvin M., and Arnold S. Feldman, "Status Perspective and Achievement: Education and Class Structure in Puerto Rico," *American Sociological Review*, 21 (August, 1956), pp. 464–472. See p. 467.

6. IMPORTANCE OF EDUCATION, PERCEPTION OF

Tumin and Feldman; see category 5 above.

7. MORALE, GENERAL

Weinberg, Carl, "Achievement and School Attitudes of Adolescent Boys as Related to Behavior and Occupational Status of

Families," *Social Forces*, 42 (May, 1964), pp. 462–466. See p. 464.

8. POSTGRADUATE EDUCATION (NURSING), ATTITUDE TOWARD

Deutscher, Irwin, and Ann Montague, "Professional Education and Conflicting Value Systems: The Role of Religious Schools in the Educational Aspirations of Nursing Students," *Social Forces*, 35 (December, 1956), pp. 126–131. See p. 127.

9. POWER RATING IN CHILDREN'S GROUP

Gold, Martin, "Power in the Classroom," *Sociometry*, 21 (March, 1958), pp. 50–60. See pp. 52–53.

10. PUBLIC EDUCATION, ATTITUDE TOWARD

Cramer, M. Richard, "School Desegregation and New Industry: The Southern Community Leaders' Viewpoint," *Social Forces*, 41 (May, 1963), pp. 384–389. See p. 388.

11. QUITTING SCHOOL, ATTITUDE TOWARD

McDill, Edward L., "A Comparison of Three Measures of Attitude Intensity," *Social Forces*, 38 (December, 1959), pp. 95–99. See p. 95.

12. SCHOOL MORALE

Weinberg; see category 7 above.

13. SCHOOL SPIRIT SENTIMENT

Selvin, Hanan C., and Warren O. Hagstrom, "The Empirical Classification of Formal Groups," *American Sociological Review*, 28 (June, 1963), pp. 399–411. See p. 405.

14. SCHOOL SUPERINTENDENCIES, PRESTIGE OF

Mason, Ward S., and Neal Gross, "Intra-occupational Prestige Differentiation: The School Superintendency," *American Sociological Review*, 20 (June, 1955), pp. 326–331. See p. 327.

15. SORORITIES AND FEMALE HOUSING UNITS, PRESTIGE OF

Nagel, Donald, and Judith Hidding, "Perceived Assignment of Prestige Variables within the Social Fraternity-Sorority System on a College Campus," unpublished, 1958.

Johnson, Margo, "A Study of Prestige Ranking among University Women," unpublished, 1961.

Barnlund, Dean C., and Carrol Harland, "Propinquity and Prestige as Determinants of Communication Networks," *Sociometry*, 26 (December, 1963), pp. 467–479. See p. 476.

16. STUDENT VALUE HIERARCHY

Wallace, Walter L., "Institutional and Life-Cycle Socialization of College Freshmen," *American Journal of Sociology*, 70 (November, 1964), pp. 303–318. See p. 305.

EDUCATION: BEHAVIOR IN AND CHARACTERISTICS OF

1. ACADEMIC PERFORMANCE

Greeley, Andrew M., "Influence of the 'Religious Factor' on Career Plans and Occupational Values of College Graduates," *American Journal of Sociology*, 68 (May, 1963), pp. 658–671. See p. 661.

2. GRADUATE SCHOOL, INDEX OF INTEGRATION IN

Gottlieb, David, "Processes of Socialization in American Graduate Schools," *Social Forces*, 40 (December, 1961), pp. 124–131. See p. 126.

3. GRADUATE STUDENTS, INDEX OF SPECIFIC ENCOURAGEMENT TO

Gottlieb, p. 130; see category 2 above.

4. LEVEL AND QUALITY OF FORMAL EDUCATION

Wilensky, Harold L., "Mass Society and Mass Culture: Interdependence or Independence?" *American Sociological Review*, 29 (April, 1964), pp. 173–197. See p. 184.

5. QUALITY OF A COLLEGE

Greeley; see category 1 above.

6. ROLE DEFINITION OF TEACHER, CONSENSUS ABOUT

Gross, Neal, Ward Mason, and Alexander McEachern, *Explorations in Role Analysis: Studies of the School Superintendency Role*, New York: John Wiley and Sons, 1958, pp. 116–163.

Bible, Bond L., and James D. McComas, "Role Consensus and Teacher Effectiveness," *Social Forces*, 42 (December, 1963), pp. 225–233. See p. 228.

7. ROLE EXPECTATION OF TEACHER

Bible and McComas (1963); see category 6 above.

8. ROLE PERFORMANCE OF TEACHER

Bible and McComas (1963); see category 6 above.

9. SELECTIVITY OF EDUCATIONAL INSTITUTIONS

Clignet, Remi P., and Philip Foster, "Potential Elites in Ghana and the Ivory Coast: A Preliminary Comparison," *American Journal of Sociology,* 70 (November, 1964), pp. 349–362. See p. 353.

10. SOCIAL STATUS STRUCTURE (PRESTIGE) OF A SCHOOL

Reiss, Albert J., Jr., and Albert L. Rhodes, "The Distribution of Juvenile Delinquency in the Social Class Structure," *American Sociological Review,* 26 (October, 1961), pp. 720–732. See p. 725.

11. TEACHER EFFECTIVENESS

Bible and McComas (1963); see category 6 above.

FAMILY: INTERPERSONAL RELATIONS AND AUTHORITY

SEE ALSO

Family: Perceptions of and Attitudes toward Personality Traits: Motives and Needs

1. ACTIVITIES PROHIBITED TO WIVES

Back, Kurt W., Reuben Hill, and J. Mayone Stycos, "Interviewer Effect on Scale Reproducibility," *American Sociological Review*, 20 (August, 1955), pp. 443–446. See p. 443.

2. ADJUSTMENT TO FAMILY AND PEERS

Bowerman, Charles E., and John W. Kinch, "Changes in Family and Peer Orientation of Children between the 4th and 10th Grades," *Social Forces*, 37 (March, 1959), pp. 206–211. See pp. 209–210.

3. ADJUSTMENT TO OTHER FAMILY MEMBERS

Stryker, Sheldon, "Role-Taking Accuracy and Adjustment," *Sociometry*, 20 (December, 1957) pp. 286–296. See p. 288.

4. ADOLESCENT INDEPENDENCE

Nye, F. Ivan, "Adolescent-Parent Adjustment—Socio-Economic Level as a Variable," *American Sociological Review*, 16 (June, 1951), pp. 341–349. See p. 344.

Landis, Paul, and Carol L. Stone, "The Relationship of Parental Authority Patterns to Teenage Adjustments," Bulletin No. 538, Washington Agricultural Experiment Station, Pullman, Wash.: State College of Washington, 1952.

Psathas, George, "Ethnicity, Social Class and Adolescent Independence from Parental Control," *American Sociological Review*, 22 (August, 1957), pp. 415–423. See pp. 416–417.

5. ADOLESCENT INDEPENDENCE: ACTIVITIES WITH STATUS IMPLICATIONS

Psathas (1957), p. 420; see category 4 above.

6. ADOLESCENT INDEPENDENCE: PARENTAL REGARD FOR JUDGMENT

Psathas (1957), p. 420; see category 4 above.

7. ADOLESCENT INDEPENDENCE: PERMISSIVENESS IN AGE-RELATED ACTIVITIES

Psathas (1957), p. 420; see category 4 above.

8. ADOLESCENT INDEPENDENCE: PERMISSIVENESS IN OUTSIDE ACTIVITIES

Psathas (1957), p. 420; see category 4 above.

9. AGREEMENT BETWEEN PARENTS AND OFFSPRING

Stryker; see category 3 above.

10. AUTHORITARIAN PARENT-YOUTH RELATIONS

Elder, Glen H., Jr., "Family Structure and Educational Attainment: A Cross-National Analysis," *American Sociological Review*, 30 (February, 1965), pp. 81–96. See p. 83.

Elder, Glen H., Jr., "Role Relations, Sociocultural Environments, and Autocratic Family Ideology," *Sociometry*, 28 (June, 1965), pp. 173–196.

11. CHILD-REARING PRACTICES: AUTONOMY

See also categories 17 and 57 below.

Rosen, Bernard C., and Roy D'Andrade, "The Psychosocial Origins of Achievement Motivation," *Sociometry*, 22 (September, 1959), pp. 185–218. See p. 203.

Hoffman, Lois Wladis, Sidney Rosen, and Ronald Lippitt, "Parental Coerciveness, Child Autonomy, and Child's Role at School," *Sociometry*, 23 (March, 1960), pp. 15–22. See p. 16.

12. CHILD-REARING PRACTICES: CASUAL TREATMENT

Sewell, William H., Paul H. Mussen, and Chester W. Harris, "Relationships among Child Training Practices," *American Sociological Review*, 20 (April, 1955), pp. 137–148. See pp. 144–145.

13. CHILD-REARING PRACTICES: CONSISTENCY OF DISCIPLINE

McCord, William, Joan McCord, and Alan Howard, "Early Familial Experiences and Bigotry," *American Sociological Review*, 25 (October, 1960), pp. 717–722. See p. 720.

14. CHILD-REARING PRACTICES: DISCIPLINE (MCCORD, MCCORD, HOWARD)

McCord, McCord, and Howard; see category 13 above.

15. CHILD-REARING PRACTICES: DISCIPLINE (YARROW, SCOTT, DELEEUW, HEINIG)

Yarrow, Marian R., Phyllis Scott, Louise deLeeuw, and Christine Heinig, "Child-Rearing in Families of Working and Nonworking Mothers," *Sociometry*, 25 (June, 1962), pp. 122–140. See pp. 138–139.

16. CHILD-REARING PRACTICES: EMOTIONAL RELATIONSHIPS OF PARENT AND CHILD

Yarrow, Scott, deLeeuw, and Heinig; see category 15 above.

17. CHILD-REARING PRACTICES: INDEPENDENCE TRAINING (WINTERBOTTOM)

See also category 10 in Achievement Motivation.

See also category 11 above.

Winterbottom, Marian, "The Relation of Need for Achievement to Learning in Independence and Mastery," in John Atkinson (ed.), *Motives in Fantasy, Action and Society*, Princeton, N.J.: D. Van Nostrand, 1958, pp. 453–478. See pp. 455–461.

Rosen, Bernard C., "Race, Ethnicity, and the Achievement Syndrome," *American Sociological Review*, 24 (February, 1959), pp. 47–60. See p. 51.

Rosen, Bernard C., "Socialization and Achievement Motivation in Brazil," *American Sociological Review*, 27 (October, 1962), pp. 612–625. See p. 617.

18. CHILD-REARING PRACTICES: INDEPENDENCE TRAINING (YARROW, SCOTT, DELEEUW, HEINIG)

Yarrow, Scott, deLeeuw, and Heinig; see category 15 above.

19. CHILD-REARING PRACTICES: NONINSISTENCE

Sewell, Mussen, and Harris; see category 12 above.

20. CHILD-REARING PRACTICES: NONPUNITIVE TREATMENT

Sewell, Mussen, and Harris; see category 12 above.

21. CHILD-REARING PRACTICES: PARENTAL COERCIVENESS

Hoffman, Rosen, and Lippitt (1960); see category 11 above.

22. CHILD-REARING PRACTICES: PARENT-CHILD INTERACTION

Rosen and D'Andrade (1959); see category 11 above.

23. CHILD-REARING PRACTICES: PARENT-CHILD INTERACTION

Sewell, Mussen, and Harris; see category 11 above.

24. CHILD-REARING PRACTICES: PARENTAL SANCTIONS

See also categories 14 and 15 above.

Rosen and D'Andrade (1959); see category 11 above.

25. CHILD-REARING PRACTICES: PERMISSIVENESS IN EARLY FEEDING

Sewell, Mussen, and Harris; see category 12 above.

26. CHILD-REARING PRACTICES: PERMISSIVENESS IN TOILET TRAINING

Sewell, Mussen, and Harris; see category 12 above.

27. CHILD-REARING PRACTICES: PROMOTION OF INDEPENDENCE

See also categories 17 and 18 above.

Sewell, Mussen, and Harris; see category 12 above.

28. CHILD-REARING PRACTICES: REARING ENVIRONMENT

Yarrow, Scott, deLeeuw, and Heinig, p. 140; see category 15 above.

29. CHILD-REARING PRACTICES: SELF-RELIANCE TRAINING

See also category 18 above.

Rosen and D'Andrade (1959); see category 11 above.

30. CHILD-REARING PRACTICES: TRADITIONAL DEVELOPMENTAL CHILD-REARING PATTERN

Straus, Murray A., "Childhood Experience and Emotional Security in the Context of Sinhalese Social Organization," *Social Forces*, 33 (December, 1954), pp. 152–160. See p. 155.

31. COMMUNICATIONS WITH SPOUSE

Back, Hill, and Stycos, p. 444; see category 1 above.

32. COMPLEMENTARY NEEDS

See Personality Traits: Motives and Needs.

33. DEPENDENCE ON OTHER FAMILY MEMBERS

Stryker, Sheldon, *Attitude Ascription in Adult Married Offspring-Parent Relationships: A Study of the Social Psychological*

Theory of G. H. Mead, unpublished Ph.D. dissertation, University of Minnesota, 1955, pp. 66–69.

Stryker, Sheldon, "Relationships of Married Offspring and Parent: A Test of Mead's Theory," *American Journal of Sociology,* 62 (November, 1956), pp. 308–319. See p. 311.

Stryker (1957); see category 3 above.

34. DIVISION OF LABOR IN HOUSEHOLD TASKS

Blood, Robert O., Jr., and Robert L. Hamblin, "The Effect of the Wife's Employment on the Family Power Structure," *Social Forces,* 36 (May, 1958), pp. 347–352. See pp. 350–351.

35. ENTREPRENEURIAL FAMILY STATUS

Ladinsky, Jack, "Careers of Lawyers, Law Practice, and Legal Institutions," *American Sociological Review,* 28 (February, 1963), pp. 47–54. See p. 49.

36. FAMILY ADJUSTMENT

Rundquist, Edward A., and Raymond F. Sletto, *Personality in the Depression,* Minneapolis, Minn.: University of Minnesota Press, 1936, p. 24.

Ramsey, Charles E., and Lowry Nelson, "Change in Values and Attitudes toward the Family," *American Sociological Review,* 21 (October, 1956), pp. 605–609. See p. 607.

37. FAMILY ADJUSTMENT: FEELING THAT PARENTS EXPECT TOO MUCH FROM THEIR CHILDREN

Ramsey and Nelson (1956); see category 36 above.

38. FAMILY ADJUSTMENT: HOME AS A PLEASANT PLACE TO BE

Ramsey and Nelson (1956); see category 36 above.

39. FAMILY ADJUSTMENT: INTIMACY-WILLINGNESS TO EXCHANGE CONFIDENCES

Ramsey and Nelson (1956); see category 36 above.

40. FAMILY ADJUSTMENT: SENSE OF AGREEMENT BETWEEN PARENT AND CHILD ON IDEALS

Ramsey and Nelson (1956); see category 36 above.

41. FAMILY ADJUSTMENT: SENSE OF OBLIGATION TO THE FAMILY

Ramsey and Nelson (1956); see category 36 above.

42. FAMILY AGREEMENT ON SOCIAL MOBILITY

Strodtbeck, Fred L., "The Family as a Three-Person Group," *American Sociological Review*, 19 (February, 1954), pp. 23–29. See p. 24.

43. FAMILY INTERACTION: EMOTIONALITY

Bales, Robert F., *Interaction Process Analysis*, Cambridge, Mass.: Addison-Wesley, 1950, pp. 1–29.

Leik, Robert, "Instrumentality and Emotionality in Family Interaction," *Sociometry*, 26 (June, 1963), pp. 131–145. See p. 136.

44. FAMILY INTERACTION: INSTRUMENTALITY

Bales (1950); see category 43 above.

Leik (1963); see category 43 above.

45. FAMILY INTERACTION: SOCIAL-EMOTIONAL ASPECTS OF INTERACTION

Parsons, Talcott, and Robert F. Bales, *Family, Socialization and Interaction Process*, Glencoe, Ill.: The Free Press, 1955, pp. 260–261.

Farber, Bernard, "An Index of Marital Integration," *Sociometry*, 20 (June, 1957), pp. 117–134. See p. 123.

46. FAMILY OPINION SURVEY: FEMALE DISAGREEMENT ESTIMATE

Kirkpatrick, Clifford, and Charles Hobart, "Disagreement, Disagreement Estimate, and Non-Empathetic Imputations for Intimacy Groups Varying from Favorite Date to Married," *American Sociological Review*, 19 (February, 1954), pp. 10–19. See p. 12.

47. FAMILY OPINION SURVEY: FEMALE NON-EMPATHY

Kirkpatrick and Hobart; see category 46 above.

48. FAMILY OPINION SURVEY: MALE DISAGREEMENT ESTIMATE

Kirkpatrick and Hobart; see category 46 above.

49. FAMILY OPINION SURVEY: MALE-FEMALE DISAGREEMENT

Kirkpatrick and Hobart; see category 46 above.

50. FAMILY OPINION SURVEY: MALE NON-EMPATHY

Kirkpatrick and Hobart; see category 46 above.

51. FAMILY PARTICIPATION

Anderson, W. A., "The Family and Individual Social Participation," *American Sociological Review*, 8 (August, 1943), pp. 420–424. See p. 420.

Young, James N., and Selz C. Mayo, "Manifest and Latent Participators in a Rural Community Action Program," *Social Forces*, 38 (December, 1959), pp. 140–145. See p. 142.

52. FAMILY TYPE: BY DIVISION OF LABOR AND DIVISION OF POWER

Gold, Martin, and Carol Slater, "Office, Factory, Store—and Family: A Study of Integration Setting," *American Sociological Review*, 23 (February, 1958), pp. 64–74. See p. 67.

53. FAMILY TYPE: BY HUSBAND'S OCCUPATION

Gold and Slater; see category 52 above.

54. FATHER-CENTERED DECISION MAKING

See also categories 59 and 83 below.

Wilkening, Eugene A., "Change in Farm Technology as Related to Familism, Family Decision Making, and Family Integration," *American Sociological Review*, 19 (February, 1954), pp. 29–37. See p. 35.

55. GENERALIZED CHILD ROLE

Emmerich, Walter, and Faye Smoller, "The Role Patterning of Parental Norms," *Sociometry*, 27 (September, 1964), pp. 382–390. See pp. 383–384.

56. GENERALIZED OBLIGATIONS

Emmerich and Smoller; see category 55 above.

57. INDEPENDENCE OF FAMILY

See also 12 and 17 above.

Strodtbeck, Fred L., "Family Interaction, Values, and Achievement," in David C. McClelland, Alfred L. Baldwin, Urie Bronfenbrenner, and Fred L. Strodtbeck, *Talent and Society*, Princeton, N.J.: D. Van Nostrand, 1958.

58. INTRAFAMILIAL CONFLICT

Heiss, Jerold S., "Premarital Characteristics of the Religiously Intermarried in an Urban Area," *American Sociological Review*, 25 (February, 1960), pp. 47–55. See p. 51.

59. JOINT INVOLVEMENT OF HUSBAND AND WIFE IN DECISIONS

See also categories 54 above and 83 below.

Wilkening, Eugene A., "Joint Decision-Making in Farm Families as a Function of Status and Role," *American Sociological Review*, 23 (April, 1958), pp. 187–192. See p. 188.

60. MARITAL AUTHORITY

Blood and Hamblin, p. 349; see category 34 above.

61. MARRIED OFFSPRING-PARENT ADJUSTMENT

Stryker, Sheldon, "The Adjustment of Married Offspring to Their Parents," *American Sociological Review*, 20 (April, 1955), pp. 149–154. See p. 149.

Stryker (1955); see category 33 above.

Stryker (1956); see category 33 above.

Stryker (1957); see category 3 above.

62. MATRIARCHAL-PATRIARCHAL CONTINUUM

Middleton, Russell, and Snell Putney, "Dominance in Decisions in the Family: Race and Class Differences," *American Journal of Sociology*, 65 (May, 1960), pp. 605–609. See p. 607.

63. MODESTY

Back, Hill, and Stycos, p. 444; see category 1 above.

64. PARENT-ADOLESCENT INTERDEPENDENCE

Elder, Glen H., Jr., "Structural Variations in the Child Rearing Relationship," *Sociometry*, 25 (September, 1962), pp. 241–262. See pp. 243–244.

Elder, Glen H., Jr., "Parental Power Legitimation and Its Effect on the Adolescent," *Sociometry*, 26 (March, 1963), pp. 50–65. See p. 55.

65. MUTUAL AID AND AFFECTION

Johnson, Cyrus M., and Alan C. Kerckhoff, "Family Norms, Social Position, and the Value of Change," *Social Forces*, 43 (December, 1964), pp. 149–156. See pp. 151–152.

66. PARENTAL AFFECTION

McCord, McCord, and Howard; see category 13 above.

67. PARENTAL AGGRESSION

McCord, McCord, and Howard; see category 13 above.

68. PARENTAL ATTITUDES

McCord, McCord, and Howard; see category 13 above.

69. PARENTAL AUTHORITY

Freeman, Howard E., and H. Ashley Weeks, "Analysis of a Problem of Treatment of Delinquent Boys," *American Journal of Sociology*, 62 (July, 1956), pp. 56–61. See pp. 57–58.

70. PARENTAL CONSTRAINT

Kohn, Melvin L., and Eleanor E. Carroll, "Social Class and the Allocation of Parental Responsibilities," *Sociometry*, 23 (December, 1960), pp. 372–392. See p. 376.

71. PARENTAL DEVIANCE

McCord, McCord, and Howard; see category 13 above.

72. PARENTAL DOMINANCE

McCord, McCord, and Howard; see category 13 above.

73. PARENTAL EXPLANATION

Elder (1963); see category 64 above.

74. PARENTAL INFLUENCE, DIFFERENTIAL

Gist, Noel P., and William S. Bennett, Jr., "Aspirations of Negro and White Students," *Social Forces*, 42 (October, 1963), pp. 40–48. See p. 47.

75. PARENTAL INFLUENCE, EMANCIPATION FROM

Heiss; see category 58 above.

76. PARENTAL POWER, TYPES OF

Elder (1962); see category 64 above.
Elder (1963); see category 64 above.

77. PARENTAL REACTION

McCord, McCord, and Howard, see category 13 above.

78. PARENTAL SUPPORTIVENESS (BOWERMAN, ELDER)

Bowerman, Charles E., and Glen H. Elder, Jr., "Variations in Adolescent Perception of Family Power Structure," *American Sociological Review*, 29 (August, 1964), pp. 551–567. See p. 563.

79. PARENTAL SUPPORTIVENESS (KOHN, CARROLL)

Kohn and Carroll, p. 375; see category 70 above.

80. PARENTAL UNIT, TYPE OF

McCord, McCord, and Howard; see category 13 above.

81. PARENTAL VALUES

McCord, McCord, and Howard; see category 13 above.

82. POSITIVE SOCIAL-EMOTIONAL RESPONSE

O'Rourke, John F., "Field and Laboratory: The Decision-Making Behavior of Family Groups in Two Experimental Conditions," *Sociometry*, 26 (December, 1963), pp. 422–435. See p. 425.

83. POWER IN MAKING FAMILY DECISIONS

See also categories 54 and 59 above.

Blood and Hamblin; see category 34 above.

84. SEX DRIVE

Wallin, Paul, "Religiosity, Sexual Gratification and Marital Satisfaction," *American Sociological Review*, 22 (June, 1957), pp. 300–305. See p. 303.

85. SUPPORTIVENESS

Strodtbeck; see category 42 above.

86. TRADITION AND AUTHORITY, FAMILY ORIENTATION TO

Suchman, Edward A., "Sociomedical Variations among Ethnic Groups," *American Journal of Sociology*, 70 (November, 1964), pp. 319–331. See pp. 323–324.

FAMILY: PERCEPTIONS OF AND ATTITUDES TOWARD

SEE ALSO

Family: Interpersonal Relations and Authority
Personality Traits: Motives and Needs

1. ADOLESCENTS' PERCEPTION OF DEPRIVATION-SATISFACTION, DIRECT

Rushing, William A., "Adolescent-Parent Relationship and Mobility Aspirations," *Social Forces*, 43 (December, 1964), pp. 157–166. See p. 162.

2. ADOLESCENTS' PERCEPTION OF DEPRIVATION-SATISFACTION, INDIRECT

Rushing, pp. 161–162; see category 1 above.

3. ATTITUDE TOWARD FAMILY

Freeman, Howard E., and H. Ashley Weeks, "Analysis of a Problem of Treatment of Delinquent Boys," *American Journal of Sociology*, 62 (July, 1956), pp. 56–61. See p. 58.

4. ATTITUDE TOWARD FAMILY RELATIONS

Dentler, Robert A., and Lawrence J. Monroe, "Social Correlates of Early Adolescent Theft," *American Sociological Review*, 26 (October, 1961), pp. 733–743. See p. 740.

5. AUTHORITARIAN FAMILY ORIENTATION

See also category 10 below.
Struening, Elmer L., and Arthur H. Richardson, "A Factor Analytic Exploration of the Alienation, Anomia and Authoritarianism Domain," *American Sociological Review*, 30 (October, 1965), pp. 768–776. See pp. 769 and 771.

6. CHILD-REARING ATTITUDES (MARTIN, WESTIE)

Martin, James G., and Frank R. Westie, "The Tolerant Personality," *American Sociological Review*, 24 (August, 1959), pp. 521–528. See p. 525.

7. CHILD-REARING ATTITUDES (MILLER, SWANSON)

Miller, Daniel R., and Guy E. Swanson, *The Changing American Parent*, New York: John Wiley and Sons, 1958, pp. 264–270.

Rosengren, William R., "Social Status, Attitudes toward Pregnancy and Child-Rearing Attitudes," *Social Forces*, 41 (December, 1962), pp. 127–134. See pp. 130–131.

8. CHILD-REARING, EXPOSURE TO LITERATURE OF

Blau, Zena Smith, "Exposure to Child-Rearing Experts: A Structural Interpretation of Class-Color Differences," *American Journal of Sociology*, 69 (May, 1964), pp. 596–608. See pp. 597–598.

Blau, Zena Smith, "Class Structure, Mobility, and Change in Child-Rearing," *Sociometry*, 28 (June, 1965), pp. 210–219. See p. 213.

9. EARLY DISSATISFACTION WITH PARENTS

Heiss, Jerold S., "Premarital Characteristics of the Religiously Intermarried in an Urban Area," *American Sociological Review*, 25 (February, 1960), pp. 47–55. See p. 51.

10. FAMILY IDEOLOGY (ADORNO, FRENKEL-BRUNSWIK, LEVINSON, SANFORD)

See also category 5 above.

Adorno, T. W., Else Frenkel-Brunswik, Daniel J. Levinson, and R. Nevitt Sanford, *The Authoritarian Personality*, New York: Harper and Brothers, 1950, pp. 339–340.

Abegglen, James C., "Subordination and Autonomy Attitudes of Japanese Workers," *American Journal of Sociology*, 63 (September, 1957), pp. 181–189. See p. 182.

11. FAMILY IDEOLOGY, TRADITIONAL

Huffman, P. E., *Authoritarian Personality and Family Ideology*, unpublished M.A. thesis, Western Reserve University, 1950.

Stryker, Sheldon, *Attitude Ascription in Adult Married Offspring-Parent Relationships: A Study of the Social Psychological Theory of G. H. Mead*, unpublished Ph.D. dissertation, University of Minnesota, 1955.

Stryker, Sheldon, "Relationships of Married Offspring and Parent: A Test of Mead's Theory," *American Journal of Sociology*, 62 (November, 1956), pp. 308–319. See p. 310.

Stryker, Sheldon, "Role-Taking Accuracy and Adjustment," *Sociometry*, 20 (December, 1957), pp. 286–296. See p. 288.

12. FAMILY TENSIONS

Morris, Ruth R., "Female Delinquency and Relational Problems," *Social Forces*, 43 (October, 1964), pp. 82–89. See p. 85.

13. ORIENTATION TOWARD FAMILY OR PEERS

See also categories 15 and 20 below.

Bowerman, Charles E., and John W. Kinch, "Changes in Family and Peer Orientation of Children between the Fourth and Tenth Grades," *Social Forces*, 37 (March, 1959), pp. 206–211. See p. 207.

14. PARENT IMAGE DIFFERENTIAL

Harburg, Ernest, *Covert Hostility: Its Social Origins and Relationship with Overt Compliance*, unpublished Ph.D. dissertation, University of Michigan, 1962.

Ginsburg, Gerald P., Noel F. McGinn, and Ernest Harburg, *Dimensions of Recalled Parent-Child Interaction*, unpublished manuscript, University of Nevada, 1964.

McGinn, Noel F., Ernest Harburg, and Stevo Julius, "Blood Pressure Reactivity and Recall of Treatment by Parents," *Journal of Personality and Social Psychology*, 1 (February, 1965), pp. 147–153. See pp. 148–149.

McGinn, Noel F., Ernest Harburg, and Gerald P. Ginsburg, "Dependency Relations with Parents and Affiliative Responses in Michigan and Guadalajara," *Sociometry*, 28 (September, 1965), pp. 305–321. See pp. 308–313.

15. PARENT-PEER CROSS PRESSURES

See also category 13 above.

Brittain, Clay V., "Adolescent Choices and Parent-Peer Cross-

Pressures," *American Sociological Review*, 28 (June, 1963), pp. 385–391. See p. 386.

16. PARENTAL INTEREST IN CHILD

Rosenberg, Morris, "Parental Interest and Children's Self-Conceptions," *Sociometry*, 26 (March, 1963), pp. 35–49. See p. 47.

17. PERCEIVED CONFLICT

Streib, Gordon F., "Family Patterns in Retirement," *Journal of Social Issues*, 14 (No. 2, 1958), pp. 46–60. See pp. 48–49.

Johnson, Cyrus M., and Alan C. Kerckhoff, "Family Norms, Social Position, and the Value of Change," *Social Forces*, 43 (December, 1964), pp. 149–156. See p. 152.

18. PERCEIVED SIMILARITY WITH FAMILY

Farber, Bernard, "An Index of Marital Integration," *Sociometry*, 20 (June, 1957), pp. 117–134. See p. 125.

19. PERCEPTION OF FAMILY

Murray, Henry A., *Thematic Apperception Test*, Cambridge, Mass: Harvard University Press, 1943.

O'Rourke, John F., "Field and Laboratory: The Decision-Making Behavior of Family Groups in Two Experimental Conditions," *Sociometry*, 26 (December, 1963), pp. 422–435. See p. 427.

20. PREDOMINANT FAMILY IDENTIFICATION

See also category 13 above.

Weinstein, Eugene A., "Family Identification of Foster Children," *Social Forces*, 38 (October, 1959), pp. 58–61. See p. 58.

21. REJECTION OF FAMILY

Sewell, William H., and A. O. Haller, "Factors in the Relationship between Social Status and the Personality Adjustment of the Child," *American Sociological Review*, 24 (August, 1959), pp. 511–520. See p. 517.

22. TRADITIONAL-DEVELOPMENTAL CONCEPTIONS OF A GOOD MOTHER, A GOOD FATHER, AND A GOOD CHILD

Duvall, Evelyn Millis, "Conceptions of Parenthood," *American*

Journal of Sociology, 52 (November, 1946), pp. 193–203. See pp. 195–196.

Connor, Ruth, Theodore B. Johannis, Jr., and James Walters, "Parent-Adolescent Relationships. II. Intra-Familial Conceptions of the Good Father, Good Mother, and Good Child," *Journal of Home Economics*, 46 (March, 1954), pp. 183–191. See p. 187.

Connor, Ruth, Theodore B. Johannis, Jr., and James Walters, "Family Recreation in Relation to Role Conceptions of Family Members," *Marriage and Family Living*, 17 (November, 1955), pp. 306–309. See pp. 307–308.

Connor, Ruth, Helen Finch Greene, and James Walters, "Agreement of Family Member Conceptions of 'Good' Parent and Child Roles," *Social Forces*, 36 (May, 1958), pp. 353–358. See p. 354.

FAMILY COHESION

SEE ALSO

Cohesion

1. EXTENDED-FAMILY ATTITUDES

Taietz, Phillip, "Conflicting Group Norms and the 'Third' Person in the Interview," *American Journal of Sociology*, 68 (July, 1962), pp. 97–104. See p. 98.

2. EXTENDED-FAMILY COHESION: CONCERN WITH FAMILY UNITY

Stuckert, Robert P., "Occupational Mobility and Family Relationships," *Social Forces*, 41 (March, 1963), pp. 301–307. See p. 306.

3. EXTENDED-FAMILY COHESION: FAMILY AS A REFERENCE GROUP

Stuckert, pp. 304–305; see category 2 above.

4. EXTENDED-FAMILY COHESION: IDENTIFICATION WITH FAMILY

Litwak, Eugene, "Occupational Mobility and Extended Family Cohesion," *American Sociological Review*, 25 (February, 1960), pp. 9–21. See pp. 16–17.

Litwak, Eugene, "Geographic Mobility and Extended Family Cohesion," *American Sociological Review*, 25 (June, 1960), pp. 385–394. See p. 388.

Stuckert, p. 304; see category 2 above.

5. FAMILISM (ROHWER)

Rohwer, Robert A., *Family Factors and Tenure Experience*, Ames, Iowa: Bulletin 375, Iowa Agricultural Experimental Station, 1950.

Wilkening, p. 31; see category 6 below.

6. FAMILISM (WILKENING)

Wilkening, Eugene A., "Change in Farm Technology as Related to Familism, Family Decision Making, and Family Integration," *American Sociological Review*, 19 (February, 1954), pp. 29–37. See p. 34.

7. FAMILY INSTABILITY

Hillery, George A., Jr., "The Negro in New Orleans: A Functional Analysis of Demographic Data," *American Sociological Review*, 22 (April, 1957), pp. 183–188. See p. 185.

8. FAMILY INTEGRATION (ANGELL)

Angell, Robert C., *The Family Encounters the Depression*, New York: Charles Scribner's Sons, 1934, pp. 14–15.
Wilkening, p. 31; see category 6 above.

9. FAMILY INTEGRATION (CAVAN)

Cavan, Ruth S., and K. Ranck, *The Family and the Depression*, Chicago, Ill.: University of Chicago, 1938, pp. 11–14.
Wilkening, p. 31; see category 6 above.

10. FAMILY INTEGRATION (HEISS)

Heiss, Jerold S., "Premarital Characteristics of the Religiously Intermarried in an Urban Area," *American Sociological Review*, 25 (February, 1960), pp. 47–55. See p. 52.

11. FAMILY INTEGRATION (HILL)

Hill, Reuben, *Families Under Stress*, New York: Harper and Brothers, 1949, pp. 130–132 and 426–428.
Wilkening, p. 31; see category 6 above.

12. FAMILY INTEGRATION (WILKENING)

Wilkening, p. 32; see category 6 above.

13. FAMILY INTEGRATION: COOPERATION OF FAMILY MEMBERS

Wilkening; see category 6 above.

14. FAMILY INTEGRATION: ESPRIT DE CORPS

Wilkening; see category 6 above.

15. FAMILY INTEGRATION: JOINT PARTICIPATION OF FAMILY MEMBERS

Wilkening; see category 6 above.

16. FAMILY INTEGRATION: RATING OF FAMILY SOLIDARITY

Wilkening; see category 6 above.

17. FAMILY SOLIDARITY

Klapp, Orrin E., "Ritual and Family Solidarity," *Social Forces*, 37 (March, 1959), pp. 212–214. See p. 214.

18. FAMILY SOLIDARITY PATTERN, TYPICAL

Geiger, Kent, "Deprivation and Solidarity in the Soviet Urban Family," *American Sociological Review*, 20 (February, 1955), pp. 57–68. See p. 59.

19. KIN INVOLVEMENT

Rossi, Alice S., "Naming Children in Middle-Class Families," *American Sociological Review*, 30 (August, 1965), pp. 499–513. See p. 501.

20. KINSHIP CONTACTS

Wilkening; see category 6 above.

HEALTH: INDIVIDUAL

SEE ALSO

Medicine and Health: Attitudes toward
Medicine and Health: Behavior in and
Characteristics of
Occupational Roles
Personal Adjustment

1. **CULTURAL-TRUISM OPINION QUESTIONNAIRE**

Anderson, Lynn R., and William J. McGuire, "Prior Reassurance of Group Consensus as a Factor in Producing Resistance to Persuasion," *Sociometry*, 28 (March, 1965), pp. 44–56. See pp. 49–50.

2. **INDIVIDUAL SOCIOMETRIC PATTERN AND MENTAL HEALTH**

Northway, Mary L., "A Plan for Sociometric Studies in a Longitudinal Programme of Research in Child Development," *Sociometry*, 17 (August, 1954), pp. 272–281. See p. 274.

3. **KNOWLEDGE ABOUT DISEASE**

Suchman, Edward A., *Socio-Cultural Variations in Illness and Medical Care*, New York: New York City Health Department, 1963.

Suchman, Edward A., "Sociomedical Variations among Ethnic Groups," *American Journal of Sociology*, 70 (November, 1964), pp. 319–331. See pp. 321–322.

4. **MEDICAL-KNOWLEDGE INDEX**

Lewis, Lionel S., "Knowledge, Danger, Certainty, and the Theory of Magic," *American Journal of Sociology*, 69 (July, 1963), pp. 7–12. See p. 10.

5. **MENTAL HEALTH**

Srole, Leo, Thomas S. Langner, Stanley T. Michael, Marvin K.

Opler, and Thomas Rennie, *Mental Health in the Metropolis*, New York: McGraw-Hill Book Co., 1962, pp. 59–66 and Appendix F.

Manis, Jerome G., Milton J. Brawer, Chester L. Hunt, and Leonard C. Kercher, "Validating a Mental Health Scale," *American Sociological Review*, 28 (February, 1963), pp. 108–116. See pp. 113–115.

Manis, Jerome, Milton J. Brawer, Chester L. Hunt, and Leonard C. Kercher, "Estimating the Prevalence of Mental Illness," *American Sociological Review*, 29 (February, 1964), pp. 84–89. See pp. 85 and 86–87.

6. MENTAL HEALTH ANALYSIS TEST

Thorpe, L. P., Willis W. Clark, and Ernest W. Tiegs, *Mental Health Analysis Manual*, Los Angeles, Calif.: California Test Bureau, 1946.

Burchinal, Lee G., "Social Status, Measured Intelligence, Achievement and Personality Adjustment of Rural Iowa Girls," *Sociometry*, 22 (March, 1959), pp. 75–80. See p. 76.

7. PATIENT INFORMATION

Seeman, Melvin, and John W. Evans, "Alienation and Learning in a Hospital Setting," *American Sociological Review*, 27 (December, 1962), pp. 772–782. See p. 775.

8. PHYSICAL-HEALTH STATUS CHECKLIST

Bellin, Seymour S., and Robert H. Hardt, "Marital Status and Mental Disorders among the Aged," *American Sociological Review*, 23 (April, 1958), pp. 155–162. See p. 158.

9. PHYSICAL SELF-MAINTENANCE

Many, Karen, "Indices of Social and Physical Self-Maintenance," Geriatrics Research Project Staff Memorandum, San Francisco, Calif.: Langley Porter Institute, 1961.

Lowenthal, Marjorie Fiske, "Social Isolation and Mental Illness in Old Age," *American Sociological Review*, 29 (February, 1964), pp. 54–70. See p. 63.

10. RISK-LEVELS MEASURE

Bellin and Hardt, p. 160; see category 8 above.

INNOVATION AND DIFFUSION

SEE ALSO

Intergroup Relations, Racial and Ethnic: Discrimination

1. ACCEPTANCE OF CHANGE

Johnson, Cyrus M., and Alan C. Kerckhoff, "Family Norms, Social Position, and the Value of Change," *Social Forces*, 43 (December, 1964), pp. 149–156. See p. 152.

2. ACCEPTANCE OF CHANGE IN FARM TECHNOLOGY: ALL PRACTICES

Wilkening, Eugene A., "Change in Farm Technology as Related to Familism, Family Decision Making, and Family Integration," *American Sociological Review*, 19 (February, 1954), pp. 29–37. See pp. 31 and 33.

3. ACCEPTANCE OF CHANGE IN FARM TECHNOLOGY: IMPROVEMENTS

Wilkening; see category 2 above.

4. ACCEPTANCE OF CHANGE IN FARM TECHNOLOGY: INNOVATIONS

Wilkening; see category 2 above.

5. ADOPTION OF FARM PRACTICES

Marsh, C. Paul, and A. Lee Coleman, "Group Influences and Agricultural Innovations: Some Tentative Findings and Hypotheses," *American Journal of Sociology*, 61 (May, 1956), pp. 588–594. See p. 589.

6. ADOPTION OF RECOMMENDED WATER-MANAGEMENT PRACTICES

Polgar, Steven, Howard Dunphy, and Bruce Cox, "Diffusion and Farming Advice: A Test of Some Current Notions," *Social Forces*, 42 (October, 1963), pp. 104–111. See p. 106.

7. ATTITUDE TOWARD DESEGREGATION

Greenfield, Robert W., "Factors Associated with Attitudes toward Desegregation in a Florida Residential Suburb," *Social Forces*, 40 (October, 1961), pp. 31–42. See p. 34.

8. ATTITUDE TOWARD SCHOOL DESEGREGATION

See also category 20 below.

Cramer, M., Richard, "School Desegregation and New Industry: The Southern Community Leader's Viewpoint," *Social Forces*, 41 (May, 1963), pp. 384–389. See p. 385.

9. ATTITUDE TOWARD SCHOOL INTEGRATION

Siegel, Sidney, and Irma Lee Shepherd, "An Ordered Metric Measure of Social Distance," *Sociometry*, 22 (December, 1959), pp. 336–342. See pp. 338–339.

10. DIFFUSION, POTENCY OF

Dodd, S. C., "Diffusion Is Predictable: Testing Probability Models for Laws of Interaction," *American Sociological Review*, 20 (August, 1955) pp. 392–401. See p. 393.

11. DIFFUSION: INTEGRATION OF COMMUNICATION STRUCTURE

Coughenour, pp. 334–335; see category 12 below.

12. DIFFUSION: LOCALITY RATE

Coughenour, C. Milton, "The Rate of Technological Diffusion Among Locality Groups," *American Journal of Sociology*, 69 (January, 1964), pp. 325–339. See p. 332.

13. DIFFUSION: STRENGTH OF SCIENTIFIC FARMING VALUE

Young, James N. and A. Lee Coleman, "Neighborhood Norms and the Adoption of Farm Practices," *Rural Sociology*, 24 (December, 1959), pp. 372–380. See pp. 374–375.

Coughenour, p. 334; see category 12 above.

14. DIFFUSION: USE OF INSTITUTIONALIZED MEDIA

Coughenour, p. 334; see category 12 above.

15. DIFFUSION: USE OF PRINTED MEDIA

Coughenour, p. 334; see category 12 above.

16. KNOWLEDGE OF KENNEDY ASSASSINATION

Spitzer, Stephan P., and Norman K. Denzin, "Levels of Knowledge in an Emergent Crisis," *Social Forces*, 44 (December 1965), pp. 234–237. See p. 235.

17. PIONEERING, ATTITUDES TOWARD

Larsen, Otto N., and Melvin L. DeFleur, "The Comparative Role of Children and Adults in Propaganda Diffusion," *American Sociological Review*, 19 (October, 1954), pp. 593–602. See p. 595.

18. PROPAGANDA DIFFUSION: DEGREE OF COMMUNICATION

Weinstein, Eugene A., and Paul N. Geisel, "Family Decision Making over Desegregation," *Sociometry*, 25 (March, 1962), pp. 21–29. See p. 25 and Appendix A.

19. READINESS TO CHANGE JOBS

Trumbo D., *An Analysis of Attitudes toward Change among the Employees of an Insurance Company*, unpublished Ph.D. dissertation, Michigan State University, 1958.

Faunce, William A., "Social Stratification and Attitude toward Change in Job Content," *Social Forces*, 39 (October, 1960), pp. 140–148. See pp. 142–143.

20. READINESS TO DESEGREGATE: GENERAL ACTION SET

See also category 8 above.

Tumin, Melvin, Paul Barton, and Bernie Burrus, "Education, Prejudice, and Discrimination: A Study in Readiness for Desegregation," *American Sociological Review*, 23 (February, 1958), pp. 41–49. See p. 44.

Tumin, Melvin, "Readiness and Resistance to Desegregation: A Social Portrait of the Hard Core," *Social Forces*, 36 (March, 1958), pp. 256–263. See pp. 257–258.

21. READINESS TO DESEGREGATE: IMAGE OF THE NEGRO

Tumin, Barton, and Burrus (1958), p. 43; see category 20 above.
Tumin (1958), p. 257; see category 20 above.

22. READINESS TO DESEGREGATE: SENTIMENT STRUCTURE

Tumin, Barton, and Burrus (1958), p. 44; see category 20 above.
Tumin (1958) p. 258; see category 20 above.

23. READINESS TO DESEGREGATE: SOCIAL IDEOLOGY

Tumin, Barton, and Burrus (1958), p. 44; see category 20 above.
Tumin (1958), p. 257; see category 20 above.

24. READINESS TO DESEGREGATE: SPECIFIC ACTION SET

Tumin, Barton, and Burrus (1958), p. 44; see category 20 above.

Tumin (1958), p. 258; see category 20 above.

25. RESISTANCE TO CHANGE

McClosky, Herbert, "Conservatism and Personality," *American Political Science Review*, 52 (March, 1958), pp. 27–45.

Carter, Roy E., Jr., and Peter Clarke, "Public Affairs Opinion Leadership among Educational Television Viewers," *American Sociological Review*, 27 (December, 1962), pp. 792–799. See p. 795.

26. RESISTANCE TO CHANGE IN A MENTAL HOSPITAL

See also Medicine and Health: Behavior in and Characteristics of.

Pearlin, Leonard I., "Sources of Resistance to Change in a Mental Hospital," *American Journal of Sociology*, 68 (November, 1962), pp. 325–334. See p. 326.

27. SOCIOCULTURAL CHANGE

Allen, Francis R., and W. Kenneth Bentz, "Toward the Measurement of Sociocultural Change," *Social Forces*, 43 (May, 1965), pp. 522–532. See pp. 524–525.

INTERESTS

SEE ALSO

Personality: General

Personality Traits: Motives and Needs

Personality Traits: Various Categories

1. INTERESTS OUTSIDE ONESELF (FACTOR H, SIXTEEN PERSONALITY FACTOR QUESTIONNAIRE)

Cattell, Raymond B., D. R. Saunders, and G. Stice, *Sixteen Personality Factor Questionnaire*, Champaign, Ill.: Institute for Personality and Ability Testing.

Haller, A. O., "Planning to Farm: A Social Psychological Interpretation," *Social Forces*, 37 (March, 1959), pp. 263–268. See p. 266.

2. INTEREST RECORD

Jones, M. C., *ICW Interest Record*, Berkeley, Calif.: Institute of Child Welfare (mimeographed).

Marks, J. B., "Interests, Leadership, and Sociometric Status Among Adolescents," *Sociometry*, 17 (November, 1954), pp. 340–349. See p. 341.

3. KUDER PREFERENCE RECORD, VOCATIONAL

Kuder, G. Frederic, *Kuder Preference Record—Vocational*, Chicago, Ill.: Science Research Associates.

Brooks, M. S., and R. S. Weynand, "Interest Preferences and Their Effect upon Academic Success," *Social Forces*, 32 (March, 1954), pp. 281–285. See p. 281.

Venable, Tom C., "The Relationship of Selected Factors to the Social Structure of a Stable Group," *Sociometry*, 17 (November, 1954), pp. 355–357. See p. 355.

4. NONVERBAL PREFERENCE TEST

Baker, Bela O., and Theodore R. Sarbin, "Differential Mediation

of Social Perception as a Correlate of Social Adjustment,"
Sociometry, 19 (June, 1956), pp. 69–83. See p. 72.

5. READING TYPE, ACTIVE-PASSIVE

Graham, Saxon, "Cultural Compatibility in the Adoption of Television," *Social Forces*, 33 (December, 1954), pp. 166–170. See p. 168.

6. RECREATION TYPE, ACTIVE-PASSIVE

Graham, p. 169; see category 5 above.

INTERGROUP RELATIONS: ETHNOCENTRISM

1. ETHNOCENTRISM (CALIFORNIA E SCALE AND MODIFICA-
TIONS, ADORNO, FRENKEL-BRUNSWIK, LEVINSON, SANFORD)

Adorno, T. W., Else Frenkel-Brunswik, Daniel J. Levinson, and R.
Nevitt Sanford, *The Authoritarian Personality*, New York:
Harper and Brothers, 1950. See especially Chapter IV, "The
Study of Ethnocentric Ideology," by Daniel J. Levinson, pp.
102–150.

Ethnocentrism "refers to group relations generally. . . . Out
groups are the objects of negative opinions and hostile attitudes;
ingroups are the objects of positive opinions and uncritically sup-
portive attitudes." (pp. 102, 104) As measures of ethnocentrism,
the authors of *The Authoritarian Personality* present several different scale forms. The Total Ethnocentrism Scale, for example,
consists of 34 items which refer to attitudes toward Negroes (subscale N), attitudes toward other minorities (subscale M), and
patriotic attitudes (subscale P). Subsequent forms of the E Scale
present fewer items, some substitutions, and various revisions in
the wording of items. Most subsequent forms also include items
from the Anti-Semitism Scale. The suggested final form of the E
Scale includes 20 items. Six of these items are devoted to anti-
Jewish sentiments, six refer to anti-Negro sentiments, and the
remaining eight concern other minorities and patriotism.

Data concerning the reliability of the scales, the means and
discriminatory power of the items, and the intercorrelations of the
various subscales are presented in relation to each of the various
forms described above. The authors' criteria of item selection

include theoretical relevance, statistical adequacy, brevity, and simplicity. On the basis of their data the authors suggest (p. 141) that "the brief ten-item E Scale [the "Fourth Form"] . . . can be used as a dependable measure of ethnocentrism. Whenever possible, however, it would appear advantageous to use a longer form which is likely to be more reliable and which can cover in a more systematic fashion various aspects of ethnocentric ideology." It also is their view that the 20-item final E Scale probably represents an acceptable balance between administrative expediency and research effectiveness.

The 20-item suggested Final Form of the E Scale (which includes nine of the ten items in the "Fourth Form") is presented below. In addition, the final item of the "Fourth Form" has been added as item 7 in subscale N. All of the items are so stated that agreement indicates ethnocentrism. An individual's total score or subscales scores may be calculated as the algebraic sum of his responses (ranging from -3 to $+3$); or the responses may be converted to positive numbers (such that $-3 = 1$; $-2 = 2$, and so on) and then summed.

THE ETHNOCENTRISM SCALE

(See Authoritarianism, category 1, for instructions and response format.)

A. JEWS

*1. One trouble with Jewish businessmen is that they stick together and prevent other people from having a fair chance in competition.
*2. I can hardly imagine myself marrying a Jew.
*3. There may be a few exceptions, but in general Jews are pretty much alike.
*4. The trouble with letting Jews into a nice neighborhood is that they gradually give it a typical Jewish atmosphere.
 5. To end prejudice against Jews, the first step is for the Jews to try sincerely to get rid of their harmful and irritating faults.
 6. There is something different and strange about Jews; it's hard to tell what they are thinking and planning, and what makes them tick.

* The asterisks indicate the items comprising the ten-item "Fourth Form" of the E Scale.

B. NEGROES

*1. Negroes have their rights, but it is best to keep them in their own districts and schools and to prevent too much contact with whites.
*2. It would be a mistake ever to have Negroes for foremen and leaders over whites.
3. Negro musicians may sometimes be as good as white musicians, but it is a mistake to have mixed Negro-white bands.
4. Manual labor and unskilled jobs seem to fit the Negro mentality and ability better than more skilled or responsible work.
5. The people who raise all the talk about putting Negroes on the same level as whites are mostly radical agitators trying to stir up conflicts.
6. Most Negroes would become overbearing and disagreeable if not kept in their place.
*7. If Negroes live poorly, it's mainly because they are naturally lazy, ignorant, and without self-control.

C. OTHER MINORITIES AND PATRIOTISM

*1. Zootsuiters prove that when people of their type have too much money and freedom, they just take advantage and cause trouble.
*2. The worst danger to real Americanism during the last 50 years has come from foreign ideas and agitators.
*3. Now that a new world organization is set up, America must be sure that she loses none of her independence and complete power as a sovereign nation.
4. Certain religious sects who refuse to salute the flag should be forced to conform to such a patriotic action, or else be abolished.
5. Filipinos are all right in their place, but they carry it too far when they dress lavishly and go around with white girls.
6. America may not be perfect, but the American Way has brought us about as close as human beings can get to a perfect society.
7. It is only natural and right for each person to think that his family is better than any other.
8. The best guarantee of our national security is for America to have the biggest army and navy in the world and the secret of the atom bomb.

Roberts, Alan H., and Milton Rokeach, "Anomie, Authoritarianism, and Prejudice: A Replication," *American Journal of Sociology*, 61 (January, 1956), pp. 355–358. See p. 357.

Riddleberger, Alice B., and Annabelle B. Motz, "Prejudice and Perception," *American Journal of Sociology*, 62 (March, 1957), pp. 498–503. See p. 499.

Pettigrew, Thomas F., "Desegregation and Its Chances for Success: Northern and Southern Views," *Social Forces*, 35 (May, 1957), pp. 339–344. See p. 339.

Abegglen, James C., "Subordination and Autonomy Attitudes of Japanese Workers," *American Journal of Sociology*, 63 (September, 1957), pp. 181–189. See p. 182.

Kaufman, Walter C., "Status, Authoritarianism, and Anti-Semitism," *American Journal of Sociology*, 62 (January, 1957), pp. 379–382. See p. 381.

Mann, John H., "The Influence of Racial Prejudice on Sociometric Choices and Perceptions," *Sociometry*, 21 (June, 1958), pp. 150–158. See p. 153.

Chapman, Loren J., and Donald T. Campbell, "The Effect of Acquiescence Response-Set upon Relationships among the F-Scale, Ethnocentrism, and Intelligence," *Sociometry*, 22 (June, 1959), pp. 153–161. See p. 154.

Silberstein, Fred B., and Melvin Seeman, "Social Mobility and Prejudice," *American Journal of Sociology*, 65 (December, 1959), pp. 258–264. See p. 259.

Friedrichs, Robert W., "Alter vs. Ego," *American Sociological Review*, 25 (August, 1960), pp. 496–508. See p. 499.

Middleton, Russell, "Prejudice and Persuasion," *American Sociological Review*, 25 (October, 1960), pp. 676–686. See p. 681.

McDill, Edward L., "Anomie, Authoritarianism, Prejudice, and Socioeconomic Status: An Attempt at Clarification," *Social Forces*, 39 (March, 1961), pp. 239–245. See p. 240.

Rhyne, Edwin Hoffman, "Racial Prejudice and Personality Scales: An Alternative Approach," *Social Forces*, 41 (October, 1962), pp. 44–53. See p. 48.

Kutner, Bernard, and Norman B. Gordon, "Cognitive Functioning and Prejudice: A Nine-Year Follow-Up Study," *Sociometry*, 27 (March, 1964), pp. 66–74. See pp. 68–69.

Feagin, Joe R., "Prejudice, Orthodoxy and the Social Situation," *Social Forces*, 44 (September, 1965), pp. 46–56. See p. 47.

2. ETHNOCENTRISM (CATTON, HONG)

Catton, William R., Jr., and Sung Chick Hong, "The Relation of

Apparent Minority Ethnocentrism to Majority Antipathy," *American Sociological Review*, 27 (April, 1962), pp. 178–191. See p. 181.

3. ETHNOCENTRISM (MCCLOSKY, SCHAAR)

McClosky, Herbert, and John H. Schaar, "Psychological Dimensions of Anomy," *American Sociological Review*, 30 (February, 1965), pp. 14–40. See pp. 33–34 and 37.

4. NATIONALISM

Martin, James G., and Frank R. Westie, "The Tolerant Personality," *American Sociological Review*, 24 (August, 1959), pp. 521–528. See p. 523.

INTERGROUP RELATIONS, NONRACIAL AND NONETHNIC

1. ARTICULATION OF AMBIENCE

Caplow, Theodore, "The Definition and Measurement of Ambiences," *Social Forces*, 34 (October, 1955), pp. 28–33. See p. 30.

2. ATTITUDES TOWARD OLD PEOPLE

Drake, Joseph T., "Some Factors Influencing Students' Attitudes toward Older People," *Social Forces*, 35 (March, 1957), pp. 266–271. See p. 267.

3. EVALUATION OF OUT-GROUPS

Triandis, Harry C., and Leigh M. Triandis, "Race, Social Class, Religion, and Nationality as Determinants of Social Distance," *Journal of Abnormal and Social Psychology*, 61 (July, 1960), pp. 110–118. See pp. 111–112.

Fishbein, Martin, "The Perceptions of Non-members: A Test of Merton's Reference Group Theory," *Sociometry*, 26 (September, 1963), pp. 271–286. See p. 276.

4. IDENTIFICATION

Havens, A. Eugene, *Social Psychological Factors Associated with the Adoption of New Technologies by Milk Producers*, unpublished Ph.D. dissertation, Ohio State University, 1962.

Lipman, Aaron, and A. Eugene Havens, "The Colombian Violencia: An Ex Post Facto Experiment," *Social Forces*, 44 (December, 1965), pp. 238–245. See p. 240.

5. INFLUENCE OF INTERACTION WITH OUT-GROUPS ON SOLIDARITY OF IN-GROUPS

Harvey, O. J., "An Experimental Investigation of Negative and Positive Relations between Small Groups through Judgmental

Indices," *Sociometry*, 19 (December, 1956), pp. 201–209. See p. 204.

6. IN-GROUP PREFERENCE (CRISWELL)

Criswell, J. N., "Sociometric Methods of Measuring Group Preferences," *Sociometry*, 6 (November, 1943), pp. 398–408. See pp. 400–403.

Miller, Delbert C., "Decision-Making Cliques in Community Power Structures: A Comparative Study of an American and an English City," *American Journal of Sociology*, 64 (November, 1958), pp. 299–310. See p. 301.

7. IN-GROUP PREFERENCE (PROCTOR, LOOMIS)

Proctor, Charles H., and Charles P. Loomis, "Analysis of Sociometric Data," in Marie Jahoda, Morton Deutsch, and Stuart Cook (eds.), *Research Methods in Social Relations, Part II*, New York: Dryden, 1951, p. 574.

Ellis, Robert A., "Social Stratification and Social Relations: An Empirical Test of the Disjunctiveness of Social Classes," *American Sociological Review*, 22 (October, 1957), pp. 560–578. See p. 576.

8. INTERCLASS FRIENDSHIP

Ellis (1957), p. 573; see category 7 above.

9. INTERGROUP ROLE CONFLICT

Getzels, J. W., and E. G. Guba, "Role, Role Conflict, and Effectiveness: An Empirical Study," *American Sociological Review*, 19 (April, 1954), pp. 164–175. See p. 167.

10. INTERPARTY COMPETITION (KEY)

Key, V. O., Jr., *American State Politics*, New York: Alfred A. Knopf, Inc., 1956, pp. 97–104.

Casstevens, Thomas W., and Charles Press, "The Context of Democratic Competition in American State Politics," *American Journal of Sociology*, 68 (March, 1963), pp. 536–543. See p. 537.

11. INTERPARTY COMPETITION (RANNEY, KENDALL)

Ranney, Austin, and Willmore Kendall, *Democracy and the American Party System*, New York: Harcourt, Brace and Co., 1956, pp. 40–56.

Casstevens and Press (1963) see category 10 above.

12. INTERPARTY COMPETITION (SCHLESINGER)

Schlesinger, Joseph A., "A Two Dimensional Scheme for Classifying the States According to Degree of Interparty Competition," *American Political Science Review*, 49 (December, 1955), pp. 1120–1128.

Casstevens and Press (1963); see category 10 above.

13. PERCEIVED THREAT OF OUT-GROUPS

Triandis and Triandis (1960); see category 3 above.

Fishbein (1963); see category 3 above.

14. SOCIAL DISTANCE (BLALOCK)

See also Medicine and Health: Behavior in and Characteristics of.

Blalock, H. M., Jr., "Status Consciousness: A Dimensional Analysis," *Social Forces*, 37 (March, 1959), pp. 243–248. See p. 244.

15. SOCIAL DISTANCE (GOSLIN)

Goslin, David A., "Accuracy of Self Perception and Social Acceptance," *Sociometry*, 25 (September, 1962), pp. 283–296. See p. 285.

16. SOCIAL DISTANCE (PHILLIPS)

Phillips, Derek L., "Rejection: A Possible Consequence of Seeking Help for Mental Disorders," *American Sociological Review*, 28 (December, 1963), pp. 963–973. See p. 967.

Phillips, Derek L., "Rejection of the Mentally Ill: The Influence of Behavior and Sex," *American Sociological Review*, 29 (October, 1964), pp. 679–687. See p. 683.

17. SOCIAL DISTANCE (WESTIE, LAUMANN)

Westie, Frank, "Negro-White Status Differentials and Social Distance," *American Sociological Review*, 17 (October, 1952), pp. 550–558. See p. 551.

Laumann, Edward O., "Subjective Social Distance and Urban Occupational Stratification," *American Journal of Sociology* 71 (July, 1965), pp. 26–36. See pp. 29–30.

18. STEREOTYPE RATING

Harvey; see category 5 above.

19. TOLERANCE (MCCLOSKY, SCHAAR)

McClosky, Herbert, and John H. Schaar, "Psychological Dimensions of Anomy," *American Sociological Review*, 30 (February, 1965), pp. 14–40. See pp. 33–34.

20. TOLERANCE (SIMMONS)

Simmons, J. L., "Tolerance of Divergent Attitudes," *Social Forces*, 43 (March, 1965), pp. 347–352. See p. 349.

INTERGROUP RELATIONS, RACIAL AND ETHNIC: CHARACTERISTICS OF

1. ABILITY TO RECOGNIZE JEWS

Savitz, Leonard D., and Richard F. Tomasson, "The Identification of Jews," *American Journal of Sociology*, 64 (March, 1959), pp. 468–475. See p. 471.

2. ACCURACY SCORE FOR OTHER RACE

Ausubel, D. P., "Reciprocity and Assumed Reciprocity of Acceptance among Adolescents, A Sociometric Study," *Sociometry*, 16 (November, 1953), pp. 339–348. See pp. 340–342.

Mann, John H., "The Influence of Racial Prejudice on Sociometric Choices and Perceptions," *Sociometry*, 21 (June, 1958), pp. 150–158. See p. 154.

3. ACCURACY SCORE FOR OWN RACE

See also category 14 below.

Mann; see category 2 above.

4. APPARENT ALLEGIANCE TO A FOREIGN POWER

Catton, William R., Jr., and Sung Chick Hong, "The Relation of Apparent Minority Ethnocentrism to Majority Antipathy," *American Sociological Review*, 27 (April, 1962), pp. 178–191. See pp. 181–182.

5. APPARENT DISPROPORTIONATE POLITICAL INFLUENCE

Catton and Hong; see category 4 above.

6. APPARENT MONOPOLISTIC HOLDING OF HIGH-STATUS JOBS

Catton and Hong; see category 4 above.

7. APPARENT UNDUE SPECIAL PRIVILEGES AND IMMUNITIES

Catton and Hong; see category 4 above.

8. AWARENESS OF GROUP HOSTILITY

Gittler, Joseph B., and Dean H. Harper, "Measuring the Awareness of the Problem of Group Hostility," *Social Forces*, 34 (December, 1955), pp. 163–167. See p. 165.

9. ETHNIC-GROUP PRESTIGE

Angell, Robert C., "Preferences for Moral Norms in Three Problem Areas," *American Journal of Sociology*, 67 (May, 1962), pp. 650–660. See p. 650.

10. ETHNIC-GROUP STATUS

Lenski, Gerhard E., "Status Crystallization: A Non-Vertical Dimension of Social Status," *American Sociological Review*, 19 (August, 1954), pp. 405–413. See pp. 406–407.

11. GENERAL CHARACTERISTICS OF NEGROES

Campbell, Ernest Q., "Some Social Psychological Correlates of Direction in Attitude Change," *Social Forces*, 36 (May, 1958), pp. 335–340. See p. 336.

12. MARGINAL PERSONALITY CHARACTERISTICS

Kerckhoff, Alan C., and T. C. McCormick, "Marginal Status and Marginal Personality," *Social Forces*, 34 (October, 1955), pp. 48–55. See pp. 51–52.

13. NEGRO-WHITE LEADERSHIP SCORES

Cox, John A., and John D. Krumboltz, "Racial Bias in Peer Ratings of Basic Airmen," *Sociometry*, 21 (December, 1958), pp. 292–299. See p. 293.

14. PERCEIVING THE RESPONSES OF OTHERS, ACCURACY IN

See also categories 3 and 4 above.

Scodel, Alvin, and Paul Mussen, "Social Perceptions of Authoritarians and Non-Authoritarians," *Journal of Abnormal and Social Psychology*, 48 (April, 1953), pp. 181–184. See pp. 181–182.

Bieri, James, "Cognitive Complexity-Simplicity and Predictive Behavior," *Journal of Abnormal and Social Psychology*, 51 (September, 1955), pp. 263–268. See pp. 264–265.

Koenig, Frederick W., and Morton B. King, Jr., "Cognitive Simplicity and Out-Group Stereotyping," *Social Forces*, 42 (March, 1964), pp. 324–327. See pp. 325–326.

15. RACIAL RECOGNITION

Morland, J., Kenneth, "Racial Recognition by Nursery School Children in Lynchburg, Virginia," *Social Forces*, 37 (December, 1958), pp. 132–141. See p. 132.

16. SIMILARITY SCORE WITH OWN RACE

Mann (1958), p. 153; see category 2 above.

INTERGROUP RELATIONS, RACIAL AND ETHNIC: DISCRIMINATION

SEE ALSO

Urban Areas, Segregation
Societal Characteristics

1. ATTITUDE TOWARD DESEGREGATION

Greenfield, Robert W., "Factors Associated with Attitudes toward Desegregation in a Florida Residential Suburb," *Social Forces*, 40 (October, 1961), pp. 31–42. See p. 34.

2. ATTITUDE TOWARD SCHOOL DESEGREGATION

See also categories 15, 16, 17, and 18 below.

Cramer, Richard M., "School Desegregation and New Industry: The Southern Community Leaders' Viewpoint," *Social Forces*, 41 (May, 1963), pp. 384–389. See p. 385.

3. ATTITUDES TOWARD SCHOOL DESEGREGATION IN FOUR HYPOTHETICAL SITUATIONS

Campbell, Ernest Q., *The Attitude Effects of Education Desegration in a Southern Community: A Methodological Study in Scale Analysis*, unpublished Ph.D. dissertation, Vanderbilt University, 1956.

Campbell, Ernest Q., "Moral Discomfort and Racial Segregation—An Examination of the Myrdal Hypothesis," *Social Forces*, 39 (March, 1961), pp. 228–234. See p. 230.

4. ATTITUDE TOWARD SCHOOL INTEGRATION

Siegel, Sidney, and Irma Lee Shepherd, "An Ordered Metric Measure of Social Distance," *Sociometry*, 22 (December, 1959), pp. 336–342. See p. 339.

5. ETHNIC REPRESENTATION IN OCCUPATIONS

Lieberson, Stanley, *Ethnic Groups and Medicine,* unpublished M.A. thesis, University of Chicago, 1958.

Lieberson, Stanley, "Ethnic Groups and the Practice of Medicine," *American Sociological Review,* 23 (October, 1958), pp. 542–549. See p. 547.

6. NEGROES IN SPECIFIC SCHOOL SITUATIONS

Campbell, Ernest Q., "Some Social Psychological Correlates of Direction in Attitude Change," *Social Forces,* 36 (May, 1958), pp. 335–340. See p. 336.

7. OVERESTIMATION OF NEGRO ARRESTS

Kephart, William M., "Negro Visibility," *American Sociological Review,* 19 (August, 1954), pp. 462–467. See p. 464.

8. OVERT BEHAVIOR TOWARD NEGROES

Linn, Lawrence S., "Verbal Attitudes and Overt Behavior: A Study of Racial Discrimination," *Social Forces,* 43 (March, 1965), pp. 353–364. See pp. 356–358.

9. PRINCIPLE OF SCHOOL SEGREGATION

Campbell; see category 6 above.

10. PUBLIC AND LEGAL RIGHTS OF NEGROES

Campbell; see category 6 above.

11. RACIAL DISCRIMINATION

Blalock, Hubert M., Jr., "Per Cent Non-White and Discrimination in the South,"*American Sociological Review,* 22 (December, 1957), pp. 677–682. See p. 679.

12. RANK ORDER OF SENSITIVITY TO DISCRIMINATION FOR NEGROES

Killian, Lewis M., and Charles M. Grigg, "Rank Orders of Discrimination of Negroes and Whites in a Southern City," *Social Forces,* 39 (March, 1961), pp. 235–239. See p. 236.

13. RANK ORDER OF DISCRIMINATION FOR WHITES

Killian and Grigg; see category 12 above.

14. READINESS TO DESEGREGATE: GENERAL ACTION SET

Tumin, Melvin, Paul Barton, and Bernie Burrus, "Education, Prejudice, and Discrimination: A Study in Readiness for Desegregation," *American Sociological Review*, 23 (February, 1958), pp. 41–49. See p. 44.

Tumin, Melvin, "Readiness and Resistance to Desegregation: A Social Portrait of the Hard Core," *Social Forces*, 36 (March, 1958), pp. 256–263. See pp. 257–258.

15. READINESS TO DESEGREGATE: IMAGE OF THE NEGRO

Tumin, Barton, and Burrus (1958), p. 43; see category 14 above.

Tumin (1958), p. 257; see category 14 above.

16. READINESS TO DESEGREGATE: SENTIMENT STRUCTURE

Tumin, Barton, and Burrus (1958), p. 44; see category 14 above.

Tumin (1958), p. 258; see category 14 above.

17. READINESS TO DESEGREGATE: SOCIAL IDEOLOGY

Tumin, Barton, and Burrus (1958), p. 44; see category 14 above.

Tumin (1958), p. 257; see category 14 above.

18. READINESS TO DESEGREGATE: SPECIFIC ACTION SET

Tumin, Barton, and Burrus (1958), p. 44; see category 14 above.

Tumin (1958), p. 258; see category 14 above.

19. REFERENCE GROUP POSITION TOWARD SEGREGATION

Campbell, p. 339; see category 6 above.

INTERGROUP RELATIONS, RACIAL AND ETHNIC: GROUP BELONGINGNESS

1. AFFILIATIONS OF MEMBERS OF ETHNIC GROUPS, CHANGE IN DIRECTION OF

Breton, Raymond, "Institutional Completeness of Ethnic Communities and the Personal Relations of Immigrants," *American Journal of Sociology*, 70 (September, 1964), pp. 193–205. See pp. 194–196.

2. AFFILIATIONS OF MEMBERS OF ETHNIC GROUPS, DIRECTION OF

Breton; see category 1 above.

3. CURRENT BEHAVIOR OF JAPANESE

Uyeki, Eugene S., "Correlates of Ethnic Identification," *American Journal of Sociology*, 65 (March, 1960), pp. 468–474. See p. 470.

4. CURRENT ORIENTATION OF JAPANESE

Uyeki; see category 3 above.

5. ETHNIC EXCLUSIVITY

Suchman, Edward A., "Sociomedical Variations among Ethic Groups," *American Journal of Sociology*, 70 (November, 1964), pp. 319–331. See pp. 323–324.

6. ETHNIC-GROUP IDENTIFICATION

Kerckhoff, Alan C., and T. C. McCormick, "Marginal Status and Marginal Personality," *Social Forces*, 34 (October, 1955), pp. 48–55. See p. 52.

Kerckhoff, Alan C., "Anomie and Achievement Motivation: A Study of Personality Development within Cultural Disorganization," *Social Forces*, 37 (March, 1959), pp. 196–202. See p. 199.

7. NEGRO IDENTIFICATION

Weinstein, Eugene, and Paul N. Geisel, "Family Decision Making over Desegregation," *Sociometry*, 25 (March, 1962), pp. 21–29. See p. 25.

8. PIONEERING IN RACE RELATIONS

Weinstein and Geisel, pp. 28–29; see category 7 above.

9. PRESUMED JAPANESENESS OF BACKGROUND

Uyeki; see category 3 above.

10. SOCIAL ORGANIZATION, COMPOSITE INDEX OF

Suchman, pp. 324–325; see category 5 above.

11. SOUTHERN IDENTIFICATION SCALE

Liu, William T., "The Marginal Catholics in the South: A Revision of Concepts," *American Journal of Sociology*, 65 (January, 1960), pp. 383–390. See p. 385.

Liu, William T., "The Community Reference System, Religiosity, and Race Attitude," *Social Forces*, 39 (May, 1961), pp. 324–328. See p. 326.

12. STICK-FIGURE TEST

Sarbin, Theodore R., and Curtis Hardyck, "Conformance in Role Perception as a Personality Variable," *Journal of Consulting Psychology*, 19 (April, 1955), pp. 109–111. See p. 109.

Fong, Stanley L. M., "Assimilation of Chinese in America: Changes in Orientation and Social Perception," *American Journal of Sociology*, 71 (November, 1965), pp. 265–273. See pp. 268–270.

INTERGROUP RELATIONS, RACIAL AND ETHNIC: PREJUDICE AND SOCIAL DISTANCE

1. ACCEPTANCE OR REJECTION BY DOMINANT GROUP

Kerckhoff, Alan C., and T. C. McCormick, "Marginal Status and Marginal Personality," *Social Forces*, 34 (October, 1955), pp. 48–55. See p. 53.

2. ACCEPTING NEGRO STUDENTS

Grafton, Thomas H., "An Attitude Scale on Accepting Negro Students," *Social Forces*, 43 (October, 1964), pp. 38–41. See p. 39.

3. ANTI-AFRICAN PREJUDICE

Pettigrew, Thomas F., "Personality and Sociocultural Factors in Intergroup Attitudes: A Cross National Comparison," *Journal of Conflict Resolution*, 2 (March, 1958), pp. 29–42. See pp. 33, 36.

Pettigrew, Thomas F., "Social Distance Attitudes of South African Students," *Social Forces*, 38 (March, 1960), pp. 246–253. See p. 246.

4. ANTI-NEGRO SENTIMENTS

See also Intergroup Relations: Ethnocentrism, category 1.

Adorno, T. W., Else Frenkel-Brunswik, Daniel J. Levinson, and R. Nevitt Sanford, *The Authoritarian Personality*, New York: Harper and Brothers, 1950. See "The Study of Ethnocentric Ideology," by Daniel J. Levinson, pp. 102–150.

Riddleberger, Alice B., and Annabelle B. Motz, "Prejudice and Perception," *American Journal of Sociology*, 62 (March, 1957), pp. 498–503. See p. 499.

Pettigrew, Thomas F., "Desegregation and Its Chances for Success: Northern and Southern Views," *Social Forces*, 35 (May, 1957), pp. 339–344. See p. 339.

Silberstein, Fred B., and Melvin Seeman, "Social Mobility and Prejudice," *American Journal of Sociology*, 65 (December, 1959), pp. 258–264. See p. 259.

Middleton, Russell, "Prejudice and Persuasion," *American Sociological Review*, 25 (October, 1960), pp. 676–686. See p. 681.

Rhyne, Edwin Hoffman, "Racial Prejudice and Personality Scales: An Alternative Approach," *Social Forces*, 41 (October, 1962), pp. 44–53. See p. 48.

Noel, Donald L., and Alphonso Pinkney, "Correlates of Prejudice: Some Racial Differences and Similarities," *American Journal of Sociology*, 69 (May, 1964), pp. 608–622. See pp. 609–610.

5. ANTI-SEMITISM (A-S SCALE, E SCALE, AND MODIFICATIONS, ADORNO, FRENKEL-BRUNSWIK, LEVINSON, SANFORD)

See also Intergroup Relations: Ethnocentrism, category 1.

Adorno, Frenkel-Brunswik, Levinson, and Sanford (1950), pp. 57–150; see category 4 above.

Kaufman, Walter C., "Status, Authoritarianism, and Anti-Semitism," *American Journal of Sociology*, 62 (January, 1957), pp. 379–382. See p. 381.

Silberstein and Seeman (1959); see category 4 above.

Middleton (1960); see category 4 above.

Rhyne (1962); see category 4 above.

6. ANTI-SEMITISM (MORSE, ALLPORT)

Morse, Nancy C., and Floyd H. Allport, "The Causality of Anti-Semitism: An Investigation of Seven Hypotheses," *Journal of Psychology*, 34 (October, 1952), pp. 197–233. See pp. 198–203.

Catton, William R., Jr., and Sung Chick Hong, "The Relation of Apparent Minority Ethnocentrism to Majority Antipathy," *American Sociological Review*, 27 (April, 1962), pp. 178–191. See p. 181.

7. ANTI-SEMITISM, COLLEGE

Segal, Bernard E., and Peter K. Thomsen, "Status Orientation and

Ethnic Sentiment among Undergraduates," *American Journal of Sociology*, 71 (July, 1965), pp. 60–67. See p. 63.

8. ANTI-SEMITISM, GENERAL

Segal and Thomsen; see category 7 above.

9. ATTITUDES TOWARD MINORITIES

Srole, Leo, "Social Integration and Certain Corollaries: An Exploratory Study," *American Sociological Review*, 21 (December, 1956), pp. 709–716. See p. 710.

10. ATTITUDES TOWARD NEGROES, SCALE I

See also category 4 above.
Linn, Lawrence S., "Verbal Attitudes and Overt Behavior: A Study of Racial Discrimination," *Social Forces*, 43 (March, 1965), pp. 353–364. See p. 356.

11. ATTITUDES TOWARD NEGROES, SCALE II

See also category 4 above
Linn, pp. 356–357; see category 10 above.

12. ATTITUDES TOWARD NEGROES: COGNITIVE

Merz, Louise E., and Leonard I. Pearlin, "The Influence of Information on Three Dimensions of Prejudice toward Negroes," *Social Forces*, 35 (May, 1957), pp. 344–351. See p. 346.

13. ATTITUDES TOWARD NEGROES: EMOTIONAL

Merz and Pearlin; see category 12 above.

14. ATTITUDES TOWARD NEGROES: MOTIVATIONAL

Merz and Pearlin; see category 12 above.

15. ATTITUDES TOWARD WHITES

Works, Ernest, "The Prejudice-Interaction Hypothesis from the Point of View of the Negro Minority Group," *American Journal of Sociology*, 67 (July, 1961), pp. 47–52. See p. 50.
Noel and Pinkney (1964); see category 4 above.

16. AUTONOMIC RESPONSES TO RACE RELATIONS STIMULI

DeFleur, Melvin L., and Frank R. Westie, "Verbal Attitudes and Overt Acts: An Experiment on the Salience of Attitudes," *American Sociological Review*, 23 (December, 1958), pp. 667–673. See p. 669.

17. INTERPRETATION OF PHOTOGRAPHED INTERRACIAL SITUATIONS

DeFleur, Melvin L., and Frank R. Westie, "The Interpretation of Interracial Situations," *Social Forces*, 38 (October, 1959), pp. 17–23. See p. 19.

18. PHILO-SEMITISM

Segal and Thomsen; see category 7 above.

19. PREJUDICE

Segal, Bernard E., "Racial Group Membership and Juvenile Delinquency," *Social Forces*, 43 (October, 1964), pp. 70–81. See p. 74.

20. PREJUDICE, ANTI-SCALE

Schuman, Howard, and John Harding, "Prejudice and the Norm of Rationality," *Sociometry*, 27 (September, 1964), pp. 353–371. See pp. 356–360.

21. PREJUDICE, COGNITIVE

Rhyne (1962); see category 4 above.

22. PREJUDICE, PICTURE TEST OF

Riddleberger and Motz (1957); see category 4 above.

23. PREJUDICE, PRO-SCALE

Schuman and Harding, see category 20 above.

24. PREJUDICE, SHORT FORM SCALE OF

Martin, James G., and Frank R. Westie, "The Tolerant Personality," *American Sociological Review*, 24 (August, 1959), pp. 521–528. See p. 522.

25. PREJUDICE, TYPOLOGY OF

Schuman and Harding, p. 362; see category 20 above.

26. RACE-ATTITUDE SCALE

Liu, William T., "The Marginal Catholics in the South: A Revision of Concepts," *American Journal of Sociology*, 65 (January, 1960), pp. 383–390. See p. 386.

Liu, William T., "The Community Reference System, Religiosity, and Race Attitude," *Social Forces*, 39 (May, 1961), pp. 324–328. See p. 326.

27. RACIAL CONFLICT

Segal and Thomsen; see category 7 above.

28. RACIAL SENSITIVITY

Segal and Thomsen; see category 7 above.

29. SALIENCE OF ATTITUDES TOWARD NEGROES

DeFleur and Westie (1958); see category 16 above.

30. SOCIAL DISTANCE (BLUNT)

Blunt, E. A. H., "Commensal and Other Restrictions of Caste," in *The Caste System of Northern India*, New York: Oxford University Press, 1931.

Mahar (1960); see category 31 below.

31. SOCIAL DISTANCE (BOGARDUS)

Bogardus, Emory S., "Measuring Social Distance," *Journal of Applied Sociology*, 9 (March-April, 1925), pp. 299–308. See p. 301.

Bogardus, Emory S., *Immigration and Race Attitudes*, New York: D. C. Heath and Company, 1928, pp. 11, 14–15.

Bogardus, Emory S., "A Social Distance Scale," *Sociology and Social Research*, 17 (January-February, 1933), pp. 265–271. See p. 265.

Bogardus (1925, p. 299) follows closely the conception of Robert E. Park by defining social distance as "the degrees and grades of understanding and feeling that persons experience regarding each other." For purposes of test administration Bogardus (1933, p. 270) also defines social distance as "the different degrees of sympathetic understanding that exist between persons." These early definitions of the concept of social distance and the efforts to measure the phenomenon referred to have resulted in a prominent research tradition within sociology. On the basis of this technique, it has been shown that people who differ in geographic location, occupation, education, and ethnicity nonetheless tend to be alike in the amount of social distance which they wish to maintain between themselves and the members of any given ethnic group.

The method under discussion consists of presenting respondents with a list of racial and ethnic groups and with seven statements which describe different degrees of social contact. It is the respondents' task to indicate for each racial or ethnic group the kinds of social contact which they would be willing to permit. Bogardus (1933) presents evidence that the seven statements describing the types of social contact represent "nearly equidistant" points along a continuum ranging from high willingness to permit social contact to low willingness to permit social contact.

The form of the Social Distance Scale and the instructions and scoring procedures presented below are adapted from Bogardus (1925, 1933). Variations of this form are still used widely.

SOCIAL DISTANCE SCALE

Please read the following descriptions of different degrees of personal "closeness" which people might be willing to permit in their relations with members of particular groups:

1. Would admit to close kinship by marriage.
2. Would admit to my club as personal chums.
3. Would admit to my street as a neighbor.
4. Would admit to my occupation in my country.
5. Would admit to citizenship in my country.
6. Would admit as visitors only to my country.
7. Would exclude from my country.

Now consider the groups of people listed below. [See page 156.] Place an "X" under the number which most nearly represents the degree of closeness (as described above) to which you would be willing to admit members of each group. Give your reaction to each group as a whole. Do not give your reaction to the best or the worst members that you have known.

The Social Distance Scale is scored by calculating the mean for each ethnic group using the numbers at the top of the seven response columns to indicate the preferred degree of social distance. The ethnic groups may then be ranked from lowest to highest average social distance, with small means signifying low social distance.

Dodd, S. C., "A Social Distance Test in the Near East," *American Journal of Sociology*, 41 (September, 1935), pp. 194–204. See p. 195.
Bogardus, Emory S., "Changes in Racial Distance," *International*

Group	1	2	3	4	5	6	7
Armenians							
Bulgarians							
Canadians							
Chinese							
Czechoslovaks							
Danes							
Dutch							
English							
French							
French-Canadians							
Finns							
Germans							
Greeks							
Hindus							
Hungarians							
Indians (American)							
Irish							
Italians							
Japanese							
Jew—German							
Jew—Russian							
Koreans							
Mexicans							
Mulattos							
Negroes							
Norwegians							
Portuguese							
Filipinos							
Poles							
Roumanians							
Russians							
Serbo-Croatians							
Scotch							
Scotch-Irish							
Spanish							
Syrians							
Swedish							
Turks							
Welsh							

Journal of Opinion and Attitude Research, 1 (December, 1947), pp. 55–62. See pp. 55–56.

Bogardus, Emory S., "Social Distance Differentials," *Sociology and Social Research*, 32 (May-June, 1948), pp. 882–887. See p. 882.

Westie, Frank R., "Negro-White Status Differentials and Social Distance," *American Sociological Review*, 17 (October, 1952), pp. 550–558. See p. 551.

Westie, Frank R., and David H. Howard, "Social Status Differentials and the Race Attitudes of Negroes," *American Sociological Review*, 19 (October, 1954), pp. 584–591. See p. 586.

Duncan, Otis D., and Stanley Lieberson, "Ethnic Segregation and Assimilation," *American Journal of Sociology*, 64 (January, 1959), pp. 364–374. See p. 372.

Bogardus, Emory S., "Race Reactions by Sexes," *Sociology and Social Research*, 43 (July-August, 1959), pp. 439–441. See p. 439.

Langworthy, Russell L., "Community Status and Influence in a High School," *American Sociological Review*, 24 (August, 1959), pp. 537–539. See p. 538.

Pettigrew (1960); see category 3 above.

Mahar, Pauline Moller, "A Ritual Pollution Scale for Ranking Hindu Castes," *Sociometry*, 23 (September, 1960), pp. 292–306. See p. 294.

Palmore, Erdman B., "Ethnophaulisms and Ethnocentrism," *American Journal of Sociology*, 67 (January, 1962), pp. 442–445. See p. 442.

Photiadis, John D., and Jeanne Biggar, "Religiosity, Education, and Ethnic Distance," *American Journal of Sociology*, 67 (May, 1962), pp. 666–673. See p. 668.

Jackson, Elton F., "Status Consistency and Symptoms of Stress," *American Sociological Review*, 27 (August, 1962), pp. 469–480. See p. 471.

Rhyne (1962); see category 4 above.

Photiadis, John D., and Arthur L. Johnson, "Orthodoxy, Church Participation, and Authoritarianism," *American Journal of Sociology*, 69 (November, 1963), pp. 244–248. See p. 244.

32. SOCIAL DISTANCE (CATTON, HONG)

Catton and Hong (1962); see category 6 above.

33. SOCIAL DISTANCE (PEARLIN)

Pearlin, Leonard I., "Shifting Group Attachments and Attitudes toward Negroes," *Social Forces*, 33 (October, 1954), pp. 47–50. See p. 48.

34. SOCIAL DISTANCE, SUMMATED DIFFERENCES TECHNIQUE

Westie (1952); see category 31 above.

Westie, Frank R., "A Technique for the Measurement of Race Attitudes," *American Sociological Review*, 18 (February, 1953), pp. 73–78.

(Professor Westie has prepared "A Note to Prospective Users of the Summated Differences Scales" which appears in print for the first time following the discussion below. The discussion describes the form in which Westie had utilized the Summated Differences Technique through 1959.)

Westie's Summated Differences Technique for measuring race attitudes has been based upon responses to four social distance scales. These scales have been intended to permit the researcher to approach the problem of attitude measurement "in a manner less direct than is true of the usual prejudice scales (1953, p. 73) and to facilitate "getting at the way the respondent actually feels rather than his notions about how he ought to feel." (1953, p. 78) The scales also have been designed to focus the researcher's attention upon social distance phenomena within separate interactional contexts: (1) residential, (2) positional, (3) physical, and (4) interpersonal. Scales (1), (3) and (4) have been measures of the degree of "closeness" or the proximity which the respondent is willing to grant particular attitude-objects. The Position Scale has measured "the extent to which the respondent is willing to have the attitude-object occupy positions of prestige and power in the community." (1953, p. 73)

Westie has specified the following attitude-objects: (1) Negroes in eight different occupations (Doctor, Lawyer, Big Business Executive, Banker, Owner-Manager of a small store, Bookkeeper, Machine Operator, and Ditch Digger), (2) Whites in the same eight occupations listed above, (3) "The Average Negro Man," and (4) "The Average White Man." Since each respondent has been asked to state how "close" he is willing to permit 18 attitude-objects (Negro Doctor, Lawyer, and so on; White Doctor, Lawyer, and so on; the "Average" Negro; the "Average" white) to approach him within 4 interactional contexts, 72 scale combinations have been presented. Also, since each of the 4 social distance scales has been composed of 6 statements indicating various points along a proximity-distance continuum, the total number of scale items has been 432.

The summated differences scores have been calculated by comparing a person's distance responses to whites and Negroes in the same occupations. If a respondent has been equally willing to have a Negro and a white doctor, for example, live next door to him, then the difference in this instance has been zero. A person's total prejudice score (which may be toward either race) has consisted of the sum of the differences between the responses to the comparable pairs of items within each of the four social distance situations. Subscores for each social distance scale have been calculated in the same manner.

ITEMS FROM THE SUMMATED DIFFERENCES SCALE

I believe I would be willing to have a Negro	Strongly agree	Agree	Undecided	Disagree	Strongly disagree
1. live in the same apartment building I live in					
2. live across the street from me					
3. live in my neighborhood					
4. live in my end of town					
5. live in my town					
6. live in my country					

I believe I would be willing to have a Negro
1. as president of the United States   [response spaces]
2. as U.S. Congressman from my district.

3. as a councilman on my city's council.   [response spaces]
4. as head of the local community chest drive.
5. as a member of a Red Cross committee in my town.
6. as a member of a national patriotic organization.

   I believe I would be willing to have a Negro
1. use the same towel that I use.   [response spaces]
2. swim in the same pool as I do.
3. have his hair cut by the same barber who cuts mine.
4. try on clothes at the store where I buy my clothes.
5. ride in the same crowded elevator I am in.
6. use lending library books I also borrow.

   I believe I would be willing to have a Negro
1. as a close, personal friend   [response spaces]
2. as a dinner guest in my home.
3. as a person I might often visit with.
4. as an acquaintance.
5. as someone I might say hello to.
6. as someone I might see on the street.

A NOTE TO PROSPECTIVE USERS OF THE SUMMATED DIFFERENCES SCALES—BY FRANK R. WESTIE

The Summated Differences Scales were developed some 18 years ago. I feel that a revision is now in order. The remarks which follow are in the spirit of an invitation to prospective users of these scales to undertake such revision.

These scales as originally constructed consisted of 432 items. When items designed to measure independent variables are added to these, the resulting interview-schedule becomes somewhat formidable. This implies a demand upon the respondent's time and patience that may go beyond many respondents' definition of "reasonable." Moreover, the peculiar format required by the "response-pad" arrangement makes the instrument quite difficult (and expensive) to reproduce. Thus I am suggesting herein various ways in which the instrument may be shortened, hopefully without compromising the discrimination-power of the scales. The user of the scales may, of course, revise them in any way he wishes to suit his own purposes.

The number of attitude-objects could be reduced by eliminating some of the occupations on the attitude-object side. For some of the socioeconomic status levels on the attitude-object side two occupations of roughly comparable level were used. Perhaps one of these occupations on each level could be eliminated without much loss. As the authors of the present volume have indicated, the scales were designed to measure social distance towards Negroes and whites in the following eight occupations: Banker, Big Business Executive, Doctor, Lawyer, Owner-Manager of a small store, Bookkeeper, Machine Operator, and Ditch Digger. I think I would retain the following of these occupations: Big Business Executive, Doctor, Bookkeeper, Machine Operator, and Ditch Digger. I am assuming that these occupations are fairly representative of the popularly used categories along the occupational prestige continuum.

By reducing the number of occupations to five and leaving out the "Average Negro" and "Average White Man" (attitude-objects which were originally included) the total number of scale items would be reduced from 432 to 240.

If the "physical aversion" scale is used it might be well to replace the most intimate item, "Use the same towel that I use," with an equally intimate one that would be less likely to alienate subjects. This item tends to evoke a lot of complaint, with the subjects arguing that they wouldn't want *anyone* to use their towel and that their rejection of this item is going to be interpreted incorrectly. A lot of explanation to the subject could be avoided if this item were replaced. A good replacement might be the item, "Drink from the same fountain as I do."

More recent findings regarding the reliability of these scales were reported by Lawrence S. Wrightsman (unpublished mimeographed statement, Peabody College, 1964). Wrightsman obtained a test-retest reliability coefficient of .804 (I presume for all four scales combined), a figure somewhat lower than I obtained in 1949–50. Users of these scales are urged to run reliability tests, particularly on persons drawn from the same population from which the experimental subjects are drawn.

Wrightsman's findings in his "Factor Analysis of 73 Personality, Attitude, and Aptitude Variables" (mimeographed) are interesting. He used fifteen scales in his analysis of the factor, "Anti-Negro Attitudes." The loadings for the Summated Differences Scales were uniformly high (.8927, .8346, .8180, and .7544), the highest of these being second only to Getzel's "PDPQ-1st Person Form" which had a loading of .8955. It follows then that these scales should be fairly valid for defining the factor "Anti-Negro Attitudes."

I believe these scales would be readily adaptable to the measurement of attitudes towards a variety of racial, ethnic and religious groups. For example, one could substitute into the "Position Scale" as attitude-objects persons of various religious backgrounds. Thus the first item in this scale might read "I believe I would be willing to have Big Business Executive (*Jewish*) as President of the United States." In subsequent repetitions of this item one would substitute "Big Business Executive (Catholic)" and "Big Business Executive (Protestant)."

The attitude-object "Big Business Executive" without religion being specified would also have to be included in order to provide a norm from which response deviations according to religion could be measured. The algebraic sum of such departures where the attitude-objects are Jewish would yield an anti-Semitism score for the particular respondent. By the same process this particular adaptation would also yield anti-Catholic and anti-Protestant scores, as well as pro-Jewish, pro-Catholic, and pro-Protestant scores, where such attitudes prevail.

I seriously doubt that prejudice can be measured in the absolute. By its nature, prejudice is an attitude that can be defined as such only in relation to the direction and magnitude (amount, intensity, salience, etc.) of the person's attitudes towards other groups, particularly his own group, *in the same situations*. The Summated Differences Technique has the peculiar advantage of measuring prejudice in such relative terms. It also has the advantage of providing a meaningful zero point on the scale of prejudice where the algebraic sum of the deviations is zero.

Westie and Howard (1954); see category 31 above.

Westie, Frank R., and Margaret L. Westie, "The Social Distance Pyramid: Relationships between Caste and Class," *American Journal of Sociology*, 63 (September, 1957), pp. 190–196. See p. 190.

DeFleur and Westie (1958); see category 16 above.

Martin, James G., and Frank R. Westie, "The Tolerant Personality," *American Sociological Review*, 24 (August, 1959), pp. 521–528. See p. 521.

DeFleur and Westie (1959), p. 18; see category 17 above.

35. TOLERANCE-INTOLERANCE

Campbell, Ernest Q., "Moral Discomfort and Racial Segregation—An Examination of the Myrdal Hypothesis," *Social Forces*, 39 (March, 1961), pp. 228–234. See p. 233.

INTERGROUP RELATIONS, RACIAL AND ETHNIC: STEREOTYPES

---

1. STEREOTYPE CHECK LIST

Katz, Daniel, and Kenneth W. Braly, "Racial Stereotypes of One Hundred College Students," *Journal of Abnormal and Social Psychology*, 28 (October-December, 1933), pp. 280–290. See p. 283.

The term *stereotype* has been defined in many different ways; but in general, as observed by Koenig and King (1964, below) "Stereotyping has commonly been treated as a broad, rigid, relatively inaccurate way of perceiving a category of persons." (p. 324) Variations in definition, however, usually have not led to corresponding variations in research procedures; consequently, the Katz and Braly stereotype check list has been the primary research tool in this field since its introduction in 1933. It is the opinion of Ehrlich and Rinehart (1965, below) that "much of our knowledge of intergroup stereotypy is based on that instrument" (p. 574) and that "The results have all been roughly congruent." (p. 565) It also is their opinion that, although the check list "is a most efficient instrument" (p. 574), the technique has led to an overestimation of the existence of intergroup hostility and that future researchers should consider the desirability of devising and utilizing other approaches.

As the list was employed by Katz and Braly (1933), respondents were asked to give "the traits which they considered most characteristic of each of the following ten groups: Germans, Italians, Negroes, Irish, English, Jews, Americans, Chinese, Japanese, and Turks." (p. 282) The following directions, description, and list of eighty-four traits are based upon the original article.

Read through the list of words [on page 165] and select those which seem to you typical of the Germans. Write as many of these words in the following space as you think are necessary to characterize these people adequately. If you do not find appropriate words [in the list] for all the typical German characteristics, you may add those which you think necessary for an adequate description. (p. 282)

When the respondent has finished characterizing the Germans, he is asked to repeat this procedure for the Italians, the Negroes, and the other remaining ethnic groups. At the end of the entire task are the following additional instructions: "Now go back over the ten lists of words which you have chosen and mark with an X the five words in each list which seem to you the most typical of the race in question."

The components of a particular stereotype and the extent to which the respondents adhere to it can be determined by percentage analysis of the data. Those traits which are most frequently listed and emphasized (by the placement of an "X" beside them) are regarded as elements of the stereotype. A perfect stereotype would result if all respondents selected for emphasis the same five traits in relation to a given ethnic group.

Katz, Daniel, and Kenneth W. Braly, "Racial Prejudice and Racial Stereotypes," *Journal of Abnormal and Social Psychology*," 30 (July-September, 1935), pp. 175–193. See p. 184.

Kusunoki, K., "Mental Characteristics of the Japanese Race as Seen by Japanese and American Students," *Japanese Journal of Applied Psychology*, 4 (1936), pp. 232–237.

Bayton, James A., "The Racial Stereotypes of Negro College Students," *Journal of Abnormal and Social Psychology*, 36 (January, 1941), pp. 97–102.

Schoenfield, Nathan, "An Experimental Study of Some Problems Relating to Stereotypes," *Archives of Psychology*, 270 (June, 1942), p. 6.

Child, Irvin L., and Leonard W. Doob, "Factors Determining National Stereotypes," *Journal of Social Psychology*, 17 (May, 1943), pp. 203–219. See pp. 205–207.

intelligent
brilliant
scientifically minded
witty
sophisticated
alert
shrewd
sly
meditative
imaginative
stupid
ignorant
superstitious
naive
industrious
lazy
honest
deceitful
unreliable
evasive
faithful
treacherous
cowardly
cruel
kind
quiet
stolid
ponderous
stubborn
impulsive
quick-tempered
suggestible
passionate
sensual
pleasure-loving
jovial
happy-go-lucky
humorless
sensitive
methodical
neat
persistent

generous
grasping
mercenary
materialistic
revengeful
quarrelsome
gluttonous
pugnacious
aggressive
conceited
boastful
ambitious
ostentatious (showy)
individualistic
talkative
loud
rude
suave
courteous
conventional
argumentative
straightforward
slovenly
suspicious
reserved
imitative
frivolous
gregarious
practical
progressive
conservative
musical
artistic
sportsmanlike
tradition-loving
efficient
religious
nationalistic
physically dirty
loyal to family ties
arrogant
radical

Meenes, M., "A Comparison of Racial Stereotypes of 1935 and 1942," *Journal of Social Psychology*, 17 (May, 1943), pp. 327–336. See pp. 328–331.

Blake, Robert, and Wayne Dennis, "The Development of Stereotypes Concerning the Negro," *Journal of Abnormal and Social Psychology*, 38 (October, 1943), pp. 525–531.

Klineberg, Otto, "Experimental Studies of Negro Personality," in Otto Klineberg (ed.), *Characteristics of the American Negro*, New York: Harper and Brothers, 1944, pp. 99–138. See p. 109.

Seago, Dorothy W., "Stereotypes: Before Pearl Harbor and After," *Journal of Psychology*, 23 (January, 1947), pp. 55–63. See pp. 56 and 60.

Bayton, James A. and Ethel Byoune, "Racio-National Stereotypes Held by Negroes," *Journal of Negro Education*, 16 (Winter, 1947), pp. 49–56. See p. 51.

Katz, Daniel and Kenneth W. Braly, "Verbal Stereotypes and Racial Prejudice," in Theodore M. Newcomb and E. L. Hartley (eds.), *Readings in Social Psychology*, New York: Henry Holt and Co., 1947, pp. 204–210.

Eysenck, H. J., and S. Crown, "National Stereotypes: An Experimental and Methodological Study," *International Journal of Opinion and Attitude Research*, 2 (1948), pp. 26–39. See p. 29.

Vinacke, W. Edgar, "Stereotyping among National-Racial Groups in Hawaii: A Study in Ethnocentrism," *Journal of Social Psychology*, 30 (November, 1949), pp. 265–279. See pp. 265 and 270.

Gilbert, G. M., "Stereotype Persistence and Change among College Students," *Journal of Abnormal and Social Psychology*, 46 (April, 1951), pp. 245–254. See p. 246.

Buchanan, William, "Stereotypes and Tensions as Revealed by the UNESCO International Poll," *International Social Science Bulletin*, 3 (Winter, 1951), pp. 515–528. See p. 518.

Buchanan, William, and Hadley Cantril, *How Nations See Each Other*, Urbana, Ill.: University of Illinois Press, 1953, p. 48.

Saenger, Gerhart, and Samuel Flowerman, "Stereotypes and Prejudiced Attitudes," *Human Relations*, 7 (May, 1954), pp. 217–238. See p. 219.

Prothro, E. Terry, "Cross Cultural Patterns of National Stereotypes," *Journal of Social Psychology*, 40 (August, 1954), pp. 53–59. See p. 55.

Bastide, Roger, "Stéréotypes et préjugés de couleur," *Sociologia*, 18 (May, 1955).

Ansari, Anwar, "A Study of the Relation between Group Stereotypes and Social Distance," *Journal of Education and Psychology*, 14 (1956), pp. 28–35.

Bastide, Roger, and Pierre van den Berghe, "Stereotypes, Norms and Interracial Behavior in São Paulo, Brazil," *American Sociological Review*, 22 (October, 1957), pp. 689–694. See p. 690.

Berreman, Joel V., "Filipino Stereotypes of Some Racial and National Minorities," *Pacific Sociological Review*, 1 (Spring, 1958), pp. 7–12.

Lambert, W. E., and Otto Klineberg, "A Pilot Study of the Origin and Development of National Stereotypes," *International Social Science Bulletin*, 11 (Summer, 1959), pp. 221–238. See pp. 228–229.

Reigrotski, Erich and Nels Anderson, "National Stereotypes and Foreign Contacts," *Public Opinion Quarterly*, 23 (Winter, 1959–1960), pp. 515–528. See p. 516.

Sinha, A., K. P. Upadhyay, and O. P. Upadhyay, "Stereotypes of Male and Female University Students in India toward Different Ethnic Groups," *Journal of Social Psychology*, 51 (February, 1960), pp. 93–102. See pp. 93 and 95.

Rath, R., and N. C. Sircar, "The Mental Pictures of Six Hindu Caste Groups about Each Other as Reflected in Verbal Stereotypes," *Journal of Social Psychology*, 51 (May, 1960), pp. 277–293. See pp. 278–280.

Bjerstedt, Åke, " 'Ego-Involved World Mindedness,' Nationality Images, and Methods of Research: A Methodological Note," *Journal of Conflict Resolution*, 4 (June, 1960), pp. 185–192. See p. 185.

Haratani, T., "Studies on Stereotypes among Japanese Students toward Themselves and Other National and Ethnic Groups," *Japanese Journal of Educational Psychology*, 8 (1960), pp. 1–17.

Rudolf, Juan, German Wettstein, and Renzo Pi, "La Formación de Estereotipos y su Relación con Los Medios de Expresión," *Revista Mexicana de Sociología*, 23 (1961), pp. 443–452.

Diab, Lutfy N., "National Stereotypes and the 'Reference Group' Concept," *Journal of Social Psychology*, 57 (August, 1962), pp. 339–351. See p. 340.

Koenig, Frederick W., and Morton B. King, Jr., "Cognitive Simplicity and Out-Group Stereotyping," *Social Forces*, 42 (March, 1964), pp. 324–327. See p. 326.

Ehrlich, Howard J., and James W. Rinehart, "A Brief Report on the Methodology of Stereotype Research," *Social Forces*, 43 (May, 1965), pp. 564–575. See pp. 568–572.

2. STEREOTYPES

Koenig and King (1964); see category 1 above.

3. STEREOTYPES OF JEWS

Ehrlich, Howard J., "Stereotyping and Negro-Jewish Stereotypes," *Social Forces*, 41 (December, 1962), pp. 171–176. See pp. 173–175.

Ehrlich, Howard J., "Instrument Error and the Study of Prejudice," *Social Forces*, 43 (December, 1964), pp. 197–206. See p. 200.

4. STEREOTYPES OF NEGROES (EHRLICH)

Ehrlich (1962); see category 3 above.

5. STEREOTYPES OF NEGROES (MIDDLETON)

Middleton, Russell, "Negro and White Reactions to Racial Humor," *Sociometry*, 22 (June, 1959), pp. 175–183. See p. 177.

INTERPERSONAL RELATIONS:
ATTITUDES TOWARD

1. ASSUMED SIMILARITY

Steiner, Ivan D., and Joan S. Dodge, "A Comparison of Two Techniques Employed in the Study of Interpersonal Perception," *Sociometry*, 20 (March, 1957), pp. 1–7. See p. 4.

2. ASSUMED SIMILARITY BETWEEN OPPOSITES

Fiedler, Fred E., "A Note on Leadership Theory: The Effect of Social Barriers between Leaders and Followers," *Sociometry*, 20 (June, 1957), pp. 87–94. See p. 89.

3. ASSUMED SIMILARITY TO LEADER

Fiedler; see category 2 above

4. BRAIN RATING

Turner, Ralph H., "Some Aspects of Women's Ambition," *American Journal of Sociology*, 70 (November, 1964), pp. 271–285. See pp. 282–283.

5. COMPETITIVE PREOCCUPATION SCALE

Turner, Ralph H., "Preoccupation with Competitiveness and Social Acceptance among American and English College Students," *Sociometry*, 23 (September, 1960), pp. 307–325. See p. 324.

Scarr, Harry A., "Measures of Particularism," *Sociometry*, 27 (December, 1964), pp. 413–432. See p. 417.

6. CONCERN WITH DETAIL

Kent, G. H., and A. J. Rosanoff, "A Study of Association in Insanity," *American Journal of Insanity*, 67 (1910), pp. 317–390.

Woodworth, R. S., and H. Schlossberg, *Experimental Psychology*, revised edition, New York: Henry Holt and Co., 1954, pp. 46–52.

Emrich, Robert, "Contrasting Disciplinary Preferences for Barnett's Types of Innovation," *Sociometry*, 22 (December, 1959), pp. 297–306. See p. 302.

7. CONFIDENCE OF BEING CHOSEN

Borgatta, Edgar F., "Analysis of Social Interaction and Sociometric Perception," *Sociometry*, 17 (February, 1954), pp. 7–32. See p. 15.

8. CONFIDENCE OF BEING LIKED

Riley, Matilda W., R. Cohn, Jackson Toby, and J. W. Riley, Jr., "Interpersonal Orientations in Small Groups: A Consideration of the Questionnaire Approach," *American Sociological Review*, 19 (December, 1954), pp. 715–724. See p. 718.

9. FRIEND RATING

Turner (1960); see category 5 above

10. INTERPERSONAL RELATIONS, PROJECTED

Murray, Henry A., *Thematic Apperception Test*, Cambridge, Mass.: Harvard University Press, 1943, p. 9.

Cartwright, Rosalind D., Julius Seeman, and Donald L. Grumman, "Patterns of Perceived Interpersonal Relations," *Sociometry*, 19 (September, 1956), pp. 166–177. See p. 167.

11. ORIENTATIONS TO INTERACTION, APPROVED

Dean, Lois R., "The Pattern Variables: Some Empirical Operations," *American Sociological Review*, 26 (February, 1961), pp. 80–90. See p. 88.

12. ORIENTATIONS TO INTERACTION, DISCREPANCY IN

Dean, p. 89; see category 11 above.

13. PERCEIVED MOTIVATION

Jones, Edward E., and Richard DeCharms, "Changes in Social Perception as a Function of the Personal Relevance of Behavior," *Sociometry*, 20 (March, 1957), pp. 75–85. See p. 77.

14. POSITIVE PROJECTED EXPANSIVENESS

Borgatta; see category 7 above.

15. PREDISPOSITION TO INTERPERSONAL CONTACT

Shuval, Judith T., "Class and Ethnic Correlates of Casual Neighboring," *American Sociological Review*, 21 (August, 1956), pp. 453–458. See p. 454.

16. PROJECTED EXPANSIVENESS

Borgatta; see category 7 above.

17. SELF-OTHER EVALUATION, CONGRUENCE OF

Couch, Carl J., *A Study of the Relationships between Self-Views and Role-Taking Accuracy*, unpublished Ph.D. dissertation, State University of Iowa, 1955.

Couch, Carl J., "Self-Attitudes and Degree of Agreement with Immediate Others," *American Journal of Sociology*, 63 (March, 1958), pp. 491–496. See p. 494.

18. SOCIAL ACCEPTANCE

James, Rita M., "Status and Competence of Jurors," *American Journal of Sociology*, 64 (May, 1959), pp. 563–570. See p. 567.

19. SOCIAL ACCEPTANCE PREOCCUPATION SCALE

Turner (1960), p. 325; see category 5.

Scarr (1964); see category 5 above

20. SOCIAL DESIRABILITY RANKING FORM

Backman, Carl W., and Paul F. Secord, "Liking, Selective Interaction, and Misperception in Congruent Interpersonal Relations," *Sociometry*, 25 (December, 1962), pp. 321–335. See p. 326.

21. SOCIAL PERCEPTION TEST

Baker, B. O., and T. R. Sarbin, "Differential Mediation of Social Perception as a Correlate of Social Adjustment," *Sociometry*, 19 (March, 1957), pp. 69–83. See p. 73.

Glaser, Daniel, "A Note on 'Differential Mediation of Social Perception as a Correlate of Social Adjustment,'" *Sociometry*, 20 (June, 1957), pp. 156–160. See pp. 156–157.

22. SOCIAL RELATIONS SCALE

Dentler, Robert A., and Lawrence J. Monroe, "Social Correlates of Early Adolescent Theft," *American Sociological Review*, 26 (October, 1961), pp. 733–743. See p. 740.

23. WHEEL RATING

Turner; see category 4 above.

INTERPERSONAL RELATIONS: CHARACTERISTICS OF

SEE ALSO

Personality Traits: Various Categories
Small Groups: Behavior and Characteristics of
Small Groups: Status and Status Relations in

1. ACCEPTANCE OF OTHERS

Gottheil, Edward, "Changes in Social Perceptions Contingent upon Competing and Cooperating," *Sociometry*, 18 (May, 1955), pp. 132–137. See p. 133.

2. AFFECTIVE RELATIONS

Shepherd, Clovis, and Irving R. Weschler, "The Relationship between Three Interpersonal Variables and Communication Effectiveness: A Pilot Study," *Sociometry*, 18 (May, 1955), pp. 102–110. See p. 105.

3. ALTERCASTING RATING

Weinstein, Eugene A., and Paul Deutschberger, "Some Dimensions of Altercasting," *Sociometry*, 26 (December, 1963), pp. 454–466. See p. 461.

4. ASCRIBED SIMILARITY, ACCEPTABLE

Lundy, Richard M., "Self-Perceptions Regarding Masculinity-Femininity and Descriptions of Same and Opposite Sex Sociometric Choices," *Sociometry*, 21 (September, 1958), pp. 238–246. See p. 240.

5. ASCRIBED SIMILARITY, TOTAL

Lundy; see category 4 above.

6. ASCRIBED SIMILARITY, UNACCEPTABLE

Lundy; see category 4 above.

7. BOUNDARY ACTIVITY

Cumming, Elaine, and Charles Harrington, "Clergyman as Counselor," *American Journal of Sociology*, 69 (November, 1963), pp. 234–243. See pp. 237–238.

8. COLINEAR ORIENTATIONS

Runkel, Phillip J., "Cognitive Similarity in Facilitating Communications," *Sociometry*, 19 (September, 1956), pp. 178–191. See p. 181.

9. COMMUNICATIONS WITH FRIENDS

Back, Kurt W., Reuben Hill, and J. Mayone Stycos, "Interviewer Effect on Scale Reproducibility," *American Sociological Review*, 20 (August, 1955), pp. 443–446. See p. 444.

10. CONFIDENCE IN ONE'S OWN ABILITIES

Blau, Peter M., "Patterns of Choice in Interpersonal Relations," *American Sociological Review*, 27 (February, 1962), pp. 41–55. See pp. 53–54.

11. COOPERATIVENESS

Weinstein and Deutschberger; see category 3 above.

12. DYADIC COMMUNICATION

Riley, Matilda W., R. Cohn, Jackson Toby, and J. W. Riley, Jr., "Interpersonal Orientations in Small Groups: A Consideration of the Questionnaire Approach," *American Sociological Review*, 19 (December, 1954), pp. 715–724. See p. 721.

13. ESTEEM FOR PSYCHIATRIC NURSES

Turk, Herman, and Theresa Turk, "Personal Sentiments in a Hierarchy," *Social Forces*, 40 (December, 1961), pp. 137–140. See p. 138.

14. EXPERIENCE AND SELF-RELIANCE

Blau; see category 10 above.

15. FRIENDSHIP

Burgess, Ernest W., "Social Relations, Activities, and Personal Adjustment," *American Journal of Sociology*, 59 (January, 1954), pp. 352–360. See pp. 353–354.

16. FRIENDSHIP, DEGREE OF

Sutcliffe, J. P., and B. D. Crabbe, "Incidence and Degrees of Friendship in Urban and Rural Areas," *Social Forces*, 42 (October, 1963), pp. 60–67. See p. 61.

17. FRIENDSHIP SOLIDARITY

Suchman, Edward A., "Sociomedical Variations Among Ethnic Groups," *American Journal of Sociology*, 70 (November, 1964), pp. 319–331. See pp. 323–324.

18. INDEPENDENCE OF PARTNER

See also Conformity and Deviance.
Willis, Richard H., "Two Dimensions of Conformity-Nonconformity," *Sociometry*, 26 (December, 1963), pp. 499–513. See p. 509.

19. INDIFFERENCE TOWARD OTHERS

Gottheil; see category 1 above.

20. INFLUENCE, EFFORTS TO

Iwao, Sumiko, "Internal versus External Criticism of Group Standards," *Sociometry*, 26 (December, 1963), pp. 410–421. See p. 417.

21. INTERACTION CHECKLIST

Backman, Carl W., and Paul F. Secord, "Liking, Selective Interaction, and Misperception in Congruent Interpersonal Relations," *Sociometry*, 25 (December, 1962), pp. 321–335. See p. 326.

22. INTERACTION PROCESS ANALYSIS

Bales, Robert F., *Interaction Process Analysis*, Cambridge, Mass.: Addison-Wesley Press, 1951.
Slater, Philip E., "Role Differentiation in Small Groups," *American Sociological Review*, 20 (June, 1955), pp. 300–310. See p. 301.
Palmore, Erdman, Henry L. Lennard, and Helen Hendin, "Similarities of Therapist and Patient Verbal Behavior in Psychotherapy," *Sociometry*, 22 (March, 1959), pp. 12–27. See p. 12.
Hare, Paul, and Robert F. Bales, "Seating Position and Small

Group Interaction," *Sociometry*, 26 (December, 1963), pp. 480–486. See p. 480.

23. INTERACTION PROCESS, DIFFICULTY IN

Bales; see category 22 above.

Borgatta, Edgar F., Robert F. Bales, and Arthur S. Couch, "Some Findings Relevant to the Great Man Theory of Leadership," *American Sociological Review*, 19 (December, 1954), pp. 755–759. See p. 758.

24. INTERACTION QUESTIONNAIRE

Blake, Robert R., Clifton C. Rhead, Bryant Wedge, and Jane S. Mouton, "Housing Architecture and Social Interaction," *Sociometry*, 19 (June, 1956), pp. 133–139. See p. 134.

25. INTERPERSONAL-BEHAVIOR CODING DEVICE

Longabaugh, Richard, "A Category System for Coding Interpersonal Behavior as Social Exchange," *Sociometry*, 26 (September, 1963), pp. 319–344. See p. 319.

26. INTERPERSONAL CHECK LIST

Leary, Timothy F., *Multilevel Measurement of Interpersonal Behavior*, Berkeley, Calif.: Psychological Consultation Service, 1956.

Dinitz, Simon, A. R. Mangus, and Benjamin Pasamanick, "Integration and Conflict in Self-Other Conceptions as Factors in Mental Illness," *Sociometry*, 22 (March, 1959), pp. 44–45. See p. 45.

Luckey, Eleanore Braun, "Marital Satisfaction and Congruent Self-Spouse Concepts," *Social Forces*, 39 (October, 1960), pp. 153–157. See pp. 154–155.

Turk, Herman, "Instrumental Values and the Popularity of Instrumental Leaders," *Social Forces*, 39 (March, 1961), pp. 252–260. See p. 254.

Smelser, William T., "Adolescent and Adult Occupational Choices as a Function of Family Socioeconomic History," *Sociometry*, 26 (December, 1963), pp. 393–409. See p. 404.

27. INTERPERSONAL CHOICE

Taguiri, Renato R., Nathan Kogan, and Jerome S. Bruner, "The

Transparency of Interpersonal Choice," *Sociometry*, 18 (December, 1955), pp. 624–635. See p. 625.

28. INTERPERSONAL COMPETENCE: AUTONOMY

Stanton, Howard R., and Eugene Litwak, "Toward the Development of a Short Form Test of Interpersonal Competence," *American Sociological Review*, 20 (December, 1955), pp. 668–674. See p. 669.

29. INTERPERSONAL CONFLICT, REACTION TO

Harburg, Ernest, *Covert Hostility: Its Social Origins and Relationships with Overt Compliance*, unpublished Ph.D. dissertation, University of Michigan, 1962.

McGinn, Noel F., Ernest Harburg, and Gerald P. Ginsburg, "Dependency Relations with Parents and Affiliative Responses in Michigan and Guadalajara," *Sociometry*, 28 (September, 1965), pp. 305–321. See pp. 314–318.

30. INTERPERSONAL ENVIRONMENT, DETERMINATION OF

Wallace, Walter L., "Institutional and Life-Cycle Socialization of College Freshmen," *American Journal of Sociology*, 70 (November, 1964), pp. 303–318. See pp. 305–306.

31. INTERPERSONAL ENVIRONMENT, GRADES-EVALUATION, BIAS IN

Wallace; see category 30 above.

32. INTERPERSONAL ROLE CONFLICT, EXTENT OF

Getzels, J. W., and E. G. Guba, "Role, Role Conflict, and Effectiveness: An Empirical Study," *American Sociological Review*, 19 (April, 1954), pp. 164–175. See pp. 167–169.

33. INTERPERSONAL ROLE CONFLICT, INTENSITY OF

Getzels and Guba; see category 32 above.

34. IRRELEVANT-RELEVANT BEHAVIOR

Rosengren, William R., "The Self in the Emotionally Disturbed," *American Journal of Sociology*, 66 (March, 1961), pp. 454–462. See p. 456.

35. LIKEABILITY (JONES, DECHARMS)

Jones, Edward E., and Richard DeCharms, "Changes in Social

Perception as a Function of the Personal Relevance of Behavior," *Sociometry*, 20 (March, 1957), pp. 75–85. See p. 77.

36. LIKEABILITY (WEINSTEIN, DEUTSCHBERGER)

Weinstein and Deutschberger, p. 462; see category 3 above.

37. LIKING

Exline, Ralph V., "Interrelations among Two Dimensions of Sociometric Status, Group Congeniality, and Accuracy of Social Perception," *Sociometry*, 23 (March, 1960), pp. 85–101. See p. 89.

38. LIKING, CHANGE IN

Singer, Jerome E., Lenor S. Radloff, and David M. Wark, "Renegades, Heretics, and Changes in Sentiment," *Sociometry*, 26 (June, 1963), pp. 178–189. See p. 183.

39. LIKING, DYADIC

Riley, Cohn, Toby, and Riley, p. 718; see category 12 above.

40. LIKING RANKING FORM

Backman and Secord; see category 21 above.

41. MUTUAL ACQUAINTANCES

Gronlund, Norman E., "Acquaintance Span and Sociometric Status," *Sociometry*, 18 (February, 1955), pp. 62–68. See p. 62.

42. MUTUALITY OF SOCIAL CHOICE

Davids, Anthony and Anita Negrin Parenti, "Personality, Social Choice, and Adults' Perception of These Factors in Groups of Disturbed and Normal Children," *Sociometry*, 21 (September, 1958), pp. 212–224. See p. 214.

43. ORIGIN-PAWN SCALE

DeCharms, Richard, Virginia Carpenter, and Aharon Kuperman, "The 'Origin-Pawn' Variable in Personal Perception," *Sociometry*, 28 (September, 1965), pp. 241–258. See pp. 248–254.

44. OTHER-RATING CHECKLIST

Backman and Secord; see category 21 above.

45. ORIENTATION TOWARD CLIENTS (BLAU)

Blau, Peter M., "Patterns of Choice in Interpersonal Relations,"

American Sociological Review, 27 (February, 1962), pp. 41–55. See p. 54.

46. ORIENTATION TOWARD CLIENTS (TURK)

Turk, Herman, "Social Cohesion through Variant Values: Evidence from Medical Role Relations," *American Sociological Review*, 28 (February, 1963), pp. 28–37. See pp. 30–31.

47. RATED EXPANSIVENESS

Borgatta, Edgar F., "Analysis of Social Interaction and Sociometric Perception," *Sociometry*, 17 (February, 1954), pp. 7–32. See p. 16.

48. REJECTION OF OTHERS

Gottheil; see category 1 above.

49. SITUATIONAL INTERPRETATION TEST

Janicki, W. P., *The Effects of Variation in Conceptual Structure on Dyadic Interaction*, unpublished Ph.D. dissertation, Princeton University, 1960.

Tuckman, Bruce W., "Personality Structure, Group Composition and Group Functioning," *Sociometry*, 27 (December, 1964), pp. 468–487. See p. 477.

50. STATUS DISCREPANCY

Lenski, Gerhard E. and John C. Leggett, "Caste, Class and Deference in the Research Interview," *American Journal of Sociology*, 65 (March, 1960), pp. 463–467. See p. 464.

51. SEMANTIC DIFFERENTIAL

Longabaugh, p. 338; see category 25 above.

52. SUSCEPTIBILITY TO INFLUENCE BY FRIENDS

Janis, Irving L., and Peter B. Field, "A Behavioral Assessment of Persuasibility: Consistency of Individual Differences," *Sociometry*, 19 (December, 1956), pp. 241–259. See pp. 253–254.

53. THREAT POTENTIAL OF INTERVIEW SCHEDULE

Williams, J. Allen, Jr., "Interviewer-Respondent Interaction: A Study of Bias in the Information Interview," *Sociometry*, 27 (September, 1964), pp. 338–352. See pp. 343 and 351–352.

JOB SATISFACTION, MORALE, AND RELATED MEASURES

SEE ALSO

Complex Organizations:
Attitudes toward and Perceptions of

1. DISSATISFACTION

Lefton, Mark, Simon Dinitz, and Benjamin Pasamanick, "Decision-Making in a Mental Hospital: Real, Perceived, and Ideal," *American Sociological Review*, 24 (December, 1959), pp. 822–829. See p. 827.

2. DISSATISFACTION WITH TASK

Day, Robert C., and Robert L. Hamblin, "Some Effects of Close and Punitive Styles of Supervision," *American Journal of Sociology*, 69 (March, 1964), pp. 499–510. See pp. 504–505.

3. FUSION WITH THE ORGANIZATION, PERCEIVED DEGREE OF

Argyris, Chris, "The Fusion of an Individual with the Organization," *American Sociological Review*, 19 (June, 1954), pp. 266–272. See p. 268.

4. HIERARCHICAL CONSENSUS REGARDING MORALE

Smith, Clagett G., and Oguz N. Ari, "Organizational Control Structure and Member Consensus," *American Journal of Sociology*, 69 (May, 1964), pp. 623–638. See pp. 629–630.

5. JOB SATISFACTION (BULLOCK)

Bullock, Robert P., *Social Factors Related to Job Satisfaction: A Technique for the Measurement of Job Satisfaction*, Columbus, Ohio: Ohio State University Bureau of Business Research, 1952. See Section II and Appendix A.

Dyer, William G., "The Interlocking of Work and Family Social

Systems among Lower Occupational Workers," *Social Forces*, 34 (March, 1956), pp. 230–233. See p. 232.

Bible, Bond L., and James D. McComas, "Role Consensus and Teacher Effectiveness," *Social Forces*, 42 (December, 1963), pp. 225–233. See p. 228.

6. JOB SATISFACTION (DAVIS)

Davis, F. James, "Conceptions of Official Leader Roles in the Air Force," *Social Forces*, 32 (March, 1954), pp. 253–258. See p. 256.

7. JOB SATISFACTION (GROSS)

Gross, Edward, "Primary Functions of the Small Group," *American Journal of Sociology*, 60 (July, 1954), pp. 24–29. See p. 26.

8. JOB SATISFACTION (KERR)

Kerr, W. A., *Tear Ballot for Industry, General Opinions*, Chicago, Ill.: Psychometric Affiliates, 1948.

Kerr, W. A., "Summary of Validity Studies of the Tear Ballot," *Personnel Psychology*, 5 (Summer, 1952), pp. 105–113. See p. 106.

Speroff, B. J., "Job Satisfaction and Interpersonal Desirability Values," *Sociometry*, 18 (February, 1955), pp. 69–72. See p. 70.

9. JOB SATISFACTION (PEARSON, BARKER, ELLIOTT)

Pearson, Judson B., Gordon H. Barker, and Rodney D. Elliott, "Sales Success and Job Satisfaction," *American Sociological Review*, 22 (August, 1957), pp. 424–427. See pp. 424–425.

10. JOB SATISFACTION (REEDER)

Reeder, Leo G., "Social Factors in Heart Disease: A Preliminary Research Report on the Relationship of Certain Social Factors to Blood Pressure in Males," *Social Forces*, 34 (May, 1956), pp. 367–371. See p. 368.

11. JOB SATISFACTION (RETTIG, JACOBSON, PASAMANICK)

Rettig, Salomon, Frank N. Jacobson, and Benjamin Pasamanick, "Status Overestimation, Objective Status and Job Satisfaction among Professions," *American Sociological Review*, 23 (February, 1958), pp. 75–81. See p. 76.

12. JOB SATISFACTION, RATING OF

Rettig, Jacobson, and Pasamanick, p. 76; see category 11 above.

Rettig, Salomon, Frank N. Jacobson, Leo DesPres, and Benjamin Pasamanick, "Rating Response Sets as a Function of Objective Status Criteria," *Sociometry*, 21 (December, 1958), pp. 281–291. See p. 284.

13. MEMBER SATISFACTION

Smith and Ari, pp. 629–631; see category 4 above.

14. MORALE (CAVAN AND COLLEAGUES)

Cavan, Ruth S., and colleagues, *Personal Adjustment in Old Age*, Chicago, Ill.: Science Research Associates, 1949, p. 50.

Maddox, George L., "Activity and Morale: A Longitudinal Study of Selected Elderly Subjects," *Social Forces*, 42 (December, 1963), pp. 195–204. See p. 197

15. MORALE (MEDALIA, MILLER)

Medalia, Nahum Z., and Delbert C. Miller, "Human Relations Leadership and the Association of Morale and Efficiency in Work Groups: A Controlled Study with Small Military Units," *Social Forces*, 33 (May, 1955), pp. 348–352. See p. 350.

16. MORALE (SURVEY RESEARCH CENTER)

Mack, Raymond W., "The Prestige System of an Air Base: Squadron Rankings and Morale," *American Sociological Review*, 19 (June, 1954), pp. 281–287. See p. 284.

17. MORALE OF ELDERLY (DEAN)

Dean, Lois R., "The Pattern Variables: Some Empirical Operations," *American Sociological Review*, 26 (February, 1961), pp. 80–90. See p. 88.

18. MORALE OF ELDERLY (LOWENTHAL)

Lowenthal, Marjorie Fiske, "Social Isolation and Mental Illness in Old Age," *American Sociological Review*, 29 (February, 1964), pp. 54–70. See p. 63.

19. MORALE OPINION SURVEY

Chesler, David J., Neil J. Van Steenberg, and Joyce E. Brueckel, "Effect on Morale of Infantry Team Replacement and Individual Replacement Systems," *Sociometry*, 18 (December, 1955), pp. 587–597. See p. 590.

20. OCCUPATIONAL SATISFACTION SCALE

Hetzler, Stanley A., "Social Mobility and Radicalism-Conservatism," *Social Forces*, 33 (December, 1954), pp. 161–166. See p. 161.

21. PERSONAL COMMITMENT TO GROUP GOALS

Gross, p. 26; see category 7 above.

22. PERSONAL ESPRIT

Gross, p. 26; see category 7 above.

23. PROFESSIONAL RECOGNITION INDEX

Glaser, Barney G., "The Local-Cosmopolitan Scientist," *American Journal of Sociology*, 69 (November, 1963), pp. 249–259. See p. 253.

24. SATISFACTION WITH THE AIR FORCE

Gross, p. 26; see category 7 above.

25. SATISFACTION WITH THE AIR SITE

Gross, p. 26; see category 7 above.

26. SATISFACTION WITH COMPANY

Bowers, David G., "Organizational Control in an Insurance Company," *Sociometry*, 27 (June, 1964), pp. 230–244. See p. 234.

27. SATISFACTION WITH INCOME

Bowers, p. 235; see category 26 above.

28. SATISFACTION WITH JOB

Bowers, p. 235; see category 26 above.

29. WORK-GROUP CONSENSUS REGARDING MORALE

Smith and Ari, pp. 629–630; see category 4 above.

LEADERSHIP, COMMUNITY AND ORGANIZATIONAL: BEHAVIOR AND CHARACTERISTICS OF

SEE ALSO

Authority: Attitudes toward and Characteristics of

1. ACQUAINTANCESHIP PATTERNS OF LEADERS

Miller, Delbert C., "Decision-Making Cliques in Community Power Structures: A Comparative Study of an American and an English City," *American Journal of Sociology*, 64 (November, 1958), pp. 299–310. See p. 302.

2. ACTIVITY OF TOP INFLUENTIALS

Hanson, Robert C., "Predicting a Community Decision: A Test of the Miller-Form Theory," *American Sociological Review*, 24 (October, 1959), pp. 662–671. See p. 665.

3. COMPETITIVENESS OF LEADERS

• Hetzler, Stanley A., "Variations in Role-Playing Patterns among Different Echelons of Bureaucratic Leaders," *American Sociological Review*, 20 (December, 1955), pp. 700–706. See p. 701.

4. CONSIDERATION (OHIO STATE LEADER BEHAVIOR DESCRIPTION QUESTIONNAIRE AND RELATED MEASURES)

Hemphill, John K., *Leader Behavior Description*, Columbus, Ohio: Personnel Research Board, Ohio State University, 1950.

Halpin, Andrew W., and Ben J. Winer, *The Leadership Behavior of the Airplane Commander*, Washington, D.C.: Human Resources Research Laboratories, Department of the Air Force, 1952.

Fleishman, Edwin A., "The Description of Supervisory Behavior,"

Journal of Applied Psychology, 37 (February, 1953), pp. 1–6.

Fleishman, Edwin A., "The Measurement of Leadership Attitudes in Industry," *Journal of Applied Psychology,* 37 (June, 1953), pp. 153–158.

Halpin, Andrew W., "The Leadership Behavior and Combat Performance of Airplane Commanders," *Journal of Abnormal and Social Psychology,* 49 (January, 1954), pp. 19–22. See pp. 19–20.

Fleishman, Edwin A., Edwin F. Harris, and Harold E. Burtt, *Leadership and Supervision in Industry,* Columbus, Ohio: Ohio State University, Bureau of Educational Research Monograph 33, 1955.

Stogdill, Ralph M., and Alvin E. Coons, eds. *Leader Behavior: Its Description and Measurement,* Columbus, Ohio: Ohio State University, Bureau of Business Research, Monograph 88, 1957.

Fleishman, Edwin A. *Manual for Administering the Leadership Opinion Questionnaire,* Chicago, Illinois: Science Research Associates, 1960.

In a series of studies beginning at Ohio State University under the direction of John K. Hemphill, Consideration was shown to be a major dimension of leader behavior. Hemphill developed the Leader Behavior Description Questionnaire (LBDQ) which was utilized and expanded in studies by members of the Personnel Research Board. An original pool of approximately 1,800 items was constructed to describe nine *a priori* dimensions of leader behavior, and from this pool 150 items were selected by judges to form the LBDQ. Further experience with these items, however, showed that the *a priori* leader-behavior dimensions were not independent and that studies of the interrelations among the dimensions might lead to the discovery of fewer and more nearly independent categories. A factor analysis undertaken by Halpin and Winer (1952) led to a regrouping of the LBDQ items into two major factors, Consideration and Initiating Structure, and two minor factors, Production Emphasis and Social Sensitivity. (A forty-item form of the LBDQ based upon the work of Halpin and Winer has been published by the Bureau of Business Research, Ohio State University, 1775 South College Road, Columbus, Ohio, 43210. This revision of the LBDQ is discussed by Stogdill and Coons (1957, above.) Consideration accounted for 49.6 per cent of the common factor variance, while Initiating Structure accounted for 33.6 per cent of the common factor variance. These major dimensions of leader behavior are described by Fleishman, Harris, and Burtt (1955, p. 27) as follows:

Consideration.—Items with high positive loadings on this factor were associated with behavior indicative of friendship, mutual trust, respect, and a certain warmth between the leader and his group. High negative loadings appeared on items which suggest that the leader is arbitrary and impersonal in his relations with group members.
Initiating Structure.—Items with high positive loadings on this factor imply that the leader organizes and defines the relationship between himself and the members of his group. He tends to define the role which he expects each member to assume, and endeavors to establish well-defined patterns of organization, channels of communication, and ways of getting the job done.

In order to determine the utility in an industrial setting of the instruments described above, Fleishman (February, 1953) conducted another factor analysis of 136 of the LBDQ items. On the basis of this analysis, a Supervisory Behavior Description (SBD) instrument was constructed. The SBD, which consists of 28 Consideration items and 20 Initiating Structure items, has been published and discussed by Fleishman (February, 1953, see p. 3), and by Fleishman, Harris, and Burtt (1955, see pp. 32–33). This instrument focuses on employees' descriptions of the behavior of their superiors toward them.

Fleishman (June, 1953) also has derived from the LBDQ an instrument for measuring leadership attitudes, the Leadership Opinion Questionnaire. This instrument is similar to the SBD, but it contains 20 Consideration items, rather than 28, and it focuses on the ways those in positions of leadership think they *ought* to behave. The LOQ has been discussed by Fleishman (June, 1953) and by Fleishman, Harris, and Burtt (1955, see pp. 32–33). The LOQ also has been published by Science Research Associates, Inc. (259 East Erie Street, Chicago, Illinois, 1960. See Fleishman,

1960, above). While there is substantial overlap between the content of the SBD and the LOQ, each instrument is based upon a separate item analysis. Also, it should be stressed that the former is appropriate to situations in which the researcher wishes to assess the actual *behavior* of supervisors, while the latter is pertinent when the researcher wishes to assess the leadership *attitudes* of a person who occupies a leadership position.

Items in the LBDQ, the SBD, and the LOQ typically are accompanied by a five-point response format. When the SBD is utilized, for example, the respondent is asked to describe the behavior of his supervisor by indicating that the supervisor Always, Often, Occasionally, Seldom, or Never "refuses to give in when people disagree with him." Or, still another example, when the LOQ is utilized, the respondent is asked to indicate in relation to the same alternatives whether he as a leader *should* "refuse to compromise a point." Responses indicating high Consideration or Initiating Structure generally are scored 4 and responses indicating low degrees of each type of leader behavior or attitudes are scored 0. Adding the responses to each item yields the total score on each dimension.

Christner, Charlotte A., and John K. Hemphill, "Leader Behavior of B-29 Commanders and Changes in Crew Members' Attitudes toward the Crew," *Sociometry*, 18 (February, 1955), pp. 82–87. See p. 82.

Halpin, Andrew W., *The Leadership Behavior of School Superintendents*, Columbus, Ohio: Ohio State University Press, 1956.

Hemphill, John K., and Alvin E. Coons, "Development of the Leader Behavior Description Questionnaire," in Ralph M. Stogdill and Alvin E. Coons (eds.), *Leader Behavior: Its Description and Measurement*. Columbus, Ohio: Ohio State University, Bureau of Business Research, Monograph 88, 1957, pp. 6–38.

Seeman, Melvin, "Social Mobility and Administrative Behavior," *American Sociological Review*, 23 (December, 1958), pp. 633–642. See p. 634.

5. INITIATING STRUCTURE (OHIO STATE LEADER BEHAVIOR DESCRIPTION QUESTIONNAIRE AND RELATED MEASURES)

Hemphill (1950); see category 4 above.
Halpin and Winer (1952); see category 4 above.
Fleishman (February, 1953); see category 4 above.
Fleishman (June, 1953); see category 4 above.
Halpin (1954); see category 4 above.
Fleishman, Harris, and Burtt (1955); see category 4 above.
Stogdill and Coons (1957); see category 4 above.
Fleishman (1960); see category 4 above.

Initiating Structure has been defined and discussed (along with Consideration) in category 4 above. The response format and scoring procedures are the same. An example of an item used for measuring the extent to which one's supervisor Initiates Structure is as follows: "He encourages overtime work" (Fleishman, Harris, and Burtt, 1955, p. 32). As in the case of Consideration, the respondent is instructed to indicate the frequency with which such behavior occurs, as by Always, Often, Occasionally, Seldom, or Never.

Christner and Hemphill (1955); see category 4 above.
Halpin (1956); see category 4 above.
Hemphill and Coons (1957); see category 4 above.
Seeman (1958); see category 4 above.

6. ISSUES OF CONCERN TO LEADERS

Barth, Ernest A. T., and Baha Abu-Laban, "Power Structure and the Negro Sub-Community," *American Sociological Review*, 24 (February, 1959), pp. 69–76. See p. 74.

7. KNOWLEDGE OF LEADERSHIP

Damarian, Fred L., and Donald T. Campbell, "Measuring Leadership Attitudes through an Information Test," unpublished, no date.
Campbell, Donald T., and Thelma H. McCormack, "Military Experience and Attitudes toward Authority," *American Jour-*

nal of Sociology, 62 (March, 1957), pp. 482–490. See pp. 483–484.

8. LEADERSHIP COOPERATION

Grusky, Oscar, "Organizational Goals and the Behavior of Informal Leaders," *American Journal of Sociology*, 65 (July, 1959), pp. 59–67. See pp. 62–65.

9. LEADERSHIP ROLE

Fanelli, A. Alexander, "A Typology of Community Leadership Based on Influence and Interaction within the Leader Subsystem," *Social Forces*, 34 (May, 1956), pp. 332–338. See p. 334.

10. NEW INDUSTRY, LEADERS' ATTITUDES TOWARD

Cramer, M. Richard, "School Desegregation and New Industry: The Southern Community Leaders' Viewpoint," *Social Forces*, 41 (May, 1963), pp. 384–389. See p. 385.

11. POWER ARRANGEMENT

Hanson, pp. 664–665; see category 2 above.

12. POWER, AWARENESS OF

Horton, John E., and Wayne E. Thompson, "Powerlessness and Political Negativism: A Study of Defeated Local Referendums," *American Journal of Sociology*, 67 (March, 1962), pp. 485–493. See p. 489.

13. POWER, CONCENTRATION OF

Hawley, Amos H., "Community Power and Urban Renewal Success," *American Journal of Sociology*, 68 (January, 1963), pp. 422–431. See p. 424.

14. POWER STRUCTURE

Whitten, Norman E., Jr., "Power Structure and Sociocultural Change in Latin American Communities," *Social Forces*, 43 (March, 1965), pp. 320–329. See p. 322.

15. SOCIAL ACTIVITY OF LEADERS

Freeman, Linton C., Thomas J. Fararo, Warner Bloomberg, Jr., and Morris H. Sunshine, "Locating Leaders in Local Communities: A Comparison of Some Alternative Approaches,"

American Sociological Review, 28 (October, 1963), pp. 791–798. See p. 795.

16. SOURCES OF POWER, ATTITUDE TOWARD

Haer, John L., "Social Stratification in Relation to Attitude Toward Sources of Power in a Community," *Social Forces*, 35 (December, 1956), pp. 137–142. See p. 139.

17. SUPERIOR-SUBORDINATE ORIENTATION

Campbell and McCormack (1957), p. 485; see category 7 above.

LEADERSHIP, COMMUNITY AND ORGAN-IZATIONAL: IDENTIFICATION OF

1. ECONOMIC DOMINANTS

Schulze, Robert O., "The Role of Economic Dominants in Community Power Structure," *American Sociological Review*, 23 (February, 1958), pp. 3–9. See p. 5.

2. INFLUENTIAL ORGANIZATIONS (BABCHUK, MARSEY, GORDON)

Babchuk, Nicholas, Ruth Marsey, and Wayne C. Gordon, "Men and Women in Community Agencies: A Note on Power and Prestige," *American Sociological Review*, 25 (June, 1960), pp. 399–403. See p. 401.

3. INFLUENTIAL ORGANIZATIONS (BARTH, ABU-LABAN)

Barth, Ernest A. T., and Baha Abu-Laban, "Power Structure and the Negro Sub-Community," *American Sociological Review*, 24 (February, 1959), pp. 69–76. See p. 71.

4. INFORMAL LEADERSHIP RANKING

Freeman, Charles, and Selz C. Mayo, "Decision Makers in Rural Community Action," *Social Forces*, 35 (May, 1957), pp. 319–322. See p. 320.

5. LEADERSHIP (DECISION-MAKING ANALYSIS APPROACHES)

Freeman and Mayo, pp. 320–321; see category 4 above.

Janes, Robert W., "A Study of a Natural Experiment in Community Action," in Marvin B. Sussman (ed.), *Community Structure and Analysis*, New York: Thomas Y. Crowell, 1959, pp. 157–172.

Freeman, Linton C., Warner Bloomberg, Jr., Stephen P. Koff, Morris H. Sunshine, and Thomas J. Fararo, *Local Commu-*

nity Leadership, Syracuse, N.Y., University College of Syracuse University, 1960.

Freeman, Linton C., Thomas J. Fararo, Warner Bloomberg, Jr., and Morris H. Sunshine, "Locating Leaders in Local Communities: A Comparison of Some Alternative Approaches," *American Sociological Review,* 28 (October, 1963), pp. 791–798. See p. 794.

Freeman, Linton C., Thomas J. Fararo, Warner Bloomberg, Jr., and Morris H. Sunshine, *Metropolitan Decision Making,* Syracuse, N.Y.: University College of Syracuse University, 1962.

6. LEADERSHIP (EVENT ANALYSIS APPROACH)

Young, James N., and Selz C. Mayo, "Manifest and Latent Participators in a Rural Community Action Program," *Social Forces,* 38 (December, 1959), pp. 140–145. See p. 141.

Miller, Delbert C., "Town and Gown: The Power Structure of a University Town," *American Journal of Sociology,* 68 (January, 1963), pp. 432–443. See p. 434.

7. LEADERSHIP (PARTICIPANT OBSERVATION APPROACH)

Agger, Robert E., and Daniel Goldrich, "Community Power Structures and Partisanship," *American Sociological Review,* 23 (August, 1958), pp. 383–392. See p. 385.

8. LEADERSHIP (REPUTATIONAL APPROACH)

Numerous variations of the reputational approach to the identification of leaders have been set forth. Although the approach is usually traced to the works of Hunter (1953, below), neighborhood leaders were identified in this manner at least three years earlier by Reid and Ehle (below). Somewhat earlier, the reputational approach was used by Warner, Hollingshead, and others not in the study of leadership, but to study community status hierarchies. (See also Socioeconomic Status: Reputational)

All variations of this technique consist essentially of asking informants to name and rank the leaders in their community. The informants may be a predesignated panel of experts or a random sample of community members, or they may be selected by that which is known as the "snowball" or "cobweb" technique. The final list of leaders usually consists either of those individuals who have received the greatest number of nominations by the informants or of all leaders whose average ranking is above a certain arbitrarily set limit.

Much additional information may be gathered in regard to the nature of leadership structure by using a question format similar to that presented on page 194.

Although the reputational approach has been the most widely used technique in the sociological study of community leadership, it has been criticized from several standpoints:

1. It has been criticized for not measuring leadership as such, but only the reputation for leadership, which may not be a valid index of power.
2. It has been criticized for incorporating an a priori assumption of a monolithic power structure—that is, some investigators have used this technique in a manner that would make it difficult to discover different groups of elites with different areas of interest. To the degree that decision areas are also investigated (as in the question format shown), this criticism may be overcome.
3. Some investigations incorporating this approach have been criticized for also incorporating an a priori assumption about group structure—assuming that the highest ranking individuals make up a ruling group rather than merely an aggregate of leaders. This criticism may be met by incorporating sociometric and interaction checks in the method (for instance, by asking, as above, "With which community leaders have you worked on the following?")
4. The approach has been criticized from the same standpoints that apply to most verbal reports—inaccuracies in respondent perceptions, a lack of agreement between the interviewer and respondent in regard to what is meant by "power" or "leadership," and the problem of establishing categories (in this case, differentiating between leaders and nonleaders).

Reid, Ira de A., and Emily Ehle, "Leadership Selection in Urban Locality Areas," *Public Opinion Quarterly*, 14 (Summer, 1950), pp. 262–284. See p. 263.

Hunter, Floyd, *Community Power Structure: A Study of Decision Makers*, Chapel Hill, N.C.: University of North Carolina Press, 1953. See pp. 262–271.

Vidich, Arthur J., and Gilbert Shapiro, "A Comparison of Participant Observation and Survey Data," *American Sociological Review*, 20 (February, 1955), pp. 28–33. See p. 30.

Olmsted, Donald W., "Organizational Leadership and Social Structure in a Small City," *American Sociological Review*, 19 (June, 1954), pp. 273–281. See p. 274.

Hunter, Floyd, Ruth Connor Schaffer, and Cecil G. Sheps, *Community Organization: Action and Inaction*, Chapel Hill, N.C.: University of North Carolina Press, 1956.

Smuckler, Ralph H., and George M. Belknap, *Leadership and Participation in Urban Political Affairs*, East Lansing, Mich.: Government Research Bureau, Michigan State University, 1956.

Agger, Robert E., and Vincent Ostrom, "Political Participation in a Small Community," in Heinz Eulau, Samuel J. Eldersveld, and Morris Janowitz (eds.), *Political Behavior*, Chicago, Ill.: The Free Press, 1956, pp. 138–148.

Belknap, George, and Ralph Smuckler, "Political Power Relations in a Mid-west City," *Public Opinion Quarterly*, 20 (Spring, 1956), pp. 73–81. See pp. 73–74.

Agger, Robert E., and Vincent Ostrom, "The Political Structure of a Small Community," *Public Opinion Quarterly*, 20 (Spring, 1956), pp. 81–89. See p. 84.

Adler, Kenneth P., and Davis Bobrow, "Interest and Influence in Foreign Affairs," *Public Opinion Quarterly*, 20 (Spring, 1956), pp. 89–101. See pp. 91–92.

Agger, Robert E., "Power Attributions in the Local Community: Theoretical and Research Considerations," *Social Forces*, 34 (May, 1956), pp. 322–331. See p. 323.

Fanelli, A. Alexander, "A Typology of Community Leadership

Based on Influence and Interaction within the Leader Subsystem," *Social Forces*, 34 (May, 1956), pp. 332–338. See p. 333.

Foskett, John M., and Raymond Hohle, "The Measurement of Influence in Community Affairs," *Research Studies of the State College of Washington*, 25 (June, 1957), pp. 148–154.

Tumin, Melvin, and Robert Rotberg, "Leaders, the Led, and the Law: A Case Study in Social Change," *Public Opinion Quarterly*, 21 (Fall, 1957), pp. 355–370. See pp. 357–359.

Schulze, Robert O., and Leonard U. Blumberg, "The Determination of Local Power Elites," *American Journal of Sociology*, 63 (November, 1957), pp. 290–296. See p. 292.

D'Antonio, William, *National Images of Business and Political Elites in Two Border Cities*, unpublished Ph.D. dissertation, Michigan State University, 1958.

Miller, Delbert C., "Industry and Community Power Structure: A Comparative Study of an American and an English City," *American Sociological Review*, 23 (February, 1958), pp. 9–15. See pp. 10–11.

Schulze (1958), p. 7; see category 1 above.

Agger and Goldrich (1958); see category 7 above.

Miller, Delbert C., "Decision-Making Cliques in Community Power Structures: A Comparative Study of an American and an English City," *American Journal of Sociology*, 64 (November, 1958), pp. 299–310. See pp. 300–301.

Barth and Abu-Laban (1959); see category 3 above.

Form, William H., and William V. D'Antonio, "Integration and Cleavage among Community Influentials in Two Border Cities," *American Sociological Review*, 24 (December, 1959), pp. 804–814. See p. 806.

Klapp, Orrin E., and L. Vincent Padgett, "Power Structure and Decision-Making in a Mexican Border City," *American Journal of Sociology*, 65 (January, 1960), pp. 400–406. See p. 401.

Sanders, Irwin T., "The Community Social Profile," *American Sociological Review*, 25 (February, 1960), pp. 75–77. See p. 76.

Form, William H., and Warren L. Sauer, "Organized Labor's

Image of Community Power Structure," *Social Forces,* 38 (May, 1960), pp. 332–341. See p. 334.

D'Antonio, William V., and Eugene C. Erickson, "The Reputational Technique as a Measure of Community Power: An Evaluation Based on Comparative and Longitudinal Studies," *American Sociological Review,* 27 (June, 1962), pp. 362–376. See p. 364.

Hanson, Robert C., "The Systemic Linkage Hypothesis and Role Consensus Patterns in Hospital-Community Relations," *American Sociological Review,* 27 (June, 1962), pp. 304–313. See pp. 306–308, and 309, 311, and 313.

Miller (1963), p. 435; see category 6 above.

Payne, Raymond, "Leadership and Perceptions of Change in a Village Confronted with Urbanism," *Social Forces,* 41 (March, 1963), pp. 264–269. See p. 266.

Bonjean, Charles M., "Community Leadership: A Case Study and Conceptual Refinement," *American Journal of Sociology,* 68 (May, 1963), pp. 672–681. See pp. 673–675.

Cramer, M. Richard, "School Desegregation and New Industry: The Southern Community Leaders' Viewpoint," *Social Forces,* 41 (May, 1963), pp. 384–389. See p. 385.

Freeman, Fararo, Bloomberg, and Sunshine (1963), p. 795; see category 5 above.

Blankenship, L. Vaughn, "Community Power and Decision Making: A Comparative Evaluation of Measurement Techniques," *Social Forces,* 43 (December, 1964), pp. 207–216. See pp. 210–211.

Miller, Delbert C., and James Dirksen, "The Identification of Visible, Concealed, and Symbolic Leaders in a Small Indiana City: A Replication of the Bonjean-Noland Study of Burlington, North Carolina," *Social Forces,* 43 (May, 1965), pp. 548–555.

Ehrlich, Howard J., and Mary Lou Bauer, "Newspaper Citation and Reputation for Community Leadership," *American Sociological Review,* 30 (June, 1965), pp. 411–415. See p. 412.

9. LEADERSHIP INDEX (BURGESS)

Burgess, Ernest W., "Social Relations, Activities, and Personal Adjustment," *American Journal of Sociology*, 59 (January, 1954), pp. 352–360. See pp. 353–354.

10. LEADERSHIP INDEX (SCHRAG)

Schrag, Clarence, "Leadership among Prison Inmates," *American Sociological Review*, 19 (February, 1954), pp. 37–42. See p. 38.

Grusky, Oscar, "Organizational Goals and the Behavior of Informal Leaders," *American Journal of Sociology*, 65 (July, 1959), pp. 59–67. See p. 61.

11. OPINION LEADERSHIP

Katz, Elihu, and Paul F. Lazarsfeld, *Personal Influence*, Glencoe, Ill.: The Free Press, 1955, p. 139.

Carter, Roy E., Jr., and Peter Clarke, "Public Affairs Opinion Leadership among Educational Television Viewers," *American Sociological Review*, 27 (December, 1962), pp. 792–799. See pp. 793–794.

12. ORGANIZATIONAL PARTICIPATION

Freeman, Fararo, Bloomberg, and Sunshine (1963), p. 796; see category 5 above.

13. RELATIVE POSITION OF COMMUNITY INFLUENTIALS

Dick, Harry R., "A Method for Ranking Community Influentials," *American Sociological Review*, 25 (June, 1960), pp. 395–399. See pp. 396–398.

LEADERSHIP, SMALL GROUP: BEHAVIOR AND CHARACTERISTICS OF

SEE ALSO

*Authority: Attitudes toward
and Characteristics of*

1. ADHERENCE TO REGULATIONS

Davis, F. James, "Conceptions of Official Leader Roles in the Air Force," *Social Forces*, 32 (March, 1954), pp. 253–258. See p. 254.

Davis, F. James, and Robert Hagedorn, "Testing the Reliability of Systematic Field Observations," *American Sociological Review*, 19 (June, 1954), pp. 345–348. See p. 345.

2. AUTOCRACY OF LEADERSHIP

Tuckman, Bruce W., "Personality Structure, Group Composition, and Group Functioning," *Sociometry*, 27 (December, 1964), pp. 469–487. See p. 480.

3. CHAIRMAN, ACTIVITIES TO KEEP HIMSELF INFORMED

Meltzer, Leo, "Comparing Relationships of Individual and Average Variables to Individual Response," *American Sociological Review*, 28 (February, 1963), pp. 117–123. See p. 118.

4. CHAIRMAN, ACTIVITIES TO MAINTAIN GROUP

Meltzer; see category 3 above.

5. CHAIRMAN, DIRECTIVE-PARTICIPATIVE ACTIVITY

Meltzer; see category 3 above.

6. CHAIRMAN, EVALUATION OF

Meltzer; see category 3 above.

7. CHAIRMAN'S EXPECTATIONS CONCERNING MEMBER ACTIVITY

Meltzer; see category 3 above.

8. COMPETENCE OF LEADER

Leik, Robert K., " 'Irrelevant' Aspects of Stooge Behavior: Implications for Leadership Studies and Experimental Methodology," *Sociometry*, 28 (September, 1965), pp. 259–271. See pp. 265–266 and 268–271.

9. CONSISTENCY IN DISCIPLINE

Davis (1954); see category 1 above.
Davis and Hagedorn (1954); see category 1 above.

10. EXTENT OF GROUP LEADERSHIP

Tuckman; see category 2 above.

11. EXTERNAL CONTROLS, APPLICATION OF

Rosengren, William R., "Symptom Manifestation as a Function of Situational Press: A Demonstration in Socialization," *Sociometry*, 22 (June, 1959), pp. 113–123. See pp. 114–115 and 117.

12. FRIENDSHIP ROLE OF LEADER

Hutchins, Edwin B., and Fred E. Fiedler, "Task-Oriented and Quasi-Therapeutic Role Functions of the Leader in Small Military Groups," *Sociometry*, 23 (December, 1960), pp. 393–406. See p. 396.

13. GROUP REFERENT

Goodchilds, Jacqueline D., "Effects of Being Witty on Position in the Social Structure of a Small Group," *Sociometry*, 22 (September, 1959), pp. 261–272. See p. 265.

14. HUMAN-RELATIONS MINDEDNESS OF LEADERS

Medalia, Nahum Z., "Unit Size and Leadership Perception," *Sociometry*, 17 (February, 1954), pp. 64–67. See p. 65.
Medalia, Nahum Z., and Delbert C. Miller, "Human Relations Leadership and the Association of Morale and Efficiency in Work Groups: A Controlled Study with Small Military Units," *Social Forces*, 33 (May, 1955), pp. 348–352. See p. 349.

15. INDIVIDUAL ASSERTIVENESS

Bales, Robert F., *Interaction Process Analysis: A Method for the*

Study of Small Groups, Cambridge, Mass.: Addison-Wesley Press, 1950.

Borgatta, Edgar F., Robert F. Bales, and Arthur S. Couch, "Some Findings Relevant to the Great Man Theory of Leadership," *American Sociological Review*, 19 (December, 1954), pp. 755–759. See p. 756.

16. INFLUENCE ATTEMPTS

Bales, Robert F. (1950), see category 15 above.

March, James G., "Influence Measurement in Experimental and Semi-Experimental Groups," *Sociometry*, 19 (December, 1956), pp. 260–271. See p. 263.

Ziller, Robert C., and Ralph V. Exline, "Some Consequences of Age Heterogeneity on Decision-Making Groups," *Sociometry*, 21 (September, 1958), pp. 198–211. See pp. 200–202.

17. INFLUENCE OF GROUP MEMBER (MARAK)

Marak, George E., Jr., "The Evolution of Leadership Structure," *Sociometry*, 27 (June, 1964), pp. 174–182. See p. 177.

18. INFLUENCE OF GROUP MEMBER (ZILLER, EXLINE)

Ziller and Exline (1958); see category 16 above.

19. INFLUENCE OVER PROBLEM SOLUTION

Schutz, W. C., *FIRO: A Three-Dimensional Theory of Interpersonal Behavior*, New York: Holt, Rinehart and Sons, 1958.

Hoffman, L. Richard, and Clagett G. Smith, "Some Factors Affecting the Behaviors of Members of Problem-Solving Groups," *Sociometry*, 23 (September, 1960), pp. 273–291. See p. 275.

20. INFORMAL ROLE OF LEADER

Hutchins and Fiedler, pp. 396–397; see category 12 above.

21. INTEREST IN THE MEN

Davis (1954); see category 1 above.

Davis and Hagedorn (1954); see category 1 above.

22. LEADER-BEHAVIOR CHECK LIST

Borg, Walter R., "The Behavior of Emergent and Designated Leaders in Situational Tests," *Sociometry*, 20 (June, 1957), pp. 95–104. See pp. 96–97.

23. LEADER DOMINATION

Bales (1950); see category 15 above.

Borgatta, Edgar F., and Leonard S. Cottrell, Jr., "On the Classification of Groups," *Sociometry*, 18 (December, 1955), pp. 665–678. See p. 666.

24. LEADER'S INTIMACY

Hall, Robert L., "Social Influence on the Aircraft Commander's Role," *American Sociological Review*, 20 (June, 1955), pp. 292–299. See p. 294.

25. LEADER'S INTIMACY, ATTITUDE TOWARD

Hall; see category 24 above.

26. LEADER'S MILITARINESS

Hall; see category 24 above.

27. LEADER'S MILITARINESS, ATTITUDE TOWARD

Hall; see category 24 above.

28. LEADER'S NURTURANCE

Hall; see category 24 above.

29. LEADER'S NURTURANCE, ATTITUDE TOWARD

Hall; see category 24 above.

30. LEADERS, CHARACTERISTICS OF

Bales (1950); see category 15 above.

Landsberger, Henry A., "Interaction Process Analysis of Professional Behavior: A Study of Labor Mediators in Twelve Labor-Management Disputes," *American Sociological Review*, 20 (October, 1955), pp. 566–575. See p. 568.

31. LEADERSHIP ABILITY, PEER RATINGS OF

Cox, John A., and John D. Krumboltz, "Racial Bias in Peer Ratings of Basic Airmen," *Sociometry*, 21 (December, 1958), pp. 292–299. See p. 293.

32. LEADERSHIP ATTEMPTS

Bales (1950); see category 15 above.

Marak (1964), p. 176; see category 17 above.

33. LEADERSHIP, COMPOSITE INDEX OF

Borgatta, Bales, and Couch (1954), p. 757; see category 15 above.

34. RELATIVE SUCCESS OF LEADERSHIP

Bass, Bernard M., "Measures of Average Influence and Change in Agreement of Rankings by a Group of Judges," *Sociometry*, 23 (June, 1960), pp. 195–202. See p. 196.

35. SUPERVISING ROLE ACTIVITIES

Schutz (1958); see category 19 above.

Hoffman and Smith (1960); see category 19 above.

36. TASK ABILITY

Borgatta, Bales, and Couch (1954), p. 756; see category 15 above.

37. TECHNICAL COMPETENCE

Evan, William M., and Morris Zelditch, Jr., "A Laboratory Experiment on Bureaucratic Authority," *American Sociological Review*, 26 (December, 1961), pp. 883–893. See p. 887.

38. THERAPEUTIC ROLE OF LEADER

Hutchins and Fiedler; see category 12 above.

39. WAY OF GIVING ORDERS

Davis (1954); see category 1 above.

Davis and Hagedorn (1954); see category 1 above.

LEADERSHIP, SMALL GROUP: IDENTIFICATION OF

SEE ALSO

Authority: Attitudes toward and Characteristics of

1. ATTRIBUTED INFLUENCE

March, James G., "Influence Measurement in Experimental and Semi-Experimental Groups," *Sociometry*, 19 (December, 1956), pp. 260–271. See p. 262.

2. CONTROL, AMOUNT OF

Bales, Robert F., *Interaction Process Analysis: A Method for the Study of Small Groups*, Cambridge, Mass.: Addison-Wesley Press, 1950.

Marak, George E., Jr., "The Evolution of Leadership Structure," *Sociometry*, 27 (June, 1964), pp. 174–182. See p. 177.

3. DEGREE OF INFLUENCE

March; see category 1 above.

4. EFFECTIVE CONSULTANTS

Couch, Carl J., and John S. Murray, "Significant Others and Evaluation," *Sociometry*, 27 (December, 1964), pp. 502–509. See p. 505.

5. EFFECTIVE TEACHERS

Couch and Murray; see category 4 above.

6. EFFECTIVE WRITERS

Couch and Murray; see category 4 above.

7. INSTRUMENTAL LEADERS

Turk, Herman, "Instrumental Values and the Popularity of Instrumental Leaders," *Social Forces*, 39 (March, 1961), pp. 252–260. See p. 255.

8. LEADER CONSENSUS

Bales (1950); see category 2 above.

Borgatta, Edgar F., and Leonard S. Cottrell, Jr., "On the Classification of Groups," *Sociometry*, 18 (December, 1955), pp. 665–678. See p. 673.

9. LEADERSHIP RATING

Borgatta, Edgar F., "Analysis of Social Interaction and Sociometric Perception," *Sociometry*, 17 (February, 1954), pp. 7–32. See pp. 15–16.

10. LEADERSHIP SELF-RATING

Borgatta; see category 9 above.

11. LEADERSHIP, SOCIOMETRIC INDEX OF (MARAK)

Marak (1964); see category 2 above.

12. LEADERSHIP, SOCIOMETRIC INDEX OF (MURPHY)

Murphy, Albert J., "A Study of the Leadership Process," *American Sociological Review*, 6 (October, 1941), pp. 674–687. See p. 678.

Theodorson, George A., "The Relationship between Leadership and Popularity Roles in Small Groups," *American Sociological Review*, 22 (February, 1957), pp. 58–67. See p. 61.

13. LEADERSHIP STRUCTURE

Bales (1950); see category 2 above.

Borgatta and Cottrell (1955); see category 8 above.

14. PREFERENCE FOR LEADER

Bjerstedt, Åke, "Sociometric Relations in Elementary School Classes," *Sociometry*, 18 (May, 1955), pp. 147–152. See p. 149.

15. SOCIAL ACCEPTABILITY OF LEADERSHIP

Borgatta, Edgar F., Robert F. Bales, and Arthur S. Couch, "Some Findings Relevant to the Great Man Theory of Leadership," *American Sociological Review*, 19 (December, 1954), pp. 755–759. See p. 757.

16. SOCIO-EMOTIONAL LEADERSHIP

Marcus, Philip M., "Expressive and Instrumental Groups: Toward a Theory of Group Structure," *American Journal of Sociology*, 66 (July, 1960), pp. 54–59. See pp. 58–59.

17. SOURCE OF IDEAS

Couch and Murray; see category 4 above.

18. TASK LEADERSHIP

Marcus, pp. 57–58; see category 16 above.

MARITAL ADJUSTMENT AND COURTSHIP

SEE ALSO

Personality Traits: Motives and Needs

Personality Traits: Various Categories

1. ACCEPTANCE OF SPOUSE'S CONTRIBUTIONS

Levinger, George, "Task and Social Behavior in Marriage," *Sociometry*, 27 (December, 1964), pp. 433–448. See p. 436.

2. ATTITUDE TOWARD MARRIAGE

Hill, Richard J., *Attitude toward Marriage*, unpublished M.A. thesis, Stanford University, 1951.

Wallin, Paul, "Marital Happiness of Parents and Their Children's Attitude to Marriage," *American Sociological Review*, 19 (February, 1954), pp. 20–23. See p. 21.

3. ATTITUDE TOWARD LIMITING NUMBER OF CHILDREN

McGinnis, Robert, "Similarity in Background Characteristics and Differential Fertility," *Social Forces*, 34 (October, 1955), pp. 67–72. See p. 69.

4. BIRTH-CONROL ATTITUDE

Liu, William T., "The Marginal Catholics in the South: A Revision of Concepts," *American Journal of Sociology*, 65 (January, 1960), pp. 383–390. See p. 386.

Liu, William T., "The Community Reference System, Religiosity, and Race Attitudes," *Social Forces*, 39 (May, 1961), pp. 324–328. See p. 326.

5. COMPLEMENTARY NEEDS

Winch, Robert F., Thomas Ktsanes, and Virginia Ktsanes, "The Theory of Complementary Needs in Mate-Selection: An Analytic and Descriptive Study," *American Sociological Review*, 19 (June, 1954), pp. 241–249.

Winch, Robert F., "The Theory of Complementary Needs in

Mate-Selection: A Test of One Kind of Complementariness," *American Sociological Review*, 20 (February, 1955), pp. 52–55. See p. 53.

6. COUPLE'S ACTIVITY LEVEL

Levinger; see category 1 above.

7. HOMOGAMY-HETEROGAMY

Kerckhoff, Alan C., "Patterns of Homogamy and the Field of Eligibles," *Social Forces*, 42 (March, 1964), pp. 289–297. See pp. 292–293.

8. INTERPERSONAL CREATIVITY

Stanton, Howard, and Eugene Litwak, "Toward the Development of a Short Form Test of Interpersonal Competence," *American Sociological Review*, 20 (December, 1955), pp. 668–674. See p. 672.

Litwak, Eugene, Gloria Count, and Edward M. Haydon, "Group Structure and Interpersonal Creativity as Factors which Reduce Errors in Prediction of Marital Adjustment," *Social Forces*, 38 (May, 1960), pp. 308–315. See p. 310.

9. INTIMACY-PERMISSIVENESS

Christensen, Harold T., and George R. Carpenter, "Value-Behavior Discrepancies Regarding Pre-Marital Coitus in Three Western Cultures," *American Sociological Review*, 27 (February, 1962), pp. 66–74. See p. 67–68.

10. MARITAL ADJUSTMENT (BURGESS, COTTRELL, LOCKE, AND MODIFICATIONS)

Hamilton, G. V., *A Research in Marriage*, New York: Albert and Bone, 1929, pp. 60–76 and 80.

Terman, Lewis M., *Psychological Factors in Marital Happiness*, New York: McGraw-Hill, 1938, pp. 48–83. See pp. 49–59.

Burgess, Ernest W. and Leonard Cottrell, *Predicting Success or Failure in Marriage*, New York: Prentice-Hall, 1939, pp. 58–74.

Substantial effort has been devoted to the problem of defining and measuring the interrelated phenomena of marital adjustment, marital success, marital happiness, marital integration, and marital satisfaction. Marital success frequently is taken to be the most comprehensive term while adjustment, happiness, integration, and satisfaction are numbered among the criteria of success; however, the most influential writers on this subject have tended to use success and adjustment interchangeably. Burgess and Wallin (1953) state, for example, that "Burgess and Cottrell called their composite criterion [of marital success] an index of marriage adjustment." According to Burgess and Cottrell, there are five principal indicators or components of marital adjustment: (1) agreement between husband and wife on critical issues, (2) presence of common interests and joint activities, (3) frequent overt demonstrations of affection, (4) low frequency of complaints about marriage, and (5) low frequency of reported unhappiness and loneliness. Each of these five indicators are reflected in the 26-item Index of Marital Adjustment constructed by Burgess and Cottrell. This index, which exhibits the influence of Hamilton (1929) and Terman (1934), has, in turn, influenced all later measures of marital adjustment listed below. Of particular interest in this connection are the 29-item adjustment test presented by Locke (1951) and the 15-item short form prepared by Locke and Wallace (1959). Both the original Burgess-Cottrell index and the Locke-Wallace short form are presented below in this category. The Burgess-Wallin measure of marital satisfaction is presented below in category 17.

Burgess and Cottrell constructed numerical scores for their Index of Marital Adjustment by (1) measuring the association between married couples' ratings of their marriages (on a scale ranging from "very unhappy" to "very happy") with the couples' responses to each item in the Index of Marital Adjustment and (2) assigning to the items weights reflecting the sizes of the coefficients of association. This method, according to the authors, "was somewhat arbitrary and not precise, but the values were crudely proportional to what appeared to be the relation existing between the answers and the happiness ratings." An individual's marital-adjustment score is calculated by summing the appropriate numerical weights as shown in the items presented in the index below.

The instructions shown below are those given by Burgess and Locke (1945).

INDEX OF MARITAL ADJUSTMENT

This form may be filled out by either the husband or wife. Frank and sincere replies are of the highest importance if the findings are to be of value to the person filling it out or for research purposes. The following points are to be kept in mind in filling out the schedule:

(1) Be sure to answer all questions.
(2) Do not leave any blanks as is sometimes done to signify a "no" reply.
(3) The word spouse is used to refer to your husband or wife.
(4) Do not confer with your spouse in answering these questions or show your answers to your spouse.

Indicate your approximate extent of agreement or disagreement with your spouse on the following things. Do this for *each item* by putting a check in the column [or space] which shows the extent of your agreement or disagreement. Check one column for each item [in the table] below.

	Always Agree	Almost Always Agree	Occa- sionally Dis- agree	Fre- quently Dis- agree	Almost Always Dis- agree	Always Dis- agree
1. Handling family finances	10	8	6	4	2	0
2. Matters of recreation	10	8	6	4	2	0
3. Religious matters	5	4	3	2	1	0
4. Demonstration of affection	10	8	6	4	2	0
5. Friends	10	8	6	4	2	0
6. Intimate relations	10	8	6	4	2	0
7. Table manners	5	4	3	2	1	0
8. Matters of conven- tionality	10	8	6	4	2	0
9. Philosophy of life	10	8	6	4	2	0
10. Ways of dealing with in-laws	10	8	6	4	2	0

11. When disagreements arise, they usually result in: husband giving in __(1); wife giving in __(1); agreement by mutual give and take __(10).
12. Do husband and wife engage in outside interests together? all of

them __(10); some of them __(10); very few of them __(1); none of them __(0).

13. In leisure time husband prefers: to be "on the go" __; to stay at home __; wife prefers: to be "on the go" __; to stay at home __ (If both husband and wife had checked "stay at home," 10 points were given; if both checked "on the go," 3 points. If they checked differently, 4 points.)

14. Do you kiss your husband (wife) every day? __(10); occasionally? __(1); almost never? __(0).

15. Do you confide in your husband (wife)? almost never __(0); rarely __(0); in most things __(10); in everything __(10).

16. Do you ever wish you had not married? frequently __(0); occasionally __(2); rarely __(4); never __(15).

17. If you had your life to live over, do you think you would: marry the same person? __(15); marry a different person? __(1); not marry at all? __(0).

18. What things annoy and dissatisfy you most about your marriage? nothing listed __(10); one listed __(7); two listed __(1); three or more listed __(0).

19. What things does you husband (wife) do that you don't like? nothing listed __(7); one listed __(5); two listed __(1); three or more listed __(0).

20. Do you often feel lonesome, even when you are with other people? yes __(0); no__(1) ?__(0).

21. Are you usually even-tempered and happy in your outlook on life? yes __(1); no __(0); ? __(0).

22. Do you often feel just miserable? yes __(0); no __(1); ? __(0).

23. Does some particular useless thought keep coming into your mind to bother you? yes __(0); no __(1); ? __(0).

24. Are you usually in good spirits? yes __(1); no __(0); ? __(0).

25. Do you often experience periods of loneliness? yes __(0); no __(1); ? __(0).

26. Are you in general self-confident about your abilities? yes __(1); no __(0); ? __(0).

In an effort to reduce the length of marital-adjustment measures without an appreciable loss in reliability and validity, Locke and Wallace constructed the short-form test shown below. The authors report a corrected split-half reliability of .90 for the short form and conclude that "a relatively small number of basic and fundamental items achieve results approximately comparable with the longer and more complex adjustment and prediction tests." As in the case of the Burgess-Cottrell measure presented above, an individual's adjustment score is calculated by adding the various weights which are indicated on the items below.

Locke, Harvey J., and Karl M. Wallace, "Short Marital-Adjustment and Prediction Tests: Their Reliability and Validity," *Marriage and Family Living*, 21 (August, 1959), pp. 251–255. See p. 252.

MARITAL-ADJUSTMENT TEST

1. Check the dot on the scale line below which best describes the degree of happiness, everything considered, of your present marriage. The middle point, "happy," represents the degree of happiness which most people get from marriage, and the scale gradually ranges on one side to those few who are very unhappy in marriage, and on the other, to those few who experience extreme joy or felicity in marriage.

0	2	7	15	20	25	35
·	·	·	·	·	·	·

Very Unhappy	Happy	Perfectly Happy

State the approximate extent of agreement or disagreement between you and your mate on the following items. Please check each column or space.

	Always Agree	Almost Always Agree	Occasionally Disagree	Frequently Disagree	Almost Always Disagree	Always Disagree
2. Handling family finances	5	4	3	2	1	0
3. Matters of recreation	5	4	3	2	1	0
4. Demonstrations of affection	8	6	4	2	1	0
5. Friends	5	4	3	2	1	0
6. Sex relations	15	12	9	4	1	0
7. Conventionality (right, good, or proper conduct)	5	4	3	2	1	0
8. Philosophy of life	5	4	3	2	1	0
9. Ways of dealing with in-laws	5	4	3	2	1	0

10. When disagreements arise, they usually result in: husband giving in ___(0); wife giving in ___(2); agreement by mutual give and take ___(10).
11. Do you and your mate engage in outside interests together? all of them ___(10); some of them ___(8); very few of them ___(3); none of them ___(0).
12. In leisure time do you generally prefer: to be "on the go" ___; to stay at home ___? Does your mate generally prefer: to be "on the go" ___; to stay at home ___? (Stay at home for both, 10 points; "on the go" for both, 3 points; disagreement, 2 points.)
13 Do you ever wish you had not married? frequently ___(0); occasionally ___(3); rarely ___(8); never ___(15).
14. If you had your life to live over, do you think you would: marry the same person ___(15); marry a different person ___(0); not marry at all ___(1)?
15. Do you confide in your mate: almost never ___(0); rarely ___(2); in most things ___(10); in everything ___(10).

Burgess, Ernest W., and Harvey J. Locke, *The Family: From Institution to Companionship*, New York: American Book Company, 1945, pp. 771–780.

Wallace, K. M., *Construction and Validation of Marital Adjustment and Prediction Scales*, unpublished Ph.D. dissertation, University of Southern California, 1947.

Locke, Harvey J., and Robert C. Williamson, *Predicting Adjustment in Marriage: A Comparison of a Divorced and a Happily Married Group*, New York: Henry Holt and Company, 1951, pp. 45–52.

Burgess, Ernest W., and Paul Wallin, *Engagement and Marriage*, New York: J. B. Lippincott Co., 1953.

Burgess, Ernest W. and Harvey J. Locke, *The Family*, New York: American Book Company, 1953, pp. 693–716.

Locke, Harvey J., and Georg Karlsson, "Marital Adjustment and Prediction in Sweden and the United States," *American Sociological Review*, 17 (February, 1952), pp. 10–17. See pp. 11–12.

Williamson, Robert C., "Socio-Economic Factors and Marital Adjustment in an Urban Setting," *American Sociological Review*, 19 (April, 1954), pp. 213–216. See p. 213.

Locke, Harvey J., and Vernon A. Snowbarger, "Marital Adjustment and Predictors in Sweden," *American Journal of Sociology*, 60 (July, 1954), pp. 51–53. See p. 51.

Reeder, Leo G., "Social Factors in Heart Disease: A Preliminary Research Report on the Relationship of Certain Social Factors to Blood Pressure in Males," *Social Forces*, 34 (May, 1956), pp. 367–371. See p. 368.

Locke, Harvey J., and Robert C. Williamson, "Marital Adjustment: A Factor Analysis Study," *American Sociological Review*, 23 (October, 1958), pp. 562–569. See p. 563.

Nimkoff, Meyer F., and C. M. Grigg, "Values and Marital Adjustment of Nurses," *Social Forces*, 37 (October, 1958), pp. 67–70. See p. 68.

Hurvitz, Nathan, "The Measurement of Marital Strain," *American Journal of Sociology*, 65 (May, 1960), pp. 610–615. See p. 613.

Luckey, Eleanore Braun, "Marital Satisfaction and Congruent Self-Spouse Concepts," *Social Forces*, 39 (October, 1960), pp. 153–157. See p. 154.

Litwak, Count, and Haydon (1960); see category 8 above.

11. MARITAL ADJUSTMENT (NYE)

Nye, F. Ivan, and Evelyn MacDougall, "The Dependent Variable in Marital Research," *Pacific Sociological Review*, 2 (Fall, 1959), pp. 67–70.

Nye, F. Ivan, "Employment Status of Mothers and Marital Conflict, Permanence, and Happiness," *Social Problems*, 6 (Winter, 1959), pp. 260–267.

Nye, F. Ivan, "Maternal Employment and Marital Interaction: Some Contingent Conditions," *Social Forces*, 40 (December, 1961), pp. 113–119. See p. 113.

12. MARITAL BREAKUP

Litwak, Eugene, "Group Pressure and Family Breakup: A Study of German Communities," *American Journal of Sociology*, 61 (January, 1956), pp. 345–354. See p. 346.

13. MARITAL HAPPINESS (FARBER)

See also category 15 below.

Farber, Bernard, "An Index of Marital Integration," *Sociometry*, 20 (June, 1957), pp. 117–134. See p. 130.

14. MARITAL HAPPINESS (TERMAN)

Terman, Lewis M. (1938), pp. 48–83; see category 10 above.

Luckey (1960); see category 10 above.

15. MARITAL INTEGRATION (FARBER)

Reeder (1956); see category 10 above.

Farber (1957); see category 13 above.

16. MARITAL PREDICTION

Locke and Snowbarger (1954); see category 10 above.

17. MARITAL SATISFACTION (BURGESS, WALLIN)

Burgess and Wallin (1953), pp. 488–489; see category 10 above.

A discussion of the relationship of the concept of marital satisfaction to closely related concepts such as marital success and marital adjustment has been presented in category 10 above. As used by Burgess and Wallin, general or over-all satisfaction is a criterion of marital success and is "a composite feeling of contentment with the relationship as a whole." These authors also have developed and presented a measure of specific satisfaction and dissatisfactions with the marriage relation.

Below are the instructions and items for the Burgess and Wallin measure of an individual's general marital satisfaction and the individual's conception of his spouse's general satisfaction. Various weights accompany each item and are shown in parentheses. An individual's total score is the algebraic sum of the appropriate item weights.

GENERAL MARITAL SATISFACTION

Place a check (√) *before* any of the following statements which represent your feelings about your marriage or your mate. *Check as many or as few* as describe your feelings.

1. ___My marriage is successful but not extraordinarily so. (1)
2. ___My mate and I are well mated. (2)
3. ___If it weren't for fear of hurting my mate, I would leave him (her). (−1)

4. __Frankly, our marriage has not been successful. (−1)
5. __My marriage has given me a new enthusiasm for life. (5)
6. __Although my marriage has its good points, they are outweighed by its bad ones. (−1)
7. __My marriage could be worse and it could be better. (−1)
8. __On the basis of my marriage at least, I think a person is a fool to marry. (−1)
9. __My marriage is less successful than the average. (−1)
10. __My marriage is perhaps a little less successful than most marriages. (−1)
11. __I wouldn't call my marriage a perfect success, but I'm pretty well content with it. (1)
12. __I feel that as times go on my marriage will mean less and less to me. (−1)
13. __Although my marriage has been only moderately successful, its good elements more than compensate for the bad. (1)
14. __My marriage is not a great success but it could be much worse. (−1)
15. __My marriage could not be more successful. (5)
16. __My marriage has been a great disappointment to me. (−1)
17. __I've gotten more out of marriage than I expected. (1)
18. __My friends mean more to me than my mate. (−1)
19. __Marrying my mate was the biggest mistake I ever made. (−1)
20. __My marriage is as successful as any I know. (4)
21. If you had your life to live over, do you think you would (check): marry the same person (4) certainly __; (3) probably __; (2) possibly __; (1) marry a different person __; (0) not marry at all __.
22. If *your mate* had life to live over do you think mate would (check): marry you (4) certainly __; (3) probably __; (2) possibly__; (1) marry a different person __; (0) not marry at all __.
23. How satisfied, on the whole, are you with your marriage? (check): (9) entirely satisfied __; (7) very much satisfied __; (6) satisfied __; (5) somewhat satisfied __; (3) somewhat dissatisfied __; (2) dissatisfied __; (1) very much dissatisfied __; (0) entirely dissatisfied __.
24. How satisfied, on the whole, is your mate with your marriage? (check): (9) entirely satisfied __; (7) very much satisfied __; (6) satisfied __; (5) somewhat satisfied __; (3) somewhat dissatisfied __; (0) entirely dissatisfied __.
25. Do you ever regret your marriage? (check): (0) frequently __; (1) occasionally__; (2) rarely__; (5) never__.
26. Do you think your mate ever regrets having married you? (check): (0) frequently __; (1) occasionally __; (2) rarely __; (5) never __.

Wallin, Paul, "Religiosity, Sexual Gratification, and Marital Satisfaction," *American Sociological Review*, 22 (June, 1957), pp. 300–305. See pp. 302–303.

Burchinal, Lee G., "Marital Satisfaction and Religious Behavior," *American Sociological Review*, 22 (June, 1957), pp. 306–310. See p. 306.

Burchinal, Lee G., Glenn R. Hawkes, and Bruce Gardner, "Personality Characteristics and Marital Satisfaction," *Social Forces*, 35 (March, 1957), pp. 218–227. See p. 219.

Wallin, Paul, and Alexander L. Clark, "Religiosity, Sexual Gratification and Marital Satisfaction in the Middle Years of Marriage," *Social Forces*, 42 (March, 1964), pp. 303–309. See p. 306.

Clark, Alexander L., and Paul Wallin, "Women's Sexual Responsiveness and the Duration and Quality of Their Marriages," *American Journal of Sociology*, 71 (September, 1965), pp. 187–196. See p. 192.

18. MARITAL SATISFACTION

Includes: achievement of marital goals, affection, communication frequency, couple's decision-making balance, couple's division of labor, estimate of spouse's happiness, general sexual relationship, global happiness, husband's desired frequency of sexual relations, husband's social-emotional role, husband's work, use of leisure, wife's desired frequency of sexual relations, wife's social-emotional role, and wife's work

Levinger, p. 445; see category 1 above.

19. MARITAL STRAIN

Hurvitz; see category 10 above.

20. MARITAL UNHAPPINESS

Farber; see category 13 above.

21. PERSONAL CHARACTERISTICS, CHANGE IN CONSENSUS ON, BETWEEN SEXES

Hill, Reuben, "Campus Values in Mate Selection," *Journal of Home Economics*, 37 (November, 1945), pp. 554–558. See p. 554.

Christensen, Harold T., *Marriage Analysis*, New York: Ronald Press, 1950, pp. 255–258.

McGinnis, Robert, "Campus Values in Mate Selection: A Repeat Study," *Social Forces*, 36 (May, 1958), pp. 368–373. See p. 369–370.

22. PERSONAL CHARACTERISTICS DESIRED IN A MARRIAGE PARTNER

Hill (1945); see category 21 above.

Christensen (1950); see category 21 above.

McGinnis (1958); see category 21 above.

23. PREMARITAL SEXUAL PERMISSIVENESS

Reiss, Ira L., "Sociological Studies of Sexual Standards," in George Winokur (ed.), *Determinants of Human Sexual Behavior*, Springfield, Ill.: Charles C Thomas, 1963, pp. 101–141. See pp. 114–122.

Reiss, Ira L., "The Scaling of Premarital Sexual Permissiveness," *Journal of Marriage and the Family*, 26 (May, 1964), pp. 188–198.

Reiss, Ira L., "Premarital Sexual Permissiveness Among Negroes and Whites," *American Sociological Review*, 29 (October, 1964), pp. 688–689. See p. 689.

24. PREMARITAL SEXUAL PERMISSIVENESS, FEMALE

Reiss (May, 1964); see category 23 above.

Reiss (October, 1964); see category 23 above.

Reiss, Ira L., "Social Class and Premarital Sexual Permissiveness: A Re-Examination," *American Sociological Review*, 30 (October, 1965), pp. 747–756. See p. 748.

25. PREMARITAL SEXUAL PERMISSIVENESS, MALE

Reiss (May, 1964); see category 23 above.

Reiss (October, 1964); see category 23 above.

Reiss (1965); see category 24 above.

26. ROMANTICISM (DEAN)

Dean, Dwight G., "Romanticism and Emotional Maturity: A Preliminary Study," *Marriage and Family Living*, 23 (February, 1961), pp. 44–45.

Dean, Dwight G., "Romanticism and Emotional Maturity: A Further Exploration," *Social Forces*, 42 (March, 1964), pp. 298–303. See p. 298.

27. ROMANTICISM (GROSS)

Gross, Llewellyn, "A Belief Pattern Scale for Measuring Attitudes toward Romanticism," *American Sociological Review*, 9 (October, 1944), pp. 463–472. See p. 472.

Hobart, Charles W., "The Incidence of Romanticism during Courtship," *Social Forces*, 36 (May, 1958), pp. 363–367. See p. 363.

28. ROMANTICISM (THEODORSON)

Theodorson, George A., "Romanticism and Motivation to Marry in the United States, Singapore, Burma, and India," *Social Forces*, 44 (September, 1965), pp. 17–27. See pp. 20–22.

MARITAL AND FAMILY ROLES

1. DEVIATION OF MARITAL ROLE EXPECTATION

Hurvitz, Nathan, "The Measurement of Marital Strain," *American Journal of Sociology*, 65 (May, 1960), pp. 610–615. See p. 612.

2. DEVIATION OF PERFORMANCE OF MARITAL ROLES

Hurvitz; see category 1 above.

3. MARITAL ROLES INVENTORY

Hurvitz, p. 611; see category 1 above.

4. MARITAL ROLE TENSION

Farber, Bernard, and L. S. Blackman, "Marital Role Tensions and Number and Sex of Children," *American Sociological Review*, 21 (October, 1956), pp. 596–601. See p. 598.

5. MATERNAL ROLE EFFECTIVENESS

Swinehart, James W., "Socio-economic Level, Status Aspiration, and Maternal Role," *American Sociological Review*, 28 (June, 1963), pp. 391–399. See p. 395.

6. PARENTAL ROLE IN FAMILY

McCord, William, Joan McCord, and Alan Howard, "Early Familial Experiences and Bigotry," *American Sociological Review*, 25 (October, 1960), pp. 717–722. See p. 720.

7. ROLE CONCEPT: AGGRESSION TOWARD MOTHER IN CHILD REARING

Leslie, Gerald R., and Kathryn P. Johnsen, "Changed Perceptions of the Maternal Role," *American Sociological Review*, 28 (December, 1963), pp. 919–928. See p. 923.

8. ROLE CONCEPT: ENCOURAGEMENT OF SELF-DIRECTION IN CHILDREN

Leslie and Johnsen; see category 7 above.

9. ROLE CONCEPT: SEX AND MODESTY TRAINING OF CHILDREN

Leslie and Johnsen; see category 7 above.

10. ROLE CONCEPTION ADJECTIVE CHECK LIST

Sarbin, T. R., *Personality Word Card*, Berkeley, Calif.: University of California Press, no date.

McKee, John P., and Alex C. Sherriffs, "Men's and Women's Beliefs, Ideals, and Self-concepts," *American Journal of Sociology*, 64 (January, 1959), pp. 356–363. See p. 357.

11. ROLE CONCEPTION INVENTORY

Motz, Anabelle B., "A Role Conception Inventory: A Tool for Research," *American Sociological Review*, 17 (August, 1952), pp. 465–471. See pp. 466–467.

Weil, Mildred W., "An Analysis of the Factors Influencing Married Women's Actual or Planned Work Participation," *American Sociological Review*, 26 (February, 1961), pp. 91–96. See p. 92.

12. ROLE CONCEPTIONS AMONG FAMILY MEMBERS, CONSISTENCY OF

See also Family: Perceptions of and Attitudes toward, category 22

Connor, Ruth, Helen Finch Greene, and James Walters, "Agreement of Family Member Conceptions of 'Good' Parent and Child Roles," *Social Forces*, 36 (May, 1958), pp. 353–358. See p. 354.

13. ROLE PERFORMANCE: AGGRESSION TOWARD MOTHER IN CHILD REARING

Leslie and Johnsen; see category 7 above.

14. ROLE PERFORMANCE: ENCOURAGEMENT OF SELF-DIRECTION IN CHILDREN

Leslie and Johnsen; see category 7 above.

15. ROLE PERFORMANCE: SEX AND MODESTY TRAINING IN CHILDREN

Leslie and Johnsen; see category 7 above.

16. ROLE-TAKING ACCURACY

Stryker, Sheldon, "Role-Taking Accuracy and Adjustment," *Sociometry*, 20 (December, 1957), pp. 286–296. See p. 288.

17. SEX ROLE CONSERVATISM

Sutcliffe, J. P., and M. Haberman, "Factors Influencing Choice in Role Conflict Situations," *American Sociological Review*, 21 (December, 1956), pp. 695–703. See p. 702.

MEDICINE AND HEALTH: ATTITUDES TOWARD

SEE ALSO

Health: Individual
Medicine and Health: Behavior in and Characteristics of Occupational Roles
Personal Adjustment

1. **APPRECIATION OF NURSING-HOME PROFESSION AND PATIENTS**

Scott, Frances G., "Factors in the Personal Adjustment of Institutionalized and Non-Institutionalized Aged," *American Sociological Review*, 20 (October, 1955), pp. 538–546. See p. 539.

2. **CLIENT ORIENTATION**

Turk, Herman, "Social Cohesion through Variant Values: Evidence from Medical Role Relations," *American Sociological Review*, 28 (February, 1963), pp. 28–37. See pp. 30–31.

3. **COMMITMENT TO STRATIFIED ORDER IN HOSPITALS**

Seeman, Melvin, and John W. Evans, "Stratification and Hospital Care: I. The Performance of the Medical Interne," *American Sociological Review*, 26 (February, 1961), pp. 67–80. See pp. 69–70.

4. **DEATH, ATTITUDES TOWARD**

Faunce, William A., and Robert L. Fulton, "The Sociology of Death: A Neglected Area of Research," *Social Forces*, 36 (March, 1958), pp. 205–209. See p. 207.

5. **ETIOLOGY OF MENTAL ILLNESS, ATTITUDE TOWARD**

Freeman, Howard E., "Attitudes toward Mental Illness among

Relatives of Former Mental Patients," *American Sociological Review*, 26 (February, 1961), pp. 59–66. See p. 61.

6. EXPECTATIONS OF ROLE IMPORTANCE

Turk, p. 33; see category 2 above.

7. EXPECTATIONS OF PROFESSIONAL ACTIVITY

Turk, pp. 32–33; see category 2 above.

8. EXPECTED AUTHORITY RELATIONS

Turk, p. 34; see category 2 above.

9. HOSPITAL BOARDS AND VOLUNTARY ASSOCIATIONS, PRESTIGE OF

Moore, Joan W., "Patterns of Women's Participation in Voluntary Organizations," *American Journal of Sociology*, 66 (May, 1961), pp. 592–598. See p. 592.

10. HOSPITAL STATUS EVALUATIONS

Dinitz, Simon, Mark Lefton, and Benjamin Pasamanick, "Status Perceptions in a Mental Hospital," *Social Forces*, 38 (December, 1959), pp. 124–128. See p. 125.

11. HOSTILITY TOWARD MEDICAL PROFESSION

Gamson, William A., and Howard Schuman, "Some Undercurrents in the Prestige of Physicians," *American Journal of Sociology*, 68 (January, 1963), pp. 463–470. See p. 465.

12. MEDICAL STUDENTS' CHOICES OF FACULTY MEMBERS

Back, Kurt W., Robert E. Coker, Thomas G. Donnelly, and Bernard S. Phillips, "Public Health as a Career of Medicine: Secondary Choice within a Profession," *American Sociological Review*, 23 (October, 1958), pp. 533–541. See p. 538.

13. MENTAL HOSPITALS, ATTITUDE TOWARD

Freeman; see category 5 above.

14. NORMALCY OF FORMER PATIENTS AFTER MENTAL ILLNESS, ATTITUDE TOWARD

Freeman; see category 5 above.

15. NURSING, INTEREST IN

Shuval, Judith T., "Perceived Role Components of Nursing in

Israel," *American Sociological Review*, 28 (February, 1963), pp. 37–46. See p. 40.

16. OBEISANCE TO AUTHORITY

Pearlin, Leonard, and Morris Rosenberg, "Nurse-Patient Social Distance and the Structural Context of a Mental Hospital," *American Sociological Review*, 27 (February, 1962), pp. 56–65. See p. 61.

17. ORIENTATION TOWARD PSYCHOTHERAPY

Grusky, Oscar, "Organizational Goals and the Behavior of Informal Leaders," *American Journal of Sociology*, 65 (July, 1959), pp. 59–67. See p. 64.

18. POSTGRADUATE EDUCATION IN NURSING, ATTITUDE TOWARD

Deutscher, Irwin, and Ann Montague, "Professional Education and Conflicting Value Systems: the Role of Religious Schools in the Educational Aspirations of Nursing Students," *Social Forces*, 35 (December, 1956), pp. 126–131. See p. 127.

19. PREFERENCE FOR FIFTEEN MEDICAL ACTIVITIES

Cohart, E. M., and W. R. Willard, "A Time Study Method for Public Health—the Yale Study," *Public Health Reports*, 70 (June, 1955), pp. 570–576. See pp. 571–573.

Cohart, E. M., and W. R. Willard, "Functional Distribution of Working Time in Five County Health Departments," *Public Health Reports*, 70 (June, 1955), pp. 713–719. See pp. 714–718.

Back, Coker, Donnelly, and Phillips (1958); see category 12 above.

20. PREGNANCY, ATTITUDES TOWARD

Rosengren, William A., "Social Sources of Pregnancy as Illness or Normality," *Social Forces*, 39 (March, 1961), pp. 260–267. See p. 262.

Rosengren, William R., "Some Social Psychological Aspects of Delivery Room Difficulties," *Journal of Nervous and Mental Disease*, 132 (June, 1961), pp. 515–521. See pp. 515–517.

Rosengren, William A., "Social Instability and Attitudes toward Pregnancy as a Social Role," *Social Problems*, 9 (Spring, 1962), pp. 371–378. See pp. 371–372.

Rosengren, William R., "Social Status, Attitudes toward Pregnancy and Child-Rearing Attitudes," *Social Forces*, 41 (December, 1962), pp. 127–134. See p. 130.

21. RESPONSIBILITY OF PATIENTS FOR THEIR CONDITION, ATTITUDE TOWARD

Freeman; see category 5 above.

22. SKEPTICISM OF MEDICAL CARE

Suchman, Edward A., *Socio-Cultural Variations in Illness and Medical Care*, New York: New York City Health Department, 1963.

Suchman, Edward A., "Sociomedical Variations among Ethnic Groups," *American Journal of Sociology*, 70 (November, 1964), pp. 319–331. See pp. 321–322.

23. SPIRITUAL-TEMPORAL ORIENTATIONS TOWARD DEATH

Faunce and Fulton, pp. 207–208; see category 4 above.

MEDICINE AND HEALTH, BEHAVIOR IN AND CHARACTERISTICS OF

SEE ALSO

Health: Individual
Medicine and Health: Attitudes toward
Occupational Roles
Personal Adjustment

1. ARATIONALITY IN HEALTH PRACTICES

Lewis, Lionel, *Arationality in Human Behavior: A Study of Health Practices*, unpublished Ph.D. dissertation, Yale University, 1961.

Lewis, Lionel, and Joseph Lopreato, "Arationality, Ignorance, and Perceived Danger in Medical Practices," *American Sociological Review*, 27 (August, 1962), pp. 508–514. See p. 509.

Lewis, Lionel, "Knowledge, Danger, Certainty, and the Theory of Magic," *American Journal of Sociology*, 69 (July, 1963), pp. 7–12. See p. 9.

2. COHESION BETWEEN DIFFERENT PROFESSIONALS

Turk, Herman, "Social Cohesion through Variant Values: Evidence from Medical Role Relations," *American Sociological Review*, 28 (February, 1963), pp. 28–37. See pp. 31–32.

3. DEPENDENCY IN ILLNESS

Suchman, Edward A., *Socio-Cultural Variations in Illness and Medical Care*, New York: New York City Health Department, 1963.

Suchman, Edward A., "Sociomedical Variations Among Ethnic Groups," *American Journal of Sociology*, 70 (November, 1964), pp. 319–331. See pp. 321–323.

4. DOMESTIC ACTIVITY OF MENTALLY ILL WIVES

Angrist, Shirley S., *Social Factors in the Outcome of Mental Hospitalization,* unpublished Ph.D. dissertation, Ohio State University, 1960.

Lefton, Mark, Shirley Angrist, Simon Dinitz, and Benjamin Pasamanick, "Social Class, Expectations, and Performance of Mental Patients," *American Journal of Sociology,* 68 (July, 1962), pp. 79–87. See p. 81.

5. HOSPITAL OCCUPATIONAL STRUCTURE

D'Antonio, William V., and Julian Samora, "Occupational Stratification in Four Southwestern Communities: A Study of Ethnic Differential Employment in Hospitals," *Social Forces,* 41 (October, 1962), pp. 17–25. See pp. 22–23.

6. HOSPITAL WARD STRATIFICATION

Seeman, Melvin, John W. Evans, and L. E. Rogers, "The Measurement of Stratification in Formal Organizations," *Human Organization,* 19 (Summer, 1960), pp. 90–96. See pp. 90–94.

Seeman, Melvin, and John W. Evans, "Stratification and Hospital Care: I. The Performance of the Medical Interne," *American Sociological Review,* 26 (February, 1961), pp. 67–80. See p. 69.

Seeman, Melvin, and John W. Evans, "Stratification and Hospital Care: II. The Objective Criteria of Performance," *American Sociological Review,* 26 (April, 1961), pp. 193–204. See p. 195.

7. LINKS WITH THE MEDICAL COMMUNITY

See also Innovation and Diffusion.

Coleman, James, Elihu Katz, and Herbert Menzel, "The Diffusion of Innovation among Physicians," *Sociometry,* 20 (December, 1957), pp. 253–270. See p. 254.

8. PATIENT DISTURBANCE IN A MENTAL HOSPITAL

Wallace, Anthony F. C., and Harold A. Rashkis, "The Relation of Staff Consensus to Patient Disturbance on Mental Hospital Wards," *American Sociological Review,* 24 (December, 1959), pp. 829–835. See p. 831.

9. PATIENT INFORMATION

Seeman, Melvin, and John W. Evans, "Alienation and Learning in a Hospital Setting," *American Sociological Review*, 27 (December, 1962), pp. 772–782. See p. 775.

10. PERFORMANCE OF MENTALLY ILL WIVES

Lefton, Angrist, Dinitz, and Pasamanick (1962); see category 4 above.

11. PERSONAL DISTANCE OF PATIENTS AND MEDICAL PERSONNEL

Pearlin, Leonard I., and Morris Rosenberg, "Nurse-Patient Social Distance and the Structural Context of a Mental Hospital," *American Sociological Review*, 27 (February, 1962), pp. 56–65. See p. 58.

Pearlin, Leonard I., "Sources of Resistance to Change in a Mental Hospital," *American Journal of Sociology*, 68 (November, 1962), pp. 325–334. See pp. 326–327.

12. POSTHOSPITAL PERFORMANCE OF MENTAL PATIENTS

Adler, Leta M., "Patients of a State Mental Hospital: The Outcome of Their Hospitalization," in Arnold Rose (ed.), *Mental Health and Mental Disorders*, New York: W. W. Norton and Co., 1955, pp. 501–523.

Freeman, Howard E., and Ozzie G. Simmons, "Mental Patients in the Community: Family Settings and Performance Levels," *American Sociological Review*, 23 (April, 1958), pp. 147–154. See p. 150.

Freeman, Howard E., and Ozzie G. Simmons, "Social Class and Posthospital Performance Levels," *American Sociological Review*, 24 (June, 1959), pp. 345–351. See p. 347.

13. PREVENTIVE MEDICAL BEHAVIOR

Suchman (1963); see category 3 above.
Suchman (1964); see category 3 above.

14. PSYCHOLOGICAL BEHAVIOR OF MENTALLY ILL WIVES

Lefton, Angrist, Dinitz, and Pasamanick (1962); see category 4 above.

15. PUNITIVENESS ON HOSPITAL WARDS

Banks, E. P., "Methodological Problems in the Study of Psychiatric Wards," *Social Forces*, 34 (March, 1956), pp. 277–280. See p. 280.

16. **QUALITY OF PATIENT CARE ON HOSPITAL WARDS**

Seeman and Evans (February, 1961), p. 70; see category 6 above.

17. **REPUTED KNOWLEDGE OF PATIENTS**

Evans, John W., *Stratification, Alienation and the Hospital: A Study in the Social Psychology of Chronic Illness*, Columbus, Ohio: Ohio State University Engineering Experiment Station Bulletin Number 184, November, 1960.

Seeman and Evans, pp. 775–776; see category 9 above.

18. **RESISTANCE TO CHANGE IN A MENTAL HOSPITAL**

Pearlin (November, 1962); see category 11 above.

19. **SENSITIVITY, AFFECTIVE**

Palmore, Erdman, Henry L. Lennard, and Helen Hendin, "Similarities of Therapist and Patient Verbal Behavior in Psychotherapy," *Sociometry*, 22 (March, 1959), pp. 12–23. See p. 19.

20. **SENSITIVITY, EVALUATIVE**

Palmore, Lennard, and Hendin; see category 19 above.

21. **SENSITIVITY, PATIENT**

Palmore, Lennard, and Hendin, p. 16; see category 19 above.

22. **SENSITIVITY, PRIMARY SYSTEM**

Palmore, Lennard, and Hendin, p. 18; see category 19 above.

23. **SENSITIVITY, THERAPIST**

Palmore, Lennard, and Hendin, p. 16; see category 19 above.

24. **SICK ROLE, ACCEPTANCE OF**

Suchman (1963); see category 3 above.
Suchman (1964); see category 3 above.

25. **SICK ROLE, EXPECTATIONS OF**

Rosengren, William R., "Social Sources of Pregnancy as Illness or Normality," *Social Forces*, 39 (March, 1961), pp. 260–267. See p. 262.

26. **SICK ROLE, INCLINATION TO ADOPT**

Phillips, Derek L., "Self-Reliance and the Inclination to Adopt the

Sick Role," *Social Forces*, 43 (May, 1965), pp. 555–563. See p. 558.

27. SICK ROLE, TENDENCY TO ADOPT

Mechanic, David, and Edmund H. Volkart, "Stress, Illness Behavior, and the Sick Role," *American Sociological Review*, 26 (February, 1961), pp. 51–58. See p. 55.

28. SIMULTANEOUS USE OF NEW DRUG BY DOCTORS

See also Innovation and Diffusion.
Coleman, Katz, and Menzel, p. 265; see category 7 above.

29. SOCIAL DISTANCE TOWARD MENTAL PATIENTS

See also 33 below.
See also Intergroup Relations, Nonracial and Nonethnic.
Phillips, Derek L., "Rejection: A Possible Consequence of Seeking Help for Mental Disorders," *American Sociological Review*, 28 (December, 1963), pp. 963–972. See p. 987.
Phillips, Derek L., "Rejection of the Mentally Ill: The Influence of Behavior and Sex," *American Sociological Review*, 29 (October, 1964), pp. 679–687. See p. 697.

30. SOCIAL PARTICIPATION OF MENTALLY ILL WIVES

Lefton, Angrist, Dinitz, and Pasamanick (1962); see category 4 above.

31. SOCIALIZATION ACTIVITY INDEX

Kandler, Harriet M., and Robert W. Hyde, "Socialization Activity Index for a Mental Hospital," *Nursing World*, 125 (1951), pp. 343–345.
Banks (1956), p. 279; see category 15 above.

32. STAFF CONSENSUS IN A MENTAL HOSPITAL

Wallace and Rashkis, p. 830; see category 8 above.

33. STATUS DISTANCE OF PATIENTS AND MEDICAL PERSONNEL

See also category 29 above.
Pearlin and Rosenberg (1962), p. 58; see category 11 above.
Pearlin (1962), p. 328; see category 11 above.

34. SUBJECTIVE KNOWLEDGE OF PATIENT SATISFACTION

Seeman and Evans, p. 776; see category 9 above.

MENTAL ABILITY

1. ABSTRACT REASONING

Kutner, Bernard, and Norman B. Gordon, "Cognitive Functioning and Prejudice: A Nine-Year Follow-Up Study," *Sociometry*, 27 (March, 1964), pp. 66–74. See p. 68.

2. AMERICAN COUNCIL ON EDUCATION PSYCHOLOGICAL EXAMINATION FOR COLLEGE FRESHMEN

Thurstone, L. L., and Thelma Gwinn Thurstone, *American Council on Education Psychological Examination for College Freshmen*, Princeton, N.J.: Educational Testing Service.

This test (which is available in several editions) consists of six components, three of which involve quantitative ability and three of which involve verbal ability. The titles of the three quantitative-ability components and their respective lengths are as follows: (1) Arithmetical Reasoning, 20 items; (2) Number Series, 30 items; and (3) Figure Analogies, 30 items. The titles of the three verbal-ability components and their respective lengths are as follows: (1) Same-Opposite, 50 items; (2) Completion, 30 items; and (3) Verbal Analogies, 40 items. Although each of the six components yields a separate score, it is recommended that the quantitative ability scores and the verbal ability scores be combined into two principal subscores.

Copies of this test may be purchased from the Educational Testing Service, Cooperative Test Division, 20 Nassau Street, Princeton, New Jersey, 08540. For further information concerning the test, see the extensive bibliography (535 citations) and references to reviews in Oscar K. Buros, *The Sixth Mental Measurements Yearbook*, Highland Park, N.J.: The Gryphon Press, 1965, pp. 680–683.

Brooks, Melvin S., and Robert S. Weymand, "Interest Preferences and Their Effect upon Academic Success," *Social Forces*, 32 (March, 1954), pp. 281–285. See p. 281.

Venable, Tom C., "The Relationship of Selected Factors to the Social Structure of a Stable Group," *Sociometry*, 17 (November, 1954), pp. 355–357. See p. 355.

Guetzkow, Harold, and William R. Dill, "Factors in the Organizational Development of Task-Oriented Groups," *Sociometry*, 20 (September, 1957), pp. 175–205. See p. 176.

Videbeck, Richard, and Alan P. Bates, "An Experimental Study of Conformity to Role Expectations," *Sociometry*, 22 (March, 1959), pp. 1–11. See p. 4.

Hall, Robert L., and Ben Willerman, "The Educational Influence of Dormitory Roommates," *Sociometry*, 26 (September, 1963), pp. 294–318. See p. 296.

Eckland, Bruce K., "Social Class and College Graduation: Some Misconceptions Corrected," *American Journal of Sociology*, 70 (July, 1964), pp. 36–50. See p. 47.

Eckland, Bruce K., "Academic Ability, Higher Education, and Occupational Mobility," *American Sociological Review*, 30 (October, 1965), pp. 735–746. See p. 738.

3. ARITHMETIC ABILITY

French, John W., *Kit of Selected Tests for Reference Aptitude and Achievement Factors*, Princeton, N.J.: Educational Testing Service, 1954.

Singer (1964); see category 30 below.

4. ARMED FORCES QUALIFICATION TEST

Hall, Robert L., "Group Performance under Feedback that Confounds Responses of Group Members," *Sociometry*, 20 (December, 1957), pp. 297–305. See p. 298.

Rosenburg, Seymour, "The Maintenance of a Learned Response in Controlled Interpersonal Conditions," *Sociometry*, 22 (June, 1959), pp. 124–138. See p. 127.

5. CARD SORTING TEST, DETAIL

Emrich, Robert, "Contrasting Disciplinary Preferences for Barnett's Types of Innovation," *Sociometry*, 22 (December, 1959), pp. 297–306. See pp. 300–301.

6. CARD SORTING TEST, RELATIONSHIP

Emrich; see category 5 above.

7. CALIFORNIA TEST OF MENTAL MATURITY

Peck, Robert F., and Cono Galliani, "Intelligence, Ethnicity, and Social Roles in Adolescent Society," *Sociometry*, 25 (March, 1962), pp. 64–72. See p. 65.

8. COLLEGE ENTRANCE EXAMINATION BOARD SCHOLASTIC APTITUDE TEST

Chapman, Loren J., and Donald T. Campbell, "The Effect of Acquiescence Response-Set Upon Relationships Among the F Scale, Ethnocentrism, and Intelligence," *Sociometry*, 22 (June, 1959), pp. 153–161. See p. 155.

Wallace, Walter L., "Institutional and Life-Cycle Socialization of College Freshmen, *American Journal of Sociology*, 70 (November, 1964), pp. 303–318. See p. 306.

9. CRITICAL THINKING APPRAISAL

Kutner and Gordon; see category 1 above.

10. EDUCATIONAL PROGRESS, SEQUENTIAL TEST OF

Weinberg, Carl, "Achievement and School Attitudes of Adolescent Boys as Related to Behavior and Occupational Status of Families," *Social Forces*, 42 (May, 1964), pp. 462–466. See p. 464.

11. GENERAL CLASSIFICATION TEST

Altman, Irwin, and William H. Haythorn, "Interpersonal Exchange in Isolation," *Sociometry*, 28 (December, 1965), pp. 411–426. See p. 414.

12. GOTTSCHALDT FIGURES

Deutsch, Morton, and Leonard Solomon, "Reactions to Evaluations by Others as Influenced by Self-Evaluations," *Sociometry*, 22 (June, 1959), pp. 93–112. See p. 100.

13. GRADUATE RECORD EXAMINATION

Graduate Record Examination, Princeton, N.J.: Educational Testing Service.

Tuckman, Bruce W., "Personality Structure, Group Composition, and Group Functioning," *Sociometry*, 27 (December, 1964), pp. 469–487. See p. 478.

14. HENMON-NELSON TEST OF MENTAL ABILITY

Henmon, V. A. C., and M. J. Nelson, *Henmon-Nelson Test of Mental Ability*, Boston: Houghton-Mifflin Co.

Sewell, William H., A. O. Haller, and Murray A. Straus, "Social Status and Educational and Occupational Aspiration," *American Sociological Review*, 22 (February, 1957), pp. 67–73. See p. 70.

Crockett, Harry J., Jr., "A Study of Some Factors Affecting the Decision of Negro High School Students to Enroll in Previously All-White High Schools, St. Louis, 1955," *Social Forces*, 35 (May, 1957), pp. 351–356. See p. 353.

Sewell, William H., "Community of Residence and College Plans," *American Sociological Review*, 29 (February, 1964), pp. 24–38. See p. 27.

Sewell, William H., and Alan M. Orenstein, "Community of Residence and Occupational Choice," *American Journal of Sociology*, 70 (March, 1965), pp. 551–563. See p. 554.

15. INTELLECTUAL TALENTS BATTERY

Ziller, Robert C., and Ralph V. Exline, "Some Consequences of Age Heterogeneity in Decision-Making Groups," *Sociometry*, 21 (September, 1958), pp. 198–211. See p. 201.

16. IOWA SILENT READING TEST

Crockett (1957); see category 14 above.

17. JOINT VOCABULARY TEST

Levinger, George, "Task and Social Behavior in Marriage," *Sociometry*, 27 (December, 1964), pp. 433–448. See pp. 436 and 446.

18. LAW APPLICATION TEST

Moore, Omar K., and Scarvia B. Anderson, "Search Behavior in Individual and Group Problem Solving," *American Sociological Review*, 19 (December, 1954), pp. 702–714. See p. 706.

19. MATHEMATICAL SOPHISTICATION

Hayes, Donald P., "Item Order and Guttman Scales," *American Journal of Sociology*, 70 (July, 1964), pp. 51–58. See pp. 52–54.

20. OBJECT SORTING TEST

Bolles, Marjorie, G. Rosin, and Carney Landis, "Psychological Performance Tests as Prognostic Agents for the Efficacy of Insulin Therapy in Schizophrenia," *Psychiatric Quarterly*, 12 (1938), pp. 733–737. See pp. 733–735.

Kutner and Gordon (1964); see category 1 above.

21. OHIO STATE UNIVERSITY PSYCHOLOGICAL TEST

Pihlblad, C. T., and C. L. Gregory, "Selective Aspects of Migration among Missouri High School Graduates," *American Sociological Review*, 19 (June, 1954), pp. 314–324. See p. 314.

Pihlblad, C. T., and C. L. Gregory, "The Role of Test Intelligence and Occupational Background as Factors in Occupational Choice," *Sociometry*, 19 (September, 1956), pp. 192–199. See p. 192.

Stuckert, Robert P., "A Configurational Approach to Prediction," *Sociometry*, 21 (September, 1958), pp. 225–237. See p. 227.

22. OTIS TESTS OF MENTAL ABILITY

Otis, Arthur S., *Otis Tests of Mental Ability*, all forms, New York: Harcourt, Brace and World, Inc.

Westoff, Charles F., Philip C. Sagi, and E. Lowell Kelly, "Fertility through Twenty Years of Marriage: A Study of Predictive Possibilities," *American Sociological Review*, 23 (October, 1958), pp. 549–556. See p. 551.

Burchinal, Lee G., "Social Status, Measured Intelligence, Achievement, and Personality Adjustment of Rural Iowa Girls," *Sociometry*, 22 (March, 1959), pp. 75–80. See p. 76.

Manheim, Henry L., "Intergroup Interaction as Related to Status and Leadership Differences between Groups," *Sociometry*, 23 (December, 1960), pp. 415–427. See p. 417.

23. QUICK WORD VOCABULARY TEST

Borgatta, Edgar F., and Raymond J. Corsini, *The Quick Word Test*, New York: The World Book Company, 1960.

Freeman, Howard E., "Attitudes toward Mental Illness among Relatives of Former Patients," *American Sociological Review*, 26 (February, 1961), pp. 59–66. See p. 63.

Teele, James E., "Suicidal Behavior, Assaultiveness, and Socialization Principles," *Social Forces*, 43 (May, 1965), pp. 510–518. See p. 513.

24. SRA PRIMARY MENTAL ABILITIES

Thurstone, L. L., and Thelma Gwinn Thurstone, SRA *Primary Mental Abilities*, Chicago, Ill.: Science Research Associates, Inc.

Borgatta, Edgar F., "Analysis of Social Interaction and Sociometric Perception," *Sociometry*, 17 (February, 1954), pp. 7–32. See p. 24.

Borgatta, Edgar F., Robert F. Bales, and Arthur S. Couch, "Some Findings Relevant to the Great Man Theory of Leadership," *American Sociological Review*, 19 (December, 1954), pp. 755–759. See p. 756.

Thorpe, J. G., "An Investigation into Some Correlates of Sociometric Status within School Classes," *Sociometry*, 18 (February, 1955), pp. 49–61. See p. 50.

Borgatta, E. F., and Leonard S. Cottrell, Jr., "On the Classification of Groups," *Sociometry*, 18 (December, 1955), pp. 409–442. See p. 410.

25. SCRAMBLED WORDS TEST

Deutsch and Solomon; see category 12 above.

26. SENTENCE COMPLETION TEST

Schroder, H. M., and S. Streufert, *The Measurement of Four Systems of Personality Structure Varying in Level of Abstractness: Sentence Completion Method*, Princeton, N.J.: Princeton University, Technical Report No. 11, 1962, p. 33.

Tuckman (1964), p. 477; see category 13 above.

27. STANFORD-BINET INTELLIGENCE SCALE

Getzels, Jacob W., and Philip W. Jackson, "Family Environment and Cognitive Style: A Study of the Sources of Highly Intelligent and of Highly Creative Adolescents," *American Sociological Review*, 26 (June, 1961), pp. 351–359. See p. 352.

Smelser, William T., "Adolescent and Adult Occupational Choices as a Function of Family Socioeconomic History," *Sociometry*, 26 (December, 1963), pp. 393–409. See p. 399.

28. TERMAN-MCNEMAR TEST OF MENTAL ABILITY

Terman, Lewis M., and Quinn McNemar, *Terman-McNemar Test of Mental Ability*, New York: Harcourt, Brace and World, Inc.

Crockett (1957); see category 14 above.

29. TEST OF G: CULTURE FAIR

Cattell, Raymond B., and A. K. S. Cattell, *Test of g: Culture Fair*, Champaign, Ill.: Institute for Personality and Ability Testing.

Haller, A. O., "Planning to Farm: A Social Psychological Interpretation," *Social Forces*, 37 (March, 1959), pp. 263–268. See p. 266.

Haller, A. O., and C. E. Butterworth, "Peer Influences on Levels of Occupational and Educational Aspiration," *Social Forces*, 38 (May, 1960), pp. 289–295. See p. 292.

Haller, A. O., and Shailer Thomas, "Personality Correlates of the Socioeconomic Status of Adolescent Males," *Sociometry*, 25 (December, 1962), pp. 398–404. See pp. 399–400.

30. VOCABULARY

French (1954); see category 3 above.

Singer, Jerome E., "The Use of Manipulative Strategies: Machiavellianism and Attractiveness," *Sociometry*, 27 (June, 1964), pp. 128–150. See pp. 129–130.

31. WECHSLER-BELLEVUE INTELLIGENCE SCALE

Wechsler, David, *Wechsler-Bellevue Intelligence Scale*, New York: Psychological Corporation.

Smelser (1963); see category 27 above.

Levinger (1964), p. 436; see category 17 above.

32. WIDE RANGE ACHIEVEMENT TEST

Jastak, Joseph and Sidney Bijou, *Wide Range Achievement Test*, New York: Psychological Corporation.

Burchinal (1959); see category 22 above.

MISCELLANEOUS CATEGORIES

1. **ATTRIBUTED SUCCESS OR FAILURE**

Rosenthal, Robert, Gordon W. Persinger, Linda Vikan-Kline, and Kermit Foote, "The Effect of Early Data Returns on Data Subsequently obtained by Outcome-Biased Experimenters," *Sociometry*, 26 (December, 1963), pp. 487–498. See p. 490.

2. **AUTONOMIC BALANCE, SALIVARY PH**

Thorpe, J. G., "Some Evidence on Northway's Autonomic Hypothesis," *Sociometry*, 17 (August, 1954), pp. 282–284.

3. **AUTONOMIC BALANCE, SUBLINGUAL TEMPERATURE**

Thorpe; see category 2 above.

4. **BACKGROUND CHARACTERISTICS, INDEX OF**

Greeley, Andrew M., "Influence of the 'Religious Factor' on Career Plans and Occupational Values of College Graduates," *American Journal of Sociology*, 68 (May, 1963), pp. 658–671. See p. 663.

5. **BEHAVIOR SCORE (8 SCALES)**

Tupes, E. C., "Relationships between Behavior Trait Ratings by Peers and Later Officer Performance of U.S.A.F. Officer Candidate School Graduates," Lackland Air Force Base, Texas, Air Force Personnel and Training Research Center Document No. AD 134257, 1957.

Tupes, E. C., A. Carp, and W. R. Borg, "Performance in Role-Playing Situations as Related to Leadership and Personality Measures," *Sociometry*, 21 (September, 1958), pp. 165–179. See pp. 167–171.

6. **CHANGE WITHIN HISTORICAL PERIODS**

Adler, Franz, "A Quantitative Study in the Sociology of Knowledge," *American Sociological Review*, 19 (February, 1954), pp. 42–48. See pp. 42–44.

7. CONSERVATISM OF SOCIAL SETTING

Reiss, Ira L., "Social Class and Premarital Sexual Permissiveness: A Re-examination," *American Sociological Review*, 30 (October, 1965), pp. 747–756. See pp. 750–752.

8. CORRESPONDENCE OF THINKER'S WORK WITH EPISTEMOLOGICAL TYPES

Adler p. 42; see category 6 above.

9. DIFFERENTIATION SCORE (OF RATERS)

Baker, B. O., and T. R. Sarbin, "Differential Mediation of Social Perception as a Correlate of Social Adjustment," *Sociometry*, 19 (June, 1956), pp. 69–83. See p. 77.

10. DRAMATIZATION OF MALE INITIATION CEREMONIES, DEGREES OF

Young, Frank W., "The Function of Male Initiation Ceremonies," *American Journal of Sociology*, 67 (January, 1962), pp. 379–391. See p. 385.

11. FREEDOM WITHIN HISTORICAL PERIODS

Adler, pp. 42–44; see category 6 above.

12. HIGH SCHOOL CHILDREN, RELATIVE INFLUENCE OF

Langworthy, Russell, "Community Status and Influence in a High School," *American Sociological Review*, 24 (August, 1959), pp. 537–539. See pp. 538–539.

13. HONESTY OF POLICEMEN, ATTITUDE TOWARD

McDill, Edward L., "A Comparison of Three Measures of Attitude Intensity," *Social Forces*, 38 (December, 1959), pp. 95–99. See p. 95.

14. HONESTY OF POLICEMEN, INTENSITY OF ATTITUDE TOWARD

McDill, p. 96; see category 13 above.

15. HYPOTHETICAL MURDER CASE, ATTITUDE TOWARD

Sears, David O., "Biased Indoctrination and Selectivity of Exposure to New Information," *Sociometry*, 28 (December, 1965), pp. 363–376. See p. 366.

16. JUNGLE SCALE

Feagin, Joe R., "Prejudice, Orthodoxy and the Social Situation,"

Social Forces, 44 (September, 1965), pp. 46–56. See pp. 47 and 54.

17. LIBERALISM OF SOCIAL SETTING

Reiss; see category 7 above.

18. NUCLEAR WAR CASUALTIES, NUMBER WILLING TO SUSTAIN

Putney, Snell, and Russell Middleton, "Some Factors Associated with Student Acceptance or Rejection of War," *American Sociological Review,* 27 (October, 1962), pp. 655–667. See p. 657.

19. NUCLEAR WEAPONS, DEGREE OF PROVOCATION DEEMED NECESSARY TO JUSTIFY USE OF

Putney and Middleton; see category 18 above.

20. NUCLEAR WEAPONS, KNOWLEDGE OF

Putney and Middleton; see category 18 above.

21. POLICEMEN, STEREOTYPING OF (2 MEASURES)

Preiss, Jack J., and Howard J. Ehrlich, *The State Policeman: Studies in Role Theory,* mimeographed, 1963.

Ehrlich, Howard J., "Instrument Error and the Study of Prejudice," *Social Forces,* 43 (December, 1964), pp. 197–206. See p. 200.

22. PROBABILITY EXPECTATIONS

Brim, Orville G., Jr., "Attitude Content-Intensity and Probability Expectations," *American Sociological Review,* 20 (February, 1955), pp. 68–76. See p. 69.

23. RELATIVE PROPENSITY OF WORKERS IN A GIVEN INDUSTRY TO STRIKE ON A PARTICULAR ISSUE

Knowles, K. G. J. C., "Strike-Proneness and Its Determinants," *American Journal of Sociology,* 60 (November, 1954), pp. 213–229. See p. 223.

24. SCIENCE, ATTITUDE TOWARD

Remmers, H. H., "High School Students Look at Science," Poll No. 50, the Purdue Opinion Panel, Division of Educational Reference, Purdue University, 17, November, 1957.

Burchinal, Lee G., "Rurality, Item Bias, and the Application of

Scientific Methodology to Human Behavior," *American Sociological Review*, 25 (April, 1960), pp. 257–260. See p. 257.

25. SECURITY WITHIN HISTORICAL PERIODS

Adler; see category 6 above.

26. SHOPPING AREAS, ATTITUDE TOWARD

Jonassen, Christen T., "Relationship of Attitudes and Behavior in Ecological Mobility," *Social Forces*, 34 (October, 1955), pp. 64–67. See p. 65.

27. SHOPPING HABIT SCALE

Jonassen; see category 26 above.

28. SOCIAL INTEGRATION, PROFESSIONAL

Coleman, James, Elihu Katz, and Herbert Menzel, "The Diffusion of Innovation among Physicians," *Sociometry*, 20 (December, 1957), pp. 253–270. See p. 254.

29. USE OF CONCEALED LISTENING DEVICES IN SOCIAL SCIENCE RESEARCH, ATTITUDES ABOUT

Burchard, Waldo W., "A Study of Attitudes toward the Use of Concealed Devices in Social Science Research," *Social Forces*, 36 (December, 1957), pp. 111–116. See p. 113.

NEIGHBORHOOD: ATTITUDES TOWARD AND CHARACTERISTICS OF

1. **ATTITUDES TOWARD PRESENT RESIDENCE**

Munson, Byron E., "Attitudes toward Urban and Suburban Residence in Indianapolis," *Social Forces*, 35 (October, 1956), pp. 76–80. See p. 76.

2. **MOBILITY POTENTIAL**

Rossi, Peter H., *Why Families Move: A Study in the Social Psychology of Urban Residential Mobility*, Glencoe, Ill.: The Free Press, 1955.

Leslie, Gerald R., and Arthur H. Richardson, "Life-Cycle, Career Pattern, and the Decision to Move," *American Sociological Review*, 26 (December, 1961), pp. 894–902. See p. 895.

3. **NEIGHBORHOOD SOCIAL INTIMACY**

Form, William H., Joel Smith, Gregory P. Stone, and James Cowhig, "The Compatibility of Alternative Approaches to the Delimitation of Urban Sub-Areas," *American Sociological Review*, 19 (August, 1954), pp. 434–440. See p. 437.

Smith, Joel, William H. Form, and Gregory P. Stone, "Local Intimacy in a Middle-Sized City," *American Journal of Sociology*, 60 (November, 1954), pp. 276–284. See p. 278.

4. **NEIGHBORHOOD, COMPLAINTS ABOUT**

Leslie and Richardson (1961); see category 2 above.

5. **NEIGHBORHOOD INTEGRATION: CONCERN WITH NEIGHBORHOOD UNITY**

Stuckert, Robert P., "Occupational Mobility and Family Relationships," *Social Forces*, 41 (March, 1963), pp. 301–307. See p. 306.

6. NEIGHBORHOOD INTEGRATION: NEIGHBORS AS A REFERENCE GROUP

See also 8 below.

Stuckert; see category 5 above.

7. NEIGHBORHOOD, SATISFACTION WITH

Swinehart, James W., "Socio-Economic Level, Status Aspiration, and Maternal Role," *American Sociological Review* (June, 1963), pp. 391–399. See p. 393.

8. NEIGHBORHOOD REFERENCE ORIENTATION

See also category 6 above.

Fellin, Phillip, *A Study of the Effects of Reference Group Orientations and Bureaucratic Careers on Neighborhood Cohesion*, unpublished Ph.D. dissertation, University of Michigan, 1961, pp. 89–99.

Fellin, Phillip, and Eugene Litwak, "Neighborhood Cohesion under Conditions of Mobility," *American Sociological Review*, 28 (June, 1963) pp. 364–376. See p. 371.

9. NEIGHBORHOOD, STAGES OF

Litwak, Eugene, "Voluntary Associations and Neighborhood Cohesion," *American Sociological Review*, 26 (April, 1961), pp. 258–271. See p. 267.

10. NEIGHBORING BEHAVIOR, ACTUAL

Shuval, Judith T., "Class and Ethnic Correlates of Casual Neighboring," *American Sociological Review*, 21 (August, 1956), pp. 453–458. See pp. 455–456.

11. NEIGHBORLINESS

Wallin, Paul, "A Guttman Scale for Measuring Women's Neighborliness," *American Journal of Sociology*, 59 (November, 1953), pp. 243–246.

Greer, Scott, "Urbanism Reconsidered: A Comparative Study of Local Areas in a Metropolis," *American Sociological Review*, 21 (February, 1956), pp. 19–25. See p. 20.

Fava, Sylvia Fleis, "Suburbanism as a Way of Life," *American Sociological Review*, 21 (February, 1956), pp. 34–37. See p. 37.

NORMS

1. ACHIEVEMENT NORMS

Freeman, Howard E., and H. Ashley Weeks, "Analysis of a Problem of Treatment of Delinquent Boys," *American Journal of Sociology*, 62 (July, 1956), pp. 56–61. See p. 58.

2. AFFECTIVITY—AFFECTIVE NEUTRALITY ORIENTATION

Loomis, Charles P., and John C. McKinney, "Systemic Differences between Latin-American Communities of Family Farms and Large Estates," *American Journal of Sociology*, 61 (March, 1956), pp. 404–412. See pp. 410–411.

3. AGE NORMS: APPEARANCE

Neugarten, Bernice L., Joan W. Moore, and John C. Lowe, "Age Norms, Age Constraints, and Adult Socialization," *American Journal of Sociology*, 70 (May, 1965), pp. 710–717. See pp. 713–714.

4. AGE NORMS: CONSUMPTIVE BEHAVIOR

Neugarten, Moore, and Lowe; see category 3 above.

5. AGE NORMS: THE FAMILY CYCLE

Neugarten, Moore, and Lowe; see category 3 above.

6. AGE NORMS: OCCUPATIONAL CAREER

Neugarten, Moore, and Lowe; see category 3 above.

7. AGE NORMS: RECREATION

Neugarten, Moore, and Lowe; see category 3 above.

8. ASCRIBED NORMS

Freeman and Weeks; see category 1 above.

9. ASCRIPTION-ACHIEVEMENT ORIENTATION

Loomis and McKinney; see category 2 above.

10. CONFORMITY TO FICTITIOUS NORM

Emerson, Richard M., "Power-Dependence Relations: Two Experiments," *Sociometry,* 27 (September, 1964), pp. 282–298. See p. 284.

11. DIFFUSENESS-SPECIFICITY ORIENTATION

Loomis and McKinney; see category 2 above.

12. FAMILISTIC-CONTRACTUAL ORIENTATION

Loomis and McKinney; see category 2 above.

13. GROUP NORM

Bates, Alan P., and Jerry S. Cloyd, "Toward the Development of Operations for Defining Group Norms and Member Roles," *Sociometry,* 19 (March, 1956), pp. 26–39. See pp. 29–30.

14. LAW AND ORDER

Freeman and Weeks; see category 1 above.

15. NORM ORIENTATION

Bowerman, Charles E., and John W. Kinch, "Changes in Family and Peer Orientation of Children between the 4th and 10th Grades," *Social Forces,* 37 (March, 1959), pp. 206–211. See p. 207.

16. NORMATIVE DIMENSION OF SELF-BLAME

Henry, Andrew F., "Family Role Structure and Self Blame," *Social Forces,* 35 (October, 1956), pp. 34–38. See pp. 34–36.

17. NORMS, INFLUENCE OF ON INDIVIDUAL JUDGMENT

Sherif, Muzafer, "A Study of Some Social Factors in Perception," *Archives of Psychology,* 27 (July, 1935). See p. 17.

Sherif, Muzafer, *The Psychology of Social Norms,* New York: Harper and Brothers, 1936, pp. 3 and 32–43.

Sherif, Muzafer, "An Experimental Approach to the Study of Attitudes," *Sociometry,* 1 (July, 1937), pp. 90–98. See p. 91.

Sherif, Muzafer, "Group Influences upon the Formation of Norms and Attitudes," in Theodore M. Newcomb and Eugene L. Hartley (eds.), *Readings in Social Psychology,* New York: Henry Holt and Company, 1947, pp. 77–90. See pp. 79–84.

Walter, Norman, "A Study of the Effects of Conflicting Suggestions upon Judgments in the Autokinetic Situation," *Sociometry,* 18 (May, 1955), pp. 138–146. See pp. 138–139.

18. PARTICULARISM-UNIVERSALISM ORIENTATION

Loomis and McKinney; see category 2 above.

19. SOCIAL NORMS

Stouffer, Samuel, "An Analysis of Conflicting Social Norms," *American Sociological Review*, 14 (December, 1949), pp. 707–717. See pp. 708–710.

Stoodley, Bartlett H., "A Cross-Cultural Study of Structure and Conflict in Social Norms," *American Journal of Sociology*, 65 (July, 1959), pp. 39–48. See pp. 40–41.

Stouffer, Samuel, and Jackson Toby, "Role Conflict and Personality," *American Journal of Sociology*, 56 (March, 1951), pp. 395–406. See pp. 396–405.

Sutcliffe, J. P., and M. Haberman, "Factors Influencing Choice in Role Conflict Situations," *American Sociological Review*, 21 (December, 1956), pp. 695–703. See pp. 696–697.

20. TRADITIONAL-RATIONAL ORIENTATION

Loomis and McKinney; see category 2 above.

21. UNDESIRABILITY OF BEHAVIOR

McGarvey, H. R., "Anchoring Effects in the Absolute Judgment of Verbal Materials," *Archives of Psychology*, 39 (May, 1943). See pp. 52–55.

Cohen, Edwin, "Stimulus Conditions as Factors in Social Change," *Sociometry*, 20 (June, 1957), pp. 135–144. See p. 136.

22. UNIVERSALISTIC-PARTICULARISTIC ORIENTATION

Laulicht, Jerome, "Role Conflict, the Pattern Variable Theory, and Scalogram Analysis," *Social Forces*, 33 (March, 1955), pp. 250–254. See pp. 251–252.

OCCUPATIONAL ROLES

SEE ALSO

Complex Organizations: Attitudes toward and Perceptions of

Complex Organizations: Characteristics of

Job Satisfaction, Morale, and Related Measures

1. ATTITUDES TOWARD WORK

Abegglen, James C., "Subordination and Autonomy Attitudes of Japanese Workers," *American Journal of Sociology*, 63 (September, 1957) pp. 181–189. See pp. 182–183.

2. BUREAUCRATIC ROLE CONCEPTION

Corwin, Ronald G., "The Professional Employee: A Study of Conflict in Nursing Roles," *American Journal of Sociology*, 66 (May, 1961), pp. 604–615. See p. 610.

3. CLIENT ORIENTATION

Wilensky, Harold L., "The Professionalization of Everyone?" *American Journal of Sociology*, 70 (September, 1964), pp. 137–158. See p. 154.

4. DISCIPLINE-INITIATIVE

Borgatta, Edgar F., "Attitudinal Concomitants to Military Statuses," *Social Forces*, 33 (May, 1955), pp. 342–347. See p. 345.

5. JOB SIMILARITY OF SELF WITH OTHERS

Meltzer, Leo, "Comparing Relationships of Individual and Average Variables to Individual Response," *American Sociological Review*, 28 (February, 1963), pp. 117–123. See p. 118.

6. OCCUPATIONAL CHOICE

Sewell, William H., and Alan M. Orenstein, "Community of

Residence and Occupational Choice," *American Journal of Sociology*, 70 (March, 1965), pp. 551–563. See p. 554.

7. OCCUPATIONAL ROLE AMBIGUITY

Reeder, Leo G., "Social Factors in Heart Disease: A Preliminary Research Report on the Relationship of Certain Social Factors to Blood Pressure in Males," *Social Forces*, 34 (May, 1956), pp. 367–371. See p. 368.

8. OCCUPATIONAL STATUS

Shepherd, C., and I. R. Weschler, "The Relation between Three Interpersonal Variables and Communication Effectiveness," *Sociometry*, 18 (May, 1955), pp. 103–110. See p. 105.

9. OCCUPATIONAL STATUS, DETERMINATENESS IN

Mack, Raymond W., "Occupational Determinateness: A Problem and Hypotheses in Role Theory," *Social Forces*, 35 (October, 1956), pp. 20–25. See p. 22.

10. ORIENTATION TO PUBLIC ASSISTANCE

Blau, Peter M., "Patterns of Choice in Interpersonal Relations," *American Sociological Review*, 27 (February, 1962), pp. 41–55. See p. 53.

11. PERFORMANCE RATING

Evan, William M., and Morris Zelditch, Jr., "A Laboratory Experiment on Bureaucratic Authority," *American Sociological Review*, 26 (December, 1961), pp. 883–893. See p. 887.

12. PERFORMANCE SCORE

Pelz, Donald C., and colleagues, *Human Relations in a Research Organization*, Ann Arbor, Mich.: Institute for Social Research, University of Michigan, 1953.

Glaser, Barney G., "The Local-Cosmopolitan Scientist," *American Journal of Sociology*, 69 (November, 1963), pp. 249–259. See p. 252.

13. PHYSICIAN'S INTEREST IN PATIENT'S WELFARE

Suchman, Edward A., *Socio-Cultural Variations in Illness and Medical Care*, New York: New York City Health Department, 1963.

Suchman, Edward A., "Sociomedical Variations among Ethnic

Groups," *American Journal of Sociology*, 70 (November, 1964), pp. 319–331. See p. 322.

14. PROFESSIONAL ACTIVITY, EXPECTATIONS OF

Turk, Herman, "Social Cohesion through Variant Values: Evidence from Medical Role Relations," *American Sociological Review*, 28 (February, 1963), pp. 28–37. See pp. 32–33.

15. PROFESSIONAL-DISCIPLINE ORIENTATION

Wilensky, pp. 152–155; see category 3 above.

16. PROFESSIONAL ROLE CONCEPTION

Corwin, p. 609; see category 2 above.

17. PROMOTION ORIENTATION SCALE

Borgatta; see category 4 above.

18. RESPONSIBILITY IN OCCUPATION

Reeder; see category 7 above.

19. RESPONSIBILITY IN WORK

Schwartz, Richard D., "Functional Alternatives to Inequality," *American Sociological Review*, 20 (August, 1955), pp. 424–430. See p. 428.

20. ROLE CENTRALITY WITHIN THE INDUSTRY

Meltzer; see category 5 above.

21. ROLE CONCEPTION

Lefton, Mark, Simon Dinitz, and Benjamin Pasamanick, "Decision-Making in a Mental Hospital: Real, Perceived, and Ideal," *American Sociological Review*, 24 (December, 1959), pp. 822–829. See p. 826.

22. ROLE CONCEPTION INVENTORY

Corwin, Ronald, Marvin J. Taves, and J. Eugene Haas, "Social Requirements for Occupational Success: Internalized Norms and Friendship," *Social Forces*, 39 (October, 1960), pp. 135–140. See p. 135.

23. ROLE CONCEPTION, BREADTH OF

Thomas, Edwin J., "Role Conceptions and Organizational Size," *American Sociological Review*, 24 (February, 1959), pp. 30–37. See p. 32.

24. ROLE CONCEPTIONS, CONSENSUS ON

Corwin, Taves, and Haas, p. 136; see category 22 above.

25. ROLE CONCEPTIONS: ADHERENCE TO REGULATIONS

Davis, F. James, "Conceptions of Official Leader Roles in the Air Force," *Social Forces*, 32 (March, 1954) pp. 253–258. See p. 254.

Davis, F. James, and Robert Hagedorn, "Testing the Reliability of Systematic Field Observations," *American Sociological Review*, 19 (June, 1954), pp. 345–348. See p. 345.

26. ROLE CONCEPTIONS: CONSISTENCY IN DISCIPLINARY MATTERS

Davis (1954); see category 25 above.

Davis and Hagedorn (1954); see category 25 above.

27. ROLE CONCEPTIONS: INTEREST IN THE MEN

Davis (1954); see category 25 above.

Davis and Hagedorn (1954); see category 25 above.

28. ROLE CONCEPTIONS: WAY OF GIVING ORDERS

Davis (1954); see category 25 above.

Davis and Hagedorn (1954); see category 25 above.

29. ROLE CONFLICT

Gullahorn, John T., "Measuring Role Conflict," *American Journal of Sociology*, 61 (January, 1956), pp. 299–303. See p. 300.

Gullahorn, John T., and Jeanne E. Gullahorn, "Role Conflict and Its Resolution," *Sociological Quarterly*, 4 (Winter, 1963), pp. 32–48. See pp. 38–43.

Gullahorn, John T., and Jeanne E. Gullahorn, "Some Computer Applications in Social Science," *American Sociological Review*, 30 (June, 1965), pp. 353–365. See pp. 357–358.

30. ROLE CONFLICT, UNRESOLVED

Gullahorn (1956); see category 29 above.

31. ROLE CONSENSUS

Thomas; see category 23 above.

32. ROLE EXPECTANCIES: AGGRESSIVENESS

Wispe, Lauren G., "A Sociometric Analysis of Conflicting Role-

Expectancies," *American Journal of Sociology*, 61 (September, 1955), pp. 134–137. See p. 135.

33. ROLE EXPECTANCIES: INTELLIGENCE

Wispe; see category 32 above.

34. ROLE EXPECTANCIES: SYMPATHY

Wispe; see category 32 above.

35. ROLE EXPECTATIONS

Hanson, Robert C., "The Systemic Linkage Hypothesis and Role Consensus Patterns in Hospital-Community Relations," *American Sociological Review*, 27 (June, 1962), pp. 304–313. See pp. 307 and 309.

36. ROLE IMPORTANCE

Turk; see category 14 above.

37. ROLE INTEGRATION: DURATION OF FRIENDSHIP

Wilensky, Harold L., "Orderly Careers and Social Participation: The Impact of Work History on Social Integration," *American Sociological Review*, 26 (August, 1961), pp. 521–539. See p. 529.

38. ROLE INTEGRATION: FRIENDSHIP CIRCLES

Wilensky; see category 37 above.

39. ROLE INTEGRATION: OVERLAPPING FRIENDSHIP AND MEMBERSHIP

Wilensky; see category 37 above.

40. ROLE INTEGRATION: WORK ASSOCIATES AND LEISURE-TIME FRIENDS

Wilensky; see category 37 above.

41. ROLE PERFORMANCE OF MEDICAL INTERNE, REPUTATIONAL

Seeman, Melvin and John W. Evans, "Stratification and Hospital Care: I. The Performance of the Medical Interne," *American Sociological Review*, 26 (February, 1961), pp. 67–80. See pp. 70 and 75–78.

42. ROLE PERFORMANCE OF MEDICAL INTERNE, SUBJECTIVE

Seeman and Evans, pp. 70–72; see category 41 above.

43. ROLE PREROGATIVES, DESIRED

Lefton, Dinitz, and Pasamanick, p. 824; see category 21 above.

44. ROLE PREROGATIVES, PERCEIVED

Lefton, Dinitz, and Pasamanick, p. 824; see category 21 above.

45. SCIENTIFIC PRODUCTIVITY

Crane, Diana, "Scientists at Major and Minor Universities: A Study of Productivity and Recognition," *American Sociological Review*, 30 (October, 1965), pp. 699–714. See p. 702.

46. SERVICE ROLE CONCEPTION

Corwin; see category 2 above.

47. STATUS AND PRESTIGE OF COOPERATING PROFESSIONAL GROUPS

Dinitz, Simon, Mark Lefton, and Benjamin Pasamanick, "Status Perceptions in a Mental Hospital," *Social Forces* 38 (December, 1959), pp. 124–128. See p. 125.

48. SUCCESS OF STAFF NURSES

Corwin, Taves, and Haas, p. 136; see category 22 above.

PERSONAL ADJUSTMENT

SEE ALSO

Marital Adjustment and Courtship
Medicine and Health: Attitudes toward
Medicine and Health: Behavior in and Characteristics of

1. ADJUSTMENT TO OLD AGE

Phillips, Bernard S., "A Role Theory Approach to Adjustment in Old Age," *American Sociological Review*, 22 (April, 1957), pp. 212–217. See p. 213.

2. ADULT ATTITUDE INVENTORY

Scott, Frances G., "Factors in Personal Adjustment of Institutionalized and Noninstitutionalized Aged," *American Sociological Review*, 20 (October, 1955), pp. 538–546. See p. 541.

3. ANXIETY (CHRISTIE, BUDNITZKY)

Christie, Richard, and Stanley Budnitzky, "A Short Forced-Choice Anxiety Scale," *Journal of Consulting Psychology*, 21 (December, 1957), p. 501.

Scarr, Harry A., "Measures of Particularism," *Sociometry*, 27 (December, 1964), pp. 413–432. See p. 417.

Back, Kurt W., and Keith E. Davis, "Some Personal and Social Situational Factors Relevant to the Consistency and Prediction of Conforming Behavior," *Sociometry*, 28 (September, 1965), pp. 227–240. See p. 229.

4. ANXIETY (HAJDA)

Hajda, Jan, "Alienation and Integration of Student Intellectuals," *American Sociological Review*, 26 (October, 1961), pp. 758–777. See p. 777.

5. ANXIETY (PALMAR SWEAT METHOD)

Mowrer, O. Hobart, *Psychotherapy: Theory and Research*, New York: Ronald Press, 1953, pp. 591–640.

Steiner, Ivan F., and Homer H. Johnson, "Authoritarianism and Conformity," *Sociometry*, 26 (March, 1963), pp. 21–34. See p. 28.

6. ANXIETY (SCHIFF)

Schiff, Herbert, "Judgmental Response Sets in the Perception of Sociometric Status," *Sociometry*, 17 (August, 1954), pp. 207–227. See p. 212.

7. ANXIETY, LEVEL OF

Hare, A. Paul, and Robert F. Bales, "Seating Position and Small Group Interaction," *Sociometry*, 26 (December, 1963), pp. 480–486. See p. 485.

8. ANXIETY, MANIFEST (BARTH)

Hayes, Donald P., "Item Order and Guttman Scales," *American Journal of Sociology*, 70 (July, 1964), pp. 51–58. See p. 52.

9. ANXIETY, MANIFEST (MCCLOSKY, SCHAAR)

McClosky, Herbert, and John H. Schaar, "Psychological Dimensions of Anomy," *American Sociological Review*, 30 (February, 1965), pp. 14–40. See p. 29.

10. ANXIETY, MANIFEST (TAYLOR)

Taylor, Janet A., "A Personality Scale of Manifest Anxiety," *Journal of Abnormal and Social Psychology*, 48 (April, 1953), pp. 285–290.

Hutchins, Edwin B., and Fred E. Fiedler, "Task-Oriented and Quasi-Therapeutic Role Functions of the Leader in Small Military Groups," *Sociometry*, 23 (September, 1960), pp. 393–406. See p. 399.

11. ANXIETY-WORRIES CHECK LIST

Montague, Joel B., Jr., "A Study of Anxiety among English and American Boys," *American Sociological Review*, 20 (December, 1955), pp. 685–689. See p. 687.

12. ARMY ADJUSTMENT INVENTORY

Havron, M. D., R. J. Fay, and D. M. Goodacre, III, "Research on the Effectiveness of Small Military Units," PRS Report No. 885, Institute for Research on Human Relations, 1951.

Hutchins and Fiedler (1960); see category 10 above.

13. BEWILDERMENT

McClosky and Schaar, p. 24; see category 9 above.

14. CALIFORNIA TEST OF PERSONALITY

See also Personality: General, category 3.

Thorpe, Louis P., Willis W. Clark, and Ernest W. Tiegs, *California Test of Personality*, Los Angeles, Calif.: California Test Bureau.

Each of the five forms of the *California Test of Personality* (Primary, Elementary, Intermediate, Secondary, and Adult) is "designed to identify and reveal the status of certain highly important factors in personality and social adjustment." The test consists of two principal components and yields a total of 15 adjustment scores. The first component, self-adjustment, consists in turn of the following six subtests: self-reliance, sense of personal worth, sense of personal freedom, feeling of belonging, withdrawing tendencies, and nervous symptoms. Scores may be calculated for the individual subtests and for the total self-adjustment component.

The second component, social adjustment, also consists of six subtests as follows: social standards, social skills, antisocial tendencies, family relations, school relations, occupation relations, and community relations. Again, scores may be calculated for the individual subtests and for the entire social-adjustment component. A fifteenth score—total adjustment—combines the self-adjustment and social-adjustment components.

Each subtest of this instrument consists of 15 questions which are to be answered by circling "yes" or "no." An example taken from the self-reliance portion of the test is as follows: "Do you usually do something about it if somebody steps in front of you in line? Yes No"

The test also includes an "Interests and Activities Questionnaire" which is not scored as part of the adjustment measures. The *Manual of Directions* presents definitions of the various components, directions for administering and scoring the test, information on reliability and validity, and directions for preparing and interpreting respondents' profiles.

The various forms of the *California Test of Personality* may be purchased from the California Test Bureau, Del Monte Research Park, Monterey, California 93940. For an extensive bibliography (166 citations) and references to reviews of the instrument, see Oscar K. Buros, *The Sixth Mental Measurements Yearbook*, Highland Park, N.J.: Gryphon Press, 1964, pp. 175–176.

Martinson, F. M., "Ego Deficiency as a Factor in Marriage," *American Sociological Review*, 20 (April, 1955), pp. 161–164. See p. 162.

Sewell, W. H., and A. O. Haller, "Social Status and Personality Adjustment of the Child," *Sociometry*, 19 (June, 1956), pp. 114–121. See p. 116.

Burchinal, Lee G., Glenn R. Hawkes, and Bruce Gardner, "Adjustment Characteristics of Rural and Urban Children," *American Sociological Review*, 22 (February, 1957), pp. 81–87. See p. 82.

Jenkins, Wesley W., "An Experimental Study of the Relationship of Legitimate and Illegitimate Birth Status to School and Personal and Social Adjustment of Negro Children," *American Journal of Sociology*, 64 (September, 1958), pp. 169–173. See p. 169.

Sewell, William H., and A. O. Haller, "Factors in the Relationship between Social Status and the Personality Adjustment of the Child," *American Sociological Review*, 24 (August, 1959), pp. 511–520. See pp. 512–513.

15. EMOTIONAL MATURITY (BELL)

Bell, Hugh M., *The Adjustment Inventory*, Palo Alto, Calif.: Consulting Psychologists Press, Inc.

Dean, Dwight G., "Romanticism and Emotional Maturity: A Preliminary Study," *Marriage and Family Living*, 23 (February, 1961). pp. 44–45.

Dean (1964); see category 17 below.

16. EMOTIONAL MATURITY (DEAN)

Includes the following separate dimensions: anger, attitude toward learning, authority, communication, egocenteredness-sociocenteredness, emotional security, integration, intellectual maturity, judgment, man-woman relationships, responsibility, self control, social poise, stress.

Dean (1964); see category 17 below.

17. EMOTIONAL MATURITY (EILBERT)

Eilbert, Leo, "A Tentative Definition of Emotional Immaturity Utilizing the Critical Incident Technique," *Personnel and Guidance*, 35 (May, 1957), pp. 554–567. See pp. 555–560.

Dean, Dwight G., "Romanticism and Emotional Maturity: A Further Exploration," *Social Forces*, 42 (March, 1964), pp. 298–303. See pp. 300–301.

18. EMOTIONAL STATUS

Nefzger, M. Dean, and Abraham M. Lilienfeld, "Item Reliability and Related Factors in a Community Survey of Emotionality," *Sociometry*, 22 (September, 1959), pp. 236–246. See pp. 238–239.

19. FRUSTRATION

Rosenzweig, Saul, *Rosenzweig Picture-Frustration Study*, St. Louis, Mo.: The Author.

Lindzey, Gardner, and James A. Urdan, "Personality and Social Choice," *Sociometry*, 17 (February, 1954), pp. 47–63. See p. 47.

Sutcliffe, J. P., and M. Haberman, "Factors Influencing Choice in Role Conflict Situations," *American Sociological Review*, 21 (December, 1956), pp. 695–703. See p. 700.

Harvey, O. J., "Personality Factors in Resolution of Conceptual Incongruities," *Sociometry*, 25 (December, 1962), pp. 336–352. See p. 339.

20. FRUSTRATION, ANAL

Straus, Murray A., "Anal and Oral Frustration in Relation to Sinhalese Personality," *Sociometry*, 20 (March, 1957), pp. 21–31. See p. 27.

21. FRUSTRATION, ORAL

Straus, p. 24; see category 20 above.

22. FRUSTRATION, PERCEIVED

Wiggins, James A., "Interaction Structure, Frustration, and the Extensiveness and Intensity of Aggression," *Sociometry*, 28 (March, 1965), pp. 89–99. See p. 94.

23. FRUSTRATION-DEPRESSION

Freeman, Howard E., and Ozzie G. Simmons, "Wives, Mothers, and the Posthospital Performance of Mental Patients," *Social Forces*, 37 (December, 1958), pp. 153–159. See p. 155.

24. GENERAL ADJUSTMENT

Grusky, Oscar, "Organizational Goals and the Behavior of Informal Leaders," *American Journal of Sociology*, 65 (July, 1959), pp. 59–67. See p. 63.

25. GUILT

McClosky and Schaar, pp. 30–31; see category 9 above.

26. HOSTILITY

McClosky and Schaar, pp. 31–32; see category 9 above.

27. INCLINATION TO ADOPT THE SICK ROLE

Mechanic, David, and Edmund H. Volkart, "Stress, Illness Behavior, and the Sick Role," *American Sociological Review*, 26 (February, 1961), pp. 51–58. See p. 55.

28. INSECURITY

See also category 60 below.

Lipman, Aaron, and A. Eugene Havens, "The Colombian Violencia: An Ex Post Facto Experiment," *Social Forces*, 44 (December, 1965), pp. 238–245. See pp. 239–240.

29. LIFE SATISFACTION

McClosky and Schaar, pp. 24 and 30–31; see category 9 above.

30. MALADJUSTMENT (DAVIDS, PARENTI)

Davids, Anthony, and Anita Negrin Parenti, "Personality, Social Choice, and Adults' Perception of These Factors in Groups of Disturbed and Normal Children," *Sociometry*, 21 (September, 1958), pp. 212–224. See p. 214.

31. MALADJUSTMENT (FISHER)

Fisher, Seymour, "Patterns of Personality and Some of Their Determinants," *Psychological Monographs*, 64 (1950), p. 264.

De Vos, George, and Horace Miner, "Algerian Culture and Personality in Change," *Sociometry*, 21 (December, 1958), pp. 255–268. See p. 257.

32. MENTAL MATURITY (SULLIVAN, CLARK, TIEGS)

Sullivan, Elizabeth T., Willis W. Clark, and Ernest W. Tiegs, *California Short-Form Test of Mental Maturity* (all forms), Los Angeles, Calif.: The California Test Bureau.

Sewell and Haller (1956); see category 14 above.

33. NERVOUS SYMPTOMS (THORPE, CLARK, TIEGS)

Thorpe, Clark, and Tiegs; see category 14 above.

Sewell and Haller (1959), p. 517; see category 14 above.

34. NEUROPSYCHIATRIC SCREENING ADJUNCT (STAR)

Star, Shirley A., "The Screening of Psychoneurotics in the Army: Technical Development of Tests," and "The Screening of Psychoneurotics: Comparison of Psychiatric Diagnoses and Test Scores at All Induction Stations," in Samuel A. Stouffer, *et. al.*, *Measurement and Prediction*, Vol. IV in *Studies in Social Psychology in World War II*, Princeton, N.J.: Princeton University Press, 1950, pp. 486–567.

Rose, Arnold M., "Neuropsychiatric Breakdown in the Garrison Army and in Combat," *American Sociological Review*, 21 (August, 1956), pp. 480–488. See p. 480.

Nefzger and Lilienfeld (1959), p. 238; see category 18 above.

Rosenberg, Morris, "The Dissonant Religious Context and Emotional Disturbance," *American Journal of Sociology*, 68 (July, 1962), pp. 1–10. See p. 2.

35. NEUROTIC INVENTORY

Thurstone, L. L., and Thelma G. Thurstone, "Neurotic Inventory," *Journal of Social Psychology*, 1 (February, 1930), pp. 3–30. See pp. 4–14.

Burgess, Ernest W., and Paul Wallin, *Engagement and Marriage*, Chicago, Ill.: J. B. Lippincott and Co., 1953, pp. 523–537 and 804–806.

Burchinal, Lee G., Glenn R. Hawkes, and Bruce Gardner, "Personality Characteristics and Marital Satisfaction," *Social Forces*, 35 (March, 1957), pp. 218–222. See p. 219.

Wallin, Paul, "Religiosity, Sexual Gratification, and Marital Satisfaction," *American Sociological Review*, 22 (June, 1957), pp. 300–305. See p. 304.

36. NEUROTIC SELF-DEPRECIATION

Ktsanes, Thomas, "Mate Selection on the Basis of Personality Type: A Study Utilizing an Empirical Typology of Personality," *American Sociological Review*, 20 (October, 1955), pp. 547–551. See p. 550.

37. NEUROTICISM (CORNELL SCREENING DEVICE)

Friedrichs, Robert W., "Alter vs. Ego," *American Sociological Review*, 25 (August, 1960), pp. 496–508. See p. 499.

38. NEUROTICISM (HATHAWAY, MCKINLEY)

Hathaway, Starke R., and J. Charnley McKinley, *Minnesota Multiphasic Personality Inventory*, Minneapolis, Minn.: University of Minnesota Press, 1943.

Nettler, Gwynn, and J. R. Huffman, "Political Opinion and Personal Security," *Sociometry*, 20 (March, 1957), pp. 51–65. See p.56.

39. NEUROTICISM: ANNOYANCES TEST

Thorpe, J. G., "An Investigation into Some Correlates of Sociometric Status within School Classes," *Sociometry*, 18 (February, 1955), pp. 49–61. See p. 50.

40. NEUROTICISM: DEJECTION

Suchman, Edward A., Bernard S. Phillips, and Gordon F. Streib, "An Analysis of the Validity of Health Questionnaires," *Social Forces*, 36 (March, 1958), pp. 223–232. See p. 225.

41. NEUROTICISM: DEPRESSIVE AFFECT

Rosenberg (1962); see category 34 above.

42. NEUROTICISM: INTERESTS TEST

Thorpe, p. 51; see category 39 above.

43. NEUROTICISM: MAUDSLEY MEDICAL QUESTIONNAIRE (EYSENCK MODIFICATION)

Eysenck, H. J., *Dimensions of Personality*, London: Methuen, 1947, pp. 64–65.

Thorpe (1955), p. 51; see category 39 above.

44. NEUROTICISM: SENTENCE COMPLETION TEST

Thorpe; see category 39 above.

45. NEUROTICISM: SYMPTOM LEVEL MEASURE

Gurin, Gerald, Joseph Veroff, and Sheila Feld, *Americans View Their Mental Health*, New York: Basic Books, Inc., 1960, p. 420.

Jackson, Elton F., "Status Consistency and Symptoms of Stress," *American Sociological Review*, 27 (August, 1962), pp. 469–480. See p. 472.

46. NEUROTICISM: WAYS TO BE DIFFERENT TEST

Thorpe; see category 39 above.

47. NEUROTICISM: WORD LIKES AND DISLIKES TEST

Thorpe; see category 39 above.

48. NEUROTICISM: WORRIES AND ANXIETIES TEST

Thorpe; see category 39 above.

49. OBSESSIVENESS

McClosky and Schaar, pp. 28–29; see category 9 above.

50. PARANOIA

McClosky and Schaar, pp. 31–32; see category 9 above.

51. PERSONAL ADJUSTMENT (BELL)

Bell; see category 15 above.

Martinson, F. M. (1955); see category 14 above.

Westoff, Charles F., Philip C. Sagi, and E. Lowell Kelley, "Fertility Through Twenty Years of Marriage: A Study of Predictive Possibilities," *American Sociological Review*, 23 (October, 1958), pp. 549–556. See p. 551.

52. PERSONAL ADJUSTMENT (BERNREUTER)

Bernreuter, Robert G., *The Personality Inventory*, Palo Alto, Calif.: Consulting Psychologists Press, Inc.

Tate, Mildred T., and Virginia A. Musick, "Adjustment Problems of College Students," *Social Forces*, 33 (December, 1954), pp. 182–185. See p. 182.

53. PERSONAL ADJUSTMENT (CAVAN, BURGESS, HAVIGHURST, GOLDHAMER)

Cavan, Ruth S., Ernest W. Burgess, Robert J. Havighurst, and Herbert Goldhamer, *Personal Adjustment in Old Age*, Chicago, Ill.: Science Research Associates, 1949, pp. 111–120.

Maddox, George L., "Activity and Morale: A Longitudinal Study of Selected Elderly Subjects," *Social Forces*, 42 (December, 1963), pp. 195–204. See p. 197.

54. PERSONAL ADJUSTMENT (FOX)

Fox, Vernon, *The Effect of Juvenile Institutionalization on Adjustment in Prison*, unpublished M.A. thesis, Michigan State College, 1943, Chapter 6.

Fox, Vernon, "The Effect of Counseling on Adjustment in Prison," *Social Forces*, 32 (March, 1954), pp. 285–289. See p. 287.

55. PERSONAL ADJUSTMENT (HATHAWAY, MCKINLEY)

Hathaway and McKinley; see category 38 above.

Schiff (1954), p. 211; see category 6 above.

56. PERSONAL ADJUSTMENT (HAVIGHURST)

Havighurst, Robert J., "The Social Competence of Middle-Aged People," *Genetic Psychology Monographs*, 56 (November, 1957), pp. 297–375. See pp. 349–373.

Havighurst, Robert L., "The Leisure Activities of the Middle Aged," *American Journal of Sociology*, 63 (September, 1957), pp. 152–162. See p. 156.

Havighurst, Robert L., and Kenneth Feigenbaum, "Leisure and Life-Style," *American Journal of Sociology*, 64 (January, 1959), pp. 396–404. See p. 397.

Donald, Marjorie N., and Robert J. Havighurst, "The Meanings of Leisure," *Social Forces*, 37 (May, 1959), pp. 355–360. See p. 359.

57. PERSONAL ADJUSTMENT (KLOPFER, KELLEY)

Schiff, p. 212; see category 6 above.

58. PERSONAL ADJUSTMENT, COMPOSITE

Schiff p. 213; see category 6 above.

59. PERSONAL ADJUSTMENT, TEACHER'S RATINGS

Schiff, p. 212; see category 6 above.

60. SECURITY-INSECURITY INVENTORY

Maslow, A. N., E. Hirsch, M. Stein, and I. Honigmann, "A Clinically Derived Test for Measuring Psychological Security-Insecurity," *Journal of General Psychology*, 33 (July, 1945), pp. 21–41. See pp. 22–28.

Lindzey and Urdan (1954), p. 49; see category 19 above.

Nettler and Huffman (1957), p. 53; see category 38 above.

61. SOCIAL INTEGRATION

Freeman, Howard E. and Ozzie G. Simmons, "Social Class and Posthospital Performance Levels," *American Sociological Review*, 24 (June, 1959), pp. 345–351. See p. 347.

62. STABILITY-DISORGANIZATION

McClosky and Schaar, p. 29; see category 9 above.

63. STRESS

Mechanic and Volkart, p. 54; see category 27 above.

PERSONALITY: GENERAL

SEE ALSO

Personality Traits: Creativity
Personality Traits: Dominance
Personality Traits: Masculinity-Femininity
Personality Traits: Motives and Needs
Personality Traits: Sociability-Withdrawal
Personality Traits: Various Categories
Values

1. CALIFORNIA BEHAVIOR INVENTORY FOR NURSERY SCHOOL CHILDREN

Koch, Helen L., "Some Personality Correlates of Sex, Sibling Position, and Sex of Sibling among Five and Six Year Old Children," *Genetic Psychology Monographs*, 52 (August, 1955), pp. 3–50. See pp. 9–10.

Brim, Orville G., Jr., "Family Structure and Sex Role Learning by Children: A Further Analysis of Helen Koch's Data," *Sociometry*, 21 (March, 1958), pp. 1–16. See p. 6.

2. CALIFORNIA PSYCHOLOGICAL INVENTORY

See also Crime and Delinquency, category 7.

Gough, Harrison G., *California Psychological Inventory*, Palo Alto, Calif.: Consulting Psychologists Press, 1956.

Vincent, Clark E., "Socioeconomic Status and Familial Variables in Mail Questionnaire Responses," *American Journal of Sociology*, 69 (May, 1964), pp. 647–653. See pp. 647–649.

3. CALIFORNIA TEST OF PERSONALITY

See also Personal Adjustment, category 14.

Thorpe, Louis P., Willis W. Clark, and Ernest W. Tiegs, *Califor-

nia Test of Personality, Los Angeles, Calif.: California Test Bureau.

Straus, Murray A., "Anal and Oral Frustration in Relation to Sinhalese Personality," *Sociometry*, 20 (March, 1957), pp. 21–31. See p. 23.

Haller, A. O. and Shailer Thomas, "Personality Correlates of the Socioeconomic Status of Adolescent Males," *Sociometry*, 25 (December, 1962), pp. 398–404. See p. 400.

4. FELS CHILD BEHAVIOR SCALES

Koch (1955); see category 1 above.

Brim (1958); see category 1 above.

5. GORDON PERSONAL PROFILE

Gordon, Leonard V., *Gordon Personal Profile*, Tarrytown N.Y.: Harcourt, Brace and World, Inc.

Backman, Carl W., Paul F. Secord, and Jerry R. Pierce, "Resistance to Change in the Self-Concept as a Function of Consensus among Significant Others," *Sociometry*, 26 (March, 1963), pp. 102–111. See p. 106.

6. GUILFORD-ZIMMERMAN TEMPERAMENT SURVEY

Guilford, J. P., and Wayne S. Zimmerman, *The Guilford-Zimmerman Temperament Survey*, Beverly Hills, Calif.: Sheridan Supply Company.

Hoffman, L. Richard, "Similarity of Personality: A Basis of Interpersonal Attraction?" *Sociometry*, 21 (December, 1958), pp. 300–308. See p. 301.

Hoffman, L. Richard, and Clagett G. Smith, "Some Factors Affecting the Behaviors of Members of Problem-Solving Groups," *Sociometry*, 23 (September, 1960), pp. 273–291. See p. 274.

Hoffman, L. Richard, "A Note on Ratings versus Choices as Measures of Group Attraction," *Sociometry*, 25 (September, 1962), pp. 313–320. See pp. 314–316.

7. INNER-DIRECTED, OTHER-DIRECTED

See also categories 9, 10, 11, and 24–32 below.

Bell, Elaine Graham, *Inner-Directed and Other-Directed Attitudes*, unpublished Ph.D. dissertation, Yale University, 1955.

Linton, Harriet, and Elaine Graham, "Personality Correlates of Persuasibility," in Carl I. Hovland and Irving L. Janis (eds.), *Personality and Persuasibility*, New Haven, Conn.: Yale University Press, 1959, pp. 69–101. See pp. 79–83.

Sofer, Elaine Graham, "Inner-Direction, Other-Direction, and Autonomy: A Study of College Students," in Seymour Lipset and Leo Lowenthal (eds.), *Culture and Social Character*, New York: The Free Press, 1961, pp. 316–348.

Back, Kurt W. and Keith E. Davis, "Some Personal and Social Situational Factors Relevant to the Consistency and Prediction of Conforming Behavior," *Sociometry*, 28 (September, 1965), pp. 227–240. See pp. 228–229, and 231.

8. MYERS-BRIGGS TYPE INDICATOR

Myers, Isabel Briggs and Katharine C. Briggs, *Myers-Briggs Type Indicator*, Princeton, N.J.: Educational Testing Service.

Hobart, Charles W., and Nancy Fahlberg, "The Measurement of Empathy," *American Journal of Sociology*, 70 (March, 1965), pp. 595–603. See p. 601.

9. OTHER-DIRECTEDNESS

See also category 7 above and categories 9, 11, and 24–32 below.

Guba, E. G., and J. W. Getzels, "The Construction of an Other-Directedness Instrument, with Some Preliminary Data on Validity," paper read before the American Psychological Association, September, 1954.

Peterson (1964), p. 195; see category 24 below.

10. OTHER-DIRECTEDNESS: ENDORSEMENTS

See also categories 7 and 9 above and categories 11 and 24–32 below.

Dornbusch, Sanford M., and Lauren C. Hickman, "Other-Directedness in Consumer-Goods Advertising: A Test of Riesman's Historical Theory," *Social Forces*, 38 (December, 1959), pp. 99–102. See p. 100.

11. OTHER-DIRECTEDNESS: INTERPERSONAL SATISFACTIONS

Dornbusch and Hickman; see category 10 above.

12. PERSONALITY DESCRIPTION BLANK

Hathaway, Starke R., and J. C. McKinley, *The Minnesota*

Multiphasic Inventory, Minneapolis, Minn.: University of Minnesota Press, 1943.

Lundy, Richard M., "Assimilative Projection and Accuracy of Prediction in Interpersonal Perceptions," *Journal of Abnormal and Social Psychology,* 52 (January, 1956), pp. 33–38. See pp. 34–35.

Lundy, Richard M., "Self Perceptions and Descriptions of Opposite Sex Sociometric Choices," *Sociometry,* 19 (December, 1956), pp. 272–277. See p. 273.

13. PERSONALITY INVENTORY (ANDERSON, MCGUIRE)

Anderson, Lynn R., and William J. McGuire, "Prior Reassurance of Group Consensus as a Factor in Producing Resistance to Persuasion," *Sociometry,* 28 (March, 1965), pp. 44–56. See p. 51.

14. PERSONALITY INVENTORY (BERNREUTER)

Bernreuter, Robert G., *The Personality Inventory,* Palo Alto, Calif.: Consulting Psychologists Press, Inc.

Tate, Mildred T., and Virginia A. Musick, "Adjustment Problems of College Students," *Social Forces,* 33 (December, 1954), pp. 182–185. See p. 182.

Westoff, Charles F., Philip C. Sagi, and E. Lowell Kelly, "Fertility Through Twenty Years of Marriage: A Study of Predictive Possibilities," *American Sociological Review,* 23 (October, 1958), pp. 549–556. See p. 551.

15. PERSONALITY RATING SCALE

Northway, Mary L., and Joyce Detweiler, "Children's Perception of Friends and Nonfriends," *Sociometry,* 18 (December, 1955), pp. 527–531. See p. 528.

16. PERSONALITY TRAITS: AZZAGEDDI TEST

Davids, Anthony, and Henry A. Murray, "Preliminary Appraisal of an Auditory Projective Technique for Studying Personality and Cognition," *American Journal of Orthospychiatry,* 25 (July, 1955), pp. 543–554. See p. 545.

Davids, Anthony, and Anita Negrin Parenti, "Personality, Social Choice and Adults' Perception of These Factors in Groups of Disturbed and Normal Children," *Sociometry,* 21 (September, 1958), pp. 212–229. See p. 214.

17. PERSUASIBILITY

Janis, Irving L. and Peter B. Field, "A Behavioral Assessment of Persuasibility: Consistency of Individual Differences," *Sociometry*, 19 (December, 1956), pp. 241–259. See pp. 242–248.

18. PROFILE OF CHARACTERIZATION

Maisonneuve, Jean, "A Contribution to the Sociometry of Mutual Choices," *Sociometry*, 17 (February, 1954), pp. 33–46. See p. 36.

19. PROJECTIVE TEST OF PERSONALITY

O.S.S. Assessment Staff, *Assessment of Men*, New York: Rinehart and Co., Inc., 1948, pp. 58–202.

Lindzey, Gardner, and James A. Urdan, "Personality and Social Choice," *Sociometry*, 17 (February, 1954), pp. 47–63. See p. 49.

20. RATING SCALE OF PERSONALITY TRAITS

Maisonneuve, p. 34; see category 18 above.

21. SIXTEEN PERSONALITY FACTOR QUESTIONNAIRE

Cattell, Raymond B., D. R. Saunders, and G. Stice, *Sixteen Personality Factor Questionnaire*, Champaign, Ill.: Institute for Personality and Ability Testing.

Winch, Robert F. and Douglas M. More, "Quantitative Analysis of Qualitative Data on the Assessment of Motivation: Reliability, Congruence, and Validity," *American Journal of Sociology*, 61 (March, 1956), pp. 445–452. See p. 447.

Haller and Thomas (1962), pp. 399–400; see category 3 above.

22. ROGERS PERSONALITY TEST

Rogers, Carl, *Measuring Personality Adjustment in Children Nine to Thirteen Years of Age*, New York: Teachers College, Columbia University, 1931.

Burchinal, Lee G., Glenn R. Hawkes, and Bruce Gardner, "Adjustment Characteristics of Rural and Urban Children," *American Sociological Review*, 22 (February, 1957), pp. 81–87. See p. 85.

23. RORSCHACH PERSONALITY ASSESSMENT

Straus (1957), p. 23; see category 3 above.

Nash, Dennison J., and Alvin W. Wolfe, "The Stranger in Laboratory Culture," *American Sociological Review*, 22 (August, 1957), pp. 400–405. See p. 401.

24. SOCIAL CHARACTER (GROSS)

See also categories 7, 9, and 10 above and categories 25–32 below.

Gross, Herbert W., *The Relationship between Insecurity, Self-Acceptance, Other Direction, and Conformity Under Conditions of Differential Social Pressure*, unpublished Ph.D. dissertation, University of Buffalo, 1959.

Peterson, Richard A., "Dimensions of Social Character: An Empirical Exploration of the Riesman Typology," *Sociometry*, 27 (June, 1964), pp. 194–207. See p. 197.

25. SOCIAL CHARACTER (KASSARJIAN)

Kassarjian, Waltrud M., "A Study of Riesman's Theory of Social Character," *Sociometry*, 25 (September, 1962), pp. 213–230. See pp. 216–217.

Peterson (1964); see category 24 above.

26. SOCIAL CHARACTER: AFFILIATION-ACHIEVEMENT

Peterson, p. 200; see category 24 above.

27. SOCIAL CHARACTER: EXTROVERSION-INTROVERSION

Peterson, pp. 200–201; see category 24 above.

28. SOCIAL CHARACTER: PERSONAL PRINCIPLES

Peterson, p. 200; see category 24 above.

29. SOCIAL CHARACTER: PRAGMATISM

Peterson, p. 201; see category 24 above.

30. SOCIAL CHARACTER: SELF-OTHER SOURCES OF SOCIALIZATION

Peterson, p. 201; see category 24 above.

31. SOCIAL CHARACTER: STRUGGLE

Peterson, p. 201; see category 24 above.

32. SOCIAL CHARACTER: TASK FOCUS

Peterson, p. 200; see category 24 above.

33. THEMATIC APPERCEPTION TEST

Murray, Henry A., *Thematic Apperception Test*, Cambridge, Mass.: Harvard University Press, 1943.

Lindzey and Urdan (1954), p. 48; see category 19 above.

34. THURSTONE TEMPERAMENT SCHEDULE

Thurstone, L. L., *Thurstone Temperament Schedule*, Chicago, Ill.: Science Research Associates, 1954, pp. 1–4.

Lindzey and Urdan (1954), p. 48; see category 19 above.

Manheim, Henry L., "Intergroup Interaction as Related to Status and Leadership Differences between Groups," *Sociometry*, 23 (September, 1960), pp. 415–427. See p. 417.

PERSONALITY TRAITS: CREATIVITY

1. CREATIVITY (GUILFORD)

Guilford, J. P.,*A Revised Structure of Intellect*, Reports from the Psychological Laboratory, No. 19, Los Angeles: University of Southern California, April, 1957. See pp. 14–15.

Getzels, Jacob W., and Philip W. Jackson, "Family Environment and Cognitive Style: A Study of the Sources of Highly Intelligent and of Highly Creative Adolescents," *American Sociological Review*, 26 (June, 1961), pp. 351–359. See p. 352.

2. CREATIVITY (SEEMAN)

Seeman, Melvin, "The Intellectual and the Language of Minorities," *American Journal of Sociology*, 64 (July, 1958), pp. 25–35. See p. 34.

3. INTERPERSONAL CREATIVITY

Foote, Nelson N., and Leonard S. Cottrell, Jr., *Identity and Interpersonal Competence: A New Direction in Family Research*, Chicago: University of Chicago Press, 1955. See p. 63.

Stanton, Howard, and Eugene Litwak, "Toward the Development of a Short Form Test of Interpersonal Competence," *American Sociological Review*, 20 (December, 1955), pp. 668–674. See p. 672.

Litwak, Eugene, Gloria Count, and Edward M. Haydon, "Group Structure and Interpersonal Creativity as Factors which Reduce Errors in the Prediction of Marital Adjustment," *Social Forces*, 38 (May, 1960), pp. 308–315. See pp. 314–315.

4. MCCALLUM FORM BOARD TEST OF CREATIVITY

McCallum, Margaret E., *An Experimental Study of Creativity in the Pre-School Child*, unpublished M.A. thesis, University of Toronto, 1954.

Northway, Mary L., and Margaret McCallum Rooks, "Creativity and Sociometric Status in Children," *Sociometry*, 18 (December, 1955), pp. 194–201. See p. 196.

PERSONALITY TRAITS: DOMINANCE

SEE ALSO

Personality: General

1. ASCENDANCE

Guilford, J. P. and Wayne S. Zimmerman, *The Guilford-Zimmerman Temperament Survey*, Beverly Hills, Calif.: Sheridan Supply Company.

Berkowitz, Leonard, "Personality and Social Position," *Sociometry*, 19 (December, 1956), pp. 210–222. See p. 211.

Guilford, J. P. and Wayne S. Zimmerman, "Fourteen Dimensions of Temperament," *Psychological Monographs*, 70 (No. 10, 1956), pp. 1–26. See p. 10.

Tuckman, Bruce W., "Personality Structure, Group Composition and Group Functioning," *Sociometry*, 27 (December, 1964), pp. 469–489. See p. 478.

2. DOMINANCE (BERNREUTER)

Bernreuter, Robert G., *The Personality Inventory*, Palo Alto, Calif.: Consulting Psychologists Press, Inc.

Bernreuter, Robert G., "The Theory and Construction of the Personality Inventory," *Journal of Social Psychology*, 4 (1933), pp. 387–404. See pp. 389–394.

Heer, David M., "Dominance and the Working Wife," *Social Forces*, 36 (May, 1958), pp. 341–347. See p. 344.

3. DOMINANCE (CATTELL)

Cattell, Raymond B., *Description and Measurement of Personality*, New York: World Book Co., 1956.

Freeman, Howard E., and Ozzie G. Simmons, "Wives, Mothers, and the Posthospital Performance of Mental Patients," *Social Forces*, 37 (December, 1958), pp. 153–159. See p. 156.

4. DOMINANCE (GOUGH, MCCLOSKY, MEIHL)

See also Crime and Delinquency, category 7.

Gough, Harrison G., Herbert McClosky, and P. E. Meehl, "A Personality Scale for Dominance," *Journal of Abnormal and Social Psychology*, 46 (July, 1951), pp. 360–366. See pp. 361–366.

Lindzey, Gardner, and James A. Urdan, "Personality and Social Choice," *Sociometry*, 17 (February, 1954), pp. 47–63. See p. 49.

Gough, Harrison G., *California Psychological Inventory*, Palo Alto, Calif.: Consulting Psychologists Press, Inc., 1956.

Vincent, Clark E., "Socioeconomic Status and Familial Variables in Mail Questionnaire Responses," *American Journal of Sociology*, 69 (May, 1964), pp. 647–653. See pp. 647–649.

McClosky, Herbert, and John H. Schaar, "Psychological Dimensions of Anomy," *American Sociological Review*, 30 (February, 1965), pp. 14–40. See pp. 30–31.

5. DOMINANCE (LEARY)

Leary, Timothy, *Interpersonal Diagnosis of Personality*, New York: Ronald Press, 1957.

Smelser, William T., "Adolescent and Adult Occupational Choices as a Function of Family Socioeconomic History," *Sociometry*, 26 (December, 1963), pp. 393–409. See pp. 405–406.

6. DOMINANCE (HARE, BALES)

Hare, A. Paul, and Robert F. Bales, "Seating Position and Small Group Interaction, *Sociometry*, 26 (December, 1963), pp. 480–486. See pp. 481–482.

7. DOMINANCE (HEISS)

Heiss, Jerold S., "Degree of Intimacy and Male-Female Interaction," *Sociometry*, 25 (June, 1962), pp. 197–208. See p. 200.

8. DOMINANCE (MURRAY)

Murray, Henry A. (ed.), *Explorations in Personality*, New York: Oxford University Press, 1938.

Winch, Robert F., Thomas Ktsanes, and Virginia Ktsanes, "The Theory of Complementary Needs in Mate Selection: An Analytic and Descriptive Study," *American Sociological Review*, 19 (June, 1954), pp. 241–249. See p. 241.

Ktsanes, Thomas, "Mate Selection on the Basis of Personality Type: A Study Utilizing an Empirical Typology of Personality," *American Sociological Review*, 20 (October, 1955), pp. 547–551. See p. 548.

Winch, Robert F., "The Theory of Complementary Needs in Mate Selection: Final Results on the Test of the General Hypothesis," *American Sociological Review*, 20 (October, 1955), pp. 552–555. See p. 552.

9. DOMINANCE (ROSENGREN)

Rosengren, William R., "The Self in the Emotionally Disturbed," *American Journal of Sociology*, 66 (March, 1961), pp. 454–462. See p. 456.

PERSONALITY TRAITS: MASCULINITY-FEMININITY

1. ANTIFEMININITY IN MEN

Allen, Dean A., "Antifemininity in Men," *American Sociological Review*, 19 (October, 1954), pp. 591–593. See p. 592.

2. MASCULINITY-FEMININITY (BRIM)

Brim, Orville G., Jr., "Family Structure and Sex Role Learning by Children: A Further Analysis of Helen Koch's Data," *Sociometry*, 21 (March, 1958), pp. 1–16. See pp. 6–7.

3. MASCULINITY-FEMININITY (GOUGH)

See also Crime and Delinquency, Category 7.

Gough, Harrison G., "Identifying Psychological Femininity," *Educational Psychological Measurement*, 12 (Autumn, 1952), pp. 427–439. See pp. 429–430.

Lindzey, Gardner, and James A. Urdan, "Personality and Social Choice," *Sociometry*, 17 (February, 1954), pp. 47–63. See p. 49.

Gough, Harrison G., *California Psychological Inventory*, Palo Alto, Calif.: Consulting Psychological Press, 1956.

Vincent, Clark E., "Socioeconomic Status and Familial Variables in Mail Questionnaire Responses," *American Journal of Sociology*, 69 (May, 1964), pp. 647–653. See pp. 647–649.

4. MASCULINITY-FEMININITY (HATHAWAY, MCKINLEY)

Hathaway, Starke R., and J. C. McKinley, *The Minnesota Multiphasic Inventory*, Minneapolis, Minn.: University of Minnesota Press, 1943.

Lundy, Richard M., "Self-Perceptions Regarding Masculinity-Femininity and Descriptions of Same and Opposite Sex Sociometric Choices," *Sociometry*, 21 (September, 1958), pp. 238–246. See p. 239.

5. MASCULINITY-FEMININITY (KUDER)

Kuder, G. F., *Kuder Preference Record—Vocational,* Chicago, Ill.: Science Research Associates, 1946.

Martinson, Floyd M., "Ego Deficiency as a Factor in Marriage," *American Sociological Review,* 20 (April, 1955), pp. 161–164. See p. 163.

6. MASCULINITY-FEMININITY (TERMAN, MILES)

Terman, Lewis M., and Catharine C. Miles, *Manual of Information and Directions for Use of Attitude-Interest Analysis Test* (M-F Test), New York: McGraw-Hill Book Co., 1938, pp. 1–19.

Parker, Frederick B., "A Comparison of the Sex Temperaments of Alcoholic and Moderate Drinkers," *American Sociological Review,* 24 (June, 1959), pp. 366–374. See pp. 368–369.

6. PSYCHOLOGICAL FEMININITY

Ferdinand, Theodore N., "Psychological Femininity and Political Liberalism," *Sociometry,* 27 (March, 1964), pp. 75–87. See pp. 78–79.

7. SEX ROLE CONSERVATISM

Sutcliffe, J. P., and M. Haberman, "Factors Influencing Choice in Role Conflict Situations," *American Sociological Review,* 21 (December, 1956), pp. 695–703. See p. 702.

PERSONALITY TRAITS: MOTIVES AND NEEDS

SEE ALSO

Achievement Motivation

Marital Adjustment and Courtship

Personality: General

1. AFFILIATION MOTIVE

Murray, Henry A., *Thematic Apperception Test*, Cambridge, Mass.: Harvard University Press, 1943.

Shipley, Thomas E., Jr., and Joseph Veroff, "A Projective Measure of Need for Affiliation," in John W. Atkinson (ed.), *Motives in Fantasy, Action, and Society*, Princeton, N.J.: D. Van Nostrand, 1958, pp. 83–94.

Crockett (1962); see category 28 below.

2. COMPLEMENTARY NEEDS

See categories 24, 25, and 26 below.

Murray (1943), see category 1 above.

Winch and More (1956); see category 3 below.

3. COVERT MOTIVATION (MODIFIED TAT)

Aron, Betty, *A Manual for Analysis of the Thematic Apperception Test*, Berkeley, Calif.: Willis E. Berg, 1949.

Winch, Robert F., and Douglas M. More, "Quantitative Analysis of Qualitative Data in the Assessment of Motivation: Reliability, Congruence, and Validity," *American Journal of Sociology*, 61 (March, 1956), pp. 445–452. See p. 447.

4. EXPRESSED AFFECTION

Schutz, William C., *FIRO: A Three Dimensional Theory of Interpersonal Behavior*, New York: Rinehart and Co., 1958, pp. 57–66.

Scarr, Harry A., "Measures of Particularism," *Sociometry*, 27 (December, 1964), pp. 413–432. See p. 417.

5. EXPRESSED CONTROL

Schutz (1958); see category 4 above.
Scarr (1964); see category 4 above.

6. EXPRESSED INCLUSION

Schutz (1958); see category 4 above.
Scarr (1964); see category 4 above.

7. GRATIFICATION DEFERMENT

Rosengren, William R., "The Self in the Emotionally Disturbed," *American Journal of Sociology*, 66 (March, 1961), pp. 454–462. See p. 456.

8. GRATIFICATION DEFERMENT: AFFILIATION

Straus, Murray A., "Deferred Gratification, Social Class, and the Achievement Syndrome," *American Sociological Review*, 27 (June, 1962), pp. 326–335. See p. 329.

9. GRATIFICATION DEFERMENT: AGGRESSION

Straus; see category 8 above.

10. GRATIFICATION DEFERMENT: CONSUMPTION

Straus; see category 8 above.

11. GRATIFICATION DEFERMENT: ECONOMIC INDEPENDENCE

Straus; see category 8 above:

12. GRATIFICATION DEFERMENT: SEXUAL EXPRESSION

Straus; see category 8 above.

13. MOBILITY MOTIVATION

Burgess, E. W., G. C. Hoyt, and C. R. Manley, "The Construction of Scales for the Measurement of Migration after Retirement," *Sociometry*, 18 (December, 1955), pp. 360–367. See pp. 361–362.

14. MOTIVATION TO ADVANCE KNOWLEDGE

Glaser, Barney G., "The Local-Cosmopolitan Scientist," *American Journal of Sociology*, 69 (November, 1963), pp. 249–259. See p. 251.

15. MOTIVATIONAL COMMITMENT—VALUATION OF MEMBER-
SHIP

Kelley, Harold H., and Edmund H. Volkart, "The Resistance to
Change in Group Anchored Attitudes," *American Sociological Review*, 17 (August, 1952), pp. 453–465. See p. 459.

Emerson, Richard M., "Power-Dependence Relations: Two Experiments," *Sociometry*, 27 (September, 1964), pp. 282–298.
See p. 284.

16. NEED AFFILIATION

French, Elizabeth G., and Irene Chadwick, "Some Characteristics
of Affiliation Motivation," *Journal of Abnormal and Social
Psychology*, 52 (May, 1956), pp. 296–300. See pp. 296–297.

Berkowitz, Leonard, and Robert C. Howard, "Reactions to Opinion Deviates as Affected by Affiliation Need (n) and Group
Member Interdependence," *Sociometry*, 22 (March, 1959),
pp. 81–91. See p. 82.

17. NEED ASSESSMENT

Secord, Paul F., and Carl W. Backman, "Interpersonal Congruency, Perceived Similarity, and Friendship," *Sociometry*, 27
(June, 1964), pp. 115–127. See pp. 118–120.

18. NEED COMPLEMENTARITY

Schutz (1958); see category 4 above.

Kerckhoff, Alan, and Keith E. Davis, "Value Consensus and Need
Complementarity in Mate Selection," *American Sociological
Review*, 27 (June, 1962), pp. 295–303. See p. 297.

19. NEED DEPENDENCY

Murray (1943); see category 1 above.

Shipley, T. E., and J. Veroff, "A Projective Measure of Need
Affiliation," *Journal of Experimental Psychology*, 43 (May,
1952), pp. 349–356. See pp. 349–352.

Shipley and Veroff (1958); see category 1 above.

Mills, Theodore M., "The Coalition Pattern in Three Person
Groups," *American Sociological Review*, 19 (December,
1954), pp. 657–667. See p. 667.

20. NEED INTENSITY

Ktsanes, Thomas, "Mate Selection on the Basis of Personality Type: A Study Utilizing an Empirical Typology of Personality," *American Sociological Review*, 20 (October, 1955), pp. 547–551. See p. 548.

21. NEED INVIOLACY

McClosky, Herbert, and John H. Schaar, "Psychological Dimensions of Anomy," *American Sociological Review*, 30 (February, 1965), pp. 14–40. See pp. 30–31.

22. NEED FOR SELF ENHANCEMENT

Murray (1943); see category 1 above.

McClelland, David C., John W. Atkinson, Russell Clark, and Edgar Lowell, *The Achievement Motive*, New York: Appleton-Century-Crofts, 1953, pp. 146–151.

Shipley and Veroff (1958); see category 1 above.

Mills (1954); see category 19 above.

23. NEEDS FOR SELF ASSERTION

Hoffman, Lois Wladis, Sidney Rosen, and Ronald Lippitt, "Parental Coerciveness, Child Autonomy, and Child's Role at School," *Sociometry*, 23 (March, 1960), pp. 15–22. See p. 19.

24. PERSONAL PREFERENCE SCHEDULE

Edwards, Allen L., *Edwards Personal Preference Schedule*, New York: The Psychological Corporation, 1954.

The *Edwards Personal Preference Schedule* (PPS) is designed to measure the 15 personality variables set forth by Murray and his associates (Henry A. Murray, ed., *Explorations in Personality*, New York: Oxford University Press, 1938). These variables are as follows: (1) Achievement (ach); (2) Deference (def); (3) Order (ord); (4) Exhibition (exh); (5) Autonomy (aut); (6) Affiliation (aff); (7) Intraception (int); (8) Succorance (suc); (9) Dominance (dom); (10) Abasement (aba); (11) Nurturance (nur); (12) Change (chg); (13) Endurance (end); (14) Heterosexuality (het); and (15) Aggression (agg).

The PPS consists of 225 "pairs of statements about things that you may or may not like; about ways in which you may or may not feel." The subject is asked to choose one of two alternatives indicating which of the members of each pair of statements most nearly describes his preferences or feelings. Edwards provides the following example:

A I like to talk about myself to others.
B I like to work toward some goal that I have set for myself.

In this manner "Each of the 15 personality variables in the PPS is paired twice with each of the other variables."

The instructions for scoring the PPS are given in a separate manual which accompanies the test. The manual also includes information on plotting the results, interpretation of the scores, norms, reliability, and validity.

Copies of the PPS and the accompanying manual may be purchased from The Psychological Corporation, 304 East 45th Street, New York, New York 10017. For an extensive bibliography concerning the PPS (326 citations), and for reviews and assessments of the PPS, see Oscar K. Buros (ed.), *The Sixth Mental Measurements Yearbook*, Highland Park, N.J.: Gryphon Press, 1965, pp. 381–387.

Bowerman, Charles E., and Barbara R. Day, "A Test of a Theory of Complementary Needs as Applied to Couples during Courtship," *American Sociological Review*, 21 (October, 1956), pp. 602–605. See p. 603.

Back, Kurt W., R. E. Coker, Jr., T. G. Donnelly, and B. S. Phillips, "Public Health as a Career of Medicine: Secondary Choice within a Profession," *American Sociological Review*, 23 (October, 1958), pp. 533–541. See p. 536.

Backman, Carl W., Paul F. Secord, and Jerry R. Pierce, "Resistance to Change in the Self-Concept as a Function of Consensus among Significant Others," *Sociometry*, 26 (March, 1963), pp. 102–111. See pp. 105–106.

Levinger, George, "Task and Social Behavior in Marriage," *Sociometry*, 27 (December, 1964), pp. 433–448. See pp. 442–443.

Altman, Irwin, and William H. Haythorn, "Interpersonal Exchange in Isolation," *Sociometry*, 28 (December, 1965), pp. 411–426. See pp. 414 and 420.

25. PERSONALITY NEEDS: CASE HISTORY ANALYSIS

Winch R. F., "The Theory of Complementary Needs in Mate-Selection: Final Results on the Test of the General Hypothesis," *American Sociological Review*, 20 (October, 1955), pp. 552–555. See p. 552.

26. PERSONALITY NEEDS: CONTENT ANALYSIS

Winch; see category 25 above.

27. PERSONALITY NEEDS: TAT

Winch, R. F., Thomas Ktsanes, and Virginia Ktsanes, "The Theory of Complementary Needs in Mate Selection: An Analytic and Descriptive Study," *American Sociological Review*, 19 (June, 1954), pp. 241–249. See p. 248.

Winch; see category 25 above.

28. POWER MOTIVES (MODIFIED TAT)

Murray (1943); see category 1 above.

Shipley and Veroff (1958); see category 1 above.

Crockett, Harry J., Jr., "The Achievement Motive and Differential Occupational Mobility in the United States," *American Sociological Review*, 27 (April, 1962), pp. 191–204. See p. 199.

29. TASK MOTIVATION

Turk, Herman, "Instrumental Values and the Popularity of Instrumental Leaders," *Social Forces*, 39 (May, 1961), pp. 252–260. See p. 255.

30. WANTED AFFECTION

Schutz (1958); see category 4 above.

Sarbin, Theodore R., and Vernon L. Allen, "Role Enactment, Audience Feedback, and Attitude Change," *Sociometry*, 27 (June, 1964), pp. 183–193. See p. 185.

Scarr (1964); see category 4 above.

31. WANTED CONTROL

Schutz (1958); see category 4 above.

Scarr (1964); see category 4 above.

32. WANTED INCLUSION

Schutz (1958); see category 4 above.

Sarbin and Allen (1964); see category 30 above.

Scarr (1964); see category 4 above.

PERSONALITY TRAITS: SOCIABILITY-WITHDRAWAL

SEE ALSO
Personality: General

1. ANTI-SOCIAL TENDENCIES

Thorpe, Louis P., Willis W. Clark, and Ernest W. Tiegs, *California Test of Personality*, Los Angeles, Calif.: California Test Bureau.

Photiadis, John D., and Jeanne Biggar, "Religiosity, Education, and Ethnic Distance," *American Journal of Sociology*, 67 (May, 1962), pp. 666–672. See p. 669.

Photiadis, John D., and Arthur L. Johnson, "Orthodoxy, Church Participation and Authoritarianism," *American Journal of Sociology*, 69 (November, 1963), pp. 244–248. See p. 244.

2. NARCISSISTIC-OTHER ORIENTED

Rosengren, William R., "The Self in the Emotionally Disturbed," *American Journal of Sociology*, 66 (March, 1961), pp. 454–462. See p. 456.

3. REJECTING-AFFILIATIVE

Rosengren; see category 2 above.

4. SOCIABILITY (GOUGH)

See also Crime and Delinquency, category 7.

Gough, Harrison G., *California Psychological Inventory*, Palo Alto, Calif.: Consulting Psychologists Press, Inc., 1956.

Vincent, Clark E., "Socioeconomic Status and Familial Variables in Mail Questionnaire Responses," *American Journal of Sociology*, 69 (May, 1964), pp. 647–653. See pp. 647–649.

5. SOCIABILITY (GUILFORD, ZIMMERMAN)

Guilford, J. P., and Wayne S. Zimmerman, *The Guilford-*

Zimmerman Temperament Survey, Beverly Hills, Calif.: Sheridan Supply Company.

Friedrichs, Robert W., "Alter vs. Ego," *American Sociological Review,* 25 (August, 1960), pp. 496–508. See p. 499.

6. SOCIABILITY (KELLY)

Kelly, E. Lowell, "A 36 Trait Personality Rating Scale," *Journal of Psychology,* 9 (January, 1940), pp. 97–102. See pp. 97–98.

Westoff, Charles F., Philip C. Sagi, and E. Lowell Kelly, "Fertility through Twenty Years of Marriage: A Study of Predictive Possibilites," *American Sociological Review,* 23 (October, 1958), pp. 549–556. See p. 554.

7. SOCIABILITY COMPLEX

Levine, Gene Norman, and Leila A. Sussmann, "Social Class and Sociability in Fraternity Pledging," *American Journal of Sociology,* 65 (January, 1960), pp. 391–399. See p. 393.

8. WITHDRAWAL

Langner, Thomas S., and Stanley T. Michael, *Life Stress and Mental Health,* London and New York: The Free Press of Glencoe, Collier-Macmillan Limited, 1963, p. 43.

Freeman, Howard E., and Ozzie G. Simmons, "Wives, Mothers, and the Posthospital Performance of Mental Patients," *Social Forces,* 37 (December, 1958), pp. 153–159. See p. 155.

9. WITHDRAWAL TENDENCIES

Thorpe, Clark, and Tiegs; see category 1 above.

Photiadis and Biggar (1962); see category 1 above.

Photiadis and Johnson (1963); see category 1 above.

PERSONALITY TRAITS: VARIOUS CATEGORIES

SEE ALSO

Interpersonal Relations
Marital Adjustment and Courtship
Personality: General
Self Image, Self Concept, and Related Measures

1. ACQUIESCENCE

McClosky, Herbert, and John H. Schaar, "Psychological Dimensions of Anomy," *American Sociological Review*, 30 (February, 1965), pp. 14–40. See p. 27.

2. ACTIVITY-PASSIVITY

Rosengren, William R., "The Self in the Emotionally Disturbed," *American Journal of Sociology*, 66 (March, 1961), pp. 454–462. See p. 456.

Shuval, Judith T., "Value Orientations of Immigrants to Israel," *Sociometry*, 26 (June, 1963), pp. 247–259. See p. 251.

3. ALTRUISM

Friedrichs, Robert W., "Alter vs. Ego," *American Sociological Review*, 25 (August, 1960), pp. 490–508. See pp. 498–499.

4. ATTRACTIVENESS

Leik, Robert K., " 'Irrelevant' Aspects of Stooge Behavior: Implications for Leadership Studies and Experimental Methodology," *Sociometry*, 28 (September, 1965), pp. 259–271. See pp. 266–267.

5. AUTISM

Geiger, Kent, and Robert Sokol, "Social Norms in Television

Watching," *American Journal of Sociology*, 65 (September, 1959), pp. 174–181. See p. 178.

6. AUTONOMY-COERCIVENESS

Hoffman, Lois Wladis, Sidney Rosen, and Ronald Lippitt, "Parental Coerciveness, Child Autonomy, and Child's Role at School," *Sociometry*, 23 (March, 1960), pp. 15–22. See pp. 16–17.

7. BLAME, CLOSURE ON

Henry, Andrew F., "Family Role Structure and Self Blame," *Social Forces*, 35 (October, 1956), pp. 34–38. See p. 37.

8. BLAME OTHER

Henry (1956), p. 34; see category 7 above.

Rosengren (1961); see category 2 above.

9. BLAME SELF

Henry; see category 7 above.

10. COGNITIVE CONSISTENCY

Rosenberg, M. J., "Cognitive Structure and Attitudinal Affect," *Journal of Abnormal and Social Psychology*, 53 (November, 1956), pp. 367–372. See pp. 367–368.

Scott, William A., "Cognitive Consistency, Response Reinforcement and Attitude Change," *Sociometry*, 22 (September, 1959), pp. 219–229. See p. 222.

11. CONTEMPT FOR WEAKNESS

McClosky and Schaar, pp. 31–32 and 37; see category 1 above.

12. CRUELTY

Nettler, Gwynn, "Cruelty, Dignity, and Determinism," *American Sociological Review*, 24 (June, 1959), pp. 375–384. See p. 378.

13. DEFENSIVENESS

Smith, Ewart E., "The Effects of Clear and Unclear Role Expectations on Group Productivity and Defensiveness," *Journal of Abnormal and Social Psychology*, 55 (September, 1957), pp. 213–217.

Goodchilds, Jacqueline D., and Ewart E. Smith, "The Effects of

Unemployment as Mediated by Social Status," *Sociometry*, 26 (September, 1963), pp. 287–293. See p. 290.

14. DISTRUST OF PEOPLE

Rosenberg, Morris, *Occupations and Values*, New York: The Free Press of Glencoe, 1957.

Elder, Glen H., Jr., "Role Relations, Sociocultural Environment, and Autocratic Family Ideology," *Sociometry*, 28 (June, 1965), pp. 173–196. See p. 192.

15. DOGMATISM

See also Authoritarianism.

Rokeach, Milton, *The Open and Closed Mind*, New York: Basic Books, 1960, pp. 71–80.

As conceived by Rokeach, "The primary purpose of this scale is to measure individual differences in openness or closedness of belief systems." (p. 71) The term dogmatism is used to signify the extent to which an individual has "an authoritarian outlook on life, an intolerance toward those with opposing beliefs, and a sufferance of those with similar beliefs." (p. 4) Hence, the Dogmatism Scale may be thought of as a general measure of authoritarianism, intolerance, and closedmindedness.

Rokeach discusses five forms of the Dogmatism Scale (Forms A-E) but presents only the 66 items comprising Form D, 40 items of which comprise Form E. Short forms of this scale are to be found in papers by Schulze (1962) and Troldahl and Powell (1965), cited below.

This scale attempts to measure many different aspects of dogmatism. Rokeach discusses several basic dimensions and subdimensions of open and closed belief systems and strives to present items reflecting the properties of each. For example, items 3–8 (below) are designed to measure (p. 74) "the coexistence of contradictions within the belief system;" items 11–14 are intended to measure (p. 75) "beliefs regarding the aloneness, isolation, and helplessness of man;" while items 58–60 (p. 79) focus upon "attitude toward the past, present, and future." The subdimensions of this scale are not scored, however, as separate scales. Agreement with any item is scored as "closed," disagreement is scored as "open," and the sum of the scores on all items yields the respondent's level of dogmatism.

Rokeach reports a corrected odd-even reliability of .91 for Form D of the Dogmatism Scale and corrected reliabilities ranging from .68 to .93 for Form E.

Below are given the instructions and items for Forms D and E of The Dogmatism Scale.

THE DOGMATISM SCALE

The following is a study of what the general public thinks and feels about a number of important social and personal questions. The best answer to each statement below is your *personal opinion*. We have tried to cover many different and opposing points of view; you may find yourself agreeing strongly with some of the statements, disagreeing just as strongly with others, and perhaps uncertain about others; whether you agree or disagree with any statement, you can be sure that many people feel the same as you do.

Mark each statement in the left margin according to how much you agree or disagree with it. Please mark every one. Write +1, +2, +3, or −1, −2, −3, depending on how you feel in each case.

+1: I AGREE A LITTLE −1: I DISAGREE A LITTLE
+2: I AGREE ON THE WHOLE −2: I DISAGREE ON THE WHOLE
+3: I AGREE VERY MUCH −3: I DISAGREE VERY MUCH

*1. The United States and Russia have just about nothing in common.
2. Communism and Catholicism have nothing in common.
3. The principles I have come to believe in are quite different from those believed in by most people.
4. In a heated discussion people have a way of bringing up irrelevant issues rather than sticking to the main issue.
*5. The highest form of government is a democracy and the highest form of democracy is a government run by those who are most intelligent.
*6. Even though freedom of speech for all groups is a worthwhile goal, it is unfortunately necessary to restrict the freedom of certain political groups.
7. While the use of force is wrong by and large, it is sometimes the only way possible to advance a noble ideal.
8. Even though I have a lot of faith in the intelligence and wisdom of the common man, I must say that the masses behave stupidly at times.
    * The items marked by asterisks comprise Form E of the scale.

*9. It is only natural that a person would have a much better acquaintance with ideas he believes in than with ideas he opposes.

10. There are certain "isms" which are really the same even though those who believe in these "isms" try to tell you they are different.

*11. Man on his own is a helpless and miserable creature.

*12. Fundamentally, the world we live in is a pretty lonesome place.

*13. Most people just don't give a "damn" for others.

*14. I'd like it if I could find someone who would tell me how to solve my personal problems.

*15. It is only natural for a person to be rather fearful of the future.

*16. There is so much to be done and so little time to do it in.

*17. Once I get wound up in a heated discussion I just can't stop.

*18. In a discussion I often find it necessary to repeat myself several times to make sure I am being understood.

*19. In a heated discussion I generally become so absorbed in what I am going to say that I forget to listen to what the others are saying.

20. In a discussion I sometimes interrupt others too much in my eagerness to put across my own point of view.

*21. It is better to be a dead hero than to be a live coward.

22. My hardest battles are with myself.

23. At times I think I am no good at all.

24. I am afraid of people who want to find out what I'm really like for fear they'll be disappointed in me.

*25. While I don't like to admit this even to myself, my secret ambition is to become a great man, like Einstein, or Beethoven or Shakespeare.

*26. The main thing in life is for a person to want to do something important.

*27. If given the chance I would do something of great benefit to the world.

28. If I had to choose between happiness and greatness, I'd choose greatness.

29. It's all too true that people just won't practice what they preach.

30. Most people are failures and it is the system which is responsible for this.

31. I have often felt that strangers were looking at me critically.

32. It is only natural for a person to have a guilty conscience.

33. People say insulting and vulgar things about me.

34. I am sure I am being talked about.

*35. In the history of mankind there have probably been just a handful of really great thinkers.

*36. There are a number of people I have come to hate because of the things they stand for.

*37. A man who does not believe in some great cause has not really lived.

*38. It is only when a person devotes himself to an ideal or cause that life becomes meaningful.

*39. Of all the different philosophies which exist in this world there is probably only one which is correct.

*40. A person who gets enthusiastic about too many causes is likely to be a pretty "wishy-washy" sort of person.

*41. To compromise with our political opponents is dangerous because it usually leads to the betrayal of our own side.

*42. When it comes to differences of opinion in religion we must be careful not to compromise with those who believe differently from the way we do.

*43. In times like these, a person must be pretty selfish if he considers primarily his own happiness.

44. To compromise with our political opponents is to be guilty of appeasement.

*45. The worst crime a person could commit is to attack publicly the people who believe in the same thing he does.

*46. In times like these it is often necessary to be more on guard against ideas put out by people or groups in one's own camp than by those in the opposing camp.

*47. A group which tolerates too much differences of opinion among its own members cannot exist for long.

*48. There are two kinds of people in this world: those who are for the truth and those who are against the truth.

*49. My blood boils whenever a person stubbornly refuses to admit he's wrong.

*50. A person who thinks primarily of his own happiness is beneath contempt.

*51. Most of the ideas which get printed nowadays aren't worth the paper they are printed on.

52. I sometimes have a tendency to be too critical of the ideas of others.

*53. In this complicated world of ours the only way we can know what's going on is to rely on leaders or experts who can be trusted.

*54. It is often desirable to reserve judgment about what's going on until one has had a chance to hear the opinions of those one respects.

*55. In the long run the best way to live is to pick friends and associates whose tastes and beliefs are the same as one's own.

56. There's no use wasting your money on newspapers which you know in advance are just plain propaganda.
57. Young people should not have too easy access to books which are likely to confuse them.
*58. The present is all too often full of unhappiness. It is only the future that counts.
59. It is by returning to our glorious and forgotten past that real social progress can be achieved.
60. To achieve the happiness of mankind in the future it is sometimes necessary to put up with injustices in the present.
*61. If a man is to accomplish his mission in life it is sometimes necessary to gamble "all or nothing at all."
*62. Unfortunately, a good many people with whom I have discussed important social and moral problems don't really understand what's going on.
*63. Most people just don't know what's good for them.
64. There is nothing new under the sun.
65. To one who really takes the trouble to understand the world he lives in, it's an easy matter to predict future events.

Schulze, Rolf H. K., "A Shortened Version of the Rokeach Dogmatism Scale," *Journal of Psychological Studies*, 13 (1962), pp. 93–97.

Powell, Frederic A., "Open and Closed-Mindedness and the Ability to Differentiate Source and Message," *Journal of Abnormal and Social Psychology*, 65 (July, 1962), pp. 61–64. See pp. 61–62.

Troldahl, Verling C., *Mediated Communication and Personal Influence: A Field Experiment*, unpublished Ph.D. dissertation, University of Minnesota, 1963.

Tuckman, Bruce W., "Personality Structure, Group Composition, and Group Functioning," *Sociometry*, 27 (December, 1964), pp. 469–487. See p. 478.

Troldahl, Verling C., and Frederic A. Powell, "A Short-Form Dogmatism Scale for Use in Field Studies," *Social Forces*, 44 (December, 1965), pp. 211–214.

Altman, Irwin, and William H. Haythorn, "Interpersonal Exchange in Isolation," *Sociometry*, 28 (December, 1965), pp. 411–426. See p. 414.

16. EMPATHY

Dymond, Rosalind F., "A Scale for Measurement of Empathic Ability," *Journal of Consulting Psychology*, 13 (April, 1949), pp. 127–133. See p. 127.

Vernon, Glenn M., and Robert L. Stewart, "Empathy as a Process in the Dating Situation," *American Sociological Review*, 22 (February, 1957), pp. 48–52. See p. 49.

Hobart, Charles W. and Nancy Fahlberg, "The Measurement of Empathy," *American Journal of Sociology*, 70 (March, 1965), pp. 595–603. See p. 595.

17. EMPATHY, COMPOUNDED

Hobart and Fahlberg (1965), pp. 600–601; see category 16 above.

18. EMPATHY, DEVIATION

Hobart and Fahlberg (1965), pp. 595, 597, and 601; see category 16 above.

19. EMPATHY, REFINED

Hastorf, A. H., and I. E. Bender, "A Caution Respecting the Measurement of Empathic Ability," *Journal of Abnormal and Social Psychology*, 47 (April, 1952), pp. 574–576.

Hobart and Fahlberg (1965), pp. 597–598, and 601; see category 16 above.

20. EMPATHY RATIO

Hobart and Fahlberg (1965), pp. 600–601; see category 16 above.

21. FAITH IN PEOPLE (MCCLOSKY, SCHAAR)

McClosky and Schaar, pp. 33–34; see category 1 above.

22. FAITH IN PEOPLE (ROSENBERG)

See also category 60 below.

Rosenberg, Morris, "Misanthropy and Political Ideology," *American Sociological Review*, 21 (December, 1956), pp. 690–695. See p. 690.

Rosenberg (1957); see category 14 above.

Elder (1965); see category 14 above.

23. FATALISM

Quinney, Richard, "Political Conservatism, Alienation, and Fatalism: Contingencies of Social Status and Religious Fundamentalism," *Sociometry*, 27 (September, 1964), pp. 372–381. See p. 380.

24. GOAL TENACITY

Schiff, Herbert, "Judgmental Response Sets in the Perception of Sociometric Status," *Sociometry*, 17 (August, 1954), pp. 207–227. See p. 214.

25. HAPPINESS

Lindzey, Gardner, and James A. Urdan, "Personality and Social Choice," *Sociometry*, 17 (February, 1954), pp. 47–63. See p. 49.

Golding, H. J., "On the Avowal and Projection of Happiness," *Journal of Personality*, 23 (September, 1954), pp. 30–47. See pp. 34–36.

26. HOSTILITY

Hoffman, Rosen, and Lippitt, p. 19; see category 6 above.

27. INFLEXIBILITY

McClosky and Schaar, pp. 28–29; see category 1 above.

28. INHIBITION

Slater, Phillip E., "Contrasting Correlates of Group Size," *Sociometry*, 21 (June, 1958), pp. 129–139. See p. 136.

29. INTERNAL-EXTERNAL CONTROL

See also Anomia and Alienation.

Rotter, Julian B., Melvin Seeman, and Shepard Liverant, "Internal versus External Control of Reinforcements: A Major Variable of Behavior Theory," in N. F. Washburne (ed.), *Decisions, Values, and Groups*, vol. 2, New York: Macmillan Co., 1962, pp. 473–516.

DeCharms, Richard, Virginia Carpenter, and Aharon Kuperman, "The 'Origin-Pawn' Variable in Personal Perception," *Sociometry*, 28 (September, 1965), pp. 241–258. See pp. 248–252 and 253.

30. INTOLERANCE OF HUMAN FRAILTY

McClosky and Schaar, pp. 31–32; see category 1 above.

31. INTELLECTUALITY

McClosky and Schaar, pp. 26–27; see category 1 above.

32. LIE SCALE

Hathaway, Starke R., and J. C. McKinley, *The Minnesota Multiphasic Personality Inventory*, Minneapolis, Minn.: University of Minnesota Press, 1943.

Meehl, Paul E., and Starke R. Hathaway, "The K Factor as a Suppressor Variable on the Minnesota Multiphasic Personality Inventory," *Journal of Applied Psychology*, 30 (October, 1946), pp. 525–564.

Smith, Ewart E., "Defensiveness, Insight and the K Scale," *Journal of Consulting Psychology*, 23 (June, 1959), pp. 275–277.

Heilbrun, Alfred B., Jr., "The Psychological Significance of the MMPI K Scale in a Normal Population," *Journal of Consulting Psychology*, 25 (December, 1961), pp. 486–491.

Nye, F. Ivan, and Alan E. Bayer, "Some Recent Trends in Family Research," *Social Forces*, 41 (March, 1963), pp. 290–301. See pp. 298–299.

33. MACHIAVELLIANISM

Christie, Richard, and Robert K. Merton, "Procedures for the Sociological Study of the Value Climate of Medical Schools," *Journal of Medical Education*, 33 (October, 1958), pp. 125–153.

Exline, Ralph, John Thibaut, Carole Brannon, and Peter Gumpert, "Visual Interaction in Relation to Machiavellianism and an Unethical Act" (Abstract), *American Psychologist*, 16 (July, 1961), p. 396.

Kutner, Bernard, and Norman B. Gordon, "Cognitive Functioning and Prejudice: A Nine-Year Follow-Up Study," *Sociometry*, 27 (March, 1964), pp. 66–74. See p. 68.

Singer, Jerome E., "The Use of Manipulative Strategies: Machiavellianism and Attractiveness," *Sociometry*, 27 (June, 1964), pp. 128–150. See pp. 129, and 130–131.

Tuckman (1964); see category 15 above.

34. MATURE NURTURANCE

Ktsanes, Thomas, "Mate Selection on the Basis of Personality

Type: A Study Utilizing an Empirical Typology of Personality," *American Sociological Review*, 20 (October, 1955), pp. 547–551. See p. 550.

35. MYSTICISM

McClosky and Schaar, pp. 26–27; see category 1 above.

36. NONVERBAL-VERBAL

Rosengren (1961); see category 2 above.

37. OPTIMISM

Kelly, E. Lowell, "A 36 Trait Personality Rating Scale," *Journal of Psychology*, 9 (January, 1940), pp. 97–102. See pp. 97–100.

Westoff, Charles F., Philip C. Sagi, and E. Lowell Kelly, "Fertility through Twenty Years of Marriage: A Study of Predictive Possibilities," *American Sociological Review*, 23 (October, 1958), pp. 549–556. See p. 554.

38. PARTICULARISM

Stouffer, Samuel A., and Jackson Toby, "Role Conflict and Personality," in Talcott Parsons and Edward A. Shils (eds.), *Toward a General Theory of Action*, Cambridge, Mass.: Harvard University Press, 1951, p. 82.

Scarr, Harry A., "Measures of Particularism," *Sociometry*, 27 (December, 1964), pp. 413–432. See pp. 413 and 418.

39. PERSUASIBILITY

Janis, Irving L., and Peter B. Field, "A Behavioral Assessment of Persuasibility: Consistency of Individual Differences," *Sociometry*, 19 (December, 1956), pp. 241–259. See p. 252. See pp. 242–248.

40. PESSIMISM

McClosky and Schaar, p. 24; see category 1 above.

41. POSSESSIVENESS

Freeman, Richard V., and Harry M. Grayson, "Maternal Attitudes in Schizophrenia," *Journal of Abnormal and Social Psychology*, 50 (January, 1955), pp. 45–53. See pp. 45–46.

Freeman, Howard E., and Ozzie G. Simmons, "Wives, Mothers, and the Posthospital Performance of Mental Patients," *Social Forces*, 37 (December, 1958), pp. 153–159. See p. 156.

42. PROJECTION

Scodel, Alvin, and Paul Mussen, "Social Perceptions of Authoritarians and Non-Authoritarians," *Journal of Abnormal and Social Psychology*, 48 (April, 1953), pp. 181–184. See p. 183.

Bieri, James, "Cognitive Complexity-Simplicity and Predictive Behavior," *Journal of Abnormal and Social Psychology*, 51 (September, 1955), pp. 263–268. See pp. 264–265.

Koenig, Frederick W., and Morton B. King, Jr., "Cognitive Simplicity and Out-Group Stereotyping," *Social Forces*, 42 (March, 1964), pp. 324–327. See pp. 325–326.

43. PROPENSITY TO CONSUME

Pfouts, Ralph W., and Erle T. Curtis, "Limitations of the Economic Base Analyses," *Social Forces*, 36 (May, 1958), pp. 303–310. See p. 309.

44. PROPENSITY TO SAVE

Pfouts and Curtis; see category 43 above.

45. REPRESSION-SENSITIZATION

Hathaway and McKinley (1943); see category 32 above.

Altrocchi, John, Oscar A. Parsons, and Hilda Dickoff, "Changes in Self-Ideal Discrepancy in Repressors and Sensitizers," *Journal of Abnormal and Social Psychology*, 61 (July, 1960), pp. 67–72. See p. 68.

Altrocchi, John, "Interpersonal Perceptions of Repressors and Sensitizers and Component Analysis of Assumed Dissimilarity Scores," *Journal of Abnormal and Social Psychology*, 62 (May, 1961), pp. 528–534. See p. 529.

Byrne, Donn, "The Repression-Sensitization Scale: Rationale, Reliability, and Validity," *Journal of Personality*, 29 (September, 1961), pp. 334–349. See pp. 336–338.

Turk, Herman, "Norms, Persons, and Sentiments," *Sociometry*, 26 (June, 1963), pp. 163–177. See pp. 165–167.

46. RIGIDITY (GOUGH, SANFORD)

Gough, Harrison G., and Robert N. Sanford, "Rigidity as a Psychological Variable," unpublished manuscript, University of

California Institute of Personality Assessment and Research, 1952.

Tuckman (1964); see category 15 above.

47. RIGIDITY (MCCLOSKY, SCHAAR)

McClosky and Schaar, pp. 28–29; see category 1 above.

48. RIGIDITY (RORSCHACH TECHNIQUE, FISHER METHOD OF SCORING)

Fisher, S., "Patterns of Personality and Some of Their Determinants," *Psychological Monographs*, 64 (No. 1, 1950). See pp. 6–8.

De Vos, George, and Horace Miner, "Algerian Culture and Personality in Change," *Sociometry*, 21 (December, 1958), pp. 255–268. See p. 258.

49. RIGIDITY (SROLE, LANGNER, AND COLLEAGUES)

Freeman and Simmons (1958), p. 155; see category 41 above.

Langner, Thomas S., and Stanley T. Michael, *Life Stress and Mental Health*, London and New York: The Free Press of Glencoe, Collier-Macmillan, Ltd., 1963, pp. 43–45.

50. ROLE CONFLICT

See also 38 above.

Stouffer, Samuel A. and Jackson Toby, "Role Conflict and Personality," *American Journal of Sociology*, 56 (March, 1951), pp. 395–406. See pp. 396–399.

Zurcher, Louis A., Jr., Arnold Meadow, and Susan Lee Zurcher, "Value Orientation, Role Conflict, and Alienation from Work: A Cross-Cultural Study," *American Sociological Review*, 30 (August, 1965), pp. 539–548. See pp. 542–543.

51. SOCIAL DESIRABILITY (CHRISTIE)

Singer (1964), pp. 128 and 130–131; see category 33 above.

52. SOCIAL DESIRABILITY (CHRISTIE, BUDNITSKY)

Christie, Richard, and Stanley Budnitsky, "A Short Forced-Choice Anxiety Scale," *Journal of Consulting Psychology*, 21 (December, 1957), p. 501.

Scarr (1964), p. 417; see category 38 above.

53. SOCIAL DESIRABILITY (MARLOWE, CROWNE)

Marlowe, D., and D. P. Crowne, "Social Desirability and Response to Perceived Situational Demands," *Journal of Consulting Psychology*, 25 (April, 1961), pp. 109–115. See pp. 110–111.

Seeman, Melvin, "Alienation and Social Learning in a Reformatory," *American Journal of Sociology*, 69 (November, 1963), pp. 270–280. See p. 273.

54. SUCCORANCE-NURTURANCE

Rosengren (1961); see category 2 above.

55. SUSCEPTIBILITY TO INFLUENCE

Janis and Field, p. 242; see category 39 above.

56. SUPERSTITION

Martin, James G., and Frank R. Westie, "The Tolerant Personality," *American Sociological Review*, 24 (August, 1959), pp. 521–528. See p. 523.

57. THREAT-COMPETITION

Martin and Westie, p. 525; see category 56 above.

58. TOTALITARIANISM

See also Authoritarianism.
McClosky and Schaar, pp. 32–33; see category 1 above.

59. TRUST AND OPTIMISM

See also category 37 above.
Struening, Elmer L. and Arthur H. Richardson, "A Factor Analytic Exploration of the Alienation, Anomia and Authoritarianism Domain," *American Sociological Review*, 30 (October, 1965), pp. 768–776. See pp. 769 and 771.

60. TRUST OF OTHERS

See also categories 21 and 22 above.
Freeman, Howard E. and H. Ashley Weeks, "Analysis of a Problem of Treatment of Delinquent Boys," *American Journal of Sociology*, 62 (July, 1956), pp. 56–61. See p. 57.

POLITICAL ATTITUDES

SEE ALSO

Alienation and Anomia

1. AWARENESS

McClosky, Herbert, and John H. Schaar, "Psychological Dimensions of Anomy," *American Sociological Review*, 30 (February, 1965), pp. 14–40. See pp. 26–27.

2. CONSERVATISM (ADORNO, FRENKEL-BRUNSWIK, LEVINSON, SANFORD)

Adorno, T. W., Else Frenkel-Brunswik, Daniel J. Levinson, and R. Nevitt Sanford, *The Authoritarian Personality*, New York: Harper and Brothers, 1950, pp. 163 and 169.

Litt, Edgar, "Jewish Ethno-Religious Involvement and Political Liberalism," *Social Forces*, 39 (May, 1961), pp. 328–332. See p. 329.

Middleton, Russell, and Snell Putney, "Student Rebellion against Parental Political Beliefs," *Social Forces*, 41 (May, 1963), pp. 377–383. See p. 379.

3. CONSERVATISM (MCCLOSKY)

McClosky, Herbert, "Conservatism and Personality," *American Political Science Review*, 52 (March, 1958), pp. 27–45. See pp. 29–34.

McClosky began his development of a measure of political conservatism by examining the writings of conservative thinkers. Despite differences in language and detail, McClosky reported finding "astonishing agreement" in conservative expressions with respect to the essential characteristics of the position. These characteristics were taken as a set of representative principles. McClosky's description (p. 29) of the level of this representation was as follows:

We have concentrated upon those attitudes and values that continually recur among acknowledged conservative thinkers and that appear to comprise the invariant elements of the conservative outlook. By the same token, we have tried to avoid attitudes or opinions that seemed to us situationally determined and which, for that reason, appear to be secondary and unstable correlates of liberal or conservative tendencies.

The responses of a large urban sample to 43 items, constructed so as to reflect the identified conservative principles, were analyzed. The original analysis resulted in a twelve-item scale. Additional refinement has led to the development of the nine-item instrument presented below which McClosky refers to as a measure of "classical conservatism."

Conservatism, as measured by the McClosky scale, has been found to be related to a variety of other variables. In his original discussion, McClosky reported relationships between conservatism and measures of intelligence, social-psychological characteristics, and personality factors. The findings of other studies have tended to confirm the existence of such relationships. For example, Photiadis and Biggar reported significant zero-order correlations between conservatism and social distance, religious orthodoxy, extrinsic religious belief, education, anomia, status concern, authoritarianism, withdrawal tendencies and antisocial tendencies. (See Photiadis and Biggar, 1962, below, Table 1, p. 670.)

Respondents are asked to "agree" or "disagree" with each of the nine items in the scale. An "agree" response is a conservative response; the total score is the number of items with which the respondent agrees.

THE CONSERVATISM SCALE

If you start trying to change things very much, you usually make them worse.

No matter how we like to talk about it, political authority really comes not from us, but from some higher power.

It's better to stick by what you have than to be trying new things you don't really know about.

A man doesn't really get to have much wisdom until he's well along in years.

I prefer the practical man any time to the man of ideas.

If something grows up over a long time, there will always be much wisdom in it.

I'd want to know that something would really work before I'd be willing to take a chance on it.

All groups can live in harmony in this country without changing the system in any way.

We must respect the work of our forefathers and not think that we know better than they did.

Middleton, Russell, "Ethnic Prejudice and Susceptibility to Persuasion," *American Sociological Review*, 25 (October, 1960), pp. 679–686. See p. 681.

Putney, Snell, and Russell Middleton, "Dimensions and Correlates of Religious Ideologies," *Social Forces*, 39 (May, 1961), pp. 285–290. See p. 286.

Photiadis, John D., and Jeanne Biggar, "Religiosity, Education and Ethnic Distance," *American Journal of Sociology*, 67 (May, 1962), pp. 666–672. See p. 669.

Middleton and Putney (1963); see category 2 above.

Photiadis, John D., and Arthur L. Johnson, "Orthodoxy, Church Participation, and Authoritarianism," *American Journal of Sociology*, 69 (November, 1963), pp. 244–248. See p. 244.

4. CONSERVATISM (QUINNEY)

Quinney, Richard, "Political Conservatism, Alienation, and Fatalism: Contingencies of Social Status and Religious Fundamentalism," *Sociometry*, 27 (September, 1964), pp. 374–381. See p. 376.

5. CONSERVATISM (SELVIN, HAGSTROM)

Selvin, Hanan C., and Warren O. Hagstrom, "The Empirical Classification of Formal Groups," *American Sociological Review*, 28 (June, 1963), pp. 399–411. See p. 405.

6. CONSERVATISM OF STATE LEGISLATORS

McRae, Duncan, Jr., "The Role of the State Legislator in Massachusetts," *American Sociological Review*, 19 (April, 1954), pp. 185–194. See p. 190.

McRae, Duncan, Jr., "Roll Call Votes and Leadership in the Massachusetts House of Representatives," *Public Opinion Quarterly*, 20 (Fall, 1956), pp. 543–588. See p. 548–549.

7. DEMOCRATIC CREED

Prothro, James W., and Charles M. Grigg, "Fundamental Principles of Democracy," *The Journal of Politics*, 22 (May, 1960), pp. 276–294. See pp. 282–283.

Litt, Edgar, "Civic Education, Community Norms, and Political Indoctrination," *American Sociological Review*, 28 (February, 1963), pp. 69–75. See p. 75.

8. DIRECTION OF STUDENT ATTITUDE IN RELATION TO PARENTS' POLITICAL ATTITUDE

Middleton and Putney, p. 380; see category 2 above.

9. DOMESTIC POLITICAL ORIENTATION

See also Work Value Orientations.

Trow, Martin, *Right Wing Radicalism and Political Intolerance: A Study of Support for McCarthy in a New England Town*, unpublished Ph.D. dissertation, Columbia University, 1957.

Trow, Martin, "Small Businessmen, Political Tolerance, and Support for McCarthy," *American Journal of Sociology*, 64 (November, 1958), pp. 270–281. See pp. 274–275.

10. ECONOMIC EQUALITY, ATTITUDE TOWARD

Nowak, Stefan, "Egalitarian Attitudes of Warsaw Students," *American Sociological Review*, 25 (April, 1960), pp. 219–231. See p. 220.

11. ELITISM, INEQUALITARIANISM

McClosky and Schaar, pp. 33–34; see category 1 above.

12. ETHNIC POLITICAL INFLUENCE, DISPROPORTIONATE

Catton, William R., Jr., and Sung Chick Hong, "The Relation of Apparent Minority Ethnocentrism to Majority Antipathy," *American Sociological Review*, 27 (April, 1962), pp. 178–191. See p. 181.

13. FEDERAL GOVERNMENT CONTROL, ATTITUDE TOWARD

Meltzer, Leo, "Comparing Relationships of Individual and Average Variables to Individual Response," *American Sociological Review*, 28 (February, 1963), pp. 117–123. See p. 119.

14. GOVERNMENT INTERVENTION, ATTITUDE TOWARD

Street, David, and John C. Leggett, "Economic Deprivation and

Extremism: A Study of Unemployed Negroes," *American Journal of Sociology*, 67 (July, 1961), pp. 53–57. See pp. 55–56.

15. **KNOWLEDGE OF CAMPAIGN INFORMATION QUIZ**

McCormick, Thomas C., and J. Richard Wahl, "Predicting Election Turnout: A Test of a Behavior Hypothesis," *American Journal of Sociology*, 61 (July, 1955), pp. 39–47. See pp. 40 and 46.

16. **LEFT WING, SCALE OF**

McClosky and Schaar, pp. 32–33; see category 1 above.

17. **LIBERALISM (CENTERS)**

Centers, Richard, *The Psychology of Social Classes*, Princeton, N.J.: Princeton University Press, 1949, pp. 55–64.
Litt (1961); see category 2 above.

18. **LIBERALISM (FERDINAND)**

Ferdinand, Theodore N., "Psychological Femininity and Political Liberalism," *Sociometry*, 27 (March, 1964), pp. 75–87. See pp. 78–79, 81 and 85–86.

19. **LIBERALISM (FUCHS)**

Fuchs, Lawrence H., *The Political Behavior of American Jews*, Glencoe, Ill.: The Free Press, 1956.
Litt (1961); see category 2 above.

20. **LIBERALISM (PATTERSON)**

Patterson, Samuel C., "Inter-Generational Occupational Mobility and Legislative Voting Behavior," *Social Forces*, 43 (October, 1964), pp. 90–93. See p. 92.

21. **LIBERALISM (KAHL, HAMBLIN AND MODIFICATIONS)**

Kahl, Joseph A., and Robert C. Hamblin, *Socio-Economic Status and Ideological Attitudes: A Non-Linear Pattern*, privately mimeographed, 1961.
Schmitt, David R., "An Attitudinal Correlate of Status Congruency of Married Women," *Social Forces*, 44 (December, 1965), pp. 190–195. See p. 193.

22. **LIBERALISM (SIMMONS)**

Simmons, J. L., *The Relationships between Liberalism, Aliena-*

tion, and Personality Disturbances, unpublished Ph.D. dissertation, State University of Iowa, 1963, Appendix A.

Simmons, J. L., "Tolerance of Divergent Attitudes," *Social Forces,* 43 (March, 1965), pp. 347–352. See pp. 348–349.

23. MCCARTHY, SENATOR JOSEPH, ATTITUDE TOWARD

Trow (1957); see category 9 above.

Trow (1958), p. 271; see category 9 above.

24. MEMBER LOYALTY OF LEAGUE OF WOMEN VOTERS MEMBERS

Smith, Clagett G., and Michael E. Brown, "Communication Structure and Control Structure in a Volutionary Association," *Sociometry,* 27 (December, 1964), pp. 448–468. See pp. 457–458.

25. MISTRUST OF PUBLIC OFFICIALS

Horton, John E., and Wayne E. Thompson, "Powerlessness and Political Negativism: A Study of Defeated Local Referendums," *American Journal of Sociology,* 67 (March, 1962), pp. 485–493. See p. 489.

26. PACIFIST SENTIMENT

Putney, Snell, and Russell Middleton, "Some Factors Associated with Student Acceptance or Rejection of War," *American Sociological Review,* 27 (October, 1962), pp. 655–667. See pp. 657 and 658.

27. PARTISANSHIP

Wallace, David, "Some Functional Aspects of Stability and Change in Voting," *American Journal of Sociology,* 69 (September, 1963), pp. 161–170. See p. 163.

28. PASSIVITY IN POLITICAL ISSUES

Almond, Gabriel, and Sydney Verba, *The Civic Culture,* Princeton, N.J.: Princeton University Press, 1963, p. 231.

Elder, Glen H., Jr., "Role Relations, Sociocultural Environments, and Autocratic Family Ideology," *Sociometry,* 28 (June, 1965), pp. 173–196. See p. 192.

29. POLITICAL ACTIVITY

Litt (1963); see category 7 above.

30. POLITICAL ALIENATION (HORTON, THOMPSON)

See also Alienation.

Thompson, Wayne E., and John E. Horton, "Political Alienation as a Force in Political Action," *Social Forces*, 38 (March, 1960), pp. 190–195. See pp. 191–192.

Horton and Thompson (1962); see category 25 above.

31. POLITICAL ALIENATION (ZIMMER)

See also Alienation.

McDill, Edward L., and Jeanne Clare Ridley, "Status, Anomia, Political Alienation, and Political Participation," *American Journal of Sociology*, 67 (September, 1962), pp. 205–213. See p. 208.

32. POLITICAL APATHY: BEHAVIOR APATHY

Dean, Dwight G., "Alienation and Political Apathy," *Social Forces*, 38 (March, 1960), pp. 185–189. See pp. 187–188.

33. POLITICAL APATHY: INFLUENCE APATHY

Dean; see category 32 above.

34. POLITICAL APATHY: INTEREST APATHY

Dean; see category 32 above.

35. POLITICAL CHAUVINISM

Litt (1963); see category 7 above.

36. POLITICAL CONVENTIONALITY

Middleton and Putney (1963), p. 382; see category 2 above.

37. POLITICAL CYNICISM

McClosky and Schaar, p. 24; see category 1 above.

38. POLITICAL FUNCTION

Litt (1963); see category 7 above.

39. POLITICAL FUTILITY, FEELINGS OF

McClosky and Schaar, pp. 24, 30–31, and 35; see category 1 above.

40. POLITICAL INFORMATION, LEVEL OF

Hastings, Philip K., "The Voter and the Non-Voter," *American Journal of Sociology*, 62 (November, 1956), pp. 302–307. See p. 305.

41. POLITICAL NORMLESSNESS

Neal, Arthur and Salomon Rettig, "Dimensions of Alienation among Manual and Non-manual Workers," *American Sociological Review*, 28 (August, 1963), pp. 599–608. See p. 603.

42. POLITICAL-ECONOMIC OPINION

Nettler, Gwynn, and James R. Huffman, "Political Opinion and Personal Security," *Sociometry*, 20 (March, 1957), pp. 51–66. See pp. 53–55.

43. POLITICAL ORIENTATION

Wilensky, Harold L., "The Labor Vote: A Local Union's Impact on the Political Conduct of Its Members," *Social Forces*, 35 (December, 1956), pp. 111–120. See pp. 115–116.

44. POLITICAL PROCESS SCALE

Litt (1963); see category 7 above.

45. PREFERENCE FOR CHANGE IN THE DISTRIBUTION OF POWER

Goffman, Irwin W., "Status Consistency and Preference for Change in Power Distribution," *American Sociological Review*, 22 (June, 1957), pp. 275–281. See pp. 277–278.

46. POLITICAL TOLERANCE (STOUFFER)

Stouffer, Samuel A., *Communism, Conformity and Civil Liberties*, New York: Doubleday and Co., 1955, p. 139.

Lipset, Seymour Martin, "Democracy and Working-Class Authoritarianism," *American Sociological Review*, 24 (August, 1959), pp. 482–501. See p. 486.

47. POLITICAL TOLERANCE (TROW)

Trow (1957); see category 9 above.

Trow (1958), p. 272; see category 9 above.

48. UNFAVORABLE ATTITUDES TOWARD POLITICS

McCormick and Wahl; see category 15 above.

49. RIGHT WING, SCALE OF

McClosky and Schaar, pp. 32–33; see category 1 above.

POLITICAL BEHAVIOR

SEE ALSO

Community Leadership

1. EFFECTIVENESS OF LEAGUE OF WOMEN VOTERS

Tannenbaum, Arnold S., "Control and Effectiveness in a Voluntary Organization," *American Journal of Sociology*, 68 (July, 1961), pp. 33–46. See p. 38.

Smith, Clagett G., and Michael E. Brown, "Communication Structure and Control Structure in a Voluntary Association," *Sociometry*, 27 (December, 1964), pp. 448–468. See p. 457.

2. EXTENT OF PARTICIPATION (IN LEAGUE OF WOMEN VOTERS ACTIVITIES

March, James G., "Group Norms and the Active Minority," *American Sociological Review*, 19 (December, 1954), pp. 733–741. See p. 735.

3. INTERPARTY COMPETITION (KEY)

Key, V. O., Jr., *Southern Politics*, New York: Alfred A. Knopf, 1950. See pp. 302–306.

Key, V. O., Jr., *American State Politics*, New York: Alfred A. Knopf, 1956. See pp. 97–104.

Casstevens, Thomas W., and Charles Press, "The Context of Democratic Competition in American State Politics," *American Journal of Sociology*, 68 (March, 1963), pp. 536–543. See p. 537.

Cutright, Phillips, "Casstevens and Press, 'The Context of Democratic Competition in American State Politics,'" *American Journal of Sociology*, 69 (November, 1963), pp. 291–292. See p. 292.

4. INTERPARTY COMPETITION (RANNEY, KENDALL)

Ranney, Austin, and Willmore Kendall, "The American Party

Systems," *American Political Science Review*, 48 (June, 1954), pp. 477–485. See pp. 482–484.

Ranney, Austin, and Willmore Kendall, *Democracy and the American Party System*, New York: Harcourt, Brace and World, 1956, pp. 18–39.

Casstevens and Press (1963), p. 537; see category 3 above.

5. INTERPARTY COMPETITION (SCHLESINGER)

Schlesinger, Joseph A., "A Two Dimensional Scheme for Classifying the States According to Degree of Interparty Competition," *American Political Science Review*, 49 (December, 1955), pp. 1120–1128. See p. 1123.

Schlesinger, Joseph A., "The Structure of Competition for Office in the American States," *Behavioral Science*, 5 (July, 1960), pp. 197–210. See pp. 198–199.

Casstevens and Press (1963), pp. 536–537; see category 3 above.

6. PARTICIPATION IN LOCAL GOVERNMENT

Greer, Scott, and Peter Orleans, "The Mass Society and the Parapolitical Structure," *American Sociological Review*, 27 (October, 1962), pp. 634–646. See p. 639.

7. PARTY LOYALTY OF LEGISLATORS

MacRae, Duncan, Jr., "The Role of the State Legislator in Massachusetts," *American Sociological Review*, 19 (April, 1954), pp. 185–194. See pp. 192–193.

8. POLITICAL ACTIVITY

Maccoby, Herbert, "The Differential Political Activity of Participants in a Voluntary Association," *American Sociological Review*, 23 (October, 1958), pp. 524–532. See p. 527.

9. POLITICAL PARTICIPATION

Woodward, Julian L., and Elmo Roper, "Political Activity of American Citizens," in Heinz Eulau, Samuel J. Eldersveld, and Morris Janowitz (eds.), *Political Behavior*, Glencoe, Ill.: The Free Press, 1956, pp. 133–137. See pp. 134–135.

Erbe, William, "Social Involvement and Political Activity: A Replication and Elaboration," *American Sociological Review*, 29 (April, 1964), pp. 198–215. See p. 202.

10. PRECINCT COMMITTEEMEN PERFORMANCE RATINGS

Cutright, Phillips, and Peter H. Rossi, "Grass Roots Politicians and the Vote," *American Sociological Review*, 23 (April, 1958), pp. 171–179. See p. 178.

11. PRECINCT INPUT OF POLITICAL CANDIDATES

Cutright, Phillips, and Peter H. Rossi, "Party Organization in Primary Elections," *American Journal of Sociology*, 69 (November, 1958), pp. 262–269. See p. 264.

12. RATE OF CHANGE IN PARTY MEMBERSHIP

Marsh, Robert M., and William L. Parish, "Modernization and Communism: A Re-test of Lipset's Hypotheses," *American Sociological Review*, 30 (December, 1965), pp. 934–942. See p. 939.

13. SUPPORT OF POLITICAL CANDIDATES BY PRECINCT CAPTAINS

Cutright and Rossi; see category 11 above.

14. SUPREME COURT JUSTICES' DECISIONS SCALES

Ten scales are set forth.

Bernard, Jessie, "Dimensions and Axes of Supreme Court Decisions: A Study in the Sociology of Conflict," *Social Forces*, 34 (October, 1955), pp. 19–27. See p. 20.

15. VOTING APATHY

Dean, Dwight G., "Alienation and Political Apathy," *Social Forces*, 38 (March, 1960), pp. 185–189. See pp. 187–188.

16. VOTING BEHAVIOR

Johnson, Benton, "Ascetic Protestantism and Political Preference in the Deep South," *American Journal of Sociology*, 69 (January, 1964), pp. 359–366. See p. 362.

17. VOTING INDEX ON LABOR MANAGEMENT ISSUES FOR LEGISLATORS

Massachusetts State Federation of Labor, "Official Labor Record of Senators and Representatives, 1951–52," Boston, 1952.

MacRae, Duncan, and Edith K. MacRae, "Legislators' Social Status and Their Votes," *American Journal of Sociology*, 66 (May, 1961), pp. 599–603. See pp. 600–601.

RELIGION: ATTITUDE TOWARD, PARTIC-IPATION IN, AND CHARACTERISTICS OF

SEE ALSO

Complex Organizations: Characteristics of

1. ADHERENCE TO CHURCH DOCTRINE

Liu, William T., "The Marginal Catholics in the South: A Revision of Concepts," *American Journal of Sociology*, 65 (January, 1960), pp. 383–390. See p. 386.

Liu, William T., "The Community Reference System, Religiosity, and Race Attitudes," *Social Forces*, 39 (May, 1961), pp. 324–328. See p. 326.

2. APOSTASY

Greeley, Andrew M., "Influence of the 'Religious Factor' on Career Plans and Occupational Values of College Graduates," *American Journal of Sociology*, 68 (May, 1963), pp. 658–671. See p. 668.

3. ASCETICISM

Goldstein, Bernice, and Robert L. Eichhorn, "The Changing Protestant Ethic: Rural Patterns in Health, Work, and Leisure," *American Sociological Review*, 26 (August, 1961), pp. 557–565. See pp. 560–561.

4. CALVINISM

McClosky, Herbert, and John H. Schaar, "Psychological Dimensions of Anomy," *American Sociological Review*, 30 (February, 1965), pp. 14–40. See pp. 33–34.

5. CHURCH, ATTITUDE TOWARD

Thurstone, L. L., and E. J. Chave, *The Measurement of Attitudes*, Chicago, Ill.: University of Chicago Press, 1929, pp. 60–65.

Lipman, Aaron, and A. Eugene Havens, "The Colombian Violencia: An Ex Post Facto Experiment," *Social Forces*, 44 (December, 1965), pp. 238–245. See p. 240.

6. CHURCH ORTHODOXY

Vernon, Glenn K., "Background Factors Related to Church Orthodoxy," *Social Forces*, 34 (March, 1956), pp. 252–254. See p. 252.

7. CHURCH PARTICIPATION (LIU)

Liu (1961), p. 325; see category 1 above.

8. CHURCH PARTICIPATION (PHOTIADIS, BIGGAR)

Photiadis, John D., and Jeanne Biggar, "Religiosity, Education, and Ethnic Distance," *American Journal of Sociology*, 67 (May, 1962), pp. 666–672. See p. 668.

Photiadis, John D., and Arthur L. Johnson, "Orthodoxy, Church Participation, and Authoritarianism," *American Journal of Sociology*, 69 (November, 1963), pp. 244–248.

Photiadis, John D., "The American Business Creed and Denominational Identification," *Social Forces*, 44 (September, 1965), pp. 92–100. See p. 95.

9. CHURCH-SECT

Dynes, Russell R., "Church-Sect Typology and Socio-Economic Status," *American Sociological Review*, 20 (October, 1955), pp. 555–560. See pp. 556–557.

Dynes, Russell R., "The Consequences of Sectarianism for Social Participation," *Social Forces*, 35 (May, 1957), pp. 331–334. See p. 331.

10. ETHICAL JUDGMENTS ABOUT RELIGION

Rettig, Salomon, and Benjamin Pasamanick, "Differences in Structure and Severity of Moral Judgments by Students and by a Community Sample: Some Observations on Ethical Relativity," *Ohio Journal of Science*, 62 (November, 1962), pp. 317–325.

Rettig, Salomon, "Invariance of Factor Structure of Ethical Judgments by Indian and American College Students," *Sociometry*, 27 (March, 1964), pp. 96–113. See pp. 99–109.

11. EXTRINSIC-INTRINSIC BELIEF

Wilson, Cody, "Extrinsic Religious Values and Prejudice," *Jour-*

nal of Abnormal and Social Psychology, 60 (March, 1960), pp. 286–288. See p. 286.

Photiadis and Biggar (1962); see category 8 above.

Photiadis and Johnson (1963), p. 244; see category 8 above.

12. FANATICISM

Putney, Snell, and Russell Middleton, "Dimensions and Correlates of Religious Ideologies," *Social Forces*, 39 (May, 1961), pp. 285–290. See p. 286.

13. FUNDAMENTALISM

Dynes (1955); see category 9 above.

Feagin, Joe R., "Prejudice, Orthodoxy and the Social Situation," *Social Forces*, 44 (September, 1965), pp. 46–56. See pp. 47–48.

14. GOD, ATTITUDE TOWARD

Friedrichs, Robert W., "Alter Versus Ego: An Exploratory Assessment of Altruism," *American Sociological Review*, 25 (August, 1960), pp. 496–508. See p. 499.

15. INSTITUTIONAL STRENGTH OF CHURCHES

Hallenbeck, Wilbur C., *Minneapolis Churches and Their Comity Problems*, New York: Institute of Social and Religious Research, 1929. See Appendix Table IV.

Chapin, F. Stuart, "The Optimum Size of Institutions: A Theory of the Large Group," *American Journal of Sociology*, 62 (March, 1957), pp. 449–460. See pp. 451–452.

16. JEWISH ETHNO-RELIGIOUS INVOLVEMENT

Litt, Edgar, "Jewish Ethno-Religious Involvement and Political Liberalism," *Social Forces*, 39 (May, 1961), pp. 328–332. See pp. 329–330.

17. OVERT CONFORMITY TO CHURCH TEACHINGS

Photiadis, John D., "Overt Conformity to Church Teaching as a Function of Religious Belief and Group Participation," *American Journal of Sociology*, 70 (January, 1965), pp. 423–428. See p. 424.

18. PARENTAL RELIGIOUS TRADITIONALISM

Rosen, Bernard C., "The Reference Group Approach to the Parental Factor in Attitude and Behavior Formation," *Social Forces*, 34 (December, 1955), pp. 137–144. See p. 139.

19. PERMISSIBLE BEHAVIOR OF MINISTERS

Glock, Charles Y., and Benjamin B. Ringer, "Church Policy and the Attitudes of Ministers and Parishioners on Social Issues," *American Sociological Review*, 21 (April, 1956), pp. 148–156. See p. 150.

20. RADICALISM, RELIGIOUS

Hammond, Philip E., and Robert E. Mitchell, "Segmentation of Radicalism—The Case of the Protestant Campus Minister," *American Journal of Sociology*, 71 (September, 1965), pp. 133–143. See p. 136.

21. RELIGION, IMPORTANCE OF

Putney and Middleton (1961), pp. 286–287; see category 12 above.

22. RELIGIOSITY (ANGELL)

Angell, Robert C., "Preferences for Moral Norms in Three Problem Areas," *American Journal of Sociology*, 67 (May, 1962), pp. 650–660. See p. 651.

23. RELIGIOSITY (MARTIN, WESTIE)

Martin, James G., and Frank R. Westie, "The Tolerant Personality," *American Sociological Review*, 24 (August, 1959), pp. 521–528. See p. 525.

24. RELIGIOSITY (PHOTIADIS, BIGGAR)

Photiadis and Biggar (1962); see category 8 above.

Photiadis and Johnson (1963); see category 8 above.

25. RELIGIOUS ATTENDANCE

Suchman, Edward A., "Sociomedical Variations among Ethnic Groups," *American Journal of Sociology*, 70 (November, 1964), pp. 319–331. See pp. 323–324.

26. RELIGIOUS BELIEF

Photiadis (1965), p. 424; see category 17 above.

27. RELIGIOUS BELIEFS, ADOLESCENT'S ATTITUDE TOWARD

Rosen; see category 18 above.

28. RELIGIOUS CONDUCT OF ADOLESCENTS

Rosen; see category 18 above.

29. RELIGIOUS CONVENTIONALITY

Putney, Snell, and Russell Middleton, "Rebellion, Conformity, and Parental Religious Ideologies," *Sociometry*, 24 (June, 1961), pp. 125–135. See p. 126.

30. RELIGIOUS FEELINGS

Salisbury, W. Seward, "Faith, Ritualism, Charismatic Leadership and Religious Behavior," *Social Forces*, 34 (March, 1956), pp. 241–245. See p. 243.

31. RELIGIOUS FUNDAMENTALISM

Lamar, Ralph E., *Fundamentalism and Selected Social Factors in the Southern Appalachian Region*, unpublished M.S. thesis, University of Kentucky, 1962.

Quinney, Richard, "Political Conservatism, Alienation, and Fatalism: Contingencies of Social Status and Religious Fundamentalism," *Sociometry*, 27 (September, 1964), pp. 372–381. See p. 374.

32. RELIGIOUS IDEOLOGY

Goldsen, Rose K., Morris Rosenberg, Robin M. Williams, Jr., and Edward A. Suchman, *What College Students Think*, Princeton, N.J.: D. Van Nostrand Co., 1960, p. 154

Scarr, Harry A., "Measures of Particularism," *Sociometry*, 27 (December, 1964), pp. 413–432. See p. 417.

33. RELIGIOUS OBSERVANCE DISSIMILARITY

Matras, Judah, "Religious Observance and Family Formation in Israel: Some Intergenerational Changes," *American Journal of Sociology*, 69 (March, 1964), pp. 464–475. See p. 468.

34. RELIGIOUS ORTHODOXY (PUTNEY, MIDDLETON)

Middleton, Russell, "Ethnic Prejudice and Susceptibility to Persuasion," *American Sociological Review*, 25 (October, 1960), pp. 679–686.

Putney and Middleton (1961); see category 12 above.

Putney and Middleton based their analysis of religious attitudes on the assumption that religiosity is a complex, multidimensional phenomenon. According to their analysis, only one of these dimensions—the ideological—is related to religious beliefs as such.

The authors argue further that religious ideology itself is composed of four attitudinal dimensions: orthodoxy, fanaticism, importance, and ambivalence.

Measures of each of the dimensions of religious ideology were developed by Putney and Middleton (1961 above). Of these, the six-item scale of religious orthodoxy has been the most frequently employed. This Likert-type, summated-rating instrument is scored according to the following weighted response categories: 7—strong agreement; 6—moderate agreement; 5—slight agreement; 4—no answer or don't know; 3—slight disagreement; 2—moderate disagreement; 1—strong disagreement. A total score is achieved by summing the weighted responses to each of the items.

THE RELIGIOUS ORTHODOXY ITEMS

The six items of the scale can be presented following some standard introduction (see, for example, the discussion of the Dogmatism Scale). The items are as follows:

1. I believe that there is a physical Hell where men are punished after death for the sins of their lives.
2. I believe there is a supernatural being, the Devil, who continually tries to lead men into sin.
3. To me the most important work of the church is the saving of souls.
4. I believe that there is a life after death.
5. I believe there is a Divine plan and purpose for every living person and thing.
6. The only benefit one receives from prayer is psychological. ["reverse" scored]

Putney and Middleton (1961); see category 29 above.
Photiadis and Biggar (1962); see category 8 above.
Photiadis and Johnson (1963); see category 8 above.
Photiadis (1965); see category 8 above.

35. RELIGIOUS ORTHODOXY (STRUENING, RICHARDSON)

Struening, Elmer L., and Arthur H. Richardson, "A Factor Analytic Exploration of the Alienation, Anomia and Authoritarianism Domain," *American Sociological Review*, 30 (October, 1965), pp. 768–776. See pp. 769 and 771.

36. RELIGIOUS PRACTICES, ADOLESCENT'S ATTITUDE TOWARD

Rosen; see category 18 above.

37. RELIGIOUSNESS

Kadushin, Charles, "Individual Decisions to Undertake Psycho-therapy," *Administrative Science Quarterly*, 3 (December, 1958), pp. 379–411. See p. 393.

Kadushin, Charles, *Steps on the Way to a Psychiatric Clinic*, Ann Arbor, Mich.: University Microfilms, 1960.

Kadushin, Charles, "Social Distance Between Client and Professional," *American Journal of Sociology*, 67 (March, 1962), pp. 517–531. See p. 522.

38. SOCIAL STATUS OF PROTESTANT DENOMINATIONS (BURCHINAL)

Burchinal, Lee G., "Some Social Status Criteria and Church Membership and Church Attendance," *Journal of Social Psychology*, 49 (February, 1959), pp. 53–64. See pp. 54–55.

Dillingham, Harry C., "Protestant Religion and Social Status," *American Journal of Sociology*, 70 (January, 1965), pp. 416–422. See pp. 417–419.

39. SOCIAL STATUS OF PROTESTANT DENOMINATIONS (DILLINGHAM)

Dillingham; see category 38 above.

40. SOCIOECONOMIC STATUS OF PRESBYTERIES

Dornbusch, Sanford M., and Roger D. Irle, "The Failure of Presbyterian Union," *American Journal of Sociology*, 64 (January, 1959), pp. 352–355. See p. 353.

SELF-IMAGE, SELF-CONCEPT, AND RELATED MEASURES

SEE ALSO

Personality Traits: Various Categories

1. ASPIRED SELF IDENTITY

Sherwood, John J., "Self Identity and Referent Others," *Sociometry*, 28 (March, 1965), pp. 66–81. See pp. 71 and 73.

2. CONSISTENCY OF PERCEIVED FEEDBACK

Schwartz, Michael, and Sandra S. Tangri, "A Note on Self-Concept as an Insulator against Delinquency," *American Sociological Review*, 30 (December, 1965), pp. 922–926. See p. 924.

3. GENERALIZED OTHER

Dymond, Rosalind F., "A Scale for the Measurement of Empathetic Ability," *Journal of Consulting Psychology*, 13 (1949), pp. 127–133. See pp. 128–129.

Miyamoto, S. Frank, and Sanford M. Dornbusch, "A Test of Interactionist Hypotheses of Self-conception," *American Journal of Sociology*, 61 (March, 1956), pp. 399–403. See pp. 400–401.

4. HAPPINESS, AVOWAL OF

Lindzey, Gardner, and James A. Urdan, "Personality and Social Choice," *Sociometry*, 17 (February, 1954), pp. 47–63. See p. 49.

Goldings, Herbert J., "On the Avowal and Projection of Happiness," *Journal of Personality*, 23 (September, 1954), pp. 30–47. See pp. 34–35.

5. HAPPINESS, SELF-EVALUATION OF

Cavan, Ruth S., Ernest W. Burgess, Robert J. Havighurst, and

Herbert Goldhamer, *Personal Adjustment in Old Age*, Chicago, Ill.: Science Research Associates, 1949, pp. 111–136.

Burgess, Ernest W., "Social Relations, Activities and Personal Adjustment," *American Journal of Sociology*, 59 (January, 1954), pp. 352–360. See p. 358.

6. IDEAL-SELF (LUNDY)

Lundy, R. M., W. Katkovsky, R. L. Cromwell, and D. J. Shoemaker, "Self Acceptability and Descriptions of Sociometric Choices," *Journal of Abnormal and Social Psychology*, 51 (September, 1955), pp. 260–262.

Lundy, Richard M., "Assimilative Projection and Accuracy of Prediction in Interpersonal Perceptions," *Journal of Abnormal and Social Psychology*, 52 (January, 1956), pp. 33–38. See pp. 34–35.

Lundy, Richard M., "Self Perceptions and Descriptions of Opposite Sex Sociometric Choices," *Sociometry*, 19 (December, 1956), pp. 272–277. See pp. 273–274.

7. IDEAL SELF (SARBIN)

Sarbin, T. R., *Personality Work Card*, Berkeley, Calif.: University of California Press, no date.

McKee, John P., and Alex C. Sherriffs, "Men's and Women's Beliefs, Ideals, and Self-Concepts," *American Journal of Sociology*, 64 (January, 1959), pp. 356–363. See p. 357.

8. INTERPERSONAL PERCEPTION

Fiedler, Fred E., "A Note on. Leadership Theory: The Effect of Social Barriers between Leaders and Followers," *Sociometry*, 20 (June, 1957), pp. 87–94. See p. 89.

9. PUBLIC EVALUATION, OBJECTIVE MEASURE OF

Sherwood ; see category 1 above.

10. PUBLIC EVALUATION, SUBJECTIVE MEASURE OF

Sherwood ; see category 1 above.

11. PUBLIC IDENTITY, OBJECTIVE INDEX OF

Sherwood ; see category 1 above.

12. PUBLIC IDENTITY, SUBJECTIVE INDEX OF

Sherwood; see category 1 above.

13. REAL SELF

Sarbin; see category 7 above.

McKee and Sherriffs (1959); see category 7 above.

14. REFLECTED SELF

Backman, Carl W., and Paul F. Secord, "Liking, Selective Interaction, and Misperceptions in Congruent Interpersonal Relations," *Sociometry*, 25 (December, 1962), pp. 321–335. See p. 326.

15. RESPONSE OF OTHERS TO SELF, ACTUAL

Dymond (1949); see category 3 above.

Miyamoto and Dornbusch (1956); see category 3 above.

16. RESPONSE OF OTHERS TO SELF, PERCEIVED

Dymond (1949); see category 3 above.

Miyamoto and Dornbusch (1956); see category 3 above.

17. ROLE ANALYSIS

Turner, Ralph H., "Self and Other in Moral Judgment," *American Sociological Review*, 19 (June, 1954), pp. 249–259. See p. 251.

18. SELF (BACKMAN, SECORD)

Backman and Secord; see category 14 above.

19. SELF (LUNDY)

Lundy, Katkovsky, Cromwell, and Shoemaker (1955); see category 6 above.

Lundy (Jan. 1956); see category 6 above.

Lundy (Dec. 1956); see category 6 above.

20. SELF-ACCEPTANCE

Freeman, Howard E., and H. Ashley Weeks, "Analysis of a Program of Treatment of Delinquent Boys," *American Journal of Sociology*, 62 (July, 1956), pp. 56–61. See pp. 57–58.

21. SELF-ADJUSTMENT TO MINORITY STATUS

Seeman, Melvin, "The Intellectual and the Language of Minorities," *American Journal of Sociology*, 64 (July, 1958), pp. 25–35. See p. 34.

22. SELF-ATTITUDES

Tagiuri, R., "Relational Analysis: An Extension of Sociometric

Method with Emphasis upon Social Perception," *Sociometry*, 15 (February-May, 1952), pp. 91–104.

Mills, Theodore M., "The Coalition Pattern in Three Person Groups," *American Sociological Review*, 19 (December, 1954), pp. 657–667. See p. 660.

23. SELF-ATTITUDES, TWENTY-STATEMENTS TEST OF

McPartland, Thomas S., *The Self and Social Structure: An Empirical Approach*, unpublished Ph.D. dissertation, State University of Iowa, 1953.

Kuhn, Manford H., and Thomas S. McPartland, "An Empirical Investigation of Self-Attitudes," *American Sociological Review*, 19 (February, 1954), pp. 68–76. See p. 69.

Couch, Carl J., "Self-Attitudes and Degree of Agreement with Immediate Others," *American Journal of Sociology*, 63 (March, 1958), pp. 491–496. See p. 492.

24. SELF-ATTRIBUTE, GENERALITY OF

Sherwood; see category 1 above.

25. SELF-ATTRIBUTE, PERCEIVED SALIENCE OF

Sherwood; see category 1 above.

26. SELF-COMPETENCE, FEELINGS OF

Douvan, Elizabeth, and Alan M. Walker, "The Sense of Effectiveness in Public Affairs," *Psychological Monographs*, 70 (1956).

Centers, Richard, "An Examination of the Riesman Social Character Typology: A Metropolitan Survey," *Sociometry*, 25 (September, 1962), pp. 231–240. See p. 235.

27. SELF-CONCEPT (HARVEY, KELLEY, SHAPIRO)

Harvey O. J., Harold H. Kelley, and Martin M. Shapiro, "Reactions of Unfavorable Evaluations of the Self Made by Other Persons," *Journal of Personality*, 25 (June, 1957), pp. 393–411. See pp. 397–399.

Harvey, O. J., "Personality Factors in Resolution of Conceptual Incongruities," *Sociometry*, 25 (December, 1962), pp. 336–352. See p. 338.

28. SELF-CONCEPT (OSGOOD, SUCI, TANNENBAUM AND MODIFICATIONS)

Osgood, Charles E., George J. Suci, and Percy H. Tannenbaum,

The Measurement of Meaning, Urbana, Ill.: University of Illinois Press, 1957, pp. 216–271.

Schwartz and Tangri (1965); see category 2 above.

29. SELF-CONCEPT (TENNESSEE DEPARTMENT OF MENTAL HEALTH)

Manual for the TDMH Self-Concept Scale, Tennessee Department of Mental Health, mimeographed.

Deutsch, Morton, and Leonard Solomon, "Reactions to Evaluations by Others as Influenced by Self-Evaluations," *Sociometry,* 22 (June, 1959), pp. 93–112.

30. SELF-CONCEPT AND SIGNIFICANT OTHERS, DISCREPANCY BETWEEN

Schwartz and Tangri; see category 2 above.

31. SELF-CONCEPTION

Dymond (1949); see category 3 above.

Miyamoto and Dornbusch (1956); see category 3 above.

32. SELF-CONCEPTION INSTRUMENT, CRITICIZED ITEMS

Videbeck, Richard, "Self-Conception and the Reactions of Others," *Sociometry,* 23 (December, 1960), pp. 351–359. See p. 353.

Maehr, Martin L., Josef Mensing, and Samuel Nafzger, "Concept of Self and the Reactions of Others," *Sociometry,* 25 (December, 1962), pp. 353–357. See p. 354.

33. SELF-CONCEPTION INSTRUMENT, RELATED ITEMS

Videbeck (1960); see category 32 above.

Maehr, Mensing, and Nafzger (1962); see category 32 above.

34. SELF-CONCEPTION INSTRUMENT, UNRELATED ITEMS

Videbeck (1960); see category 32 above.

Maehr, Mensing, and Nafzger (1962); see category 32 above.

35. SELF-CONFIDENCE (HOFFMAN)

Hoffman, Lois W., Sidney Rosen, and Ronald Lippitt, "Parental Coerciveness, Child Autonomy, and Child's Role at School," *Sociometry,* 23 (March, 1960), pp. 15–21. See p. 20.

36. SELF-CONFIDENCE (MCCLOSKY, SCHAAR)

McClosky, Herbert, and John H. Schaar, "Psychological Dimensions of Anomy," *American Sociological Review*, 30 (February, 1965), pp. 14–40. See pp. 30–31.

37. SELF-DISCLOSURE, BREADTH OF

Jourard, Sidney M., and Paul Lasakow, "Some Factors in Self-Disclosure," *Journal of Abnormal and Social Psychology*, 56 (January, 1958), pp. 91–98. See pp. 91–93.

Altman, Irwin, and William H. Haythorn, "Interpersonal Exchange in Isolation," *Sociometry*, 28 (December, 1965), pp. 411–426. See pp. 416–419.

38. SELF-DISCLOSURE, DEPTH OF

Jourard and Lasakow (1958), see category 37 above.

Altman and Haythorn (1965), pp. 415–416; see category 37 above.

39. SELF-ESTEEM (DAY, HAMBLIN)

Day, Robert C., and Robert L. Hamblin, "Some Effects of Close and Punitive Styles of Supervision," *American Journal of Sociology*, 69 (March, 1964), pp. 499–510. See pp. 504–506.

40. SELF-ESTEEM (DECHARMS, ROSENBAUM)

DeCharms, Richard, and M. E. Rosenbaum, "Status Variables and Matching Behavior," *Journal of Personality*, 28 (December, 1960), pp. 492–502. See p. 495.

Day and Hamblin (1964); see category 39 above.

41. SELF-ESTEEM (ROSENBERG)

Rosenberg, Morris, "The Dissonant Religious Context and Emotional Disturbance," *American Journal of Sociology*, 58 (July, 1962), pp. 1–10. See p. 2.

Rosenberg, Morris, "The Association between Self-Esteem and Anxiety," *Journal of Psychiatic Research*, 1 (1962), pp. 135–152.

Rosenberg, Morris, "Parental Influence and Children's Self-Conceptions," *Sociometry*, 26 (March, 1963), pp. 35–49. See pp. 35–36.

42. SELF-EVALUATION (GOODCHILDS, SMITH)

Goodchilds, Jacqueline D., and Ewart E. Smith, "The Effects of Unemployment as Mediated by Social Status," *Sociometry*, 26 (September, 1963), pp. 287–293. See p. 289.

43. SELF-EVALUATION (SHERWOOD)

Sherwood; see category 1 above.

44. SELF-HATRED

Segal, Bernard E., "Racial Group Membership and Juvenile Delinquency," *Social Forces*, 43 (October, 1964), pp. 70–81. See p. 74.

45. SELF-IDENTITY

Sherwood; see category 1 above.

46. SELF-IMAGE

Street, David, *Inmate Social Organization: A Comparative Study of Juvenile Correctional Institutions*, unpublished Ph.D. dissertation, University of Michigan, 1962. See pp. 213–224.

Street, David, "The Inmate Group in Custodial and Treatment Settings," *American Sociological Review*, 30 (February, 1965), pp. 40–55. See pp. 47 and 51–54.

47. SELF-IMAGE OF ONE'S BODY

Dentler, Robert A., and Lawrence J. Monroe, "Social Correlates of Early Adolescent Theft," *American Sociological Review*, 26 (October, 1961), pp. 733–743. See p. 740.

48. SELF-IMAGE OF ORIENTATIONS TO INTERACTION

Dean, Lois R., "The Pattern Variables: Some Empirical Operations," *American Sociological Review*, 26 (February, 1961), pp. 80–90. See p. 88.

49. SELF-PERCEPTION, ASSUMED SIMILARITY

Steiner, Ivan D., and Joan S. Dodge, "A Comparison of Two Techniques Employed in the Study of Interpersonal Perception," *Sociometry*, 20 (March, 1957), pp. 1–7. See p. 2.

50. SELF-RANK

Reeder, Leo G., George A. Donohue, and Arturo Biblarz, "Conceptions of Self and Others," *American Journal of Sociology*, 66 (September, 1960), pp. 153–159. See p. 154.

51. SELF-RATING (DEUTSCH, SOLOMON)

Deutsch and Solomon (1959); see category 29 above.

52. SELF-RATING (LINDZEY, URBAN)

Lindzey and Urdan (1954); see category 4 above.

53. SELF-REFERENT

Goodchilds, Jacqueline D., "Effects of Being Witty on Position in the Social Structure of a Small Group," *Sociometry*, 22 (September, 1959), pp. 261–272. See p. 265.

54. STABILITY OF SELF

Lindzey and Urdan (1954); see category 4 above.

55. USEFULNESS, SELF-EVALUATION OF

Cavan, Burgess, Havighurst and Goldhamer (1949); see category 5 above.

Burgess (1954); see category 5 above.

SMALL GROUPS: ATTITUDES TOWARD, IDENTIFICATION WITH, AND PERCEPTIONS OF

1. ACCEPTABILITY OF CO-WORKER

Kelley, Harold H., and Martin M. Shapiro, "An Experiment on Conformity to Group Norms Where Conformity is Detrimental to Group Achievement," *American Sociological Review*, 19 (December, 1954), pp. 667–677. See p. 669.

2. ACCEPTANCE BY GROUP MEMBERS

Kelley and Shapiro, p. 671; see category 1 above.

3. ANGER WITH CO-WORKERS

Kelley and Shapiro; see category 1 above.

4. ATTEMPTS TO BE LIKED

Schutz, W. C., *FIRO: A Three-Dimensional Theory of Interpersonal Behavior*, New York: Rinehart and Company, Inc., 1958.

Hoffman, L. Richard, and Clagett G. Smith, "Some Factors Affecting the Behaviors of Members of Problem-Solving Groups," *Sociometry*, 23 (September, 1960), pp. 273–291. See p. 275.

5. ATTRACTION TO GROUP

Hoffman, L. Richard, "Similarity of Personality: A Basis for Interpersonal Attraction," *Sociometry*, 21 (December, 1958), pp. 300–308. See p. 302.

6. COMMITMENT TO GROUP GOALS

Gross, Edward, "Primary Functions of the Small Group," *American Journal of Sociology*, 60 (July, 1954), pp. 24–29. See p. 26.

7. CONTRIBUTION TO GROUP HARMONY

Olmsted, Michael S., "Orientation and Role in the Small Group," *American Sociological Review*, 19 (December, 1954), pp. 741–751. See p. 747.

8. DESIRE TO REMAIN IN GROUP

Kelley and Shapiro; see category 1 above.

9. DISCUSSIONAL INVOLVEMENT

Bales, Robert F., *Interaction Process Analysis: A Method for the Study of Small Groups*, Cambridge, Mass.: Addison-Wesley Press, 1950.

Borgatta, Edgar F., and Leonard S. Cottrell, Jr., "On the Classification of Groups," *Sociometry*, 18 (December, 1955), pp. 665–678. See pp. 673–674.

10. ENJOYMENT OF PARTICIPATION

Kelley and Shapiro; see category 1 above.

11. EMOTIONALLY INHIBITED NEUTRALITY

Bales (1950); see category 9 above.
Borgatta and Cottrell (1955), p. 666; see category 9 above.

12. EVALUATION, PROBLEMS OF

Bales (1950); see category 9 above.

Psathas, George, "Phase Movement and Equilibrium Tendencies in Interaction Process in Psychotherapy Groups," *Sociometry*, 23 (June, 1960), pp. 177–194. See p. 184.

13. FRIENDLY ATMOSPHERE IN GROUP

Bales (1950); see category 9 above.

Borgatta, Edgar F., Robert F. Bales, and Arthur S. Couch, "Some Findings Relevant to the Great Man Theory of Leadership," *American Sociological Review*, 19 (December, 1954), pp. 755–759. See p. 758.

14. GROUP, ATTITUDE TOWARD

Shelley, Harry P., "Focused Leadership and Cohesiveness in Small Groups," *Sociometry*, 23 (June, 1960), pp. 209–216. See p. 212.

15. GROUP COORDINATION, PERCEPTIONS OF

Meltzer, Leo, "Comparing Relationships of Individual and Average Variables to Individual Response," *American Sociological Review*, 28 (February, 1963), pp. 117–123. See p. 118.

16. GROUP EXPECTATIONS, LEVEL OF

Emerson, Richard M., "Power-Dependence Relations: Two Experiments," *Sociometry*, 27 (September, 1964), pp. 282–298. See p. 284.

17. GROUP EXPERIENCE, ATTITUDE TOWARD

Brandon, Arlene C., *The Relevance of Expectation as an Underlying Factor in Status Congruence*, unpublished Ph.D. dissertation, University of California, Berkeley, 1964.

Brandon, Arlene C., "Status Congruence and Expectations," *Sociometry*, 28 (September, 1965), pp. 272–288. See pp. 282–283.

18. GROUP IDENTIFICATION

Bales (1950); see category 9 above.

Borgatta and Cottrell (1955), p. 672; see category 9 above.

19. GROUP MEETINGS, REACTIONS TO

Slater, Philip E., "Contrasting Correlates of Group Size," *Sociometry*, 21 (June, 1958), pp. 129–139. See p. 130.

20. GROUP MOTIVATION, DEGREE OF

Tuckman, Bruce W., "Personality Structure, Group Composition, and Group Functioning," *Sociometry*, 27 (December, 1964), pp. 469–487. See p. 480.

21. GROUP ORIENTATION

Bowerman, Charles E., and John W. Kinch, "Changes in Family and Peer Orientation of Children Between the Fourth and Tenth Grades," *Social Forces*, 37 (March, 1959), pp. 206–211. See p. 207.

22. GROUP SATISFACTION

Ziller, Robert C., and Ralph V. Exline, "Some Consequences of Age Heterogeneity in Decision-Making Groups," *Sociometry*, 21 (September, 1958), pp. 198–211. See p. 201.

23. GROUP SIZE, ATTITUDE TOWARD

Slater; see category 19 above.

24. **IDENTIFICATION WITH GROUP MEMBERS**

Meltzer, see category 15 above.

25. **INTERACTIVE INVOLVEMENT**

Bales (1950); see category 9 above.
Borgatta and Cottrell (1955); see category 9 above.

26. **INVOLVEMENT ACTIVITY**

Bales (1950); see category 9 above.
Borgatta and Cottrell (1955), p. 672; see category 9 above.

27. **MATURITY**

Bales (1950); see category 9 above.
Borgatta and Cottrell (1955), p. 675; see category 9 above.

28. **ORIENTATION, PROBLEMS OF**

Bales (1950); see category 9 above.
Psathas (1960); see category 12 above.

29. **OTHER'S PERFORMANCE, RATING OF**

Leik, Robert K., " 'Irrelevant' Aspects of Stooge Behavior: Implications for Leadership Studies and Experimental Methodology," *Sociometry*, 28 (September, 1965), pp. 259–271. See pp. 261–264.

30. **OTHERS, ATTITUDE TOWARD**

Mills, Theodore M., "The Coalition Pattern in Three Person Groups," *American Sociological Review*, 19 (December, 1954), pp. 657–667. See p. 660.

31. **PERSONAL INVOLVEMENT WITH GROUP**

Olmsted, Donald W., "Inter-Group Similarities of Role Correlates," *Sociometry*, 20 (March, 1957), pp. 8–20. See p. 12.

32. **POSITIVITY OF INTERACTION (DERIVED FROM BALES)**

O'Rourke, John F., "Field and Laboratory: The Decision-Making Behavior of Family Groups in Two Experimental Conditions," *Sociometry*, 26 (December, 1963), pp. 422–435. See p. 428.

33. **REFERENCE GROUP ORIENTATION**

Rosen, Bernard C., "Conflicting Group Membership: A Study of Parent-Peer Group Cross-Pressures," *American Sociological Review*, 20 (April, 1955), pp. 155–161. See p. 158.

34. SOCIAL-EMOTIONAL REACTIONS

Bales (1950); see category 9 above. (1950a)

Bales, Robert F., "A Set of Categories for the Analysis of Small Group Interaction," *American Sociological Review*, 15 (April, 1950), pp. 257–263. See pp. 258–261. (1950b)

A measure of social-emotional reactions in small-group situations, like a large number of other measures in such settings, has been derived from the system of Interaction Process Analysis formulated by Bales. Interaction Process Analysis is based upon a set of twelve categories which provides "a general-purpose framework for observation which can be used to obtain a series of standard indices regarding the structure and dynamics of interaction in any small group" (Bales, 1950a, p. 33).

The twelve categories of this system resulted from a conceptual analysis of within group interaction. According to Bales' model, the properties of interaction include a number of fundamental dimensions. Using a social-systems theoretical orientation, Bales defined these basic dimensions, and then addressed the problem of obtaining measures for each. The core of the measurement system is "a way of classifying behavior act by act, as it occurs in small face-to-face groups, and a series of ways of analyzing the data to obtain indices descriptive of group process, and derivatively, of factors influencing that process." (Bales, 1950b, p. 258)

The twelve categories and the major areas within which each was classified by Bales are presented in Table 1 p. 331.

A second combination of the twelve categories was suggested by Bales for the analysis of "system problems." This combination is as follows:

I. *Problems of orientation or communication.* Combine categories 6 and 7.

II. *Problems of evaluation.* Combine categories 5 and 8.

III. *Problems of control.* Combine categories 4 and 9.

IV. *Problems of decision.* Combine categories 3 and 10.

V. *Problems and tension-management or tension-reduction.* Combine categories 2 and 11.

VI. *Problems of integration or reintegration.* Combine categories 1 and 12.

TABLE 1. BALES'S CATEGORIES FOR OBSERVATION OF INTERACTION WITHIN SMALL GROUPS

Major Problem Area	*Category*
A. Social-Emotional Area: Positive Reactions	1. *Shows solidarity*, raises other's status, gives help, reward. 2. *Shows tension release*, jokes, laughs, shows satisfaction. 3. *Agrees*, shows passive acceptance, understands, concurs, complies.
B. Task Area: Attempted Answers	4. *Gives suggestion*, direction, implying autonomy for other. 5. *Gives opinion*, evaluation, analysis, expresses feeling, wish. 6. *Gives orientation*, information, repeats, clarifies, confirms.
C. Task Area: Asks Questions	7. *Asks for orientation*, information, repetition, confirmation. 8. *Asks for opinion*, evaluation, analysis, expression of feeling. 9. *Asks for suggestion*, direction, possible ways of action.
D. Social-Emotional Area: Negative Reactions	10. *Disagrees*, shows passive rejection, formality, withholds help. 11. *Shows tension*, asks for help, withdraws out of field. 12. *Shows antagonism*, deflates other's status, defends or asserts self.

The above system of categories has been utilized in a variety of ways (see for example categories 9, 11, 12, 13, 18, 25, 26, 27, and 28, above, and category 38 below). Among these applications has been the measurement of the social-emotional reactions of members in the group. For example, O'Rourke (1963) employed the combination of Bales's categories 1, 2, and 3 to measure positive social-emotional acts within family groups, and his categories 10, 11 and 12 to measure negative acts in such groups. Similarly, Mills (1954) used the same combinations of categories to assess positive and negative reactions within three-person groups.

TABLE 2. FORM FOR OBSERVATION OF SMALL GROUP INTERACTION USING BALES'S CATEGORIES

Category	1	2	3	4	. . .
	Time Periods				
1. Shows solidarity					
2. Shows tension release					
3. Agrees					
4. Gives suggestions					
5. Gives opinion	6–4				
6. Gives orientation		6–4			
7. Asks for orientation	4–6				
8. Asks for opinion					
9. Asks for suggestions					
10. Disagrees					
11. Shows tension					
12. Shows antagonism					

To facilitate the observational and recording process, Bales and his associates developed the Interaction Recorder. While this device does make the observer's task less burdensome, it is not a necessity. A *trained* observer using a form of the type presented in Table 2 can record the interaction process with considerable efficiency.

Suppose a researcher is observing a six-member group which has 30 minutes to solve a given task. The form might be set up with 10 time periods of 3 minutes each. If during the first time period, member 6 says to member 4, "I believe that this piece of the puzzle does not fit anywhere," a 6–4 would be recorded opposite category 5 under the first time period. If 4 then says to 6, "I don't get what you mean," a 4–6 is noted opposite category 7. Then at the beginning of the second time period, suppose Mr. 6 explains what he has in mind to Mr. 4. A 6–4 is recorded opposite category 6 under the second time period.

The form presented here is merely suggestive. It should be modified in line with the particular aims of the researcher. Regardless of the form used, considerable training is required before a researcher can observe interaction reliably. (See Bales, 1950a, Chapter 3.) In training himself or other observers, the researcher will find Bales's detailed description of his categories extremely helpful (Bales [1950a], "Appendix: Definitions of the Categories").

Mills (1954) p. 659; see category 30 above.

Philip, Hugh and Dexter Dunphy, "Developmental Trends in Small Groups," *Sociometry*, 22 (June, 1959), pp. 162–174. See p. 165.

Psathas (1960); see category 12 above.

O'Rourke (1963); see category 32 above.

35. SOCIOMETRIC PERCEPTION, ACCURACY OF

Gronlund, Norman E., "Sociometric Status and Sociometric Perception," *Sociometry*, 18 (May, 1955), pp. 122–128. See p. 123.

36. TASK ENJOYMENT

DeCharms, Richard, Virginia Carpenter, and Aharon Kuperman, "The 'Origin-Pawn' Variable in Personal Perception," *Sociometry*, 28 (September, 1965), pp. 241–258. See pp. 248, 250, and 252–254.

37. TASK-ORIENTED PERCEPTUAL ACCURACY

Cronbach, Lee J., "Processes Affecting Scores on 'Understanding of Others' and 'Assumed Similarity,' " *Psychological Bulletin*, 52 (May, 1955), pp. 177–193. See pp. 180–181.

Exline, Ralph V., "Interrelations among Two Dimensions of Sociometric Status, Group Congeniality and Accuracy of Social Perception," *Sociometry*, 23 (March, 1960), pp. 85–101. See pp. 88–89.

38. TENSION-NEUTRAL ACTIVITY

Bales (1950); see category 9 above.
Borgatta and Cottrell (1955), p. 671; see category 9 above.

39. UNIT SATISFACTION

Harvey, O. J., "Reciprocal Influence of the Group and Three Types of Leaders in an Unstructured Situation," *Sociometry*, 23 (March, 1960), pp. 57–68. See p. 60.

40. VALUATION OF MEMBERSHIP

Kelley and Shapiro; see category 1 above.

41. WORKING IN GROUPS, ATTITUDE TOWARD

Exline (1960), p. 87; see category 37 above.

SMALL GROUPS: BEHAVIOR AND INTERACTION IN

1. AGGRESSIVENESS

Thorpe, J. G., "Some Evidence on Northway's Autonomic Hypotheses," *Sociometry*, 17 (August, 1954), pp. 282–284. See p. 283.

2. ASSIGNMENT TO ROLES IN CLASS PLAY

Bower, Eli M., *A Process for Early Identification of Emotionally Disturbed Children*, Sacramento, Calif.: California State Department of Education, Bulletin 27, 1958, pp. 107–108. See footnote 9.

Dentler, Robert and Lawrence J. Monroe, "Social Correlates of Early Adolescent Theft," *American Sociological Review*, 26 (October, 1961), pp. 733–743. See p. 739.

3. CLIQUES, EXTENT OF

Carlson, Earl R., "Clique Structure and Member Satisfaction in Groups," *Sociometry*, 23 (December, 1960), pp. 327–337. See p. 330.

4. CLIQUES, NUMBER OF

Carlson; see category 3 above.

5. CLIQUES, MEMBERS IN

Carlson; see category 3 above.

6. CLIQUES, RATIO OF NUMBER TO GROUP SIZE

Carlson; see category 3 above.

7. COHESIVENESS

Suchman, Edward A., "Sociomedical Variations among Ethnic Groups," *American Journal of Sociology*, 70 (November, 1964), pp. 319–331. See pp. 323–324.

8. COMMUNICATION, AMOUNT AND DIRECTION OF

Bales, Robert F., *Interaction Process Analysis: A Method for the Study of Small Groups*, Cambridge, Mass.: Addison-Wesley Press, 1950.

Sampson, Edward E., and Arlene C. Brandon, "The Effects of Role and Opinion Deviation on Small Group Behavior," *Sociometry*, 27 (September, 1964), pp. 261–281. See pp. 268–269.

9. CONTRIBUTION OF IDEAS

Schutz, W. C., *FIRO: A Three-Dimensional Theory of Interpersonal Behavior*, New York: Rinehart and Company, Inc., 1958.

Hoffman, L. Richard, and Clagett G. Smith, "Some Factors Affecting the Behaviors of Members of Problem-Solving Groups," *Sociometry*, 23 (September, 1960), pp. 273–291. See p. 275.

10. CONTRIBUTION OF FACTS

Olmsted, Michael S., "Orientation and Role in the Small Group," *American Sociological Review*, 19 (December, 1954), pp. 741–751. See p. 747.

11. CONTROL, PROBLEMS OF

Bales (1950); see category 8 above.

Psathas, George, "Phase Movement and Equilibrium Tendencies in Interaction Process in Psychotherapy Groups," *Sociometry*, 23 (June, 1960), pp. 177–194. See p. 184.

12. COOPERATIVENESS-CONTROL

Borgatta, Edgar F., Leonard S. Cottrell, Jr., and Henry J. Meyer, "On the Dimensions of Group Behavior," *Sociometry*, 19 (December, 1956), pp. 223–240. See pp. 226–227.

13. CULTURE FORMATION

Rose, Edward, and William Felton, "Experimental Histories of Culture," *American Sociological Review*, 20 (August, 1955), pp. 383–392. See p. 383.

14. DISAGREEMENT BETWEEN ACCOMPLICES

Steiner, Ivan D., and Homer H. Johnson, "Authoritarianism and

Conformity," *Sociometry*, 26 (March, 1963), pp. 21–34. See p. 28.

15. DISTRIBUTION OF ACTIVITY

Bales (1950); see category 8 above.

Olmsted (1954), p. 745; see category 10 above.

16. EXPANSIVENESS, POSITIVE

Borgatta, Edgar F., "Analysis of Social Interaction and Sociometric Perception," *Sociometry*, 17 (March, 1954), pp. 7–32. See p. 18.

17. EXPANSIVENESS, PROJECTED

Borgatta; see category 16 above.

18. EXPANSIVENESS IN INTERACTION

Bales (1950); see category 8 above.

Borgatta (1954); see category 16 above.

19. EXPERIMENTER AWARENESS

Berkowitz, Leonard, Sharon B. Klanderman, and Richard Harris, "Effects of Experimenter Awareness and Sex of Subject and Experimenter on Reactions to Dependency Relationship," *Sociometry*, 27 (September, 1964), pp. 327–337. See p. 332.

20. EXPRESSIVE-MALINTEGRATIVE BEHAVIOR

Bales (1950); see category 8 above.

Manheim, Henry L., "Intergroup Interaction as Related to Status and Leadership Differences between Groups," *Sociometry*, 23 (December, 1960), pp. 415–427. See p. 421.

21. FOLLOWING ACTS RECEIVED

Bales (1950); see category 8 above.

Marak, George E., Jr., "The Evolution of Leadership Structure," *Sociometry*, 27 (June, 1964), pp. 174–182. See pp. 176–177.

22. GROUP CONFLICT, EXTENT OF

Tuckman, Bruce W., "Personality Structure, Group Composition, and Group Functioning," *Sociometry*, 27 (December, 1964), pp. 469–487. See pp. 479–480.

23. GROUP CONFLICT, INTENSITY OF

Tuckman, p. 479; see category 22 above.

24. GROUP CONFLICT, OVERALL MEASURE

Tuckman, p. 480; see category 22 above.

25. GROUP COOPERATION, AMOUNT OF

Tuckman; see category 22 above.

26. GROUP DECISION MECHANISMS, ABSTRACTNESS OF

Tuckman, p. 480; see category 22 above.

27. GROUP EFFECTIVENESS

Hutchins, Edwin B., and Fred E. Fiedler, "Task-Oriented and Quasi-Therapeutic Role Functions of the Leader in Small Military Groups," *Sociometry*, 23 (December, 1960), pp. 393–406. See p. 398.

28. GROUP MEMBERSHIP

Rosen, Bernard C., "Conflicting Group Membership: A Study of Parent-Peer Group Cross-Pressures," *American Sociological Review*, 20 (April, 1955), pp. 155–161. See p. 155.

29. GROUP STRUCTURE, ABSTRACTNESS OF

Tuckman, p. 479; see category 22 above.

30. HUMOR

Goodchilds, Jacqueline D., "Effects of Being Witty on Position in the Social Structure of a Small Group," *Sociometry*, 22 (September, 1959), pp. 261–272. See pp. 262–263.

31. INSTRUMENTAL ACTIVITY

Bales (1950); see category 8 above.

Mills, Theodore M., "The Coalition Pattern in Three Person Groups," *American Sociological Review*, 19 (December, 1954), pp. 657–667. See p. 659.

32. INTEGRATION

Gross, Edward, "Primary Functions of the Small Group," *American Journal of Sociology*, 60 (July, 1954), pp. 24–29. See p. 25.

33. INTELLECTUAL COMPULSIVENESS

Bales (1950); see category 8 above.

Borgatta, Edgar F., and Leonard S. Cottrell, Jr., "On the Classification of Groups," *Sociometry*, 18 (December, 1955), pp. 665–678. See p. 666.

34. INTERACTION, AMONG JURORS

James, Rita M., "Status and Competence of Jurors," *American Journal of Sociology*, 64 (May, 1959), pp. 563–570. See p. 565.

35. INTERACTION, FREQUENCY OF

Gross, p. 26; see category 32 above.

36. INTERACTION, PATTERNS OF

Rosengren, William R., "Symptom Manifestations as a Function of Situational Press: A Demonstration in Socialization," *Sociometry*, 22 (June, 1959), pp. 113–123. See p. 115.

37. INTERACTION, QUANTITY OF

Bales (1950); see category 8 above.

Bates, Alan P., and Jerry S. Cloyd, "Toward the Development of Operations for Defining Group Norms and Member Roles," *Sociometry*, 19 (March, 1956), pp. 26–39. See p. 29.

38. INTERACTION WITH HIGH-STATUS GROUPS

Bell, Gerald D., "Processes in the Formation of Adolescents' Aspirations," *Social Forces*, 42 (December, 1963), pp. 179–186. See p. 183.

39. INITIATION OF ACTION

Bales (1950); see category 8 above.

Slater, Philip E., "Role Differentiation in Small Groups," *American Sociological Review*, 20 (June, 1955), pp. 300–310. See p. 301.

Leik, Robert K., "Type of Group and the Probability of Initiating Acts," *Sociometry*, 28 (March, 1965), pp. 57–65. See p. 60.

40. MEMBERSHIP-SELF-STRUCTURED COMMITMENT

Borgatta, Cottrell, and Meyer; see category 12 above.

41. NOTICEABILITY

Davids, Anthony, and Anita Negrin Parenti, "Personality, Social Choice, and Adults' Perception of These Factors in Groups of Disturbed and Normal Children," *Sociometry*, 21 (September, 1958), pp. 212–224. See p. 214.

42. OBJECTING BEHAVIOR

Rosengren, p. 114; see category 36 above.

43. PARTICIPATION, IN DISCUSSION

Schutz (1958); see category 9 above.

Hoffman and Smith (1960); see category 9 above.

44. PARTICIPATION, IN GROUP

Hawkins, Charles H., "Interaction Rates of Jurors Aligned in Factions," *American Sociological Review*, 27 (October, 1962), pp. 689–691. See p. 689.

45. PARTICIPATION, TOTAL

Bales (1950); see category 8 above.

March, James G., "Influence Measurement in Experimental and Semi-Experimental Groups," *Sociometry*, 19 (December, 1956), pp. 260–271. See p. 263.

46. PERFORMANCE (BURNSTEIN, ZAJONC)

Burnstein, Eugene, and Robert B. Zajonc, "Individual Task Performance in a Changing Social Structure," *Sociometry*, 28 (March, 1965), pp. 16–29. See pp. 18–25.

47. PERFORMANCE (HALL)

Hall, Robert L., "Group Performance under Feedback that Confounds Responses of Group Members," *Sociometry*, 20 (December, 1957), pp. 297–305. See p. 299.

48. PERFORMANCE (LANZETTA, ROBY)

Lanzetta, John T., and Thornton B. Roby, "Group Performance as a Function of Work-Distribution Patterns and Task Load," *Sociometry*, 19 (June, 1956), pp. 95–104. See p. 100.

49. PERFORMANCE, ADEQUACY OF

Weinstein, Eugene A., and Paul Deutschberger, "Some Dimensions of Altercasting," *Sociometry*, 26 (December, 1963), pp. 454–466. See p. 462.

50. PERFORMANCE, RANKING

Burnstein and Zajonc; see category 46 above.

51. PERFORMANCE, ROUTINE DECISIVE

Bales (1950); see category 8 above.

Borgatta and Cottrell (1955); see category 33 above.

52. PERSONAL RELATIONS, PROMOTION OF

Schutz (1958); see category 9 above.

Hoffman and Smith (1960); see category 9 above.

53. PRIMARY-SECONDARY GROUPNESS

Borgatta, Cottrell, and Meyer; see category 12 above.

54. PRODUCTION

Berkowitz, Klanderman, and Harris p. 331; see category 19 above.

55. PROVIDES INFORMATION

Bales (1950); see category 8 above.

Philip, Hugh, and Dexter Dunphy, "Developmental Friends in Small Groups," *Sociometry*, 22 (June, 1959), pp. 162–174. See p. 165.

56. RATIONAL-IRRATIONAL PLAY

Vinacke, W. Edgar, and Abe Arkoff, "An Experimental Study of Coalitions in the Triad," *American Sociological Review*, 22 (August, 1957), pp. 406–414. See p. 412.

57. RECEIVES ACTION

Bales (1950); see category 8 above.

Slater (1955); see category 39 above.

58. RECEIVERS OF SOCIOMETRIC CHOICES, CHARACTERISTICS OF

Lundy, Richard M., "Self-Perceptions Regarding Masculinity-Femininity and Descriptions of Same and Opposite Sex Sociometric Choices," *Sociometry*, 21 (September, 1958), pp. 238–246. See p. 240.

59. RECESSIVENESS

Thorpe; see category 1 above.

60. RELEVANCY OF BEHAVIOR

Rosengren; see category 36 above.

61. ROLE APPROPRIATENESS

Meltzer, Leo, "Comparing Relationships of Individual and Average Variables to Individual Response," *American Sociological Review*, 28 (February, 1963), pp. 117–123. See p. 118.

62. ROLE BEHAVIOR

Mann, John H., and Carola Honroth Mann, "The Effects of Role-Playing Experience on Role-Playing Ability," *Sociometry*, 22 (March, 1959), pp. 64–74. See p. 68.

63. ROLE DESCRIPTION

Bates and Cloyd, pp. 29–30; see category 37 above.

64. ROLE DIFFERENTIATION

Hall; see category 47 above.

65. ROLE ENACTMENT

Mann and Mann; see category 62 above.

66. ROLE EXPECTATIONS

Videbeck, Richard, and Alan P. Bates, "An Experimental Study of Conformity to Role Expectations," *Sociometry*, 22 (March, 1959), pp. 1–11. See pp. 4–5.

67. ROLE PERFORMANCE, QUALITY OF

Mann and Mann; see category 62 above.

68. ROLE PLAYING

Mann and Mann; see category 62 above.

69. ROLE STABILITY

Meltzer; see category 61 above.

70. SEEKS INFORMATION

Bales (1950); see category 8 above.
Philip and Dunphy (1959); see category 55 above.

71. SIZE-FORMALITY FACTOR

Borgatta, Cottrell, and Meyer; see category 12 above.

72. SOCIAL INTERACTION PATTERN, FACTOR ANALYSIS

Factors: social euphoria, communication facilitation, disagreement, tension, ego defensiveness, antagonism responsiveness, low interactor high rate, middle interactor high rate, middle interactor agreement, high interactor evaluative behavior, middle interactor control #1, middle interactor control #2, high interactor control, low interactor compliance, and low interactor control)

Borgatta, Edgar F., "The Analysis of Patterns of Social Interaction," *Social Forces*, 44 (September, 1965), pp. 27–34. See p. 32.

73. SOCIAL ROLE

McGuire, Carson, "The Textown Study of Adolescents," *Texas Journal of Science*, 8 (September, 1956), pp. 264–274. See pp. 266–272.

McGuire, C., G. White, and A. C. Murphy, "Adolescent Attitudes and Expectations," *Research Memorandum* No. 6, Laboratory of Human Behavior, Department of Educational Psychology, University of Texas, April, 1957.

Peck, Robert F., and Cono Galliani, "Intelligence, Ethnicity, and Social Roles in Adolescent Society," *Sociometry*, 25 (March, 1962), pp. 64–72.

74. SPECIALIZATION, TENDENCY TOWARD

Slater (1955); see category 39 above.

75. SUGGESTING BEHAVIOR

Rosengren; see category 36 above.

76. SUPPORT OF AN ISSUE

Iwao, Sumiko, "Internal versus External Criticism of Group Standards," *Sociometry*, 26 (December, 1963), pp. 410–421. See p. 417.

77. SUPPORT RATE

Mills, Theodore M., "Power Relations in Three-Person Groups," *American Sociological Review*, 18 (August, 1953), pp. 351–357. See p. 352.

Scott, Frances Gillespie, "Family Group Structure and Patterns of Social Interaction," *American Journal of Sociology*, 68 (September, 1962), pp. 214–228. See p. 216.

Turk, Theresa, and Herman Turk, "Group Interaction in a Formal Setting: The Case of the Triad," *Sociometry*, 25 (March, 1962), pp. 48–55. See p. 51.

78. SUPPORTING BEHAVIOR

Rosengren; see category 36 above.

79. TASK ABILITY

Marak, p. 176; see category 21 above.

80. TASK-RELEVANT COOPERATION

Tuckman; see category 22 above.

SMALL GROUPS: STATUS AND STATUS RELATIONS IN

SEE ALSO
Interpersonal Relations: Attitudes toward
Interpersonal Relations: Characteristics of

1. ACQUAINTANCE

March, James G., "Influence Measurement in Experimental and Semi-Experimental Groups," *Sociometry*, 19 (December, 1956), pp. 260–271. See p. 261.

2. AFFECTIVE STATUS

Maisonneuve, Jean, "A Contribution to the Sociometry of Mutual Choices," *Sociometry*, 17 (March, 1954), pp. 33–46. See p. 36.

3. ANTAGONISM

Harvey, O. J., "An Experimental Investigation of Negative and Positive Relations Between Small Groups Through Judgmental Indices," *Sociometry*, 19 (December, 1956), pp. 201–209. See p. 203.

4. ASSOCIATION

Dentler, Robert A., and Lawrence J. Monroe, "Social Correlates of Early Adolescent Theft," *American Sociological Review*, 26 (October, 1961), pp. 733–743. See p. 737.

5. ATTRIBUTED STATUS

Sherif, Muzafer, Jack B. White, and O. J. Harvey, "Status in Experimentally Produced Groups," *American Journal of Sociology*, 60 (January, 1955), pp. 370–379. See p. 376.

6. FRIENDSHIP

Harvey (1956); see category 3 above.

Olmsted, Donald W., "Inter-group Similarities of Role Correlates," *Sociometry*, 20 (March, 1957), pp. 8–20. See p. 12.

7. INFORMAL STATUS

Harvey, O. J., "Reciprocal Influence of the Group and Three Types of Leaders in an Unstructured Situation," *Sociometry*, 23 (March, 1960), pp. 57–88. See p. 60.

8. PRESTIGE

Larsen, Otto N., and Richard J. Hill, "Social Structure and Interpersonal Communication," *American Journal of Sociology*, 63 (March, 1958), pp. 497–505. See p. 498.

9. PRODUCTIVITY STATUS

Exline, Ralph V., "Interrelations among Two Dimensions of Sociometric Status, Group Congeniality and Accuracy of Social Perception," *Sociometry*, 23 (March, 1960), pp. 85–101. See p. 90.

10. SOCIAL WORTH

Jackson, Jay M., "Reference Group Processes in a Formal Organization," *Sociometry*, 22 (December, 1959), pp. 307–327. See p. 311.

11. SOCIOMETRIC STATUS AND STRUCTURE (POPULARITY, LIKING OR DISLIKING ANOTHER, REJECTION, PERSONAL PREFERENCE, PERSONAL CHOICE, AND THE LIKE)

Moreno, Jacob L., *Who Shall Survive? A New Approach to the Problem of Human Interrelations*, Washington, D.C.: Nervous and Mental Diseases Publishing Co., 1934, Monograph No. 58.

Unlike most of the techniques included in this volume, the measurement of sociometric status and structure cannot be discussed in terms of a specific instrument or index. What is involved here is an orientation which leads the researcher to ask subjects for a type of information. The focus of this orientation is on the interpersonal relations existing between individual members of a given group or collectivity.

Jennings has described the "sociometric test" (1953, below, p. 65) as allowing "the individual to become an agent in his own behalf, to give his personal feeling for others in the form of choice for functioning with them within the group of which he and they are members." Since interpersonal relations are studied within the context of a defined group, the exact phrasing of sociometric questions tends to be tailored to the social setting being investigated. Thus, the originator of this type of questioning, Jacob L. Moreno (1934), asked school children to name their preferences for study companions. Twenty-four years later, Larsen and Hill asked campers who they would like to have as cabin mates (see Larsen and Hill, 1958). The "sense" of the question and the "importance" of the choice are situationally dependent. This quality alone has given great variety to the sociometric-type questions that researchers have asked.

A second factor contributing to the variety characterizing this general approach is the range of theoretical problems which researchers using these techniques have addressed. Sometimes the interest has been in the status of individual group members. Thus, an individual might be a "sociometric star" (a receiver of many choices), or "sociometric isolate" (a receiver of no choices), or at some point in between. Other researchers have employed sociometric instruments in analyzing communication networks, diffusion of behavior, conformity, and so on. In such research, emphasis tends to be given to clique formation and reciprocal choice behavior rather than to individual status alone. For example, Johnstone and Katz studied mutual friendship choices in their attempt to account for preferences in popular music among teen-age girls. (See Johnstone and Katz, 1957, below).

A third source of variation within the sociometric approach stems from the strategy the researcher employs in combining the basic choice data into a single, summary measure. Arbitrary combinations have been employed (see, again, Larsen and Hill, 1958, p. 498), as have more sophisticated procedures. The more sophisticated procedures have included both matrix analysis (see Proctor and Loomis, 1951, below) and scale analysis (see Riley, Riley, and

Toby, 1954, below). The selection of the analytic procedure influences the nature of the resulting measure.

Because of this great variation, it is impossible to discuss sociometric techniques both briefly and fully. The following examples illustrate the types of sociometric questions which have been asked and the contexts within which such data have been secured.

1. Theodorson, in his research on leadership and popularity, studied adult discussion-group members. At the end of the discussion meetings, members rated each other from −4 (dislike) to +4 (like) on the question: "How much do you like each person?" (Theodorson, 1957, below)

2. In their study of interpersonal orientations, Riley, Cohn, Toby, and Riley (1954, below) asked high school students the following two questions: (a) "Who in the grade do you personally like best?" (b) "Who in the grade do you think likes you best?"

3. Kerckhoff, Back, and Miller (1965, below) found channels of interpersonal relations to be important in the spread of hysterical reactions within a factory. Channels of interpersonal relations were identified by asking workers to name their three best friends in the plant.

4. Riley and her associates measured the status of high-school students by employing the H-technique for scale analysis. Each student was asked to name those among his fellows whom (1) he thought popular, (2) he admired, (3) he liked, (4) he confided in, (5) he chose to have fun with, and (6) he talked to about movies. H-technique analysis resulted in a scale containing four contrived items and having a reproducibility of 99 per cent. (Riley, Riley, and Toby, 1954, below.)

5. In determining the relative degree of ethnocentrism for different ethnic groups, Lundberg and Dickson (February, 1952, and July, 1952, below) asked high-school students the following sociometric questions:

a. Name three students whom you would like to have represent your high school next week at a big national meeting of high school students.

b. If all the students were asked to help on a school picnic, which three students would you like to work with?
c. If you could have a *date* with *anyone in this school*, which three people would you choose?
d. Who are your three best friends in this high school (boys or girls)?
e. It is an obvious fact that we do not like everyone equally well. List here the names of students in this high school whom you don't like so well, wouldn't like to run around with, or feel that your personalities clash.
f. If you think any of the students you listed in question d will choose you as one of their best friends, place an X in front of their names.

6. Harrison White (1961, below) analyzed the relationships between organization conflict and sociometric structure in the "Forthright" Corporation, a medium-sized metallurgical company. The data he secured from his sample of company managers included responses to the following questions:

a. Could you list the two or three managers with whom you have the most dealings in the course of your work?
b. Do any of your personal friends work at [Forthright]? Who? How regularly do you see them away from work?
c. Would you single out the one or two people in [Forthright] whose ideas about business policy and procedure are most similar and congenial to yours?
d. Who do you guess might single you out as one of those with similar ideas about business policy and procedure?
e. Who is the individual in [Forthright] whom you most respect for great knowledge? For ability to deal effectively with people?
f. With what persons in [Forthright] do you find it most uncomfortable to associate?—not that you dislike them, just that you find it awkward to deal with them.
g. Who might think you were one of the people it was most uncomfortable to associate with?

The content of the questions asked, then, depends upon both the researcher's problem and the situation within which that problem is being investigated. A complete discussion of the types of sociometric questions that have been used and the types of measures which have been constructed on the basis of data derived from such questions would require a separate volume of considerable length. For those wishing to pursue this topic further, the earlier summaries of sociometric measurement by Lindzey and

Borgatta (see Lindzey and Borgatta, 1954, below) and by Moreno and his associates (see Moreno and colleagues, 1960, below) will be of considerable value.

Proctor, Charles H., and Charles P. Loomis, "Analysis of Sociometric Data," Chapter 17 in Marie Jahoda, Morton Deutsch, and Stuart W. Cook, *Research Methods in Social Relations*, Part Two, New York: Dryden Press, 1951. See pp. 561–585.

Lundberg, George A., and Lenore Dickson, "Selective Association among Ethnic Groups in a High School Population," *American Sociological Review*, 17 (February, 1952), pp. 23–35. See pp. 23–24.

Lundberg, George A., and Lenore Dickson, "Inter-Ethnic Relations in a High School Population," *American Journal of Sociology*, 58 (July, 1952), pp. 1–10. See p. 2.

Northway, Mary L., *A Primer of Sociometry*, Toronto: University of Toronto Press, 1952, p. 26.

Jennings, Helen Hall, "The Significance of Choice in Human Behavior," Chapter 6 in Dorwin Cartwright and Alvin Zander (eds.), *Group Dynamics*, Evanston, Ill.: Row, Peterson and Co., 1953, pp. 62–69.

Riley, Matilda White, John W. Riley, Jr., and Jackson Toby, *Sociological Studies in Scale Analysis*, New Brunswick, N.J.: Rutgers University Press, 1954, pp. 390–409.

Borgatta, Edgar F., "Analysis of Social Interaction and Sociometric Perception," *Sociometry*, 17 (March, 1954), pp. 7–32. See p. 15.

Lindzey, Gardner, and James A. Urdan, "Personality and Social Choice," *Sociometry*, 17 (March, 1954), pp. 47–63. See p. 47.

Lindzey, Gardner, and Edgar F. Borgatta, "Sociometric Measurement," Chapter 11 in Gardner Lindzey (ed.), *Handbook of Social Psychology*, volume I, Cambridge, Mass.: Addison-Wesley Publishing Co., 1954, pp. 405–448.

Northway, Mary L., "A Plan for Sociometric Studies in a Longitudinal Programme of Research in Child Development," *Sociometry*, 17 (August, 1954), pp. 272–281. See p. 273.

Cole, David, " 'Rational Argument' and 'Prestige-Suggestion' as

Factors Influencing Judgment," *Sociometry*, 17 (December, 1954), pp. 350–354. See p. 350.

Emerson, Richard M., "Deviation and Rejection: An Experimental Replication," *American Sociological Review*, 19 (December, 1954), pp. 688–693. See p. 689.

Marks, J. B., "Interests, Leadership and Sociometric Status among Adolescents," *Sociometry*, 17 (December, 1954), pp. 340–349. See p. 341.

Olmsted, Michael S., "Orientation and Role in the Small Group," *American Sociological Review*, 19 (December, 1954), pp. 741–751. See p. 748.

Riley, Matilda White, Richard Cohn, Jackson Toby, and John W. Riley, Jr., "Interpersonal Orientations in Small Groups: A Consideration of the Questionnaire Approach," *American Sociological Review*, 19 (December, 1954), pp. 715–724. See p. 718.

Venable, Tom C., "The Relationship of Selected Factors to the Social Structure of a Stable Group," *Sociometry*, 17 (December, 1954), pp. 355–357. See p. 356.

Gronlund, Norman E., "Acquaintance Span and Sociometric Status," *Sociometry*, 18 (February, 1955), pp. 62–68. See p. 64.

Muldoon, John F., "The Concentration of Liked and Disliked Members in Groups and the Relationship of the Concentrations to Group Cohesiveness," *Sociometry*, 18 (February, 1955), pp. 73–81. See p. 75.

Speroff, B. J., "Job Satisfaction and Interpersonal Desirability Values," *Sociometry*, 18 (February, 1955), pp. 69–72. See p. 70.

Bjerstedt, Åke, "Sociometric Relations in Elementary School Classes," *Sociometry*, 18 (May, 1955), pp. 147–152. See p. 149.

Gronlund, Norman E., "Sociometric Status and Sociometric Perception," *Sociometry*, 18 (May, 1955), pp. 122–128. See pp. 122–123.

Speroff, B. J., "The Stability of Sociometric Choice among Kindergarten Children," *Sociometry*, 18 (May, 1955), pp. 129–131. See p. 129.

Northway, Mary L., and Joyce Detweiler, "Children's Perception of Friends and Non-Friends," *Sociometry*, 18 (December, 1955), pp. 527–531. See p. 528.

Northway, Mary L., and Margaret McCallum Rooks, "Creativity and Sociometric Status in Children," *Sociometry*, 18 (December, 1955), pp. 450–457. See p. 452.

Banks, E. P., "Methodological Problems in the Study of Psychiatric Wards," *Social Forces*, 34 (March, 1956), pp. 277–280. See p. 278.

Theodorson, George A., "The Relationship between Leadership and Popularity Roles in Small Groups," *American Sociological Review*, 22 (February, 1957), pp. 58–67. See p. 61.

Johnstone, John, and Elihu Katz, "Youth and Popular Music: A Study in the Sociology of Taste," *American Journal of Sociology*, 62 (March, 1957), pp. 563–568. See p. 567.

Larsen and Hill (1958), p. 498; see category 8 above.

Riley, Matilda White, and Richard Cohn, "Control Networks in Informal Groups," *Sociometry*, 21 (March, 1958), pp. 30–49. See pp. 35 and 43–44.

Berkun, Mitchell, and Tor Meeland, "Sociometric Effects of Race and of Combat Performance," *Sociometry*, 21 (June, 1958), pp. 145–149. See p. 145.

Davids, Anthony, and Anita Negrin Parenti, "Personality, Social Choice, and Adults' Perception of These Factors in Groups of Disturbed and Normal Children," *Sociometry*, 21 (September, 1958), pp. 212–224. See pp. 213 and 214.

Exline (1960); see category 9 above.

Moreno, Jacob L. and colleagues, *The Sociometry Reader*, Glencoe, Ill.: The Free Press, 1960.

Turk, Herman, "Instrumental Values and the Popularity of Instrumental Leaders," *Social Forces*, 39 (March, 1961), pp. 252–260. See p. 255.

White, Harrison, "Management Conflict and Sociometric Structure," *American Journal of Sociology*, 67 (September, 1961), pp. 185–199. See p. 192.

Turk, Herman, and Theresa Turk, "Personal Sentiments in a Hierarchy," *Social Forces*, 40 (December, 1961), pp. 137–140. See p. 138.

Steiner, Ivan D., and Homer H. Johnson, "Authoritarianism and Conformity," *Sociometry*, 26 (March, 1963), pp. 21–34. See p. 28.

Kerckhoff, Alan C., Kurt W. Back, and Norman Miller, "Sociometric Patterns in Hysterical Contagion," *Sociometry*, 28 (March, 1965), pp. 2–15. See pp. 8–13.

12. STATUS CONSENSUS

Slater, Philip E., "Role Differentiation in Small Groups," *American Sociological Review*, 20 (June, 1955), pp. 300–310. See p. 301.

13. STATUS INSECURITY

Emerson, Richard M., "Power-Dependence Relations: Two Experiments," *Sociometry*, 27 (September, 1964), pp. 282–298. See p. 285.

14. STATUS RANKING

Sherif, White, and Harvey (1955); see category 5 above.

Bonney, Merl E., "A Study of Constancy of Sociometric Ranks Among College Students Over a Two-Year Period," *Sociometry*, 18 (December, 1955), pp. 531–542. See p. 532.

Katz, Elihu, William L. Libby, Jr., and Fred L. Strodtbeck, "Status Mobility and Reactions to Deviance and Subsequent Conformity," *Sociometry*, 27 (September, 1964), pp. 245–260. See p. 249.

SOCIAL MOBILITY AND
RELATED MEASURES

SEE ALSO

Achievement
Achievement Motivation
Aspirations

1. CAREER MOBILITY

Seeman, Melvin, "Social Mobility and Administrative Behavior," *American Sociological Review*, 23 (December, 1958), pp. 633–642. See p. 636.

2. CAREER PATTERNS

Gusfield, Joseph R., "Occupational Roles and Forms of Enterprise," *American Journal of Sociology*, 66 (May, 1961), pp. 571–580. See p. 574.

3. CLASS MOBILITY, INTERGENERATIONAL

Blau, Zena Smith, "Exposure to Child-Rearing Experts: A Structural Interpretation of Class-Color Differences," *American Journal of Sociology*, 69 (May, 1964), pp. 596–608. See p. 603.

4. GENERATIONAL OCCUPATIONAL MOBILITY SCORE (GOMS)

Tumin, Melvin M., and Arnold S. Feldman, "Theory and Measurement of Occupational Mobility," *American Sociological Review*, 22 (June, 1957), pp. 281–288. See pp. 283–284.

Geschwender, James A., "Theory and Measurement of Occupational Mobility: A Re-examination," *American Sociological Review*, 26 (June, 1961), pp. 451–452.

5. DEMAND MOBILITY

Rogoff, Natalie, *Recent Trends in Occupational Mobility*, New York: The Free Press of Glencoe, 1953, pp. 29–33.

Marsh, Robert M., "Values, Demand, and Social Mobility," *American Sociological Review*, 28 (August, 1963), pp. 565–575. See p. 566.

6. INTERGENERATIONAL CLIMBING OF COUPLE

Wilensky, Harold L., "Mass Society and Mass Culture: Interdependence or Independence?" *American Sociological Review*, 29 (April, 1964), pp. 173–197. See p. 185.

7. JOB HISTORY

Wilensky, Harold L., "Orderly Careers and Social Participation: The Impact of Work History on Social Integration in the Middle Mass," *American Sociological Review*, 26 (August, 1961), pp. 521–539. See p. 525.

Ladinsky, Jack, "Careers of Lawyers, Law Practice, and Legal Institutions," *American Sociological Review*, 28 (February, 1963), pp. 47–54. See p. 50.

8. JOB MOBILITY

Manley, Charles R., Jr., "The Migration of Older People," *American Journal of Sociology*, 59 (January, 1954), pp. 324–331. See p. 329.

9. MOBILITY POTENTIAL

Leslie, Gerald R., and Arthur H. Richardson, "Life-Cycle, Career Pattern, and the Decision to Move," *American Sociological Review*, 26 (December, 1961), pp. 894–902. See p. 895.

10. OCCUPATIONAL MOBILITY, CAREER (CENSUS, EDWARDS RELATED)

Goldstein, Sidney, "Migration and Occupational Mobility in Norristown, Pennsylvania," *American Sociological Review*, 20 (August, 1955), pp. 402–408. See p. 405.

Mack, Raymond W., Raymond J. Murphy, and Seymour Yellin, "The Protestant Ethic, Level of Aspiration, and Social Mobility: An Empirical Test," *American Sociological Review*, 21 (June, 1956), pp. 295–300. See p. 298.

Mack, Raymond W., "Occupational Ideology and the Determinate Role," *Social Forces*, 35 (October, 1957), pp. 37–44. See p. 42.

Meier, Dorothy L., and Wendell Bell, "Anomia and Differential Access to the Achievement of Life Goals," *American Sociological Review*, 24 (April, 1959), pp. 189–202. See p. 202.

Breed, Warren, "Occupational Mobility and Suicide among White Males," *American Sociological Review*, 28 (April, 1963), pp. 179–188. See p. 184.

11. OCCUPATIONAL MOBILITY, CAREER (NORTH, HATT RELATED)

Reiss, Albert J., Jr., "Occupational Mobility of Professional Workers," *American Sociological Review*, 20 (December, 1955), pp. 693–700. See p. 694.

Westoff, Charles E., Marvin Bressler, and Philip C. Sagi, "The Concept of Social Mobility: An Empirical Inquiry," *American Sociological Review*, 25 (June, 1960), pp. 375–385. See p. 380.

Wilensky (1961), p. 527; see category 7 above.

Breed (1963), p. 184; see category 10 above.

Bressler, Marvin, and Charles F. Westoff, "Catholic Education, Economic Values and Achievement," *American Journal of Sociology*, 69 (November, 1963), pp. 225–233. See p. 228.

12. OCCUPATIONAL MOBILITY, INTERGENERATIONAL (CAMPBELL, GURIN, MILLER)

Campbell, Angus, Gerald Gurin, and Warren E. Miller, *The Voter Decides*, Evanston, Ill.: Row, Peterson and Co., 1954, p. 226.

Jackson, Elton F., and Harry J. Crockett, Jr., "Occupational Mobility in the United States: A Point Estimate and Trend Comparison," *American Sociological Review*, 29 (February, 1964), pp. 5–15. See pp. 11–15.

13. OCCUPATIONAL MOBILITY, INTERGENERATIONAL (CENSUS, EDWARDS RELATED)

The twelve citations listed below all use the Census index of occupations by socioeconomic groups (see Socioeconomic Status: Occupation, category 25) as their point of departure in measuring intergenerational mobility. Because the manner in which the Census categories are used varies considerably, none is singled out here for detailed presentation.

Mack, Murphy, and Yellin (1956), p. 298; see category 10 above.

Lystad, Mary H., "Social Mobility Among Selected Groups of Schizophrenic Patients," *American Sociological Review*, 22 (June, 1957), pp. 288–292. See p. 289.

Mack (1957), p. 42; see category 10 above.

Curtis, Richard F., "Note on Occupational Mobility and Union Membership in Detroit: A Replication," *Social Forces*, 38 (October, 1959), pp. 69–71. See p. 70.

Curtis, Richard F., "Occupational Mobility and Urban Social Life," *American Journal of Sociology*, 65 (December, 1959), pp. 296–298. See p. 297.

Litwak, Eugene, "Occupational Mobility and Extended Family Cohesion," *American Sociological Review*, 25 (February, 1960), pp. 9–21. See p. 14.

Litwak, Eugene, "Reference Group Theory, Bureaucratic Career, and Neighborhood Primary Group Cohesion," *Sociometry*, 23 (March, 1960), pp. 72–84. See p. 78.

Curtis, Richard F., "Occupational Mobility and Church Participation," *Social Forces*, 38 (May, 1960), pp. 315–319. See p. 317.

Litwak, Eugene, "Voluntary Associations and Neighborhood Cohesion," *American Sociological Review*, 26 (April, 1961), pp. 258–271. See p. 268.

Breed (1963), p. 183; see category 10 above.

Duncan, Otis Dudley, and Robert W. Hodge, "Education and Occupational Mobility: A Regression Analysis," *American Journal of Sociology*, 68 (May, 1963), pp. 629–644. See p. 630.

Curtis, Richard F., "Differential Association and the Stratification of the Urban Community," *Social Forces*, 42 (October, 1963), pp. 68–77. See p. 71.

14. OCCUPATIONAL MOBILITY, INTERGENERATIONAL (CENTERS)

Centers, Richard, "Occupational Mobility of Urban Occupational Strata," *American Sociogical Review*, 13 (April, 1948), pp. 197–203. See p. 198.

Centers, Richard, "Marital Selection and Occupational Strata,"

American Journal of Sociology, 54 (May, 1949), pp. 530–535. See p. 535.
Jackson and Crockett (1964), pp. 6, 7, and 12; see category 12 above.

15. OCCUPATIONAL MOBILITY, INTERGENERATIONAL (GLASS)

Glass, D. V. (ed.), *Social Mobility in Britain*, New York: The Free Press of Glencoe, 1954, pp. 79–159.
White, Harrison C., "Cause and Effect in Social Mobility Tables," *Behavioral Science*, 7 (January, 1963), pp. 14–27.
Goodman, Leo A., "On the Statistical Analysis of Mobility Tables," *American Journal of Sociology*, 70 (March, 1965), pp. 564–585. See pp. 565 and 571.

16. OCCUPATIONAL MOBILITY, INTERGENERATIONAL (NORTH, HATT RELATED)

The ten citations listed below measure intergenerational mobility in a similar manner only in that they all use the North-Hatt occupational prestige scores (see Socioeconomic Status: Occupation, category 6) as their point of departure. Because the manner in which the scores are used varies considerably, none is presented in detail here.

Davis, James A., "Status Symbols and the Measurement of Status Perception," *Sociometry*, 19 (September, 1956), pp. 154–165. See p. 162.
Adams, Stuart, "Origins of American Occupational Elites, 1900–55," *American Journal of Sociology*, 62 (January, 1957), pp. 360–368. See p. 361.
Seeman (1958), p. 636; see category 1 above.
Westoff, Bressler, and Sagi (1960), p. 380; see category 11 above.
Crockett, Harry J., Jr., "The Achievement Motive and Differential Occupational Mobility in the United States," *American Sociological Review*, 27 (April, 1962), pp. 191–204. See pp. 195–204.
Breed (1963), p. 183; see category 10 above.
Bressler and Westoff (1963), p. 228; see category 11 above.
Jackson and Crockett (1964); see category 12 above.

Neal, Arthur G., and Melvin Seeman, "Organizations and Power-lessness: A Test of the Mediation Hypothesis," *American Sociological Review*, 29 (April, 1964), pp. 216–225. See p. 219.

Patterson, Samuel C., "Inter-Generational Occupational Mobility and Legislative Voting Behavior," *Social Forces*, 43 (October, 1964), pp. 90–93. See p. 91.

17. OCCUPATIONAL MOBILITY, INTERGENERATIONAL (PIHLBLAD, GREGORY)

Pihlblad, C. T., and C. L. Gregory, "The Role of Test Intelligence and Occupational Background as Factors on Occupational Choice," *Sociometry*, 19 (September, 1956), pp. 192–199. See p. 194.

18. OCCUPATIONAL MOBILITY, INTERGENERATIONAL (SVALA-STOGA)

Svalastoga, Kaare, *Prestige, Class, and Mobility*, London: William Heineman, Ltd., 1959, pp. 288–299.

White (1963), pp. 14–27; see category 15 above.

Goodman (1965), p. 571; see category 15 above.

19. OCCUPATIONAL MOBILITY, INTERGENERATIONAL (SIMS RE-LATED)

Sims, Verner M., "A Technique for Measuring Social Class Identification," *Educational and Psychological Measurement*, 11 (Winter, 1951), pp. 541–548. See pp. 542–545.

Perrucci, Robert, "The Significance of Intra-Occupational Mobil-ity: Some Methodological and Theoretical Notes, Together with a Case Study of Engineers," *American Sociological Review*, 26 (December, 1961), pp. 874–883. See p. 880.

20. OCCUPATIONAL MOBILITY OF IMMIGRANTS TO ISRAEL

Shuval, Judith T., "Value Orientations of Immigrants to Israel," *Sociometry*, 26 (June, 1963), pp. 247–259. See pp. 253–254.

21. OCCUPATIONAL MOBILITY IN WEST GERMANY

Janowitz, Morris, "Social Stratification and Mobility in West Ger-many," *American Journal of Sociology*, 64 (July, 1958), pp. 6–24. See p. 7.

22. PAY MOBILITY

Manley, pp. 328–329; see category 8 above.

23. PERCEIVED SOCIAL MOBILITY

Lopreato, Joseph, "Social Stratification and Mobility in a South Italian Town," *American Sociological Review*, 26 (August, 1961), pp. 585–596. See p. 595.

24. SOCIAL DISTANCE MOBILITY

Rogoff (1953), pp. 29–33; see category 5 above.

Marsh (1963), p. 566; see category 5 above.

25. SOCIAL MOBILITY

(Factors: occupational mobility, financial mobility, residential mobility, and mobility perceptions and aspirations)

Westoff, Bressler, and Sagi (1960), pp. 380–382; see category 11 above.

26. SOCIAL MOBILITY, CAREER

Rosengren, William R., "Social Sources of Pregnancy as Illness or Normality," *Social Forces*, 39 (March, 1961), pp. 260–267. See p. 263.

27. SOCIAL MOBILITY, INTERGENERATIONAL (HOLLINGSHEAD)

Hollingshead, August B., Robert Ellis, and E. Kirby, "Social Mobility and Mental Illness," *American Sociological Review*, 19 (October, 1954), pp. 577–584. See p. 579.

28. SOCIAL MOBILITY, INTERGENERATIONAL (WARNER RELATED)

Mack, Murphy, and Yellin (1956), p. 298; see category 10 above.

Mack (1957), p. 42; see category 10 above.

Smelser, William T., "Adolescent and Adult Occupational Choices as a Function of Family Socioeconomic History," *Sociometry*, 26 (December, 1963), pp. 393–409. See p. 395.

29. SOCIAL MOBILITY IN ITALY

Lopreato, p. 592; see category 23 above.

SOCIAL PARTICIPATION

1. ACTIVENESS OF UNION MEMBER

Wilensky, Harold L., "The Labor Vote: A Local Union's Impact on the Political Conduct of Its Members," *Social Forces*, 35 (December, 1956) pp. 111–120. See p. 115.

2. ACTIVITY

Cavan, Ruth S., and Colleagues, *Personal Adjustment in Old Age*, Chicago, Ill.: Science Research Associates, 1949, p. 50.

Maddox, George L., "Activity and Morale: A Longitudinal Study of Selected Elderly Subjects," *Social Forces*, 42 (December, 1963), pp. 195–204. See p. 197.

3. FRIENDSHIP PARTICIPATION, EXTENT OF

Blau, Zena Smith, "Structural Constraints on Friendship in Old Age," *American Sociological Review*, 26 (June, 1961), pp. 429–439. See p. 430.

4. GENERAL COMMUNITY PARTICIPATION SCALE

Foskett, John M., "Social Structure and Social Participation," *American Sociological Review*, 20 (August, 1955), pp. 431–438. See p. 432.

Agger, Robert E., "Power Attributions in the Local Community: Theoretical and Research Considerations," *Social Forces*, 34 (May, 1956), pp. 322–331. See p. 323.

5. GREGARIOUSNESS

Katz, Elihu, and Paul F. Lazarsfeld, *Personal Influence*, Glencoe, Ill.: The Free Press, 1955.

Carter, Roy E., Jr., and Peter Clarke, "Public Affairs Opinion Leadership among Educational Television Viewers," *American Sociological Review*, 27 (December, 1962), pp. 792–799. See pp. 797–798.

6. LIFE SPACE, PERCEIVED

Cumming, Elaine, Lois R. Dean, David S. Newell, and Isabel McCaffrey, "Disengagement—A Tentative Theory of Aging," *Sociometry*, 23 (March, 1960), pp. 23–35. See p. 27.

7. LIFE SPACE, SOCIAL

Williams, Richard H., and Martin B. Loeb, "The Adult's Social Life Space and Successful Aging: Some Suggestions for a Conceptual Framework," paper read at the annual meeting of the American Gerontological Society, 1956.

Cumming, Dean, Newell, and McCaffrey (1960), p. 26; see category 6 above.

8. MEMBERSHIP INVOLVEMENT

Simpson, Richard L. and William H. Gulley, "Goals, Environmental Pressures, and Organizational Characteristics," *American Sociological Review*, 27 (June, 1962), pp. 344–351. See p. 348.

9. ORGANIZATIONAL MEMBERSHIP STRUCTURE

Agger, Robert E., and Daniel Goldrich, "Community Power Structure and Partisanship," *American Sociological Review*, 23 (August, 1958), pp. 383–392. See p. 384.

10. ORIENTATIONS TO INTERACTION

Dean, Lois R., "The Pattern Variables: Some Empirical Operations," *American Sociological Review*, 26 (February, 1961), pp. 80–90. See p. 85.

11. OWN ACTIVITY ON COMMITTEE PROJECTS

Meltzer, Leo, "Comparing Relationships of Individual and Average Variables to Individual Response," *American Sociological Review*, 28 (February, 1963), pp. 117–123. See p. 118.

12. PARTICIPATION

Clark, John P., "Measuring Alienation within a Social System," *American Sociological Review*, 24 (December, 1959), pp. 849–852. See p. 851.

13. PARTICIPATION IN COMMUNITY POLICY-MAKING, COMPOS-
ITE INDEX OF

Agger and Goldrich, p. 389; see category 9 above.

14. PARTICIPATION IN VOLUNTARY RELATIONSHIPS

Lenski, Gerhard E., "Social Participation and Status Crystallization," *American Sociological Review*, 21 (August, 1956), pp.
458–464. See p. 461.

15. RECREATION SCORE

Burgess, Ernest W., "Social Relations, Activities, and Personal
Adjustment," *American Journal of Sociology*, 59 (January,
1954), pp. 352–360. See p. 355.

16. SOCIAL INVOLVEMENT

Hastings, Philip K., "The Voter and Non-Voter," *American Journal of Sociology*, 62 (November, 1956), pp. 302–307. See p.
304.

17. SOCIAL ISOLATION (LOWENTHAL)

Lowenthal, Marjorie Fiske, "Social Isolation and Mental Illness in
Old Age," *American Sociological Review*, 29 (February,
1964), pp. 54–70. See pp. 56–63.

18. SOCIAL ISOLATION (MEIER, BELL)

Meier, Dorothy L., and Wendell Bell, "Anomia and Differential
Access to the Achievement of Life Goals," *American Sociological Review*, 24 (April, 1959), pp. 189–202. See p. 202.

19. SOCIAL PARTICIPATION (ADLER)

Adler, Leta M., "Patients of a State Mental Hospital: The Outcome of Their Hospitalization," in Arnold Rose (ed.), *Mental Health and Mental Disorder*, New York: W. W. Norton
& Co., 1955, pp. 501–523.

Freeman, Howard E., and Ozzie G. Simmons, "Mental Patients in
the Community: Family Settings and Performance Levels,"
American Sociological Review, 23 (April, 1958), pp. 147–154.
See p. 150.

Freeman, Howard E., and Ozzie G. Simmons, "The Social Integration of Former Mental Patients," *International Journal of
Social Psychiatry*, 4 (Spring, 1959), pp. 264–271. See p. 264.

20. SOCIAL PARTICIPATION (ANGRIST)

Angrist, Shirley S., *Social Factors in the Outcome of Mental Hospitalization*, unpublished Ph.D. dissertation, Ohio State University, 1960.

Lefton, Mark, Shirley Angrist, Simon Dinitz, and Benjamin Pasamanick, "Social Class, Expectations, and Performance of Mental Patients," *American Journal of Sociology*, 68 (July, 1962), pp. 79–87. See p. 81.

21. SOCIAL PARTICIPATION (BELL)

Bell, Wendell, "Anomie, Social Isolation, and the Class Structure," *Sociometry*, 20 (June, 1956), pp. 105–116. See p. 107.

22. SOCIAL PARTICIPATION (CHAPIN AND MODIFICATIONS)

Chapin, F. Stuart, "A Quantitative Scale for Rating the Home and Social Environment of Middle Class Families in an Urban Community," *Journal of Educational Psychology*, 19 (February, 1928), pp. 99–111. See pp. 100–101.

Chapin, F. Stuart, *Social Participation Scale*, Minneapolis, Minn.: University of Minnesota Press, 1937. Reprinted in F. Stuart Chapin, *Experimental Designs in Sociological Research* (Revised Edition), New York: Harper and Brothers, 1955, pp. 276–278.

Chapin, F. Stuart, "Social Participation and Social Intelligence," *American Sociological Review*, 4 (April, 1939), pp. 157–166. See pp. 158–159.

The Social Participation Scale was developed in 1928 to measure "the degree of a person's or family's participation in community groups and institutions." (Chapin, 1937/1955, p. 276) Chapin included five organizational activities in his measure: organizational memberships, attendance, contributions, committee memberships and office holding. These five activities were assigned arbitrary weights, and the sum of the weighted activities was taken as an index of participation.

For example, suppose a husband belongs to six organizations or clubs, attends five, contributes to three, is a member of two committees and holds one officership. His score would be computed as follows:

$$S.P. = 6(1) + 5(2) + 3(3) + 2(4) + 1(5) = 38$$

If the researcher is interested in family rather than individual participation, the score for the wife would be added to that of the husband, and the sum divided by two. Chapin has called this total score for a family "the group setting index of the family." (Chapin, 1928, p. 101)

In his original discussion of the measure, Chapin reported correlations between the "group setting score" and (1) a cultural possessions score based on the presence in the home of books, newspapers, periodicals, musical instruments, and the like $(r = .68)$, (2) a measure of family income $(r = .64)$ and (3) a measure of a family's material possessions $(r = .63)$. (Chapin, 1928, p. 106) In later studies, social participation was found to correlate with socioeconomic status, income, and occupation. (Chapin, 1939, pp. 159–160) Several studies have been made of the reliability of the Social Participation Scale with reliability coefficients between .89 and .95 being reported. (Chapin, 1928, p. 159 and Chapin, 1937/1955, p. 276)

Directions for Using the Social Participation Scale

1. List by name the organizations with which the husband and wife are affiliated (at the *present time*) as indicated by the five types of participation No. 1 to No. 5 across the top of the schedule. [See page 365.] It is not necessary to enter the date at which the person became a member of the organization. It is important to enter L if the membership is in a purely local group, and to enter N if the membership is in a local unit of some state or national organization.

2. An organization means some active and organized grouping, usually but not necessarily in the community or neighborhood of residence, such as club, lodge, business or political or professional or religious organization, labor union, etc.; subgroups of a church or other institution are to be included separately *provided they are organized* as more or less independent entities.

3. Record under attendance the mere fact of attendance or non-attendance without regard to the number of meetings attended (corrections for the number attended *have not* been found to influence the final score sufficiently to justify such labor).

4. Record under contributions the mere fact of financial contributions or absence of contributions, and *not the amount* (corrections for

amount of contributions *have not* been found to influence the final score sufficiently to justify such labor).

5. Previous memberships, committee work, offices held, etc., should *not* be counted or recorded or used in computing the final score.
6. Final score is computed by counting each membership as 1, each attended as 2, each contributed to as 3, each committee membership as 4, and each office held as 5. If both parents are living

SOCIAL PARTICIPATION SCALE

Address_____ Case No._____

HUSBAND

Age_____Education_____Race or Nationality_____
Occupation_____Income_____

Name of Organization	1. Member*	2. Attendance	3. Financial Contributions	4. Member of Committees (Not Names)	5. Offices Held
1.					
2.					
3.					
4.					
5.					
6.					
7.					
8.					
9.					
10.					
Totals					

WIFE

The schedule for the Wife is the same as the schedule for the Husband.
Date_____ Investigator_____

* Enter L if purely local group; enter N if a local unit of a state or national organization.

Distribution of total scores from a representative sample of an urban population, a J-curve; skewed to higher scores of 100 and over; mode at 0 to 11 points.

regularly in the home, add their total scores and divide the sum by two. The result is the mean social participation score of the family. In case only one parent lives in the home, as widow, widower, etc., the sum of that one person's participations is the score for the family (unless it is desired to obtain scores on children also).

Anderson, W. A., "The Family and Individual Social Participation," *American Sociological Review*, 8 (August, 1943), pp. 420–424. See p. 420.

Anderson, W. A., "Family Social Participation and Social Status Self-Rating," *American Sociological Review*, 11 (June, 1946), pp. 253–258. See p. 256.

Chapin, F. Stuart, *Experimental Designs in Sociological Research*, New York: Harper and Bros., 1947, pp. 196–197.

Webber, Irving L., "The Organized Social Life of the Retired in Two Florida Communities," *American Journal of Sociology*, 59 (January, 1954), pp. 340–346. See p. 340.

Olmsted, Donald W., "Organizational Leadership and Social Structure in a Small City," *American Sociological Review*, 19 (June, 1954), pp. 273–281. See p. 273.

Reeder, Leo G., "Social Factors in Heart Disease: A Preliminary Research Report on the Relationship of Certain Social Factors to Blood Pressure in Males," *Social Forces*, 34 (May, 1956), pp. 367–371. See p. 368.

Evan, William M., "Dimensions of Participation in Voluntary Associations," *Social Forces*, 35 (December, 1957), pp. 148–153. See p. 151.

Miller, Delbert C., "Industry and Community Power Structure: A Comparative Study of an American and an English City," *American Sociological Review*, 23 (February, 1958), pp. 9–15. See p. 13.

Liu, William T., "The Marginal Catholics in the South: A Revision of Concepts," *American Journal of Sociology*, 65 (January, 1960), pp. 383–390. See p. 386.

Mizruchi, Ephraim H., "Social Structure and Anomia," *American Sociological Review*, 25 (October, 1960), pp. 645–654. See p. 649.

Liu, William T., "The Community Reference System, Religiosity, and Race Attitude," *Social Forces*, 39 (May, 1961), pp. 324–328. See p. 326.

Polgar, Steven, Howard Dunphy, and Bruce Cox, "Diffusion and Farming Advice: A Test of Some Current Notions," *Social Forces*, 42 (October, 1963), pp. 104–111. See p. 107.

Coughenour, C. Milton, "The Rate of Technological Diffusion among Locality Groups," *American Journal of Sociology*, 69 (January, 1964), pp. 325–339. See p. 334.

Erbe, William, "Social Involvement and Political Activity: A Replication and Elaboration," *American Sociological Review*, 29 (April, 1964), pp. 198–215. See p. 205.

Photiadis, John D., "Overt Conformity to Church Teaching as a Function of Religious Belief and Group Participation," *American Journal of Sociology*, 70 (January, 1965), pp. 423–428. See p. 424.

23. SOCIAL PARTICIPATION (HIRABAYASHI, ISHAQ)

Hirabayashi, Gordon H., and My Ishaq, "Social Change in Jordan: A Quantitative Approach in a Non-Census Area," *American Journal of Sociology*, 64 (July, 1958), pp. 36–40. See p. 38.

24. SOCIAL PARTICIPATION (KOHN)

Kohn, Melvin L., and John A. Clausen, "Social Isolation and Schizophrenia," *American Sociological Review*, 20 (June, 1955), pp. 265–273. See p. 267.

25. SOCIAL PARTICIPATION (LARSON)

Larson, Olaf F., "Rural Community Patterns of Social Participation," *Social Forces*, 16 (March, 1938), pp. 385–388. See p. 385.

Mather, William G., "Income and Social Participation," *American Sociological Review*, 6 (June, 1941), pp. 380–383. See p. 380.

Reissman, Leonard, "Class, Leisure, and Social Participation," *American Sociological Review*, 19 (February, 1954), pp. 76–84. See p. 80.

26. SOCIAL PARTICIPATION (TEELE)

Teele, James E., "Measures of Social Participation," *Social Problems*, 10 (Summer, 1962), pp. 31–39.

Teele, James E., "Suicidal Behavior, Assaultiveness, and Socialization Principles," *Social Forces*, 43 (May, 1965), pp. 510–518. See p. 512.

27. SOCIAL PARTICIPATION (YOUNG, MAYO)

Young, James N., and Selz C. Mayo, "Manifest and Latent Participators in a Rural Community Action Program," *Social Forces*, 38 (December, 1959), pp. 140–145. See p. 141.

28. SOCIAL PARTICIPATION, RANGE OF PRIMARY

Wilensky, Harold L., "Orderly Careers and Social Participation: The Impact of Work History on Social Integration in the Middle Mass," *American Sociological Review*, 26 (August, 1961), pp. 521–539. See p. 528.

Wilensky, Harold L., "Mass Society and Mass Culture: Interdependence or Independence?" *American Sociological Review*, 29 (April, 1964), pp. 173–197. See p. 185.

29. SOCIAL PARTICIPATION, RANGE OF SECONDARY

Wilensky (1961); see category 28 above.

30. SOCIAL PARTICIPATION, VITALITY OF OBJECTIVE

Wilensky (1961), p. 526; see category 28 above.

31. SOCIAL PARTICIPATION: ATTACHMENT TO THE COMMUNITY

Wilensky (1961), pp. 527–528; see category 28 above.

32. SOCIAL PARTICIPATION: EARLY FARM ISOLATION

Wilensky (1964), p. 184; see category 28 above.

33. SOCIAL PARTICIPATION: EFFECTIVE MEDIATING ATTACHMENTS

Wilensky (1961); see category 28 above.
Wilensky (1964), p. 186; see category 28 above.

34. SOCIAL PARTICIPATION: EVERYDAY ACTIVITIES

Havighurst, Robert J., "The Leisure Activities of the Middle-Aged," *American Journal of Sociology*, 63 (September, 1957), pp. 152–162. See p. 156–157.

Havighurst, Robert J., "The Social Competence of Middle-Aged People," *Genetic Psychology Monographs*, 56 (November, 1957), pp. 297–395.

Donald, Marjorie N., and Robert J. Havighurst, "The Meanings of Leisure," *Social Forces*, 37 (May, 1959), pp. 355–360. See p. 356.

35. SOCIAL PARTICIPATION: FREQUENCY OF CONTACT AND TIME SPENT

Wilensky (1961), p. 526; see category 28 above.

36. SOCIAL PARTICIPATION: LEISURE ACTIVITIES

Havighurst (September, 1957); see category 34 above.

Havighurst, Robert J., and Kenneth Feigenbaum, "Leisure and Life-Style," *American Journal of Sociology*, 64 (January, 1959), pp. 396–404. See p. 396.

Donald and Havighurst (1959); see category 34 above.

37. SOCIAL PARTICIPATION: NUMBER OF MEMBERSHIPS

Wilensky (1961), p. 526; see category 28 above.

38. SOCIAL PARTICIPATION: ROLE INTEGRATION

Wilensky (1961); see category 28 above.

39. WIVES' SOCIAL PARTICIPATION

Wilkening, Eugene A., "Joint Decision-Making in Farm Families as a Function of Status and Role," *American Sociological Review*, 23 (April, 1958), pp. 187–192. See p. 189.

SOCIETAL CHARACTERISTICS

SEE ALSO

Urban Areas: *Metropolitan Areas and Dominance*
Urban Areas: *Segregation*
Urban Areas: *Socioeconomic Status*
Urban Areas: *Urbanization (Family Status)*
Urban Areas: *Various Categories*

1. AGRICULTURAL EMPLOYMENT LEVEL

Cutright, Phillips, "National Political Development: Measurement and Analysis," *American Sociological Review*, 28 (April, 1963), pp. 253–264. See p. 259.

2. AUTONOMY-INTEGRATION OF CULTURES

March, James G., "Group Autonomy and Internal Group Control," *Social Forces*, 33 (May, 1955), pp. 322–326. See p. 323.

3. CHANGING AGE DISTRIBUTION IN GENERAL POPULATIONS

Anderson, O. W., "A Suggested Single Index for a Measure of Changing Age Distributions in General Populations," *Social Forces*, 33 (October, 1954), pp. 86–87. See p. 86.

4. COMMUNICATIONS DEVELOPMENT

Cutright, p. 257; see category 1 above.

5. CONJUNCTIVE MARITAL AFFILIATION

Ackerman, Charles, "Affiliations: Structural Determinants of Differential Divorce Rates," *American Journal of Sociology*, 69 (July, 1963), pp. 13–20. See p. 16.

6. CULTURAL DEVELOPMENT

Rose, Edward, and Gary Willoughby, "Culture Profiles and Emphases," *American Journal of Sociology*, 63 (March, 1958), pp. 476–490. See p. 485.

7. CULTURAL ELEMENT

Whitten, Norman E., Jr., "Power Structure and Sociocultural Change in Latin American Communities," *Social Forces*, 43 (March, 1965), pp. 320–329. See pp. 322–323.

8. CULTURAL MODERNITY

Rose and Willoughby; see category 6 above.

9. CULTURAL CATEGORIES

Rose and Willoughby; p. 483, see category 6 above.

10. DIVISION OF LABOR: SEXUAL

Heath, Dwight B., "Sexual Division of Labor and Cross-Cultural Research," *Social Forces*, 37 (October, 1958), pp. 77–79. See p. 77.

11. DIVISION OF LABOR: INDUSTRIAL DIVERSIFICATION

Gibbs, Jack P., and Walter T. Martin, "Urbanization, Technology, and the Division of Labor: International Patterns," *American Sociological Review*, 27 (October, 1962), pp. 667–677. See pp. 670–672.

Mehta, Surinder K., "The Correlates of Urbanization," *American Sociological Review*, 28 (August, 1963), pp. 609–614. See pp. 609–611.

12. ECONOMIC DEVELOPMENT

Cutright, p. 257; see category 1 above.

13. EDUCATION LEVEL

Cutright, p. 259; see category 1 above.

14. EXCESSIVE EMPHASES OF CULTURES ON PRIMITIVE ACTIVITIES

Rose and Willoughby, p. 485; see category 6 above.

15. EXTERNAL DISPERSION OF OBJECTS OF CONSUMPTION

Gibbs and Martin (1962), p. 673; see category 11 above.
Mehta (1963), p. 610; see category 11 above.

16. EXTERNAL DISPERSION OF OBJECTS OF CONSUMPTION, RELATIVE

Gibbs, Jack P., and Walter T. Martin, "Urbanization and Natural Resources: A Study in Organizational Ecology," *American Sociological Review*, 23 (June, 1958), pp. 266–277. See p. 272.

17. INDUSTRIALIZATION, RATE OF

Marsh, Robert M., and William L. Parish, "Modernization and Communism: A Re-Test of Lipset's Hypotheses," *American Sociological Review*, 30 (December, 1965), pp. 934–942. See p. 939.

18. INDUSTRIALIZATION: NUMBER OF PERSONS EMPLOYED IN MANUFACTURING

Allen, Francis R., "Civil Defense and Regions: An Exploratory Study," *Social Forces*, 36 (March, 1958), pp. 239–246. See p. 242.

19. INDUSTRIALIZATION: VALUE ADDED BY MANUFACTURING

Allen; see category 18 above.

20. LABOR-FORCE PARTICIPATION RATE

Hauser, Phillip M., "Changes in the Labor-Force Participation of the Older Worker," *American Journal of Sociology*, 59 (January, 1954), pp. 312–323. See p. 312.

21. LABOR-FORCE PARTICIPATION RATE, CHANGE IN

Hauser; see category 20 above.

22. LIFE EXPECTATIONS, AGE-SPECIFIC

Madigan, Francis C., and Rupert B. Vance, "Differential Sex Mortality: A Research Design," *Social Forces*, 35 (March, 1957), pp. 193–199. See p. 197.

23. LITERACY

Cutright, Phillips, "Political Structure, Economic Development, and National Social Security Programs," *American Journal of Sociology*, 70 (March, 1965), pp. 537–550. See p. 541.

24. MANIPULATORY POTENTIAL OF SOCIETAL MEMBERS

March, p. 324; see category 2 above.

25. MIGRATION, NET

Hitt, Homer L., "The Role of Migration in Population Change among the Aged," *American Sociological Review*, 19 (April, 1954), pp. 194–200. See p. 196.

Hitt, Homer L., "Migration between the South and Other Regions, 1949 to 1950," *Social Forces*, 36 (October, 1957), pp. 9–16. See p. 11.

26. MIGRATION, SELECTIVE

Johnson, Elmer H., "Methodological Note on Measuring Selection in Differential Migration," *Social Forces*, 33 (March, 1955), pp. 289–292. See p. 291.

27. NATIONAL ENERGY CONSUMPTION

Cutright; see category 23 above.

28. NATIONAL INTEGRATION

Goode, William J., "Illegitimacy, Anomie, and Cultural Penetration," *American Sociological Review*, 26 (December, 1961), pp. 910–925. See pp. 922–923.

29. NATIONAL POLITICAL REPRESENTATIVENESS

Cutright, pp. 541, 549–550, and Appendix B; see category 23 above.

30. NATIONAL POLITICAL REPRESENTATIVENESS, RELATIVE CHANGE IN

Cutright, pp. 544–545; see category 23 above.

31. NATIONAL PRESTIGE

Shimbori, Michiya, Hideo Ikeda, Tsuyoshi Ishida, and Moto Kondo, "Measuring a Nation's Prestige," *American Journal of Sociology*, 69 (July, 1963), pp. 63–68. See pp. 65–67.

32. NATIONAL SOCIAL INSURANCE PROGRAM COMPLETION

Cutright, pp. 544–545; see category 23 above.

33. NATIONAL SOCIAL INSURANCE PROGRAM EXPERIENCE

Cutright, pp. 540–541; see category 23 above.

34. OCCUPATIONAL GROUPS, HOMOGENEITY OF

Blau, Peter M., "The Flow of Occupational Supply and Recruitment," *American Sociological Review*, 30 (August, 1965), pp. 475–490. See p. 488.

35. POLITICAL DEVELOPMENT

Cutright, pp. 256–257; see category 1 above.

36. POPULATION REPLACEMENT INDEX

Hawley, Amos H., "Rural Fertility in Central Luzon," *American Sociological Review*, 20 (February, 1955), pp. 21–27. See p. 22.

37. PRINCIPAL PHASES OF CULTURE

Rose and Willoughby, p. 484; see category 6 above.

38. SOCIAL DEVELOPMENT

Naroll, Raoul, "A Preliminary Index of Social Development," *American Anthropologist*, 58 (August, 1956), pp. 687–715. See pp. 691–703.

Rose and Willoughby (1958), p. 476; see category 6 above.

39. SOCIAL DIFFERENTIATION, FERTILITY

Broom, Leonard, and Jack P. Gibbs, "Social Differentiation and Status Interrelations: The Maori-Pakeha Case," *American Sociological Review*, 29 (April, 1964), pp. 258–265. See p. 262–263.

40. SOCIAL DIFFERENTIATION, INDUSTRY IN WHICH EMPLOYED

Broom and Gibbs, pp. 260–262; see category 39 above.

41. SOCIAL DIFFERENTIATION, INFANT MORTALITY

Broom and Gibbs, pp. 262–263: see category 39 above.

42. SOCIAL DIFFERENTIATION, OCCUPATIONAL

Broom and Gibbs, pp. 260–262; see category 39 above.

43. SOCIAL DIFFERENTIATION, RELIGIOUS

Broom and Gibbs, p. 260; see category 39 above.

44. SOCIETAL COMPLEXITY (FREEMAN, WINCH)

Freeman, Linton C., and Robert F. Winch, "Societal Complexity: An Empirical Test of a Typology of Societies," *American Journal of Sociology*, 62 (March, 1957), pp. 461–466. See pp. 463 and 466.

Freeman, Linton C., *An Empirical Test of Folk-Urbanism*, unpublished Ph.D. dissertation, Northwestern University, 1957.

Young, Frank W., and Ruth C. Young, "The Sequence and Direction of Community Growth: A Cross-Cultural Generalization," *Rural Sociology*, 27 (December, 1962), pp. 374–386. See pp. 378–379.

Schwartz, Richard D., and James C. Miller, "Legal Evolution and Societal Complexity," *American Journal of Sociology*, 70 (September, 1964), pp. 159–169. See pp. 160–161.

45. SOCIETAL COMPLEXITY (OSMOND)

Osmond, Marie W., "Toward Monogamy: A Cross-Cultural Study of Correlates of Type of Marriage," *Social Forces*, 44 (September, 1965), pp. 8–16. See pp. 14–15.

46. SOCIETAL LEGAL EVOLUTION

Schwartz and Miller (1964); see category 44 above.

47. SOCIETAL TYPES

Hatt, Paul K., Nellie Louise Farr, and Eugene Weinstein, "Types of Population Balance," *American Sociological Review*, 20 (February, 1955), pp. 14–21. See p. 16.

48. STRIKE-PRONENESS, REGIONAL-INDUSTRIAL RATIOS

Knowles, K. G. J. C., "Strike-Proneness and Its Determinants," *American Journal of Sociology*, 60 (November, 1954), pp. 213–239. See p. 219.

49. TECHNOLOGICAL DEVELOPMENT, VARIOUS MEASURES

(Includes measures such as earnings attributable to economic development, median income, per capita consumption of inanimate energy—for productive or all purposes and based upon differing energy sources, per capita income, and the value of capital goods)

Ogburn, William F., "Population, Private Ownership, Technology, and the Standard of Living," *American Journal of Sociology*, 56 (January, 1951), pp. 314–319. See p. 317.

Ogburn, William F., "Technology and the Standard of Living in the United States," *American Journal of Sociology*, 60 (January, 1955), pp. 380–386. See p. 384.

Ogburn, William F., and Francis R. Allen, "Technological Development and Per Capita Income," *American Journal of Sociology*, 65 (September, 1959), pp. 127–131. See p. 128.
Gibbs and Martin (1962), p. 672; see category 11 above.
Mehta (1963), p. 611; see category 11 above.

50. URBANISM

Queen, Stuart A., and David B. Carpenter, *The American City*, New York: McGraw-Hill Book Co., 1953, pp. 29–33.
Flittie, Edwin G., "Fertility and Mortality in the Rocky Mountain West," *American Sociological Review*, 22 (April, 1957), pp. 189–193. See p. 191.

51. URBANIZATION (CUTRIGHT)

Cutright, p. 541; see category 23 above.

52. URBANIZATION (DAVIS)

Davis, Kingsley, *The Population of India and Pakistan*, Princeton, N.J.: Princeton University Press, 1951, p. 129.

Davis takes the per cent of a country's population residing in places of a given size or larger as an indicator of the degree to which that country is urbanized. While Davis has employed several methods to analyze urbanization, his easily computed index of urbanization appears to be the most widely used of the approaches he has suggested.

The Davis Index of Urbanization can be most readily described in terms of examples. The table (p. 377) presents the required data for the 1940 populations of Chile and the United States. To compute the Index of Urbanization, simply add the percentages in rows A, B, C, and D, and divide by 4. For Chile in 1940:

$$IU = \frac{44.8 + 41.1 + 34.3 + 23.1}{4} = 35.8$$

For the United States in 1940:

$$IU = \frac{52.7 + 47.6 + 40.1 + 28.8}{4} = 42.3$$

An advantage of this particular index is that it gives greater weight to the larger urban places. Since the population of each larger place is included in each category preceding it, the index emphasizes the direct relationship between town and city size and the frequency with which urban characteristics occur.

TABLE 1. Per Cent of the Population in Cities by Size Class for Chile and the United States, 1940 [Adapted from Davis (1951), Table 45, page 129.]

Size Class of Cities	Chile (per cent)	United States (per cent)
A. 5,000 and over	44.8	52.7
B. 10,000 and over	41.1	47.6
C. 25,000 and over	34.3	40.1
D. 100,000 and over	23.1	28.8
Index of Urbanization	35.8	42.3

Gibbs and Martin (1958), p. 271; see category 16 above.

Gibbs, Jack P., and Kingsley Davis, "Conventional Versus Metropolitan Data in the International Study of Urbanization," *American Sociological Review*, 23 (October, 1958), pp. 505–514. See p. 505.

International Urban Research, *The World's Metropolitan Areas*, Berkeley and Los Angeles: University of California Press, 1959, pp. 6–33.

Gibbs and Martin (1962), pp. 672–673; see category 11 above.

Mehta (1963), p. 610; see category 11 above.

53. URBANIZATION (FERGUSON)

Ferguson, C. E., "A Statistical Study of Urbanization," *Social Forces*, 37 (October, 1958), pp. 19–26. See p. 21.

54. URBANIZATION (HYMAN, COHEN)

Hyman, Ray, and Elizabeth G. Cohen, "Water-Witching in the United States," *American Sociological Review*, 22 (December, 1957), pp. 719–724. See p. 723.

55. URBANIZATION (MCRAE)

McRae, Duncan, Jr., "Religious and Socioeconomic Factors in the

French Vote, 1946–56," *American Journal of Sociology,* 64 (November, 1958), pp. 290–298. See pp. 291–292.

56. URBANIZATION (MEHTA)

Mehta (1963), p. 613; see category 11 above.

57. URBANIZATION: PERCENT OF POPULATION RESIDING IN LOCALITIES OF VARIOUS SIZES

Gibbs and Martin (1958), p. 271; see category 16 above.

Gibbs and Davis (1958); see category 52 above.

Gibbs and Martin (1962), pp. 675–676; see category 11 above.

Mehta (1963), p. 610; see category 11 above.

58. URBANIZATION: PERCENT OF POPULATION RESIDING IN METROPOLITAN AREAS

Gibbs and Martin (1962), pp. 672–673; see category 11 above.

59. WATER WITCHING, CORRELATES OF

Hyman and Cohen, p. 723; see category 54 above.

SOCIOECONOMIC STATUS:
COMPOSITE, OBJECTIVE

1. ADULT SOCIAL CLASS

Elder, Glenn H., Jr., "Family Structure and Educational Attainment: A Cross-National Analysis," *American Sociological Review*, 30 (February, 1965), pp. 81–96. See p. 85.

2. AUTOMOBILE INDEX

French, Cecil L., "Correlates of Success in Retail Selling," *American Journal of Sociology*, 66 (September, 1960), pp. 128–134. See p. 130.

3. CLASS BOUNDARIES

Landecker, Werner S., "Class Boundaries," *American Sociological Review*, 25 (December, 1960), pp. 868–877. See pp. 871–874.

4. CLASS POSITION

Segal, Bernard E., "Racial Group Membership and Juvenile Delinquency," *Social Forces*, 43 (October, 1964), pp. 70–81. See p. 73.

5. DWELLING RATING (KAHL)

Kahl, Joseph A., *Adolescent Ambition*, unpublished Ph.D. dissertation, Harvard University, 1952.

McRae, Duncan, Jr., and Edith K. MacRae, "Legislators' Social Status and Their Votes," *American Journal of Sociology*, 66 (May, 1961), pp. 599–603. See p. 599.

6. DWELLING RATING (MCKEE)

McKee, James B., "Changing Patterns of Race and Housing: A Toledo Study," *Social Forces*, 41 (March, 1963), pp. 253–260. See p. 256.

7. DWELLING RATING (TILLY)

Tilly, Charles, "Occupational Rank and Grade of Residence in a Metropolis," *American Journal of Sociology*, 67 (November, 1961), pp. 323–330. See p. 326.

8. ECONOMIC ELITE, IDENTIFICATION OF

Polsby, Nelson, "Three Problems in the Analysis of Community Power," *American Sociological Review*, 24 (December, 1959), pp. 796–803. See p. 800.

9. EXTRA-BUREAUCRATIC STATUS ADVANTAGE (FOR CHINESE)

Marsh, Robert M., "Formal Organization and Promotion in a Pre-Industrial Society," *American Sociological Review*, 26 (August, 1961), pp. 547–556. See p. 555.

10. FARM ECONOMIC CLASS

United States Census of Agriculture, 1954, Vol. 1, pt. 16, p. xxii.
Mayo, Selz C., C. Horace Hamilton, and Charles W. Pettus, "Sources of Variation in the Level of Living of Farm Operators in the United States," *Social Forces*, 39 (May, 1961), pp. 338–346. See p. 338.

11. FARM OPERATOR LEVEL-OF-LIVING INDEX

Cowhig, James D., *Farm Operator Level of Living Indexes for Counties of the United States*, United States Department of Agriculture, Statistical Bulletin 321, 1962, pp. 21–24.
Cowhig, James D., and Calvin L. Beale, "Socio-Economic Differences between White and Non-White Farm Populations of the South," *Social Forces*, 42 (March, 1964), pp. 354–362. See p. 356.

12. FRIENDS' STATUS

Campbell, Ernest Q., and C. Norman Alexander, "Structural Effects and Interpersonal Relationships," *American Journal of Sociology*, 71 (November, 1965), pp. 284–289. See p. 287.

13. HOME INDEX SCORE

Gough, Harrison G., "A Short Social Status Inventory," *Journal of Educational Psychology*, 40 (January, 1949), pp. 52–56. See pp. 53–55.

Burchinal, Lee G., "Social Status, Measured Intelligence, Achievement, and Personality Adjustment of Rural Iowa Girls," *Sociometry*, 22 (March, 1959), pp. 75–80. See p. 76.

14. HOUSEHOLD RATING

Bellin, Seymour S., and Robert H. Hardt, "Marital Status and Mental Disorders among the Aged," *American Sociological Review*, 23 (April, 1958), pp. 155–162. See p. 158.

15. HOUSING STATUS

Windham, Gerald O., "Pre-Adult Socialization and Selected Status Achievement Variables," *Social Forces*, 42 (May, 1964), pp. 456–461. See p. 460.

16. INDEX OF CLASS POSITION

Ellis, Robert A., W. Clayton Lane, and Virginia Olesen, "The Index of Class Position: An Improved Intercommunity Measure of Stratification," *American Sociological Review*, 28 (April, 1963), pp. 271–277. See pp. 272–274.

Ellis, Robert A., and W. Clayton Lane, "Structural Supports for Upward Mobility," *American Sociological Review*, 28 (October, 1963), pp. 743–756. See p. 745.

Lewis, Lionel S., "Class and the Perception of Class," *Social Forces*, 42 (March, 1964), pp. 336–340. See p. 338.

17. TWO-FACTOR AND THREE-FACTOR INDEXES OF SOCIAL POSITION (HOLLINGSHEAD)

Hollingshead, August B., Two Factor Index of Social Position (copyrighted 1957), privately printed, 1965, Yale Station, New Haven, Connecticut.

Hollingshead, August B., and Frederick C. Redlich, *Social Class and Mental Illness*, New York: John Wiley, 1958. See pp. 387–397.

"The Index of Social Position was developed to meet the need for an objective, easily applicable procedure to estimate positions individuals occupy in the status structure of the community." (1958 above, p. 387) Both the two- and three-factor forms of the index have been used extensively.

This index was developed first by examining a number of studies previously conducted of the New Haven, Connecticut, social structure and by supplementing this knowledge through study of a cross-sectional random sample of 552 households. According to Hollingshead and Redlich, "This study provided detailed data on the size of the family, participation in economic, religious, educational, and leisure-time institutions, as well as the members' values, attitudes, aspirations, standard of living, ideas of the future, and their frustrations, desires, hopes, and fears." (1958, p. 388)

Two sociologists familiar with the community's social structure examined each family's schedule in detail and, working independently, placed each into one of five class or social levels. Independent agreement was obtained in 96 per cent of the cases. The investigators re-examined those cases where there was disagreement and assigned these families to a class by mutual agreement. Criteria used in class assignment were (p. 390):

. . . (a) where a family lived, (b) the way it made its living, and (c) its tastes, its cultural orientation, and the way it spent its leisure time. After considerable additional discussion, the conclusion was reached that the educational level of the head of the household was probably a good single index to the general area of cultural and social values exhibited in the answers the respondent had given to questions about their associations and leisure time activities.

Thus, it was decided to use as specific indicators of class position, the family's address, the occupation of its head, and the years of school completed.

A. *The Residential Scale*. This was a six-point scale based upon ecological research done by Maurice R. Davie and brought up-to-date by Jerome K. Myers. It will not be described in detail since it is applicable only to New Haven. The data used enabled the investigators to rank respondents (on the basis of address) on a six-position scale that ranged from the finest homes to the poorest tenements.

B. *The Occupational Scale*. This seven-point scale is described in some detail in Socioeconomic Status: Occupational, category 32. The seven scale positions are:

1. Higher executives of large concerns, proprietors, and major professionals.
2. Business managers, proprietors of medium-sized businesses, and lesser professionals.
3. Administrative personnel, owners of small businesses, and minor professionals.
4. Clerical and sales workers, technicians, and owners of little businesses.
5. Skilled manual employees.
6. Machine operators and semiskilled employees.
7. Unskilled employees.

C. *The Educational Scale*. This scale also was divided into seven positions:

1. Professional (M.A., M.S., M.E., M.D., Ph.D, L.L.B., and the like).
2. Four-year college graduate (A.B., B.S., B.M.).
3. 1-3 years college (also business schools).
4. High school graduate.
5. 10-11 years of school (part high school).
6. 7-9 years of school.
7. Under 7 years of school.

The exact score a family head received on each of the four variables (the three listed above and judged class position) was placed in a matrix, and the families were ranked on the basis of scale patterns. This procedure enabled the investigators "to delineate areas of complete agreement between our clinical judgments of class position and the objective scores of a family on the three-criterion scales." (1958, p. 392) Score patterns gave the investigators clues as to where to cut the continuum of scores in a meaningful way. The continuum was cut at the points where the greatest amount of variation existed between the four variables.

To determine how to combine and weight the three criterion variables, correlations and a multiple-regression equation were computed to determine the relationship among all four variables (including judged class position) The multiple-regression equation suggested the best approximate weights for each criterion variable were: residence, 6; education, 5; and occupation, 9. Multiplying each scale position score by its approximate weight "yields a distribution of scores ranging from a theoretical low of 20 to a theoretical high of 134, and representing a continuum from the very highest class to the very lowest." (1958, p. 394)

Thus, to compute a Three-factor Index of Social Position score, a family's address, its head's exact occupational pursuit, and the years of school he has completed are necessary data. The appropriate scale score is assigned to each and then each score is multiplied by the appropriate weight. For example, the score of a family whose head works at a clerical job, is a high school graduate, and lives in a middle-rank residential area would be computed thus (1958, p. 396):

Factor	Scale Value	×	Factor Weight	=	Partial Score
Residence	3		6		18
Occupation	4		9		36
Education	4		5		20
Index of Social Position Score					74

Using the heterogeneity criterion mentioned above, the range of scores for each class was determined as follows:

Class	Range of Scores
I	20–31
II	32–55
III	56–86
IV	87–115
V	116–134

Thus, the hypothetical family discussed above would be placed in Class III.

THE TWO-FACTOR INDEX

Because of the difficulty in obtaining residential information where adequate ecological maps do not exist, a two-factor variation of the Index of Social Position has been used widely. This index utilizes only the occupational and educational scales discussed above. They are used in the same manner except the factor weights have been changed. When only two factors are used, occupation is given a weight of 7 and education is given a weight of 4. Thus, if one were to compute a score on the Two-factor Index of Social Position for the manager of a Safeway store who had completed high school and one year of business college, the following would be approximate:

Factor	Scale Score	×	Factor Weight	=	Partial Score
Occupation	3		7		21
Education	3		4		12
Index of Social Position Score					33

The range of scores in each class on the Two-Factor Index is as follows:

Class	Range of Scores
I	11–17
II	18–31
III	32–47
IV	· 48–63
V	64–77

Hollingshead (1957 above) notes,

The various combinations of scale score for occupation and education are reproducible in the Guttman sense for there is no overlap between education-occupation combinations. If an individual's education and occupation are known, one can calculate his score. Conversely, if one knows an individual's score, he can calculate both occupational position and educational level.

Hollingshead and others "have made extensive studies of the reliability of scoring, and the validity of the Index on over one hundred variables."

Hollingshead, August B., and Frederick C. Redlich, "Social Stratification and Psychiatric Disorders," *American Sociological Review*, 18 (April, 1953), pp. 163–169. See p. 165.

Hollingshead, August B., and Frederick C. Redlich, "Social Stratification and Schizophrenia," *American Sociological Review*, 19 (June, 1954), pp. 302–306. See p. 302.

Hollingshead, August B., Robert Ellis, and E. Kirby, "Social Mobility and Mental Illness," *American Sociological Review*, 19 (October, 1954), pp. 577–584. See p. 579.

Hollingshead, August B., and L. Z. Freeman, "Social Class and the Treatment of Neurotics," *The Social Welfare Forum*, 1955, New York: Columbia University Press, pp. 194–205. See p. 195.

Hollingshead, August B., and Frederick C. Redlich, "Social Mobility and Mental Illness," *American Journal of Psychiatry*, 112 (September, 1955), pp. 179–185. See pp. 180–182.

Rosen, Bernard C., "The Achievement Syndrome: A Psychocultural Dimension of Social Stratification," *American Sociological Review*, 21 (April, 1956), pp. 203–211. See p. 204.

Psathas, George, "Ethnicity, Social Class and Adolescent Independence from Parental Control," *American Sociological Review*, 22 (August, 1957), pp. 415–423. See p. 417.

Strodtbeck, Fred L., Margaret R. McDonald, and Bernard C. Rosen, "Evaluation of Occupations: A Reflection of Jewish and Italian Mobility Differences," *American Sociological Review*, 22 (October, 1957), pp. 546–553. See p. 547.

Ellis, Robert A., "Social Stratification and Social Relations: An Empirical Test of the Disjunctiveness of Social Classes," *American Sociological Review*, 22 (October, 1957), pp. 570–578. See p. 571.

Kohn, Melvin L., "Social Class and Parental Values," *American Journal of Sociology*, 64 (January, 1959), pp. 337–351. See p. 338.

Rosen, Bernard C., "Race, Ethnicity, and the Achievement Syndrome," *American Sociological Review*, 24 (February, 1959), pp. 47–60. See p. 48.

Smith, Bulkeley, Jr., "The Differential Residential Segregation of Working-Class Negroes in New Haven," *American Sociological Review*, 24 (August, 1959), pp. 529–533. See p. 530.

Rosen, Bernard C., and Roy D'Andrade, "The Psychosocial Origins of Achievement Motivation," *Sociometry*, 22 (September, 1959), pp. 185–218. See p. 189.

Mizruchi, Ephraim H., "Social Structure and Anomia in a Small

City," *American Sociological Review*, 25 (October, 1960), pp. 645–654. See p. 647.

Kohn, Melvin L., and Eleanor E. Carroll, "Social Class and the Allocation of Parental Responsibilities," *Sociometry*, 23 (December, 1960), pp. 372–392. See p. 374.

Lawson, Edwin D., and Walter E. Boek, "Correlations of Indexes of Families' Socio-economic Status," *Social Forces*, 39 (December, 1960), pp. 149–152. See p. 150.

Wechsler, Henry, "Community Growth, Depressive Disorders, and Suicide," *American Journal of Sociology*, 67 (July, 1961), pp. 9–16. See p. 15.

Rosen, Bernard C., "Family Structure and Achievement Motivation," *American Sociological Review*, 26 (August, 1961), pp. 574–585. See p. 576.

Yarrow, Marian R., Phyllis Scott, Louise deLeeuw, and Christine Heinig, "Child-Rearing in Families of Working and Non-working Mothers," *Sociometry*, 25 (June, 1962), pp. 122–140. See p. 124.

Lefton, Mark, Shirley Angrist, Simon Dinitz, and Benjamin Pasamanick, "Social Class, Expectations, and Performance of Mental Patients," *American Journal of Sociology*, 68 (July, 1962), pp. 79–87. See p. 82.

Lewis, Lionel S., and Joseph Lopreato, "Arationality, Ignorance, and Perceived Danger in Medical Practices," *American Sociological Review*, 27 (August, 1962), pp. 508–514. See p. 508.

Rosen, Bernard C., "Socialization and Achievement Motivation in Brazil," *American Sociological Review*, 27 (October, 1962), pp. 612–624. See p. 613.

Lewis, Lionel S., "Knowledge, Danger, Certainty, and the Theory of Magic," *American Journal of Sociology*, 69 (July, 1963), pp. 7–12. See p. 9.

Ellis, Lane, and Olesen (September, 1963), pp. 271–277; see category 16 above.

Bell, Gerald D., "Processes in the Formation of Adolescents' Aspirations," *Social Forces*, 42 (December, 1963), pp. 179–186. See p. 182.

Leslie, Gerald R., and Kathryn P. Johnsen, "Changed Perceptions of the Maternal Role," *American Sociological Review*, 28 (December, 1963), pp. 919–928. See p. 923.

Rosen, Bernard C., "The Achievement Syndrome and Economic Growth in Brazil," *Social Forces*, 42 (March, 1964), pp. 341–354. See p. 345.

Levinger, George, "Task and Social Behavior in Marriage," *Sociometry*, 27 (December, 1964), pp. 433–448. See pp. 442 and 446.

18. INDEX OF STATUS CHARACTERISTICS (WARNER AND MODIFICATIONS)

Warner, W. Lloyd, Marchia Meeker, and Kenneth Eells, *Social Class in America*, Chicago, Ill.: Science Research Associates, 1949, pp. 131–185.

The Index of Status Characteristics is based upon data concerning four status characteristics, each of which is divided into categories as described below:

A. *Occupation.* This modification of the Census-Edwards scheme is discussed in more detail elsewhere in this volume (see Socioeconomic Status: Occupational, category 38). The seven general categories used are (1949, pp. 140–141):

1. Major professionals, proprietors and managers of businesses valued at $75,000 and over, regional divisional managers of large financial and industrial enterprises, certified public accountants, and "gentlemen farmers."
2. Minor professionals, proprietors and managers of businesses valued at $20,000 to $75,000, assistant managers and office and department managers of large businesses, assistants to executives, accountants, salesmen of real estate and insurance, postmasters, and large-farm owners.
3. Semiprofessionals, owners and managers of businesses valued at $5,000 to $20,000, all minor officials of businesses, auto salesmen, bank clerks and cashiers, postal clerks, secretaries to execu-

tives, supervisors of railroad companies, telephone companies, and the like, justices of the peace, and contractors.

4. Managers and proprietors of businesses valued at $2,000 to $5,000, stenographers, bookkeepers, rural mail clerks, railroad ticket agents, sales people in dry-goods stores, factory foremen; electricians, plumbers, and carpenters who own their own businesses; watchmakers; dry-cleaning workers, butchers, sheriffs, railroad engineers, and conductors.

5. Managers and proprietors of businesses valued at $500 to $2,000, dime-store clerks, hardware salesmen, beauty operators, telephone operators, carpenters, plumbers, electricians (apprentice), timekeepers, linemen, telephone or telegraph or radio repairmen, medium-skill workers, barbers, firemen, butcher's apprentices, practical nurses, policemen, seamstresses, cooks in restaurants, bartenders, and tenant farmers.

6. Managers and proprietors of businesses valued at less than $500, moulders, semiskilled workers, assistants to carpenters, baggagemen, night policemen and watchmen, taxi and truck drivers, gas-station attendants, waitresses, and small tenant farmers.

7. Heavy labor, migrant work, odd-job men, miners, janitors, scrubwomen, newsboys, and migrant farm laborers.

B. *Source of Income.* According to Warner, Meeker, and Eells (p. 139), "While socioeconomic scales have generally paid greater attention to the amount of income, the source of income is an equally good or better determinant of status." Source of income was classified as follows on a seven-point scale (pp. 139–142):

1. *Inherited wealth.* Families are so classified who live on money made by a previous generation (including money derived from savings and investments or business enterprises inherited from an earlier generation).

2. *Earned wealth.* Families or individuals are so classified if they live on savings or investments earned by the present generation. This category implies considerable wealth, for the individual lives on interest from capital and has amassed sufficient money so that he does not need to work.

Composite, Objective · 389

3. *Profits and fees*. This includes money which is paid to professional men for services and advice. It also includes money made by owners of businesses for sale of goods and royalties paid to writers, musicians, and the like.
4. *Salary*. This is a regular income paid for services on a monthly or yearly basis. This category also includes the commission type of salary paid to salesmen.
5. *Wages*. This is distinguished from salary since the amount is determined by an hourly rate.
6. *Private relief*. This includes money paid by friends or relatives for the sake of friendship or because of family ties. It also includes money given by churches, associations, or the like, when the agency does not reveal the names of those receiving help.
7. *Public relief and nonrespectable income*. This includes money received from a government agency or from some semipublic charity organization which does not mind revealing the names of those getting help. A nonrespectable income includes money made from illegal occupations such as gambling or prostitution.

Retired persons are assigned the source of income on which they were dependent while working and persons receiving incomes from more than one source are classified according to chief source.

C. *House Type*. Following the leads of other studies, especially the Yankee City study, "it was felt that house type was related to social status and that if the houses of the community were classified, this material might be used in conjunction with other information to indicate the general status of a family within a community." (1949, p. 143) Using size and condition as basic criteria and validating the results by comparing assigned house type with other status criteria, the following scale was set forth (pp. 149–150):

1. *Excellent house*. This includes only houses which are very large single-family dwellings in good repair and surrounded by large lawns and yards which are landscaped and well cared for. These

houses have an element of ostentation with respect to size, architectural style, and general condition of yards and lawns.

2. *Very good houses.* Roughly, this includes all houses which do not quite measure up to the first category. The primary difference is one of size. They are slightly smaller, but still larger than utility demands for the average family.

3. *Good houses.* In many cases they are only slightly larger than utility demands. They are more conventional and less ostentatious than the two higher categories.

4. *Average houses.* One-and-a-half to two-story wood-frame and brick single-family dwellings. Conventional style, with lawns well cared for but not landscaped.

5. *Fair houses.* In general, this includes houses whose condition is not quite as good as those houses given a 4 rating. It also includes smaller houses in excellent condition.

6. *Poor houses.* In this, and the category below, size is less important than condition in determining evaluation. Houses in this category are badly run-down but have not deteriorated sufficiently that they cannot be repaired. They suffer from lack of care but do not have the profusion of debris which surrounds houses in the lowest category.

7. *Very poor houses.* All houses which have deteriorated so far that they cannot be repaired. They are considered unhealthy and unsafe to live in.

Using this classification, houses intended for one family but converted into multiple-family dwellings are given a rating one point lower than the rating arrived at on the basis of the total structure. Apartments in regular apartment buildings are ranked by condition and single apartments further ranked by size.

D. *Dwelling Area.* This factor "takes cognizance of the fact that most towns are divided into a series of ecological areas which are considered to have unequal prestige and unequal value, both socially and economically." (1949, p. 151) General appearance (as assessed by a field worker) was used as the basic criterion for rating neighborhoods. This was validated by comparing dwelling-area ratings with the class characteristics of residents of these areas. A description of the levels and each category follows (pp. 153–154):

1. *Very high.* In most towns and small cities this includes but one area. Residents, aware that this area has a high status reputation, remark that "no one can live here unless his family has lived in the community for at least three generations." The best houses in town are located in such an area. The streets are wide and clean and have many trees.

2. *High.* Dwelling areas felt to be superior and well above average but a little below the top. There are fewer mansions and pretentious houses in such districts than in the first. However, the chief difference is one of reputation.

3. *Above average.* A little above average in social reputation and to the eye of the scientific observer. This is an area of nice but not pretentious houses. The streets are kept clean and the houses are well cared for. It is known as a "nice place to live" but "society doesn't live here."

4. *Average.* These are areas of workingmen's homes which are small and unpretentious but neat in appearance. In these areas live "the respectable people in town who don't amount to much but never give anybody any trouble."

5. *Below average.* All the areas in this group are undesirable because they are close to factories, or because they include the business section of town, or are close to the railroad. There are more run-down houses here because there are people living in these areas who "don't know how to take care of things." They are more congested and heterogeneous than those above. It is said that "all kinds of people live here, and you don't know who your neighbors will be."

6. *Low.* These areas are run-down and semislums. The houses are set close together. The streets and yards are often filled with debris and in some of the smaller towns some of the streets are not paved.

7. *Very low.* Slum districts, the areas with the poorest reputation in town, not only because of unpleasant and unhealthy geographical positions—for example, being near a garbage dump

or a swamp—but also because of the social stigma attached to those who live there. The houses are little better than shacks. The people are referred to by such terms as "squatters along the canal," and are said to be lazy, shiftless, ignorant, and immoral. This general reputation is assigned to most people living in such sections regardless of their abilities or accomplishments.

To determine the relationships between the status characteristics, their appropriate weightings, and ultimately class assignment based on ISC scores, Warner and his associates compared status-characteristic rankings with one another and with class assignment by the reputational (Evaluative Participation) approach for 303 families. A multiple-regression equation was then used as the basis for computing the weights assigned to each status characteristic used to construct index scores as follows:

Status Characteristic	Weight
Occupation	4
Source of Income	3
House Type	3
Dwelling Area	2

Thus, partial scores for the index are computed by multiplying the rating (1-7 on each characteristic) by the appropriate weight. The total index score is simply the sum of the four products. Thus, an Index of Status Characteristics score for a doctor living in an excellent house in the best area of town would be computed as follows:

Characteristic	Scale Position	× Weight	= Partial Score
Occupation	1	4	4
Source of Income	3	3	9
House Type	1	3	3
Dwelling Area	1	2	2
Index of Status Characteristics Score			18

According to Warner, this weighted total of four status characteristics may be used to assign individuals or families to social classes "with a considerable degree of accuracy." The following sets of scores are used for such assignments:

Weighted Total of Four Status Characteristics	Revised I.S.C.	Predicted Social Class Placement	Equivalent E.P. Rating
12	A++	Upper	1++
13–17	A+	Upper	1+
18–22	A–	Upper	1–
23–27	B++	Upper-Middle	2++
28–32	B+	Upper-Middle	2+
33–37	B–	Upper-Middle	2–
38–41	C++	Lower-Middle	3++
42–46	C+	Lower-Middle	3+
47–51	C–	Lower-Middle	3–
52–56	D++	Upper-Lower	4++
57–61	D+	Upper-Lower	4+
62–66	D–	Upper-Lower	4–
67–71	E++	Lower-Lower	5++
72–75	E+	Lower-Lower	5+
76–84	E–	Lower-Lower	5–

The + designations are used to specify more clearly placements within classes. "Thus a B++ designated a person whose Index of Status Characteristics indicated that his most likely social class placement was in the upper-middle class and that he was most likely near the top of that class, on the borderline of being in the upper class." (1949, p. 184)

Further refinement of the Index of Status Characteristics for ethnic groups is discussed in Warner, Meeker, and Eells, pp. 186–199.

Stone, Gregory P., "City Shoppers and Urban Identification: Observations on the Social Psychology of City Life," *American Journal of Sociology*, 60 (July, 1954), pp. 36–45. See p. 41.

Hochbaum, Godfrey, John G. Darley, E. D. Monachesi, and Charles Bird, "Socioeconomic Variables in a Large City," *American Journal of Sociology*, 61 (July, 1955), pp. 31–38. See p. 34.

White, R. Clyde, "Social Class Differences in the Uses of Leisure," *American Journal of Sociology*, 61 (September, 1955), pp. 145–150. See p. 145.

Haer, John L., "A Test of the Unidimensionality of the Index of

Status Characteristics," *Social Forces*, 34 (October, 1955), pp. 56–58. See p. 56.

Haer, John L., "A Comparative Study of the Classification Techniques of Warner and Centers," *American Sociological Review*, 20 (December, 1955), pp. 689–692. See p. 690.

Reeder, Leo G., "Social Differentials in Mode of Travel, Time and Cost in the Journey to Work," *American Sociological Review*, 21 (February, 1956), pp. 56–63. See p. 57.

Fanelli, A. Alexander, "Extensiveness of Communication Contacts and Perceptions of the Community," *American Sociological Review*, 21 (August, 1956), pp. 439–445. See p. 442.

Haer, John L., "Social Stratification in Relation to Attitude toward Sources of Power in a Community," *Social Forces*, 35 (December, 1956), pp. 137–142. See p. 139.

Wilensky, Harold L., "The Labor Vote: A Local Union's Impact on the Political Conduct of Its Members," *Social Forces*, 35 (December, 1956), pp. 111–120. See p. 117.

Gottlieb, David, "The Neighborhood Tavern and the Cocktail Lounge: A Study of Class Differences," *American Journal of Sociology*, 62 (May, 1957), pp. 559–562. See p. 559.

Scott, John C., Jr., "Members and Participation in Voluntary Associations," *American Sociological Review*, 22 (June, 1957), pp. 315–326. See p. 317.

Havighurst, Robert J., "The Leisure Activities of the Middle-Aged," *American Journal of Sociology*, 65 (September, 1957), pp. 152–162. See p. 153.

Westie, Frank R., and Margaret L. Westie, "The Social-Distance Pyramid: Relationships between Caste and Class," *American Journal of Sociology*, 61 (September, 1957), pp. 190–196. See p. 190.

Freeman, Howard E., Edwin Novak, and Leo G. Reeder, "Correlates of Membership in Voluntary Associations," *American Sociological Review*, 22 (October, 1957), pp. 528–533. See p. 529.

Haer, John L., "Predictive Utility of Five Indices of Social Stratification," *American Sociological Review*, 22 (October, 1957), pp. 541–546. See p. 542.

Haer, John L., "An Empirical Study of Social Class Awareness," *Social Forces*, 36 (December, 1957), pp. 117–121. See p. 118.

Janes, Robert W., "A Technique for Describing Community Structure through Newspaper Analysis," *Social Forces*, 37 (December, 1958), pp. 102–109. See p. 103.

Donald, Marjorie N., and Robert J. Havighurst, "The Meanings of Leisure," *Social Forces*, 37 (May, 1959), pp. 355–360. See p. 356.

Form, William H., and Julius Rivera, "Work Contacts and International Evaluations: The Case of a Mexican Border Village," *Social Forces*, 37 (May, 1959), pp. 334–339. See p. 337.

Freeman, Howard E., and Ozzie G. Simmons, "Social Class and Posthospital Performance Levels," *American Sociological Review*, 24 (June, 1959), pp. 345–351. See p. 347.

Lawson and Boek (1960), pp. 149–152. See category 17 above.

Freeman, Howard E., "Attitudes toward Mental Illness among Relatives of Former Patients," *American Sociological Review*, 26 (February, 1961), pp. 59–66. See p. 63.

Glenn, Norval, "Negro Prestige Criteria: A Case Study in the Bases of Prestige," *American Journal of Sociology*, 68 (May, 1963), pp. 645–657. See p. 649.

Swinehart, James W., "Socio-economic Level, Status Aspiration, and Maternal Role," *American Sociological Review*, 28 (June, 1963), pp. 391–399. See p. 393.

Ellis, Lane, and Olesen (April, 1963), p. 271; see category 16 above.

Teele, James E., "Suicidal Behavior, Assaultiveness, and Socialization Principles," *Social Forces*, 43 (May, 1965), pp. 510–518. See p. 512.

19. LEISURE STYLE AS A STATUS CRITERION: EXTERNAL SYMBOLS

Wilensky, Harold L., "Mass Society and Mass Culture: Interdependence or Independence?" *American Sociological Review*, 29 (April, 1964), pp. 173–197. See p. 186.

20. **LEISURE STYLE AS A STATUS CRITERION: FACTOR OF TASTE**

Wilensky (1964), p. 186; see category 19 above.

21. **LEVEL OF LIVING SCALE**

Wilkening, Eugene A., "Joint Decision-Making in Farm Families as a Function of Status and Role," *American Sociological Review*, 23 (April, 1958), pp. 187–192. See p. 189.

22. **NEGRO SOCIAL CLASS**

Bell, Robert R., "Lower Class Negro Mothers' Aspirations for Their Children," *Social Forces*, 43 (May, 1965), pp. 493–500. See p. 496.

23. **ROOM CONDITION SCORE**

Mann, Peter H., "The Concept of Neighborliness," *American Journal of Sociology*, 60 (September, 1954), pp. 163–168. See p. 167.

24. **SCHOOL STATUS**

Campbell and Alexander, p. 287; see category 12 above.

25. **SOCIAL CLASS**

Hardt, Robert H., and Sherwin J. Feinhandler, "Social Class and Mental Hospitalization Prognosis," *American Sociological Review*, 24 (December, 1959), pp. 815–821. See p. 817.

26. **SOCIAL CLASS IN BRAZIL**

Hutchinson, Bertram, and Carlo Castaldi, "A Hierarquia de Prestígio das Oçupacões," in Bertram Hutchinson, Carolina Martuscelli Bori, Juarez Rubens, Brandão Lopes, and Carlo Castaldi, *Mobilidade e Trabalho*, Rio de Janeiro: Centro Brasileiro des Pesquisas Educacionais, 1960.

Rosen (1964), p. 345; see category 17 above.

27. **SOCIAL CLASS STATUS**

Landis, Judson R., and Frank R. Scarpitti, "Perceptions Regarding Value Orientation and Legitimate Opportunity: Delinquents and Non-Delinquents," *Social Forces*, 44 (September, 1965), pp. 83–91. See p. 85.

28. **SOCIAL RANK**

Williams, J. Allen, Jr., "Interviewer-Respondent Interaction: A

Study of Bias in the Information Interview," *Sociometry,* 27 (September, 1964), pp. 338–352. See p. 342.

29. SOCIAL STATUS (BLOOM)

Bloom, Richard, Martin Whiteman, and Martin Deutsch, "Race and Social Class as Separate Factors Related to Social Environment," *American Journal of Sociology,* 70 (January, 1965), pp. 471–476. See pp. 471–472.

30. SOCIAL STATUS (QUINNEY)

Quinney, Richard, "Political Conservatism, Alienation, and Fatalism: Contingencies of Social Status and Religious Fundamentalism," *Sociometry,* 27 (September, 1964), pp. 372–381. See p. 374.

31. SOCIOECONOMIC RANKS OF CENSUS TRACTS (USED AS INDIVIDUAL MEASURE)

French, p. 130; see category 2 above.

32. SOCIOECONOMIC STATUS (BELL)

Bell, Wendell, "Anomie, Social Isolation, and the Class Structure," *Sociometry,* 20 (June, 1957), pp. 105–116. See p. 108.

33. SOCIOECONOMIC STATUS (BURCHINAL)

Burchinal (1959), p. 76; see category 13 above.

34. SOCIOECONOMIC STATUS (CHAPIN)

Chapin, F. Stuart, "A Quantitative Scale for Rating the Home and Social Environment of Middle Class Families in an Urban Community," *Journal of Educational Psychology,* 19 (February, 1928), pp. 99–111. See pp. 100–109.

Mann, Peter H. (1954), p. 165; see category 23 above.

Minnis, Mhyra S., "The Relationship of the Social Structure of an Indian Community to Adult and Juvenile Delinquency," *Social Forces,* 41 (May, 1963), pp. 395–403. See p. 397.

Ellis, Lane, and Olesen (April, 1963), p. 271; see category 16 above.

35. SOCIOECONOMIC STATUS (CHAPMAN, SIMS)

Chapman, J. Crosby, and V. M. Sims, "The Quantitative Measurement of Certain Aspects of Socio-economic Status," *Journal of Educational Psychology*, 16 (September, 1925), pp. 380–390. See pp. 381–382 and 390.

Westoff, Charles F., Philip C. Sagi, and Lowell E. Kelly, "Fertility through Twenty Years of Marriage: A Study in Predictive Possibilities," *American Sociological Review*, 23 (October, 1958), pp. 549–556. See p. 551.

36. SOCIOECONOMIC STATUS (COLEMAN)

Coleman, Richard, unpublished working paper in the files of the Committee of Human Development.

Havighurst, Robert J., and Kenneth Feigenbaum, "Leisure and Life-Style," *American Journal of Sociology*, 64 (January, 1959), pp. 396–404. See p. 399.

37. SOCIOECONOMIC STATUS (DENTLER, MONROE)

Dentler, Robert A., and Lawrence J. Monroe, "Social Correlates of Early Adolescent Theft," *American Sociological Review*, 26 (October, 1961), pp. 733–743. See p. 736.

38. SOCIOECONOMIC STATUS (DUNCAN, HODGE)

Duncan, Otis D., and Robert W. Hodge, "Education and Occupational Mobility: A Regression Analysis," *American Journal of Sociology*, 68 (May, 1963), pp. 629–644. See p. 631.

39. SOCIOECONOMIC STATUS (ERBE)

Erbe, William, "Social Involvement and Political Activity: A Replication and Elaboration," *American Sociological Review*, 29 (April, 1964), pp. 198–215. See p. 204.

40. SOCIOECONOMIC STATUS (GOODCHILDS, SMITH)

Goodchilds, Jacqueline D., and Ewart E. Smith, "The Effects of Unemployment as Mediated by Social Status," *Sociometry*, 26 (September, 1963), pp. 287–293. See p. 289.

41. SOCIOECONOMIC STATUS (GREELEY)

Greeley, Andrew M., "Influence of the 'Religious Factor' on Career Plans and Occupational Values of College Graduates," *American Journal of Sociology*, 68 (May, 1963), pp. 658–671. See p. 664.

42. SOCIOECONOMIC STATUS (JITODAI)

Jitodai, Ted T., "Migrant Status and Church Attendance," *Social Forces*, 43 (December, 1964), pp. 241–248. See p. 243.

43. SOCIOECONOMIC STATUS (KADUSHIN)

Kadushin, Charles, *Steps on the Way to a Psychiatric Clinic*, Ann Arbor, Mich.: University Microfilms, 1960, pp. 201–204 and Appendix II.

Kadushin, Charles, "Social Distance between Client and Professional," *American Journal of Sociology*, 67 (March, 1962), pp. 517–531. See p. 523.

44. SOCIOECONOMIC STATUS (LANGWORTHY)

Langworthy, Russell L., "Community Status and Influence in a High School," *American Sociological Review*, 24 (August, 1959), pp. 537–539. See p. 538.

45. SOCIOECONOMIC STATUS (LENSKI, LANDECKER)

Axelrod, Morris, "Urban Structure and Social Participation," *American Sociological Review*, 21 (February, 1956), pp. 13–18. See p. 17.

46. SOCIOECONOMIC STATUS (MCCLOSKY, SCHAAR)

McClosky, Herbert, and John H. Schaar, "Psychological Dimensions of Anomy," *American Sociological Review*, 30 (February, 1965), pp. 14–40. See p. 36.

47. SOCIOECONOMIC STATUS (MEIER, BELL)

Meier, Dorothy L., and Wendell Bell, "Anomia and Differential Access to the Achievement of Life Goals," *American Sociological Review*, 24 (April, 1959), pp. 189–202. See pp. 201–202.

48. SOCIOECONOMIC STATUS (MILLS)

Mills, Theodore M., "The Coalition Pattern in Three Person Groups," *American Sociological Review*, 19 (December, 1954), pp. 657–667. See pp. 663–664.

49. SOCIOECONOMIC STATUS (MINNIS)

Minnis, Mhyra S., "Selected Social Problems of Fort Hall Reservation," *Sociology and Social Research*, 46 (July, 1962), pp. 436–445. See pp. 437–438.

Minnis (1963), p. 402; see category 34 above.

50. SOCIOECONOMIC STATUS (NAM)

Nam, Charles B., *Methodology and Scores of Socioeconomic Status*, working paper number 15, Washington, D.C.: United States Bureau of the Census, 1963.

Nam, Charles B., and Mary G. Powers, "Variation in Socioeconomic Structures by Race, Residence and the Life Cycle," *American Sociological Review*, 30 (February, 1965), pp. 97–103. See p. 97.

51. SOCIOECONOMIC STATUS (OMARI)

Omari, Thompson Peter, "Factors Associated with Urban Adjustment of Rural Southern Migrants," *Social Forces*, 35 (October, 1956), pp. 47–53. See p. 49.

52. SOCIOECONOMIC STATUS (ROSENGREN)

Rosengren, William R., "Social Status, Attitudes toward Pregnancy and Child-Rearing Attitudes," *Social Forces*, 41 (December, 1962), pp. 127–134. See p. 130.

53. SOCIOECONOMIC STATUS (SCHATZMAN, STRAUSS)

Schatzman, Leonard, and Anselm Strauss, "Social Class and Modes of Communication," *American Journal of Sociology*, 60 (January, 1955), pp. 329–338. See p. 330.

54. SOCIOECONOMIC STATUS (SEWELL AND MODIFICATIONS)

Sewell, William H., *The Construction and Standardization of a Scale for the Measurement of Socio-Economic Status of Oklahoma Farm Families*, Oklahoma A. and M. College Agricultural Experiment Station, Technical Bulletin No. 9, 1940.

Sewell (p. 20) follows Chapin in defining socioeconomic status as "the position that an individual or family occupies with reference to the prevailing average standards of cultural possessions, effective income, material possessions and participation in the group activities of the community." In order to measure these components of socioeconomic status, Sewell first assembled more than 200 items. These items were further examined and 123 of them were administered to a "representative" sample of 800 Oklahoma farm families. The criterion of internal consistency was then employed as the basis for selecting items for the final scale form from among the 123 investigated. Of these items, 36 were retained because of their superior ability to differentiate families classified on the basis of responses to the original 123 items. Responses to each item were weighted on the basis of the response distributions found among the 800 families: "For this purpose the sigma method of scoring was used. This method assigns weights to items in reverse relation to their frequency in the population. . . . Items that are more common are considered less important in differentiating the various levels and receive lower scores." (p. 43)

The items making up the scale and weights assigned responses are as follows:

Score	Scale Items	Score if Y	Score if N
___	1. Construction of house:		

Brick, stucco, etc.,   Unpainted frame
or painted frame   or other
Score: 5   3

___ 2. Room-person ratio: (Number of rooms?__ ÷ Number of persons?__ = __)
Ratio: Below 1.00 1.00–1.99 2.00–2.99 3.00 and up
Score: 3   5   7   9

		Y	N
___	3. Separate dining room? Y–N	6	3
___	4. Separate kitchen? Y–N	6	3
___	5. Separate living room? Y–N	6	3
___	6. Living room floors finished? Y–N	7	4
___	7. Living room woodwork finished? Y–N	5	2
___	8. Living room wall construction:		

                                    Building paper
Plaster Wallboard Ceiling or no inside wall
Score: 6   3   4   2

		Y	N
___	9. Living room walls decorated? Y–N	5	2
___	10. Living room floor covering:		

                          Linoleum or
Rugs or carpets bare floors
Score: 6   3

___ 11. Shades and curtains or drapes on living room windows?
Y–N   5   2

Score	Scale Items	Score if	
		Y	N

___ 12. Living room lounge:

	Divan, davenport, or studio couch	Day bed or couch	Bed, cot, or none
Score:	6	5	3

___ 13. Lighting facilities:

	Electric	Gas, mantle, or pressure	Oil lamps, others or none
Score:	8	6	3

___ 14. Water piped into house? Y–N   8   4
___ 15. Kitchen sink? Y–N   7   4
___ 16. Linoleum on kitchen floor? Y–N   5   2
___ 17. Power washer? Y–N   6   3
___ 18. Refrigerator:

	Mechanical	Ice	Other or none
Score:	8	6	3

___ 19. Radio? Y–N   6   3
___ 20. Telephone? Y–N   6   3
___ 21. Automobile? (other than truck) Y–N   5   2
___ 22. Furniture insured? Y–N   7   4
___ 23. Family takes a daily newspaper? Y–N   6   3
___ 24. Number of magazines regularly taken?___

Number:	0–1	2–3	4–5	6 and up
Score:	3	5	7	8

___ 25. Approximate number of books in the home?___

Number:	0–7	8–49	50–99	100 and up
Score:	3	5	7	8

___ 26. Wife's education? (grades completed)___

Number:	0–7	8	9–11	12	13 and up
Score:	2	4	6	7	8

___ 27. Husband's education? (grades completed)___

Number:	0–7	8	9–11	12	13 and up
Score:	3	5	6	7	8

___ 28. Husband's life insured? Y–N   6   3
___ 29. Husband a church member? Y–N   5   3
___ 30. Husband attends church? (1/4 of meetings) Y–N   5   2
___ 31. Husband attends Sunday school? (1/4 of meetings) Y–N   6   3
___ 32. Husband a member of a farm cooperative? Y–N   8   4
___ 33. Wife a church member? Y–N   5   2
___ 34. Wife attends church? (1/4 of meetings) Y–N   5   2
___ 35. Wife attends Sunday school? (1/4 of meetings) Y–N   6   3
___ 36. Wife a member of an extension or P.T.A. group? Y–N   8   4
___ Scale Score

A family's socioeconomic status score is the sum of the scores on the separate questions. More specific instructions and definitions of the items used in the scale are found in Sewell (1940), Appendix H.

The scale has been validated in several ways: by comparing the scale scores of 257 Oklahoma farm families with scores obtained from the same sample on four other socioeconomic-status scales, by calculating a multiple correlation based on the above data, and by comparing mean socioeconomic-status scale scores of 1,190 Oklahoma farm families with their assignment in one of the following farm tenure groups: owners, tenants, or laborers.

Reliability was determined through the use of the split-half method, the test-retest method and by comparing scores assigned to 60 families by two independent interviewers.

Sewell, William H., "A Short Form of the Farm Family Socio-Economic Status Scale," *Rural Sociology*, 8 (June, 1943), pp. 161–170.

Sewell, William H., and A. O. Haller, "Factors in the Relationship between Social Status and the Personality Adjustment of the Child," *American Sociological Review*, 24 (August, 1959), pp. 511–520. See p. 512.

Haller, A. O., and Shailer Thomas, "Personality Correlates of the Socioeconomic Status of Adolescent Males," *Sociometry*, 25 (December, 1962), pp. 398–404. See p. 400.

Minnis (1963), p. 397; see category 34 above.

Ellis, Lane, and Olesen (April, 1963), pp. 272–273; see category 16 above.

Sewell, William H., "Community of Residence and College Plans," *American Sociological Review*, 29 (February, 1964), pp. 24–38. See p. 27.

Sewell, William H., and Alan M. Orenstein, "Community of Residence and Occupational Choice," *American Journal of Sociology*, 70 (March, 1965), pp. 551–563. See p. 554.

55. SOCIOECONOMIC STATUS (SROLE)

Srole, Leo, "Social Integration and Certain Corollaries: An Exploratory Study," *American Sociological Review*, 21 (December, 1956), pp. 709–716. See p. 715.

56. SOCIOECONOMIC STATUS (STRAUS)

Straus, Murray A., "Deferred Gratification, Social Class, and the Achievement Syndrome," *American Sociological Review*, 27 (June, 1962), pp. 326–335. See p. 331.

57. SOCIOECONOMIC STATUS (SUCHMAN)

Suchman, Edward A., "Sociomedical Variations among Ethnic Groups," *American Journal of Sociology*, 70 (November, 1964), pp. 319–331. See pp. 326–327.

58. SOCIOECONOMIC STATUS (VINCENT)

Vincent, Clark E., "Ego Involvement in Sexual Relations: Implications for Research on Illegitimacy," *American Journal of Sociology*, 65 (December, 1959), pp. 287–295. See p. 289.

59. SOCIOECONOMIC STATUS (WHITE)

White, Martha S., "Social Class, Child Rearing Practices, and Child Behavior," *American Sociological Review*, 22 (December, 1957), pp. 704–712. See p. 706.

60. SOCIOECONOMIC STATUS (WILLIAMS)

Williams, James H., "Close Friendship Relations of Housewives Residing in an Urban Community," *Social Forces*, 36 (May, 1958), pp. 358–362. See p. 359.

61. SOCIOECONOMIC STATUS (WILLIE)

Willie, Charles V., "Age Status and Residential Stratification," *American Sociological Review*, 25 (April, 1960), pp. 260–264. See p. 260.

62. SOCIOECONOMIC STATUS (WINDHAM)

Windham, p. 460; see category 15 above.

63. SOCIOECONOMIC STATUS (YOUNG, MAYO)

Young, James N., and Selz C. Mayo, "Manifest and Latent Participators in a Rural Community Action Program," *Social Forces*, 38 (December, 1959), pp. 140–145. See p. 142.

64. SOCIOECONOMIC STATUS IN INDIA

Rahudker, W. B., "A Scale for Measuring Socio-economic Status of India Farm Families," *Nagpur Agricultural College Magazine*, 34 (1960).

Dasgupta, Satadal, "Communication and Innovation in Indian Villages," *Social Forces*, 43 (March, 1965), pp. 330–337. See pp. 335–336.

65. SOCIOECONOMIC STATUS IN LEBANON

Armstrong, Lincoln, and Gordon K. Hirabayashi, "Social Differentiation in Selected Lebanese Villages," *American Sociological Review*, 21 (August, 1956), pp. 425–434. See pp. 429–430.

66. STATUS (SCARR)

Scarr, Harry A., "Measures of Particularism," *Sociometry*, 27 (December, 1964), pp. 413–432. See p. 417.

67. STATUS (SCHMITT)

Schmitt, David R., "An Attitudinal Correlate of the Status Congruency of Married Women," *Social Forces*, 44 (December, 1965), pp. 190–195. See p. 192.

68. STUDENT STATUS

Campbell and Alexander, p. 287; see category 12 above.

SOCIOECONOMIC STATUS: COMPOSITE, SUBJECTIVE AND OBJECTIVE

1. SOCIAL CLASS

Blau, Zena Smith, "Structural Constraints on Friendship in Old Age," *American Sociological Review*, 26 (June, 1961), pp. 429–439. See p. 433.

2. SOCIAL STATUS (DAVIS)

Davis, James A., "Status Symbols and the Measurement of Status Perception," *Sociometry*, 19 (September, 1956), pp. 154–165. See p. 155.

3. SOCIAL STATUS (SCUDDER, ANDERSON)

Scudder, Richard, and C. Arnold Anderson, "Migration and Vertical Occupational Mobility," *American Sociological Review*, 19 (June, 1954), pp. 329–334. See p. 329.

4. SOCIOECONOMIC STATUS (FORD)

Ford, Thomas R., "Status, Residence, and Fundamentalist Religious Beliefs in the Southern Appalachians," *Social Forces*, 39 (October, 1960), pp. 41–49. See p. 44.

5. SOCIOECONOMIC STATUS (KAHL, DAVIS)

Kahl, Joseph A., and James A. Davis, "A Comparison of Indexes of Socio-economic Status," *American Sociological Review*, 20 (June, 1955), pp. 317–325. See pp. 320–321.

6. SOCIOECONOMIC STATUS (VAUGHAN)

Vaughan, Charles L., "A Scale for Assessing Socio-Economic Status in Survey Research," *Public Opinion Quarterly*, 22 (Spring, 1958), pp. 19–34. See pp. 20–34.

Middleton, Russell, "Ethnic Prejudice and Susceptibility to Persuasion," *American Sociological Review,* 25 (October, 1960), pp. 679–686. See p. 681.

Putney, Snell, and Russell Middleton, "Dimensions and Correlates of Religious Ideologies," *Social Forces,* 39 (May, 1961), pp. 285–290. See p. 287.

SOCIOECONOMIC STATUS: OCCUPATIONAL

SEE ALSO
Social Mobility and Related Measures

1. OBJECTIVE PROFESSIONAL STATUS

Rettig, Salomon, Frank N. Jacobson, and Benjamin Pasamanick, "Status Overestimation, Objective Status, and Job Satisfaction among Professions," *American Sociological Review*, 23 (February, 1958), pp. 75–81. See p. 76.

Rettig, Salomon, Frank N. Jacobson, Leo DesPres, and Benjamin Pasamanick, "Rating Response Sets as a Function of Objective Status Criteria," *Sociometry*, 21 (December, 1958), pp. 281–291. See p. 284.

2. OCCUPATIONAL EVALUATION SCALE

Three subscales: prestige, attractiveness, competence required.

Burnstein, Eugene, Robert Moulton, and Paul Liberty, Jr., "Prestige versus Excellence as Determinants of Role Attractiveness," *American Sociological Review*, 28 (April, 1963), pp. 212–219. See p. 215.

3. OCCUPATIONAL PRESTIGE (GAMSON, SCHUMAN)

Gamson, William A., and Howard Schuman, "Some Undercurrents in the Prestige of Physicians," *American Journal of Sociology*, 68 (January, 1963), pp. 463–470. See p. 465.

4. OCCUPATIONAL PRESTIGE (GARBIN, BATES)

Garbin, Albeno P., and Frederick L. Bates, "Occupational Prestige: An Empirical Study of Its Correlates," *Social Forces*, 40 (December, 1961), pp. 131–136. See p. 133.

5. OCCUPATIONAL PRESTIGE (HETZLER)

Hetzler, Stanley A., "Social Mobility and Radicalism-Conservatism," *Social Forces*, 33 (December, 1954), pp. 161–166. See p. 161.

6. OCCUPATIONAL PRESTIGE (NORTH, HATT AND MODIFICATIONS)

See also category 29 below.

North, Cecil C., and Paul K. Hatt, "Jobs and Occupations: A Popular Evaluation," *Opinion News*, 9 (September, 1947), pp. 3–13.

Hodge, Robert W., Paul M. Siegel, and Peter H. Rossi, "Occupational Prestige in the United States, 1925–1963," *American Journal of Sociology*, 70 (November, 1964), pp. 286–302.

Among the most widely used measures of occupational prestige or occupational status are those based more or less directly on the National Opinion Research Center's well-known 1947 study. NORC interviewers asked a nationally representative sample of 2,920 adults and youths to rate 90 occupations. Specifically, respondents were asked to classify occupations as being of (1) excellent standing, (2) good standing, (3) average standing, (4) somewhat below average standing, or (5) poor standing. Respondents were also given a "don't know" alternative. For each occupation, the "don't know" responses were excluded and a mean score was computed by assigning a value of 100 to each "excellent" rating, 80 to each "good" rating, 60 to each "average" rating, 40 to each "somewhat below average" rating, and 20 to each "poor" rating. The average scores ranged from 96 (for U.S. Supreme Court Justice) to 33 (for shoe shiner). The set of 90 scores has been used in various ways in subsequent research to assess respondents' socioeconomic status. The uses have ranged from simple high or low status assignment based on the scale scores (see Angell, 1962, below) to indexes where one component is based upon the NORC occupational prestige score (see Bloom, Whiteman and Deutsch, 1965, below).

In 1963, the National Opinion Research Center conducted a replication of the 1947 study. Using the same sampling procedures and questions, the second study was based on 651 interviews. The smaller sample was justified because of the stability of prestige positions of occupations from subgroup to subgroup in the 1947 study. The major result of the 1963 restudy "is summarized in the product-moment correlation coefficient of .99 between the scores in 1947 and the scores in 1963." Although this seems to indicate that recent studies using prestige or status measures based on the 1947 NORC study are valid, both sets of scores are here summarized (from Hodge, Siegel, and Rossi, 1964 above, pp. 289, 290–292).

Myers, Jerome K., "Assimilation to the Ecological and Social Systems of a Community," *American Sociological Review*, 15 (June, 1950), pp. 367–372. See p. 370.

Reissman, Leonard, "Class, Leisure, and Social Participation," *American Sociological Review*, 19 (February, 1954), pp. 76–84. See pp. 79–82.

Lenski, Gerhard E., "Status Crystallization: A Non-vertical Dimension of Social Status," *American Sociological Review*, 19 (August, 1954), pp. 405–413. See pp. 406, 409, and 416.

Kahl, Joseph A., and James A. Davis, "A Comparison of Indexes of Socio-economic Status," *American Sociological Review*, 20 (June, 1955), pp. 317–325. See pp. 319–323.

Dynes, Russell R., "Church-Sect Typology and Socio-Economic Status," *American Sociological Review*, 20 (October, 1955), pp. 555–560. See pp. 558–560.

Brown, Morgan C., "The Status of Jobs and Occupations as Evaluated by an Urban Negro Sample," *American Sociological Review*, 20 (October, 1955), pp. 561–566. See pp. 564–565.

McCormack, Thelma Herman, "The Druggists' Dilemma: Problem of a Marginal Occupation," *American Journal of Sociology*, 61 (January, 1956), pp. 308–315. See pp. 310, and 313–314.

Clarke, Alfred C., "The Use of Leisure and Its Relation to Levels of Occupational Prestige," *American Sociological Review*, 21 (June, 1956), pp. 301–307. See pp. 301–302.

TABLE 1. DISTRIBUTION OF PRESTIGE RATINGS, UNITED STATES, MARCH, 1947

	Excel-lent*	Good	Aver-age	Below Aver-age	Poor	Don't Know†	NORC Score	Rank
U.S. Supreme Court justice	83	15	2	—	—	3	96	1
Physician	67	30	3	—	—	1	93	2.5
Nuclear physicist	48	39	11	1	1	51	86	18
Scientist	53	38	8	1	—	7	89	8
Government scientist	51	41	7	1	—	6	88	10.5
State governor	71	25	4	—	—	1	93	2.5
Cabinet member in the federal government	66	28	5	1	—	6	92	4.5
College professor	53	40	7	—	—	1	89	8
U.S. representative in Congress	57	35	6	1	1	4	89	8
Chemist	42	48	9	1	—	7	86	18
Lawyer	44	45	9	1	1	1	86	18
Diplomat in the U.S. foreign service	70	24	4	1	1	9	92	4.5
Dentist	42	48	9	1	—	—	86	18
Architect	42	48	9	1	—	6	86	18
County judge	47	43	9	1	—	1	87	13
Psychologist	38	49	12	1	—	15	85	22
Minister	52	35	11	1	1	1	87	13
Member of the board of directors of a large corporation	42	47	10	1	—	5	86	18
Mayor of a large city	57	36	6	1	—	1	90	6
Priest	51	34	11	2	2	6	86	18
Head of a department in a state government	47	44	8	—	1	3	87	13
Civil engineer	33	55	11	1	—	5	84	23
Airline pilot	35	48	15	1	1	3	83	24.5
Banker	49	43	8	—	—	1	88	10.5
Biologist	29	51	18	1	1	16	81	29
Sociologist	31	51	16	1	1	23	82	26.5
Instructor in public schools	28	45	24	2	1	1	79	34
Captain in the regular army	28	49	19	2	2	2	80	31.5
Accountant for a large business	25	57	17	1	—	3	81	29
Public school teacher	26	45	24	3	2	—	78	36
Owner of a factory that employs about 100 people	30	51	17	1	1	2	82	26.5
Building contractor	21	55	23	1	—	1	79	34
Artist who paints pictures that are exhibited in galleries	40	40	15	3	2	6	83	24.5
Musician in a symphony orchestra	31	46	19	3	1	5	81	29
Author of novels	32	44	19	3	2	9	80	31.5
Economist	25	48	24	2	1	22	79	34
Official of an international labor union	26	42	20	5	7	11	75	40.5
Railroad engineer	22	45	30	3	—	1	77	37.5
Electrician	15	38	43	4	—	1	73	45

* Bases for the 1947 occupational ratings are 2,920 less "don't know" and "not answered" for each occupational title.
† Base is 2,920 in all cases.
— Less than 0.5 per cent.
Source of the 1947 Distributions: Albert J. Reiss, Jr. and others, *Occupations and Social Status*, New York: Free Press of Glencoe, 1961, Table ii-9.

[continued, next left-hand page]

TABLE 2. DISTRIBUTION OF PRESTIGE RATINGS, UNITED STATES, JUNE, 1963

	Per Cent							
	Excellent‡	Good	Average	Below Average	Poor	Don't Know§	NORC Score	Rank
U.S. Supreme Court justice	77	18	4	1	1	1	94	1
Physician	71	25	4	—	—	1	93	2
Nuclear physicist	70	23	5	1	1	10	92	3.5
Scientist	68	27	5	—	—	2	92	3.5
Government scientist	64	30	5	—	1	2	91	5.5
State governor	64	30	5	—	1	1	91	5.5
Cabinet member in the federal government	61	32	6	1	1	2	90	8
College professor	59	35	5	—	—	1	90	8
U.S. representative in Congress	58	33	6	2	—	2	90	8
Chemist	54	38	8	—	—	3	89	11
Lawyer	53	38	8	—	—	—	89	11
Diplomat in the U.S. foreign service	57	34	7	1	1	3	89	11
Dentist	47	47	6	—	—	—	88	14
Architect	47	45	6	—	—	2	88	14
County judge	50	40	8	1	—	1	88	14
Psychologist	49	41	8	1	—	6	87	17.5
Minister	53	33	13	1	1	1	87	17.5
Member of the board of directors of a large corporation	42	51	6	1	—	1	87	17.5
Mayor of a large city	46	44	9	1	1	—	87	17.5
Priest	52	33	12	2	1	6	86	21.5
Head of a department in a state government	44	48	6	1	1	1	86	21.5
Civil engineer	40	52	8	—	—	2	86	21.5
Airline pilot	41	48	11	1	—	1	86	21.5
Banker	39	51	10	1	—	—	85	24.5
Biologist	38	50	11	—	—	6	85	24.5
Sociologist	35	48	15	1	1	10	83	26
Instructor in public schools	30	53	16	1	—	—	82	27.5
Captain in the regular army	28	55	16	2	—	1	82	27.5
Accountant for a large business	27	55	17	1	—	—	81	29.5
Public school teacher	31	46	22	1	—	—	81	29.5
Owner of a factory that employs about 100 people	28	49	19	2	1	1	80	31.5
Building contractor	22	56	20	1	—	—	80	31.5
Artist who paints pictures that are exhibited in galleries	28	45	20	5	2	4	78	34.5
Musician in a symphony orchestra	25	45	25	3	1	3	78	34.5
Author of novels	26	46	22	4	2	5	78	34.5
Economist	20	53	24	2	1	12	78	34.5
Official of an international labor union	21	53	18	5	3	5	77	37
Railroad engineer	19	47	30	3	1	1	76	39
Electrician	18	45	34	2	—	—	76	39

‡ Bases for the 1963 occupational ratings are 651 less "don't know" and "not answered" for each occupational title.

§ Base is 651 in all cases.

— Less than 0.5 per cent.

[continued, next right-hand page]

TABLE 1 (CONTINUED)
1947 DISTRIBUTION OF PRESTIGE RATINGS

	Per Cent							
	Excel-lent*	Good	Aver-age	Below Aver-age	Poor	Don't Know†	NORC Score	Rank
County agricultural agent	17	53	28	2	—	5	77	37.5
Owner-operator of a printing shop	13	48	36	3	—	2	74	42.5
Trained machinist	14	43	38	5	—	2	73	45
Farm owner and operator	19	46	31	3	1	1	76	39
Undertaker	14	43	36	5	2	2	72	47
Welfare worker for a city government	16	43	35	4	2	4	73	45
Newspaper columnist	13	51	32	3	1	5	74	42.5
Policeman	11	30	46	11	2	1	67	55
Reporter on a daily newspaper	9	43	43	4	1	2	71	48
Radio announcer	17	45	35	3	—	2	75	40.5
Bookkeeper	8	31	55	6	—	1	68	51.5
Tenant farmer—one who owns live-stock and machinery and manages the farm	10	37	40	11	2	1	68	51.5
Insurance agent	7	34	53	4	2	2	68	51.5
Carpenter	5	28	56	10	1	—	65	58
Manager of a small store in a city	5	40	50	4	1	1	69	49
A local official of a labor union	7	29	41	14	9	11	62	62
Mail carrier	8	26	54	10	2	—	66	57
Railroad conductor	8	30	52	9	1	1	67	55
Traveling salesman for a wholesale concern	6	35	53	5	1	2	68	51.5
Plumber	5	24	55	14	2	1	63	59.5
Automobile repairman	5	21	58	14	2	—	63	59.5
Playground director	7	33	48	10	2	4	67	55
Barber	3	17	56	20	4	1	59	66
Machine operator in a factory	4	20	53	20	3	2	60	64.5
Owner-operator of a lunch stand	4	24	55	14	3	1	62	62
Corporal in the regular army	5	21	48	20	6	3	60	64.5
Garage mechanic	4	21	57	17	1	—	62	62
Truck driver	2	11	49	29	9	—	54	71
Fisherman who owns his own boat	3	20	48	21	8	7	58	68
Clerk in a store	2	14	61	20	3	—	58	68
Milk route man	2	10	52	29	7	1	54	71
Streetcar motorman	3	16	55	21	5	2	58	68
Lumberjack	2	11	48	29	10	8	53	73
Restaurant cook	3	13	44	29	11	1	54	71
Singer in a nightclub	3	13	43	23	18	6	52	74.5
Filling station attendant	1	9	48	34	8	1	52	74.5
Dockworker	2	7	34	37	20	8	47	81.5
Railroad section hand	2	9	35	33	21	3	48	79.5
Night watchman	3	8	33	35	21	1	47	81.5
Coal miner	4	11	33	31	21	2	49	77.5
Restaurant waiter	2	8	37	36	17	1	48	79.5
Taxi driver	2	8	38	35	17	1	49	77.5
Farm hand	3	12	35	31	19	1	50	76

* Bases for the 1947 occupational ratings are 2,920 less "don't know" and "not answered" for each occupational title.
† Base is 2,920 in all cases.
— Less than 0.5 per cent.

[continued, next left-hand page]

TABLE 2 (CONTINUED)
1963 DISTRIBUTIONS OF PRESTIGE RATINGS

	Per Cent							
	Excel-lent‡	Good	Aver-age	Below Aver-age	Poor	Don't Know§	NORC Score	Rank
County agricultural agent	13	54	30	2	1	4	76	39
Owner-operator of a printing shop	13	51	34	2	—	2	75	41.5
Trained machinist	15	50	32	4	—	—	75	41.5
Farm owner and operator	16	45	33	5	—	1	74	44
Undertaker	16	46	33	3	2	3	74	44
Welfare worker for a city government	17	44	32	5	2	2	74	44
Newspaper columnist	10	49	38	3	1	1	73	46
Policeman	16	38	37	6	2	—	72	47
Reporter on a daily newspaper	7	45	44	3	1	1	71	48
Radio announcer	9	42	44	5	1	1	70	49.5
Bookkeeper	9	40	45	5	1	—	70	49.5
Tenant farmer—one who owns live-stock and machinery and manages the farm	11	37	42	8	3	1	69	51.5
Insurance agent	6	40	47	5	2	—	69	51.5
Carpenter	7	36	49	8	1	—	68	53
Manager of a small store in a city	3	40	48	7	2	—	67	54.5
A local official of a labor union	8	36	42	9	5	4	67	54.5
Mail carrier	7	29	53	10	1	—	66	57
Railroad conductor	6	33	48	10	3	—	66	57
Traveling salesman for a wholesale concern	4	33	54	7	3	2	66	57
Plumber	6	29	54	9	2	—	65	59
Automobile repairman	5	25	56	12	2	—	64	60
Playground director	6	29	46	15	4	3	63	62.5
Barber	4	25	56	13	2	1	63	62.5
Machine operator in a factory	6	24	51	15	4	1	63	62.5
Owner-operator of a lunch stand	4	25	57	11	3	1	63	62.5
Corporal in the regular army	6	25	47	15	6	2	62	65.5
Garage mechanic	4	22	56	15	3	—	62	65.5
Truck driver	3	18	54	19	5	—	59	67
Fisherman who owns his own boat	3	19	51	19	8	4	58	68
Clerk in a store	1	14	56	22	6	—	56	70
Milk route man	3	12	55	23	7	1	56	70
Streetcar motorman	3	16	46	27	8	2	56	70
Lumberjack	2	16	46	29	7	3	55	72.5
Restaurant cook	4	15	44	26	11	—	55	72.5
Singer in a nightclub	3	16	43	24	14	3	54	74
Filling station attendant	2	11	41	34	11	—	51	75
Dockworker	2	9	43	33	14	3	50	77.5
Railroad section hand	3	10	39	29	18	2	50	77.5
Night watchman	3	10	39	32	17	1	50	77.5
Coal miner	3	13	34	31	19	2	50	77.5
Restaurant waiter	2	8	42	32	16	—	49	80.5
Taxi driver	2	8	39	31	18	1	49	80.5
Farm hand	3	12	31	32	22	—	48	83

‡ Bases for the 1963 occupational ratings are 651 less "don't know" and "not answered" for each occupational title.

§ Base is 651 in all cases.

— Less than 0.5 per cent.

[continued, next right-hand page]

TABLE 1 (CONTINUED)
1947 DISTRIBUTION OF PRESTIGE RATINGS

	Per Cent							
	Excel-lent*	Good	Aver-age	Below Aver-age	Poor	Don't Know†	NORC Score	Rank
Janitor	1	7	30	37	25	1	44	85.5
Bartender	1	6	32	32	29	4	44	85.5
Clothes presser in a laundry	2	6	35	36	21	2	46	83
Soda fountain clerk	1	5	34	40	20	2	45	84
Sharecropper—one who owns no live-stock or equipment and does not manage farm	1	6	24	28	41	3	40	87
Garbage collector	1	4	16	26	53	2	35	88
Street sweeper	1	3	14	29	53	1	34	89
Shoe shiner	1	2	13	28	56	2	33	90
Average	22	31	30	11	7	4	70	—

* Bases for the 1947 occupational ratings are 2,920 less "don't know" and "not answered" for each occupational title.
† Base is 2,920 in all cases.
— Less than 0.5 per cent.

Kenkel, William F., "The Relationship between Status Consistency and Politico-Economic Attitudes," *American Sociological Review*, 21 (June, 1956), pp. 365–368. See pp. 365–366.

Davis, James A., "Status Symbols and the Measurement of Status Perception," *Sociometry*, 19 (September, 1956), pp. 154–165. See pp. 157 and 160.

Empey, LaMar T., "Social Class and Occupational Aspiration: A Comparison of Absolute and Relative Measurement," *American Sociological Review*, 21 (December, 1956), pp. 703–709. See pp. 705–706.

Haller, A. O., and William H. Sewell, "Farm Residence and Levels of Educational and Occupational Aspiration," *American Journal of Sociology*, 62 (January, 1957), pp. 407–411. See pp. 408–410.

Sewell, William H., A. O. Haller, and Murray A. Straus, "Social Status and Educational and Occupational Aspiration," *American Sociological Review*, 22 (February, 1957), pp. 67–73. See p. 69.

Dynes, Russell R., "The Consequences of Sectarianism for Social Participation," *Social Forces*, 35 (May, 1957), pp. 331–334. See pp. 332–333.

TABLE 2 (CONTINUED)
1963 DISTRIBUTIONS OF PRESTIGE RATINGS

| | Per Cent | | | | | | | |
	Excel-lent‡	Good	Aver-age	Below Aver-age	Poor	Don't Know§	NORC Score	Rank
Janitor	1	9	35	35	19	1	48	83
Bartender	1	7	42	28	21	2	48	83
Clothes presser in a laundry	2	7	31	38	22	1	45	85
Soda fountain clerk	—	5	30	44	20	1	44	86
Sharecropper—one who owns no livestock or equipment and does not manage farm	1	8	26	28	37	2	42	87
Garbage collector	2	5	21	32	41	1	39	88
Street sweeper	1	4	17	31	46	1	36	89
Shoe shiner	—	3	15	30	51	2	34	90
Average	22	32	29	11	6	2	71	—

‡ Bases for the 1963 occupational ratings are 651 less "don't know" and "not answered" for each occupational title.
§ Base is 651 in all cases.
— Less than 0.5 per cent.

Blau, Peter M., "Occupational Bias and Mobility," *American Sociological Review*, 22 (August, 1957), pp. 392–399. See p. 393.

Kahl, Joseph A., *The American Class Structure*, New York: Rinehart and Company, 1957, pp. 259–261.

Nye, F. Ivan, James F. Short, Jr., and Virgil J. Olson, "Socioeconomic Status and Delinquent Behavior," *American Journal of Sociology*, 58 (January, 1958), pp. 381–389. See p. 384.

Janowitz, Morris, "Social Stratification: Mobility in West Germany," *American Journal of Sociology*, 64 (July, 1958), pp. 6–24. See p. 12.

Westoff, Charles F., Philip C. Sagi, and E. Lowell Kelly, "Fertility through Twenty Years of Marriage: A Study in Predictive Possibilities," *American Sociological Review*, 23 (October, 1958), pp. 549–556. See pp. 551–552.

Rosen, Bernard C., "Race, Ethnicity and the Achievement Syndrome," *American Sociological Review*, 24 (February, 1959), pp. 47–60. See pp. 58–59.

Haller, A. O., "Planning to Farm: A Social Psychological Interpretation," *Social Forces*, 37 (March, 1959), pp. 263–268. See p. 266.

Gross, Edward, "The Occupational Variable as a Research Category," *American Sociological Review*, 24 (October, 1959), pp. 640–649. See p. 642.

Reissman, Leonard, *Class in American Society*, New York: Free Press of Glencoe, 1959, pp. 401–404.

More, Douglas M., "A Note on Occupational Origins of Health Service Professions," *American Sociological Review*, 25 (June, 1960), pp. 403–404.

Dean, Dwight, "Alienation and Political Apathy," *Social Forces*, 38 (March, 1960), pp. 185–189. See p. 188.

Haller, A. O., and C. E. Butterworth, "Peer Influence on Levels of Occupational and Educational Aspirations," *Social Forces*, 38 (May, 1960), pp. 289–295. See p. 292.

More, Douglas M., and Nathan Kohn, Jr., "Some Motives for Entering Dentistry," *American Journal of Sociology*, 66 (July, 1960), pp. 48–53. See pp. 49–50.

French, Cecil L., "Correlates of Success in Retail Selling," *American Journal of Sociology*, 66 (September, 1960), pp. 128–134. See p. 129.

Porterfield, Austin L., and Jack P. Gibbs, "Occupational Prestige and Social Mobility of Suicides in New Zealand," *American Journal of Sociology*, 66 (September, 1960), pp. 147–152. See pp. 147–148.

Simpson, Richard L., and Ida H. Simpson, "Correlates and Estimation of Occupational Prestige," *American Journal of Sociology*, 66 (September, 1960), pp. 135–140. See p. 136.

Faunce, William A., "Social Stratification and Attitude toward Change in Job Content," *Social Forces*, 39 (December, 1960), pp. 140–148. See p. 144.

Sarapata, Adam, and Wlodzimierz Wesolowski, "The Evaluation of Occupations of Warsaw Inhabitants," *American Journal of Sociology*, 66 (May, 1961), pp. 581–591. See p. 591.

Dean, Dwight G., "Alienation: Its Meaning and Measurement," *American Sociological Review*, 26 (October, 1961), pp. 753–758. See p. 757.

Greenfield, Robert W., "Factors Associated with Attitudes toward Desegregation in a Florida Residential Suburb," *Social Forces*, 40 (October, 1961), pp. 31–42. See p. 35.

Tilly, Charles, "Occupational Rank and Grade of Residence in a Metropolis," *American Journal of Sociology*, 68 (November, 1961), pp. 323–330. See p. 325.

Crockett, Harry J., Jr., "The Achievement Motive and Differential Occupational Mobility in the United States," *American Sociological Review*, 27 (April, 1962), pp. 191–204. See p. 196.

Angell, Robert C., "Preferences for Moral Norms in Three Problem Areas," *American Journal of Sociology*, 67 (May, 1962), pp. 650–660. See p. 650.

Dean, Dwight G., and Jon A. Reeves, "Anomie: A Comparison of a Catholic and a Protestant Sample," *Sociometry*, 25 (June, 1962), pp. 209–212. See p. 211.

Straus, Murray A., "Deferred Gratification, Social Class and the Achievement Syndrome," *American Sociological Review*, 27 (June, 1962), pp. 326–335. See pp. 331 and 333.

Jackson, Elton F., "Status Consistency and Symptoms of Stress," *American Soicological Review*, 27 (August, 1962), pp. 469–480. See p. 471.

Stuckert, Robert P., "Occupational Mobility and Family Relationships," *Social Forces*, 41 (March, 1963), pp. 301–307. See p. 303.

Burnstein, Moulton, and Liberty (April, 1963), p. 217; see category 2 above.

Gusfield, Joseph R., and Michael Schwartz, "The Meanings of Occupational Prestige: Reconsideration of the NORC Scale," *American Sociological Review*, 28 (April, 1963), pp. 265–271. See p. 269.

Glenn, Norval D., "Negro Prestige Criteria: A Case Study in the Bases of Prestige," *American Journal of Sociology*, 68 (May, 1963), pp. 645–657. See p. 649.

Gist, Noel P., and William S. Bennett, Jr., "Aspiration of Negro and White Students," *Social Forces*, 42 (October, 1963), pp. 40–48. See p. 41.

Sessoms, H. Douglas, "An Analysis of Selected Variables Affecting Outdoor Recreation Patterns," *Social Forces*, 42 (October, 1963), pp. 112–115. See p. 113.

Smelser, William T., "Adolescent and Adult Occupational Choice as a Function of Family Socioeconomic History," *Sociometry*, 26 (December, 1963), pp. 393–409. See p. 400.

Bennett, William S., Jr., and Noel P. Gist, "Class and Family Influences on Student Aspirations," *Social Forces*, 43 (December, 1964), pp. 167–173. See p. 169.

Bloom, Richard, Martin Whiteman, and Martin Deutsch, "Race and Social Class as Separate Factors Related to Social Environment," *American Journal of Sociology*, 70 (January, 1965), pp. 471–476. See p. 472.

Rhodes, Albert Lewis, Albert J. Reiss, Jr., and Otis Dudley Duncan, "Occupational Segregation in a Metropolitan School System," *American Journal of Sociology*, 70 (May, 1965), pp. 682–694. See p. 686.

Landis, Judson R., and Frank R. Scarpitti, "Perceptions Regarding Value Orientations and Legitimate Opportunity: Delinquents and Non-Delinquents," *Social Forces*, 44 (September, 1965), pp. 83–91. See p. 85.

7. OCCUPATIONAL PRESTIGE (MEASURED BY SEMANTIC DIFFERENTIAL)

Osgood, Charles E., George J. Suci, and Percy H. Tannenbaum, *The Measurement of Meaning*, Urbana, Ill.: University of Illinois Press, 1957.

Gusfield and Schwartz (1963), p. 267; see category 6 above.

8. OCCUPATIONAL PRESTIGE (SMITH)

Smith, Mapheus, "An Empirical Scale of Prestige Status of Occupations," *American Sociological Review*, 8 (April, 1943), pp. 185–192. See pp. 187–188.

Empey (1956), pp. 705–706; see category 6 above.

Nye, Short, and Olson (1958), pp. 384–388; see category 6 above.

Straus (1962), p. 331; see category 6 above.

9. OCCUPATIONAL PRESTIGE (WOOD)

Wood, Arthur Lewis, "Informal Relations in the Practice of Criminal Law," *American Journal of Sociology*, 62 (July, 1956), pp. 48–55. See p. 52.

10. OCCUPATIONAL PRESTIGE RANKING BY CHILDREN

Weinstein, Eugene A., "Weights Assigned by Children to Criteria of Prestige," *Sociometry*, 19 (June, 1956), pp. 126–132. See pp. 127–129.

11. OCCUPATIONAL PRESTIGE RANKINGS BY DENTAL STUDENTS

More and Kohn (1960), pp. 48–53; see category 6 above.

12. OCCUPATIONAL PRESTIGE OF NURSES, TEACHERS, AND SOCIAL WORKERS

Deutscher, Irwin, "The Stereotype as a Research Tool," *Social Forces*, 37 (October, 1958), pp. 55–60. See p. 58.

13. OCCUPATIONAL PRESTIGE, SITUS RANKINGS

McTavish, Donald G., "The Differential Prestige of Situs Categories," *Social Forces*, 41 (May, 1963), pp. 363–368. See p. 365.

14. OCCUPATIONAL PRESTIGE IN AUSTRALIA

Taft, Ronald, "The Social Grading of Occupations in Australia," *British Journal of Sociology*, 4 (June, 1953), pp. 181–188.
Porterfield and Gibbs (1960), p. 148; see category 6 above.

15. OCCUPATIONAL PRESTIGE IN DENMARK

Svalastoga, K., E. Høgh, M. Pedersen, and E. Schild, "Differential Class Behavior in Denmark," *American Sociological Review*, 21 (August, 1956), pp. 435–439. See pp. 435–436.

16. OCCUPATIONAL PRESTIGE IN GHANA (TWO MEASURES)

Clignet, Remi P., and Philip Foster, "Potential Elites in Ghana and the Ivory Coast: A Preliminary Comparison," *American Journal of Sociology*, 70 (November, 1964), pp. 349–362. See p. 360.

17. OCCUPATIONAL PRESTIGE IN GREAT BRITAIN

Hall, John, and D. C. Caradog Jones, "Social Grading of Occupations," *British Journal of Sociology*, 1 (March, 1950), pp. 31–55. See pp. 35–37.

Moser, C. A., and John R. Hall, "The Social Grading of Occupations," in D. V. Glass (ed.), *Social Mobility in Britain*, Glencoe, Ill.: The Free Press, 1954, pp. 29–50.

Collison, Peter, "Occupation, Education and Housing in an English City," *American Journal of Sociology*, 65 (May, 1960), pp. 588–597. See pp. 588–589.

Porterfield and Gibbs (September, 1960), p. 148; see category 6 above.

18. OCCUPATIONAL PRESTIGE IN INTERNATIONAL COMPARISONS

Inkeles, Alex, and Peter H. Rossi, "National Comparisons of Occupational Prestige," *American Journal of Sociology*, 61 (January, 1956), pp. 329–339. See pp. 330–332 and 334–337.

19. OCCUPATIONAL PRESTIGE IN JAPAN AND THE UNITED STATES (THREE RATINGS)

Ramsey, Charles E., and Robert J. Smith, "Japanese and American Perceptions of Occupations," *American Journal of Sociology*, 65 (March, 1960), pp. 475–482. See pp. 476–478.

20. OCCUPATIONAL PRESTIGE IN NEW ZEALAND

Congalton, A. A., "Social Grading of Occupations in New Zealand," *British Journal of Sociology*, 4 (March, 1953), pp. 45–49.

Porterfield and Gibbs (1960); see category 6 above.

21. OCCUPATIONAL PRESTIGE IN THE PHILIPPINES

Tiryakian, Edward A., "The Prestige Evaluation of Occupations in an Underdeveloped Country: The Philippines," *American Journal of Sociology*, 68 (January, 1958), pp. 390–399. See pp. 392–394.

22. OCCUPATIONAL PRESTIGE IN POLAND

Sarapata and Wesolowski (1961); see category 6 above.

23. OCCUPATIONAL PRESTIGE IN SWEDEN AND THE UNITED STATES (FOUR RANKINGS)

McDonagh, Edward C., Sven Wermlund, and John F. Crowther,

"Relative Professional Status as Perceived by American and Swedish University Students," *Social Forces*, 38 (October, 1959), pp. 65–69. See pp. 67–68.

24. OCCUPATIONAL PRESTIGE IN THE SOVIET UNION

Rossi, Peter H., and Alex Inkeles, "Multidimensional Ratings of Occupations," *Sociometry*, 20 (September, 1957), pp. 234–251. See pp. 235 ff.

25. OCCUPATIONAL STATUS (CENSUS, EDWARDS AND MODIFICATIONS)

See also categories 26, 32, and 38 below.

Edwards, Alba M., *Alphabetical Index of Occupations by Industries and Socio-Economic Groupings*, Washington, D.C.: Government Printing Office, 1937.

Edwards, Alba M., *A Social-Economic Grouping of the Gainfully Employed Workers of the United States, 1930*, Washington, D.C.: Government Printing Office, 1938, pp. 1–6.

Edwards, Alba M., *U.S. Census of Population, 1940: Comparative Occupational Statistics, 1870–1940*, Washington, D.C.: Government Printing Office, 1943.

U.S. Bureau of the Census, *1960 Census of Population: Classified Index of Occupations and Industries*, Washington, D.C.: Government Printing Office, 1960.

The Census (Alba M. Edwards) index of occupations by social-economic groups has been the most frequently used measure set forth in this inventory. Including modifications (see categories 26, 32, and 38 below), it has been used 131 times in the sources covered by this inventory.

Although, when used as a measure of socioeconomic status, the classification scheme employs only one item of information (occupation), its inclusion in this inventory is justified by the rationale for its construction: "Edwards maintained that these categories were the most practical means for making a rough scale of occupations that would increase in prestige, education, and income as one ascended step by step. He had no way to validate his claim about prestige, but showed that with one or two exceptions, average figures for each group for education and income did follow a cumulative scale." (See Kahl, 1953, pp. 64-69, below.)

The basic categories now used by the Bureau of the Census (a slight modification of those originally presented by Edwards) are:

1. Professional, technical and kindred workers
2. Managers, Officials and Proprietors
   a. Nonfarm managers, officials, and proprietors
   b. Farmers and farm managers
3. Clerical and sales workers
   a. Clerical and kindred workers
   b. Sales workers
4. Craftsmen, foremen, and kindred workers
5. Operatives and kindred workers
6. Unskilled, service, and domestic workers
   a. Private household workers
   b. Service workers, except private household
   c. Farm laborers and foremen
   d. Laborers, except farm and mine

Occupations listed under each category (U.S. Bureau of the Census, 1960, above) are indicated below:

CENSUS OCCUPATIONAL CLASSIFICATION

PROFESSIONAL, TECHNICAL, AND KINDRED WORKERS

Accountants and auditors
Actors and actresses
Airplane pilots and navigators
Architects
Artists and art teachers
Athletes
Authors
Chemists
Chiropractors
Clergymen
College presidents, professors, and instructors (not elsewhere cited)
College presidents and deans

Dancers and dancing teachers
Dentists
Designers
Dietitians and nutritionists
Draftsmen
Editors and reporters
Engineers, aeronautical
Engineers, chemical
Engineers, civil
Engineers, electrical
Engineers, industrial
Engineers, mechanical
Engineers, metallurgical, and metallurgists

Engineers, mining
Engineers, sales
Engineers (n.e.c.)
Entertainers (n.e.c.)
Farm and home management advisers
Foresters and conservationists
Funeral directors and embalmers
Lawyers and judges
Librarians
Musicians and music teachers
Natural scientists (n.e.c.)
  Agricultural scientists
  Biological scientists
  Geologists and geophysicists
  Mathematicians
  Physicists
  Miscellaneous natural scientists
Nurses, professional
Nurses, student professional
Optometrists
Osteopaths
Personnel and labor relations workers
Pharmacists
Photographers
Physicians and surgeons

Public relations men and publicity writers
Radio operators
Recreation and group workers
Religious workers
Social and welfare workers, except group
Social scientists
  Economists
  Psychologists
  Statisticians and actuaries
  Miscellaneous social scientists
Sports instructors and officials
Surveyors
Teachers, elementary schools
Teachers, secondary schools
Teachers (n.e.c.)
Technicians, medical and dental
Technicians, electrical and electronic
Technicians, other engineering and physical sciences
Technicians (n.e.c.)
Therapists and healers (n.e.c.)
Veterinarians
Professional, technical, and kindred workers (n.e.c.)

FARMERS AND FARM MANAGERS

Farmers (owners and tenants)

Farm managers

MANAGERS, OFFICIALS, AND PROPRIETORS, EXCEPT FARM

Buyers and department heads, store
Buyers and shippers, farm products
Conductors, railroad
Credit men
Floor men and floor managers, store
Inspectors, public administration
Managers, officials, and proprietors (n.e.c.)

Managers and superintendents, building
Officers, pilots, pursers, and engineers, ship
Officials and administrators (n.e.c.), public administration
Officials, lodge, society, union, etc.
Postmasters
Purchasing agents and buyers (n.e.c.)

Occupational · 425

CLERICAL AND KINDRED WORKERS

Agents (n.e.c.)
Attendants and assistants, library
Attendants, physician's and dentist's offices
Baggagemen, transportation
Bank tellers
Bookkeepers
Cashiers
Collectors, bill and account
Dispatchers and starters, vehicle
Express messengers and railway mail clerks
File clerks
Insurance adjusters, examiners, and investigators
Mail carriers

Messengers and office boys
Office machine operators
Payroll and timekeeping clerks
Postal clerks
Receptionists
Secretaries
Shipping and receiving clerks
Stenographers
Stock clerks and storekeepers
Telegraph messengers
Telegraph operators
Telephone operators
Ticket, station, and express agents
Typists
Clerical and kindred workers (n.e.c.)

SALES WORKERS

Advertising agents and salesmen
Auctioneers
Demonstrators
Hucksters and peddlers
Insurance agents, brokers, and underwriters

Newsboys
Real estate agents and brokers
Stock and bond salesmen
Salesmen and sales clerks (n.e.c.)

CRAFTSMEN, FOREMEN, AND KINDRED WORKERS

Bakers
Blacksmiths
Boilermakers
Bookbinders
Brickmasons, stonemasons, and tile setters
Cabinetmakers
Carpenters
Cement and concrete finishers
Compositors and typesetters
Cranemen, derrickmen, and hoistmen
Decorators and window dressers
Electricians
Electrotypers and stereotypers
Engravers, except photoengravers

Excavating, grading, and road machinery operators
Foremen (n.e.c.)
Forgemen and hammermen
Furriers
Glaziers
Heat treaters, annealers, and temperers
Inspectors, scalers, and graders, log and lumber
Inspectors (n.e.c.)
Jewelers, watchmakers, goldsmiths, and silversmiths
Job setters, metal
Linemen and servicemen, telegraph, telephone, and power

Locomotive engineers
Locomotive firemen
Loom fixers
Machinists
Mechanics and repairmen, air conditioning, heating, and refrigeration
Mechanics and repairmen, airplane
Mechanics and repairmen, automobile
Mechanics and repairmen, office machine
Mechanics and repairmen, radio and television
Mechanics and repairmen, railroad and car shop
Mechanics and repairmen (n.e.c.)
Millers, grain, flour, feed, etc.
Millwrights
Molders, metal
Motion picture projectionists
Opticians, and lens grinders and polishers
Painters, construction and maintenance

Paperhangers
Pattern and model makers, except paper
Photoengravers and lithographers
Piano and organ tuners and repair men
Plasterers
Plumbers and pipe fitters
Pressmen and plate printers, printing
Rollers and roll hands, metal
Roofers and slaters
Shoemakers and repairers, except factory
Stationary engineers
Stone cutters and stone carvers
Structural metal workers
Tailors and tailoresses
Tinsmiths, coppersmiths, and sheet metal workers
Toolmakers, and die makers and setters
Upholsterers
Craftsmen and kindred workers (n.e.c.)
Members of the armed forces

OPERATIVES AND KINDRED WORKERS[1]

Apprentice auto mechanics
Apprentice bricklayers and masons
Apprentice carpenters
Apprentice electricians
Apprentice machinists and toolmakers
Apprentice mechanics, except auto
Apprentice plumbers and pipe fitters

Apprentices, building trades (n.e.c.)
Apprentices, metalworking trades (n.e.c.)
Apprentices, printing trades
Apprentices, other specified trades
Apprentices, trade not specified
Asbestos and insulation workers
Assemblers
Attendants, auto service and parking

[1] Mine laborers are included in the major group "Operators and Kindred Workers."

Blasters and powdermen
Boatmen, canalmen, and lock keepers
Brakemen, railroad
Bus drivers
Chairmen, rodmen, and axmen, surveying
Checkers, examiners, and inspectors, manufacturing
Conductors, bus and street railway
Deliverymen and routemen
Dressmakers and seamstresses, except factory
Dyers
Filers, grinders, and polishers, metal
Fruit, nut, and vegetable graders and packers, except factory
Furnacemen, smeltermen, and pourers
Graders and sorters, manufacturing
Heaters, metal
Knitters, loopers, and toppers, textile
Laundry and dry cleaning operatives

Meat cutters, except slaughter and packing house
Milliners
Mine operatives and laborers (n.e.c.)
Motormen, mine, factory, logging camp, etc.
Motormen, street, subway, and elevated railway
Oilers and greasers, except auto
Packers and wrappers (n.e.c.)
Painters, except construction and maintenance
Photographic process workers
Power station operators
Sailors and deck hands
Sawyers
Sewers and stitchers, manufacturing
Spinners, textile
Stationary firemen
Switchmen, railroad
Taxicab drivers and chauffeurs
Truck and tractor drivers
Weavers, textile
Welders and flame-cutters
Operatives and kindred workers (n.e.c.)

PRIVATE HOUSEHOLD WORKERS

Baby sitters, private household
Housekeepers, private household
Laundresses, private household

Private household workers (n.e.c.)

SERVICE WORKERS, EXCEPT PRIVATE HOUSEHOLD

Attendants, hospital and other institutions
Attendants, professional and personal service (n.e.c.)
Attendants, recreation and amusement
Barbers
Bartenders

Bootblacks
Boarding and lodging house keepers
Chambermaids and maids, except private household
Charwomen and cleaners
Cooks, except private household
Counter and fountain workers

Elevator operators
Hairdressers and cosmetologists
Housekeepers and stewards, except private household
Janitors and sextons
Kitchen workers (n.e.c.), except private household
Midwives
Porters
Practical nurses
Protective service workers
  Firemen, fire protection

Guards, watchmen, and doorkeepers
Marshals and constables
Policemen and detectives
Sheriffs and bailiffs
Watchmen (crossing) and bridge tenders
Ushers, recreation and amusement
Waiters and waitresses
Service workers, except private household (n.e.c.)

FARM LABORERS AND FOREMEN

Farm foremen
Farm laborers, wage workers
Farm laborers, unpaid family workers

Farm service laborers, self-employed

LABORERS, EXCEPT FARM AND MINE[1]

Carpenters' helpers, except logging and mining
Fishermen and oystermen
Garage laborers, and car washers and greasers
Gardeners, except farm, and groundskeepers

Longshoremen and stevedores
Lumbermen, raftsmen, and woodchoppers
Teamsters
Truck drivers' helpers
Warehousemen (n.e.c.)
Laborers (n.e.c.)

OCCUPATION NOT REPORTED

[Necessarily has no specific listings]

Weeks, H. Ashley, "Differential Divorce Rates by Occupations," *Social Forces*, 21 (March, 1943), pp. 334–337. See p. 334.

McGuire, Carson, "Supplement to *Social Class in America*," Chicago, Ill.: Committee on Human Development, University of Chicago, 1950, mimeographed.

Goode, William J., "Economic Factors and Marital Stability," *American Sociological Review*, 16 (December, 1951), pp. 802–812. See p. 804.

[1] Mine laborers are included in the major group "Operatives and Kindred Workers."

Sewell, William H., and Bertram L. Ellenbogen, "Social Status and the Measured Intelligence of Small City and Rural Children," *American Sociological Review*, 17 (October, 1952), pp. 612–616. See p. 613.

Kahl (1957), pp. 64–69; see category 6 above.

Harlan, William H., "Community Adaptation to the Presence of Aged Persons: St. Petersburg, Florida," *American Journal of Sociology*, 59 (January, 1954), pp. 332–339. See pp. 336–339.

Turner, Ralph H., "Occupational Patterns of Inequality," *American Journal of Sociology*, 59 (March, 1954), pp. 437–447. See pp. 438–442 and 444.

Montague, Joel B., Jr., and Bernard Pustilnik, "Prestige Ranking of Occupations in an American City with Reference to Hall's and Jones' Study," *British Journal of Sociology*, 5 (June, 1954), pp. 154–160. See pp. 157–158.

Smigel, Erwin O., "Trends in Occupational Sociology in the United States: A Survey of Postwar Research," *American Sociological Review*, 19 (August, 1954), pp. 398–404. See p. 399.

Goldstein, Sidney, "City Directories as Sources of Migration Data," *American Journal of Sociology*, 60 (September, 1954), pp. 169–176. See pp. 172–173 and 176.

Vincent, Clark E., "The Unwed Mother and Sampling Bias," *American Sociological Review*, 19 (October, 1954), pp. 562–567. See p. 564.

Westoff, Charles F., "Differential Fertility in the United States, 1900–1952," *American Sociological Review*, 19 (October, 1954), pp. 549–561. See pp. 556–561.

Graham, Saxon, "Cultural Compatibility in the Adoption of Television," *Social Forces*, 33 (December, 1954), pp. 166–170. See p. 167.

Vidich, Arthur J., and Gilbert Shapiro, "A Comparison of Participant Observation and Survey Data," *American Sociological Review*, 20 (February, 1955), pp. 28–33. See pp. 31–32.

Duncan, Otis D., and Beverly Duncan, "Residential Distribution and Occupational Stratification," *American Journal of Sociol-*

ogy, 60 (March, 1955), pp. 493–503. See pp. 496–499 and 501.

Morse, Nancy C., and Robert S. Weiss, "The Function and Meaning of Work and the Job," *American Sociological Review*, 20 (April, 1955), pp. 191–198. See pp. 195–198.

Ogburn, William F., "Implications of the Rising Standard of Living in the United States," *American Journal of Sociology*, 60 (May, 1955), pp. 541–546. See p. 542.

Kahl and Davis (June, 1955), p. 318; see category 6 above.

Goldstein, Sidney, "Migration and Occupational Mobility in Norristown, Pennsylvania," *American Sociological Review*, 20 (August, 1955), pp. 402–408. See p. 404.

Kephart, William M., "Occupational Level and Marital Disruption," *American Sociological Review*, 20 (August, 1955), pp. 456–465. See pp. 458–459 and 461–464.

United States Bureau of the Census, *Current Population Reports, Consumer Income*, Washington, D.C.: Government Printing Office, October, 1955, p. 24.

Dynes (October, 1955), pp. 558–559; see category 6 above.

Gusfield, Joseph R., "Social Structure and Moral Reform: A Study of the Woman's Christian Temperance Union," *American Journal of Sociology*, 61 (November, 1955), pp. 221–232. See p. 231.

Montague, Joel B., Jr., "A Study of Anxiety among English and American Boys," *American Sociological Review*, 20 (December, 1955), pp. 685–689. See pp. 685–686.

Miller, Herman, *Income of the American People*, New York: John Wiley and Sons, 1955, pp. 55–58 and 166.

Axelrod, Morris, "Urban Structure and Social Participation," *American Sociological Review*, 21 (February, 1956), pp. 13–18. See pp. 15–16.

Bell, Wendell, and Maryanne T. Force, "Urban Neighborhood Types and Participation in Formal Associations," *American Sociological Review*, 21 (February, 1956), pp. 25–34. See pp. 30–31.

Duncan, Beverly, "Factors in Work-Residence Separation: Wage and Salary Workers, Chicago, 1951," *American Sociological*

Review, 21 (February, 1956), pp. 48–56. See pp. 49–50.

Reeder, Leo G., "Social Differentials in Mode of Travel, Time and Cost in the Journey to Work," *American Sociological Review*, 21 (February, 1956), pp. 56–63. See p. 58.

Toby, Jackson, "Orientation to Education as a Factor in the School Maladjustment of Lower-Class Children," *Social Forces*, 35 (March, 1957), pp. 259–266. See pp. 260–261.

Deasy, Leila Calhoun, "Socio-economic Status and Participation in the Poliomyelitis Vaccine Trial," *American Sociological Review*, 21 (April, 1956), pp. 185–191. See pp. 186–187.

Bell, Wendell, and Maryanne T. Force, "Social Structure and Participation in Different Types of Formal Associations," *Social Forces*, 34 (May, 1956), pp. 345–350. See pp. 345–346.

Reeder, Leo G., "Social Factors in Heart Disease: A Preliminary Research Report on the Relationship of Certain Social Factors to Blood Pressure in Males," *Social Forces*, 34 (May, 1956), pp. 367–371. See p. 369.

Sewell, William H., and A. O. Haller, "Social Status and Personality Adjustment of the Child," *Sociometry*, 19 (June, 1956), pp. 114–125. See pp. 116–118.

Pihlblad, C. T., and C. L. Gregory, "The Role of Test Intelligence and Occupational Background as Factors in Occupational Choice," *Sociometry*, 19 (September, 1956), pp. 192–199. See pp. 193–194.

More, Douglas M., "Social Origins and Occupational Adjustment," *Social Forces*, 35 (October, 1956), pp. 16–19. See p. 19.

Munson, Byron E., "Attitudes toward Urban and Suburban Residence in Indianapolis," *Social Forces*, 35 (October, 1956), pp. 76–80. See p. 76.

Peters, William S., "A Method of Deriving Geographic Patterns of Associated Demographic Characteristics within Urban Areas," *Social Forces*, 35 (October, 1956), pp. 62–68. See pp. 64–67.

Wilensky, Harold L., "The Labor Vote: A Local Union's Impact on the Political Conduct of Its Members," *Social Forces*, 35

(December, 1956), pp. 111–120. See p. 117.

Kahl (1957), pp. 64–69; see category 6 above.

Burchinal, Lee G., Glenn R. Hawkes, and Gardner Bruce, "Personality Characteristics and Marital Satisfaction," *Social Forces*, 35 (March, 1957), pp. 218–222. See p. 219.

Stephenson, Richard M., "Mobility Orientation and Stratification of 1,000 Ninth Graders," *American Sociological Review*, 22 (April, 1957), pp. 204–212. See pp. 206–207.

Lystad, Mary H., "Social Mobility among Selected Groups of Schizophrenic Patients," *American Sociological Review*, 22 (June, 1957), pp. 288–292. See p. 289.

Kolko, Gabriel, "Economic Mobility and Social Stratification," *American Journal of Sociology*, 68 (July, 1957), pp. 30–38. See pp. 32–34.

Ianni, Francis A. J., "Residential and Occupational Mobility as Indices of the Acculturation of an Ethnic Group," *Social Forces*, 36 (October, 1957), pp. 65–72. See pp. 68–70.

Pihlblad, C. T., and C. L. Gregory, "Occupation and Patterns of Migration," *Social Forces*, 35 (October, 1957), pp. 56–64. See p. 58.

Johnson, Elmer H., "Selective Factors in Capital Punishment," *Social Forces*, 35 (December, 1957), pp. 165–169. See p. 168.

Strodtbeck, Fred L., Rita M. James, and Charles Hawkins, "Social Status in Jury Deliberations," *American Sociological Review*, 22 (December, 1957), pp. 713–719. See pp. 713–718.

Gold, Martin, and Carol Slater, "Office, Factory, Store—and Family: A Study of Integration Setting," *American Sociological Review*, 23 (February, 1958), pp. 64–74. See p. 66.

Powell, Elwin H., "Occupation, Status and Suicide: Toward a Redefinition of Anomie," *American Sociological Review*, 23 (April, 1958), pp. 131–139. See pp. 135–137.

Heer, David, "Dominance and the Working Wife," *Social Forces*, 36 (May, 1958), pp. 341–347. See p. 342.

Wright, Charles R., and Herbert H. Hyman, "Voluntary Association Memberships of American Adults: Evidence from National Sample Surveys," *American Sociological Review*, 23 (June, 1958), pp. 284–294. See p. 289.

Janowitz (July, 1958), pp. 7–10; see category 6 above.

Wilhelm, Sidney, and Gideon Sjoberg, "The Social Characteristics of Entertainers," *Social Forces*, 37 (October, 1958), pp. 71–76. See p. 72.

Duncan, Otis Dudley, and Stanley Lieberson, "Ethnic Segregation and Assimilation," *American Journal of Sociology*, 64 (January, 1959), pp. 364–374. See p. 365.

Bowerman, Charles E., and John W. Kinch, "Changes in Family and Peer Orientation of Children between the Fourth and Tenth Grades," *Social Forces*, 37 (March, 1959), pp. 206–211. See p. 209.

Lee, Ann, and Everett Lee, "The Future Fertility of the American Negro," *Social Forces*, 37 (March, 1959), pp. 228–231. See p. 230.

Morris, Richard T., and Raymond J. Murphy, "The Situs Dimension in Occupational Structure," *American Sociological Review*, 24 (April, 1959), pp. 231–239. See p. 231.

Nam, Charles B., "Nationality Groups and Social Stratification in America," *Social Forces*, 37 (May, 1959), pp. 328–333. See p. 328.

Nefzger, M. Dean, and Abraham M. Lilienfeld, "Item Reliability and Related Factors in a Community Survey of Emotionality," *Sociometry*, 22 (September, 1959), pp. 236–246. See p. 240.

Reiss, Albert J., Jr., "Rural-Urban and Status Differences in Interpersonal Contacts," *American Journal of Sociology*, 65 (September, 1959), pp. 182–195. See p. 183.

Zimmer, Basil G., and Amos H. Hawley, "The Significance of Membership in Associations," *American Journal of Sociology*, 65 (September, 1959), pp. 196–201. See p. 199.

Heberle, Rudolph, "The Changing Social Stratification in the South," *Social Forces*, 38 (October, 1959), pp. 42–50. See p. 46.

Gross (October, 1959), pp. 640–649; see category 6 above.

Sharp, Harry, and Allan Feldt, "Some Factors in a Probability Sample Survey of a Metropolitan Community," *American Sociological Review*, 24 (October, 1959), pp. 650–661. See p. 657.

Yeracaris, Constantine A., "Differentials in the Relationship between Values and Practices in Fertility," *Social Forces*, 38 (December, 1959), pp. 153–158. See p. 154.

Lewis, Gordon F., "A Comparison of Some Aspects of the Backgrounds and Careers of Small Businessmen and American Business Leaders," *American Journal of Sociology*, 65 (January, 1960), pp. 348–355. See p. 350.

Vincent, Clark E., "Unmarried Fathers and the Mores," *American Sociological Review*, 25 (February, 1960), pp. 40–46. See p. 41.

Lazerwitz, Bernard, "Metropolitan Community Residential Belts, 1950 and 1956," *American Sociological Review*, 25 (April, 1960), pp. 245–252. See p. 249.

Olson, Philip, "On Occupational Classification," *American Sociological Review*, 25 (April, 1960), pp. 267–269.

Gross, Edward, "Reply to Olson," *American Sociological Review*, 25 (April, 1960), p. 269.

Lawson, Edwin D., and Walter Boek, "Correlation of Indexes of Families' Socio-economic Status," *Social Forces*, 39 (October, 1960), pp. 149–152. See p. 150.

Schwarzweller, Harry K., "Values and Occupational Choice," *Social Forces*, 39 (October, 1960), pp. 126–135. See p. 128.

Feldman, Arnold S., and Charles Tilly, "The Interaction of Social and Physical Space," *American Sociological Review*, 25 (December, 1960), pp. 877–884. See p. 881.

Winsborough, Hal H., "Occupational Composition and the Urban Hierarchy," *American Sociological Review*, 25 (December, 1960), pp. 894–897. See p. 895.

Weil, Mildred W., "An Analysis of the Factors Influencing Married Women's Planned or Actual Work Participation," *American Sociological Review*, 26 (February, 1961), pp. 91–96. See p. 92.

Heer, David M., "The Marital Status of Second-Generation Americans," *American Sociological Review*, 26 (April, 1961), pp. 258–271. See p. 240.

Litwak, Eugene, "Voluntary Associations and Neighborhood Cohesion," *American Sociological Review*, 26 (April, 1961), pp. 258–271. See p. 268.

Lazerwitz, Bernard, "Some Factors Associated with Variations in Church Attendance," *Social Forces*, 39 (May, 1961), pp. 301–309. See p. 307.

Smith, James O., and Gideon Sjoberg, "Origins and Career Patterns of Leading Protestant Clergymen," *Social Forces*, 39 (May, 1961), pp. 290–296. See pp. 291 and 293.

Reiss, Albert J., Jr., and Albert Lewis Rhodes, "The Distribution of Juvenile Delinquency in the Social Class Structure," *American Sociological Review*, 26 (October, 1961), pp. 720–732. See p. 721.

Form, William H., and James A. Geschwender, "Social Reference Basis of Job Satisfaction: The Case of Manual Workers," *American Sociological Review*, 27 (April, 1962), pp. 228–237. See p. 230.

Haber, Lawrence D., "Age and Integration Setting: A Re-Appraisal of *The Changing American Parent*," *American Sociological Review*, 27 (October, 1962), pp. 682–689. See p. 683.

Duncan, Otis Dudley, and Robert W. Hodge, "Education and Occupational Mobility: A Regression Analysis," *American Journal of Sociology*, 68 (May, 1963), pp. 629–644. See p. 631.

Curtis, Richard F., "Differential Association and the Stratification of the Urban Community," *Social Forces*, 42 (October, 1963), pp. 68–77. See p. 71.

Galle, Omer R., "Occupational Composition and the Metropolitan Hierarchy: The Inter- and Intra-Metropolitan Division of Labor," *American Journal of Sociology*, 69 (November, 1963), pp. 260–269. See p. 263.

Rhodes, Lewis, "Anomia, Aspiration, and Status," *Social Forces*, 42 (May, 1964), pp. 434–440. See p. 436.

Weinberg, Carl, "Achievement and School Activities of Adolescent Boys as Related to Behavior and Occupational Status of

Families," *Social Forces*, 42 (May, 1964), pp. 462–466. See pp. 464–465.

Rhodes, Reiss, and Duncan (May, 1965), pp. 683–684; see category 6 above.

26. OCCUPATIONAL STATUS (CENSUS RELATED)

The following use occupation as an index of socioeconomic status, but neither refer to the Edwards scheme nor use the same sets of categories, although they employ similar categories. Each citation uses a *different* set of categories.

Lipset, Seymour Martin, Reinhard Bendix, and F. Theodore Malm, "Job Plans and Entry into the Labor Market," *Social Forces*, 33 (March, 1955), pp. 224–232. See pp. 226–230.

Zimmer, Basil G., "Participation of Migrants in Urban Structures," *American Sociological Review*, 20 (April, 1955), pp. 218–224. See p. 219.

MacKinnon, William J., and Richard Centers, "Authoritarianism and Urban Stratification," *American Journal of Sociology*, 61 (May, 1956), pp. 610–620. See pp. 616–617.

Agger, Robert E., "Power Attributions in the Local Community: Theoretical and Research Considerations," *Social Forces*, 34 (May, 1956), pp. 322–331. See pp. 327–329.

Nash, Dennison J., "The Socialization of an Artist: The American Composer," *Social Forces*, 35 (May, 1957), pp. 307–313. See p. 309.

Smith, Charles U., and James W. Prothro, "Ethnic Differences in Authoritarian Personality," *Social Forces*, 35 (May, 1957), pp. 334–338. See p. 335.

MacKinnon, William, and Richard Centers, "Social-Psychological Factors in Public Orientation toward an Out-Group," *American Journal of Sociology*, 63 (January, 1958), pp. 415–419. See pp. 417–418.

Blood, Robert O., Jr., and Robert L. Hamblin, "The Effect of the Wife's Employment on the Family Power Structure," *Social Forces*, 36 (May, 1958), pp. 347–352. See p. 348.

Agger, Robert E., and Daniel Goldrich, "Community Power

Structure and Partisanship," *American Sociological Review*, 23 (August, 1958), pp. 383–392. See pp. 386–388.

Form, William H., and Julius Rivera, "Work Contacts and International Evaluations: The Case of a Mexican Border Village," *Social Forces*, 37 (May, 1959), pp. 334–339. See p. 335.

Thompson, Wayne E., and John E. Horton, "Political Alienation as a Force in Political Action," *Social Forces*, 38 (March, 1960), pp. 190–195. See p. 192.

Slater, Carol, "Class Differences in Definition of Role and Membership in Voluntary Associations among Urban Married Women," *American Journal of Sociology*, 65 (May, 1960), pp. 616–619. See pp. 616–617.

Inkeles, Alex, "Industrial Man: The Relation of Status to Experience, Perception, and Value," *American Journal of Sociology*, 66 (July, 1960), pp. 1–31. See p. 10.

Anderson, C. Arnold, "A Skeptical Note on the Relation of Vertical Mobility to Education," *American Journal of Sociology*, 66 (May, 1961), pp. 560–570. See p. 565.

Wilensky, Harold L., "Orderly Careers and Social Participation: The Impact of Work History on Social Integration in the Middle Mass," *American Sociological Review*, 26 (August, 1961), pp. 521–539.

McKee, James B., "Changing Patterns of Race and Housing: A Toledo Study," *Social Forces*, 41 (March, 1963), pp. 253–260. See p. 257.

27. OCCUPATIONAL STATUS (COUNTS)

Counts, George S., "Social Status of Occupations: A Problem in Vocational Guidance," *School Review*, 33 (January, 1925), pp. 16–27. See pp. 17–18.

Adams, Stuart, "Trends in Occupational Origins of Business Leaders," *American Sociological Review*, 19 (October, 1954), pp. 541–548. See p. 543.

28. OCCUPATIONAL STATUS (DEEG, PATERSON)

Deeg, M. E., and D. G. Paterson, "Changes in Social Status of Occupations," *Occupations*, 25 (January, 1947), pp. 205–208.

Adams (1954), pp. 543–546; see category 27 above.

29. OCCUPATIONAL STATUS (DUNCAN)

Duncan, Otis Dudley, "A Socioeconomic Index for All Occupations," in Albert J. Reiss, Jr., Otis D. Duncan, Paul K. Hatt, and C. C. North, *Occupations and Social Status*, Glencoe, Ill.: The Free Press, 1961, pp. 109–161 and Appendix B.

Noting the widespread use of the NORC occupational prestige scores (see category 6 above) by researchers in social stratification, Duncan has indicated that a major limitation of their use is that such scores are available "only for occupations encompassing, in the aggregate, less than half of the labor force." Because of this and other limitations, Duncan decided "to approach the problem of constructing the occupational socioeconomic index in terms of the relationship between the NORC prestige ratings and socioeconomic characteristics of the occupations." The problem, then, was to

. . . obtain a socioeconomic index for each of the occupations in the detailed classification of the 1950 Census of Population. This index is to have both face validity, in terms of its constituent variables, and sufficient predictive efficiency with respect to the NORC occupational prestige ratings that it can serve as an acceptable substitute for them in any research where it is necessary to grade or rank occupations in the way that the NORC score does but where some of the occupations are not on the NORC list. (p. 115)

After explaining the logical relationship of education and income to occupation and noting that each of these are influenced by age, Duncan turned to census data to construct his index. Each occupation was given an education weight (X_2) based on the percentage of those in the occupation who were high-school graduates. Income weights (X_3) were determined by the percentage of those in each occupation reporting incomes of $3,500 or more in 1949. Because age is related to both of these variables, the education and income indicators were then adjusted to control for different age distributions in different occupations. Occupational scores on each of these indicators were compared with NORC prestige scores (X_1) for the 45 occupations on the NORC list that are reasonably equivalent to census titles (Duncan, 1961, pp. 124–125):

The prestige variable is rather highly related to each predictor, as is suggested by the zero-order correlations: $r_{12} = 0.84$, and $r_{13} = 0.85$. The relationship between the two predictors is summarized by the correlation $r_{23} = 0.72$ . . . Combining the two predictors in a linear multiple-regression equation produces a multiple correlation appreciably larger than either zero-order correlation: $R_{1(23)} = 0.91$. . . . The multiple-regression equation expressing the estimated prestige rating, $\hat{X}_1$ as a function of the two predictors is as follows: $\hat{X}_1 = 0.59\ X_2 + 0.55\ X_3 - 6.0$.

The value of $\hat{X}_1$, then, is the socioeconomic index score assigned by Duncan to each occupation. Duncan notes that although "the index weights were derived from data on only the forty-five occupations for which prestige ratings were available, the index can be calculated for any occupation for which education and income data are given in the census reports." (p. 125) This is then done for the 446 occupations listed in the Detailed Classification of the Bureau of the Census (1950). Scores also are transformed to the metric of the NORC (North, Hatt) index scores, and population decile scores are given. The latter were included as approximations to a normative scale: "Thus, occupations scored '10' include the (approximately) 10 per cent of this population (male experienced civilian labor force in 1950) with the highest-ranking occupations." (pp. 128–129) For a complete listing of the three sets of scores, see Appendix B in *Occupations and Social Status* (1961). The user should be warned that this Appendix does not suffice, by itself, as an occupational coding guide (see McTavish, 1964, below).

Current work at NORC is expected to provide an equally complete set of occupational prestige scores, so that Duncan's index, in the future, may no longer be needed to approximate prestige, but can be taken to represent the more strictly socioeconomic component thereof.

Clark, John P., and Eugene P. Wenninger, "Socioeconomic Class and Areas as Correlates of Illegal Behavior among Juveniles," *American Sociological Review*, 27 (December, 1962), pp. 826–834. See p. 828.

Clark, John P., and Eugene P. Wenninger, "Goal Orientations and Illegal Behavior among Juveniles," *Social Forces*, 42 (October, 1963), pp. 49–59. See p. 51.

Erbe, William, "Social Involvement and Political Activity: A Replication and Elaboration," *American Sociological Review*, 29 (April, 1964), pp. 198–215. See p. 203.

McTavish, Donald G., "A Method for More Reliably Coding Detailed Occupations into Duncan's Socio-Economic Categories," *American Sociological Review*, 29 (June, 1964), pp. 402–406.

Eckland, Bruce K., "Social Class and College Graduation: Some Misconceptions Corrected," *American Journal of Sociology*, 70 (July, 1964), pp. 36–50. See p. 43.

Blau, Peter M., "The Flow of Occupational Supply and Recruitment," *American Sociological Review*, 30 (August, 1965), pp. 475–490. See p. 476.

Eckland, Bruce K., "Academic Ability, Higher Education, and Occupational Mobility," *American Sociological Review*, 30 (October, 1965), pp. 735–746. See p. 739.

Reiss, Ira L., "Social Class and Premarital Sexual Permissiveness: A Re-examination," *American Sociological Review*, 30 (October, 1965), pp. 747–756. See p. 749.

30. OCCUPATIONAL STATUS (FREEDMAN)

Freedman, Ronald, *Recent Migration to Chicago*, Chicago, Ill.: University of Chicago Press, 1950, pp. 26–27.

Hillery, George A., Jr., "The Negro in New Orleans: A Functional Analysis of Demographic Data," *American Sociological Review*, 22 (April, 1957), pp. 183–188. See p. 185.

31. OCCUPATIONAL STATUS (HANSEN)

Lundberg, George A., "Occupations and 'Class' Alignments in the United States, 1870–1950," *Social Forces*, 34 (December, 1955), pp. 128–130.

Hansen, Alvin H., "Industrial Class Alignments in the United States," *Journal of the American Statistical Association*, 17 (December, 1920), pp. 422–424.

32. OCCUPATIONAL STATUS (HOLLINGSHEAD)

Hollingshead, August B., Two Factor Index of Social Position (copyrighted 1957), privately printed, 1965, Yale Station, New Haven, Connecticut.

Hollingshead's occupational-status scale is part of his Two Factor Index of Social Position (see Socioeconomic Status: Composite, Objective, category 17), although it is sometimes used by itself as an indicator of respondents' class or status positions. It is a modification of the Edwards-Census occupational classification scheme (see category 25 above, and category 38 below). As Hollingshead indicates, "The essential differences between the Edwards system and the one used is that Edwards does not differentiate among kinds of professionals or the sizes and economic strengths of businesses." The 7 category scale below ranks professions into different groups and businesses by their size and value:

1. *Higher Executives of Large Concerns, Proprietors, and Major Professionals*

A. *Higher Executives* (Value of corporation $500,000 and above as rated by Dun and Bradstreet)

Bank
  Presidents
  Vice-Presidents
  Assistant Vice-Presidents
Business
  Directors
  Presidents

Business
  Vice-Presidents
  Assistant Vice-Presidents
  Executive Secretaries
  Research Directors
  Treasurers

B. *Proprietors* (Value over $100,000 by Dun and Bradstreet)

Brokers
Contractors
Dairy owners

Farmers
Lumber dealers

C. *Major Professionals*

Accountants (CPA)
Actuaries
Agronomists
Architects
Artists, portrait
Astronomers
Auditors
Bacteriologists
Chemical Engineers
Chemists
Clergymen (professional trained)
Dentists

Economists
Engineers (college graduates)
Foresters
Geologists
Judges (superior courts)
Lawyers
Metallurgists
Military: commissioned officers, major and above
Officials of the Executive Branch of Government, Federal, State, Local: e.g. Mayor, City man-

ager, City plan director, Internal Revenue director
Physicians
Physicists, Research
Psychologists, practicing
Symphony conductor
Teachers, university, college
Veterinarians (veterinary surgeons)

2. Business Managers, Proprietors of Medium-Sized Businesses, and Lesser Professionals

A. *Business Managers in Large Concerns* (Value $500,000)

Advertising directors
Branch managers
Brokerage salesmen
Directors of purchasing
District managers
Executive assistants
Export managers, international concerns
Farm managers
Government officials, minor, e.g. Internal Revenue agents
Manufacturer's representatives
Office managers
Personnel managers
Police chief; Sheriff
Postmaster
Production managers
Sales engineers
Sales managers, national concerns
Store managers

B. *Proprietors of Medium Businesses* (Value $35,000–$100,000)

Advertising
Clothing store
Contractors
Express company
Farm owners
Fruits, wholesale
Furniture business
Jewelers
Poultry business
Real estate brokers
Rug business
Store
Theater

C. *Lesser Professionals*

Accountants (not C.P.A.)
Chiropodists
Chiropractors
Correction officers
Director of Community House
Engineers (not college graduate)
Finance writers
Health educators
Labor relations consultants
Librarians
Military: commissioned officers, Lieutenant, Captain
Musicians (symphony orchestra)
Nurses
Opticians
Optometrists, D.O.
Pharmacists
Public health officers (M.P.H.)
Research assistants, university (full-time)
Social workers

Occupational · 443

3. Administrative Personnel, Owners of Small Businesses, and Minor Professionals

A. *Administrative Personnel*

Advertising agents
Chief clerks
Credit managers
Insurance agents
Managers, departments
Passenger agents, railroad
Private secretaries
Purchasing agents
Sales representatives
Section heads, Federal, State and Local governmental offices
Section heads, large businesses and industries
Service managers
Shop managers
Store managers (chain)
Traffic managers

B. *Small Business Owners* ($6,000–$35,000)

Art gallery
Auto accessories
Awnings
Bakery
Beauty shop
Boatyard
Brokerage, insurance
Car dealers
Cattle dealers
Cigarette machines
Cleaning shops
Clothing
Coal businesses
Contracting businesses
Convalescent homes
Decorating
Dog supplies
Dry goods
Engraving business
Feed
Finance companies, local
Fire extinguishers
Five and dime
Florist
Food equipment
Food products
Foundry
Funeral directors
Furniture
Garage
Gas station
Glassware
Grocery, general
Hotel proprietors
Jewelry
Machinery brokers
Manufacturing
Monuments
Music
Package stores (liquor)
Paint contracting
Poultry
Real estate
Records and radios
Restaurant
Roofing contractor
Shoe
Signs
Tavern
Taxi company
Tire shop
Trucking
Trucks and tractors
Upholstery
Wholesale outlets
Window shades

C. *Semiprofessionals*

Actors and showmen
Army, Master Sergeant
Artists, commercial
Appraisers (estimators)
Clergymen (not professionally trained)
Concern managers
Deputy sheriffs
Dispatchers, railroad
Interior decorators
Interpreters, courts
Laboratory assistants
Landscape planners
Morticians

Navy, Chief Petty Officer
Oral Hygienists
Physiotherapists
Piano teachers
Publicity and public relations
Radio, TV announcers
Reporters, court
Reporters, newspapers
Surveyors
Title searchers
Tool designers
Travel agents
Yard masters, railroad

D. *Farmers*

Farm owners ($20,000–$35,000)

4. *Clerical and Sales Workers, Technicians, and Owners of Little Businesses* (Value under $6,000)

A. *Clerical and Sales Workers*

Bank clerks and tellers
Bill collectors
Bookkeepers
Business machine operators, offices
Claims examiners
Clerical or stenographic
Conductors, railroad
Factory storekeepers

Factory supervisors
Post Office clerks
Route managers
Sales clerks
Sergeants and petty officers, military services
Shipping clerks
Supervisors, utilities, factories
Supervisors, toll stations

B. *Technicians*

Dental technicians
Draftsmen
Driving teachers
Expeditor, factory
Experimental tester
Instructors, telephone company, factory
Inspectors, weights, sanitary, railroad, factory
Investigators
Laboratory technicians

Locomotive engineers
Operators, PBX
Proofreaders
Safety supervisors
Supervisors of maintenance
Technical assistants
Telephone company supervisors
Timekeepers
Tower operators, railroad
Truck dispatchers
Window trimmers (stores)

C. *Owners of Little Businesses* ($3,000–$6,000)

Flower shop

Grocery

News stand

Tailor shop

D. *Farmers*

Owners (Value $10,000–$20,000)

5. *Skilled Manual Employees*

Auto body repairers
Bakers
Barbers
Blacksmiths
Bookbinders
Boilermakers
Brakemen, railroad
Brewers
Bulldozer operators
Butchers
Cabinet makers
Cable splicers
Carpenters
Casters (founders)
Cement finishers
Cheese makers
Chefs
Compositors
Diemakers
Diesel engine repair and
   maintenance (trained)
Diesel shovel operators
Electricians
Engravers
Exterminators
Firemen, city
Firemen, railroad
Fitters, gas, steam
Foremen, construction,
   dairy
Gardners, landscape
   (trained)
Glass blowers
Glaziers
Gunsmiths
Gauge makers
Hair stylists

Heat treaters
Horticulturists
Linemen, utility
Linotype operators
Lithographers
Locksmiths
Loom fixers
Machinists (trained)
Maintenance foremen
Linoleum layers (trained)
Masons
Masseurs
Mechanics (trained)
Millwrights
Moulders (trained)
Painters
Paperhangers
Patrolmen, railroad
Pattern and model makers
Piano builders
Piano tuners
Plumbers
Policemen, city
Postmen
Printers
Radio, television
   maintenance
Repairmen, home appliances
Rope splicers
Sheetmetal workers
   (trained)
Shipsmiths
Shoe repairmen (trained)
Stationary engineers
   (licensed)
Stewards, club
Switchmen, railroad

Tailors (trained)
Teletype operators
Tool makers
Track supervisors, railroad
Tractor-trailer trans.
Typographers

Upholsters (trained)
Watchmakers
Weavers
Welders
Yard supervisors, railroad

Small Farmers

Owners (Value under
$10,000)

Tenants who own farm
equipment

6. *Machine Operators and Semiskilled Employees*

Aides, hospital
Apprentices, electricians,
printers, steam fitters,
toolmakers
Assembly line workers
Bartenders
Bingo tenders
Bridge tenders
Building superintendents
(construction)
Bus drivers
Checkers
Coin machine fillers
Cooks, short order
Deliverymen
Dressmakers, machine
Elevator operators
Enlisted men, military
services
Filers, sanders, buffers
Foundary workers
Garage and gas station
attendants
Greenhouse workers
Guards, doorkeepers,
watchmen
Hairdressers
Housekeepers
Meat cutters and packers
Meter readers
Operators, factory
machines

Oilers, railroad
Practical nurses
Pressers, clothing
Pump operators
Receivers and checkers
Roofers
Set-up men, factories
Shapers
Signalmen, railroad
Solderers, factory
Sprayers, paint
Steelworkers (not skilled)
Stranders, wire machines
Strippers, rubber factory
Taxi drivers
Testers
Timers
Tire moulders
Trainmen, railroad
Truck drivers, general
Waiters-waitresses ("better
places")
Weighers
Welders, spot
Winders, machine
Wiredrawers, machine
Wine bottlers
Wood workers, machine
Wrappers, stores and
factories

Farmers

Smaller tenants who own little equipment

7. Unskilled Employees

Amusement park workers (bowling alleys, pool rooms)
Ash removers
Attendants, parking lots
Cafeteria workers
Car cleaners, railroad
Carriers, coal
Countermen
Dairy workers
Deck hands
Domestics
Farm helpers
Fishermen (clam diggers)
Freight handlers
Garbage collectors
Grave diggers
Hod carriers
Hog killers
Hospital workers, unspecified
Hostlers, railroad
Janitors (sweepers)
Laborers, construction

Laborers, unspecified
Laundry workers
Messengers
Platform men, railroad
Peddlers
Porters
Relief, public, private
Roofer's helpers
Shirt folders
Shoe shiners
Sorters, rag and salvage
Stage hands
Stevedores
Stock handlers
Street cleaners
Struckmen, railroad
Unemployed (no occupation)
Unskilled factory workers
Waitresses ("Hash Houses")
Washers, cars
Window cleaners
Woodchoppers

Farmers

Share croppers

Hollingshead, August B., and Frederick C. Redlich, *Social Class and Mental Illness: A Community Study*, New York: John Wiley and Sons, 1958, pp. 390–391.

Hunt, Raymond G., Orville Gursslin, and Jack L. Roach, "Social Status and Psychiatric Science in a Child Guidance Clinic," *American Sociological Review*, 23 (February, 1958), pp. 81–83. See p. 81.

Lawson and Boek (1960), pp. 149–152; see category 25 above.

Maccoby, Eleanor E., "Class Differences in Boys' Choices of Authority Roles," *Sociometry*, 25 (March, 1962), pp. 117–119. See p. 117.

Simpson, Richard L., "Parental Influence, Anticipatory Socialization and Social Mobility," *American Sociological Review*, 27 (August, 1962), pp. 517–522. See p. 519.

Ellis, Robert A., and W. Clayton Lane, "Structural Supports for Upward Mobility," *American Sociological Review*, 28 (October, 1963), pp. 743–756. See p. 745.

Kerckhoff, Alan C., "Patterns of Homogamy and the Field of Eligibles," *Social Forces*, 42 (March, 1964), pp. 289–297. See p. 292.

33. OCCUPATIONAL STATUS (IOWA DIVISION OF VITAL STATISTICS OCCUPATIONAL CODE)

Burchinal, Lee B., and Loren E. Chancellor, "Survival Rates among Religiously Homogamous and Interreligious Marriages," *Social Forces*, 41 (May, 1963), pp. 353–362. See p. 356.

34. OCCUPATIONAL STATUS (KAHL)

Kahl, Joseph A., "Educational and Occupational Aspirations of 'Common Man' Boys," *Harvard Educational Review*, 23 (Summer, 1953), pp. 186–203. See p. 188.

Bordua, David, "Educational Aspirations and Parental Stress on College," *Social Forces*, 38 (March, 1960), pp. 262–269. See p. 264.

35. OCCUPATIONAL STATUS (KINSEY)

Kinsey, A. C., W. B. Pomeroy, and C. E. Martin, *Sexual Behavior in the Human Male*, Philadelphia, Penn.: W. B. Saunders Co., 1948, pp. 77–79.

West, S. Stewart, "Sibling Configurations of Scientists," *American Journal of Sociology*, 66 (November, 1960), pp. 268–274. See p. 269.

36. OCCUPATIONAL STATUS (NICHOLS, KING)

Nichols, Ralph R., and Morton B. King, Jr., *Social Effects of Government Land Purchase*, Bulletin 390, State College, Miss.: Agricultural Experiment Station, June, 1943.

King, Morton B., Jr., "Socioeconomic Status and Sociometric Choice," *Social Forces*, 39 (March, 1961), pp. 199–206. See p. 201.

37. OCCUPATIONAL STATUS (UNESCO)

UNESCO, Première Mission du Groupe de Planification de l'Éducation en Côte d'Ivoire, Paris: UNESCO, 1963, p. 19.

UNESCO, Situation et Perspectives de l'Emploi dans le Cadre du Plan Décennal de Développement, 1963, Table IIH (mimeographed).

Clignet and Foster (1964), pp. 355–356; see category 16 above.

38. OCCUPATIONAL STATUS (WARNER)

Warner, W. Lloyd, Marchia Meeker, and Kenneth Eells, *Social Class in America: A Manual of Procedure for the Measurement of Social Status*, Chicago, Ill.: Science Research Associates, 1949, pp. 123, 132–138, 140–141, and 149–150.

A frequently used revision of the Census classification of occupations by social-economic groupings is Warner's modification (which he also uses in his Index of Status Characteristics—see Socioeconomic Status: Composite, Objective, category 38).

Warner thought it seemed "advisable to subdivide some of the occupational groups in the Edwards' classification, and . . . to combine certain of the categories. In making these changes the primary criteria were level of skill that a job required and prestige value attached to a job." (1949 above, p. 133)

The *major* departure from the Edwards classification is in regard to professionals and proprietors. Using Dun and Bradstreet ratings, Warner thought it meaningful to subdivide proprietors to avoid the dilemma of "giving equal rating to the owner of the smallest neighborhood store and the owner of the largest factory." Similarly, while Edwards included all ranks of professionals in one category, Warner thought it was more meaningful to subdivide them on the basis of skill and prestige (apparently operationally defined by the amount of training required for a profession). Large proprietors and "top professionals" were then placed in the same category. The revised scale, as set forth by Warner (above, pp. 140–141), is presented below.

WARNER'S REVISED SCALE FOR RATING OCCUPATION

RATING 1

Professionals: Lawyers; doctors; dentists; engineers; judges; high school superintendents; veterinarians; ministers (graduated from divinity school); chemists, etc., with postgraduate training; architects.
Proprietors and Managers: Businesses valued at $75,000 and over.
Businessmen: Regional and divisional managers of large financial and industrial enterprises.
Clerks and Kindred Workers, etc.: Certified public accountants.
Manual Workers: None in this rating.
Protective and Service Workers: None in this rating.
Farmers: Gentlemen farmers.

RATING 2

Professionals: High school teachers; trained nurses; chiropodists; chiropractors; undertakers; ministers (some training); newspaper editors; librarians (graduate).
Proprietors and Managers: Businesses valued at $20,000 to $75,000.
Businessmen: Assistant managers and office and department managers of large businesses; assistants to executives; etc.
Clerks and Kindred Workers, etc.: Accountants; salesmen of real estate; salesmen of insurance; postmasters.
Manual Workers: None in this rating.
Protective and Service Workers: None in this rating.
Farmers: Large farm owners; farm owners.

RATING 3

Professionals: Social workers; grade school teachers; optometrists; librarians (not graduate); undertakers' assistants; ministers (no training).
Proprietors and Managers: Businesses valued at $5,000 to $20,000.
Businessmen: All minor officials of businesses.
Clerks and Kindred Workers, etc.: Auto salesmen; bank clerks and cashiers; postal clerks; secretaries to executives; supervisors of railroad, telephone, etc.; justices of the peace.
Manual Workers: Contractors.
Protective and Service Workers: None in this rating.
Farmers: None in this rating.

RATING 4

Professionals: None in this rating.
Proprietors and Managers: Businesses valued at $2,000 to $5,000.
Businessmen: None in this rating.

Clerks and Kindred Workers, etc.: Stenographers; bookkeepers; rural mail clerks; railroad ticket agents; people in dry goods stores; etc.
Manual Workers: Factory foremen; electricians; plumbers; carpenters; watchmakers (own businesses).
Protective and Service Workers: Dry cleaners; butchers; sheriffs; railroad engineers and conductors.
Farmers: None in this rating.

RATING 5

Professionals: None in this rating.
Proprietors and Managers: Businesses valued at $500 to $2,000.
Businessmen: None in this rating.
Clerks and Kindred Workers, etc.: Dime store clerks; hardware salesmen; beauty operators; telephone operators.
Manual Workers: Carpenters; electricians (apprentice); timekeepers; linemen, telephone or telegraph; radio repairmen; medium-skill workers.
Protective and Service Workers: Barbers; firemen; butcher's apprentices; practical nurses; policemen; seamstresses; cooks in restaurants; bartenders.
Farmers: Tenant farmers.

RATING 6

Professionals: None in this rating.
Proprietors and Managers: Businesses valued at less than $500.
Businessmen: None in this rating.
Clerks and Kindred Workers, etc.: None in this rating.
Manual Workers: Moulders; semiskilled workers; assistants to carpenters; etc.
Protective and Service Workers: Baggage men; night policemen and watchmen; taxi and truck drivers; gas station attendants; waitresses in restaurants.
Farmers: Small tenant farmers.

Rating 7

Professionals: None in this rating.
Proprietors and Managers: None in this rating.
Businessmen: None in this rating.
Clerks and Kindred Workers, etc.: None in this rating.
Manual Workers: Heavy labor; migant work; odd-job men; miners.
Protective and Service Workers: Janitors; scrubwomen; newsboys.
Farmers: Migrant farm workers.

Warner, W. Lloyd, and Mildred Hall Warner, *What You Should Know about Social Class*, Chicago, Ill.: Science Research Associates, 1953, pp. 23–25.

Havighurst, Robert J., and Allison Davis, "A Comparison of the Chicago and Harvard Studies of Social Class Differences in Child Rearing," *American Sociological Review*, 20 (August, 1955), pp. 438–442. See p. 439.

Scudder, Richard, and C. Arnold Anderson, "Range of Acquaintance and of Repute as Factors in Prestige Rating Methods of Studying Social Status," *Social Forces*, 32 (March, 1954), pp. 248–253. See p. 252.

Scudder, Richard, and C. Arnold Anderson, "Migration and Vertical Occupational Mobility," *American Sociological Review*, 19 (June, 1954), pp. 329–334. See p. 330.

Westie, Frank R., and David H. Howard, "Social Status Differentials and the Race Attitudes of Negroes," *American Sociological Review*, 19 (October, 1954), pp. 584–591. See p. 587.

Kahl and Davis (1955), pp. 319–323; see category 6 above.

Wilensky (1956), p. 117; see category 25 above.

Goffman, Irwin W., "Status Consistency and Preference for Change in Power Distribution," *American Sociological Review*, 22 (June, 1957), pp. 275–281. See p. 277.

Littman, Richard A., Robert C. A. Moore, and John Pierce-Jones, "Social Class Differences in Child-Rearing: A Third Community for Comparison with Chicago and Newton," *American Sociological Review*, 22 (December, 1957), pp. 694–704. See p. 695.

Salisbury, W. Seward, "Religion and Secularization," *Social Forces*, 36 (March, 1958), pp. 197–205. See p. 198.

Kanin, Eugene, Jr., and David H. Howard, "Postmarital Consequences of Premarital Sex Adjustments," *American Sociological Review*, 23 (October, 1958), pp. 556–562. See p. 557.

Morland, J. Kenneth, "Racial Recognition by Nursery School Children in Lynchburg, Virginia," *Social Forces*, 37 (December, 1958), pp. 132–141. See p. 132.

Morland, J. Kenneth, "Educational and Occupational Aspirations of Mill and Town School Children in a Southern Community," *Social Forces*, 39 (December, 1960), pp. 169–175. See p. 173.

Smelser (1963), p. 395; see category 6 above.

Emmerich, Walter, and Faye Smoller, "The Role Patterning of Parental Norms," *Sociometry*, 27 (September, 1964), pp. 382–390. See p. 385.

39. OCCUPATIONAL STATUS IN AUSTRALIA

Tien, H. Yuan, "The Social Mobility-Fertility Hypothesis Reconsidered: An Empirical Study," *American Sociological Review*, 26 (April, 1961), pp. 247–257. See p. 250.

40. OCCUPATIONAL STATUS IN DENMARK

Goldstein, Sidney, "Some Economic Consequences of Suburbanization in the Copenhagen Metropolitan Area," *American Journal of Sociology*, 68 (March, 1963), pp. 551–564. See p. 558.

41. OCCUPATIONAL STATUS IN GERMANY

Lipset, Seymour Martin, "Democracy and Working-Class Authoritarianism," *American Sociological Review*, 24 (August, 1959), pp. 482–501. See p. 485.

42. OCCUPATIONAL STATUS IN GREAT BRITAIN

Census 1951, England and Wales: County Report, London: H.M. Stationery Office, 1954, p. 47, Table 27.

Collison, Peter, and John Mogey, "Residence and Social Class in Oxford," *American Journal of Sociology*, 64 (May, 1959), pp. 599–605. See p. 599.

Collison (1960), p. 558; see category 17 above.

43. OCCUPATIONAL STATUS IN INDIA

Gist, Noel P., "Caste Differentials in South India," *American Sociological Review*, 19 (April, 1954), pp. 126–137. See pp. 130–131.

Gist, Noel P., "Occupational Differentiation in South India," *Social Forces*, 33 (December, 1954), pp. 129–138. See p. 131.

44. OCCUPATIONAL STATUS IN JAMAICA

Broom, Leonard, "The Social Differentiation of Jamaica," *American Sociological Review*, 19 (April, 1954), pp. 115–125. See p. 122.

45. OCCUPATIONAL STATUS IN LEBANON

Armstrong, Lincoln, and Gordon K. Hirabayashi, "Social Differentiation in Selected Lebanese Villages," *American Sociological Review*, 21 (August, 1956), pp. 425–434. See p. 430.

46. OCCUPATIONAL STATUS IN NEW ZEALAND

Congalton, A. A., and R. J. Havighurst, "Status Ranking of Occupations in New Zealand," *Australia Journal of Psychology*, 6 (1954), pp. 10–15.

Sutcliffe, J. P., and M. Haberman, "Factors Influencing Choice in Role Conflict Situations," *American Sociological Review*, 21 (December, 1956), pp. 695–703. See pp. 700–702.

47. OCCUPATIONAL STATUS IN NORWAY

Park, George K., and Lee Soltow, "Politics and Social Structure in a Norwegian Village," *American Journal of Sociology*, 67 (September, 1961), pp. 152–164. See pp. 156–157.

48. OCCUPATIONAL STATUS IN THE PHILIPPINES

Hawley, Amos H., "Rural Fertility in Central Luzon," *American Sociological Review*, 20 (February, 1955), pp. 21–27. See pp. 23–24.

49. OCCUPATIONAL STATUS IN POLAND

Nowak, Stefan, "Egalitarian Attitudes of Warsaw Students," *American Sociological Review*, 25 (April, 1960), pp. 219–231. See p. 221.

50. OCCUPATIONAL STATUS IN THE SOVIET UNION (FIELD)

Field, Mark G., "Former Soviet Citizens' Attitudes toward the Soviet, the German and the American Medical Systems," *American Sociological Review*, 20 (December, 1955), pp. 674–679. See p. 676.

51. OCCUPATIONAL STATUS IN THE SOVIET UNION (GEIGER)

Geiger, Kent, "Deprivation and Solidarity in the Soviet Urban Family," *American Sociological Review*, 20 (February, 1955), pp. 57–68. See pp. 61–66.

52. OCCUPATIONAL STATUS OF NEGROES AND WHITES

Glenn (1963), pp. 646–647; see category 6 above.

Glenn, Norval D., "Occupational Benefits to Whites from the

Subordination of Negroes," *American Sociological Review*, 28 (June, 1963), pp. 443–448. See p. 444.

Glenn, Norval D., "The Relative Size of the Negro Population and Negro Occupational Status," *Social Forces*, 43 (October, 1964), pp. 42–49. See p. 44.

53. OCCUPATIONAL STATUS OF WOMEN

Vincent, Clark E., "Ego Involvement in Sexual Relationships: Implications for Research on Illegitimacy," *American Journal of Sociology*, 65 (December, 1959), pp. 287–295. See p. 291.

54. PROFESSIONAL RATING TECHNIQUE

Rettig, Jacobson, and Pasamanick (February, 1958), p. 75; see category 1 above.

Rettig, Salomon, Frank N. Jacobson, and Benjamin Pasamanick, "The Magnetic Board Rating Technique," *Journal of Psychology*, 45 (July, 1958), pp. 201–206. See pp. 201–204.

Rettig, Jacobson, DesPres, and Pasamanick (December, 1958), pp. 283–284; see category 1 above.

55. SOCIAL CLASS IDENTIFICATION OCCUPATIONAL RATING SCALE

Sims, Verner M., "A Technique for Measuring Social Class Identification," *Educational and Psychological Measurement*, 11 (Winter, 1951), pp. 541–548. See pp. 542–545.

Perrucci, Robert, "The Significance of Intra-Occupational Mobility: Some Methodological and Theoretical Notes, Together with a Case Study of Engineers," *American Sociological Review*, 26 (December, 1961), pp. 874–883. See p. 880.

56. SOCIAL DISTANCE OF OCCUPATIONS

Laumann, Edward O., "Subjective Social Distance and Urban Occupational Stratification," *American Journal of Sociology*, 71 (July, 1956), pp. 26–36. See pp. 29–30.

SOCIOECONOMIC STATUS: REPUTATIONAL

Note: This conceptual class differs from the Occupational Prestige categories in that specific individuals or families are rated, rather than status indicators.

1. SOCIOECONOMIC STATUS: INTERVIEWER RATING

Thompson, Wayne E., and John E. Horton, "Political Alienation as a Force in Political Action," *Social Forces*, 38 (March, 1960), pp. 190–195. See p. 192.

2. SOCIAL CLASS: JUDGES OR INFORMANTS (TECHNIQUES VARY)

Hollingshead, August B., *Elmtown's Youth*, New York: John Wiley and Sons, 1949, pp. 27–41.

A number of technically different attempts to measure socioeconomic status reputationally have a common point of departure—the method employed by Hollingshead in his study of Elmtown.

The basic assumption underlying this approach (pp. 27–28) is the belief that "local values . . . . define position, standing or class in a more functional way than an arbitrarily imposed factor such as a single criterion index."

Hollingshead noted several months after the field work started that Elmtown residents divided the social structure into strata and identified families as falling within each stratum. Fifty interviews were then analyzed to see how 30 families were classified and to learn why each family was classified as it was. Different informants placed the 30 families in similar, if not identical, positions. The names of the heads of these 30 families were then typed on cards which were taken to 25 community residents who were asked (p. 30): "(1) to tell how representative they believed these families were of the different positions . . . in the community; and (2) to place each family where they believed it belonged in terms of its 'station,' 'peg,' or 'standing.' " Nineteen of the 25 informants divided the cards into five groups. The raters agreed with one another on 77 per cent of their ratings and 91 per cent of this agreement was concentrated on 21 families. Hollingshead then used those 20 families where there was greatest agreement as a control list to be compared with other families. Twelve long-time Elmtown residents were then asked to classify the 20 names on this control list, judging each on the following points (p. 31):

(a) The way the family lived.
(b) Income and possessions.
(c) Participation in community affairs.
(d) Prestige or standing in the community.

Ten of the twelve raters divided the families into five groups. The classifications by these raters were highly correlated with the classifications of these same 20 families by the original set of informants. Eight of the first group of 25 raters were then asked to equate 53 new families with the 20 families on the control list. More specifically, each judge was asked "to equate each of the 53 families which he knew personally with the family on the control list which he believed it most closely approximated with respect to the way the family lived, income and possessions, participation or non-participation in community affairs, and general standing or prestige." (p. 32) Twenty-nine of the families were known and rated by all eight judges. The ratings on these 29 families were then split into two series by random sortings on the eight different ratings. The ratings of one group were then correlated with those of the other by strata. The five correlation coefficients "were high enough to indicate that the rating device was reliable." (p. 32) Thus, it was decided that the use of a control list of families and raters could be used to describe the social structure of the community.

Four criteria were used in the selection of raters (p. 33): "(1) persons who had a child or close relative in the study were eliminated; (2) those who had been used in the preliminary tests were excluded; (3) only adults who had resided in the community 20 years or more were considered; and (4) raters had to appear to be stable in their station." Twenty-five raters and 31 aides were selected to rate 535 families. Each rater was given a box of cards showing the name and address of each family and the control list (arranged alphabetically). Each rater was asked to tell the investigator as much as possible about each family he was rating. After giving this information to the investigator the rater then named the family on the control list he believed the family in question most closely approximated. The average informant knew 75 families well enough to rate them.

Next, a rating schedule was constructed which indicated how each rater had equated each family with relation to the families on the control list. To translate these ratings into numerical values, the families on the control list were weighted as follows (p. 36): "Class I was given a weight of 1; Class II, 2, . . . and Class V, 5." Then the total rated score awarded by the several raters to each family was divided by the number of raters. This mean score was then assigned to each family as its class score. Weighted intervals assigned to each class were as follows: Class I, 0.51–1.50; Class II, 1.51–2.50, and so on.

Hollingshead noted (pp. 39–40): "Generally speaking, placement of families tended to be uniform from rater to rater when the rater and the rated belonged to the same class, were well known to each other, and when the family being rated was stable in its position."

The method was further validated by comparing the rating of 134 Elmtown families with their social class placement using Warner's Index of Evaluated Participation. The agreement between the two methods was "so high that it should be clear that the two stratification techniques as used by independent investigators produced a valid and reliable index of stratification in the samples studied." (p. 41)

Scudder, Richard, and C. Arnold Anderson, "Range of Acquaintance and of Repute as Factors in Prestige Rating Methods of

Studying Social Status," *Social Forces*, 32 (March, 1954), pp. 248–253. See p. 248.

Hoult, Thomas Ford, "Experimental Measurement of Clothing as a Factor in Some Social Ratings of Selected American Men," *American Sociological Review*, 19 (June, 1954), pp. 324–328. See p. 325.

Lasswell, Thomas E., "A Study of Social Stratification Using an Area Sample of Raters," *American Sociological Review*, 19 (June, 1954), pp. 310–313. See pp. 310–312.

Vidich, Arthur J., and Gilbert Shapiro, "A Comparison of Participant Observation and Survey Data," *American Sociological Review*, 20 (February, 1955), pp. 28–33. See p. 29.

Sewell, William H., and A. O. Haller, "Social Status and Personality Adjustment of the Child," *Sociometry*, 19 (June, 1956), pp. 114–121. See pp. 116–117.

Ellis, Robert A., "Social Stratification and Social Relations: An Empirical Test of the Disjunctiveness of Social Classes," *American Sociological Review*, 22 (October, 1957), pp. 570–578. See pp. 572–574.

Sewell, William H., and A. O. Haller, "Factors in the Relationship between Social Status and the Personality Adjustment of the Child," *American Sociological Review*, 24 (August, 1959), pp. 511–520. See p. 512.

Lopreato, Joseph, *Effects of Emigration on the Social Structure of a Calabrian Community*, unpublished Ph.D. dissertation, Yale University, 1960, Appendix III.

Lopreato, Joseph, "Social Stratification and Mobility in a South Italian Town," *American Sociological Review*, 26 (August, 1961), pp. 585–596. See pp. 587–588.

STATUS CONCERN

1. CONCERN WITH FAMILY'S SOCIAL STATUS

Sewell, William H., and A. O. Haller, "Factors in the Relationship between Social Status and the Personality Adjustment of the Child," *American Sociological Review*, 24 (August, 1959), pp. 511–520. See p. 516.

2. STATUS CONCERN (KAUFMAN, INCLUDING SHORT FORMS)

Kaufman, Walter C., "Status, Authoritarianism, and Anti-Semitism," *American Journal of Sociology*, 62 (January, 1957), pp. 379–383. See p. 381.

Kaufman defines status concern (p. 380) as "the value placed on symbols of status and on the attainment of higher status." To measure this phenomenon, the ten items listed below are presented to respondents. An individual's status-concern score is the algebraic sum of his responses (ranging from −3 to +3) to the items.

THE STATUS–CONCERN SCALE

The following statements refer to opinions regarding a number of social groups and issues, about which some people agree and others disagree. Please mark each statement in the left-hand margin according to your agreement or disagreement, as follows:

+1: slight support, agreement   −1: slight opposition, disagreement

+2: moderate support, agreement   −2: moderate opposition, disagreement

+3: strong support, agreement   −3: strong opposition, disagreement

1. The extent of a man's ambition to better himself is a pretty good indication of his character.
2. In order to merit the respect of others, a person should show the desire to better himself.

3. One of the things you should consider in choosing your friends is whether they can help you make your way in the world.
4. Ambition is the most important factor in determining success in life.
5. One should always try to live in a highly respectable residential area, even though it entails sacrifices.
6. Before joining any civic or political association, it is usually important to find out whether it has the backing of people who have achieved a respected social position.
7. Possession of proper social etiquette is usually the mark of a desirable person.
8. The raising of one's social position is one of the more important goals in life.
9. It is worth considerable effort to assure one's self of a good name with the right kind of people.
10. An ambitious person can almost always achieve his goals.

Although an analysis of pretest responses did not meet the 90 per cent reproducibility criterion for a Guttman scale, a "quasi-scalable" pattern, in which no systematic error patterns were evident, was observed. Kaufman also noted (p. 381) that, "The differences between means of high and low scorers were significant at the .01 level for each item, and the split-half reliability, corrected for double-length, was .78."

Middleton, Russell, "Ethnic Prejudice and Susceptibility to Persuasion," *American Sociological Review*, 25 (October, 1960), pp. 679–686. See p. 681.
Putney, Snell, and Russell Middleton, "Dimensions and Correlates of Religious Ideologies," *Social Forces*, 39 (May, 1961), pp. 285–290. See p. 287.
Photiadis, John D., and Jeanne Biggar, "Religiosity, Education, and Ethnic Distance," *American Journal of Sociology*, 67 (May, 1962), pp. 666–672. See p. 669.
Putney, Snell, and Russell Middleton, "Some Factors Associated with Student Acceptance or Rejection of War," *American Sociological Review*, 27 (October, 1962), pp. 655–667. See pp. 657–658.
Photiadis, John D., and Arthur L. Johnson, "Orthodoxy, Church

Participation, and Authoritarianism," *American Journal of Sociology*, 69 (November, 1963), pp. 244–248. See p. 246.

3. STATUS CONSCIOUSNESS

(Six dimensions or factors: job aspirations, proper behavior, organizational membership, social distance, respect for status, conspicuous consumption.)

Blalock, H. M., Jr., "Status Consciousness: A Dimensional Analysis," *Social Forces*, 37 (March, 1959), pp. 243–248. See p. 246.

4. STATUS ORIENTATION

Litwak, Eugene, *Primary Group Instruments of Social Control*, unpublished Ph.D. dissertation, Columbia University, 1958.

Litwak, Eugene, "Occupational Mobility and Extended Family Cohesion," *American Sociological Review*, 25 (February, 1960), pp. 9–21. See p. 18.

STATUS CONSISTENCY AND
RELATED MEASURES

1. INTEGRATION OF OCCUPATIONAL STATUS WITH AGE

Brenner, Berthold, "Suicide and Occupation," *American Sociological Review*, 23 (October, 1958), p. 579.

2. MARITAL INTEGRATION (SEX-ETHNIC CONSISTENCY)

Gibbs, Jack P., and Walter T. Martin, "Status Integration and Suicide in Ceylon," *American Journal of Sociology*, 64 (May, 1959), pp. 585–591. See p. 588.

3. OCCUPATIONAL STATUS CONSISTENCY

Hodge, Robert W., "The Status Consistency of Occupational Groups," *American Sociological Review*, 27 (June, 1962), pp. 336–343. See p. 339.

4. PERCEPTUAL INCONGRUITY OF CLASS STATUS

Curtis, Richard F., "Differential Association and the Stratification of the Urban Community," *Social Forces*, 42 (October, 1963), pp. 68–77. See p. 71.

5. STATUS CONGRUENCY

Schmitt, David R., "An Attitudinal Correlate of Status Congruency of Married Women," *Social Forces*, 44 (December, 1965), pp. 190–195. See pp. 192–193.

6. STATUS CONSISTENCY (GOFFMAN)

Goffman, Irwin W., "Status Consistency and Preference for Change in Power Distribution," *American Sociological Review*, 22 (June, 1957), pp. 275–281. See p. 277.

7. STATUS CONSISTENCY (KENKEL)

Kenkel, William F., "The Relationship between Status Consistency and Politico-economic Attitudes," *American Sociological Review*, 21 (June, 1956), pp. 365–368. See p. 365.

Lenski, Gerhard E., "Comment on Kenkel's Communication," *American Sociological Review*, 21 (June, 1956), pp. 368–369.

8. STATUS CONSISTENCY (NAM, POWERS)

Nam, Charles B., and Mary G. Powers, "Variation in Socioeconomic Structure by Race, Residence and the Life Cycle," *American Sociological Review*, 30 (February, 1965), pp. 97–103. See pp. 97–98.

9. STATUS CRYSTALLIZATION (LENSKI)

Lenski, Gerhard E., "Status Crystallization: A Non-Vertical Dimension of Social Status," *American Sociological Review*, 19 (August, 1954), pp. 405–413. See pp. 406–409.
Lenski, Gerhard E., "Comment," *Public Opinion Quarterly*, 28 (Summer, 1964), pp. 326–330.

Status Crystallization, or status consistency, exists when units occupy the same or similar relative positions in several vertical hierarchies. For operational purposes, Lenski originally (1954) selected four vertical hierarchies because of their great importance in the national system of stratification and because of the relative ease with which necessary information relating to them could be obtained: the income hierarchy, the occupation hierarchy, the education hierarchy, and the ethnic hierarchy.

To develop comparable scores for each vertical hierarchy, frequency distributions are used. "Using these distributions as a basis, scores were assigned for each of the various positions (or intervals) in each hierarchy on the basis of the midpoint of the percentile range for that position (or interval)." (p. 407) Lenski illustrates this procedure for the income hierarchy of his sample of 624 Detroit area residents (see Table 1).

In this manner comparable scores may be obtained for each of the four hierarchies. A quantitative measure of status crystallization is computed by taking the square root of the sum of the squared deviations from the mean of the four hierarchy scores of the individual (or family) and subtracting this figure from one hundred. For example, if an individual's percentile score in the occupational hierarchy is 66, in the educational hierarchy is 41, in

TABLE 1

Annual Income of Family Head	Number of Respondents	Cumulative Percentile Range	Assigned Score
$10,000 or more	29	95.4–100.0	98
8,000–9,999	15	93.0– 95.3	94
7,000–7,999	19	90.0– 92.9	91
6,000–6,999	58	80.7– 89.9	85
5,000–5,999	82	67.6– 80.6	74
4,000–4,999	137	45.6– 67.5	57
3,000–3,999	191	15.0– 45.5	30
2,000–2,999	57	5.9– 14.9	10
1,000–1,999	21	2.5– 5.8	4
1– 999	10	0.9– 2.4	2
No income	5	0.0– 0.8	0
Total	624*		

* This figure includes only those who were themselves currently in the labor force or respondents who were members of families in which the head was in the labor force, and for whom income data were available.

the income hierarchy is 59, and in the ethnic hierarchy is 34, his status crystallization score would be computed as follows:

Hierarchy	Percentile Score	d	d^2
Occupation	66	16	256
Education	41	− 9	81
Income	59	9	81
Ethnic	34	−16	256
	200		674

$$\bar{X} = 50 \qquad \sqrt{674} = 26$$

Status Crystallization Score $= 100 - 26 = 74$

The more highly consistent or crystallized an individual's status, the more closely his crystallization score, of course, approaches 100; the less consistent, or crystallized, his status, the more closely his score approaches zero.

More recently (1964) Lenski has proposed a much simpler method of testing for the effects of status inconsistency. This newer method avoids certain of the statistical difficulties inherent

466 · *Status Consistency*

in the earlier method, and furthermore, is grounded in basic statistical theory. He has noted that one can set up a simple test to determine whether the relationship between two status variables and a stress measure is simply additive (in which case there is no inconsistency effect) or whether it involves a nonadditive, interactive element as well. This procedure involves setting up a table where the rows and columns represent roughly comparable status levels for different vertical hierarchies and where the cells are the percentage of respondents displaying the predicted consequence of status inconsistency. As Table 2 indicates, if there were no interaction effect (or if the relationship were simply additive), "the magnitude of the percentage differences between the rows should be the same regardless of column and vice versa, except insofar as distorted by sampling error, measurement error, and the like." (1964, p. 327)

TABLE 2. ADDITIVE MODEL OF THE RELATIONSHIP
BETWEEN THREE VARIABLES
Percentage Displaying Predicted Pattern of Action with
Respect to y

	Variable x_1		
Variable x_2	*High*	*Medium*	*Low*
High	a	b	c
Medium	$a + d$	$b + d$	$c + d$
Low	$a + e$	$b + e$	$c + e$

Lenski further notes (1964, pp. 327–328): "if the relationship were purely additive, then in any body of data we would predict that the sum of the percentages in any pair of consistent status cells would equal the sum of the percentages in the corresponding pair of inconsistent status cells." Thus, letting Hh represent the consistently high status cell; Mm, the consistently medium status cell; Ll, the consistently low status cell; Hm and Mh, the cells that combine high and medium status, and so on, if the relationship were additive, it could be represented as follows (1964, p. 328):

$$Hh + Mm = Hm + Mh = a + b + d$$
$$Mm + Ll = Ml + Lm = b + c + d + e$$
$$Hh + Ll = Hl + Lh = a + c + e$$

On the other hand, if there is an interactive effect generating stress (or related in this manner to any dependent variable entered in the cells of the table), "then the sums of pairs of inconsistent cells should be greater than the sums of the corresponding consistent cells." (1964, p. 328) Specifically, one would predict:

$$Hh + Mm < Hm + Mh$$
$$Mm + Ll < Ml + Lm$$
$$Hh + Ll < Hl + Lh$$

Kenkel (June, 1956), p. 366; see category 7 above.

Lenski, Gerhard E., "Social Participation and Status Crystallization," *American Sociological Review*, 21 (August, 1956), pp. 458–464. See p. 461.

Jackson, Elton F., "Status Consistency and Symptoms of Stress," *American Sociological Review*, 27 (August, 1962), pp. 469–480. See pp. 471–472.

Beshers, James M., "Urban Social Structure as a Single Hierarchy," *Social Forces*, 41 (March, 1963), pp. 233–239. See p. 234.

Landecker, Werner S., "Class Crystallization and Class Consciousness," *American Sociological Review*, 28 (April, 1963), pp. 219–229. See p. 220.

Curtis (1963), p. 68; see category 4 above.

Schmitt (1965), pp. 192–193; see category 5 above.

10. STATUS INTEGRATION

Gibbs, Jack P., and Walter T. Martin, "A Theory of Status Integration and Its Relationship to Suicide," *American Sociological Review*, 23 (April, 1958), pp. 140–147. See pp. 143–144.

Brenner (1958), p. 579; see category 1 above.

Gibbs, Jack P., and Walter T. Martin, "On Status Integration and Suicide Rates in Tulsa," *American Sociological Review*, 24 (June, 1959), pp. 392–396. See p. 393.

11. STATUS TENSION

Reeder, Leo G., "Social Factors in Heart Disease: A Preliminary Research Report on the Relationship of Certain Social Factors to Blood Pressure in Males," *Social Forces*, 34 (May, 1956), pp. 367–371. See p. 369.

URBAN AREAS: METROPOLITAN AREAS AND DOMINANCE

SEE ALSO
Societal Characteristics

1. **METROPOLITAN ACTIVITY, LOCAL**

Carroll, Robert L., "The Metropolitan Influence of the 168 Standard Metropolitan Area Central Cities," *Social Forces*, 42 (December, 1963), pp. 166–173. See pp. 166–167.

2. **METROPOLITAN ACTIVITY, REGIONAL**

Carroll; see category 1 above.

3. **METROPOLITAN AREAS, DELIMITATION OF**

Gibbs, Jack P. and Kingsley Davis, "Conventional Versus Metropolitan Data in the International Study of Urbanization," *American Sociological Review*, 23 (October, 1958), pp. 504–514. See p. 506.

Gibbs, Jack P., and Leo F. Schnore, "Metropolitan Growth: An International Study," *American Journal of Sociology*, 66 (September, 1960), pp. 160–170. See p. 160.

4. **METROPOLITAN DOMINANCE**

Vance, Rupert B., and Sarah Smith, "Metropolitan Dominance and Integration," in Rupert B. Vance and N. J. Demerath (eds.), *The Urban South*, New York: Van Rees, 1954, pp. 114–135.

Carroll, p. 166; see category 1 above.

5. **METROPOLITAN DOMINANCE POTENTIAL**

Pappenfort, Donnell M., "The Ecological Field and the Metropolitan Community: Manufacturing and Management," *American Journal of Sociology*, 64 (January, 1959), pp. 380–385. See p. 383.

6. PERCEIVED SALES PRESSURE

DeFleur, Melvin L., and John Crosby, "Analyzing Metropolitan Dominance," *Social Forces*, 35 (October, 1956), pp. 68–75. See p. 70.

7. PERFORMANCE OF INTEGRATIVE SERVICES BY METROPOLITAN AREAS

Carroll, p. 169: see category 1 above.

8. PRICE ADVANTAGE

DeFleur and Crosby, p. 71; see category 6 above.

9. SPEED OF SERVICE

DeFleur and Crosby, p. 71; see category 6 above.

10. UNAWARENESS OF ALTERNATIVE OUTLETS

DeFleur and Crosby, p. 71; see category 6 above.

11. WHOLESALE ACTIVITY

DeFleur and Crosby, p. 69; see category 6 above.

URBAN AREAS: SEGREGATION

SEE ALSO

Intergroup Relations, Racial and Ethnic:
Discrimination
Societal Characteristics

1. OCCUPATIONAL CONCENTRATION

Turner, Ralph H., "Occupational Patterns of Inequality," *American Journal of Sociology*, 59 (March, 1954), pp. 437–447. See p. 437.

2. OCCUPATIONAL DIFFERENTIATION, CRUDE

Gibbs, Jack P., "Occupational Differentiation of Negroes and Whites in the United States," *Social Forces*, 44 (December, 1965), pp. 159–165. See p. 161.

3. OCCUPATIONAL DIFFERENTIATION, STANDARDIZED

Gibbs, pp. 163–164; see category 2 above.

4. PATTERNS OF OCCUPANCY AND INTERRACIAL CONTACTS

Works, Ernest, "The Prejudice-Interaction Hypothesis from the Point of View of the Negro Minority Group," *American Journal of Sociology*, 67 (July, 1961), pp. 47–52. See p. 49.

5. SEGREGATION (COWGILL, COWGILL)

See also Duncan, Duncan and Modifications, category 6 below; Jahn, Schmid, Schrag, category 7 below; and Shevky, Williams, Bell and Modifications, category 8 below.

Cowgill, Donald O., and Mary S. Cowgill, "An Index of Segregation Based on Block Statistics," *American Sociological Review*, 16 (December, 1951), pp. 825–831.

Professor Donald Cowgill has expressed to us in a personal communication (December, 1966) the opinion that methodological developments in the measurement of residential segregation have superseded his own earlier efforts; and that, consequently, researchers should be directed to some more recent sources. He suggests particularly the treatment of these matters by Duncan and Duncan as revealed in the excellent work by Karl E. Taeuber and Alma F. Taeuber, *Negroes in Cities*, Chicago, Ill.: Aldine Publishing Company, 1965. The reader should find Appendix A, "The Measurement of Residential Segregation," pp. 195–245 in *Negroes in Cities*, especially helpful in attempting to understand the development of segregation indexes within sociology.

Duncan, Otis Dudley, and Beverly Duncan, "A Methodological Analysis of Segregation Indexes," *American Sociological Review*, 20 (April, 1955), pp. 210–217. See p. 211.

Cowgill, Donald O., "Trends in Residential Segregation of Nonwhites in American Cities, 1940–50," *American Sociological Review*, 21 (February, 1956), pp. 43–47. See p. 43.

Cowgill, Donald O., "Segregation Scores for Metropolitan Areas," *American Sociological Review*, 27 (June, 1962), pp. 400–402. See p. 400.

Duncan, Otis Dudley, and Beverly Duncan, "Measuring Segregation," *American Sociological Review*, 28 (February, 1963), p. 133.

Cowgill, Donald O., "In Defense of a Segregation Index," *American Sociological Review*, 28 (June, 1963), pp. 453–454.

Taeuber, Karl F., "On Assessing Segregation Indexes," *American Sociological Review*, 28 (June, 1963), p. 454.

6. SEGREGATION (DUNCAN, DUNCAN AND MODIFICATIONS)

See also Cowgill, Cowgill, category 5 above; Jahn, Schmid, Schrag, category 7 below; and Shevky, Williams, Bell and Modifications, category 8 below.

Duncan, Otis Dudley, and Beverly Duncan, "Residential Distribution and Occupational Stratification," *American Journal of Sociology*, 60 (March, 1955), pp. 493–503.

The index of segregation was developed by Duncan and Duncan in connection with their investigations of the spatial aspect of stratification phenomena. The orientation of their work was that of comparative urban ecology, and the techniques developed were seen as being applicable to a wide range of ecological problems.

The index of segregation is, in a sense, a special case of the index of dissimilarity. Because of this relationship, it is convenient to treat the index of dissimilarity prior to discussing the measure of segregation.

The index of dissimilarity measures differences in the areal distributions of occupational groups. Suppose a city is divided into five area units (census tracts, predetermined sectors, or even blocks could be used as the area units). For each occupational group, the percentage of workers in that group residing in each area is determined. "The index of dissimilarity between two occupation groups is then one-half the sum of the absolute values of the differences between the respective distributions, taken area by area." (p. 494) Consider the data in Table 1. The index of dissimilarity between occupation X and occupation Y is one-half of 60 or 30 per cent.

The Duncans have argued that this index can be interpreted as a "measure of displacement." That is, 30 per cent of the workers in occupation X would have to move to different areas in order to make their areal distribution identical with that of occupation Y.

"When the index of dissimilarity is computed between one occupation group and all other occupations combined (i.e., total employed males except those in the given occupation group), it is referred to as an *index of segregation*." (p. 494) A convenient computational procedure is suggested by the Duncans. Suppose 10

TABLE 1. PERCENTAGE OF TWO OCCUPATIONAL
GROUPS RESIDING IN EACH OF FIVE AREAS

Area	Occupation X	Occupation Y	Absolute Difference
I	20	10	10
II	20	10	10
III	30	20	10
IV	15	40	25
V	15	20	5
Total	100	100	60

TABLE 2. PERCENTAGES OF OCCUPATIONAL GROUP X
AND OF ALL EMPLOYED MALES RESIDING IN
EACH OF FIVE AREAS

Area	Occupation X	Total Employed Males	Absolute Difference
I	20	30	10
II	20	30	10
III	30	20	10
IV	15	10	5
V	15	10	5
Total	100	100	40

per cent of the total male labor force is employed in occupation X. Consider the data presented in Table 2.

The index of segregation can be computed by the following equation:

$$IS = \frac{\text{Absolute Difference}}{2(1 - P)}$$

where P = the proportion of males employed in occupation X.

In the example given,

$$IS = \frac{40}{2(1 - 0.10)} = 22.2$$

The index of segregation has been used to compare the areal distributions of ethnic (see Lieberson, 1958, below) and social-class groups (see Collison and Mogey, 1959, below), as well as those of occupational groups.

Duncan and Duncan (1955); see category 5 above.
Cowgill (1956), p. 43; see category 5 above.
Lieberson, Stanley, "Ethnic Groups and the Practice of Medicine," *American Sociological Review*, 23 (October, 1958), pp. 542–549. See p. 544.
Duncan, Otis Dudley, and Stanley Lieberson, "Ethnic Segregation and Assimilation," *American Journal of Sociology*, 64 (January, 1959), pp. 364–374. See p. 365.
Collison, Peter, and John Mogey, "Residence and Social Class in

Oxford," *American Journal of Sociology*, 64 (May, 1959), pp. 599–605. See p. 604.

Collison, Peter, "Occupation, Education, and Housing in an English City," *American Journal of Sociology*, 65 (May, 1960), pp. 588–597. See p. 588.

Lieberson, Stanley, "The Impact of Residential Segregation on Ethnic Assimilation," *Social Forces*, 40 (October, 1961), pp. 52–57. See p. 53.

Lieberson, Stanley, "Suburbs and Ethnic Residential Patterns," *American Journal of Sociology*, 67 (May, 1962), pp. 673–681. See p. 674.

Cowgill (1962); see category 5 above.

Glenn, Norval, "Negro Prestige Criteria: A Case Study in the Bases of Prestige," *American Journal of Sociology*, 68 (May, 1963), pp. 645–657. See p. 651.

Lieberson, Stanley, "The Old-New Distinction and Immigrants in Australia," *American Sociological Review*, 28 (August, 1963), pp. 550–565. See pp. 557 and 559.

Lieberson, Stanley, *Ethnic Patterns in American Cities*, New York: Free Press of Glencoe, 1963.

Taeuber, Karl E., and Alma F. Taeuber, "The Negro as an Immigrant Group: Recent Trends in Racial and Ethnic Segregation in Chicago," *American Journal of Sociology*, 69 (January, 1964), pp. 374–382. See pp. 376–377.

Uyeki, Eugene S., "Residential Distribution and Stratification, 1950–1960," *American Journal of Sociology*, 69 (March, 1964), pp. 491–498. See p. 493.

7. SEGREGATION (JAHN, SCHMID, SCHRAG)

See also Cowgill, Cowgill, category 5 above; Duncan, Duncan and Modifications, category 6 above; and Shevky, Williams, Bell and Modifications, category 8 below.

Jahn, Julius, Calvin F. Schmid, and Clarence Schrag, "The Measurement of Ecological Segregation," *American Sociological Review*, 12 (June, 1947), pp. 293–303.

The indices of ecological segregation developed by Jahn, Schmid, and Schrag were derived from a consideration of two underlying assumptions. First, if no segregation exists, then the members of a minority group should be distributed randomly throughout the various census tracts of a city. For example, if ten per cent of a city's population is Negro and there is no segregation, then each census tract would be expected to have a Negro population of approximately ten per cent.

A second assumption was made with respect to complete segregation. A city is completely segregated if minority and majority groups are located so that no member of one group resides in a tract in which there are members of the other group.

Given these two assumptions, Jahn, Schmid, and Schrag argued that any index of segregation should meet two basic conditions and have certain additional characteristics. Their argument (pp. 293–294) is as follows:

First, "no segregation" exists if the proportion of Negroes to the number of persons in any given census tract is equal to the proportion of Negroes in the total population of the city. The "segregation score" for any tract, area (combination of census tracts), or city which fulfills this specification should be zero. Second, "complete segregation" exists if the Negroes reside only in census tracts in which there are no non-Negroes. Any tract, area (combination of tracts), or city which fulfills this specification should have a "segregation score" of 100. Hence, the range of possible scores should be 0 to 100.

In addition to these two basic stipulations, a satisfactory measure of ecological segregation should (1) be expressed as a single quantitative value so as to facilitate such statistical procedures as comparison, classification, and correlation; (2) be relatively easy to compute; (3) not be distorted by the size of the total population, the proportion of Negroes, or the area of a city; (4) be generally applicable to all cities; and (5) differentiate degrees of segregation in such a way that the distribution of intermediate scores cover most of the possible range between the extremes of 0 and 100.

The authors have developed four indices which meet the above conditions. In the following, each index will be defined and then a computational illustration will be provided. The discussion, like the original treatment by Jahn, Schmid, and Schrag, will deal with the ecological segregation of Negroes. The indices can be applied to any spatially ordered phenomenon including minority or nativity groups, social classes, educational or occupational groups, and so on.[1]

INDEX 1

Index 1 is based upon the difference between the proportions of Negroes and non-Negroes in that area of the city having the highest concentration of Negro residents. The following notation is employed:

N = total population of the city
N_a = total Negro population of the city
N_b = total non-Negro population of the city
N_1 = total population of Area 1
N_{1a} = Negro population of Area 1
N_{1b} = non-Negro population of Area 1
N_2 = total population of Area 2
N_{2a} = Negro population of Area 2
N_{2b} = non-Negro population of Area 2

In order to determine Area 1, the census tracts of the city are ranked from highest to lowest according to the proportion of the tract that is Negro. Area 1 is that subset of tracts beginning with the tract having the highest proportion Negro and adding successively ranked tracts until Area 1 includes a total population equal to the total Negro population of the city; that is, until $N_1 = N_a$.

Area 2 consists of the remaining census tracts.

Index 1 is then defined as follows:

$$I_1 = \left(\frac{N_{1a}}{N_a} - \frac{N_{1b}}{N_b}\right) 100$$

Suppose City X contains 10 census tracts having the characteristics reported in Table 1. These very nice hypothetical tracts each contain 100 people and already have been ranked in the order required in computing Index 1.

Area 1 must contain a total population approximately equal

[1] In this discussion, some modifications of the original equations have been introduced. The notation used also differs slightly from that employed by Jahn, Schmid, and Schrag. These changes were introduced in the effort to simplify the treatment of these indices.

to the total Negro population of City X. In our example, the first four tracts contain 400 people, and the total Negro population is 400. Thus, Area 1 consists of tracts 1 through 4. Given this:

$$N_a = 400 \qquad N_{1a} = 275$$
$$N_b = 600 \qquad N_{1b} = 125$$

$$I_1 = \left(\frac{275}{400} - \frac{125}{600}\right) 100 = 48$$

TABLE 1. DISTRIBUTION OF NEGROES AND NON-NEGROES IN CITY X BY CENSUS TRACT

Census Tract	Number of Negroes	Number Non-Negroes	Total Population
1	90	10	100
2	75	25	100
3	60	40	100
4	50	50	100
5	45	55	100
6	30	70	100
7	20	80	100
8	15	85	100
9	15	85	100
10	0	100	100
Total	400	600	1000

INDEX 2

Index 2 is defined as the standard deviation of the observed percentages of Negroes in the various tracts divided by the standard deviation of the distribution which would occur if there were complete segregation.

In computing Index 2, Jahn, Schmid, and Schrag advised the construction of a frequency distribution in which the class intervals represent the percentage of Negroes in each tract, and the frequencies the respective number of tracts in each class interval. With contemporary computer techniques such a step is no longer necessary. Using the percentage Negro as input data removes the chance of grouping error. (p. 297)

First, the percentage of each tract which is Negro is computed. Next the standard deviation of these percentages is determined. Third, the standard deviation of the percentage distribution under the hypothetical conditions of complete segregation is calculated using the following equation:

$$S_c = \sqrt{\frac{p(q)^2 + q(p)^2}{100}}$$

where p = the mean of the distribution of the percentage Negro in each Census tract of the set, and
$q = 100 - p$.

If we let S_a stand for the standard deviation of the observed percentages, then I_2 is defined as follows:

$$I_2 = \frac{S_a}{S_c}(100)$$

In our hypothetical City X,

$$S_c = \sqrt{\frac{40(60)^2 + 60(40)^2}{100}} = 49$$

and

$$S_a = 27.6$$

For City X, then:

$$I_2 = \frac{27.6}{49}(100) = 56.3$$

INDEX 3

The third measure discussed by Jahn, Schmid, and Schrag is based upon an "index of concentration" developed by the Italian statistician Corrado Gini. Index 3 is defined as the ratio of the Gini index computed for observed proportions of Negroes in the various tracts to the index which would obtain if there were complete segregation.

In order to compute Index 3, the various census tracts are entered on a work sheet in rank order. In contrast to Index 1, here the researcher enters first the tract having the lowest proportion of

TABLE 2. FORM FOR COMPUTING THE
GINI INDEX FOR CITY X

Census Tract (1)	Proportion of Total Population in Tract (2)	Proportion of Negroes in Tract (3)	Cumulative Proportion of Negroes (4)	Two Point Totals of Column 4 (5)	Column 2 Times Column 5 (6)
10	.10	.0000	.0000	.0000	.00000
9	.10	.0375	.0375	.0375	.00375
8	.10	.0375	.0750	.1125	.01125
7	.10	.0500	.1250	.2000	.02000
6	.10	.0750	.2000	.3250	.03250
5	.10	.1125	.3125	.5125	.05125
4	.10	.1250	.4375	.7500	.07500
3	.10	.1500	.5875	1.0250	.10250
2	.10	.1875	.7750	1.3625	.13625
1	.10	.2250	1.0000	1.7750	.17750
Totals	1.00	1.000	——	——	.61000

Negroes. For our hypothetical City X, this has been done in Table 2. Once the tracts are entered in the proper order, Index 3 is computed as follows:

1. Construct column 4 in the Table by accumulating the proportions in column 3.
2. Construct column 5. The first entry in column 5 is the same as the first entry in column 4. The second entry in column 5 is the sum of the first and second entries in column 4 (.0000 + .0375). The third entry in column 5 is the sum of the second and third entries in column 4 (.0375 + .0750). The fourth entry in column 5 is the sum of the third and fourth entries in column 4 (.0750 + .1250), and so on.
3. Construct column 6 by multiplying the entry in column 2 by the corresponding entry in column 5.
4. Sum column 6.
5. The Gini index for the observed proportions is then given by:

$$G_a = 1 - \Sigma \text{ (column 6)}$$

480 · Urban Areas

6. The Gini index for the hypothetical condition of complete segregation is obtained by:

$$G_c = 1 - \frac{N_a}{N}$$

where N_a is the total Negro population and N is the total population of the city.

7. Index 3 can then be obtained as follows:

$$I_3 = \frac{G_a}{G_c} (100)$$

In our example:

$$G_a = 1 - .61 = .39$$
$$G_c = 1 - \frac{400}{1000} = .60$$
$$I_3 = \frac{.39}{.60} (100) = 65$$

INDEX 4

Index 4 is defined as the sum of the differences (disregarding signs) between observed numbers of Negroes residing in the various census tracts and the numbers that would occur if there were no segregation, divided by the sum of the differences that would occur if there were complete segregation.

Here again a computation form is used in obtaining the value of the index (see Table 3). The basic data are entered into columns 1, 2, and 3. Computation, then, proceeds as follows:

1. The "expected number" of Negroes in each tract is computed by multiplying the population of the tract by the proportion of Negroes in the city's population.

$$N_e = N_t \left(\frac{N_a}{N} \right)$$

where N_e = "expected number" of Negroes,
N_t = population of the tract,
N_a = total Negro population of the city, and
N = total population of the city

TABLE 3. FORM FOR COMPUTING INDEX 4 FOR CITY X

Census Tract (1)	Population of Tract (2)	Number of Negroes in Tract (3)	Expected Number of Negroes in Tract (4)	Absolute Difference ($|d|$) between Column 3 and Column 4 (5)
1	100	90	40	50
2	100	75	40	35
3	100	60	40	20
4	100	50	40	10
5	100	45	40	5
6	100	30	40	10
7	100	20	40	20
8	100	15	40	25
9	100	15	40	25
10	100	0	40	40
Total	1,000	400	400	240

These "expected numbers" are entered in column 4. In our example, because the population of each tract is the same, the expected number of Negroes in each tract is the same. In real cities, of course, the researcher would not be this fortunate.

2. Compute column 5 by subtracting column 4 from column 3. Disregard the signs of the differences (that is, take the absolute differences between columns 4 and 3).
3. Sum column 5 to obtain $\Sigma|d|$.
4. Index 4 can then be computed by the following equation:

$$I_4 = \left[\frac{\Sigma\,|d|}{2N_a\left(1 - \dfrac{N_a}{N}\right)} \right] 100$$

For City X

$$I_4 = \left[\frac{240}{2(400)\left(1 - \dfrac{400}{1000}\right)} \right] 100 = 50$$

As can be seen from the example, the various indices give different "values" for segregation. Jahn, Schmid, and Schrag determined the correlations among the four indices and these findings are summarized in Table 4. Given the fact that the indices are not perfectly intercorrelated, which one should be employed? The answer given by the authors was: "The utility, value or application of a particular index is dependent upon the problem or purpose at hand. There is no 'best' index in any absolute sense." (p. 303) There has been some discussion of this position (see, for example, below: Hornseth, 1947; Jahn, Schmid, and Schrag, 1948; Williams, 1948; and Jahn, 1950). And Professor Jahn has advised us in a personal communication that he has recently developed a new approach to the problem based upon an application of statistical decision theory (see Julius A. Jahn, "The Statistical Design and Analysis of an Experiment to Measure the Effectiveness and Costs of a Health and Welfare Program," *Proceedings of the American Statistical Association*, 1965, pp. 42–50).

TABLE 4. INTERCORRELATIONS
AMONG THE FOUR JAHN-
SCHMID-SCHRAG INDICES
OF SEGREGATION*

	Index		
Index	*2*	*3*	*4*
1	.91	.60	.59
2		.50	.48
3			.96

* Adapted from Jahn, Schmid, and Schrag, 1947, Chart I, p. 301. The correlation between indexes 1 and 2 is based on data from 44 cities. All other intercorrelations are based on data from 25 cities. The original data were taken from the 1940 U.S. Census.

Hornseth, Richard, "A Note on 'The Measurement of Ecological Segregation' by Julius Jahn, Calvin F. Schmid, and Clarence Schrag," *American Sociological Review*, 12 (October, 1947), pp. 603–604.

Jahn, Julius, Calvin F. Schmid, and Clarence Schrag, "Rejoinder to Dr. Hornseth's Note on 'The Measurement of Ecological Segregation,' " *American Sociological Review,* 13 (April, 1948), pp. 216–217.

Williams, Josephine J., "Another Commentary on So-Called Segregation Indices," *American Sociological Review,* 13 (June, 1948), pp. 298–304.

Jahn, Julius, "The Measurement of Ecological Segregation: Derivation of an Index Based on the Criterion of Reproducibility," *American Sociological Review,* 15 (February, 1950), pp. 100–104. See pp. 102–103.

Cowgill and Cowgill (1951), p. 825; see category 5 above.

Duncan and Duncan (1955), p. 212; see category 5 above.

8. SEGREGATION (SHEVKY, WILLIAMS, BELL AND MODIFICATIONS)

See also Cowgill, Cowgill, category 5 above; Duncan, Duncan and Modifications, category 6 above; and Jahn, Schmid, Schrag, category 7 above.

Shevky, Eshref, and Marilyn Williams, *The Social Areas of Los Angeles,* Berkeley and Los Angeles, Calif.: The University of California Press, 1949.

Shevky, Eshref, and Wendell Bell, *Social Area Analysis: Theory, Illustrative Application and Computational Procedures,* Stanford, Calif.: Stanford University Press, 1955.

This measure of segregation is one of three dimensions of social area analysis. For the reader's convenience, all three dimensions are summarized below. For citations to the remaining dimensions, see also: Urban Areas: Socioeconomic Status, category 14; and Urban Areas: Urbanization (Family Status).

Social area analysis was originally formulated by Shevky and Williams to provide for the systematic organization of the masses of census data which are available with respect to urban areas. The objective of the Shevky and Williams investigation was to understand the aggregation that constituted Los Angeles in terms of a more general system of relationships which was characteristic of contemporary, urban, industrial society.

The strategy that emerged from the analysis of Los Angeles was further specified in the later work of Shevky and Bell. This summary of the procedure is based upon the restatement of rationale and technique which appears in the Shevky and Bell monograph. Starting from a set of "postulates concerning industrial society," Shevky and Bell identify three sets of general trends which they believe to be descriptive of the changing character of modern society. The trends so identified are: (1) changes in the distribution of skills, (2) changes in the organization of productive activity, and (3) changes in the composition of the population. Consideration of these three trends led to the formulation of three general constructs: *social rank* or economic status, *urbanization* or family status, and *segregation* or ethnic status. These three concepts refer to "structural reflections of change which can be used as factors for the study of social differentiation and stratification at a particular time in modern society." (Shevky and Bell, pp. 3–5)

With these concepts so defined, the authors turned to the task of developing indexes of each. "These derived measures indicate aspects of urban population which are most clearly indicative of the changing distribution of skills, the changing organization of productive activity (especially the changing structure of the family), and the changing composition of the population." (Shevky and Bell, p. 5)

The data required in the computation of the three indexes, and in the determination of the social areas based upon these three measures, are available in the United States Bureau of the Census volumes reporting census tract statistics. The computational procedures are as follows (pp. 54–58):

I. INDEXES OF SOCIAL RANK, URBANIZATION, AND SEGREGATION

In some instances, modifications are required by these techniques depending on the reporting procedures used in a particular census. These modifications are not difficult and usually are obvious. See Shevky and Bell, pp. 54–57, for examples of such modifications.

A. SOCIAL RANK COMPONENTS

1. *Occupation ratio* (total number of craftsmen . . . , operatives . . . , and laborers . . . per 1,000 employed persons . . .):

a. Add:
   (1) "Craftsmen, foremen, and kindred workers"
   (2) "Operatives and kindred workers"
   (3) "Laborers" . . .
b. Subtract the total number of persons with "Occupation not reported" from the total number of persons "Employed." . . .
c. Divide the total number of craftsmen . . . , operatives . . . , and laborers by the above difference.
d. Multiply the above quotient by 1,000.

2. *Occupation standard score:* Substitute in standard score formula:

$$\text{Occupation score} = 100 - [x \ (r - o)]$$

where $x = .1336898$,
   $o = 0$,
   $r =$ occupation ratio for each census tract.

3. *Education ratio* (number of persons who have completed no more than grade school per 1,000 persons 25 years old and over):
a. Add number of persons 25 years old and over who have had only eight years of schooling or less.
b. Subtract the total number of persons with "School years not reported" from the total number of "Persons 25 years old and over."
c. Divide the total number of persons completing only elementary school or less by the above difference.
d. Multiply the quotient by 1,000.

4. *Education standard score:* Substitute in standard score formula:

$$\text{Education score} = 100 - [x(r - o)]$$

where $x = .1298701$,
   $o = 130$,
   $r =$ education ratio for each census tract.

5. *Social rank index:* Compute a simple average of the occupation and education standard scores. The average is the index of social rank.

B. URBANIZATION COMPONENTS

1. *Fertility ratio* (number of children under 5 years per 1,000 females age 15 through 44):
a. Record total number of persons "Under 5 years." . . .
b. Add the number of females in the age range 15 through 44.
c. Divide the total number of children under 5 by the total number of females age 15 through 44.
d. Multiply the quotient by 1,000.

2. *Fertility standard score:* Substitute in standard score formula:

$$\text{Fertility score} = 100 - [x(r - o)]$$

486 · *Urban Areas*

where x = .1661130,

  o = 9,

  r = fertility ratio for each census tract.

3. *Women in the labor force ratio* (the number of females in the labor force per 1,000 females 14 years old and over):

a. Record number of females "14 years old and over" who are in the "Labor force."

b. Divide the above by the total number of females "14 years old and over."

c. Multiply the quotient by 1,000.

4. *Women in the labor force standard score*: Substitute in standard score formula:

$$\text{Women in the labor force score} = x(r - o)$$

where x = .2183406,

  o = 86,

  r = women in the labor force ratio for each census tract.

5. *Single-family detached dwelling units ratio* (the number of single-family dwelling units per 1,000 dwelling units of all types):

a. Record number of "1 dwelling unit, detached (includes trailers)" in 1950 census. (The definition in 1940 was "1-family detached" dwelling units.)

b. Divide by total of "All dwelling units."

c. Multiply the quotient by 1,000.

6. *Single-family detached dwelling units standard score*: Substitute in standard score formula:

$$\text{SFDU score} = 100 - [x(r - o)]$$

where x = .1006441,

  o = 6,

  r = single-family detached dwelling units ratio.

7. *Urbanization Index*: Compute a simple average of the fertility, women in the labor force, and single-family dwelling units standard scores. The average is the index of urbanization.

C. THE INDEX OF SEGREGATION

1. Add the number of persons designated "Negro"; "Other Races"; and "foreign-born white" from "Poland," "Czechoslovakia," "Hungary," "Yugoslavia," "U.S.S.R.," "Lithuania," "Finland," "Rumania," "Greece," "Italy," "Other Europe," "Asia," "French Canada," "Mexico," and "Other America." . . .

2. Divide the above sum by the total population in each tract.

3. Multiply the above quotient by 100 to obtain the index of segregation for each census tract.

II. CONSTRUCTION OF THE SOCIAL AREAS

A. DIVISIONS IN THE INDEX OF SOCIAL RANK

Divide the census tracts into four groups on the basis of their scores on the index of social rank. Group tracts together having social rank scores of 0 to 24, 25 to 49, 50 to 74, and 75 to 100, respectively. Designate these groups of tracts as social areas of the order 1, 2, 3, and 4, respectively.

B. DIVISIONS IN THE INDEX OF URBANIZATION

Divide the census tracts into four groups on the basis of their scores on the index of urbanization. Group together tracts having urbanization scores of 0 to 24, 25 to 49, 50 to 74, and 75 to 100. Designate these groups of tracts as social areas with the order A, B, C, and D, respectively. Combining these divisions in the index of social rank, there are sixteen possible social areas. These are designated 1A, 1B, 1C, 2A, . . . 4D.

C. DIVISIONS IN THE INDEX OF SEGREGATION

Divide the census tracts into two groups on the basis of their scores on the index of segregation. Select as the cutting point the percent of the total population of the urban area represented by the combined racial and nationality groups considered subordinate. Those tracts having more than the average proportion of the combined subordinate groups designate "segregated" tracts; those tracts having less than the average proportion of the combined subordinate groups designate "not segregated." Thus, there are thirty-two possible groupings of census tracts into social areas: 1A, 1B, 1C, 1D, 2A, . . . 4D and 1AS, 1BS, 1CS, 1DS, 2AS, . . . 4DS.

Bell, Wendell, "The Social Areas of the San Francisco Bay Region," *American Sociological Review*, 18 (February, 1953), pp. 39–47. See p. 41.

Williamson, Robert C., "Socio-economic Factors and Marital Adjustment in an Urban Setting," *American Sociological Review*, 19 (April, 1954), pp. 213–216. See p. 214.

Bell, Wendell, "A Probability Model for the Measurement of Ecological Segregation," *Social Forces*, 32 (May, 1954), pp. 357–364. See p. 357.

Broom, Leonard, Helen P. Beem, and Virginia Harris, "Characteristics of 1,107 Petitioners for Change of Name," *American Sociological Review*, 20 (February, 1955), pp. 33–39. See p. 37.

Bell, Wendell, "Economic, Family, and Ethnic Status: An Empirical Test," *American Sociological Review*, 20 (February, 1955), pp. 45–52. See pp. 46–47.

Greer, Scott, "Urbanism Reconsidered: A Comparative Study of Local Areas in a Metropolis," *American Sociological Review*, 21 (February, 1956), pp. 19–25. See p. 19.

Bell, Wendell, and Maryanne T. Force, "Urban Neighborhood Types and Participation in Formal Associations," *American Sociological Review*, 21 (February, 1956), pp. 25–34. See p. 26.

Bell, Wendell, and Maryanne T. Force, "Social Structure and Participation in Different Types of Formal Associations," *Social Forces*, 34 (May, 1956), pp. 345–350. See p. 345.

Bell, Wendell, and Marion D. Boat, "Urban Neighborhood and Informal Social Relations," *American Journal of Sociology*, 62 (January, 1957), pp. 391–398. See p. 392.

Bell, Wendell, and Maryanne T. Force, "Religious Preference, Familism, and the Class Structure," *The Midwest Sociologist*, 19 (May, 1957), pp. 79–86. See p. 80.

Bell, Wendell, "Anomie, Social Isolation, and the Class Structure," *Sociometry*, 20 (June, 1957), pp. 105–116. See p. 196.

Hawley, Amos, and Otis Dudley Duncan, "Social Area Analysis: A Critical Appraisal," *Land Economics*, 33 (November, 1957), pp. 337–345.

Van Arsdol, Maurice D., Jr., Santo F. Camilleri, and Calvin F. Schmid, "The Generality of Urban Social Indexes," *American Sociological Review*, 23 (June, 1958), pp. 277–284. See p. 277.

Van Arsdol, Maurice D., Jr., Santo F. Camilleri, and Calvin F. Schmid, "An Application of the Shevky Social Area Indexes to a Model of Urban Society," *Social Forces*, 37 (October, 1958), pp. 26–32. See pp. 26–27.

Meier, Dorothy L., and Wendell Bell, "Anomia and Differential Access to the Achievement of Life Goals," *American Sociological Review*, 24 (April, 1959), pp. 189–202. See p. 193.

Farber, Bernard, and John C. Osoinach, "An Index of Socio-Economic Rank of Census Tracts in Urban Areas," *American Sociological Review*, 24 (October, 1959), pp. 630–640. See p. 630.

Bell, Wendell, "Social Areas: Typology of Urban Neighborhoods," in Marvin B. Sussman (ed.), *Community Structure and Analysis*, New York: Thomas Y. Crowell Company, 1959, pp. 61–92.

Kaufman, Walter C., and Scott Greer, "Voting in a Metropolitan Community: An Application of Social Area Analysis," *Social Forces*, 38 (March, 1960), pp. 196–204. See p. 196.

Anderson, Theodore R., and Lee L. Bean, "The Shevky-Bell Social Areas: Confirmation of Results and a Reinterpretation," *Social Forces*, 40 (December, 1961), pp. 119–124. See p. 119.

McElrath, Dennis C., "The Social Areas of Rome: A Comparative Analysis," *American Sociological Review*, 27 (June, 1962), pp. 376–391. See p. 377.

Willie, Charles V., and William B. Rothney, "Racial, Ethnic, and Income Factors in the Epidemiology of Neonatal Mortality," *American Sociological Review*, 27 (August, 1962), pp. 522–526. See p. 523.

Greer, Scott and Peter Orleans, "The Mass Society and the Parapolitical Structure," *American Sociological Review*, 27 (October, 1962), pp. 634–646. See p. 636.

Boggs, Sarah L., "Urban Crime Patterns," *American Sociological Review*, 30 (December, 1965), pp. 899–908. See p. 905.

9. SEGREGATION (ZUBRZYCKI)

Zubrzycki, Jerzy, *Immigrants in Australia: A Demographic Survey Based on the 1954 Census*, Parkville, Victoria: Melbourne University Press, 1960, pp. 79–85.

Lieberson (August, 1963), p. 559; see category 6 above.

10. SOCIAL AND DEMOGRAPHIC DIMENSIONS: RACE

Schmid, Calvin F., "Urban Crime Areas," *American Sociological Review*, 25 (August, 1960), pp. 527–542. See p. 537.

URBAN AREAS: SOCIOECONOMIC STATUS

SEE ALSO

Societal Characteristics

1. DWELLING AREA RATING

Reeder, Leo G., "Social Differentials in Mode of Travel, Time, and Cost in the Journey to Work," *American Sociological Review*, 21 (February, 1956), pp. 56–63. See pp. 57 and 62.

2. ECONOMIC PROSPERITY

Pettigrew, Thomas F., "Demographic Correlates of Border-State Desegregation," *American Sociological Review*, 22 (December, 1957), pp. 683–689. See p. 685.

3. LOW-RENT CONCENTRATION

Duncan, Otis Dudley, "Urbanization and Retail Specialization," *Social Forces*, 30 (March, 1952), pp. 267–271.

Duncan, Otis Dudley, and Beverly Duncan, "Residential Distribution and Occupational Stratification," *American Journal of Sociology*, 60 (March, 1955), pp. 493–503. See p. 495.

Uyeki, Eugene S., "Residential Distribution and Stratification, 1950–1960," *American Journal of Sociology*, 69 (March, 1964), pp. 491–498. See pp. 493–494.

4. OCCUPATIONAL STATUS OF DISTRICT

MacRae, Duncan, Jr., "Occupations and the Congressional Vote, 1940–1950," *American Sociological Review*, 20 (June, 1955), pp. 332–340. See p. 335.

5. OCCUPATIONAL STATUS OF CENSUS TRACTS

Schmid, Calvin F., Earle H. MacCannell, and Maurice D. Van Arsdol, Jr., "The Ecology of the American City: Further Comparison and Validation of Generalizations," *American*

Sociological Review, 23 (August, 1958), pp. 392–401. See p. 394.

6. OCCUPATIONAL STATUS OF PRECINCT

Heberle, Rudolph, and P. H. Howard, "An Ecological Analysis of Political Tendencies in Louisiana: the Presidential Elections of 1952," *Social Forces*, 32 (May, 1954), pp. 344–350. See p. 349.

7. QUALITY OF HOUSING OF CENSUS TRACTS

Collison, Peter, "Occupation, Education, and Housing in an English City," *American Journal of Sociology*, 65 (May, 1960), pp. 588–597. See p. 591.

8. RESIDENTIAL DESIRABILITY OF CENSUS TRACTS

Green, Norman E., "Scale Analysis of Urban Structures: A Study of Birmingham, Alabama," *American Sociological Review*, 21 (February, 1956), pp. 8–13. See p. 9.

9. SCHOOL STATUS LEVEL BY CENSUS TRACTS (WEINSTEIN)

Weinstein, Eugene A., "Weights Assigned by Children to Criteria of Prestige," *Sociometry*, 19 (June, 1956), pp. 126–132. See p. 127.

10. SCHOOL STATUS LEVEL BY CENSUS TRACT (WILSON)

Wilson, Alan B., "Residential Segregation of Social Classes and Aspirations of High School Boys," *American Sociological Review*, 24 (December, 1959), pp. 836–845. See p. 837.

11. SOCIAL AND DEMOGRAPHIC DIMENSIONS: LOW FAMILY AND ECONOMIC STATUS

Schmid, Calvin, "Urban Crime Areas: Part I," *American Sociological Review*, 25 (August, 1960), pp. 527–542. See p. 537.

12. SOCIAL AND DEMOGRAPHIC DIMENSIONS: LOW SOCIAL COHESION—LOW FAMILY STATUS

Schmid; see category 11 above.

13. SOCIAL AND DEMOGRAPHIC DIMENSIONS: LOW SOCIAL COHESION—LOW OCCUPATIONAL STATUS

Schmid; see category 11 above.

14. SOCIAL RANK

See also categories 15–23 below.

This index is discussed in full in Urban Areas: Segregation, category 8.

Shevky, Eshref, and Marilyn Williams, *The Social Areas of Los Angeles*, Berkeley and Los Angeles, Calif.: University of California Press, 1949.

Shevky, Eshref, and Wendell Bell, *Social Area Analysis: Theory, Illustrative Application and Computational Procedures*, Stanford, Calif.: Stanford University Press, 1955.

Bell, Wendell, "The Social Areas of the San Francisco Bay Region," *American Sociological Review*, 18 (February, 1953), pp. 39–47. See p. 40.

Williamson, Robert C., "Socio-Economic Factors and Marital Adjustment in an Urban Setting," *American Sociological Review*, 19 (April, 1954), pp. 357–364. See p. 357.

Broom, Leonard, Helen P. Beem, and Virginia Harris, "Characteristics of 1,107 Petitioners for Change of Name," *American Sociological Review*, 20 (February, 1955), pp. 33–39. See p. 37.

Bell, Wendell, "Economic, Family, and Ethnic Status: An Empirical Test," *American Sociological Review*, 20 (February, 1955), pp. 45–52. See pp. 46–47.

Greer, Scott, "Urbanism Reconsidered: A Comparative Study of Local Areas in a Metropolis," *American Sociological Review*, 21 (February, 1956), pp. 19–25. See p. 19.

Bell, Wendell, and Maryanne T. Force, "Urban Neighborhood Types and Participation in Formal Associations," *American Sociological Review*, 21 (February, 1956), pp. 25–34. See p. 26.

Bell, Wendell, and Maryanne T. Force, "Social Structure and Participation in Different Types of Formal Associations," *Social Forces*, 34 (May, 1956), pp. 345–350. See p. 345.

Bell, Wendell, and Marion D. Boat, "Urban Neighborhood and

Informal Social Relations," *American Journal of Sociology*, 62 (January, 1957), pp. 391–398. See p. 392.

Bell, Wendell, and Maryanne T. Force, "Religious Preference, Familism, and the Class Structure," *The Midwest Sociologist*, 19 (May, 1957), pp. 79–86. See p. 80.

Flittie, Edwin G., "Fertility and Mortality in the Rocky Mountain West," *American Sociological Review*, 22 (April, 1957), pp. 189–193. See p. 191.

Bell, Wendell, "Anomie, Social Isolation, and the Class Structure," *Sociometry*, 20 (June, 1957), pp. 105–116. See p. 106.

Van Arsdol, Maurice D., Jr., Santo F. Camilleri, and Calvin F. Schmid, "The Generality of Urban Social Indexes," *American Sociological Review*, 23 (June, 1958), pp. 277–284. See p. 277.

Van Arsdol, Maurice D., Jr., Santo F. Camilleri, and Calvin F. Schmid, "An Application of the Shevky Social Area Indexes to a Model of Urban Society," *Social Forces*, 37 (October, 1958), pp. 26–32. See pp. 26–27.

Meier, Dorothy L., and Wendell Bell, "Anomia and Differential Access to the Achievement of Life Goals," *American Sociological Review*, 24 (April, 1959), pp. 189–202. See p. 193.

Farber, Bernard, and John C. Osoinach, "An Index of Socio-Economic Rank of Census Tracts in Urban Areas," *American Sociological Review*, 24 (October, 1959), pp. 630–640. See p. 630.

Bell, Wendell, "Social Areas: Typology of Urban Neighborhoods," in Marvin B. Sussman (ed.), *Community Structure and Analysis*, New York: Thomas Y. Crowell Company, 1959, pp. 61–92.

Kaufman, Walter C., and Scott Greer, "Voting in a Metropolitan Community: An Application of Social Area Analysis," *Social Forces*, 38 (March, 1960), pp. 196–204. See p. 196.

Anderson, Theodore R., and Janice A. Egeland, "Spatial Aspects of Social Area Analysis," *American Sociological Review*, 26 (June, 1961), pp. 392–398. See p. 394.

Anderson, Theodore R., and Lee L. Bean, "The Shevky-Bell Social Areas: Confirmation of Results and a Reinterpretation," *Social Forces*, 40 (December, 1961), pp. 119–124. See p. 119.

McElrath, Dennis C., "The Social Areas of Rome: A Comparative Analysis," *American Sociological Review*, 27 (June, 1962), pp. 376–391. See p. 377.

Greer, Scott, and Peter Orleans, "The Mass Society and the Parapolitical Structure," *American Sociological Review*, 27 (October, 1962), pp. 634–646. See p. 636.

Goldstein, Sidney, and Kurt Mayer, "Population Decline and the Social and Demographic Structure of an American City," *American Sociological Review*, 29 (February, 1964), pp. 48–54. See p. 50.

Duncan, Beverly, "Devolution of an Empirical Generalization," *American Sociological Review*, 29 (December, 1964), pp. 855–862. See p. 861.

Quinney, Richard, "Mortality Differentials in a Metropolitan Area," *Social Forces*, 43 (December, 1964), pp. 222–230. See p. 223.

Boggs, Sarah L., "Urban Crime Patterns," *American Sociological Review*, 30 (December, 1965), pp. 899–908. See p. 905.

15. SOCIOECONOMIC STATUS OF BLOCKS

See also category 14 above.

Crockett, Harry J., Jr., "A Study of Some Factors Affecting the Decision of Negro High School Students to Enroll in Previously All-White High Schools, St. Louis, 1955," *Social Forces*, 35 (May, 1957), pp. 351–356. See pp. 352–353.

16. SOCIOECONOMIC STATUS OF CENSUS TRACTS (FARBER, OSOINACH)

Farber and Osoinach (1959); see category 14 above.

Muir, Donal E., and Eugene Weinstein, "The Social Debt: An Investigation of Lower-Class and Middle-Class Norms of Social Obligation," *American Sociological Review*, 27 (August, 1962), pp. 532–539. See p. 535.

17. SOCIOECONOMIC STATUS OF CENSUS TRACTS (GREEN)

See also category 14 above.

Green; see category 8 above.

18. SOCIOECONOMIC STATUS OF CENSUS TRACTS (KOHN)

See also category 14 above.

Kohn, Melvin, "Social Class and the Exercise of Parental Authority," *American Sociological Review*, 24 (June, 1959), pp. 352–366. See p. 353.

19. SOCIOECONOMIC STATUS OF CENSUS TRACTS (MABRY)

See also category 14 above.

Mabry, John H., "Census Tract Variation in Urban Research," *American Sociological Review*, 23 (April, 1958), pp. 193–196. See p. 194.

Mabry, John H., *Census Tract, Street and Road Index of Lexington and Fayette County, Kentucky*, Lexington, Ky.: Office of the City Manager, 1963.

Quinney (1964); see category 14 above.

20. SOCIOECONOMIC STATUS OF CENSUS TRACTS (MAYER, HOULT)

See also category 14 above.

Mayer, Albert J., and Thomas Ford Hoult, "Social Stratification and Combat Survival," *Social Forces*, 34 (December, 1955), pp. 155–159. See p. 156.

Rose, Arnold M., "Distance of Migration and Socioeconomic Status of Migrants," *American Sociological Review*, 23 (August, 1958), pp. 420–423. See p. 421.

21. SOCIOECONOMIC STATUS OF CENSUS TRACTS (MYERS)

See also category 14 above.

Myers, Jerome K., "Note on the Homogeneity of Census Tracts: A Methodological Problem in Urban Ecological Research," *Social Forces*, 32 (May, 1954), pp. 364–366.

22. SOCIOECONOMIC STATUS OF CENSUS TRACTS (TRYON)

See also category 14 above.

Tryon, Robert C., *Identification of Social Areas by Cluster Analysis*, Berkeley, Calif.: University of California Press, 1955.

Lowenthal, Marjorie Fiske, "Social Isolation and Mental Illness in Old Age," *American Sociological Review*, 29 (February, 1964), pp. 54–70. See p. 60.

23. SOCIOECONOMIC STATUS OF CENSUS TRACTS (WILLIE)

See also category 14 above.

Willie, Charles V., "A Research Note on the Changing Associa-

tion Between Infant Mortality and Socio-economic Status,"
Social Forces, 37 (March, 1959), pp. 211–227. See p. 222.

Willie, Charles V., and William B. Rothney, "Racial, Ethnic, and
Income Factors in the Epidemiology of Neonatal Mortality,"
American Sociological Review, 27 (August, 1962), pp.
522–526. See p. 523.

Willie, Charles V., and Anita Gershenovitz, "Juvenile Delinquency in Racially Mixed Areas," *American Sociological Review*, 29 (October, 1964), pp. 740–744. See p. 741.

24. SOCIOECONOMIC STATUS OF CITIES AND SUBURBS (SCHNORE)

Schnore, Leo F., "City-Suburban Income Differentials in Metropolitan Areas," *American Sociological Review*, 27 (April,
1962), pp. 252–255.

Schnore, Leo F., "The Socio-Economic Status of Cities and Suburbs," *American Sociological Review*, 28 (February, 1963),
pp. 76–85. See pp. 77–78.

Farley, Reynolds, "Suburban Persistence," *American Sociological
Review*, 29 (February, 1964), pp. 38–47. See pp. 40–41.

25. SOCIOECONOMIC STATUS OF CITIES AND SUBURBS (TAEU-BER, TAEUBER)

Taeuber, Karl E., and Alma F. Taeuber, "White Migration and
Socio-Economic Differences Between Cities and Suburbs,"
American Sociological Review, 29 (October, 1964), pp.
718–729. See pp. 722–723.

26. SOCIOECONOMIC STATUS OF COUNTIES

Flittie (1957); see category 14 above.

27. SOCIOECONOMIC STATUS OF MUNICIPALITIES

Dye, Thomas R., "The Local-Cosmopolitan Dimension and the
Study of Urban Politics," *Social Forces*, 41 (March, 1963),
pp. 239–246. See p. 241.

URBAN AREAS: URBANIZATION
(FAMILY STATUS)

Shevky, Eshref, and Marilyn Williams, *The Social Areas of Los Angeles*, Berkeley and Los Angeles, Calif.: University of California Press, 1949.

Shevky, Eshref, and Wendell Bell, *Social Area Analysis: Theory, Illustrative Application and Computational Procedures*, Stanford, Calif.: Stanford University Press, 1955.

This dimension of the Shevky-Williams-Bell system of social area analysis is called, variously, urbanization or family status. The index is discussed fully in Urban Areas: Segregation, category 8. For the specific uses and citations of the index, see the references listed under Urban Areas: Socioeconomic Status, category 14.

URBAN AREAS: VARIOUS CATEGORIES

SEE ALSO

Societal Characteristics

1. CENTRALIZATION (DUNCAN, DUNCAN AND MODIFICATIONS)

Duncan, Otis Dudley, and Beverly Duncan, "Residential Distribution and Occupational Stratification," *American Journal of Sociology*, 60 (March, 1955), pp. 493–503. See p. 495.

The index of centralization measures the extent to which a "given occupation tends to be 'decentralized,' or on the average located farther away from the city center than all other occupations." (p. 495) The computational procedures for this index are related to those for the Duncans' indices of dissimilarity and segregation, which are discussed in another part of this volume (see Urban Areas: Segregation, category 6) and are even more similar to the Duncans' index of low-rent concentration (for citations see Urban Areas: Socioeconomic Status, category 3).

The index of centralization is obtained in the following manner: (1) classify census tracts into intervals according to their distance from the center of the city; (2) compute the percentage distribution of residences by zonal intervals "for each occupation group and for all occupations combined" (p. 495); (3) cumulate the distributions from the central to the peripheral zones; (4) evaluate the formula

$$IC = \frac{\Sigma X_{i-1} Y_i - \Sigma X_i Y_{i-1}}{1 - P}$$

where $X_i =$ the cumulated percentage of the given occupation through the ith zonal interval,

$Y_i =$ the cumulated percentage of all occupations combined, and

P = the proportion of the total male employed labor force included in the given occupation.

This procedure is illustrated below utilizing the hypothetical data below. Assume that 10 per cent of the total male labor force is employed in occupation X.

PERCENTAGES AND CUMULATIVE PERCENTAGES OF OCCUPATIONAL GROUP X AND OF ALL EMPLOYED MALES RESIDING IN EACH OF FIVE ZONES

Zone	Occupation X	Cumulative Percentage	Total Employed Males	Cumulative Percentage
I	30	30	40	40
II	20	50	25	65
III	15	65	20	85
IV	20	85	10	95
V	15	100	5	100

$$IC = \frac{27,665 - 27,720}{1 - 0.10} = \frac{-55}{.90} = -61.11$$

The index of centralization varies between 100 and -100, with high positive scores denoting a high degree of centralization.

Redick, Richard W., "Population Growth and Distribution in Central Cities, 1940–50," *American Sociological Review*, 21 (February, 1956), pp. 38–43. See p. 40.

Duncan, Otis Dudley, and Stanley Lieberson, "Ethnic Segregation and Assimilation," *American Journal of Sociology*, 64 (January, 1959), pp. 364–374. See p. 365.

Pappenfort, Donnel M., "The Ecological Field and the Metropolitan Community: Manufacturing and Management," *American Journal of Sociology*, 64 (January, 1959), pp. 380–385. See p. 381.

Collison, Peter, and John Mogey, "Residence and Social Class in Oxford," *American Journal of Sociology*, 64 (May, 1959), pp. 599–605. See p. 603.

Collison, Peter, "Occupation, Education, and Housing in an English City," *American Journal of Sociology*, 65 (May, 1960), pp. 588–597. See p. 595.

Uyeki, Eugene S., "Residential Distribution and Stratification, 1950–60," *American Journal of Sociology*, 69 (March, 1964), pp. 491–498. See p. 495.

2. COMMUNICATION PROBABILITY IN DIFFERENT ETHNIC SEGMENTS

Greenberg, Joseph H., "The Measurement of Linguistic Diversity," *Language*, 32 (January-March, 1956), pp. 109–115.

Lieberson, Stanley, "An Extension of Greenberg's Measures of Linguistic Diversity," *Language*, 40 (October-December, 1964), pp. 526–531.

Lieberson, Stanley, "Bilingualism in Montreal: A Demographic Analysis," *American Journal of Sociology*, 71 (July, 1965), pp. 10–25. See pp. 13–14.

3. CRIME OCCURRENCE (FOUR FACTORS)

Boggs, Sarah L., "Urban Crime Patterns," *American Sociological Review*, 30 (December, 1965), pp. 899–908. See pp. 904–908.

4. DEMOGRAPHICALLY HOMOGENEOUS AREAS

Smith, Joel, "A Method for the Classification of Areas on the Basis of Demographically Homogeneous Populations," *American Sociological Review*, 19 (April, 1954), pp. 201–207. See p. 204.

5. EDUCATIONAL STATUS

Schmid, Calvin F., and Charles E. Nobbe, "Socioeconomic Differentials Among Nonwhite Races," *American Sociological Review*, 39 (December, 1965), pp. 909–922. See p. 912.

6. EQUAL APPORTIONMENT OF STATE LEGISLATURES

Jacob, Herbert, "The Consequences of Malapportionment: A Note of Caution," *Social Forces*, 43 (December, 1964), pp. 256–261. See pp. 257–258.

7. RURAL DOMINANCE OF STATE LEGISLATURES

Jacob; see category 6 above.

8. SOCIAL AND DEMOGRAPHIC DIMENSIONS: ATYPICAL CRIME PATTERN

Schmid, Calvin F., "Urban Crime Areas, Part I," *American Sociological Review*, 25 (August, 1960), pp. 527–542. See p. 537.

9. SOCIAL AND DEMOGRAPHIC DIMENSIONS: LOW MOBILITY GROUPS

Schmid; see category 8 above.

10. SOCIAL AND DEMOGRAPHIC DIMENSIONS: POPULATION MOBILITY

Schmid; see category 8 above.

11. SOCIOECONOMIC STATUS

Nam, Charles B., *Methodology and Scores of Socioeconomic Status*, Washington, D.C.: U.S. Bureau of the Census, Working Paper No. 15, 1963.

Schmid and Nobbe (1965), p. 918; see category 5 above.

12. SPECIALIZATION OF CENSUS TRACTS

Peters, William S., "A Method of Deriving Geographic Patterns of Associated Demographic Characteristics within Urban Areas," *Social Forces*, 35 (October, 1956), pp. 62–68. See p. 64.

Peters, William S., "Cluster Analysis in Urban Demography," *Social Forces*, 37 (October, 1958), pp. 38–44. See p. 39.

13. URBANISM

Jonassen, Christen T., "Functional Unities in Eighty-Eight Community Systems," *American Sociological Review*, 26 (June, 1961), pp. 399–407. See p. 401.

14. URBAN SUBAREAS: DEMOGRAPHIC

Form, William H., Joel Smith, Gregory P. Stone, and James Cowhig, "The Compatibility of Alternative Approaches to the Delimitation of Urban Sub-Areas," *American Sociological Review*, 19 (August, 1954), pp. 434–440. See p. 435.

15. URBAN SUBAREAS: ECOLOGICAL

Form, Smith, Stone, and Cowhig, p. 434; see category 14 above.

16. URBAN SUBAREAS: SOCIAL INTIMACY

Form, Smith, Stone, and Cowhig, p. 436; see category 14 above.

17. URBAN UNDERREPRESENTATION IN STATE LEGISLATURES

Jacob; see category 6 above.

18. WORK-RESIDENCE SEPARATION

Duncan, Beverly, "Factors in Work-Residence Separation: Wage and Salary Workers, Chicago, 1951," *American Sociological Review*, 21 (February, 1956), pp. 48–56. See p. 49.

19. ZONAL REDISTRIBUTION

Duncan (1952); see category 1 above.

Redick (1956); see category 1 above.

VALUES

SEE ALSO

Achievement Motivation
Norms
Personality: General
Work-Value Orientations

1. ACTIVISTIC-PASSIVISTIC ORIENTATION

See also categories 25 and 44 below.

Kluckhohn, Florence R., "Dominant and Substitute Profiles of Cultural Orientations," *Social Forces*, 28 (May, 1950), pp. 376–393.

Rosen, Bernard C., "The Achievement Syndrome: A Psychocultural Dimension of Social Stratification," *American Sociological Review*, 21 (April, 1956), pp. 203–211. See pp. 207–208.

Rosen, Bernard C., "Race, Ethnicity, and the Achievement Syndrome," *American Sociological Review*, 24 (February, 1959), pp. 47–60. See p. 54.

Rosen, Bernard C., "The Achievement Syndrome and Economic Growth in Brazil," *Social Forces*, 42 (March, 1964), pp. 341–354. See p. 348.

2. BIRTH CONTROL, ETHICAL JUDGMENT ABOUT

Rettig, Salomon, and Benjamin Pasamanick, "Differences in Structure and Severity of Moral Judgments by Students and by a Community Sample: Some Observations on Ethical Relativity," *Ohio Journal of Science*, 62 (November, 1962), pp. 317–325. See p. 320.

Rettig, Salomon, "Invariance of Factor Structure of Ethical Judgments by Indian and American College Students," *Sociometry*, 27 (March, 1964), pp. 96–113. See pp. 97–110.

3. COLLECTIVE MORALITY

Rettig, Salomon, and Benjamin Pasamanick, "The Decline in Collective Morality of College Students, 1929–58," mimeographed, no date.

Rettig, Salomon, and Benjamin Pasamanick, "Invariance in Factor Structure of Moral Value Judgments from American and Korean College Students," *Sociometry*, 25 (March, 1962), pp. 73–84. See pp. 75–79.

4. CONCEPTUAL SYSTEM (THIS I BELIEVE TEST)

Brook, Rupert, *Personality Correlates Associated with Differential Success of Affiliation with Alcoholics Anonymous*, unpublished Ph.D. dissertation, University of Colorado, 1962.

Felknar, Catherine, and O. J. Harvey, *Cognitive Determinants of Concept Formation and Attainment*, Technical Report 10, Contract NONR 1147(07), University of Colorado, 1963.

Harvey, O. J., *Cognitive Determinants of Role Playing*, Technical Report 3, Contract NONR 1147(07), University of Colorado, 1963.

Harvey, O. J., *Self Systems, Anomie and Self Esteem*, Technical Report 9, Contract NONR 1147(07), University of Colorado, 1963.

Harvey, O. J., "Some Cognitive Determinants of Influencibility," *Sociometry*, 27 (June, 1964), pp. 208–221. See pp. 212–213.

5. CONSCIENTIOUS OBJECTORS, ATTITUDE TOWARD

Glock, Charles Y., and Benjamin B. Ringer, "Church Policy and the Attitudes of Ministers and Parishioners on Social Issues," *American Sociological Review*, 21 (April, 1956), pp. 148–156. See p. 150.

6. DETERMINISM SCALE

Nettler, Gwynn, "Cruelty, Dignity, and Determinism," *American Sociological Review*, 24 (June, 1959), pp. 375–384. See p. 378.

7. DOMESTIC VALUE CONSENSUS

Farber, Bernard, "An Index of Marital Integration," *Sociometry*, 20 (June, 1957), pp. 117–134. See p. 119.

Kerckhoff, Alan C., and Keith E. Davis, "Value Consensus and

Need Complementarity in Mate Selection," *American Sociological Review*, 27 (June, 1962), pp. 295–303. See p. 297.

8. ECONOMIC MORALITY

Rettig and Pasamanick (no date); see category 3 above.

Rettig, Salomon, and Benjamin Pasamanick, "Changes in Moral Values among College Students: A Factorial Study," *American Sociological Review*, 24 (December, 1959), pp. 856–863. See pp. 862–863.

Rettig, Salomon, and Benjamin Pasamanick, "Differences in the Structure of Moral Values of Students and Alumni," *American Sociological Review*, 25 (August, 1960), pp. 550–555. See p. 550.

Rettig, Salomon, and Benjamin Pasamanick, "Moral Value Structure and Social Class," *Sociometry*, 24 (March, 1961), pp. 21–35. See pp. 25–27.

Rettig and Pasamanick (1962); see category 3 above.

9. ETHICAL ACTIVITY, VALUE OF

Gordon, Robert A., James F. Short, Jr., Desmond S. Cartwright, and Fred L. Strodtbeck, "Values and Gang Delinquency: A Study of Street-Corner Groups," *American Journal of Sociology*, 69 (September, 1963), pp. 109–128. See p. 111.

10. ETHICAL COMMITMENT

Thomas, Edwin J., "Role Conceptions and Organizational Size," *American Sociological Review*, 24 (February, 1959), pp. 30–37. See p. 32.

11. ETHICAL RELATIVISM

Rettig and Pasamanick (1962); see category 2 above.
Rettig (1964); see category 2 above.

12. EXPLOITATIVE-MANIPULATIVE MORALITY

Rettig and Pasamanick (no date); see category 3 above.
Rettig and Pasamanick (1959); see category 8 above.
Rettig and Pasamanick (1960); see category 8 above.
Rettig and Pasamanick (1961); see category 8 above.
Rettig and Pasamanick (1962); see category 3 above.

13. EXTRINSIC REWARD ORIENTATION

Rosenberg, Morris, *Occupations and Values,* Glencoe, Ill.: The Free Press, 1957. See pp. 10–11, 33, and 95–108.

Schwarzweller, Harry K., "Values and Occupational Choice," *Social Forces,* 39 (December, 1960), pp. 126–135. See p. 133.

14. FAMILY MORALITY

Rettig and Pasamanick (no date); see category 3 above.
Rettig and Pasamanick (1959); see category 8 above.
Rettig and Pasamanick (1960); see category 8 above.
Rettig and Pasamanick (1961); see category 8 above.
Rettig and Pasamanick (1962); see category 3 above.

15. FAMILY VALUE POSITION

Litwak, Eugene, *Primary Group Instruments of Social Control,* unpublished Ph.D. dissertation, Columbia University, 1958, pp. 43–47.

Litwak, Eugene, "Voluntary Associations and Neighborhood Cohesion," *American Sociological Review,* 26 (April, 1961), pp. 258–271. See p. 269.

16. FERTILITY VALUE

Yeracaris, Constantine A., "Differentials in the Relationship between Values and Practices in Fertility," *Social Forces,* 38 (December, 1959), pp. 153–158. See p. 153.

17. GENERAL (BASIC) MORALITY

Rettig and Pasamanick (no date); see category 3 above.
Rettig and Pasamanick (1959); see category 8 above.
Rettig and Pasamanick (1960); see category 8 above.
Rettig and Pasamanick (1961); see category 8 above.
Rettig and Pasamanick (1962); see category 3 above.

18. GOAL ORIENTATION

Clark, John P. and Eugene P. Wenninger, "Goal Orientations and Illegal Behavior among Juveniles," *Social Forces,* 42 (October, 1963), pp. 49–59. See p. 52.

19. GOAL ORIENTATION, LOWER-CLASS CULTURE

Clark and Wenninger; see category 18 above.

20. GOAL ORIENTATION, MIDDLE-CLASS STANDARDS

Clark and Wenninger; see category 18 above.

21. GOVERNMENT CONTROL, ATTITUDE TOWARD

Glock and Ringer; see category 5 above.

22. HUMAN RIGHTS, ATTITUDE TOWARD

Glock and Ringer; see category 5 above.

23. ILLICIT SEX, ETHICAL JUDGMENTS ABOUT

Rettig and Pasamanick (1962); see category 2 above.
Rettig (1964); see category 2 above.

24. IMMIGRATION, ATTITUDE TOWARD

Glock and Ringer; see category 5 above.

25. INDIVIDUALISTIC-FAMILISTIC ORIENTATION

See also categories 1 above and 44 below.
Kluckhohn (1950); see category 1 above.
Rosen (1956); see category 1 above.
Rosen (1959); see category 1 above.
Rosen (1964); see category 1 above.

26. INFINITE VALUES, IDENTIFICATION PROCEDURE

Catton, William R., Jr., "Exploring Techniques for Measuring Human Values," *American Sociological Review,* 19 (February, 1954), pp. 49–55. See p. 53.

27. INFINITE VALUES, PAIRED COMPARISONS PROCEDURE

Catton; see category 26 above.

28. INFINITE VALUES, RANK ORDER PROCEDURE

Catton; see category 26 above.

29. INNER-OTHER DIRECTED CONTINUUM

Olmstead, Michael S., "Character and Social Role," *American Journal of Sociology,* 63 (July, 1957), pp. 49–57. See p. 52.

30. INNER-OTHER DIRECTEDNESS

Dornbusch, Sanford M. and Lauren C. Hickman, "Other-Directedness in Consumer-Goods Advertising: A Test of Riesman's Historical Theory," *Social Forces,* 38 (December, 1959), pp. 99–102. See p. 100.

31. INNER-OTHER SOCIAL PREFERENCE

Kassarjian, Waltraud M., "A Study of Riesman's Theory of Social Character," *Sociometry*, 25 (September, 1962), pp. 213–230. See pp. 226–230.

Centers, Richard, "An Examination of the Riesman Social Character Typology: A Metropolitan Survey," *Sociometry*, 25 (September, 1962), pp. 231–240. See p. 235.

32. INTERMARRIAGE, ATTITUDE TOWARD

Glock and Ringer; see category 5 above.

33. LABOR, ATTITUDE TOWARD

Glock and Ringer; see category 5 above.

34. LEISURE ACTIVITY, VALUE OF

Gordon, Short, Cartwright, and Strodtbeck; see category 9 above.

35. LOCAL-COSMOPOLITAN

Dye, Thomas R., "The Local-Cosmopolitan Dimension and the Study of Urban Politics," *Social Forces*, 41 (March, 1963), pp. 239–246. See p. 241.

36. MORAL IDEALS

Scott, William A., "Empirical Assessment of Values and Ideologies," *American Sociological Review*, 24 (June, 1959), pp. 299–310. See pp. 302–303.

37. MORAL JUDGMENT

Turner, Ralph H., "Self and Other in Moral Judgment," *American Sociological Review*, 19 (June, 1954), pp. 249–259. See pp. 250–256 and 259.

38. MORAL JUDGMENTS

Crissman, Paul, "Temporal Changes and Sexual Difference in Moral Judgments," *Journal of Social Psychology*, 16 (August, 1942), pp. 29–38. See pp. 29–31.

Crissman, Paul, "Temporal Changes and Sexual Difference in Moral Judgments," *University of Wyoming Publication*, 15 (July, 1950), pp. 57–68.

Rettig and Pasamanick (1959), pp. 856–857; see category 8 above.

39. MORALITY-IMMORALITY

Sutcliffe, J. P., and M. Haberman, "Factors Influencing Choice in Role Conflict Situations," *American Sociological Review*, 21 (December, 1956), pp. 695–703. See p. 702.

40. NATIONAL GOALS

Carter, Roy E., Jr., "An Experiment in Value Measurement," *American Sociological Review*, 21 (April, 1956), pp. 156–163. See pp. 157–158 and 161–163.

41. PEOPLE ORIENTATION

Rosenberg (1957); see category 13 above.

Schwarzweller (1960); see category 13 above.

42. PERSONAL VALUES

Scott, William A., "Cognitive Consistency, Response Reinforcement, and Attitude Change," *Sociometry*, 22 (September, 1959), pp. 219–229. See pp. 223–224.

43. POLITICAL ROLE OF THE CHURCH, ATTITUDE TOWARD

Glock and Ringer; see category 5 above.

44. PRESENT-FUTURE ORIENTATION

See also categories 1 and 25 above.

Kluckhohn (1950); see category 1 above.

Rosen (1956); see category 1 above.

Rosen (1959); see category 1 above.

Rosen (1964); see category 1 above.

45. PUBLIC DEPENDENCY, ORIENTATION TOWARD

Anderson, C. Leroy, "Development of an Objective Measure of Orientation toward Public Dependence," *Social Forces*, 44 (September, 1965), pp. 107–113. See p. 112.

46. PURITANICAL MORALITY

Rettig and Pasamanick (no date); see category 3 above.

Rettig and Pasamanick (1959); see category 8 above.

Rettig and Pasamanick (1960); see category 8 above.

Rettig and Pasamanick (1961); see category 8 above.

Rettig and Pasamanick (1962); see category 3 above.

47. RELIGIOUS MORALITY

Rettig and Pasamanick (no date); see category 3 above.

Rettig and Pasamanick (1959); see category 8 above.
Rettig and Pasamanick (1960); see category 8 above.
Rettig and Pasamanick (1961); see category 8 above.
Rettig and Pasamanick (1962); see category 3 above.

48. RURAL LIVING, OPINION ABOUT

Anderson, W. A., "Rural Living Opinion Scale (Short Form)," A *Study of the Values in Rural Living*, Part IV, Cornell University Agricultural Experiment Station, Department of Rural Sociology, Rural Sociology Publication 22, September, 1949.

Fava, Sylvia Fleis, "Suburbanism as a Way of Life," *American Sociological Review*, 21 (February, 1956), pp. 34–37. See p. 37.

49. SELECTIVE VALUES

Magistretti, Franca, "Sociological Factors in the Structuring of Industrial Workers' Teams," *American Journal of Sociology*, 60 (May, 1955), pp. 536–540. See p. 537.

50. SELF-EXPRESSION ORIENTATION

Rosenberg (1957); see category 13 above.
Schwarzweller (1960); see category 13 above.

51. SOCIOMETRIC VALUES

Eng, Erling W., "An Approach to the Prediction of Sociometric Choice," *Sociometry*, 17 (November, 1954), pp. 329–339. See p. 330.

52. STUDENT VALUE HIERARCHY

Wallace, Walter L., "Institutional and Life-Cycle Socialization of College Freshmen," *American Journal of Sociology*, 70 (November, 1964), pp. 303–318. See p. 305.

53. TASK VALUES

Turk, Herman, "Instrumental Values and the Popularity of Instrumental Leaders," *Social Forces*, 39 (March, 1961), pp. 252–260. See p. 254.

54. UNDERDOG MORALITY

Rettig and Pasamanick (1962); see category 2 above.
Rettig (1964); see category 2 above.

55. UNITED NATIONS, ATTITUDE TOWARD

Glock and Ringer; see category 5 above.

56. VALUE ANALYSIS

Eng; see category 51 above.

57. VALUE ORIENTATION

Landis, Judson R., Simon Dinitz, and Walter C. Reckless, "Implementing Two Theories of Delinquency: Value Orientation and Awareness of Limited Opportunity," *Sociology and Social Research*, 47 (July, 1963), pp. 408–416.

Landis, Judson R., and Frank R. Scarpitti, "Perceptions Regarding Value Orientation and Legitimate Opportunity: Delinquents and Non-Delinquents," *Social Forces*, 44 (September, 1965), pp. 83–91. See pp. 84–85.

58. VALUE PROFILE

Bales, Robert F. and Arthur S. Couch, "The Value Profile: A Factor Analytic Study of Value Statements," paper read at the 54th annual meeting of the American Sociological Society, 1959.

Bales, Robert F., and Arthur S. Couch, "The Value Profile Form F," unpublished, no date.

Marak, George E., Jr., "The Evolution of Leadership Structure." *Sociometry*, 27 (June, 1964), pp. 174–182. See p. 176.

Peterson, Richard A., "Dimensions of Social Character: An Empirical Exploration of the Riesman Typology," *Sociometry*, 27 (June, 1964), pp. 194–207. See p. 197.

Scott, Frances G., "Family Group Structure and Patterns of Social Interaction," *American Journal of Sociology*, 68 (September, 1962), pp. 214–228. See p. 215.

59. VALUE RELEVANCE

Turner, Ralph H., "Reference Groups of Future-Oriented Men," *Social Forces*, 34 (December, 1955), pp. 130–136. See p. 131.

60. VALUES, STUDY OF

Allport, Gordon W., Phillip E. Vernon, and Gardner Lindzey, *Study of Values*, Boston, Mass.: Houghton Mifflin Co., 1960.

Study of Values, based upon Eduard Spranger's *Types of Men,* "aims to measure the relative prominence of six basic interests or motives in personality: the *theoretical, economic, aesthetic, social, political,* and *religious.*"

The test is divided into two parts. Part I presents 30 "controversial statements or questions" such as the following: "The main object of scientific research should be the discovery of truth rather than its practical application. (a) yes; (b) no." The respondent is asked to indicate the strength of his agreement with one or the other alternative by answering respectively either 3, 0; 0, 3; 2, 1; or 1, 2. Part II of the test presents 15 "situations or questions . . . followed by four possible attitudes or answers." The subject is asked to rank the response alternatives according to his personal preferences, giving 4 to his first choice and 3, 2, and 1 respectively to the remaining choices.

Each page of the test booklet is so arranged that the subject's responses when summed yield six separate subtotals. Each of these subtotals, in turn, contributes to one of the six total scores for each of the six value areas listed above. The six value totals may then be plotted on a graph which results in a profile of the individual's theoretical, economic, aesthetic, social, political, and religious values.

Copies of *Study of Values* and accompanying instruction booklets may be purchased from Houghton Mifflin Company, 2 Park Street, Boston, Mass. 02107. For an extensive bibliography concerning *Study of Values* (280 citations) and for reviews and assessments of *Study of Values,* see Oscar K. Buros (ed.), *The Sixth Mental Measurements Yearbook,* Highland Park, N.J.: The Gryphon Press, 1965, pp. 381–387.

Back, Kurt W., Robert E. Coker, Jr., Thomas G. Donnelly, and Bernard S. Phillips, "Public Health as a Career in Medicine: Secondary Choices Within a Profession," *American Sociological Review,* 23 (October, 1958), pp. 533–541. See p. 536.

Lindzey, Gardner, and James A. Urdan, "Personality and Social Choice," *Sociometry,* 17 (February, 1954), pp. 47–63. See p. 49.

Nimkoff, Meyer F., and Charles M. Grigg, "Values and Marital Adjustment of Nurses," *Social Forces*, 37 (October, 1958), pp. 67–70. See p. 68.

Schellenberg, James A., "Homogamy in Personal Values and the 'Field of Eligibles,' " *Social Forces*, 39 (December, 1960), pp. 157–162. See pp. 159–160.

Schuman, Howard, and John Harding, "Prejudice and the Norm of Rationality," *Sociometry*, 27 (September, 1964), pp. 353–371. See p. 366.

61. WAR, ATTITUDE TOWARD

Glock and Ringer; see category 5 above.

62. WAR, ETHICAL JUDGMENT ABOUT

Rettig and Pasamanick (1962); see category 2 above.

Rettig (1964); see category 2 above.

63. WAYS TO LIVE

Morris, Charles, and Lyle V. Jones, "Value Scales and Dimensions," *Journal of Abnormal and Social Psychology*, 51 (November, 1955), pp. 523–535. See pp. 524–532.

Morris, Charles W., *Varieties of Human Value*, Chicago, Ill.: University of Chicago Press, 1956, pp. 15–19.

Jones, Lyle V., and R. Darrell Bock, "Multiple Discriminant Analysis Applied to 'Ways to Live' Ratings from Six Cultural Groups," *Sociometry*, 23 (June, 1960), pp. 162–176. See p. 162.

WORK-VALUE ORIENTATIONS

SEE ALSO
Aspirations
Occupational Roles
Values

1. ANTI-GOVERNMENT-REGULATION VALUES (STRAUS)

Photiadis, John D., "The American Business Creed and Denominational Identification," *Social Forces*, 44 (September, 1965), pp. 92–100. See p. 94.

2. ANTI-LABOR-ORIENTATION VALUES (STRAUS)

Photiadis; see category 1 above.

3. ANTI-WELFARE-STATE VALUES (STRAUS)

Photiadis; see category 1 above.

4. ATTITUDE TOWARD MOBILITY

Seeman, Melvin, "Social Mobility and Administrative Behavior," *American Sociological Review*, 23 (December, 1958), pp. 633–642. See p. 635.

Silberstein, Fred B., and Melvin Seeman, "Social Mobility and Prejudice," *American Journal of Sociology*, 55 (November, 1959), pp. 258–264. See p. 259.

Neal, Arthur G., and Melvin Seeman, "Organizations and Powerlessness: A Test of the Mediation Hypothesis," *American Sociological Review*, 29 (April, 1964), pp. 216–225. See p. 219.

5. CAREER-ORIENTATIONS ANCHORAGE

Tausky, Curt, and Robert Dubin, "Career Anchorage: Managerial Mobility Motivations," *American Sociological Review*, 30 (October, 1965), pp. 725–735. See pp. 726–729.

6. CAREERIST ORIENTATION

Wilensky, Harold L., "The Professionalization of Everyone?" *American Journal of Sociology*, 70 (September, 1964), pp. 137–158. See pp. 152–154.

7. CHANGE IN CAREER PREFERENCE

Gottlieb, David, "Processes of Socialization in American Graduate Schools," *Social Forces*, 40 (December, 1961), pp. 124–131. See p. 126.

8. COMMITMENT TO WORK VALUES

Westoff, Charles F., Marvin Bressler, and Philip C. Sagi, "The Concept of Social Mobility: An Empirical Inquiry," *American Sociological Review*, 25 (June, 1960), pp. 375–385. See p. 382.

Westoff, Charles F., Robert G. Potter, Jr., Philip C. Sagi, and Elliot G. Mishler, *Family Growth in Metropolitan America*, Princeton: Princeton University Press, 1961, pp. 383–400.

Bressler, Marvin, and Charles F. Westoff, "Catholic Education, Economic Values, and Achievement," *American Journal of Sociology*, 69 (November, 1963), pp. 225–233. See p. 228.

Segal, Bernard E., and Peter K. Thomsen, "Status Orientation and Ethnic Sentiments among Undergraduates," *American Journal of Sociology*, 71 (July, 1965), pp. 60–67. See p. 63.

9. COMPETITION VALUES (STRAUS)

Photiadis; see category 1 above.

10. COMPETITIVE MOBILITY ORIENTATION

Seeman (1958); see category 4 above.

Neal, Arthur G., and Salomon Rettig, "Dimensions of Alienation among Manual and Non-Manual Workers," *American Sociological Review*, 28 (August, 1963), pp. 599–608. See p. 603.

11. DIGNITY OF WORK VALUES (STRAUS)

Photiadis; see category 1 above.

12. FACTORS INFLUENCING CHOICE OF A PROFESSION

Back, Kurt W., Robert E. Coker, Jr., Thomas G. Donnelly, and Bernard S. Phillips, "Public Health as a Career of Medicine:

Secondary Choice within a Profession," *American Sociological Review*, 23 (October, 1958), pp. 533–541. See p. 541.

Stiles, W. W., and Lois C. Watson, "Motivation of Persons Electing Public Health as a Career," *American Journal of Public Health*, 45 (December, 1955), pp. 1563–1568. See pp. 1563–1565.

13. GENERAL DRIVE TO GET AHEAD

Westoff, Bressler, and Sagi (1960), p. 381; see category 8 above.
Bressler and Westoff (1963); see category 8 above.

14. IMPORTANCE ATTACHED TO GETTING AHEAD

Westoff, Bressler, and Sagi (1960), p. 381; see category 8 above.
Bressler and Westoff (1960); see category 8 above.
Westoff, Potter, Sagi, and Mishler (1961); see category 8 above.

15. INDEX OF SUCCESS THEMES

Rubin, Morton, "Localism and Related Values Among Negroes in a Southern Rural Community," *Social Forces*, 36 (March, 1958), pp. 263–267. See p. 264.

16. INDIVIDUALISM VALUES (STRAUS)

Photiadis; see category 1 above.

17. INVESTMENT VALUES (STRAUS)

Photiadis; see category 1 above.

18. LEISURE ORIENTATION

Segal and Thomsen (1965); see category 8 above.

19. MATERIALISM AND PRACTICALITY VALUES (STRAUS)

Photiadis; see category 1 above.

20. MOBILITY-ACHIEVEMENT SCALE

Seeman (1958); see category 4 above.
Neal and Rettig (1963); see category 10 above.
Silberstein and Seeman (1959); see category 4 above.

21. MOBILITY COMMITMENT RELATIVE TO COMMUNAL VALUES

Seeman (1958); see category 4 above.
Neal and Rettig (1963); see category 10 above.

22. MOBILITY COMMITMENT RELATIVE TO INTRINSIC VALUES

Seeman (1958); see category 4 above.

Neal and Rettig (1963); see category 10 above.

23. OCCUPATIONAL CAREER

Neugarten, Bernice L., Joan W. Moore, and John C. Lowe, "Age Norms, Age Constraint and Adult Socialization," *American Journal of Sociology*, 70 (May, 1965), pp. 710–717. See p. 713.

24. OCCUPATIONAL PREFERENCE INSTRUMENT

Morlock, James E., *Predicting Delinquency in a Homogeneous Group of Pre-Adolescent Boys*, unpublished Ph.D. dissertation, Ohio State University, 1947.

Reckless, Walter C., Simon Dinitz, and Ellen Murray, "Self-Concept as an Insulator Against Delinquency," *American Sociological Review*, 21 (December, 1956), pp. 744–746. See p. 744.

25. OPTIMUM SIZE VALUES (STRAUS)

Photiadis; see category 1 above.

26. PERSONAL FREEDOM AND RESPONSIBILITY INDEX AND PLANNING AND CONTROL INDEX

Neal and Rettig (1963); see category 10 above.

27. PREFERENCE FOR WORK

Wilensky, Harold L., "Mass Society and Mass Culture: Interdependence or Independence?" *American Sociological Review*, 29 (April, 1964), pp. 173–197. See p. 185.

28. STATUS SATISFACTION, LEVEL OF HUSBAND'S

Westoff, Bressler, and Sagi (1960), pp. 381–382; see category 8 above.

29. RISK-WILLINGNESS VALUES (STRAUS)

Photiadis; see category 1 above.

30. VALUE DEPRIVATION, EXPECTED

Phillips, Bernard S., "Expected Value Deprivation and Occupational Preference," *Sociometry*, 27 (June, 1964), pp. 151–160. See pp. 153–155.

31. VALUE OF CLOSE PATIENT RELATIONSHIPS

Phillips; see category 30 above.

32. VALUE OF CONTINUED LEARNING
Phillips; see category 30 above.
33. VALUE OF HELPING PEOPLE
Phillips; see category 30 above.
34. VALUE OF HIGH INCOME
Phillips; see category 30 above.
35. VALUE OF HOURS NOT EXTREMELY LONG
Phillips; see category 30 above.
36. VALUE OF INVOLVEMENT WITH COMPLEX PROBLEMS
Phillips; see category 30 above.
37. VALUE OF PRESTIGE AMONG COLLEAGUES
Phillips; see category 30 above.
38. VALUE OF RESEARCH ACTIVITIES
Phillips; see category 30 above.
39. VALUE OF UTILIZING ABILITIES
Phillips; see category 30 above.
40. VALUE OF WORK WITHOUT GREAT PHYSICAL EXERTION
Phillips; see category 30 above.
41. WILLINGNESS TO SACRIFICE IDEOLOGICAL VALUES TO GET AHEAD
Westoff, Bressler, and Sagi (1960), p. 381; see category 8 above.
Bressler and Westoff (1960); see category 8 above.
42. WILLINGNESS TO SACRIFICE SOCIAL INTERESTS TO GET AHEAD
Bressler and Westoff (1960); see category 8 above.
43. WORK BELIEFS CHECK LIST
Haller, A. O., *The MSU Work Beliefs Check List*, Department of Sociology and Anthropology, Michigan State University, 1957.
Haller, A. O., "Planning to Farm: A Social Psychological Interpretation," *Social Forces*, 37 (March, 1959), pp. 263–268. See p. 265.
44. WORK ORIENTATION INDEX
Riedel, D. C., *Personal Adjustment to Perceived and Medically*

Established Heart Disease, unpublished Ph.D. dissertation, Purdue University, 1958.

Goldstein, Bernice, and Robert L. Eichhorn, "The Changing Protestant Ethic: Rural Patterns in Health, Work, and Leisure," *American Sociological Review,* 26 (August, 1961), pp. 557–565. See p. 558.

Dick, Harry R., 198
Dickoff, Hilda, 297
Dickson, Lenore, 347–348, 349
Dill, William R., 233
Dillingham, Harry C., 317
Dinitz, Simon, 41, 94, 95, 97, 98, 176, 180, 224, 228, 229, 231, 250, 253, 363, 387, 512, 518
Dirksen, James, 197
Dodd, Stuart Carter, 128, 155
Dodge, Joan S., 169, 324
Donald, Marjorie N., 263, 369, 396
Donnelly, Thomas G., 85, 224, 225, 282, 513, 516–517
Donohue, George A., 85, 324
Doob, Leonard W., 164
Dornbusch, Sanford M., 72, 267, 317, 318, 320, 322, 324, 508
Douvan, Elizabeth, 321
Drake, Joseph T., 138
Dubin, Robert, 515
Duncan, Beverly, ix, 13, 430–431, 431–432, 471, 472–474, 475, 484, 491, 495, 499–500, 503
Duncan, Otis Dudley, viii, ix, xiii, 13, 157, 356, 399, 420, 430–431, 434, 436, 437, 439–440, 471, 472–474, 475, 484, 489, 491, 499–500, 503
Dunphy, Dexter, 333, 341, 342
Dunphy, Howard, 127, 367
Duvall, Evelyn Millis, 120–121
Dye, Thomas R., 497, 509
Dyer, William G., 180–181
Dymond, Rosalind F., 293, 318, 319, 322
Dynes, Russell R., 41, 312, 313, 411, 416, 431

Eager, Joan, 52
Eckland, Bruce K., 233, 441
Edwards, Alba M., 355–356, 423–429, 450
Edwards, Allen L., vii, 13, 14, 15, 19, 281–282
Eells, Kenneth, 388–394, 450–452
Egeland, Janice A., 494
Ehle, Emily, 192, 195

Ehrlich, Howard J., 163, 168, 197, 241
Eichhorn, Robert L., 311, 520
Eilbert, Leo, 258
Elder, Glen H., Jr., 108, 114, 115, 288, 293, 305, 379
Eldersveld, Samuel J., 195, 309
Ellenbogen, Bertram L., 430
Elliott, Rodney D., 181
Ellis, Robert A., 18, 39, 66, 139, 359, 381, 385–386, 387, 396, 398, 404, 449, 460
Emerson, Richard M., 88, 245–246, 280, 328, 350, 352
Emmerich, Walter, 113, 454
Empey, LaMar T., 42, 416, 420
Emrich, Robert, 170, 233, 234
Eng, Erling W., 512
Erbe, William, 28, 36, 309, 367, 399, 441
Erickson, Eugene C., 197
Eulau, Heinz, 195, 309
Evan, William M., 203, 249, 366
Evans, John W., 38, 74, 126, 223, 228, 229, 230, 252
Exline, Ralph V., 178, 201, 235, 295, 328, 333, 334, 345, 351
Eysenck, H. J., 166, 261

Fahlberg, Nancy, 267, 293
Fanelli, A. Alexander, 68, 189, 195, 395
Fararo, Thomas J., 189, 191, 192, 197, 198
Farber, Bernard, 92, 112, 120, 214–215, 217, 220, 490, 494, 495, 505
Farley, Reynolds, 497
Farr, Nellie Louise, 375
Faunce, William A., 2n, 129, 223, 226, 418
Fava, Sylvia Fleis, 244, 511
Fay, R. J., 255
Feagin, Joe R., 89, 136, 240–241, 313
Feder, Gloria J., 88
Feigenbaum, Kenneth, 263, 369, 399
Feinhandler, Sherwin J., 397
Feld, Sheila, 21, 22, 262

Goodacre, D. M., III, 255
Goodchilds, Jacqueline D., 200, 287–288, 323, 325, 338, 399
Goode, William J., 373, 429
Goodman, Leo A., 357, 358
Gordon, Leonard V., 266
Gordon, Norman B., 56, 136, 232, 234, 236, 295
Gordon, Robert A., 506, 509
Gordon, Wayne C., 191
Goslin, David A., 140
Gottheil, Edward, 173, 175, 179
Gottlieb, David, 105, 395, 516
Gough, Harrison G., vi, 13, 14, 93, 94, 95, 265, 274, 276, 284, 297, 380
Grafton, Thomas H., 150
Graham, Elaine, 267
Graham, Saxon, 132, 430
Grayson, Harry M., 296
Greeley, Andrew M., 105, 239, 311, 399
Green, Norman E., 492, 495
Greenberg, Joseph H., 501
Greene, Helen Finch, 121, 221
Greenfield, Robert W., 128, 145, 419
Greer, Scott, 244, 309, 489, 490, 493, 494, 495
Gregory, C. L., 236, 358, 432, 433
Grigg, Charles M., 36, 146, 214, 303, 514
Gronlund, Norman E., 178, 333, 350
Gross, Edward, 65, 83, 181, 183, 326, 338, 339, 418, 434, 435
Gross, Herbert W., 270
Gross, Llewellyn, 219
Gross, Neal, 103, 105
Grumman, Donald L., 170
Grusky, Oscar, 58, 79, 85, 86, 189, 198, 225, 259
Guba, E. G., 139, 177, 267
Guetzkow, Harold, 233
Guilford, J. P., 266, 271, 272, 273, 284–285
Gullahorn, Jeanne E., 251
Gullahorn, John T., 251
Gulley, William H., 59, 73, 80, 361

Gumpert, Peter, 295
Gurin, Gerald, 22, 262, 355
Gursslin, Orville, 438
Gusfield, Joseph R., 353, 419, 420, 431

Haas, J. Eugene, 250, 251, 253
Haber, Lawrence D., 436
Haberman, M., 52, 89, 222, 247, 258, 277, 455, 510
Haer, John L., 62, 190, 394–395, 396
Hagedorn, Robert B., 87, 199, 200, 201, 203, 251
Hagood, Margaret Jarman, 3
Hagstrom, Warren O., 23, 66, 103, 302
Hajda, Jan, 28, 254
Hakerlein, Bernard J., 88
Hall, John R., 421–422
Hall, Richard H., 59, 78, 79, 80, 81
Hall, Robert L., 32, 65, 202, 233, 340, 342
Hallenbeck, Wilbur C., 313
Haller, Archie O., 19, 39, 41, 42, 120, 131, 235, 238, 257, 260, 266, 269, 404, 416, 417–418, 460, 461, 519
Halpin, Andrew W., 184, 185–186, 187, 188
Hamblin, Robert L., 82, 111, 114, 116, 180, 304, 323
Hamilton, G. V., 208–209
Hamilton, Horace, 380
Hammond, Philip E., 314
Hansen, Alvin H., 441
Hanson, Robert C., 184, 189, 197, 252
Haratani, T., 168
Harburg, Ernest, 119, 177
Harding, John, 153, 513
Hardt, Robert H., 126, 381, 397
Hardyck, Curtis, 149
Hare, Paul A., 175, 255, 274
Harlan, William H., 430
Harland, Carrol, 103
Harper, Dean H., 143
Harrington, Charles, 174
Harris, Chester W., 108, 109, 110

Lipset, Seymour Martin, 54, 267, 307, 437, 454
Lipsitz, Lewis, 56
Litt, Edgar, 67, 102, 300, 303, 304, 305, 306, 307, 313
Littman, Richard A., 453
Litwak, Eugene, 122, 177, 208, 214, 244, 272, 356, 436, 463, 507
Liu, William T., 73, 149, 153, 207, 311, 312, 366, 367
Liverant, Shephard, v, 28, 294
Locke, Harvey J., vii, xiii, xiv, 13, 209–214, 215
Loeb, Martin B., 361
Longabaugh, Richard, 176, 179
Loomis, Charles P., 65, 139, 245, 246, 247, 346, 349
Lopes, Brandao, 397
Lopreato, Joseph, 227, 359, 387, 460
Lowe, John C., 245, 518
Lowell, Edgar, 19, 20–22, 281
Lowenthal, Leo, 267
Lowenthal, Marjorie Fiske, 36, 38, 126, 182, 362, 496
Luckey, Eleanore Braun, 176, 214, 215
Lundberg, George A., 347–348, 349, 441
Lundy, Richard M., 173, 268, 276, 319, 320, 341
Lystad, Mary H., 356, 433

Mabry, John H., 496
McCaffrey, Isabel, 361
McCallum, Margaret E., 272
MacCannell, Earle H., 491–492
McClelland, David C., v, 13, 20–22, 24, 26, 113, 281
McClosky, Herbert, vii, xiv, 11, 14, 18, 30, 37, 56, 95, 130, 137, 141, 255, 256, 259, 262, 264, 274, 281, 286, 287, 293, 294, 295, 296, 298, 299, 300–302, 303, 304, 306, 307, 311, 322, 400
Maccoby, Eleanor E., 438–439
Maccoby, Herbert, 309
McComas, James D., 105, 106, 181

McCord, Joan, 109, 114, 115, 116, 220
McCord, William, 109, 114, 115, 116, 220
McCormack, Thelma H., 53, 188, 190, 411
McCormick, Thomas C., 143, 148, 150, 304, 307
McDill, Edward L., 35, 36, 37, 38, 55, 103, 136, 240, 306
McDonagh, Edward C., 422, 423
McDonald, Margaret R., 386
MacDougall, Evelyn, 214
McEachern, Alexander, 105
McElrath, Dennis C., 490, 495
McGarvey, H. R., 247
McGinn, Noel F., 119, 177
McGinnis, Robert, 207, 218
McGuire, Carson, 343, 429
McGuire, William J., 125, 268
Mack, Raymond W., 81, 182, 249, 354, 356, 359
McKee, James B., 379, 438
McKee, John P., 221, 319, 320
McKinley, J. C., 261, 263, 267, 276, 295, 297
McKinney, John C., 245, 246, 247
MacKinnon, William J., 52, 53, 437
McLemore, S. Dale, 4n
McNemar, Quinn, 238
McPartland, Thomas, 87, 321
McRae, Duncan, Jr., 302, 309–310, 377–378, 379, 491
McRae, Edith K., 310, 379
McTavish, Donald G., 421, 440, 441
Madden, Richard, 17
Maddox, George L., 182, 263, 360
Madigan, Francis C., 372
Maehr, Martin L., 322
Magistretti, Franca, 511
Mahar, Pauline Moller, 154, 157
Maisonneuve, Jean, 269, 344
Malm, F. Theodore, 437
Mangus, A. R., 176
Manheim, Henry L., 236, 271, 337
Manis, Jerome G., 62, 126
Manley, Charles R., Jr., 279, 354, 359

Morgan, Christiana D., 20
Morland, Kenneth J., 144, 453–454
Morlock, James E., 518
Morris, Charles W., 514
Morris, Richard T., 434
Morris, Ruth R., 119
Morrison, H. William, 26
Morse, Nancy C., 151, 431
Moser, C. A., 422
Motz, Annabelle B., 135, 150, 153, 221
Moulton, Robert, 23, 26, 409, 419
Mouton, Jane S., 176
Mowrer, O. Hobart, 254
Muir, Donal E., 495
Mulder, Mauk, 60
Muldoon, John F., 64, 350
Mulford, Harold, 87
Munson, Byron E., 243, 432
Murphy, A. C., 343
Murphy, Albert J., 205
Murphy, Raymond J., 354, 356, 359, 434
Murray, Ellen, 94, 95, 97, 518
Murray, Henry A., v, 13, 19, 20, 120, 170, 268, 270, 274, 278, 280, 281, 283
Murray, John S., 204, 206
Musick, Virginia A., 262, 268
Mussen, Paul H., 108, 109, 110, 143, 297
Myers, Isabel Briggs, 267
Myers, Jerome K., 382, 411, 496

Nafzger, Samuel, 322
Nam, Charles B., 401, 434, 465, 502
Naroll, Raoul, 374
Nash, Dennison J., 270, 437
Neal, Arthur G., xiv, 14, 28–30, 36, 37, 38, 307, 358, 515, 516, 517, 518
Nefzger, M. Dean, 258, 260, 434
Nelson, Lowry, 111
Nelson, M. J., 235
Nettler, Gwynn v, xiv, 14, 30–33, 87, 89, 90, 93, 98, 100, 261, 264, 287, 307, 505
Neugarten, Bernice L., 245, 518
Newcomb, Theodore M., 246

Newell, David S., 361
Nichols, Ralph R., 449
Nimkoff, Meyer F., 214, 514
Nobbe, Charles E., 501, 502
Noel, Donald L., 151, 152
North, Cecil C., viii, 3n, 11–12, 13, 15, 41, 357, 410–417, 439–440
Northway, Mary L., 125, 268, 272, 349, 350–351
Novak, Edwin, 395
Nowak, Stefan, 303, 455
Nye, F. Ivan, vi, xiv, 95, 96–97, 107, 214, 295, 417, 420

Ogburn, William F., 375, 376, 431
Older, H. J., 47, 51
Oleson, Virginia, 381, 387, 396, 398, 404
Olmsted, Donald W., 195, 329, 345, 366
Olmsted, Michael S., 327, 336, 337, 350, 508
Olson, Philip, 435
Olson, Virgil J., 96, 97, 417, 420
Omari, Thompson Peter, 68, 401
O'Neil, W. M., 52
Opler, Marvin K., 125–126
Orenstein, Alan M., 235, 248–249, 404
Orleans, Peter, 309, 490, 495
O'Rourke, John F., 116, 120, 329, 331, 333
Osgood, Charles E., 82, 321, 420
Osmond, Marie W., 375
Osoinach, John C., 490, 494, 495
Ostrom, Vincent, 195
Otis, Arthur S., 236
Ott, J. Steven, 73

Padgett, L. Vincent, 196
Palmore, Erdman B., 157, 175, 230
Pappenfort, Donnell M., 469, 500
Parenti, Anita Negrin, 178, 259, 268, 339, 351
Parish, William L., 310, 372
Park, George K., 455
Park, Robert E., 154
Parker, Frederick B., 277
Parsons, Oscar A., 297

509, 510, 511, 514, 516, 517, 518
Rhead, Clifton C., 176
Rhodes, Albert L., 106, 420, 436, 437
Rhodes, Lewis, 37, 436
Rhyne, Edwin Hoffman, 55, 136, 151, 153, 157
Richardson, Arthur H., 27, 33, 37, 56, 62, 117, 243, 299, 316, 354
Riddleberger, Alice B., 135, 150, 153
Ridley, Jeanne Clare, 36, 38, 306
Riedel, D. C., 519–520
Riley, John W., Jr., 87, 170, 174, 178, 346–347, 349, 350
Riley, Matilda White, 78, 87, 170, 174, 178, 346–347, 349, 350, 351
Rinehart, James W., 163, 168
Ringer, Benjamin, 314, 505, 507, 508, 509, 510, 512, 514
Rivera, Julius, 45, 396, 438
Rivera, Raymond, 98, 99, 100
Roach, Jack L., 438
Roberts, Alan H., 35, 52, 135
Robertson, Richard J., 18
Robinson, James A., 72
Roby, Thornton B., 340
Rogers, Carl, 269
Rogers, L. E., 228
Rogoff, Natalie, 353, 359
Rohwer, Robert A., 122
Rokeach, Milton, vii, xiii, xiv, 14, 35, 52, 135, 288–292
Rooks, Margaret McCallum, 272, 351
Roper, Elmo, 309
Rosanoff, A. J., 169
Rose, Arnold M., 35, 36, 93, 229, 260, 496
Rose, Edward, 336, 370–371, 374
Rosen, Bernard C., 20, 22, 23, 24, 26, 41, 108, 109, 110, 313–314, 317, 329, 338, 397, 417, 504, 508, 510
Rosen, Sidney, 108, 281, 287, 294, 322, 386, 387, 388

Rosenbaum, M. E., 323
Rosenberg, Morris, 2, 59, 120, 225, 229, 231, 260, 261, 288, 293, 315, 323, 507, 510, 511
Rosenburg, M. J., 287
Rosenburg, Seymour, 233
Rosengren, William R., 42, 65, 118, 177, 200, 225, 226, 230, 275, 279, 284, 286, 287, 296, 299, 339, 341, 343, 359, 401
Rosenthal, Robert, 239
Rosenzweig, Saul, 258
Rosin, G., 236
Rossi, Alice S., 124
Rossi, Peter H., xiii, xiv, 243, 310, 410–417, 422, 423
Rotberg, Robert, 196
Rothney, William B., 490, 497
Rotter, Julian B., v, 28, 294
Roy, Prodipto, 44, 45
Rubens, Juarez, 397
Rubin, Morton, 69, 517
Ruch, Giles M., 17
Rudolf, Juan, 168
Rundquist, Edward A., 111
Runkel, Phillip J., 173
Rushing, William A., 117

Saenger, Gerhart, 166–167
Sagi, Philip C., 17, 42, 43, 236, 262, 268, 285, 296, 355, 357, 359, 399, 417, 516, 517, 518, 519
Salisbury, W. Seward, 315, 453
Samora, Julian, 228
Sampson, Edward E., 336
Sanders, Irwin T., 196
Sanford, Fillmore H., 47, 51
Sanford, R. Nevitt, xiii, 46, 56, 118, 133–135, 150, 151, 297, 300
Sarapata, Adam, 418, 422
Sarbin, Theodore R., 131–132, 149, 171, 221, 240, 283, 319, 320
Saunders, D. R., 131, 269
Sauer, Warren L., 196
Savitz, Leonard D., 142
Savorgnan, Franco, 45
Scanzoni, John, 78
Scarpitti, Frank R., 95, 97, 98, 397, 420, 512

Names · 537

INDEX OF TOPICS

541

Age:
  adjustment to, 254
  distribution in general population, 370
  integration of occupational status with, 464
  norms of, 245
  related activities, 108
Agency:
  development, 77–78
  effectiveness, 77–78
Agreement:
  in classroom, 64
  of family on social mobility, 112
  between parent and child on ideals, 111
  between parents and offspring, 108
  see also Consensus
Aggression:
  deferment of, 279
  feelings toward co-workers, 82, 326
  feelings toward supervisor, 82
  parental, 114
  toward mother in child-rearing, 220, 221
  parental, 114
  as personality trait, 281
  verbal, toward co-workers, 82
  verbal, toward supervisor, 82
Aggressiveness, 335
  as role expectancy, 251
Agricultural cooperative:
  knowledge about, 73
  members' satisfaction with, 74
Agriculture, employment level in, 370
Aid, mutual: and affection, 114
Air defense, commitment to goals of, 72
Air division squadrons, efficiency of, 79
Air Force, satisfaction with, 183
Air site, satisfaction with, 183
Alcohol:
  quantity-frequency index of intake, 87
  use, 87
  use, definitions of, 87

Alienation, 6, 27–33, 300
  Nettler measure of, 31–33
  political, 37–38, 306
  powerlessness, Neal measure of, 14, 28–30
  origin-pawn scale, 178
  see also Anomia
Allegiance, apparent, 142
Allport-Vernon-Lindzey study of values, 512–513
Altercasting, rating of, 173
Altruism, 286
Amalgamation, 44
Ambience:
  articulation of, 138
  density of, 64
Ambiguity:
  intolerance of, 56
  in occupational role, 249
Ambition, composite index of, 39
Ambivalence in religion, 316
American Council on Education Psychological Examination for College Freshmen, 13, 232
Americanization, indices of, 44
Americans, traits of, 163
Anger with co-workers, 326
Anomia, 33–37
  mention of, 27, 300
  number of measuring instruments of, 6
  Srole's scale of, 13, 33–35
  see also Alienation; Anomy
Anomy, 37
Antagonism, 344
  responsiveness, 342
Anti-Catholicism, mention of, 162
Anti-femininity in men, 276
Anti-governmental regulation value, 515
Anti-labor orientation value, 515
Anti-Protestantism, mention of, 162
Anti-Semitism, 151–152
  mention of, 162
Antisocial tendencies, 256
Anti-unionism, church, 72
Anti-welfare-state value, 515
Anxiety, 254–255
Anxiety-worries checklist, 255

Culture, Cultural:
autonomy-integration of, 370
categories of, 371
development, 370
element, 371
formation of, 336
goal orientation of lower class, 507
modernity, 371
principal phases of, 374
truism opinion questionnaire, 125
see also Norms; Values
Customs: see Norms
Cynicism, as used in the California
F-scale, 47

Davis index of urbanization, 14,
376–377
Death:
attitudes toward, 223
spiritual-temporal orientations toward, 226
Deceit, crimes of, 93
Decision(s):
centrality in, 60
joint involvement in of husband
and wife, 114
mechanisms of, in group, 338
problems of, 330
of Supreme Court, consensus and
dissent of, 91
Decision-making:
analysis of, as approach to leadership studies, 191
father-centered, 113
power of in family, 116
Defensiveness, 287
Deference, 281
Deferment of gratification, 279
Dejection, neurotic, 261
Delinquency, Delinquent, 6, 87, 93–
101
acts of, and interpersonal relations,
95
authority protest of gangs, 97
gang conflict, 98
Nye and Short delinquent-behavior
checklist, 14, 95–97
prediction for successful treatment
of, 100

Delinquency (Continued)
proneness, Gough's measure of,
13, 93–94, 95
staff perspectives of, 100
see also Crime
Democracy, creed of, 303
Denmark:
occupational prestige in, 421
occupational status in, 454
Denominations, Protestant, social
status of, 317
Dependency:
in illness, 227
need, 280
on other family members, 110
public, orientation to, 510
Depression-frustration, 259
Deprivation, expected value of, 518
Deprivation-satisfaction, adolescents'
perceptions of, 117
Desegregate, Desegregation:
attitude toward, 128
readiness to, 129, 146–147
residential, of census tracts, 492
see also Discrimination; Prejudice
Desirability:
social, 298
social ranking form, 171
Destructiveness, as used in the California F-scale, 47
Detail, concern with, 169–170
Determinism, scale of, 505
Development:
in communications, 370
cultural, 370
economic, 371, 375
political, 374
social, 374
Deviance: see Conformity; Crime;
Delinquency
Differentiation:
occupational, 471
role, 342
score of raters, 240
social, 374
see also Division of labor
Diffuseness-specificity orientation,
246

Diffusion, 127–130
  locality rate, 128
  number of measures of, 6
  potency of, 128
  of propaganda, 129
  simultaneous use of new drug by
    doctors, 231
  use of media for, 128
  see also Innovation
Dignity of work values, 516
Disagreement, 342
  between accomplices, 336
  female estimate of, 112
  male estimate of, 112
  male-female, 112
Discipline:
  belief in, 100
  consistency in, 109, 200, 251
  initiative, 60, 248
  professional orientation, 250
  see also Child rearing
Discrepancy in status: see Status,
    consistency
Discrimination, racial and ethnic,
    145–147
  for Negroes, sensitivity to, 146
  number of measures of, 6
  rank order of, for whites, 146
  mention of, 127, 471
Discussion:
  involvement in, 327
  participation in, 340
Disease, knowledge about, 125
Dispersion, external, of objects of
    consumption, 371–372
Dissatisfaction, 180
  with parents, 118
Dissent, see Consensus
Dissimilarity:
  index of, 473, 499
  in religious observance, 315
Distance, social: see Social distance
Disturbance of patients, in mental
    hospital, 228
Distrust of people, 288
  see also Faith in people; Jungle
    scale; Trust
Diversification, industrial, 371

Division of labor:
  census-tract specialization, 502
  in household tasks, 111
  industrial diversification, 371
  industry in which employed, 374
  occupational, 374, 471
  organizational, 79
  role differentiation in small groups,
    342
  sexual, 371
  specialization, tendency toward in
    small groups, 343
  specialization, as used in Udy's
    measure of administrative ra-
    tionality, 77
Doctrine of church, adherence to,
    311
Dogmatism, Rokeach's scale of, 14,
    288–292
Dominance:
  by leader, 202
  metropolitan, 469–470
  by parents, 115
  as personality trait, 7, 28, 94, 265,
    273–275, 281
  potential, 469
  rural, of state legislature, 501
  of urban areas, 93, 370, 469–470
Dominants, economic, 191
Drive to get ahead: see Achievement
    motivation; Work, value orien-
    tations
Dun and Bradstreet ratings, 442, 450
Drugs, simultaneous use of new, by
    doctors, 231
Duncan-Duncan index of centraliza-
    tion, 13, 499–500
Duncan-Duncan index of dissimilar-
    ity, mention of, 499
Duncan-Duncan index of segrega-
    tion, 13, 472–475
Duncan socioeconomic index for all
    occupations, 13, 439–441
Dwelling, rating of, 379–381
  see also Housing
Dwelling area:
  as component of Warner index of
    status characteristics, 391–393
  rating of, 491

Enthnocentrism:
  California E-scale, 13, 133–137
  degrees of, 347
  number of measures of, 6
  see also Intergroup relations
Etiology of mental illness, 223
Eunomia: *see* Anomia
Euphoria, social, 342
Event analysis, as approach to identifying leadership, 192
Evolution, societal legal, 375
Exhibition, as personality trait, 381
Expansiveness, 337
  projected, 171
  rated, 179
Expectations:
  of children by parents, 111
  for future, 40
  of group, 328
  of life, 372
  probability, 241
  of professional activity, 224
  role, 251–252
  of role importance, 224
  of role in marriage, 220
  sick role, 230
  see also Norms
Experience and self-reliance, 174
Experimenter awareness, 337
Exploitation-manipulation, morality
  of, 506
Extended family:
  attitudes of, 122
  cohesion of, 122
  see also Family
Extroversion-introversion, 270

Faculty members, medical students'
  choices of, 224
Failure, attributed, 239
Faith in people, 293
Familism, 122, 123
Familistic-contractual orientation,
  246
Family, Families, 107–124
  adjustment of, 111
  adjustment to, 107
  agreement in on social mobility,
    112

Family (*Continued*)
  authority in, 107–117
  cohesion, 6, 122–124
  concern with unity of, 122
  cooperation of members of, 123
  cycle of age norms in, 245
  decision-making power in, 116
  emotionality in interaction, 112
  entrepreneurial status, 111
  esprit de corps of, 123
  father in, 113, 120
  identification with, 120, 122
  ideology of, 118
  independence of, 113
  instability of, 123
  integration of, 123
  interaction within, 112
  interpersonal relations in, 6, 107–
    116, 117
  joint involvement of husband and
    wife in decisions, 114
  kin, involvement with, 124
  kinship contacts, 124
  mention of, 9, 10, 19, 107, 117
  morality of, 506
  mother in, 120, 220, 221
  opinion survey, 112
  orientation toward, 119
  orientation of, 116, 117
  parents in, 108–111, 114–119,
    220, 303, 313; *see also* Parents
    for detail entries
  participation of members in, 123
  perception of, 120
  as reference group, 122
  rejection of, 120
  relations, attitude toward, 117
  roles, 220–222
  sense of obligation to, 111
  social participation of, 113
  social status of, concern with, 461
  solidarity of, 123, 124
  spouse in, 110, 207
  status satisfaction of husband, 518
  tensions in, 119
  type of, 113
  value position of, 507
  wives in, 107, 228, 229, 231, 369
  see also Child; Extended family

Fanaticism, 313
  religious, 316
Farm, Farming:
  economic class, 380
  family socioeconomic status scale, 402–403
  operator level-of-living index, 380
  practices, adoption of, 127
  scientific, strength of value of, 128
  technology, change in, acceptance of, 127
Fascism, 56
  see also Authoritarianism
Fatalism, 293
Father, 113, 120
Feedback, perceived consistency of, 318
Fels child-behavior scales, 266
Femininity, 94
  psychological, 277
  see also Masculinity
Fertility, 344
  value of, 507
Flexibility:
  organizational, 80
  as personality trait, 94
Following acts received, 337
Frailty, human, intolerance of, 294
Freedom:
  within historical periods, 240
  personal, 518
  personal, sense of, 256
Friend(s), Friendship, 174, 344
  circles of, 252
  communications with, 174
  degree of, 175
  duration of, 252
  extent of participation in, 360
  influence of susceptibility to, 179
  interclass, 139
  involvement of, 84
  leisure-time and work associates, 252
  overlapping of with membership, 252
  rating of, 170
  role of leaders, 200
  solidarity of, 175

Friend(s) (Continued)
  status of, 380
  see also Small groups
Frustration, 74, 258
Frustration-depression, 259
Fundamentalism, religious, 313, 315
Fusion with organization, 180
Futility, political, 306
Future-present, orientation to, 510

Gang delinquency, dimensions of, 97–98
Gangs, delinquent: see Crime; Delinquency
General classification test, 234
Generational:
  mobility, see Social mobility
  occupational mobility score, 353
Germans, traits of, 163
Germany, occupational status in, 454
Getting ahead: see Work, value orientations
Ghana, occupational prestige in, 421
Goal(s):
  air defense, commitment to, 72
  discrepancy in, 39
  focused or diffuse, 80
  group, commitment to, 183, 326
  life, achievement of, 17
  national, 509
  orientation to, 507
  tenacity to, 294
  see also Values
God, attitude toward, 313
Gordon personal profile, 266
Gottschaldt embedded figures test, 234
Government:
  attitude toward control by, 303, 507
  attitude toward intervention by, 303
  city, satisfaction with, 69
  federal, attitude toward control by, 303
  local, participation in, 309
  see also Political, attitudes and behavior
Grades, evaluation of, 40

Graduate:
record examination, 234
school, index of integration in, 105
Gratification, deferment of, 279
Great Britain, occupational prestige in, 422
Gregariousness, 360
Group(s):
acceptance by members of, 326
acceptance or rejection by dominant, 150
adjustment of, 84
assumed similarity of, 82, 83
attitudes toward, 328, 334
attraction to, 326
awareness of hostility of, 143
belongingness to, 148–149
chairman's activities to maintain, 199
children's power rating in, 103
cohesiveness of, 65
conflict in, 337–338
conformity to pressure from, 88
consensus of regarding solution of problem, 91
contributions to harmony of, 327
cooperation in, 338
coordination, 327
decision mechanisms, abstractness of, 338
desire to remain in, 327
effectiveness of, 338
expectations of, 328
goals of, commitment to, 183, 326
harmony of, 327
of high status, interaction with, 339
identification of, 328
identification with by members, 138, 329
influence of member, 201
of low mobility, 502
membership in, 338
motivation, 328
norms of, 246
occupational homogeneity of, 373
orientation of, 328
participation in, 340

Group(s) (Continued)
perceived accomplishment of, 18
personal involvement with, 329
reactions to meeting of, 328
reference, 122, 147, 244, 329
as referent, 200
sanctions in, extent of, 84
satisfaction of, 328
small, see Small groups
solidarity of, 65
professional status and prestige of, 253
Group-individual similarity, 91
Groupness, primary-secondary, 341
Guilford-Zimmerman temperament survey, 266
Guilt, 259

Happiness, 294
avowal of, 318
marital, 209, 214–215, 217
self evaluation of, 318
see also Enjoyment
Harmony of group, contribution to, 327
Hatred of self, 324
Health: see Medicine and health; Mental health; Patients
Helping people, value of, 519
Henmon-Nelson test of mental ability, 235
Heterogamy-homogamy, 10, 208
Heterosexuality, as personality trait, 281
Hierarchy of student values, 511
Historical periods:
change within, 239
freedom within, 240
security within, 242
Hollingshead occupational-status scale, 441–448
Home, as a pleasant place to be, 111
Homogamy, heterogamy, 10, 208
Honesty of policemen, 240
Hospital(s):
boards, prestige of, 224
mental, see Mental hospitals
occupational structure of, 228
punitiveness of wards, 229

League of Women Voters (*Cont.*)
  member loyalty to, 305
  participation in, 308
Learning, continued value of, 519
Lebanon:
  occupational status in, 455
  socioeconomic status in, 406
Left wing, scale of, 304
Legislators:
  conservatism of, 302
  party loyalty of, 309
  voting index of on labor-management issues, 310
Legislatures, state:
  equal apportionment of, 501
  rural dominance of, 501
  underrepresentation in, 503
Leisure:
  activities of, 369
  activity, value of, 509
  orientation of, 517
  style of, 397
Lenski status-crystallization measure, 14, 465–468
Level of living:
  of farm families, 380
  scale, 397
Liberalism, 304
  of social setting, 241
  see also Conservatism
Lie scale, 295
Life:
  expectations of, 372
  satisfaction with, 259
  social space of, 361
Likeability, Liking, 177, 178
  another, 345
  ranking form, 178
Listening devices, use of, 242
Literacy, 372
Live, ways to, 514
Living, rural, opinion about, 510
Local-cosmopolitan, 509
Locality:
  orientation to, 69
  satisfaction with, 69
Locke-Wallace short-form index of marital happiness, 209, 212–213
Love and affection, 28

Low-rent, concentration of, mention of, 499
Loyalty:
  of League of Women Voters members, 305
  of legislators to party, 309

McCallum form-board test of creativity, 272
McCarthy, Senator Joseph, attitude toward, 305
McClosky measure of conservatism, 14, 300–302
Machiavellianism, 295
Magni-complexity, as community factor, 69
Maladjustment, 259
  see also Adjustment
Management:
  central, 77
  military, problems of, 74
Manipulation potential, of societal members, 372
Manipulation-exploitation, morality of, 506
Manufacturing, number of persons employed in, 372
Marital:
  adjustment, *see* Adjustment, marital
  breakup, 214
  morality, middle class, 37
  prediction, 215
  roles, 7, 220–222
  satisfaction, 215–217
  strain, 217
Marriage:
  attitude toward, 207
  authority in, 114
  conjunctive affiliation of, 370
  integration in, 464
  patterns of, 45
  personal characteristics desired in partner, 218
  see also Courtship; Family; Needs, complementary
Masculinity-femininity, 7, 265
  as personality trait, 276–277
Mastery behavior in children, 24

Topics · 561

Materialism, values of, 517
Mathematics, sophistication in, 236
  see also Ability; Mental ability
Matriarchal-patriarchal continuum, 114
Maturity, 329
  emotional, 257–258
  mental, 260
Maudsley medical questionnaire, 261
Measurement, continuities in, 2–8
Mechanisms of group decisions, 338
Media:
  use of institutionalized, 128
  use of printed, 128
Medicine (Medical) and health, 6, 7, 125–126, 223–231
  arationality in practices of, 227
  care, skepticism of, 226
  community, links with, 228
  illness, dependency in, 227
  knowledge, 125
  mention of, 76, 125, 223, 227, 254
  personnel, distance of from patients, 231
  preventive behavior, 229
  profession, hostility toward, 224
Meetings of group, reactions to, 328
Members:
  group, identification with, 329
  involvement of, 73
  satisfaction of, 182
  union, activeness of, 360
Membership(s):
  benefits of for self-development, 74
  on committees, 363
  contact benefits of, 72
  disadvantages of, 72
  economic benefits of, 72
  of group, 338
  involvement in, 361
  number of, 369
  organizational, as status consciousness factor, 463
  in organizations, 363
  overlapping with friendship, 252
  participation, 80
  party, rate of change in, 310

Membership(s) (Continued)
  self-development, benefits of, 74
  valuation of, 279, 334
Men:
  antifemininity in, 276
  interest in the, 201, 251
Mental ability, 7, 17, 232–238
  see also Ability
Mental health:
  analysis test, 126
  and individual sociometric pattern, 125
  see also Medicine; Mental illness; Mental patients
Mental hospitals:
  attitudes toward, 224
  patient disturbance in, 228
  resistance to change in, 130, 230
  staff consensus in, 92, 231
Mental illness:
  etiology of, 223
  normalcy of patient after, 224
  of wives, 228, 229, 231
  see also Adjustment, personal; Medicine; Mental health; Mental patients
Mental patients:
  post-hospital performance of, 229
  social distance toward, 231
  see also Medicine; Mental health; Mental illness
Metropolitan areas, 93, 370, 469–470
  delimitation of, 469
  percentage of population residing in, 378
Middleton-Putney measure of religious orthodoxy, 14, 315–316
Migration, 373
Militariness of leader, 202
Military, management problems of, 74
Minister, permissible behavior of, 314
Minorities;
  attitudes toward, 133, 152
  random distribution of, 476
  status of, self adjustment to, 320
  see also Intergroup relations

Mistrust of public officials, 305
Mobility:
  population, 502
  social, see Social mobility
Modernity, cultural, 371
Modesty, 114
  training in children, 221
Monopolistic holding of high-status
    job, 142
Morale, 71, 180–183, 248
  of elderly, 182
  general, 102
  hierarchical consensus regarding,
    180
  opinion survey, 183
  school, 103
  work group, consensus regarding,
    183
  see also Job satisfaction
Morality:
  collective, 504
  economic, 505
  exploitive-manipulative, 506
  of family, 506
  general, 507
  middle-class marital, 37
  puritanical, 510
  religious, 510
  underdog, 511
  see also Values
Morality-immorality, 509
Mortality, infant, 374
Mother: see Family
Motive(s), motivation:
  achievement, see Achievement mo-
    tivation
  affiliation, 278
  covert, 278
  effects of in fantasy, 21
  of group, 328
  human, 20
  measurement of, 20
  mobility, 279
  perceived, 170
  as personality traits, 19, 30, 117,
    265, 278–283
  of power, 283
  task, 283

Municipalities, socioeconomic status
    of, 497
Murder, hypothetical case of, 240
Murray-McClelland-Atkinson meas-
    ure of achievement motivation,
    13, 19–23
Mutuality of social choice, 178
Myers-Briggs type indicator, 267
Mysticism, 296

Narcissistic-other oriented, 284
Narcotics index, 89
National Opinion Research Center
    occupational prestige scores, 11,
    12, 13, 355, 357–358, 410–417,
    439–440
Nationalism, 137
Neal measure of powerlessness, 14,
    28–30
Need(s):
  for achievement, 19–23, 281
  for affiliation, 280
  assessment, 280
  complementary, 9, 110, 207, 278,
    280
  dependency, 280
  intensity, 280
  inviolacy, 280
  as personality traits, 117, 265,
    278–283
  for self-assertion, 281
  for self-enhancement, 281
Negro(es):
  acceptance of, as students, 150
  arrests, overestimation of, 146
  attitudes toward, 133, 135, 150,
    152–154, 158
  general characteristics of, 143
  identification, 149
  image of, 129, 147
  leadership scores of, 143
  legal rights of, 146
  occupational status of, 455
  overt behavior toward, 146
  public rights of, 146
  residential segregation of, 471–490
  social class of, 397
  in specific school situations, 146

Participative-directive activity of chairman, 199
Particularism, 296
Particularism-universalism, orientation to, 247
Partisanship, 305
Partner:
  independence of, 175
  in marriage, personal characteristics desired, 218
Party:
  loyalty to, of legislators, 309
  membership of, rate of change in, 310
Passivity in political issues, 305
Passivity-activity, 286
Patient(s):
  close relationship with, value of, 518
  disturbance of, in mental hospitals, 228
  former, normality after mental illness, 224
  information, 126, 229
  nursing-home, appreciation of, 223
  personal distance of from medical personnel, 229
  quality of care of in hospital wards, 230
  reputed knowledge of, 230
  responsibility of, for condition, 226
  satisfaction of, knowledge of, 231
  sensitivity of, 230
  status distance of from medical personnel, 231
  welfare of, physicians' interest in, 248
  see also Medicine
Patriotism, see Ethnocentrism
Pay, mobility in, 359
Peer(s):
  adjustment to, 107
  group, conformity to, 89
  orientation toward, 119
Peer-parent cross pressures, 119
People:
  distrust of, 288

People (Continued)
  faith in, 283
  orientation to, 510
Perception(s), Perceiving:
  by adolescents, of deprivation-satisfaction, 117
  of complex organizations, 6, 71–75
  of education, 6, 102–104
  of family, 6, 117–121
  of information wanted from above, 73
  interpersonal, 319
  of mobility, 359
  responses of others, accuracy in, 143
  of small groups, 8, 326–335
  social, test of, 171
  sociometric, 333
  by wife, of husband's opportunity, 43
Performance:
  academic, 105
  bombardment crew, rating of, 80
  emphasis on, 77
  of marital role, deviations from, 220
  of mental patients, 229
  within organizations, 249
  organizational stations, rating of, 80
  of other, 329
  rating of, 249
  of precinct committeemen, 310
  of role, by medical interne, 252
  of roles, 221, 342
  in small groups, 340
Permissiveness:
  in age-related activities, 108
  in early feeding, 110
  in outside activities, 108
  sexual, premarital, 218
  in toilet training, 110
Personal characteristics:
  change in consensus on, 217
  desired in marriage partner, 218
Personality, 265–299
  Azzageddi test, of traits of, 268
  basic interests of, 512
  California test of, 255

Value(s) (*Continued*)
intrinsic, 518
in investment, 517
of involvement with complex problems, 519
of materialism, 517
of membership, 279, 334
on optimum size, 518
of parents, 116
personal, 510
of practicality, 517
of prestige among colleagues, 519
profile of, 512
relevance of, 512
risk-willingness, 518
selective, 511
sociometric, 511
of students, hierarchy of, 511
study of, Allport-Vernon-Lindzey, 14, 512–513
of task, 511
of utilizing abilities, 519
of work without great physical exertion, 519
mention of, 39, 265, 515
see also Morality; Work, value orientations
Vocabulary, 238
test, joint, 235
Voting, 310
apathy in, 310

War:
attitude toward, 514
ethical judgment about, 514
inevitability of, 37
Wards of hospitals, stratification of, 228
Warner index of status characteristics, 13, 388–396
Warner occupational-status measure, 13, 450–452
Water:
management practices, adoption of, 127
witching, 378
Ways to be different test, 262
Weakness, contempt for, 287

Wechsler-Bellevue intelligence scale, 238
Welfare:
as community factor, 69
of patient, physician's interest in, 249
Well-being, sense of, as a personality trait, 94
Weltanschauung, negative, 37
West Germany, occupational mobility in, 358
Westie summated-differences measure of social distance, 14, 160–162
Wheel rating, 172
Wife, Wives:
activities prohibited to, 107
mentally ill, 228, 229, 231
social participation of, 369
see also Family
Whites:
as attitude object, 159
attitudes toward, 152
occupational status of, 455
rank order of discrimination for, 146
Wholesale, activity in, 470
Wide-range achievement test, 238
Willingness:
to sacrifice ideological values to get ahead, 519
to sacrifice social interests to get ahead, 519
Winterbottom measure of achievement training, 14, 24–26
Withdrawal: *see* Sociability
Withdrawing, tendencies of, 256
Women, occupational status of, 456
Word likes and dislikes test, 262
Work:
attitudes toward, 248
beliefs check list, 519
department, evaluation of, 75
group, 61, 83, 183
orientation index, 519
preference for, 518
responsibility of, 250
separation of from residence, 503

Topics · 579

Work (*Continued*)
standards, hierarchical consensus regarding, 75
value(s), commitment to, 516
value(s), dignity of, 516
value(s), without great physical exertion, 519
value(s), promotional frustration, 74
value(s), promotional orientations, 250
value orientations, 8, 17, 39, 504, 515–520

Work (*Continued*)
see also Achievement motivation; Achievement orientation
Worker(s), working:
class consciousness of, 63
in groups, 234
propensity of to strike, 241
see also Co-workers; Employees
Worries and anxieties test, 262
Worth, personal, sense of, 256
Writers, effective, 204

Zone, redistribution by, 503